Contents

Kenneth J. Thygerson
California State University, San Bernardino

■HarperCollins*College*Publishers

To Darlene, Keith, and Kent

Acquisitions Editor: Kirsten Sandberg
Project Coordination, Text and Cover Design, Art Coordination, Electronic Page Makeup: York Production Services
Electronic Production Manager: Christine Pearson
Printer and Binder: R. R. Donnelley & Sons Co.
Cover Printer: Coral Graphics

Management of Financial Institutions

Library of Congress Cataloging-in-Publication Data

Thygerson, Kenneth J. (Kenneth James)
    Management of financial institutions / Kenneth J. Thygerson.--1st ed.
        p.   cm.
    Includes bibliographical references and index.
    ISBN 0-673-99471-6
    1. Financial institutions--Management.   I. Title.
    HG1615.T49 1995
    332.1'068--dc20

                                                        95-6660
                                                        CIP

95 96 97 98 9 8 7 6 5 4 3 2 1

*M*anagement of Financial Institutions

What do your students need to know about managing financial institutions? Should they focus, as so many textbooks do, specifically on bank management techniques, or would they be more marketable if they understood how to create and implement successful financial strategies across all types of financial intermediaries? If your students expect practical skills and tools to use immediately on the job within the financial services industry, then this is the text for your classroom. Based upon years of observing, responding to, and anticipating rapid change in the U.S. financial system, it represents one of the first major efforts to integrate financial management concepts, principles, and decision-making algorithms useful to all types of financial institutions.

While depository institutions are most prominent in the text, the book acknowledges the continuing overlap of functions performed by competing intermediaries and the declining role of depositories within the global marketplace. The text builds a framework for comprehending and thinking critically about the management of any financial institution and for applying the techniques of financial planning and management. Based on sound coverage of concepts and theories, it becomes an engaging learning tool as well as a practical resource for students who want a deep understanding of, and profitable insights into, the relationships among markets, institutions, and management.

This text takes a new approach to the material: It maintains that if students understand underlying principles, they can apply their knowledge across the board to all intermediaries—past, present, and future. This approach enables the book to cover topics relevant to all institutions—intermediation, arbitrage, financial innovation, regulation, planning, asset and liability pricing, credit risk, interest rate risk, financial claim valuation, and derivatives—first from a theoretical or conceptual perspective and then from a more practical point of view. While the book recognizes that commercial banks no longer dominate the financial landscape, it provides comprehensive coverage of the special issues concerning these commercial entities and their sister thrift institutions.

To be effective in the finance community today, students must also understand the market setting within which the institutions operate. However, too many texts present microeconomic optimization algorithms out of context; that is, they fail to explain the macroeconomic, regulatory, and competitive influences on institutions. In contrast, this book features an entire chapter on market structure and the competitive forces impacting financial institution performance in the last decade.

The book is filled with a variety of pedagogical features, based on student experience in the classroom and designed to assist students in learning efficiently and relating material to the real world.

Finally, the book includes a large number of decision-making algorithms—models for asset and liability pricing, interest rate risk management, credit risk management, branch profitability, and so forth—models that financial managers have used successfully in a variety of financial institutions. By reviewing these key decision-making tools, students can effectively transfer and apply what they have already learned in prerequisite finance courses to their study of financial markets and institutions.

Innovative Features

This book has features designed *for* students *by* students, such as special sections that highlight relevant real-world issues, worked-out example problems and self-test problems, and special coverage of international issues and ethics to meet the requirements of the AACSB.

1. *Financial claim/function matrix:* Since financial intermediaries are becoming more alike in terms of the functions they perform and the services they provide, the theory of financial intermediation allows for the development of a financial claim/function matrix. Highlighting the similarities rather than the differences among financial intermediaries, this matrix or table visually explains and compares the financial claims created by, and the functions served by, particular institutions.

2. *Credit risk management:* With so many problem loans plaguing financial institutions today, students should appreciate fully the essential tasks of intermediaries—specifically the origination of financial claims and the management of associated risks. The text features a complete chapter on credit risk management, which covers the theory and approach to diversification and the process of creating claims by focusing on the development of covenants. This is followed by chapters on individual loan credit risk evaluation and managing problem loans and investments.

3. *International activities:* The text gives students a sense of the international nature of financial institutions and markets in the chapter on commercial banks; in a separate chapter that covers foreign exchange, exchange rates, and currency risk management; and in international focus boxes throughout. Equally important is Chapter 5, which provides a macro and micro view of the international investment decision, emphasizing the global nature of capital movement so crucial today.

4. *Valuation techniques for hybrid financial claims:* Chapter 15, on the valuation of financial claims, extends valuation concepts in finance to more financial instruments and applies valuation techniques to such hybrid securities as stripped Treasury bills and mortgage securities. Chapter 17, on measuring interest rate risk, stresses mark-to-market valuation techniques, which require broader knowledge of valuation.

5. *Regulation of Financial Institutions:* The savings and loan debacle of the 1980s revealed how inadequate regulation can affect the financial system. This text devotes a chapter to the theory of regulation but focuses on those regulations common to all institutions because the system is so highly regulated.

6. *Futures, options, and swaps:* Because financial intermediaries write many financial contracts with options embedded in them, students must learn how to identify and value options. Therefore, the text stresses option pricing theory and emphasizes the role of futures and swaps in risk management.

7. *Measurement and management of interest rate risk:* Since the tools that intermediaries use to measure and manage interest rate risks are the same for all financial institutions, two chapters devoted to interest rate risk treat these topics as general subjects, with some reference to specific institutions where necessary. These chapters also incorporate more advanced valuation techniques, because more intermediaries are beginning to consider GAP, duration, and mark-to-market interest rate risk management techniques in order to remain profitable.

8. *Planning for financial institutions:* A special effort has been made to simplify the planning process exposition. Strategic, operating, and financial plans, and action steps are presented clearly with examples of their use by a wide variety of financial intermediaries. The text also provides a strong discussion of innovation.

9. *Asset and liability pricing:* Several chapters treat asset and liability pricing with special care, because financial managers of intermediaries must be able to perform this function.

10. *Financial product distribution:* The continual blending of the U.S. financial system creates many new distribution channels for financial products and services. In a unique chapter on distribution channels, students examine the financial intermediary's role as distributor of financial products and services. This chapter also includes a model for assessing the profitability of retail branches for depository institutions.

11. *Macroeconomic and structural issues affecting intermediaries:* An entire chapter raises important macroeconomic and structural issues, including the competitive forces that affect depositories.

12. *Mergers and Acquisitions:* With consolidation of the financial services industry at hand, a discussion of mergers and acquisitions is necessary and relevant.

Key Features

No text in the area of financial institution management has as many learning features as this one, and the reason is simple: The student is the consumer of this product. Making learning easier and more relevant to a career in the financial services industry are the two primary objectives of these features. Many of our students today are older, often with job experience of some kind; they appreciate solid examples of how concepts work in the real world. More importantly, these students—like most people these days—do not have the luxury of time to plod through unnecessarily long or tediously detailed discussions.

- "Learning Goals" provide the student with a brief summary of the most important concepts and problems to be found in each chapter.

- "Summary and Review" sections restate each learning goal and provide a summary response to each.

- "Checkpoints" after each major section of the text provide questions to help students make sure that they have understood the most important material before continuing.

- "Demonstration Problems" walk students through a realistic management problem and the financial tool used to solve it.

- Because of differences in teaching pedagogy, instructors will find questions, problems, projects, or case studies at the end of many chapters.

- "How It Really Works" summarize actual events involving financial institutions which illustrate material found in the textbook.

- "Management Highlights" summarize the major financial management issues that affect each institution.

- "Legal and Ethical Issues" summarize the legal and ethical issues that affect organized markets, regulatory institutions, and foreign financial institutions. The topics include profiles of Michael Milken and the junk bond market, Salomon Brothers' Treasury auction irregularities, and Lincoln Savings and Loan and Charles Keating.

- "Reading the Financial Page" features present financial tables common to various financial publications. Each of these tables includes an explanation of the data found in the table and a description of the abbreviations.

- "International Focus" sections give a worldwide perspective on investing, regulation, and financial markets.

- "Self-Test Problems" are provided to assist students in mastering the decision-making financial tools.

Supplemental Materials

A number of additional materials have been prepared and class-tested to enrich students' learning experience and to enhance faculty efficiency.

INSTRUCTOR'S MANUAL (400 PAGES) AND TRANSPARENCY MASTERS (200 + ITEMS)

A comprehensive instructor's manual provides chapter-by-chapter outlines, with teaching tips, anecdotes where appropriate, solutions to all problems and cases, and special references to the transparency masters found in the instructor's manual. Professors can provide students with the outlines to follow along during lectures, and highlight information on the most important graphs, tables, and charts found in the text. The transparency master package contains more than 200 elements, including conceptual "talking" outlines, graphs, charts, and tables, plus examples of problems and worked-out solutions for the more problem-driven and case-oriented chapters.

PRINTED AND COMPUTERIZED TEST BANK (360 PAGES)

A test bank made up of factual and conceptual problems in true/false, multiple-choice, and short essay formats has also been developed. There are over 1,500 questions in the test bank, all class-tested to ensure clarity and validity of each item. The test bank is available on disk in word for windows format.

READINGS BOOK

A companion book, *Financial Markets and Institutions: Readings,* by Kenneth J. Thygerson, is available from HarperCollins College Publishers, Inc. This book is designed specifically to accompany this text and includes 29 readings selected to complement various chapters in the text.

Acknowledgments

Textbooks are not written in a vacuum. Special acknowledgment must go to executives whom I had the pleasure to work with at several financial institutions. Kevin Villani provided much of the conceptual and operational framework for the managerial material found in the book. Kevin also assisted me greatly through his input acquired from teaching early versions of the text in his courses at the University of Southern California. Michael Lea also was responsible for a significant number of ideas that have found their way into the text. Mike's input was particularly useful in Chapters 21, 22, and 24.

The early draft chapters benefited greatly from the following reviewers:

James C. Baker, Kent State University
H. Robert Bartell, East Tennessee State University
Randall S. Billingsley, Virginia Polytechnic Institute and State University
Paul J. Bolster, Northeastern University
Elijah Brewer, Federal Reserve Bank of Chicago
Ivan T. Call, Brigham Young University
David B. Cox, University of Denver
Clifford L. Fry, University of Houston
John S. Jahera, Jr., Auburn University
Rauf Khan, California State University, San Bernardino
John Olieny, Colorado State University

Robert Schweitzer, University of Delaware
Charlene Sullivan, Purdue University
Haluk Unal, University of Maryland
James A. Verbrugge, University of Georgia.

The final draft of this particular product benefitted from the insights of the following colleagues:

James F. Gatti, University of Vermont
Sylvia C. Hudgins, Old Dominion University
Mel Jameson, University of Nevada at Las Vegas
Gary E. Kundy, Columbus College
Rose M. Prasad, Central Michigan University
Carolin D. Schellhorn, Northeastern University
Oliver G. Wood, Jr., University of South Carolina

I must also thank many of my undergraduate and graduate students at California State University, San Bernardino, who suffered the indignity of working through incomplete early versions of this text. They found numerous mathematical errors, tested the book's test bank, and provided ideas for problems. I must thank Eldon Lewis of California State University, San Bernardino, for providing a schedule that allowed me to take on this task.

I would also like to thank the team at and assembled by HarperCollins Publishers. The most important of this group was Kirsten Sandberg, who spent countless hours improving exposition and organization of ideas. The group also includes Suzanne Ivester, Tracey Topper, Ed Yarnell, and Julie Zasloff. They all helped improve the final product.

Finally, to my wife, Darlene, I truly appreciate her unwavering support.

Kenneth J. Thygerson

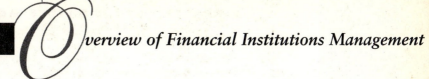

CHAPTER 1

Overview of Financial Institutions Management

Learning Goals

After studying this chapter, you should be able to:

1. Describe the process of financial intermediation and other financial services performed by financial institutions.
2. Explain the globalization of financial transactions relative to financial institutions management.
3. Explain and relate agency theory to financial institutions management and discuss some current agency issues that managers must consider.
4. Discuss some key ethical and legal issues involving the management of financial institutions.
5. Discuss government influence on financial institutions and their management.
6. Explain how financial institutions benefit from the strategic management processes of corporate planning, assessing the external environment, and assessing financial asset expected risk and returns.

Introduction

You happen to be studying the management of financial institutions in one of the more dynamic times of change, as intense as that of the 1930s. The thrift debacle, bank failures, junk bonds, unprecedented innovation in financial instruments, and expansive globalization of financial markets have all challenged the most knowledgeable and seasoned of finance professionals. Presumably, you may soon join in their endeavors.

What lies ahead? Most significant of all is change. At the beginning of most chapters, you will read about how progress in communications and data processing technology has made much of the increased global activity possible, as has the tremendous growth in the world's economies outside the United States. Trading of financial instruments now occurs around the clock in integrated markets around the world. Advancing technology and financial creativity will no doubt drive the pace and the scope of such trading activities.

In the Pacific Basin, Japan is the financial powerhouse. Its financial institutions have grown to become the largest, mea-

JAPANESE AUTO INDUSTRY MOVES TO UNITED STATES

Does buying a Honda or Toyota car mean that you are "buying foreign"? Before 1970, the answer was unambiguously *yes*. During the 1970s and 1980s, the largest Japanese auto manufacturers, responding partially to criticism that Japan's car exports to the United States were totaling the U.S. auto industry, began to open auto manufacturing plants in the United States. Initially, these plants merely assembled autos using parts imported from plants located in Japan and elsewhere. Today, however, many of these plants use a large percentage of parts manufactured in the States.

How significant is this activity? In 1992, the largest Japanese auto manufacturers—Honda, Nissan, Toyota, Mitsubishi, Mazda, and Fuji/Isuzu—had the ability to build 1.65 million cars and light trucks within the United States. This figure represents about 15–20% of total U.S. manufacturing capacity. Such foreign investments in the United States demonstrate one type of important global capital movement.

Source: Hidenada Kato, "Nissan Looking South of the Border," *Asian Weekly*, Dec. 7, 1992.

sured in terms of assets in international banking markets. Europe is also growing at a pace unanticipated ten years ago; with the economic integration of Europe and the United Kingdom, new economic forces are influencing financial markets and institutions not just in the European Community but worldwide. The North American Free Trade Agreement (NAFTA) passed by Congress in late 1993 heralds further integration of product and service markets for the western hemisphere.

THE PROCESS OF FINANCIAL INTERMEDIATION AND ROLE OF FINANCIAL INTERMEDIARIES

The most important function of finance is the allocation of capital—determining where money is spent or invested. Money is a financial asset that provides its owner with the ability to buy other income-producing assets. Since money and the assets it can control are scarce, economies must devise systems to allocate such scarce resources. The field of finance provides the tools needed to determine which investments will provide the greatest benefits. As you might expect, these investments attract the scarce capital. So who makes these capital asset allocation decisions in developed economies? Among the most influential are the managers of **financial institutions,** firms involved in one or more of the activities: of origination, brokering, servicing, and investing and issuing financial assets. Many financial institutions position themselves between savers and borrowers by issuing their own financial liabilities, such as savings deposits to savers, and lending the funds they raise to borrowers. These firms are called *financial intermediaries.* Because not all financial institutions manage asset and liability portfolios, only a subset of all financial institutions are intermediaries. Consequently, both terms will be used throughout the book.

Financial **intermediation** is a process of facilitating the flow of capital by bringing savers, called *capital surplus units (CSUs),* together with borrowers, called *capital deficit units (CDUs),* who otherwise may not have met to transact. In this process, financial intermediaries provide a variety of services that reduce costs of saving and borrowing for the participants in the economy and at the same time provide risk sharing, which reduces risks for savers.

Financial intermediation concerns the mechanisms and financial firms constituting a country's **payment system.** Such a system is essential so that businesses and individuals can undertake commercial transactions quickly, inexpensively, and safely. In developed countries, citizens often take for granted their payment system of paper and coin money, checks, credit and debit cards, and electronic money transfers. These systems use a number of financial institutions—commercial banks, thrift institutions such as savings banks, and central banks, like the U.S.'s Federal Reserve System or the United Kingdom's Bank of England—to operate efficiently. Sophisticated payment systems have evolved and continue to improve in most developed countries.

However, new or developing countries such as the former Soviet satellites and Mexico often do not have such an efficient system. Over a year after Latvia, one of three Baltic republics, received its independence from the Soviet Union, it still had no payment system for conducting its commercial and individual financial transactions. All financial transactions required either currency—coins and paper money— or **barter**—trading one product for another. Most transactions were difficult, time-consuming, and unsafe, in the criminal sense of theft and robbery. The lack of an efficient payment system significantly retarded the economic development of Latvia.

The process of intermediation also deals with the design of financial assets, the development and workings of financial markets, and the creation and management of financial institutions.

FINANCIAL ASSETS

Financial assets, also called *financial claims,* are contracts that give the owner the right to a stream of income or tangible or another financial asset. Advances in financial theory and the availability of low-cost computer power have led to the engineering and trading of a wide variety of new financial assets, with names like zeros, S&P futures, futures options, caps, swaps, swaptions, strip-Ts, CMOs, and REMICs. These assets not only facilitate the transfer of money from those with excess funds to those that have uses for funds beyond their own resources but also reduce risks borne by the investors and issuers of these assets.

FINANCIAL MARKETS

The creation and the efficient functioning of financial markets are also critical to the optimal capital allocation. Financial markets enable suppliers and users of capital to avoid a costly and time-consuming search process for each other. Financial markets are also the source of information about the price of various financial assets.

There are many different types of financial markets. Organized markets, such as the Chicago Board of Trade, exist for common stock, bonds, futures contracts, and options. As mentioned earlier, many of these markets are global; investors around the world are connected through communication and data processing systems to central markets or to other dealers. The globalization of financial market systems has pointedly promoted the international flow of capital.

FINANCIAL INSTITUTIONS

The financial landscape stretching from the United States, through the European Community, to the Pacific Rim, and back again is dotted by different types of financial institutions. Most nations have financial firms known as *depository institutions* that offer deposit services and make loans to business entities and individuals. The most common depositories worldwide are commercial banks. Some countries have specialized depositories called *thrift institutions,* such as the U.S.'s savings and loans, savings banks, and credit unions, specialized in the sense that they concentrate most of their activities on a particular financial function or financial asset. Most developed countries also have government-owned and -operated financial institutions. One of these is typically the country's **central bank,** which controls the supply of the nation's money, handles international transactions, and helps fund the government's borrowing needs.

Many developed countries also have **nondepository institutions,** firms that may provide a broad range of financial functions but do not issue deposits; the major nondepositories in the United States include finance companies, insurance companies (both life and property and casualty), investment banking firms, and pension funds. A third group of **investment-oriented intermediaries** provides various specialized asset management services. Among this group are open-end mutual funds, real estate investment trusts, and limited partnerships. There are counterparts for these nondepository institutions in most developed countries. Financial institutions are the subject of Chapter 3.

The federal government has also chartered **government sponsored enterprises (GSEs),** which provide lending services to a variety of borrowers, from college students to farmers. The largest of these GSEs fund residential mortgages. Most of the GSEs are privately owned and compete directly against other financial intermediaries.

If you studied financial institutions 10 or 20 years ago, then you probably would have defined each firm by the functions that it served in the payment system. But with deregulation, technological progress, financial innovation, and competition, there is an increasing overlap in the products and services that these firms can provide. Today, students of financial institutions management must consider the following, made possible in part by the Federal Reserve Board and legislation:

- Some bank holding companies, since 1990, can underwrite corporate securities.[1]

---

[1]Bank holding companies are corporations that hold the stock in one or more commercial banks. These corporations also hold stock in companies that are not permitted under commercial bank charters. The bank holding company is discussed in Chapter 3.

- Thrift institutions, since 1981, can provide virtually all the deposit and loan services that commercial banks do.
- Thrifts, investment brokers and dealers, and commercial banks can all sell insurance.
- Nonbank financial institutions, such as the investment banker Merrill Lynch & Co., can offer virtually all the products and services that commercial banks provide.
- Brokers and dealers can offer customers mutual funds and insurance policies.
- Commercial firms, such Sears Roebuck & Co., and industrial firms, such as General Electric Co., can offer bank-type credit cards.

With so many similarities among these institutions as well as the financial products and services they provide, this book concentrates more on what will really matter to the manager of the generic financial firm: the motivating factors of change, the underlying concepts and issues, and the decision-making algorithms—but not on industry-specific detail, which will no doubt change.

One of the most important functions performed by financial institutions is that of intermediation. One way to intermediate is to manage a customer's portfolio of financial assets; and this **portfolio management function** is the greatest source of revenue for most financial institutions.[2] In the United States, financial firms hold most of the financial assets issued by CDUs. Exhibits 1.1 and 1.2 show the total amount of credit market debt outstanding in the United States held by financial institutions and directly by households, businesses, foreigners, and government units.[3]

The exhibits clarify how significant a role financial institutions play in allocating capital. Intermediaries hold $12.3 billion of the total of $15.9 billion in credit market debt. Each day, managers of thousands of financial institutions select individual investments from tens of thousands of alternatives. This book will help you to grapple with these decisions and understand the process of intermediation relative to the capital allocation decision.

✓ Checkpoints

1-1 How does the process of intermediation work in terms of capital surplus and deficit units?

1-2 How does each of the following fit into a developed financial infrastructure:

a. Efficient payments system?

---

[2]Portfolio management involves the ownership of financial assets financed by issuing financial liabilities. The revenue from this activity is primarily interest income and the expense interest cost. This function is performed by financial intermediaries, but not by all financial institutions. Portfolio management is discussed extensively in Chapters 2 and 10.

[3]Much of the data presented in Chapters 1 and 2 come from the Federal Reserve's *Flow of Funds Accounts*. These data provide quarterly estimates of both stocks and flows of financial assets and liabilities of major economic sectors such as households, businesses, and financial institutions.

EXHIBIT 1.1

Financial Institution's Ownership Share of Credit Market Debt
December 31, 1993 (percent)

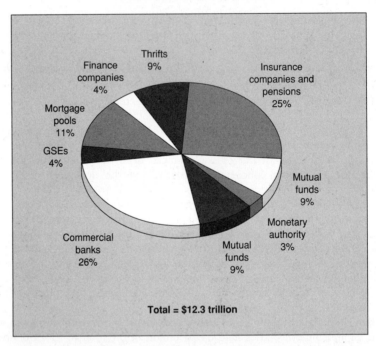

Total = $12.3 trillion

Source: *Flow of Funds Accounts,* Board of Governors of the Federal Reserve Board, March 9, 1994, p. 70

    b. Financial assets?

    c. Financial markets?

    d. Financial institutions?

1-3 What are some of the largest intermediaries in the United States?

1-4 What is the difference between depository and nondepository institutions? What are some examples of each?

1-5 What types of services, such as intermediation, do financial institutions perform?

Global Allocation of Capital

During the 1960s and 1970s, western Europe and Japan were recovering from the devastation of World War II. International trade grew rapidly. Since 1980, very powerful economic and financial forces have accelerated the global movement of capital. By 1993, the United States had net imports from other countries

EXHIBIT 1.2

Household, Business, Foreign, and Government Unit Ownership Share of Credit Market Debt
December 31, 1993 (percent)

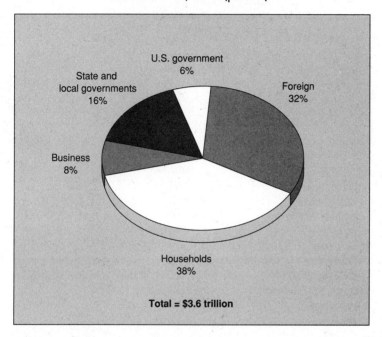

U.S. government 6%

State and local governments 16%

Foreign 32%

Business 8%

Households 38%

Total = $3.6 trillion

Source: *Flow of Funds Accounts,* Board of Governors of the Federal Reserve Board, March 9, 1994, p. 70

of $725 billion and exports to its trading partners of $662 billion. These exports represented over 10% of the U.S. gross domestic product (GDP)—the value of all domestically produced goods and services. With this growth in trade came the need to develop more effective methods for exchanging the currencies of trading partners—U.S. dollars for Japanese yen or for Deutschmarks—to facilitate these transactions.

There has been a significant increase in **foreign direct investment (FDI)**, which is the transfer of financial, managerial, and technical assets from one country to another. By year-end 1993, the United States had invested $704 billion in direct foreign investments. Foreigners, on the other hand, had invested $520 billion directly into the United States. The movement of capital around the world can largely hasten a country's growth in production output, income, and employment. Countries successful in attracting capital create more job opportunities and a greater chance for income growth for their citizens.

Matching increased trade and foreign direct investment is the growth of international trading of financial securities. At year-end 1993, U.S. residents held $479 billion in deposits and credit market instruments against foreign entities. Foreigners, however, held a staggering $1,155 billion in deposits and credit market instruments against U.S. entities. Of that amount, $738 billion was in U.S. government securities. The scale of international securities transactions is enormous: in 1992 alone, foreigners bought and sold approximately $700 billion in U.S. corporate stocks and bonds.

INTERNATIONAL ✪ FOCUS

U.S. INVESTORS FIND PACIFIC FUNDS

The rapid economic growth prospects in the Far East has propagated a rash of newly created investment funds for U.S. investors. As of July 31, 1992, investors put over $2 billion into funds specializing in investments in Far Eastern countries. Here is a brief list of the major funds available:

Name of Specific Country Fund	Assets as of July 31, 1992 (in millions)
First Philippine Fund	$105
India Growth Fund	151
Indonesia Fund	42
Japan Fund	361
Korea Fund	241
Malaysia Fund	110
ROC Taiwan Fund	252
Scudder New Asia Fund	110
Taiwan Fund	173
Thai Fund	165

The number of funds providing investment opportunities in the Far East indicates the investor demand for diverse growth opportunities. Today, through these funds, investors and their intermediaries can direct individual investment dollars into the ownership of companies in Pacific Rim countries of Korea, Japan, Malaysia, Taiwan, India, the Philippines, and Indonesia. Similar funds are available for investments in many of Europe's developed countries.

Source: Richard Phalon, "How to Pick a Far East Fund," *Forbes*, Sept. 14, 1992, pp. 528–30.

Related to increased foreign direct investing and trading is the melding of world financial markets so that capital flows easily and quickly from one country to another, depending on various economic and political events and potentially rewarding investment opportunities. This flow of capital positively affects employment and the standard of living for the citizens of each country. The changes in eastern Europe and the new republics of the former Soviet Union illustrate how the integration of formerly closed economies and financial systems with developed economies creates new challenges and opportunities for all the world. But these challenges pose a number of important questions that managers should consider:

- What changes in law and financial structure must occur to sustain an increased flow of capital from the developed countries to eastern Europe and the former Soviet Union republics toward their providing more productive uses for capital?
- What financial structure will emerge in the economic union of the European Community?
- How will the U.S. financial system progress from the thrift debacle and the many failures of commercial banks and insurance companies?
- How will the growing Pacific Basin economies, especially Japan, handle their growing asset accumulation? How will they invest these assets around the world? Who will win and who will lose in the global competition for capital?

The answers to these questions involve complex political, social, and economic forces, often beyond the control of financial institution managers but very much influencing what these managers do when making capital allocation decisions.

✓ Checkpoints

1-6 What special skills and insights must managers have when allocating capital in a global context?

1-7 What are some examples of integrated world capital markets and increased capital movement? How might further integration affect a manager's long-term business considerations?

Ethical and Legal Issues of Financial Institutions

Since the management of financial institutions involves money—often other people's money—no study of the subject would be complete without a look at ethical and legal issues. In recent years, the press—both print and electronic—have put before their audiences the words and the faces of business executives, investors, investment bankers, savings and loan executives, and others convicted of financial wrongdoing. These charges of unethical, sometimes illegal, behavior often relate to how people use information, money, or power to enrich themselves. **Ethics** refers to the agreed-upon standards of behavior or moral judgments of a community or of a society; and the definition of what is ethical differs among societies—a challenge indeed for increased globalization. Moreover, the line between unethical and illegal behavior is a fine one. **Law** reflects the general views of each society at any given point in time, and it changes with public opinion, represented by government officials. An act viewed to be marginally unethical may become unlawful, or vice versa. A quick look at laws in the United States, compared to those in many other developed foreign countries, highlights the shifting nature of ethical and legal standards.

AGENCY THEORY AND INTERMEDIARIES

Earlier in this chapter, Exhibit 1.1 revealed that financial institutions hold most credit market debt. These institutions issue the liabilities that households, businesses, and government units own; but these groups of owners are not directly involved in the financial institution's investment or allocation of those funds. The holder of deposits in banks, reserves in life companies, or reserves in pension funds, for example, does not select the investments that those intermediaries make. Likewise in corporate finance, the owner of 100 shares of stock in a company relies upon the firm's manager and board of directors to respect the owner's preferences. Creditors of a firm also rely on that firm's financial managers to fulfill the obligations of debt contracts. Owners and creditors are considered **principals**, defined as the holders of financial assets; and the financial manager and board of directors are referred to as *agents,* or representatives who actually make investment decisions on behalf of the principals of firms and financial institutions. The relationship between principal and agent is called an *agency relationship.*

Agency theory refers to the study of the agency relationship, specifically of agent behavior. Agency theory helps identify circumstances where agents do not act with the interest of their owners and debtors in mind. It guides governments in establishing financial laws and regulations to address such conflict in agency relationships. It also helps firms in devising various performance goals, incentive plans, and other means to supervise the actions of agents. All of this monitoring and controlling results in complex legal contracts, accounting systems, regular auditing and reporting, and all other measures taken toward compliance with and administration of regulation. The costs of these measures are called *agency costs*. Other examples of agency costs include the hiring of trustees to monitor corporate behavior under debt agreements and the convening of boards of directors.

A financial intermediary is, in many cases, an agent of both the CDU and the CSU—a bit different from the agent's role in a typical corporation. The federal government adds to the complexity of the agency relationship because, as an insurer of the liabilities of financial firms like depositories, it must recognize agency issues on behalf of its citizens. In effect, federal insurance of deposits shifts agency costs from the depositors themselves to the society as a whole through taxation. But, regardless of the type of firm—financial or otherwise—the costs of agency relationships are significant. Consequently, the suppliers of capital must consider the incentives under which the users of their capital operate.

ETHICS AND FINANCIAL PERFORMANCE

Although readers may spot an article here and there about how the stock market has rewarded an ethical, socially motivated, or environmentally aware firm with a higher share price, scandal is the stuff that headlines are made of. There are numerous examples of how unethical behavior has led to sharp drops in a firm's stock value due to fines, lawsuits, lost business and licenses, product recalls, or environmental cleanup costs, to name a few. As consumer confidence does not come cheaply or quickly, stockholders have a large stake in how ethically their companies conduct business.

But there are many definitions of what is ethical. One example involves the quest for corporate control, as through a leveraged buyout (LBO). An LBO is a financial transaction that takes control of a firm away from self-serving entrenched bureaucrats, some argue, for the benefit of shareholders, to mitigate an agency problem. But others label LBOs as unscrupulous cut-throat transactions designed to sell assets for immediate profit and to cut jobs. Does either view matter much to managers of financial institutions who find themselves intermediating such transactions? Another example concerns financial restructurings, especially those designed to reduce a firm's equity relative to its debt. Sometimes, increasing financial leverage severely reduces the value of outstanding bonds, so that creditors lose but have little control over their loss. In a technical sense, such transactions are usually legal but could jeopardize the firm's ability to borrow in the future. After all, who would issue a bond to such a firm, once the firm ups its leverage but downs the value of its debt? The implications behind these two examples is that corporations have stockholders as well as **stakeholders,** parties with a stake in the firm's behavior, such as creditors, employees, customers, and neighboring communities. The manager of a financial firm must consider all the stakeholders involved in a financial transaction.

In business, and especially financial businesses, ethical behavior translates into an attribute called *reputation,* as important as the quality of products and services. A firm's reputation not only attracts customers but influences the firm's standards of practice and choice of customers. Some commercial or investment banking firms may avoid dealing with a takeover firm known for excessive leverage or for massive layoffs. Management makes such decisions by considering the broader constituent groups beyond the immediate profitability of the deal. Reputation is particularly important in the business of initial public offerings (IPOs). Some investment bankers are known for their careful screening of companies wanting to go public, so as to protect potential investors from particularly risky ventures and to get generally higher prices for the IPOs they do issue. Other investment bankers have poorer reputations in this regard, and a higher percentage of their IPOs may suffer from price decline.

COMMON LEGAL AND ETHICAL ISSUES

In the United States, financial ethical issues and financial laws generally fall into four categories. The first concerns the use or misuse of information, referred to as *informational asymmetry* and relating to a transaction where the two parties involved have unequal access to information about the deal at hand. The second type, an information asymmetry of sorts, involves the manipulation or misuse of financial markets. The third, an agency problem, entails the misuse of corporate resources. The fourth, also an agency problem, concerns customers who must rely on finance professionals or **fiduciaries** for investment advice. Breaches of the fiduciary relationship are often punishable by law.

LEGAL
and
ETHICAL
ISSUES

LIMITED PARTNERSHIPS GO SOUR

In the early to mid-1980s, Prudential Securities, Inc., the large brokerage and dealership arm of Prudential Insurance Co. sold $6 billion of limited partnerships. Many of these investments did not perform as expected. In fact, investors found that the value of some of their partnerships fell 50 percent or more.

As a result, the firm's investors in energy partnerships brought a number of class action suits against Prudential. By 1993, the firm had set up reserves from profits of $400 million to settle outstanding lawsuits. But its unhappy customers were not its only problem. The Securities and Exchange Commission, state securities regulators, the Justice Department, and the National Association of Securities Dealers all launched investigations of Prudential's sales activities relating to allegations which included misleading sales practices and fraud. Many experts felt that $400 million would not cover these settlements.

The Prudential case is a good example of the risks inherent in relying on agents in the investment of money, the important ethical and legal issues involved in financial institution management, and the effects on reputation.

Source: "Pru Securities: What the Scandal May Cost," *Business Week,* July 5, 1993.

Information Asymmetry and Financial Disclosure

Most analysts expect managers and directors of firms to have better information than outsiders. How else could the firm compete strategically? Consequently, a major issue in information asymmetries deals with the accuracy, breadth, and timeliness of financial statement reporting and press releases. Investors, analysts, and managers of financial intermediaries, to name a few, all expect sound information upon which to make their capital allocation decisions but not so much detail as to divulge trade secrets and jeopardize future earnings. On the other hand, these secrets—the approval of a drug to cure AIDS or cancer, for example—could be extremely valuable because they would no doubt increase a pharmaceutical company's share price. The person with access to this information, perhaps a lab technician or a public relations specialist, calls his stock broker and buys several thousand shares of the company's stock before the press release goes out. This practice is known as *insider trading* and is illegal in the United States. What might managers of financial institutions want to consider when trading in countries where insider dealing is legal?

Another abuse of information is outright **fraud,** where people on either side of a transaction cook the data or stretch the truth to the other party for personal gain. Accusations of fraud usually involve IPOs and lending; that's why a financial firm's reputation for screening candidates is so important to potential investors.

Financial Market Manipulation

Just as there are attempts to monopolize or otherwise control markets outside the financial services industry, so too are there attempts to manipulate the financial markets. As you might expect, most forms of manipulation are illegal in some fashion. In 1991, Salomon Brothers, Inc., admitted to breaking U.S. Treasury Department rules by acquiring a large percentage of newly issued Treasury securities, forcing other security dealers to bid higher prices for the securities from Salomon Brothers to fill their already contracted orders. Salomon Brothers was fined millions of dollars, and several of their highest ranking officers lost their jobs and were subject to numerous lawsuits.

Another form of dubious dealing involves fair execution of a customer's order. Customers typically do not have access to pricing information, especially on infrequently traded securities, but a dealer does and can profit by offering excessively large bid and ask spreads. Or the dealer will place an order for his own account before that of a customer if the dealer thinks the customer's order might cause the price of the security to rise or fall. This act is called *front-running,* where the dealer profits from buying before the customer's buy order is executed and selling before a customer's sell order is executed. On occasion, dealers buy or sell assets for their own accounts at a more favorable price than that paid in transactions made for their customers' accounts. This practice is known as *self-dealing.*

Misuse of Corporate Resources

Employees and directors sometimes use corporate resources for personal enrichment. Executive compensation practices that also raise ethical issues include:

1. Large grants of executive stock options.
2. Repricing down previously issued executive stock options of firms whose stock price had fallen.
3. Guaranteed bonuses or bonuses paid when corporate performance was poor.
4. Long-term management employment contracts.

Fiduciary Responsibilities of Intermediaries

Agents of intermediaries, such as security brokers, who control corporate or customer investment funds are occasionally accused of excessively buying and selling a customer's securities to increase the broker's commissions. This activity is called *churning the account.* Other breaches of fiduciary responsibilities include selling a customer's investments at unusually high commission rates and misrepresenting the risks of investments to clients for a commission.

✓ **Checkpoints**

1-8 How can an agency relationship be viewed in the context of managing a financial institution? What are examples of several types of agents, and what agency costs are involved in each?

1-9 What types of behavior raise ethical and legal questions, and why is a financial firm's reputation important? What are stakeholders?

1-10 What are the four main types of legal and ethical issues in terms of agency relationships and information asymmetries? Give examples of each.

1-11 What are the practices of insider trading, fraud, and self-dealing, and how must managers of financial intermediaries consider them when transacting in countries where these actions are legal?

Government Effects on Financial Institutions

Central governments are very involved in their financial systems generally and with financial institutions in particular in allocating or directing the flow of capital in several ways. Primarily, they strive to:

1. Provide an efficient payments system and stable currency.
2. Finance government activities.
3. Allocate capital directly through taxation and spending tax money.
4. Facilitate capital allocation by chartering financial institutions and issuing financial guarantees.

PROVIDE AN EFFICIENT PAYMENT SYSTEM AND STABLE CURRENCY

Most economists believe that one of the most important responsibilities of government is to provide a currency in which economic participants have confidence and to manage its availability, thereby avoiding unexpected price volatility.[4] The Federal Reserve system was established in 1913 to provide stability in the money supply as well as efficiency in the payment system. Central banks, with responsibilities similar to the Federal Reserve, are key components of financial systems in most developed countries.

---

[4]The role of a central bank in facilitating the development of an efficient payment system typically includes such activities as: (1) printing and distributing currency; (2) assisting in the clearing of checks between financial institutions; (3) managing a wire transfer system for large domestic and international transactions; (4) controlling the money supply; (5) providing for the security of the payment system; and (6) managing, maintaining, and safeguarding reserves for international transactions.

FINANCE GOVERNMENT ACTIVITIES

Central governments must collect taxes and spend funds on behalf of their constituents. To do so requires a financial intermediary such as a central bank, and most new countries charter such a bank as the first step in financial system development. In the first 100 years of U.S. history, the federal government only chartered national banks in times of war, when it needed an institution to borrow funds and pay bills. Indeed, the U.S. system of nationally chartered banks was not created until the Civil War in 1863.

ALLOCATE CAPITAL THROUGH TAXATION AND SPENDING TAX MONEY

Central governments influence the allocation of savings in a number of ways, one of which is tax law. In the United States, the tax deductibility of home mortgages, federal tax-free status of state and municipal bonds, and tax-deferred nature of savings bonds all factor into the decision-making process of savers. When the tax law negatively affects after-tax interest earnings, savers opt for more profitable investment strategies and allocate their capital elsewhere.

Through public policy, central governments also use savings directly for public-purpose investments such as roads, schools, airports, and seaports. In the United States, however, the federal government also taps a large percentage of the savings pool to finance transfer payments to individuals, so as to reallocate income.

FACILITATE CAPITAL ALLOCATION THROUGH INTERMEDIARIES

Central governments also influence the allocation of capital indirectly by chartering financial institutions and by guaranteeing deposits in these institutions. By issuing charters and insuring deposits, governments can set the standard for involvement in the payment system, thereby safeguarding the system, avoiding an inequitable distribution of financial services, and maintaining confidence in the financial institutions. Stability in the financial system enables governments to implement monetary policy in a predictable way and to avoid economic depression or hyperinflation.

In the United States, the federal government guides the allocation of savings by guaranteeing deposits of certain financial institutions and then regulating how these institutions lend these deposits. The federal government also has a large number of government operated and government sponsored enterprises (GSEs) that guarantee and lend money for specific purposes. These programs, discussed in the appendix to Chapter 3, are designed to encourage investment in residential housing and other purposes deemed important by government officials.

On the other hand, in 1991 Congress passed a law prohibiting government insured deposits from being invested in high-risk corporate bonds. By doing so, the government discouraged investments in these types of businesses. Some economists argue that as a result of this type of government involvement in our financial markets, many commercial and industrial needs for savings go unfulfilled and productivity suffers.

✓ Checkpoints

1-12   What role do governments normally play in the financial system? Which of these activities are most important in creating a more efficient savings and investment process?

1-13   How do governments influence which types of investments get funded?

Management of Financial Institutions

Thus far, the savings and investment process appears relatively simple. In fact, the process is anything but that. It requires sophisticated information systems, analytical tools, and complex organizations. Today, the United States deals in international markets for goods and services that require no less than domestic markets, which are really global. Participants in these markets face new risks as well as longer hours; and managers of financial firms need a wide variety of skills to compete. A short overview of these management activities follows.

CORPORATE PLANNING: PICKING FINANCIAL FUNCTIONS AND ASSETS

Like nonfinancial organizations, financial institutions must plan. The planning begins first with an analysis of the firm's charter or state license of incorporation.[5] Many financial intermediaries obtain charters from state and federal authorities which spell out the rules under which the firm must operate. The financial institutions with the greatest number of rules include insured depositories, security brokers and dealers, insurance companies, pension funds, and investment intermediaries such as real estate investment trusts. Some financial institutions, such as finance companies, are less regulated.

Once the firm understands its allowable activities and its customers' needs, it must choose the financial functions it will perform and the asset and liability markets in which it will participate. These decisions are not straightforward or routine; they demand careful analysis of the external environment, internal capabilities, and expected risk and returns. Chapter 2 introduces readers to the **financial function/claim matrix** as one type of tool for decision making. The purpose of the matrix is to provide a systematic way to describe the financial functions that financial institutions can perform and the range of financial assets they can use. Managers must devise strategic operating and financial action plans for

---

[5]Planning is discussed extensively in Chapter 9. The discussion includes strategic, operating and financial, and action plans.

their firm. This planning necessarily involves an assessment of the external environment as well as an assessment of the expected returns and risks of the various types of investments. These are discussed in the next two sections.

ASSESSING THE EXTERNAL ENVIRONMENT

Managers must constantly assess four basic aspects of the external environment in which they operate. These are:

1. The economy.
2. The competition.
3. The regulatory and legislative climate.
4. Technological change.

The economic and competitive environments are important since they profoundly affect expected risk and returns on various financial and real assets. These assessments are crucial to making decisions about both the functions and markets in which the firm chooses to participate.

The regulatory and legislative environment significantly affects the functions and markets in which financial institutions can engage, the minimum amount of capital needed to operate the firm, the costs of certain operations that are influenced by regulations covering social issues and examination and supervision, and the impact of government's own lending activities such as GSEs.

Finally, as information-processing companies, financial institutions must keep abreast of technological change in information processing and communication relative to operations, product development, and market globalization. Chapter 6 addresses these issues in detail.

RETURN ASSESSMENT AND RISK MANAGEMENT

Financial institutions with major portfolio management activities must develop highly specialized techniques for assessing returns and risks of the financial assets and liabilities in which they choose to engage. The management activities associated with this include:

1. Determining an optimal capital structure (Chapter 10).
2. Portfolio credit risk assessment (Chapter 11).
3. Loan and investment credit risk analysis (Chapter 12).
4. Interest rate risk measurement and management (Chapters 17 and 18).
5. Cash and liquidity management (Chapter 20).
6. Asset selection and pricing (Chapter 21).
7. Liability selection and pricing (Chapter 22).
8. Foreign exchange risk management (Chapter 19).

Managers of financial institutions face the same challenges as managers outside the financial services industry. The first relates to **capital structure,** defined as the relationship between the amount of equity and debt used to finance the firm's assets. Managers of financial institutions must determine their optimal level of debt in their capital structure. They must also manage risk effectively. Primary risks involve changes in financial asset prices due to interest rate and currency price fluctuations or quality of the investments made, referred to as *credit risk.* One has only to look the failure of savings and loans, commercial banks, and insurance companies in recent years to understand the importance of risk management.

Financial institutions are the country's largest supplier of liquid assets held by individuals, businesses, and governments. Consequently, their managers must be experts in cash and liquidity management. Financial institutions generally have many investment and financing options. As a result, maximizing the return on investments given acceptable risk and minimizing the cost of financing alternatives are major functions of management. Finally, financial institutions with international operations must understand and manage foreign exchange risk.

✓ Checkpoints

1-14 What are the most important external factors to consider when making strategic decisions for a financial institution?

1-15 What regulatory and legislative issues relate to the financial services industry?

1-16 What are the primary financial management activities that managers of financial institutions must also carry out?

Careers in Financial Institutions

Financial institutions are major employers within the U.S. labor force. As of December 31, 1991, financial and real estate-related businesses provided jobs for 6.7 million people. Exhibit 1.3 provides a breakdown of the employment within financial institutions by type of financial firm. Commercial banks are the largest employers in this group, followed by insurance companies and thrifts. Real estate employment is also shown, since a large percentage of real estate employment relates to financing real estate.

Employment growth in financial institutions weakened in the early 1990s as a result of the large number of financial institution failures and consolidations. This is likely to prevail for several more years. Ironically, the growth in jobs in the financial agencies—especially those dealing with failed institutions—has grown rapidly. As always, however, the prospective employee with good training and a solid understanding of the forces impacting financial institutions has a great advantage in the job market.

EXHIBIT 1.3

Employment Share in Financial Institutions
December 31, 1991

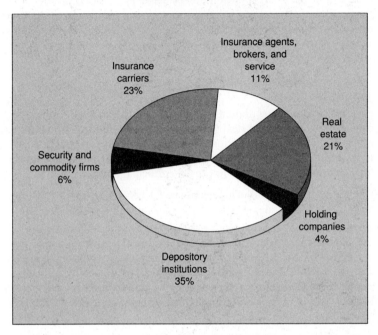

Source: *Statistical Abstract of the United States,* 1992. Department of Commerce, p. 407.

SUMMARY AND REVIEW

1. **Describe the process of financial intermediation and other financial services performed by financial institutions.**

   Intermediation, the issuing of financial liabilities to invest in other financial assets, is the most important function of financial institutions. There are many other important functions. One of the more fundamental is providing **payment services.**

2. **Explain the globalization of financial transactions relative to financial institutions management.**

   The growth in foreign trade, improved communication technologies, and economic privatization movements around the world have resulted in fast-growing globalization in financial assets, markets, and institutions.

3. **Explain and relate agency theory to financial institutions management and discuss some current agency issues that managers must consider.**

Agency theory provides the basis for understanding the potential for conflict between the owners of capital and the agents who invest capital on their behalf. These **agents** include management and directors of commercial, industrial, and financial organizations. Since agents will not necessarily act in accordance with the owner's desires, there is a need to expend substantial resources on monitoring and controlling agents. These costs are known as **agency costs.** The federal government, as an insurer of deposits, must also spend significant resources for monitoring and control.

4. **Discuss some key ethical and legal issues involving the management of financial institutions.**

   Ethical and legal issues abound in the area of financial institutions. The most common areas of abuse deal with the **misuse of information (information asymmetries),** the **manipulation of financial markets (information asymmetries), misuse of corporate resources (agent/principal issues),** and **misuse of financial resources of customers (agent/principal issues).**

5. **Discuss government influence on financial institutions and their management.**

   Governments are typically active participants in the financial system. They can impact private-sector economic units by: (1) assisting in the development of an **efficient payment system and maintenance of stable currency;** (2) creating financial institutions to **finance government activities;** (3) **allocating capital through taxation and spending;** (4) indirectly contributing to the allocation of capital by chartering financial institutions and issuing financial guarantees.

6. **Explain how financial institutions benefit from the strategic management processes of corporate planning, assessing the external environment, and assessing financial asset expected risk and returns.**

   The primary duties of the management of financial intermediaries include planning at the **strategic, operating and financial,** and **action** levels. Also involved is reviewing the external environment, including reviewing **economic and competitive trends,** the **regulatory and legislative** climate, and **technological** changes. Finally, the duties of financial intermediary management include: (1) determining the **optimal capital structure;** (2) managing **credit, currency, and interest rate risks;** (3) **pricing** and **selecting** investments and liabilities; and (4) **operating effectively,** using information processing and communication technologies.

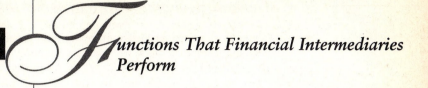

CHAPTER 2

*F*unctions That Financial Intermediaries Perform

Learning Goals

After studying this chapter, you should be able to:

1. Define the role of financial institutions within a financial system.
2. Describe the most important financial transformations made by intermediaries.
3. Describe the relationship among an intermediary's four primary functions of origination, servicing, brokerage, and portfolio management.
4. Explain how intermediaries decide which claims to buy and which to issue.
5. Show how to use the financial claim/function matrix.

Do you know what type of institution services your savings or checking account? What about your student loan, your home mortgage, or your car lease? You might be transacting with any number of different financial firms. In recent years, legislation and deregulation have allowed financial institutions to compete in the same markets by offering the same products and servicing the same customers, to the point of blurring the institutional differences among them. Yet, within each group, the individual firms differ significantly: a small commercial bank is more like a savings bank in its activities than it is like a large commercial bank, and a large commercial bank performs more like an investment banking firm. And so students of the financial services industry should focus on the similarities of products and functions before looking at the differences among aggregate data of each financial firm. This chapter provides an overview of the products and functions performed by all or most firms, and then Chapter 3 moves onto the description of the key players.

General Economic Rationales for Intermediaries

While much of the recent literature on intermediation has attempted to explain why intermediaries exist, no single explanation has reached wide acceptance. Among the important rationales are the following:

1. They reduce transaction costs.
2. They operate the payment system.
3. They monitor information important to investors.

These rationales are not mutually exclusive and provide a fairly comprehensive understanding of the intermediary and the intermediation process. They all support the hypothesis that financial markets are not perfectly efficient. **Efficient financial markets** are assumed to be markets with negligible transaction costs, perfect and costless information for borrowers and lenders, and infinite allotments in the denomination of financial claims. Relaxing these assumptions opens the opportunity to form intermediaries, go-betweens, that can perform various functions at a net cost lower than what governments, individuals, and firms could accomplish on their own.

TRANSACTION COST REDUCTION RATIONALE

One major source of improved efficiency is the reduction of transaction costs, the costs of exchanging financial products between the sellers or capital surplus units (CSUs) and the buyers or capital deficit units (CDUs). Intermediaries reduce transaction costs by originating and servicing financial claims and by managing portfolios of claims. Intermediaries create financial assets and liabilities through processes called *transformations,* conversions of one type of claim into a more marketable one. Financial institutions also reduce **search costs,** which are transaction costs incurred when finding sellers and buyers to participate in the exchange. One search process that reduces transactions costs is called *brokerage,* a function of financial firms which involves the creation of markets and dealerships to bring buyers and sellers of financial claims together.

PAYMENT SYSTEM RATIONALE

The early work of monetary economists on the subject of financial intermediation concerned the intermediary's role in creating liabilities that serve as a **medium of exchange,** any claim used to facilitate an exchange.[1] Studies concentrated on how intermediaries implemented monetary policy and created the transaction balances that central governments, households, and business units

---

[1]Students who have taken a course in money and banking in an economics department will be familiar with the emphasis placed in these courses on the role of financial institutions, especially commercial banks, in facilitating financial transactions and assisting in the implementation of monetary policy.

would use in exchange. These economists regarded commercial banks as essential to a smoothly functioning payment system, as very special economic units requiring special attention. Over time, **near monies,** the various liabilities that are not demand deposits like checking accounts but are accepted as mediums of exchange, have broadened the concept of money and liquidity.[2]

Developing countries without established financial systems appreciate the need for an efficient payment system. Without one, these countries must rely on large amounts of currency—often that of another country—or else barter goods and services. *Bartering* describes the process of exchanging of actual goods and services without the convenience of a medium of exchange.

INFORMATION-MONITORING RATIONALE

Another major rationale for the existence of intermediaries is that they collect and analyze data about potential borrowers and sellers. Intermediaries originate loans and securities that are valuable to CDUs; at the same time, they produce financial claims which are liabilities written against themselves and which are valuable to CSUs. Through financial transformations, the CDUs obtain capital on better terms than if they attempted to negotiate directly with CSUs. Similarly, the CSUs obtain investments that are more desirable than what they could obtain through direct negotiation with CDUs. For example, making sound loans requires accumulating extensive data on the prospective borrower. Data must be monitored over time to ensure that a borrower is living up to the provisions in the financial asset. Financial institutions relieve CSUs of having to perform this expensive activity by issuing liabilities against themselves that are more desirable to CSUs than what they could obtain through direct negotiation.

Delegated monitoring describes this basic rationale of intermediaries. For example, CSUs hire intermediaries to monitor the financial performance of CDUs over time. This service is particularly useful when the firm's debt is held by many CSUs. Otherwise, each CSU would have to monitor the CDU separately, which would cost substantially more than having one agent perform this function.

✓ Checkpoints

2-1   What are the three basic rationales for financial institutions?

2-2   What types of transaction costs are financial institutions most likely to reduce for their users?

2-3   If financial institutions are said to be information processing companies, what types of information do they process?

2-4   What is meant by *delegated monitoring*? What is the economic justification for establishing intermediaries that relates to this concept?

---

[2]*Near money* is a term rarely used today. Over the last several decades, the number of liabilities that can be used as a medium of exchange has expanded significantly, as has the number of financial institutions that provide these products. In addition, the growth in debit and credit cards has made a strict definition of money less important.

Financial Claim Creation and Transformation

Asset and liability transformation is the conversion of products with one set of characteristics into products with potentially very different characteristics. Through these transformations, financial institutions simultaneously create desirable financial claims issued by CDUs and others purchased by CSUs. These transformations account for most of the loans and securities such as auto loans, bonds, and business loans, and liability products such as savings accounts, life insurance reserves, and pension fund reserves of intermediaries.

Traditionally, financial experts emphasized denomination, maturity (or duration), and marketability transformations. In addition to these, intermediaries transform the credit-risk characteristics, the monetary unit or currency, the extent to which the product serves as a medium of exchange, and the efficiency of a market. Anyone who plans to work within the financial services industry—particularly as a manager of a financial firm—must understand what each transformation seeks to accomplish. The following section introduces each type, and later chapters detail how to manage each transformation.

DENOMINATION TRANSFORMATION

- Rarely does a CSU have the exact amount of funds needed by a CDU. And so the intermediary transforms the denomination. This *denomination transformation,* perhaps the most common type of transformation, involves selling liabilities in denominations that differ from those of the assets held. For instance, a mutual fund sells shares in denominations of several dollars but invests in securities worth thousands of dollars. Other examples include converting various-sized deposits into loans, and underwriting and distributing stocks and bonds in small amounts.

MATURITY OR DURATION TRANSFORMATION

- *Maturity transformation* relates to the actions of some intermediaries in issuing liabilities that have different maturities from the assets in which they invest. For example, most of the liabilities, such as demand deposits and savings accounts, of thrift institutions remain very short-term in nature, while the primary asset of the thrift is a long-term home mortgage. These maturities undergo transformation through the activities of the intermediary. Other examples include issuing long-term pension liabilities and investing in short-term bonds, and issuing long-term bonds and investing in credit card receivables.

MARKETABILITY TRANSFORMATION

- *Marketability transformation* refers to the activities of many financial institutions that hold less marketable assets and issue highly marketable liabilities. Their ability to create marketable liabilities while holding less marketable assets stems, in part, from the economies of scale in their own liquid-asset management activities, as well as certain advantages they might have. Many financial institutions are experts in generating and managing cash, which allows them to offer customers such products as transaction accounts. One such advantage is the ability some depositories have to borrow from the Federal Reserve's discount window, the Federal Home Loan Banks, or the Credit Union Liquidity Fund. These federal government credit facilities provide emergency and longer-term borrowing facilities for depositories, allowing depository institutions to hold smaller liquid-asset holdings than otherwise. Other examples include issuing marketable asset-backed bonds using less marketable installment loans, and creating standardized futures contracts.

CREDIT RISK TRANSFORMATION

- *Credit risk transformation* relates to the differences between the credit risk of an intermediary's assets and that of its liabilities. A large percentage of the assets of most financial depository institutions are below investment grade. Nevertheless, these intermediaries sell liabilities that have investment-grade ratings or the full faith and credit of the U.S. government, thanks to deposit insurance. This is a major transformation. Less well known are the securitization activities of intermediaries. These are financial claims in which intermediaries use overcollateralization to transform the credit quality of a collateralized security. Other examples include issuing senior-subordinated securities using high-risk financial claims and issuing third-party guarantees on risky debt.

CURRENCY TRANSFORMATION

- *Currency transformation* relates to alterations in the currency of financial claims. With the growth in international transactions, the need for currency transformations has grown rapidly. Much of this involves foreign exchange. Somewhat less well known has been the growth in the currency swap market. Commercial banks have been leaders in arranging for foreign institutions to swap funds in two different currencies for repayment at a later date. Other examples include selling securities issued in foreign currencies and creating a mutual fund that holds foreign securities.

PROVIDING A MEDIUM OF EXCHANGE

- *Creating mediums of exchange* relates to the payment system rationale of intermediaries, a very specific type of marketability transformation but traditionally defined separately from that transformation. There has been significant innovation in the creation of new mediums of exchange over the last several decades. The bank credit card is the preferred medium of exchange for many consumers. Other examples include providing electronic payment services and creating debit cards and pre-authorized payment services.

ENHANCING MARKET EFFICIENCY

- Many financial institutions are engaged in brokerage and security trading activities, which have as their by-product the enhancement of market efficiency.[3] Financial firms specialize in buying, selling, and brokering specific types of securities. Market efficiency is improved through the reduction in the bid-ask spread for a specific security. Other examples include trading of securities for a firm's own portfolio and dealing specified types of securities.

✓ Checkpoints

2-5   What are at least four asset and liability transformations that financial institutions perform? What products and services do intermediaries offer that involve these transformations?

2-6   How do financial intermediaries contribute to market efficiency?

The Functions of Intermediaries

To faciliate the transformations, create the many products, and provide various services, intermediaries must also perform certain basic functions. Those common to all intermediaries are origination, servicing, and brokerage of financial claims, and portfolio risk management. The first three of these functions involve information processing as their primary feature. The last, portfolio management, broadly incorporates a group of activities that includes managing all asset and liability risks. The following section considers each of these four functions separately.

FINANCIAL CLAIM ORIGINATION

From an intermediary's perspective, the creation of a financial claim may be an asset or a liability. **Origination,** called *underwriting* in the security business, involves the primary activities associated with the creation of a new financial claim—credit underwriting, document preparation, creation of covenants, as well as the processing activities related to closing the transaction. Exhibit 2.1 shows

---

[3]Enhancing market efficiency is a somewhat abstract concept. It is meant to highlight the value served by institutions active in realizing value through the trading of loans and securities. Markets with many buyers and sellers tend to have small differences between bid and ask prices. This lowers transaction costs and makes markets more efficient.

the relationship between the originating institution and the issuer and owner of a financial claim: the originating institution can create a financial claim for its own portfolio or as an agent for another third-party portfolio.

Origination also involves selecting the most cost-effective channel of distribution for attracting loan, investment, or liability customers. For a retail bank, deposit gathering might include using branch banks, telemarketing, direct mail, and an agent. Similar choices would exist for selecting a channel of distribution for a credit card. Originating a financial claim often includes the following activities, all of which are covered in later chapters from the managerial perspective:

- *Credit underwriting (or credit scoring):* Performing credit analysis to determine the riskiness of a financial claim.

EXHIBIT 2.1

Origination Function

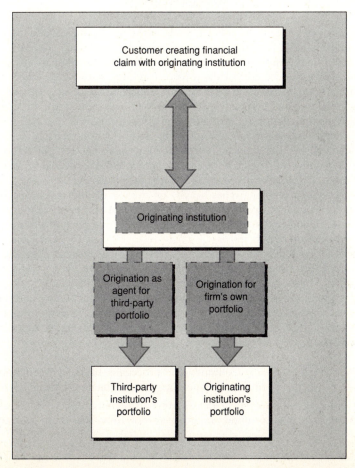

- *Financial claim documentation:* Creating legally binding documents that protect the interests of both the issuer of the claim and its purchaser.
- *Development of covenants:* Creating provisions to reduce the risks of the purchaser of a debt financial claim.
- *Collateral review:* Inspecting and appraising any collateral used to reduce the risk of a debt financial claim.
- *Loan disbursement:* Developing a process to insure that settlement of a financial transaction protects the parties to it.
- *Document control:* Developing, reviewing, and safeguarding of legal documents evidencing rights of the financial claim issuer and purchaser, such as legal documents evidencing ownership of collateral.
- *Selection of channel of distribution:* Selecting the most cost-efficient method of reaching customers for issuing or buying financial claims.

FINANCIAL CLAIM SERVICING

Servicing often means the collection and payment of principal and interest on assets and liabilities. Actually, however, it includes everything related to facilitating and monitoring financial transactions: managing the mechanisms, such as demand deposits and credit cards, for operating the nation's payment system; monitoring loans to ensure that borrowers adhere to the loan covenants; controlling collateral; and performing other problem-loan related activities. Exhibit 2.2 diagrams the relationship of the servicing function to the customer who can issue a financial claim or own one and to the servicing organization.

Someone outside the financial institution may not see its servicing responsibilities or may underestimate its importance to the intermediary. Many institutions devote most of their human resources to servicing assets and liabilities.

Financial claim servicing relies heavily on the use of information processing technology. Computers process the collection of payments on consumer and business loans and update records on the many deposit accounts, mutual fund shares, and insurance policies.

Other servicing activities include loan restructuring, repossessions and foreclosures, collateral disposition, and implementing legal remedies. Loan-servicing units within a financial intermediary must keep good records on the performance of borrowers meeting their obligations under loan contracts. This information permits the firm to respond quickly to default situations. It also can determine how to obtain the best value for repossessed and foreclosed assets. Key servicing activities are:

- *Processing payments:* Collecting and processing payments required under the provisions of financial claims such as principal and interest payments.
- *Collecting past-due payments:* Creating a system for collection of past-due payments called for under the provisions of a financial claim contract.

EXHIBIT 2.2

Servicing Function

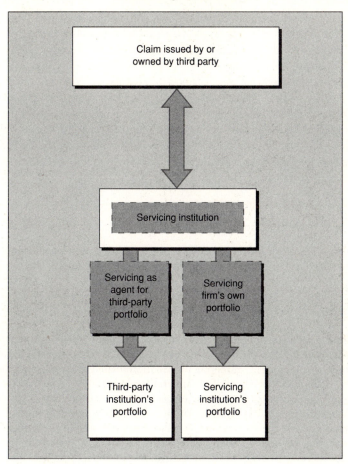

- *Controlling collateral:* Inspecting, inventorying, and appraising collateral over the life of a debt financial claim.
- *Safekeeping collateral:* Providing for the safekeeping of collateral called for under a debt financial claim.
- *Monitoring covenants and borrower's financial condition:* Providing the delegated monitoring services over the life of a financial debt claim.
- *Developing delinquency and credit-risk reports:* Providing reports and analyses to assess ongoing credit loss experience to assist in pricing loans.
- *Implementing problem-loan legal remedies:* Managing the legal issues related to collection of defaulted debt financial claims.

How

it

Really

Works

CUTTING THE COST OF SERVICING ACCOUNTS

For decades, retail depositories have experimented with electronic systems to reduce their need for costly brick and mortar offices which are primarily used to service existing accounts. Home banking, with and without computers, has largely failed. Enter Midland Bank in Britain.

Midland Bank has created Firstdirect, Britain's only retail telephone bank. Firstdirect decided that simplicity is best. They provide 24-hour telephone access to a person that will process money transfers, sell accounts, and process loan applications. The trick is that Firstdirect's staff inputs the information into computers rather than requiring customers to do it from their own computers or using touch-tone phones. The bank convinced over 400,000 customers to sign up for the service in only four years. The management claims the service lowers costs.

Source: "Dial C for Cash," *Economist,* June 19, 1993, pp. 75–76.

- *Disposing of problem-loan collateral:* Developing systems and procedures for disposing of the foreclosed and repossessed collateral.

FINANCIAL CLAIM BROKERAGE

Brokerage involves two very significant information processing functions: (1) identifying potential buyers and sellers of various financial claims the intermediary is interested in, and (2) gathering information related to establishing the market value of a particular claim. The demand for brokerage services derives from the need of financial asset portfolio managers to alter their portfolio's structure in response to changes in expectations of risk and return, liquidity, and changing conditions. They do this by buying and selling securities and other financial assets using brokerage services. Exhibit 2.3 depicts the relationship between the brokering institution and its customers: an institution can broker financial claims into and out of its own portfolio and that of third-parties or between third-parties.

Brokerage also involves reviewing various distribution channels to determine the best price for an asset or liability that the intermediary might create. By surveying competitor prices for a given financial claim, such as a loan or deposit, the brokerage function helps to answer the questions, Should the firm fund its needs with retail or wholesale funds? Should the firm originate home mortgages or purchase them in the secondary market? Other key brokerage activities include:

- *Identifying borrower needs:* Assessing and developing loan and security products that CDUs would desire.
- *Identifying saver needs:* Assessing and developing investment products that CSUs would desire.
- *Monitoring prices of financial claims:* Assessing and evaluating prices of financial claims.

EXHIBIT 2.3

Brokerage Function

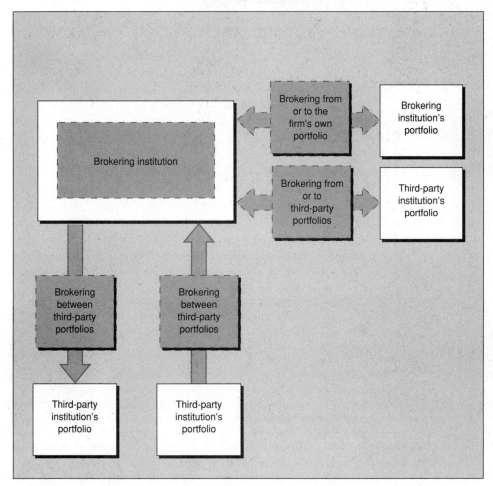

- *Monitoring other terms and conditions of the claims:* Assessing and evaluating risk factors that impact the value of financial claims.

PORTFOLIO RISK MANAGEMENT

Portfolio risk management is the heart of intermediation: the selection of assets and liabilities the firm chooses to purchase or issue. The firm considers all risk aspects of the portfolio and then performs its asset and liability transformation services by combining the information on customer needs gathered in the brokerage function with information on the status of the firm's portfolio. While many financial institutions perform origination, servicing, and brokerage functions—or some combination of them—with a portfolio of assets and liabilities, only a subset of financial institutions provides portfolio risk management services.

Portfolio risk management uses information from the brokerage function and the servicing function to help establish the firm's asset and liability strategies. Major activities of the portfolio risk management function detailed later in this book are:

- *Setting prices for assets and liabilities:* Performing financial claim valuation analyses in order to determine prices to buy and sell financial claims.
- *Managing credit risk:* Assessing credit risks for purposes of developing an optimal combination of risk and return in an investment portfolio.
- *Managing interest rate risk:* Measuring and managing the risk that the value of a firm's assets will rise or fall in value more than the firm's liabilities, creating a decline in equity.
- *Managing liquidity:* Managing cash flow.
- *Managing mortality risk:* Managing liabilities that are contingent on the life of an investor or beneficiary.
- *Performing arbitrage:* Engaging in financial claim trading with the purpose of buying in one market and selling in another at a profit.
- *Providing financial guarantees:* Using the firm's financial strength to reduce the risk of financial claims issued by another party.

Portfolio risk managers in many respects affect the other functions within the firm. They price assets and liabilities to ensure that the institution can operate profitably, and they manage interest rate risk. Analysts who provide quantitative measurements of the interest rate position of the firm submit their reports to portfolio risk managers.

Although assisted by many other groups within the firm, the portfolio risk management group must understand the credit risks inherent in the firm's asset portfolio. Again, credit risk is a portfolio concern since the risks of various types of assets differ and many assets react differently to changing general and local economic trends. Diversification reduces credit risks to manageable levels. Portfolio credit risks must also include any financial guarantees that the firm provides on securities or assets it sells or on securities it guarantees for others. In insurance companies and pension funds, the portfolio risk management group controls the mortality risk of the firm or portfolio.

✓ Checkpoints

2-7   What are the four primary functions of intermediaries?

2-8   What is the relationship of origination, servicing, and brokerage institutions to their customers and other third-parties?

2-9   What are the primary management functions related to portfolio management?

2-10   What risks must be managed in the portfolio management function?

2-11   What determines the financial functions performed by any particular intermediary?

2-12 What are the primary activities associated with origination? What are the primary activities associated with servicing? What are the primary activities associated with brokerage? What are the primary activities associated with portfolio management?

The Financial Claim/Function Matrix

The **financial claim/function** matrix, introduced in Table 2.1, puts each of the four functions, on both the asset and liability sides of the balance sheet, into a comprehensive framework.

TABLE 2.1

Financial Claim/Function Matrix for Assets

Type of Claim	Origination	Servicing	Brokerage	Portfolio Management
Government:				
United States				
Agency				
State and municipal				
Business:				
Corporate bonds				
Equities				
Income-property mortgages				
Leases				
Loans				
Household:				
Installment				
Credit card				
Residential mortgages				
Foreign:				
Government				
Business				

The financial intermediary appears as an information processing firm that gathers, handles, and analyzes data in its origination, servicing, and brokerage functions and manages a portfolio of assets and liabilities, viewed as the firm's risk management activities. Interest rate and credit risks are present whenever the firm takes a financial claim onto its balance sheet, which could be for a short time, as when trading securities. Table 2.2 provides a similar comprehensive schematic for the liability side of the intermediary's balance sheet.

Managers of any intermediary, from the most complex money center bank to the simplest mutual fund, can use the matrix to:

1. Describe the current business activities and markets served by an institution.

2. Plan for future new activities and markets when analyzing business opportunities and forecasting growth.

3. Structure a performance evaluation system, for example, by identifying costs and revenues associated with each function.

TABLE 2.2

Financial Claim/Function
Matrix for Liabilities

Type of Claim	Origination	Servicing	Brokerage	Portfolio Management
Transaction accounts:				
Demand deposits				
NOW accounts				
Money market demand accounts				
Time and savings deposits:				
Passbook accounts				
Certificates of deposit				
Other retail funding sources:				
Life insurance reserves				
Pension fund reserves				
Mutual fund shares				

4. Assist in organizational planning, such as by identifying activities associated with entering a new asset or liability market.

5. Aid in organization control, such as by outlining responsibilities and procedures necessary for regulatory compliance.

You can describe any intermediary by identifying those business transformations a firm makes and with what financial claims. Management preference, business strategy, law, and regulation really distinguish one firm from another.

AN EXAMPLE OF THE SMALL COMMERCIAL BANK

The financial claim/function matrix can be used to describe the functions of any intermediary. Consider the case of the 1st National Bank of Porter, Indiana. This bank, with $40 million in assets, is located in a small, isolated town. It has few investment options. The balance sheet is shown in Table 2.3.

Table 2.2, continued

Type of Claim	Origination	Servicing	Brokerage	Portfolio Management
Capital market funding sources:				
Collateralized debt:				
FHLB advances				
Secured bank loans				
Repos				
Asset-backed securities				
Unsecured debt:				
Negotiable CDs				
Bankers' acceptances				
Commercial paper				
Unsecured bank loans				
Debentures				

TABLE 2.3

Balance Sheet
1st National Bank of Porter, Indiana
December 31, 1995
(in millions)

Assets		Liabilities	
Cash and U.S. government		Demand deposits	$14
bonds	$12	CDs	22
Commercial loans	14		
Mortgages	11		
Auto loans	2		
Building and equipment	1	Net worth	4
Total	$40	Total	$40

Table 2.4 shows the financial claim/financial function matrix for 1st National Bank. The matrix indicates that the bank originates and services commercial business loans, mortgages, and auto loans in the primary market. The bank also acts as a market maker and portfolio manager for these assets. It also purchases government securities where it is a market maker and portfolio manager.

On the liability side of the balance sheet, the bank originates demand deposits and certificates of deposit, both of which it services.

TABLE 2.4

Financial Claim/Function Matrix for Assets and Liabilities
1st National Bank of Porter, Indiana

Type of Claim	Origination	Servicing	Brokerage	Portfolio Management
Assets				
Government:				
United States			X	X
Agency				
State and municipal				
Business:				
Corporate bonds				
Equities				

continued

Table 2.4, continued

Type of Claim	Origination	Servicing	Brokerage	Portfolio Management
Mortgages				
Leases				
Loans	X	X	X	X
Household:				
Installment	X	X	X	X
Credit card				
Mortgages	X	X	X	X
Foreign:				
Liabilities				
Demand deposits	X	X	X	X
Certificates of deposit	X	X	X	X

INDIA INSURANCE COMPANY FINANCIAL CLAIM/FUNCTION MATRIX

Table 2.5 is a financial claim/function matrix of a medium-sized life insurance company. India Insurance Company was founded in Michigan in 1925. It expanded into several other Midwest states and now does business in Illinois, Ohio, Michigan, Kentucky, and Iowa. The firm has grown to $125 million in assets. The firm writes primarily whole life policies and term insurance on individuals, relying on a small but successful in-house sales force. In recent years, due to competition in the industry, it expanded its product offering to include single premium annuities. The investment strategy of the company emphasizes very conservative investments, including high-grade corporate bonds, U.S. government and agency securities, a small amount of preferred stock, and the balance in mortgage-backed securities. The firm obtains all its assets in the secondary markets. It has, however, recently created a small commercial real estate loan department that originates small loans on office buildings and retail strip shopping centers in and around Indianapolis, where its main office is located.

Table 2.5 shows the balance sheet for the company as of December 31, 1995. The financial claim/function matrix for the India Insurance Company is shown in Table 2.6.

The financial claim/function matrix is a good reference for the activities of any intermediary.

TABLE 2.5

Balance Sheet
India Insurance Company
December 31, 1995
(in millions)

Assets		Liabilities	
Cash and U.S. and agency money market instruments	$ 9	Policy reserves:	
		Term insurance	$ 15
		Whole life	46
Corporate bonds	56	Annuities	24
Preferred stock	14	Single premium whole life	10
Mortgage securities	35		
Commercial mortgages	11	Net worth	20
Total	$125	Total	$125

TABLE 2.6

Financial Claim/Function Matrix for Assets and Liabilities
India Insurance Company

Type of Claim	Origination	Servicing	Brokerage	Portfolio Management
Assets				
Government:				
United States			X	X
Agency			X	X
State and municipal				
Business:				
Corporate securities				
Equities (preferred)			X	X
Leases				
Commercial mortgages	X	X	X	X
Mortgage securities		X	X	X
Loans				

continued

Table 2.6, *continued*

Type of Claim	Origination	Servicing	Brokerage	Portfolio Management
Household:				
Installment				
Mortgages				
Foreign:				
Liabilities				
Insurance reserves:				
Term insurance reserves	X	X		X
Whole life and annuity	X	X		X

✓ Checkpoints

2-13 What is the advantage of considering an intermediary in terms of the functions it performs?

2-14 If you were put in charge of a task force charged with establishing a unit within the commercial bank you work for to offer loans on recreational vehicles, what would you do to make sure the bank could handle this business effectively? Use the financial claim/function matrix to identify the functions you would have to put in place to handle this new activity.

SUMMARY AND REVIEW

1. **Define the role of financial institutions within a financial system.**

   The intermediary is an economic unit whose overall rationale is to **reduce transaction costs.** Reducing transaction costs is the primary rationale of financial intermediaries. Intermediaries also provide a **medium of exchange** and contribute to the smooth functioning of the payments system. **Information processing** and **delegated monitoring** are two other ways intermediaries reduce transaction costs.

2. **Describe the most important financial transformations made by intermediaries.**

   The products and services of intermediaries were discussed in terms of financial transformations. Intermediaries typically sell liabilities that are different from their assets. This process is a **financial transformation.** The products and services of intermediaries relate to the transformation of assets and liabilities. These transformations include (1) **denomination,** (2) **credit,** (3) **marketability,** (4) **currency,** (5) **maturity,** (6) **market efficiency,** and (7) **medium of exchange.**

3. **Describe the relationship among an intermediary's four primary functions of origination, servicing, brokerage, and portfolio management.**

    The following are the primary functions of intermediaries: (1) **origination,** (2) **servicing,** (3) **brokerage,** and (4) **portfolio management.** Origination involves creating financial claims. Servicing involves all the activities related to ongoing maintenance of the claims. Brokerage involves participating in financial markets so financial claims can be bought and sold. Portfolio management relates to a host of activities concerning the management of financial assets and liabilities.

4. **Explain how intermediaries decide which claims to buy and which to issue.**

    An intermediary's selection of financial claims and functions is a matter of law and regulation relating to the firm's charter and the choices of management.

5. **Show how to use the financial claim/function matrix.**

    The **financial claim/function matrix** is a schematic which describes the functions of a particular intermediary and the claims relating to each function. It is used to describe the current activities of a financial institution, to plan for new activities, to structure a performance evaluation system, and to assist in organization planning.

CASE 2.1

FINANCIAL FUNCTIONS: SOUTH REGIONAL BANK

The South Regional Bank was founded in North Carolina in the 1800s. The regional amalgamation of banks in the Southeast was exactly what the management had hoped would happen to increase the growth opportunities for the bank. It now has over 125 offices in four states. Tables C2.1 and C2.2, respectively, show the bank's statement of sources and uses of funds and a balance sheet for 1996. This statement is used to develop a financial claims/function matrix.

The bank has several other activities that may not be apparent from the statements. The bank is a major originator and seller of loans on apartments to the FNMA and FHLMC. It currently services over $650 million of such loans. In addition, the bank makes and immediately sells loans guaranteed under the federal student loan program. It does not service these loans. Finally, the bank will purchase U.S. Treasury securities for its customers. These securities are purchased in the name of the customer, and the bank does not put them on its books.

TABLE C2.1

Sources and Uses of Funds Statement for 1996
(in millions)

Category	Source	Uses
Cash	$ 12	
U.S. Treasury securities		$ 5
U.S. agency securities		12
Mortgage pass-through securities		124
Consumer loans		
Auto loans		43
R/V and boat loans		12
Credit card receivables		13
Mortgage loans		
Home mortgages	74	145
Apartment loans	34	34
Commercial mortgages		54
Business loans		
Commercial loans		143
Participations purchased (sold)		23
Municipal securities	44	15
Demand deposits	39	
Time deposits	325	
Subordinated debt	50	
Repurchase agreements		
Retained earnings	45	
Total	$623	$623

TABLE C2.2

South Regional Bank
Balance Sheet
December 31, 1996
(in millions)

Assets	
Cash due from banks	$ 324
Government and agency securities	
Treasury securities	430
Agency securities	850
State and municipal securities	332
Consumer loans	
Auto loans	724
R/V and boat loans	76
Credit card receivables	546
Mortgages	
Home mortgages	1,534
Apartment mortgages	123
Commercial mortgages	365
Business loans	
Commercial loans	2,700
Total	$8,004
Liabilities	
Demand deposits	$2,345
Time deposits	4,900
Repurchase agreement	23
Subordinated debt	50
Capital	
Retained earnings	676
Stockholder's equity	10
Total	$8,004

PROBLEMS

1. Fill out a financial claim/function matrix for the bank. Use Tables C2.1 and C2.2.

2. How did you treat the Treasury securities the bank purchases for its customers?

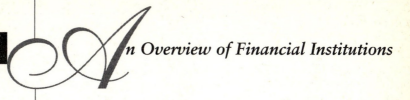

An Overview of Financial Institutions

Now that you have a framework for understanding what intermediaries do to facilitate the allocation of capital through transforming financial products, you can focus on the major financial institutions themselves. While all financial firms in general serve the four basic functions of origination, service, brokerage, and portfolio management, each institution's charter does help to distinguish one type of firm from the next, in terms of legal and regulatory constraints. The charter defines what the firm can and cannot do, and these legal parameters obviously affect the firm's operations and business strategy. And so the real differences among firms lie in the managerial talent, insight, and input into each strategic and executive decision: What financial assets and liabilities will the firm transform, and how will it transform them? What markets should the firm pursue? "Management Highlights" sections showcase some of these managerial challenges from within each type of institution, providing a better feel for the managerial differences among them.

Financial Institutions

Today, the charters of financial firms allow for considerable overlap in products and markets; in fact, many large corporate holding companies own several different types of financial institutions. But you may find further classification helpful in your study of institutions. Based on the historically dominant financial functions that intermediaries perform, four broad types of financial firms are:

1. **Depositories,** which issue government insured deposits such as savings accounts and certificates of deposit, comprising commercial banks, savings and loan associations, savings banks, and credit unions.

2. **Contractual savings institutions,** which receive periodic payments from customers to fund life insurance policies or pension reserves, comprising life insurance companies and pension funds.

3. **Specialized financial institutions,** comprising investment banking firms and finance companies which provide a range of financial functions, but do not issue government-insured deposits.

4. **Investment-oriented intermediaries,** comprising open-end mutual funds, limited partnerships, and real estate investment trusts which are chartered under special tax laws to avoid taxation of their income at the organization level.

These firms compete with one another for the same customers and with many of the same products. Large commercial **bank holding companies (BHC)** own stock in several separate companies—one example is J. P. Morgan & Co., which owns an investment banking firm that underwrites and distributes securities. Citicorp, the U.S.'s largest bank holding company, owns a number of savings and loan associations throughout the United States. Prudential Insurance Co. owns a large investment banking firm. Sears, Roebuck & Co., AT&T, and General Motors Company are all major players in the credit card market. Household Finance, a financing intermediary, possesses a large savings and loan, as does the Ford Motor Co. As handy as the above four classifications might be for pedagogical purposes, they will not help to describe the competitive global landscape.

Table 3.1 shows the total financial assets of most of the major intermediaries at year-end 1980 and 1993. The table reveals some important trends. First, depository institutions, those which issue government insured deposits, are losing market share of total financial assets relative to nondepository institutions, those that do not issue deposits. Second, the pension funds and mutual funds have become the largest sources of long-term capital in the United States.

✓ Checkpoints

3-1 What is the difference between depository and nondepository financial institutions?

3-2 What are contractual savings institutions? Why do you suppose they are called that?

| TABLE 3.1 |

Total Financial Assets of Major Financial Institutions 1980 and 1993
(dollars in billions)

	Year		
			Annual Percent Change
	1980	1993	1980–1993
Depositories:			
Commericial banks	$1,482	$3,869	7.7%
Savings and loans and savings banks	893	1,033	1.1
Credit unions	68	281	11.5
Total depositories	$2,443	$5,183	6.0%
Nondepositories:			
Life insurance companies	$ 464	$1,792	11.0%
Pension funds	668	3,401	13.3
Finance companies	243	658	8.0
Property and casualty companies	182	637	10.1
Investments banks	45	465	19.7
Mutual funds	138	1,986	22.8
Total Nondepositories	$1,558	$8,939	14.4%

Source: *Flow of Funds Accounts, Fourth Quarter 1993,* Boards of Governors of the Federal Reserve System, March 4, 1994.

Commercial Banks

With the broadest asset and liability authority granted by charter among the depositories, commercial banks are the most diversified of the U.S. depository institutions. Although commercial banks historically have emphasized their need to maintain adequate liquidity for operating the nation's payment system, many small commercial banks are simply not large enough to offer a broad range of services effectively. Therefore, their asset and liability structures, quite simple in nature, resemble those of specialized savings and loans or of savings banks. As you might expect, the larger the bank's assets, the more diversified its asset and liability structure.

Commercial banks are often classified further as community, regional, super-regional, money center, or international banks, based on size and markets served. BHCs own most large banks; by owning several other financial firms, BHCs can diversify activities and reduce risks.

- **Community banks** are banks with assets below $500 million that service medium-sized cities or rural counties and may also be located in neighborhoods of larger cities.

- **Regional banks** generally range from $500 million in assets to upwards of $10 billion. They serve large metropolitan areas or whole states.
- **Super-regional banks** are BHCs that have expanded to include multiple states and metropolitan areas and usually hold over $10 billion in assets. Examples of BHCs are First Chicago Corp. in Chicago and Bank One Corp. in Columbus, Ohio.
- **Money center or international banks** are BHCs with assets of $50 billion or more, which usually provide virtually all types of bank products and services and have significant international activities. Examples include Citicorp and Chemical Banking, both of New York, and BankAmerica in San Francisco.

ASSET STRUCTURE OF COMMERCIAL BANKS

As Exhibit 3.1 shows, commercial banks have considerable latitude in choosing the types of financial assets to hold—including securities, commercial and industrial loans, real estate loans, and loans to individuals.

EXHIBIT 3.1

Financial Assets Held by All Commercial Banks (December 1993)

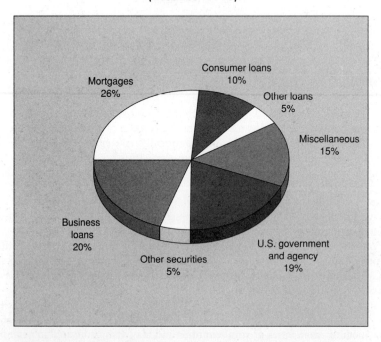

Source: *Flow of Funds Accounts, Fourth Quarter 1993*, Board of Governors of the Federal Reserve System, March 9, 1994, p. 86

Securities

Exhibit 3.1 also reveals that commercial banks hold large securities portfolios of U.S. government and other securities, equal to 19% and 5%, respectively, of their financial assets. Banks hold such large portfolios for two reasons. First, as the largest issuers of transaction accounts such as demand deposits used in transactions, commercial banks must maintain highly liquid securities to meet potential withdrawals. Second, commercial banks invest in state and local municipal bonds since these investments provide attractive after-tax yields with some exemption from federal and some state income taxation.

Business Loans

Even though many larger companies use corporate bond and commercial paper markets to finance their needs, commercial banks are by far the largest lenders to commerce and industry. Exhibit 3.1 indicates that banks issued to businesses $781 billion in loans, representing 20% of assets, provided on both a secured and unsecured basis, usually to smaller and medium-sized firms. Secured loans include accounts receivable, inventory, and equipment financing.

Mortgage Loans

Mortgage loans include residential property (both first and second mortgages), multifamily dwelling, and commercial property. Exhibit 3.1 shows how real estate lending, over the last decade, has become big business for commercial banks, with loans topping $947 billion, or 26% of total financial assets. In the next decade, industry analysts expect the residential mortgage market to grow for banks as they reduce their risk exposures in the commerical market and as savings and loans and savings banks shrink in market share.

Consumer Loans

A major growth area for banks in the last decade, **consumer loans** are those made to individuals to finance automobiles, recreational vehicles, boats, credit cards, personal needs, and any other loan not secured through real estate lending. These loans added up to $394 billion, or 10% of total financial assets.

Leases

The last major asset type is the lease. Commercial banks issue consumer leases for motor vehicles and equipment leases to businesses and not-for-profit organizations. These are classified with business loans in Exhibit 3.1. Banks offer leases rather than loans for such items partially because of the tax advantage to leasing over lending.

LIABILITY STRUCTURE OF COMMERCIAL BANKS

Deposits of consumers, governmental units, and businesses represent the primary sources of funding for banks. To augment smaller-sized deposits, commercial banks have also developed large-denomination funding sources, called

wholesale sources since firms exchange them in large dollar amounts. Examples include federal funds, repurchase agreements, negotiable certificates of deposit, and commercial paper. Exhibit 3.2 breaks down the major classes of commercial bank liabilities.

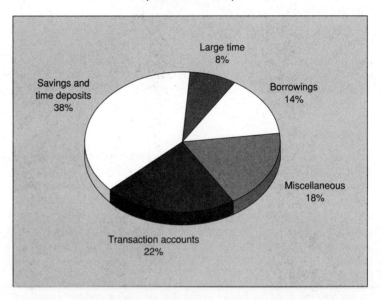

EXHIBIT 3.2

Major Liabilities of Commercial Banks
(December 1993)

Source: *Flow of Funds Accounts, Fourth Quarter 1993,* Board of Governors of the Federal Reserve System, March 9, 1994, p. 86.

Deposits

Commercial banks are by far the largest supplier of **transaction accounts,** including checking accounts, negotiable orders of withdrawal, and money market demand accounts, all of which serve as a medium of exchange. Exhibit 3.2 also depicts that these accounts totaled $783 billion or 22% of total financial liabilities.[1] Until 1980, commercial banks monopolized the market for checking ac-

---

[1]Transaction accounts include a variety of interest-paying and noninterest-paying accounts which can be used as a medium of exchange. The most popular include demand deposits, negotiable order of withdrawal accounts (NOW), and money market demand accounts (MMDA).

counts; but a series of regulatory changes opened the market door to thrift institutions and credit unions. Now banks eagerly seek transaction accounts because these accounts have low or no interest costs (although they are costly to service) and because they constitute a primary account relationship through which other products can be sold. In other words, one satisfied customer may purchase additional services.

A substantial, but steadily declining share of bank liabilities are savings deposits, often called **passbook or savings accounts,** which offer interest rates higher than interest-paying transaction accounts but lower than other interest-paying deposits. They are attractive to small savers because deposit and withdrawal transactions are relatively easy.

The largest and fastest growing category of deposit accounts, **time deposits,** includes **certificates of deposit,** offered primarily to individuals, as well as large-denomination **negotiable certificates of deposit** (CDs), offered to businesses, non-profit organizations, and governmental units. Savings and time deposits, at 38%, represent the largest percentage of commmercial bank liabilities. Large denomination negotiable CDs are issued in denominations of $100,000 or more and differ from other CDs in that investors can sell them in a secondary market. They provided 8% of total liabilities at year-end 1993.

Borrowings

Commercial banks have developed a range of wholesale funding sources, perhaps the most useful of which is federal funds. By law, all banks must hold a percentage of deposits in Federal Reserve banks; the Fed can transfer these reserves from one bank to another to adjust actual reserves to the required levels. A bank needing reserves is, in effect, the borrower, or buyer, in the federal funds market. Smaller institutions with less-sophisticated cash management procedures generally have fewer lending options and, as a consequence, hold a higher percentage of assets in liquid assets such as federal funds than do larger institutions. In terms of the transaction, the smaller firms are lenders, or sellers, of federal funds to larger institutions.

Commercial banks are also major borrowers in the **repurchase agreement,** or **repo,** market, where banks sell their securities to other institutions with the agreement to repurchase them at an agreed-upon price and time, usually overnight. Although bank activities in the Fed funds and repo markets are simply borrowing and lending transactions, they technically involve purchases and sales of assets.

To meet capital requirements, banks also borrow on a longer-term basis, using unsecured capital notes and **debentures.** Banks also hold funds for the U.S. government in the form of Treasury tax-and-loan accounts. Moreover, they take collateralized loans from the Federal Reserve Bank's discount window, typically for only a few days. In recent years, many commercial banks have become members of **Federal Home Loan Banks** (FHLBs) to enjoy further borrowing privileges.

MANAGEMENT HIGHLIGHTS

SPECIAL MANAGEMENT CONCERNS FOR COMMERCIAL BANKS

COMMUNITY BANKS

Achieving Adequate Economies of Scale in Operating Efficiency:

Smaller commercial banks have difficulty realizing processing efficiencies until they reach $50 million or more in size. Economies of scale are particularly important in determining the bank's selection of assets and liabilities to issue. Smaller-sized institutions may be too inefficient to service credit cards, for example.

Achieving Adequate Asset Portfolio Diversification:

Smaller banks cannot participate in many asset markets because they cannot assemble a portfolio of any given asset that is large enough to ensure diversification of risk. They also find that they cannot easily diversify risk by acquiring enough of a particular asset or of many different types of assets to achieve optimal diversification. This problem is discussed in Chapter 11.

Providing High-Quality Customer Service:

Community banks are very dependent on a neighborhood or small city for deposits and loans. Since they cannot offer as many services as larger banks, they must provide better customer service.

REGIONAL BANKS

Achieving an Adequate Net Interest Margin:

Moderate-sized banks confined to a region of the country may find that loan demands do not provide a high enough net interest margin without also accepting excessive credit or interest rate risks. Local supply-and-demand conditions are more important for regional institutions than for nationwide firms. This issue is addressed in Chapter 21.

Achieving Adequate Diversification of Regional Economic Business Cycle Risks:

Regional banks typically must bear excessive credit risks due to their large concentration of loan assets within one region of the country. This is a less-severe version of the same problem the smaller institutions face.

Controlling Operating Costs:

Regional banks typically must expand their loan origination activities to improve credit diversification and provide additional services to customers. This tends to increase expenses faster than revenues. As banks grow and provide additional services, they must add plant and equipment and personnel to perform servicing and origination functions. Chapter 23, on noninterest income, discusses the problem of increased operating risk related to this growth.

INTERNATIONAL BANKS

Managing Price Risks on Trading Portfolios:

International banks are generally active in trading securities for customers and their own account. This requires developing sophisticated risk-measuring and risk-management hedging systems. These institutions must develop sophisticated valuation and risk management tools. Especially important is knowledge on valuation (Chapter 15); futures, options, swaps (Chapter 16); and the management of interest rate risk (Chapters 17 and 18).

Controlling Foreign Credit Risks:

International banks must manage foreign credit risks (called *country risk*) in addition to domestic credit risks. This issue is discussed in Chapter 12.

Controlling Foreign Exchange Risks:

International banks typically trade foreign exchange in the cash and forward markets. Like securities, this trading involves substantial price risks that require developing sophisticated risk-measuring and management systems. This is discussed in Chapter 19.

Managing Off-Balance-Sheet Risks:

International banks tend to have large portfolios of off-balance sheet exposures, such as interest rate and currency swaps, foreign exchange forward positions, letters of credit, and credit guarantees that involve considerable risks. These off-balance sheet risks are discussed in Chapters 11 and 12.

INTERNATIONAL BANKING

The globalization of product and financial markets has forced large commercial banks to follow their customers to markets around the world. What commercial banks do in foreign markets are mostly the same functions they perform in their domestic market. The major issues in operating internationally relate to:

1. The existence of foreign exchange.
2. The differences in language and custom.
3. The differences in financial regulation between the host and home countries.

As international commercial banks became established, they generally expanded by selling their products to governments, businesses, and individuals in the foreign markets they entered.

The post-World War II history of international banking can be divided conveniently into three periods. The first—the 1950s to the early 1970s—was the period when U.S. banks took the lead in establishing worldwide banking operations. During this period, international banking was needed primarily to facilitate trade expansion. U.S. banks and companies dominated international markets.

During the second period—from the mid-1970s to the early 1980s—U.S. international banks took on the role of recycling the petrodollars of the Organization of Petroleum Exporting Countries (OPEC), which created huge dollar surpluses by successfully increasing the worldwide price of oil.

The third period began in the mid 1980s. Banks in Japan and Western Europe caught up and surpassed the United States in international banking. These are three main reasons why this occurred:

1. *Strong foreign currencies:* The economies in these countries performed very well during this period, and they greatly expanded international trade, creating an internal market for international banking services.

2. *Large trade surpluses:* Some of these countries, especially Japan, developed large foreign trade surpluses, which stimulated the development of foreign investment programs and facilitated the growth of their banks' international activities.

3. *Weakened domestic bank earnings:* U.S. bank earnings and capital positions began to weaken, and the shortage of capital inhibited international expansion. Many U.S. banks actually reduced their foreign presence during this period.

FUNCTIONS PERFORMED BY U.S. BANKS INTERNATIONALLY

U.S. banks participate in international markets in a number of ways. The most important activities and functions include:

- Commercial banking.
- Investment and merchant banking.
- Consumer finance.
- Security brokerage.
- Leasing.
- Trust services.
- Foreign exchange trading and hedging.

The management of these functions and activities will be discussed later.

HOW U.S.-CHARTERED BANKS ARE ORGANIZED FOR INTERNATIONAL BANKING

U.S. banks conduct global operations by using the following six organizational forms:

1. Foreign branch offices are the most common structure, because they have the same powers and capabilities as the domestic bank and need not be duplicated in a foreign subsidiary.

2. Domestic offices are most convenient but cannot provide services in the country where the customer does business. They can conduct such global activities as buying foreign loan participations, trading foreign exchange, and issuing letters of credit.

3. Foreign subsidiaries are less easy to generalize about because U.S. banks sometimes set them up to circumvent some prohibition imposed on the domestic bank by U.S. regulation. In other cases, U.S. banks buy foreign banks to obtain an immediate market presence.

4. Edge Act corporations are relatively insignificant today. The McFadden Act prohibition against interstate branches caused Congress to pass the Edge Act allowing banks to operate branches in other states as long as they accepted only foreign deposits. The number of these corporations has declined in recent years to approximately 100, partly because of the growth of interstate bank holding companies.

5. International banking facilities (IBFs) are authorized by the Federal Reserve to allow a U.S.-domiciled bank to establish a separate set of accounts for foreign deposits. This permits the U.S. bank to avoid reserve requirements and deposit insurance on these "foreign-like deposits."

6. Offshore centers are countries or cities that have developed favorable special provisions designed to attract international financial transactions. These centers provide a site for subsidiaries of foreign banks to conduct activities for their customers and benefit from low or no taxes, an absence of reserve requirements, bank secrecy, customer account secrecy in the form of numbered bank accounts, and the availability of securities or deposits that can be held in bearer form, which means without registering the owner. Some of the more popular offshore centers are the Bahamas, Bahrain, the Cayman Islands, Luxembourg, and the Netherlands Antilles.

FOREIGN BANKS OPERATING IN THE UNITED STATES

The United States has been one of the most popular markets for foreign banks. As European and Pacific Basin countries developed large export markets in the United States, banks in those countries first began to expand overseas to provide services for their customers. Since the early 1970s, there has been a rapid increase in the number of foreign banks operating in the United States. Much of the growth in the 1980s came about because of foreign bank inroads into U.S. domestic banking markets.

Foreign banks operate in the United States using the same organizational forms as U.S. banks use internationally. They participate in U.S. markets through the following structures, which are simply the foreign equivalents of the structures used by U.S. banks:

- Home offices working through correspondent banks in the United States.
- Branch offices located in the United States.
- U.S.-domiciled bank subsidiaries.
- Edge Act corporations.

✓ Checkpoints

3-3 What is the primary difference between money center and regional banks?

3-4 What are the primary assets held by commercial banks? What are their primary liabilities?

3-5 What services do commercial banks provide internationally? What organizational structures are used by U.S. and foreign banks operating outside their countries?

Thrift Institutions

Thrift institutions are similar to commercial banks except their charters offer more-restricted asset and liability authority. They also have their own regulators. These institutions all began operating in the United States as mutual institutions, designed to serve individuals by providing savings deposit services and—in the case of savings and loans and credit unions—mortgage and consumer loans, respectively. Savings and loan associations (S&Ls) and BIF-insured savings banks (SBs) thrived in the post-World War II period until the late 1970s. Savings and loans are classified differently from savings banks here because there are two government insurance corporations that insure their deposits. S&Ls, some of which are federally chartered savings banks (FSB), are insured by the Savings Association Insurance Fund (SAIF). There are also savings banks insured by the Bank Insurance Fund (BIF), which insures commercial banks.[2] Despite the highly constrained asset and liability authority of these firms, they benefited from a number of advantages the Federal government granted them which propelled their growth. These advantages were largely eliminated in the 1980s as they were granted broader asset and liability powers.

Credit unions are all mutual institutions whose primary role is to provide consumer loans and savings account services to a defined group called the *common bond*. Most credit unions were organized by employers to provide services to em-

---

[2]The situation is actually more complicated than this. Because of acquisitions across insurance company fund lines, portions of a single institution's deposits can be insured by the BIF and SAIF. As of September 30, 1993, BIF-insured institutions held $136 billion in SAIF-insured deposits, and SAIF-insured institutions held $4 billion in BIF-insured deposits.

ployees.[3] Credit unions are insured by the National Credit Union Share Insurance Fund (NCUSIF).

Beginning in the late 1970s, S&Ls and SBs fell on hard times. Record high interest rates in the early 1980s largely depleted their capital base. This was caused by their holding long-term fixed-rate mortgages as assets and financing them primarily with short-term deposits. As interest rates skyrocketed, their deposit costs rose more rapidly than the return on their assets, resulting in insolvency for many in the industry in the early 1980s. This was followed by excessive risk-taking by some of the firms and regulatory miscues that culminated in the "thrift debacle."

Exhibit 3.3 shows the total financial assets of the three major thrifts and commercial banks, covering the eight years ending in 1993. The S&Ls experienced severe profitability and capital shortage problems in the 1980s. These problems became so severe that by late 1989 the industry began to shrink and has continued to shrink well into the early 1990s. The BIF-insured savings banks also experienced operating problems in the 1980s but less severe than those of the S&Ls. Consequently, their growth in the 1985 to 1993 period actually exceeded that of the S&Ls.

EXHIBIT 3.3

Total Financial Assets of Major Depositories
(1985–1993)

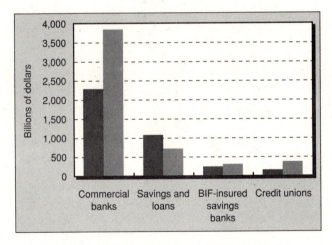

Source: *Flow of Funds Accounts, Fourth Quarter 1993,* Board of Governors of the Federal Reserve System, March 9, 1994.

Credit unions, on the other hand, have continued to prosper and grow at double-digit annual rates. The growth rate of commercial banks was moderate in the 1985 to 1993 period. They have grown faster than S&Ls, in part because they have been purchasers of savings and loan deposits from shrinking and failed S&Ls.

---

[3]The common bond used to be a well-defined group made up primarily of current employees of an organization. Over the years, Congress permitted the common bond to include family members, retired employees, and even members of community.

*L*EGAL

and

*E*THICAL

ISSUES

LINCOLN SAVINGS: SECURITY FRAUD, INFLUENCE PEDDLING, AND THE DUAL SYSTEM OF CHARTERING FINANCIAL INSTITUTIONS

No financial institution epitomized the S&L debacle more than Lincoln Savings and Loan. Lincoln S&L was purchased in 1984 by American Continental Corporation, a large-scale real estate development company run by Charles Keating. Keating, like a number of other developers, considered the California state S&L charter to be an attractive way to fund real estate development. In fact, the state's new charter permitted unlimited direct investment in real estate.

The aggressive investment activities of Lincoln and several other institutions caught the eye of the federal savings and loan regulator, the former FHLBB. The board was responsible for insuring these institutions and promulgated a regulation that restricted to 10% the investment of insured institution assets in direct real estate. Keating allegedly responded by making political contributions to several highly placed U.S. senators (known as *the Keating Five*) in return for their help in pressuring the FHLBB to back off from their regulation and later to impede the regulator's effort to gain control over Lincoln. The result was one of the most emotion-charged ethics hearings ever conducted by the Senate Ethics Committee, in which the Keating Five were asked to explain their activities concerning Lincoln.

Lincoln's officers and professional advisers also were the subjects of numerous lawsuits by public and government units. The suit that gained the most publicity related to the sale of subordinated debt in Lincoln's parent, ACC, which was sold in small denominations by using broker/dealers located in the branches of Lincoln Savings. These bondholders, many of them retirees, subsequently lost an estimated $200 million when Lincoln was taken over by the government. The suit alleged that ACC management, accountants, lawyers, and others committed negligent and fraudulent acts. This suit sent Keating to prison.

Aside from the press hype, the Lincoln situation raised several important issues:

1. It provided clear evidence of the problem caused by having state-chartered institutions insured by federal insurance funds. This problem was partially resolved through federal legislation restricting the powers of state-chartered institutions.

2. Lincoln highlighted the potential for influence peddling, given a system in which regulators have very broad powers, and recourse and redress for overzealous regulators is difficult. The Ethics Committee did not resolve that issue.

3. The sales of subordinated debt raised additional issues about the responsibilities of management, directors, lawyers, and accountants in making representations concerning securities sold to the public.

ASSETS AND LIABILITIES OF THRIFTS

S&Ls and SBs specialize in home mortgages because of their restrictive charters and historical development. Credit unions specialize in consumer loans for the same reasons. Exhibit 3.4 shows the asset structure of all thrifts as a group at year-end 1993.

The liability structure of these institutions is also specialized. All thrifts rely on deposit accounts for most of their funds because they are primarily smaller-sized institutions with little access to wholesale funding sources. S&Ls and SBs also obtain funds from Federal Home Loan Bank borrowings, and some of the larger institutions use money and capital market security sales. Exhibit 3.5 depicts the liability structure of thrifts as a group.

EXHIBIT 3.4

Financial Assets of Thrifts
(December 31, 1993)

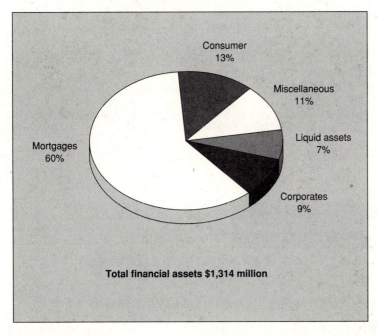

Source: *Flow of Funds Accounts, Fourth Quarter 1993,* Board of Governors of the Federal Reserve System, March 4, 1994, p. 94.

EXHIBIT 3.5

Financial Liabilities of Thrifts
(December 31, 1993)

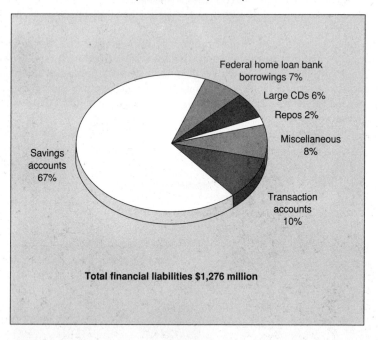

Federal home loan bank borrowings 7%

Large CDs 6%

Repos 2%

Miscellaneous 8%

Savings accounts 67%

Transaction accounts 10%

Total financial liabilities $1,276 million

Source: *Flow of Funds Accounts, Fourth Quarter 1993,* Board of Governors of the Federal Reserve System, March 4, 1994, p. 94.

MANAGEMENT HIGHLIGHTS

SPECIAL MANAGEMENT CONCERNS FOR S&LS AND SBS

ACHIEVING AN ADEQUATE NET INTEREST MARGIN

S&Ls and SBs have a large concentration of their assets in home mortgages. These assets have a modest spread over their cost of funds, making it difficult to sustain an adequate net interest margin. This thrift problem has been complicated by the rapid growth in government sponsored enterprises, as discussed in the appendix to this chapter.

CONTROLLING THE COST OF DEPOSITS

S&Ls and SBs have traditionally paid more for deposits than commercial banks. They have, therefore, cultivated a customer base that expects a higher rate of interest. In today's environment, S&Ls and SBs are not able to earn higher interest rates on assets than banks, making their high deposit rate strategy less viable. Adding to the problem is the rising cost of deposit insurance. Both these issues are discussed in Chapter 22.

CONTROLLING OPERATING EXPENSES

S&Ls and SBs will face low net interest margins for the foreseeable future. As they attempt to compete against large commercial banks, with their broad product and service offerings, thrifts find that as they add new products and services costs tend to rise faster than revenue. This dilemma is discussed in Chapter 23.

MANAGING INTEREST RATE RISK

Mortgages involve prepayment options that are difficult to hedge. This means that interest rate risk is an ever-present feature of these institutions. Even adjustable-rate mortgages are not without difficult-to-hedge provisions, such as interest rate caps, lagging rate indices, and other provisions that involve substantial risk. Chapters 17 and 18 are devoted to these issues.

CONTROLLING EXPOSURE TO LOCAL AND REGIONAL REAL ESTATE PRICE RISKS

Most S&Ls and SBs have a high concentration of assets in local markets which are exposed to regional economic real estate value cycles. These firms must successfully manage this risk. The need to diversify credit risk is discussed in Chapters 11 and 12.

MANAGEMENT HIGHLIGHTS

SPECIAL MANAGEMENT CONCERNS FOR CREDIT UNIONS

CONTROLLING CREDIT RISKS

Credit unions sometimes make consumer loans to small groups of employees who may be subject to mass layoff or strike. The lack of employment diversification of the credit unions' customer base could present credit problems. Techniques for controlling this risk are discussed in Chapter 11.

RISKS OF EMPLOYER CHANGES

Credit unions frequently find themselves with significant operating problems due to sponsor failure, merger, or facility closure. These events can result in the need to merge one credit union with another or close it altogether.

FINDING PROFESSIONAL TALENT

Credit unions start small and then grow. Sometimes it is difficult to find experienced management for a larger credit union.

BALANCING FUNDING SOURCES WITH INVESTMENTS

Because of the lack of safe loans to invest in, small credit unions typically have excess savings liabilities which leads to large holdings of liquidity which reduces interest income. The problems related to liquidity management useful to credit unions are discussed in Chapter 20.

✓ Checkpoints

3-6   What financial institutions constitute the thrift industry?
3-7   What are the primary loans made by S&Ls, SBs, and credit unions?
3-8   What are the primary liabilities of thrifts?

Life Insurance Companies and Pension Funds

Life insurance companies and **pension funds** are similar in that they both provide a source of retirement income, manage mortality risk, and are funded by systematic contractual payments which the insurance company policyholder, beneficiary, or pension plan beneficiary withdraws after a long period. As a result, both types of intermediaries grow rather steadily and can invest mostly in long-term assets.

Some families place all or a portion of their retirement savings directly with life insurance companies in the form of individual insurance policies with annuity features. In many cases, retirement savings are accumulated in pooled pension plans, and the trustees of these plans invest the funds in group annuity policies or separate investment accounts with insurance companies. Life insurance companies compete with deposit institutions, mutual funds, and securities brokers for individual retirement savings. Bank trust departments and investment advisory firms also manage pension fund assets.

LIFE INSURANCE COMPANIES

Life insurance companies are financial intermediaries that provide two primary services:

1. Mortality risk management services, insurance against the loss of income due to death.
2. Savings and investment programs, mainly for retirement, often in a single policy with premiums split between mortality and savings.

Mortality Risk

Life insurance company policyholders seek to hedge the risk of losing income by dying prematurely and the risk of outliving their assets. In both cases, the probability, called *mortality risk,* of a policyholder's dying at a certain age is highly important. Life insurance companies pool mortality risk by insuring large numbers of individuals so that the company's average mortality experience approaches that expected from the whole population or a specified segment of it.

Primary Types of Life Policies

The primary types of life policies issued by life insurance companies include:

1. **Term insurance** policies represent pure insurance. These policies provide only death benefits without an investment feature. The other policies offered by life companies have savings and investment features.
2. **Whole life insurance** policies represent insurance plus an investment feature designed in such a way as to create a level premium of the life of the policy. The level premium is made possible because the policy builds cash values, reducing the insurance amount as the individual grows older and mortality increases.
3. **Annuities** are investment-oriented policies that provide recurring payments to the policyowner in return for large periodic or lump-sum payments to the company. These are basically investments with little insurance. They are popular because the earnings on the policy's cash values are not taxed when they are earned. Pension plans frequently purchase these policies to provide pension payments.
4. **Investment-oriented** policies, sometimes called *wrap-around policies,* feature a small amount of life insurance wrapped around a large amount of invested capital. These include variable life, universal life, and variable universal life. Since policyholders can direct their premium into specific investments, for deferring taxes on the cash invested and implementing other strategies, wrap-arounds are more versatile than whole life policies.

SPECIAL MANAGEMENT CONCERNS FOR LIFE INSURANCE COMPANIES

AVOIDING PAYING EXCESSIVE INTEREST RATES ON INVESTMENT-ORIENTED POLICIES

Many life insurance companies have failed in recent years because they have guaranteed policyholders high interest rates. For example, single-premium annuities are sold partly on the basis of yield. Insurance companies that promise excessive rates are tempted to invest in risky assets such as junk bonds and commercial real estate which can produce large losses. Other life insurance companies paid excessively high rates of guaranteed investment contracts. Guaranteed investment contracts of life company liabilities are sold primarily to pension funds. The pricing of some of these investment-oriented policies is the subject of Chapter 22.

CONTROLLING THE COSTS OF DISTRIBUTION AND ADMINISTRATION

Life insurance companies spend considerable operating expenses on policy sales and distribution, administration, and servicing existing policies. These companies have invested heavily in computer technology to control costs. Distribution costs can be controlled by finding less-costly distribution channels such as those discussed in Chapter 24.

UNDERWRITING MORTALITY RISKS

Although mortality risks are generally easier to control than most other risks, a disease such as AIDS can significantly affect the mortality experience of a company if it has not properly underwritten and diversified this risk. Life companies must be expert in evaluating mortality risk and pricing it properly. This problem is beyond the scope of this book.

ACHIEVING DIVERSIFICATION IN CREDIT RISKS

Insurance companies must have large asset portfolios to diversify credit risks, providing an advantage for large life insurance companies over smaller ones. This is discussed in Chapters 11 and 12.

Asset Structure of Life Insurance Companies

In response to changes in types of insurance policies sold, managers have altered the asset structure of life insurance companies in several important ways. Due to the long-term nature of the liabilities and largely predictable cash inflows, portfolio managers within life insurance companies hold the majority of their assets in fixed-return, long-term investments such as government securities, **corporate bonds,** and **home mortgages.** At year-end 1993, these types of investments accounted for three-fourths of all life insurance company assets. Portfolio managers have gradually increased the riskiness of their portfolios by investing higher percentages of assets in common stock equities and high-yield bonds.

PENSION FUNDS

In 1950, pension funds constituted only slightly more than 5% of total financial holdings of households; but, by year-end 1993, the percentage had climbed to 30%. Now pension reserves represent the largest single class of financial assets for U.S. households and the U.S. economy's largest institutional source of long-term capital. Over the last two decades, growth of private, state, and local government pension funds has surpassed that of most other intermediaries; this growth coincides with the post-World War II population bulge, now the largest percentage of the U.S. labor force.

Managers of pension funds must grasp the following points:

1. Pension funds combined control the largest stock of long-term financial capital in the country.
2. The accounting method chosen by corporate financial managers and human resource personnel to document pension costs can make earnings of private pension plans either a major profit or loss item on the corporate balance sheet.

For organizations with certain types of pension plans, investment performance of the funds accumulated to pay future benefits can have a significant year-to-year impact on the profit and loss statement.

Types of Pension Plans

Two major types of pension plans that accumulate substantial amounts of investment funds are **private pension plans,** operated by private, profit and not-for-profit organizations; and **state and local government pension plans,** run by governmental units for their employees such as teachers, police and firemen, and municipal employees.

Pension plans are also classified by the way benefits are determined. **Defined benefit** plans provide contractually determined benefits to recipients: the employing organization must pay earned benefits irrespective of the amount of funds set aside to provide for these benefits. By law, an employer having such a plan must fund these liabilities on a current basis and make additional contributions if the investment returns on the funds are poor. The employer bears the risk of the investment, not the employee.

Defined contribution plans do not provide a fixed benefit but establish a contractual amount of contribution, typically a specified percentage (such as 10%) of an employee's income. The company automatically invests these contributions, and the employee benefits depend, in part, on investment performance. In some plans, the employee may choose among possible investments; this choice also affects the level of retirement benefits. Clearly, the employee bears much of the risk in this type of plan. Since the employer has limited liability—no liabilities beyond the initial contributions made—more companies have shifted from defined benefit to defined contribution plans.

Pension plans can also be insured and noninsured. **Insured pension programs** are funded by annuities purchased from life insurance companies, that take on the responsibility of paying promised benefits to beneficiaries. **Noninsured pension plans** are administered by trustees selected by the employer, the plan participants, or both. These trustees have a fiduciary responsibility with respect to the funds set aside to provide benefits; that is, they must oversee the investment of the funds, specify acceptable types of investments, and obtain investment management expertise. While they often designate commercial bank trust departments, investment advisory firms, and life insurance companies to perform daily duties, they are ultimately responsible for prudently investing funds accumulated to pay pension benefits.

ANAGEMENT HIGHLIGHTS

SPECIAL MANAGEMENT CONCERNS FOR PENSION FUNDS

ESTIMATING ACTUARIAL LIABILITIES

Estimating future benefits for defined benefit pension funds, especially those that provide health care, is a difficult job. These estimates rely on many assumptions about future salaries, wages, and costs. It is the job the of actuary to evaluate the obligation of the plan sponsor to the employee beneficiaries. These calculations use primarily present value techniques, as discussed in Chapter 15.

CONTROLLING REINVESTMENT RISK

As long-term investors, pension funds must reinvest considerable funds each month. Thought must be given to the reinvestment risks associated with the investment of these large recurring cash flows. Reinvestment risk, discussed in Chapter 14, concerns the risk that cash flows derived from an investment cannot be reinvested to obtain an anticipated rate.

Asset Structure of Pension Funds

Since pension benefits are typically paid many years after the funds contributed to pay them are set aside, pension funds are considered long-term investors; and managers of pensions funds may invest assets in corporate stocks, long-term bonds and mortgages, and real estate equities. Table 3.2 profiles the assets holdings of private and state and local pension funds.

| TABLE 3.2 |

Asset Structure of Private and State and Local Pension Funds
December 31, 1993
(dollars in billions)

Type of Asset	Private Pensions		State and Local Pensions	
	$ Amount	% of Total	$ Amount	% of Total
Demand deposits	$ 5	0.2%	$ 7	0.7%
Time deposits				
and Money market funds	231	9.9	10	0.9
Corporate equities	1079	46.2	506	47.5
Mutual fund shares	78	3.3	—	—
Treasuries	291	12.5	173	16.2
Agencies	110	4.7	102	19.5
Corporate bonds	298	12.8	197	18.5
Mortgages	39	1.7	12	1.1
Open market paper	20	0.9	36	3.4
Miscellaneous assets	185	7.8	22	2.2
Total	$2,336	100.0%	$1,065	100.0%

Source: *Flow of Funds Accounts, Second Quarter 1994,* Board of Governors of the Federal Reserve System, March 4, 1994, p. 96.

Growth of Pension Fund Assets

A number of factors contributed to the rapid growth of pension funds in the last several decades. The baby-boom generation added to the number of employees covered, along with the level of benefits promised. As a result, the funds set aside to pay future benefits accumulated faster. Also, the government has required employers to give employees greater vesting rights and to increase the amounts reserved in pension funds so that benefits money will be available as employees retire.

Vesting refers to the employee's right to receive benefits under a pension plan even if the employee quits or is terminated before reaching retirement age. A few plans provide for immediate vesting: employees can leave at any time without losing earned benefits. More frequently, employees must work for a minimum number of years, often three to five, before the employer-contributed earned benefits are vested. After the initial vesting period, an employee is usually vested in an increasing proportion of earned benefits as service time increases. To protect an employee from losing benefits if terminated after many years of service with an employer, congress established minimum vesting requirements for private pension plans through the **Employee Retirement Income Security Act of 1974 (ERISA).** Also because of ERISA, employers with defined benefit plans must meet minimum funding requirements in order to deduct pension fund costs from federal income tax. The ERISA requirements for earlier vesting of pension benefits and gradual funding of underfunded plans significantly increased employer contributions to private pension plans. Finally, if the sponsoring company goes bankrupt without providing sufficient funds to pay vested benefits, the federal **Pension Benefit Guarantee Corporation (PBGC)** insures benefits.

PUTTING PENSION OBLIGATIONS ON THE BALANCE SHEET

How it Really Works

ERISA has not been the only factor driving change in pension plan financing. The Financial Accounting Standards Board, through accounting standards FAS-87 and FAS-106, has had a very significant impact on how pension obligations are recorded on a company's books. FAS-87 requires that employers account for pension liabilities by using a uniform method of cost recognition. It also requires immediate recognition of liabilities. As a result, underfunded liabilities of pension funds must be recognized and reflected on the company's balance sheet. Employers with overfunded pension plans (pension plans whose assets exceed its liabilities) are required to recognize the excess funding as income over a period of time. FAS-106 requires employers to count as a current expense other types of retirement benefits, such as health benefits, paid after retirement.

During the early 1990s, the biggest impact of pension costs on corporations related to medical benefits. Imagine trying to determine the value of future medical benefits for all past and current employees—at best you can only estimate it. In 1992, IBM had to report a charge against its income of $2.26 billion to cover anticipated medical pension benefits. For 1992 General Motors Corporation had a staggering $20.8 billion write-off to cover these costs. The result is that some companies are considering revising their benefit programs to reduce medical benefits.

Source: Phyllis Feinberg, "Pension Report," *Barron's*, Nov. 18, 1991, pp. 34–45.

✓ Checkpoints

3-9 What is mortality risk, and how do life insurance companies handle it?

3-10 What are the main assets and liabilities of life insurance companies?

3-11 What is the difference between a defined benefit plan and a defined contribution plan?

a. Under which plan does the employer accept more risk?

b. Under which plan does the employee accept more risk?

Other Financial Institutions

This section describes a number of very specialized institutions, such as investment banks, finance companies, and a number of investment-oriented intermediaries, which exist to provide a wide range of investments, including:[4]

---

[4]Another important financial institution not discussed here is the mortgage banking company. These firms specialize in the origination and servicing of mortgages. In recent years they have overtaken the thrift institutions as the nation's largest originator of home mortgages. Mortgage bankers are described in the appendix to Chapter 3.

1. Open end mutual funds.
2. Limited partnerships.
3. Real estate investment trusts.

These investment-oriented intermediaries are created to (1) provide investors with access to investments for which they have limited expertise; (2) provide investors with diversified portfolios of assets; and (3) reduce transaction costs. They also benefit from income tax provisions that allow them to avoid corporate income taxation if they meet certain conditions.

INVESTMENT BANKERS

Stories like those of former investment banker Michael Milken's multimillion-dollar income, multibillion-dollar mergers and acquisitions, and highly sophisticated trading activities, and the temptations that surround money and power form the mystique surrounding investment banking. **Investment banking institutions** are complex, performing a variety of functions for both institutional and consumer customers.

Investment banking companies provide a vast array of financial services. The following is a list of the most important:

1. Originating—called underwriting by investment bankers—financial assets such as stocks and bonds.
2. Selling and distributing financial assets through brokerage and acting as dealers of specific assets.
3. Advising customers on such transactions as mergers, financial restructurings, investments, acquisitions, hostile takeovers, corporate valuations, and other major transactions.
4. Lending to customers with acceptable security collateral.

Types of Investment Bankers

Investment banks typically can be broken down into three groups.[5] The first group emphasizes retail customers, acting principally as brokers of financial assets created by other investment bankers or traded in the secondary markets. Although these firms are not active in originating financial assets for large companies, they may serve small firms in regional markets. A subset of this retail group are the **discount brokers,** which provide brokerage services primarily to household customers at discounted prices. These firms tend to offer little investment advice and emphasize low price and service. A number of commercial banks have created discount brokers as subsidiaries within their holding companies.

The second group of investment banks serves primarily the corporate sector by originating financial assets, providing financial services, and acting as broker and market maker for institutional clients.

---

[5]The classification *investment banker* is defined very broadly to include security brokers and dealers, which do not underwrite securities. For example, discount security brokers are included in this classification.

The third group consists of larger firms that have both institutional and retail orientations and provide virtually all the services discussed in this section for institutional clients yet maintain retail offices for distribution of financial assets to the household market.

LEGAL and ETHICAL ISSUES

JAPANESE INVESTMENT BANKING COMPANIES: FINANCIAL GUARANTEES FOR CUSTOMERS AND INFLUENCE PEDDLING

For industrial, commercial, and service firms in the United States, Japan has been a tough market to crack. Accusations of unfair business practices and government protection have been ongoing. In 1988 and again in 1991, the world capital markets shook with revelations that political influence peddling occurred in the higher levels of the Japanese government and that major Japanese investment banking firms gave sweetheart financial arrangements to a number of Japanese customers.

In 1988, a Japanese firm named Recruit Co.—a powerful publishing and real estate conglomerate—was accused of contributing to a large number of bureaucrats, businessmen, and senior members of one of Japan's major political parties. Recruit's officials purportedly allowed these influential people to obtain shares of stock in a firm that subsequently went public, creating a large profit for them. The trail of influence peddling eventually led to Japan's prime minister and an aide. The prime minister resigned, and the aide committed suicide.

In 1991, Japanese financial markets were again shaken by revelations that some of the largest and most prestigious investment banking firms had profited from financial guarantees on stocks held by customers against losses in order to obtain their business.

These revelations merely provided additional ammunition concerning the purported unfair symbiotic relationship between Japan's financial institutions, commercial and industrial firms, politicians, and the Japanese ministry of finance. Foreign financial service companies claim to be seriously disadvantaged in their ability to compete for financial business against the entrenched Japanese firms, with their alleged illegal business practices and cozy political relationships.

Underwriting Debt and Equity Securities

The underwriting process typically involves three primary steps. First, the underwriter and the issuer must identify the type of security to be offered. The available financing options will be compared to determine which option provides the least cost with the most issuer flexibility. This is the *supply side* of the underwriting equation. Second, the underwriters will use their customer base to determine the potential market for a new security. This is the *demand side* of the equation. The underwriter will then attempt to put a final design in place, incorporating the provisions that are important to investors and acceptable to the issuer and providing a preliminary price indication.

One of the most important decisions of a firm selling securities is the selection of the underwriter, and one important aspect of this decision is whether the underwriter will be compensated under a **competitive offer** or on a **negotiated offer** basis. The competitive offer approach allows underwriters to bid freely on the price they will charge to underwrite and distribute the securities. It is used primarily in very large security offerings and by public utilities which are sometimes required to seek competitive bids. The majority of security underwritings are priced on the negotiated bid basis. This involves direct negotiation between the security-issuing firm and prospective underwriters. This approach is used more frequently, despite evidence suggesting that the competitive bid approach is less costly to security issuers. This is an area of ongoing debate.

The issuing company's management and the underwriting firm subsequently provide additional information about the issuer to prospective investors by communicating with them face to face. In a large issue, the senior management of the company visits with potential investors from all around the country. A **syndication group,** made up of several investment banker underwriters, is formed when it is felt that the sales effort will require broader coverage of potential investors. This group may be augmented still further by bringing in smaller regional investment bankers as part of a selling group.

The next job, to price and sell the security, is typically done on an **indicative bid** basis. That is, the underwriters and other distributors of the security determine the potential buyers and estimate a price near what they think to be the final price the market will bear. They usually do this in the days just prior to the issue date. The indicated bid price normally is expressed as a spread over or under some benchmark security, in the case of debt. Needless to say, neither the issuer nor the investors know what might happen in the market from one day to the next; a sudden drop in the stock or bond market will unravel the most carefully orchestrated transaction. If the demand is strong at the indicative bid, then the issuer may feel confident that it can price slightly higher. If demand is soft, the opposite occurs.

Underwriters distribute securities on a **best efforts underwriting** or **firm commitment underwriting.** On a best efforts basis, the underwriter is legally bound only to sell what it is able to distribute through its "best efforts" and is not obligated to sell the entire issue if it is not possible. A negotiated bid or competitive bid basis puts the underwriters and other distributors on the line, since they will buy the issue and will end up owning what they do not initially sell. Under the firm commitment underwriting, the underwriter purchases the entire security issue from the issuing firm and accepts the risk of having to resell the securities. If the underwriter has difficulty selling the securities, it may have to lower the price and cut into its own fees. The most prevalent type of U.S. underwritings are done on a firm commitment basis.

LEGAL *and* **ETHICAL** ISSUES

SALOMON BROTHERS: TREASURY AUCTION IRREGULARITIES

In August 1991, Salomon Brothers Inc., one of Wall Street's leading security trading investment bankers, shocked the investment community with a press release admitting to "irregularities and rule violations in connection with its submission of bids in certain auctions of Treasury securities." This release was followed by resignations and removals of several of Salomon's highest ranking officials, lawsuits by shareholders and others, and investigations by a number of regulatory bodies. Allegations against Salomon Brothers included market manipulation, fraud, misrepresentations to federal authorities, books and records violations, and wire and mail fraud.

Salomon Brothers' violations of Treasury auction rules are related to limitations on the percentage of the total volume of a Treasury auction that could be bid by a single dealer. Salomon admitted to submitting false bids in the names of customers who had not authorized the bids in order to control more than the 35% limit. The trail led to Salomon Brothers partly because several competitors felt that they had been squeezed by Salomon's control of a larger percentage of the auction. In the Treasury market, there is an active forward cash market called the *when issued market*. Trading occurs in Treasury securities for forward delivery. Several of Salomon's competitors had sold Treasuries to customers, expecting to be able to successfully obtain them in the auction. But, they claimed, the bogus Salomon bids forced them to bid up the price of the securities in the secondary market after they were unsuccessful in obtaining them in the primary auction. Thus, they were squeezed out and forced to suffer a loss.

The result of the Salomon revelations led to allegations that many dealers routinely overbid in several of the markets for government sponsored enterprise securities. Salomon's admission put considerable pressure on the Treasury department to review the structure of its auction procedures and its adherence to a relatively small group of primary dealers. This led the Treasury department to open up the auction to more dealers in late 1991.

Source: E. J. Stevens and Diana Dumitru, "Auctioning Treasury Securities," *Economic Commentary*, Federal Reserve Bank of Cleveland, June 15, 1992.

Mergers and Acquisitions

Investment banking companies are major participants in the merger, acquisition, and financing business. Merger and acquisition activities are typically categorized into three classes:

1. Leveraged buyouts (LBOs).
2. Financial restructurings.
3. Divestitures.

SPECIAL MANAGEMENT CONCERNS FOR INVESTMENT BANKERS

CONTROLLING RISKS OF TRADING PORTFOLIOS

Investment bankers frequently carry large portfolios of securities to meet customer demands. These assets can sometimes experience huge price fluctuations, making valuation and protecting against adverse price changes particularly challenging jobs for investment bankers. The tools used to address these issued are discussed in Chapters 15 and 16.

CONTROLLING OPERATING COSTS

The security and brokerage businesses are quite cyclical. As a result, investment bankers must carefully control costs of personnel and office space. Expanding too rapidly during the boom times can lead to a rash of layoffs and operating losses during the slow periods. The operating risks associated with expansion are discussed in Chapter 23.

CONTROLLING SALARIES AND BONUSES

Investment bankers are known for their sometimes huge salaries and bonuses. Michael Milken, the "Junk Bond King," was thought to have earned over $500 million in one year. Securities traders, leveraged buyout experts, and merger and acquisition professionals frequently earn seven-figure incomes. The problem for management is to determine how much of a firm's profit is due to the individual's special effort and skill versus how much belongs to the stockholders for supplying the capital and to the firm's good reputation.

LBOs have received the greatest publicity because they have involved some of the largest financial transactions in U.S. corporate history. LBOs involve the purchase of companies using large amounts of debt. Financial restructurings—also a major activity in the 1980s—usually involve replacing a portion of a firm's equity with debt. Divestitures were also prevalent in the 1980s, as companies attempted to increase shareholder value by selling subsidiary activities that did not strategically fit with the rest of their organizations. These transactions provided significant fee income to the investment banking business.

Market-Making and Trading

Many investment bankers are involved in security trading. This activity involves three closely related activities. The first is pure brokerage. A number of securities lack marketability, are difficult to value, and may be volatile in price. For these types of assets, investment bankers usually act as brokers.

Second, for most liquid securities, the trading firm will stand ready to take a security into inventory. The objective of this trading activity is to mark up the price and find a buyer as soon as possible.

Third, investment bankers deal in **proprietary trading,** which involves taking a position in a security for the firm's own account. The firm tries to profit from buying undervalued securities.

FINANCE COMPANIES

Finance companies are the largest and least regulated financial institutions. These firms got their start by providing financial lending services to two entirely different markets. The commercial finance companies developed largely as captives to large manufacturing firms. These business customers typically needed financing for equipment purchases. Firms that sold equipment developed their own companies to finance sales. Because many of these firms were subsidiaries of large, highly capitalized manufacturing firms with strong credit ratings, they were able to obtain financing at highly favorable rates. A good credit rating is important to finance companies because they rely on open market sales of debentures and short-term commercial paper.

Another group of finance companies had their origin in the financing of lower- and moderate-income consumers. These consumer finance companies had a business strategy far different from their commercial finance company sisters. Many of these firms lend money to low- and moderate-income individuals through retail offices. The consumer finance company succeeded by segmenting the market and concentrating on the lower-income household that was unable to meet commercial bank underwriting credit standards.

Over the years, a portion of the market for unsecured personal loans—the specialty of the consumer finance company—has come to be served by credit cards. This caused many of the major consumer finance companies to alter their business strategies and find new ways to deliver their products. Some of these firms have become very large issuers of credit cards. Others have become large, diversified holding companies that have entered the depository business through acquisitions.

Asset and Liability Structures of Finance Companies

The assets of finance companies are concentrated in consumer and business loans while their liabilities are primarily open market paper, such as commercial paper and other debt, as well as loans obtained from parent companies. Exhibit 3.6 shows the percentage distribution of all U.S. finance companies' $658 billion in financial assets and $586 billion in financial liabilities as of December 31, 1993.

✓ Checkpoints

3-12 What makes investment bankers unique among our financial institutions?

3-13 How would you describe the differences between retail and corporate investment bankers?

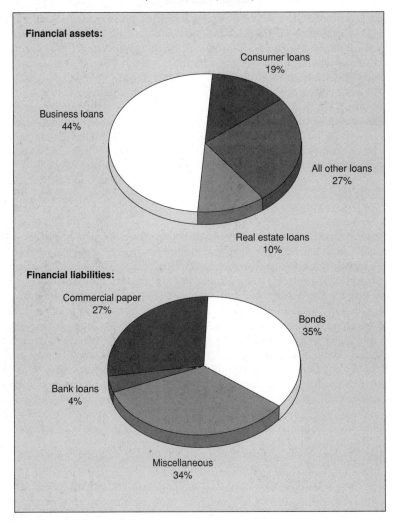

EXHIBIT 3.6

Financial Assets and Liabilities of U.S. Finance Companies
(December 31, 1993)

Financial assets:

Consumer loans
19%

Business loans
44%

All other loans
27%

Real estate loans
10%

Financial liabilities:

Commercial paper
27%

Bonds
35%

Bank loans
4%

Miscellaneous
34%

Source: *Flow of Funds Accounts, Fourth Quarter 1993,* Board of Governors of the Federal Reserve System, March 4, 1994, p. 98.

3-14 If you were issuing a new security, would your firm have more risk under a best efforts, or firm commitment agreement, with an investment banker handling the distribution?

3-15 How would you describe the asset and liability structure of finance companies? If you ran a business, what do you think you would use a finance company for?

Investment-oriented Intermediaries

Investment-oriented intermediaries comprise a group of institutions whose primary purpose is to provide portfolio management services to individual and institutional investors. The largest of these intermediaries are the open-end mutual funds. Less important are the limited partnerships and real estate investment trusts. All of these institutional forms have one thing in common: they are structured to avoid federal taxation at the intermediary level. These organizations pass their income directly to investors, where it is then taxed.

Investment-oriented intermediaries are among our country's fastest growing institutions. As individuals and institutional investors have become more experienced in managing their financial assets, they have searched out ways to diversify into more sophisticated investments. Investment-oriented intermediaries provide the vehicles to make these types of investments, pooling the funds of many investors and making available investment expertise.

OPEN-END MUTUAL FUNDS

The most successful financial intermediary, measured by growth in assets for the last 20 years, has been the **open-end mutual fund,** an intermediary that issues shares representing a pro rata ownership in a pool of assets.[6] Mutual funds provide professional portfolio management skills and asset diversification for investors through the pooling of funds.

The popularity of mutual funds derives primarily from the wide variety of different investments they make available to investors. Mutual funds provide diversified portfolios of common investments, such as money market instruments, government bonds, municipal bonds, and equities of large capitalization firms. Over the years, however, mutual funds have expanded into less-common investments, such as foreign securities, equities of small-capitalization companies, mortgage-backed securities, and high-yield bonds. Another advantage of mutual funds is their high marketability. Unlike many of the investments in which mutual funds invest, which may have poor marketability, the shares of mutual funds can be bought and sold daily at the funds' **net asset value.** The net asset value is calculated at the end of each trading day by the managers of the fund, based on the current market values of the securities held by the fund. Mutual fund management companies have also improved the popularity by offering funds conveniently through the mail or by telephone, by allowing investors to shift assets between funds, and by expanding distribution of the funds to broker/dealers that market their services directly to depository customers, sometimes in depository offices.

Today, mutual funds are the second-largest type of financial intermediary. Only commercial banks control more assets. At nearly $2 trillion on December 31, 1993, mutual funds have also been the fastest growing intermediaries—their

---

[6]Another important investment-oriented intermediary is the closed-end investment fund, typically a publicly-traded corporation that raises funds through the issuance of common stock. These funds are used to purchase stock in other corporations. These firms differ from open-end funds in that they do not stand ready to sell new shares and redeem outstanding shares at the firm's net asset value. At year-end 1993, closed-end funds had total financial assets of $79 billion.

WILL MUTUAL FUNDS BECOME THE LARGEST INTERMEDIARY

Mutual funds have become an increasing force in the money and capital markets since the mid-1970s. Consider that in 1977 mutual funds controlled assets of $77 billion, representing a mere 8% of the $945 billion in commercial bank financial assets. By November 1993, mutual funds were up to $2 trillion, or over 50% of total financial assets of commercial banks. In the interval, mutual funds surpassed the size of all thrift institutions and all life insurance companies.

One appeal of mutual funds is the wide variety of assets that investors can select. There are over 25 major fund classifications, including the major ones: money market, bonds, equities, state and municipal, and international.

Other appeals of mutual funds include marketability and diversification. Where else can the investor purchase a diversified portfolio of below-investment-grade corporate bonds and sell the entire investment with a simple phone call? The growth in mutual funds has raised a number of issues. First, there is concern that too much money will be controlled by too few investment managers. Second, there is worry that these investors might act in tandem to create more volatility in security prices. Third, mutual fund managers are starting to put pressure on corporate boards of directors and senior management when corporate performance in lagging. Clearly, fund managers are playing a more important role in determining who wins and loses the competition for capital.

How it Really Works

growth having been accelerated in recent years by the problems in the banking and thrift industries, many of which have failed or shrunk in order to improve their capital-to-assets ratios.

One of the main appeals of the mutual fund is access to professional management. Mutual funds are sold via a **prospectus**—a legal document describing the objectives of the fund, its management, and any fees charged for various services provided. It also describes in detail the fund's investment strategy.

LIMITED PARTNERSHIPS

One the most versatile types of investment-oriented financial intermediary, **limited partnerships** are composed of a general partner, who acts as the operating entity for the partnership and accepts unlimited liability for its actions, and one or more limited partners, who invest funds and accept liability only to the extent of the funds invested. Limited partnerships have the advantage of channeling income directly to the partners and thus avoiding a layer of corporate taxation. They also have one of the advantages of a corporate form of organization—limited liability for the limited partners.

Limited partnerships exist for many types of investments but are best suited for very specialized investments that require intensive management. Limited partnerships involve investments that have very long-term time horizons and volatile cash flows. They are very popular investments in real estate, oil and gas wells, loans to young companies (venture capital partnerships), and leveraged buyouts (LBO partnerships). One major drawback to the limited partnership is that it lacks marketability: few investors in limited partnerships are able to find markets for the shares they purchase. This tends to relegate limited partnership investments to a fairly small percentage of any investment portfolio.

REAL ESTATE INVESTMENT TRUSTS

The **real estate investment trust (REIT)** is an investment-oriented intermediary that, like the limited partnership, is a creature of the U.S. tax law. A REIT is a corporation, trust, or association primarily organized to own or finance real estate. It may hold income-producing real estate, invest in mortgages, finance real estate development and construction, and acquire and lease property to developers. As corporate entities, most REITs have a board of directors or trustees that is responsible to the REIT shareholders. Like the shares of most new companies, REIT shares typically are sold in a public offering. The major difference is that an initial public offering (IPO) of most companies is done after the company has established a track record. REITs, like limited partnerships, are sold based on representations made in a prospectus before they have established an investment track record. REITs are not limited to selling common stock, they may also sell preferred stock and issue warrants and debt.

The REIT has been granted a special position in the tax code. This special provision allows the REIT to be exempt from federal taxation if 95% of the income of the trust is distributed to its shareholders.[7]

✓ Checkpoints

3-16 What accounts for the very rapid growth of open-end mutual funds since the mid-1970s?

3-17 What is the investment specialty of the real estate investment trust?

3-18 What are the primary reasons for the use of the limited partnership?

SUMMARY AND REVIEW

1. **Describe the financial assets, liabilities, and functions of commercial banks.**

   Commercial banks have very a diversified asset structure. Loans are the largest asset category, amounting to 60% of total assets, and are spread between business, real estate, and consumer loans. They also invest heavily in U.S. government, agency and state and local government securities.

   Commercial banks have diversified liability structures. Banks raise funds by issuing deposits. Some banks rely on wholesale financing sources.

[7]Additional major requirements that must be met by a REIT to maintain its tax status include: (1) shares must be fully transferable; (2) there must be a minimum of 100 shareholders; (3) no more than 50% of its shares may be held by five or fewer individuals; and (4) 75% of assets and income must be derived from real estate.

2. **Explain how banks are organized for international activities.**

   Internationally, commercial banks carry out their activities using:

   1. Domestic offices.
   2. Foreign offices.
   3. Subsidiary companies located out of the country.
   4. Edge Act Corporations.
   5. International banking facilities (IBFs).

   Commercial banks perform the same services internationally that they do in the United States, except in some countries they can also be involved in underwriting and distributing securities.

3. **Describe the assets, liabilities, and functions of thrift institutions.**

   Thrift institutions are specialized depositories including savings and loans, savings banks, and credit unions. They specialize in origination, servicing, and investing in mortgage lending and consumer loans and issuing deposit liabilities to households.

4. **Compare the primary functions of life insurance companies, pension funds, investment banking firms, and finance companies.**

   Life insurance companies provide investment and mortality risk management services. **Pension funds** are the fastest growing of the major intermediaries and provide investment administration for retirement funds. They include both private and public state and local pension funds. **Investment banking firms** provide a wide variety of financial services. In fact, as a group, they provide just about every financial service except taking deposits. Their primary activities include:

   1. Underwriting financial assets such as stocks and bonds.
   2. Selling and distributing financial assets through brokerage and acting as dealers of specific assets.
   3. Advising customers on such transactions as mergers, financial restructurings, investments, acquisitions, hostile takeovers, corporate valuations, and other major transactions.
   4. Lending to customers with acceptable security collateral.

   Finance companies are the least regulated of our major intermediaries. Consumer finance companies specialize in consumer lending to individuals and secured lending to businesses.

5. **Characterize the role of investment-oriented intermediaries such as mutual funds, limited partnerships and real estate investment trusts.**

   Investment-oriented intermediaries represent a group of firms that specialize in pooling assets of investors and providing investment expertise. All these intermediaries share a common feature in that the investments they hold are not taxed at the intermediary level. These intermediaries include: (1) **open-end mutual funds**; (2) **limited partnerships**; and (3) **real estate investment trusts**.

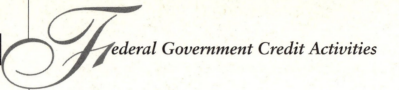

Federal Government Credit Activities

Learning Goals

After studying this appendix, you should be able to:

1. Discuss the rationale for government credit programs.
2. Describe the three primary types of government credit programs and discuss the special advantage of government sponsored enterprises.
3. Explain the activities of private financial institutions with government credit programs.
4. Describe the primary federal lending programs and the types of credit they make available.
5. Explain the impact of GSEs on private intermediaries.

The federal government is our nation's largest financial intermediary. Through its direct lending, guarantees, and sponsored enterprises, it is now about one-fifth the size of all private-sector intermediaries.

This appendix details the growth in federal government credit activities. The significance of these programs relates to the following issues:

1. The rationale for the federal government's participation in the credit markets.

2. The types of credit market programs government uses.

3. The impact that these programs have on the allocation of credit and on private-sector financial institutions.

4. The controversy surrounding the accelerated growth of these programs in the 1990s.

Rationales for Federal Government Credit Activities

Federal credit programs have four principal rationales.

1. *Reduce market imperfections:* These programs are seen as a way to reduce the impact of market imperfections. Many believe that without government involvement, certain groups of borrowers would be unable to obtain adequate credit, that worthy borrowers are not being adequately serviced— either because of an inadequate number of lenders or because lenders inaccurately view these borrowers as having excessive credit risks. Farmers and small businesses have been selected for federal credit benefits because they cannot compete effectively for credit in the private sector. Credit agencies that have been established to assist these groups include the Farm Credit Banks and the Small Business Administration loan guarantee programs.

2. *Achieve national priorities:* Credit programs have been designed to achieve major national priorities. The federal government's desire to improve and increase the nation's housing stock as outlined in the 1968 Housing Act, for example, led to the creation of the GNMA and the FHLMC. Other national priorities provided the rationale for creating the Export-Import Bank, the Rural Electrification Administration, and the Agency for International Development.

3. *Assist the disadvantaged:* Credit programs are used in conjunction with direct subsidies to assist disadvantaged groups. For example, the student loan program of the federal government provides financing for college students and includes a large direct subsidy in the form of below-market interest rates, despite extremely high default rates.

4. *Provide emergency funding:* Credit guarantees have been used for emergency loan purposes, such as the bailouts of Chrysler, Lockheed, and New York City. More recently, Congress has created agencies to raise money for the bailout of the federal insurance fund, which covers the deposits of failed thrift institutions.

✓ Checkpoints

A3-1 Why is the federal government involved in the credit markets?

A3-2 What national priorities have been identified for government credit assistance?

A3-3 How have government credit programs been used for emergency purposes?

Types of Federal Government Lending Programs

The credit programs of the federal government can be classified into the following three groups:

1. Direct loans.
2. Loan guarantees.
3. Government sponsored enterprises.

There are about 350 different government direct and guaranteed lending programs that fall under these three classifications.

DIRECT LENDING PROGRAMS

The federal government has a wide variety of programs that provide direct loans to individuals, businesses, and government units. These programs are financed through appropriated tax revenues and borrowing. Direct lending programs provide credit on more favorable terms than borrowers could obtain in the private market. This frequently means that loans can be made at interest rates that are below market rates and that credit can be extended for longer periods of time than would otherwise be available from the private sector.

Business and agriculture have been the primary beneficiaries of direct government lending programs. Business has benefited from the activities of the Export-Import Bank, Small Business Administration, Rural Electrification Administration, and the Agency for International Development. Agricultural interests have received loans from the Farmers' Home Administration and the price support programs of the Commodity Credit Corporation.

GUARANTEE PROGRAMS

Federal government loan guarantee programs guarantee the payment of principal and interest, in whole or in part, in the event the borrower defaults on a loan. These loans are originated, serviced, and funded by private-sector institutions. The loan guarantee effectively transfers the risk of default from the private-sector institution to the federal government. By providing credit on more favorable terms than would otherwise be available, loan guarantees channel financial resources to favored groups. A borrower with a government guaranteed loan can, in effect, go to the top of the credit ladder.

The largest user of loan guarantees by far is the housing sector. Home mortgages insured by the **Federal Housing Administration** and guaranteed by the **Veterans Administration** represented over 70% of government guarantees in the 1980s.

GOVERNMENT SPONSORED ENTERPRISES (GSES)

During the last decade, GSEs have become the largest federal credit program. The initial capital used to start these corporations was provided by government and private sources. In recent years, these organizations have largely converted to private ownership, but they still retain a special status in the credit markets because of their government sponsorship. The most recently created GSEs have been started as privately owned corporations with substantial government conferred advantages.

The advantages granted to GSEs include various combinations of the following:

1. The ability to issue stock and debt securities that can be held by federally regulated financial institutions, while similar securities issued by private companies are prohibited.

2. An implied guarantee from the federal government, referred to as *agency status,* which allows these agencies to borrow at interest rates below even the best-rated private borrowers.

3. Exemption from Securities and Exchange Commission registration requirements.

4. National or regional monopolies in credit-granting activities.

5.   Regulatory net worth or capital requirements that are lower than those imposed on comparable private institutions.

Through their overwhelming advantages over private-sector competitors, GSEs account for most of the rapid growth in government credit programs.

The significant role of government credit programs is evident from the fact that from 1988 through 1993, agencies and GSEs represented 17.5% of total net borrowing in the entire U.S. economy. This figure does not include government guarantee and insurance programs such as the Federal Housing Administration's mortgage insurance program, Veteran's Administration mortgage insurance program, or Small Business Administration loan guarantee programs. This growth in federal credit programs is heavily concentrated in GSEs.

Table A3.1 provides dramatic evidence of the growth of GSEs. It shows the total debt plus the securities guaranteed by each of the privately owned GSEs, including the FHLBs, the FNMA, the FHLMC, the Student Loan Marketing Association (SLMA), and the Farm Credit Banks (FCBs).

TABLE A3.1

Total Debt Plus Guaranteed Securities of the Government Sponsored Enterprises
1979–1993
(dollars in billions)

Enterprise	1993	1984	1979
FHLBs	$ 142	$ 65	$ 33
FNMA	662	120	49
FHLMC	495	81	18
SLMA	40	6	2
FCBs	53	72	33
Total	$1,392	$344	$135

Sources: *Federal Reserve Bulletin, Statistical Abstract of the United States,* and *Annual Economic Report of the President,* various issues.

These GSEs grew by over $1 trillion from 1979 through 1993, representing a compound growth rate of 18% per annum. This compares to a growth rate in total assets of all U.S. commercial banks for the same period of 8% per annum.

✓ Checkpoints

A3-4   What are the three basic types of government credit programs? How would you describe them? What is an example of each?

A3-5   What government credit programs have grown the fastest? In which credit markets are the government credit programs most active?

A3-6   What is a government sponsored enterprise? Can you name several? What advantages has Congress granted the GSEs to carry out their various missions?

A3-7 Which of these advantages seem to be the most important to GSEs in enhancing their competitive position?

Private Financial Institution Involvement with Government Credit Programs

Private-sector financial institutions have several reasons to be involved in the federal government lending programs. In fact, most of these programs rely on private-sector institutions to make them work. Financial institutions can benefit from being involved with federal lending programs through origination of assets for sale to and/or guaranteed by the government, servicing assets sold to an agency, and borrowing from or selling loans to an agency to increase liquidity. Each of these activities can generate increased profits for the private-sector institution.

ORIGINATION ACTIVITIES

Financial institutions are active in the origination of assets that carry government guarantees and loans sold to a GSE. Table A3.2 shows the major programs and institutions that are involved.

Private financial institutions profit from these programs by charging fees to originate loans and, in some cases, selling loans to the agency at a price higher than the amount funded to the borrower.

TABLE A3.2

Private-sector Participation in Originating and Servicing
Government Credit Programs

Federal Credit Program	Private Intermediaries Using the Origination and Servicing Programs
FHA mortgage insurance program and VA mortgage insurance programs	Mortgage bankers, thrifts, commercial banks
GNMA, FHA, and VA mortgage guarantee programs; FNMA and FHLMC conventional single-family and multifamily mortgage purchase programs	Mortgage bankers, thrifts, commercial banks, insurance companies
Small Business Administration loan insurance programs	Commercial banks, thrifts, finance companies
Student Loan insurance program	Commercial banks, thrifts
Federal Agricultural Mortgage Corporation farm mortgage purchase program	Commercial banks

SERVICING ACTIVITIES

Private financial institutions service loans that are purchased by government agencies or guaranteed by government agencies and sold to others. These servicing activities can represent major profit centers for the servicing institution. This is especially true in the residential mortgage market in which the government purchases or guarantees a majority of the loans originated. Financial institutions service other types of loans for federal agencies as well. Some of these programs are shown in Table A3.2.

For a large number of private financial institutions, the servicing of government guaranteed loans sold to private firms and loans sold to GSEs constitutes a major portion of their business activities. Their motivation to service these loans lies in the profit made from the servicing fees.

Liquidity-producing Activities

A number of federal lending programs are designed primarily to provide liquidity to financial institutions. There are two types of agencies that provide this service. The first type includes among its activities making loans directly to financial institutions. These include the Federal Home Loan Banks (FHLBs), the Central Liquidity Fund of the National Credit Union Administration, and the Federal Reserve Banks. The second type of liquidity-enhancing federal lending agency is one that purchases or guarantees loans, thereby increasing their marketability. Agencies designed primarily for this purpose include the GNMA, the FNMA, the FHLMC, the SLMA, and the **Federal Agricultural Mortgage Corporation.**

Of the three federal lending programs designed to provide liquidity to financial institutions, only the FHLBs are significant in terms of dollars lent. The Federal Reserve Banks' discount window and the Central Liquidity Fund are used infrequently, since most banks and credit unions hold a large percentage of assets in liquid forms. The FHLBs, by contrast, had total loans outstanding in excess of $103 billion at year-end 1993. The FHLBs provide short-term liquidity advances as well as long-term advances with maturities of up to ten years or more, primarily to S&Ls and commercial banks. The availability of longer-term advances has encouraged thrift institutions to borrow large amounts from FHLBs to fund long-term home loans. At year-end 1993, FHLB advances represented 8.5% of the total liabilities of S&Ls and federally chartered savings banks. The FIRREA of 1989 allowed commercial banks and credit unions to have access to FHLB loans when they are significantly involved in housing finance. This has encouraged growth in commercial bank and credit union borrowing from the FHLBs. On July 31, 1993, 2,229 thrifts, 1,754 commercial banks, 46 credit unions, and 14 insurance companies were members of FHLBs.

The second government-supported source of liquidity for financial institutions comes through the use of government agencies and sponsored enterprises that purchase and/or guarantee loans. Such loans are readily marketable and therefore can be converted easily to cash when necessary. The mortgage purchase and guarantee programs of GNMA, FNMA, and FHLMC have grown rapidly in the 1980s and 90s. They now account for more than 49.1% of all residential mortgage debt in the United States. Of this, FNMA and FHLMC accounted for almost 37.4% at year-end 1993, up from only 6.5% ten years earlier.

The Secondary Mortgage Market

As discussed above, the GSEs are the dominant residential mortgage finance organizations. Consequently, it is important to understand how private financial institutions interact with these organizations. Commercial banks, thrifts, and mortgage banking companies are the U.S.'s largest originators and servicers of residential mortgages. These firms originate residential mortgages with the expectation that they will be sold or swapped for mortgage-backed securities. The market for these mortgages is known as the *secondary mortgage market*. Exhibit A3.1 provides an overview of the activities involved in using the secondary mortgage market.

EXHIBIT A3.1

Overview of the Secondary Mortgage Market

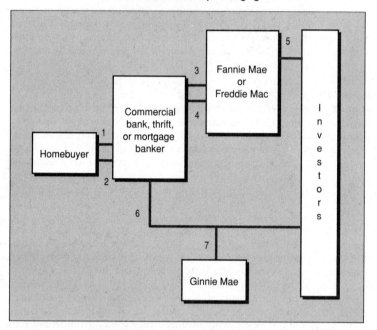

The steps involved in the process are as follows:

1. The mortgage is originated by the financial institution.

2. Monthly payments are made by the homeowner to the financial institution servicing the mortgage.

3. The mortgage is sold to Fannie Mae or Freddie Mac for cash, or a pool of mortgages is swapped to Fannie Mae or Freddie Mac for securities guaranteed by these GSEs.

4. Monthly principal and interest payments and principal prepayments are made to Fannie Mae or Freddie Mac some weeks after the servicer receives them from the homebuyer.

5. Mortgages purchased by GSEs are sold to investors, as are mortgage securities received by mortgage lenders in swap transactions.

6. FHA and VA mortgages are packed into securities with full faith and credit guaranteed by Ginnie Mae.

7. The mortgage servicer then remits principal and interest payments to the trustee for the securities, which are then remitted to investors.

The secondary mortgage market is quickly becoming the primary method by which home mortgages are financed in the United States. Thus, consumer-based financial institutions that want to provide home mortgage service to their customers must become skilled in using this market.

✓ Checkpoints

A3-8 What involvement do private-sector institutions have with government credit programs?

A3-9 Who are the major lending intermediaries that originate for government credit programs?

A3-10 What is the secondary mortgage market? Explain the primary steps in the financing of a home using the secondary mortgage market.

Primary Federal Lending Organizations and Programs

This section presents a short history of the major activities of the federal agencies that provide direct lending, guarantees, and government sponsored enterprise credit.

FARM CREDIT BANKS

The Farm Credit Banks (FCBs) are a farm credit system consisting of a number of cooperatively owned banks that provide credit to farmers. This system dates back to 1916 and was expanded during the Great Depression of the 1930s, when farmers faced severe foreclosure problems. It represented the first government sponsored credit program.

The system includes the Federal Land Banks (FLBs), Federal Intermediate Credit Banks (FICBs), and Banks for Cooperatives (BCs). Today, the capitalization for these banks comes from the farmers and farm cooperatives that borrow from them. The banks provide credit to farmers who want to purchase farm land, equipment, livestock, seed and fertilizer, and inventory for farm cooperatives. At year-end 1992, the farm credit system had $53 billion in loans outstanding.

GOVERNMENT NATIONAL MORTGAGE ASSOCIATION (GNMA)

GNMA or **Ginnie Mae** was created in 1968 to guarantee mortgage-backed securities that were backed by FHA and VA mortgages. Mortgage-backed securities were virtually unknown at the time. Today GNMA securities enjoy ready reception in the capital market because they carry the "full faith and credit" guarantee of the federal government, and their huge volume creates high marketability. As of year-end 1993, GNMA had guaranteed over $414 billion in securities. Over 1,100 lenders have participated in GNMA programs since its establishment.

GNMA does not issue securities itself; instead, it guarantees securities of private issuers. The guarantee provides that the owner of a GNMA security will have prompt receipt of scheduled monthly principal and interest payments on the underlying mortgages, as well as prepayments of principal when the mortgage borrower repays early or defaults.

FEDERAL NATIONAL MORTGAGE ASSOCIATION (FNMA)

FNMA or **Fannie Mae** is the largest of the mortgage finance GSEs. It was established in 1938 to purchase mortgages from lenders. It financed these purchases by issuing debt securities. In 1954 it became a mixed-ownership corporation, owned partly by shareholders (those organizations that sold it mortgages) and partly by the government. Then in 1968, Congress split the corporation into two entities, GNMA and FNMA, and FNMA became a privately owned entity. Today its stock is widely held and traded on the New York Stock Exchange.

FNMA operates by purchasing mortgages and issuing guaranteed mortgage-backed securities. In its purchase program, it buys FHA-insured, VA-guaranteed, and conventional mortgages on single and multifamily properties. The maximum dollar amount of each mortgage is set by law using an index. This is intended to limit the benefits of a government support program to moderate-income families. In 1992, the maximum exceeded $200,000. Loans qualifying for purchase are known as *conforming mortgages.* If a lender wishes to hold mortgages but still have the benefits of an FNMA guarantee, it can swap the mortgages for a mortgage pass-through security backed by the same mortgages. The lender, in effect, holds the same mortgages as before but now has the benefit of the greater marketability and safety of the FNMA security.

FNMA had assets of over $201 billion at year-end 1993 and, in addition, had $496 billion of guaranteed mortgage pass-through securities outstanding. These securities are not shown as debt on the FNMA balance sheet since they are not considered a direct obligation. They are not "owed" by the agency; like GNMA securities, they are merely guaranteed by the agency.

FEDERAL HOME LOAN MORTGAGE CORPORATION (FHLMC)

FHLMC or **Freddie Mac** was established in 1970 to provide a secondary market for privately insured, or conventional, mortgages. At that time, GNMA and FNMA were limited to FHA-insured and VA-guaranteed mortgages. Funds to capitalize FHLMC were provided initially by the FHLB system. In 1990, it issued stock to the public and repaid the FHLBs. FHLMC stock is widely held and traded on the NYSE.

Because of the similarity of their programs, FHLMC and FNMA are strong competitors. Over the years, FHLMC has been a major innovator in the field of mortgage-backed securities, having created the first conventional pass-through security, guaranteed mortgage security, and collateralized mortgage obligation. At year-end 1993, FHLMC had total assets of over $50 billion. It also has guaranteed mortgage-backed securities over $439 billion.

FEDERAL HOME LOAN BANKS (FHLBS)

The system of 12 FHLBs were established in 1932 to provide liquidity for savings and loan associations and savings banks and to encourage housing finance. Over the years, the system expanded its mission from providing primarily short-term loans to meet liquidity needs to longer-term credit and expanded depository services to member institutions.[1] Among the expanded list of lending services available from FHLBs are:

---

[1]The primary advantage of FHLB lending programs derives from the low cost of FHLB borrowing and resulting lending costs. Data from 1988 to 1991 show that FHLB's borrowed funds in the open market at between 1 and 51 basis points over comparable Treasury securities. This is generally a narrower spread than AAA-rated debt compared to Treasury. More on the advantages of FHLB membership is found in H. Robert Bartell Jr., *Community Bank Membership in the Federal Home Loan Bank System: A Decision Guide* (Madison: Graduate School of Banking, the University of Wisconsin, Madison, 1990).

- Short-term variable-rate loans.
- Fixed-rate and adjustable-rate long-term loans.
- Lines of credit.
- Interest rate swaps.
- Letters of credit.

The Financial Institution Reform, Recovery and Enforcement Act of 1989 (FIRREA) expanded the membership base of the banks by making it much easier for commercial banks to obtain membership in FHLBs. At year-end 1993, the FHLBs had $142 billion in loans outstanding.

STUDENT LOAN MARKETING ASSOCIATION (SLMA)

SLMA or **Sallie Mae** is the nation's largest investor in and servicer of government-insured student loans; it was established to provide a secondary market for student loans originated by commercial banks and others. SLMA stock is held by the public as well as by a group of lending institutions that originate student loans. SLMA is also the nation's largest servicer of student loans. Many originators of student loans hold loans in portfolio until the student graduates and must begin to repay it. At that point, most financial institutions sell the loans to SLMA because of the complexity and high costs of servicing the default-ridden student loans. At year-end 1993, SLMA had debt outstanding of over $40 billion.

FEDERAL HOUSING ADMINISTRATION (FHA)

This mortgage insurance agency was established by the government in 1934 to provide insurance against risk of default on home mortgages. The objective was to encourage lenders to make longer-term mortgages than the customary 5- to 15-year maturities of that period. FHA is an agency within the Department of Housing and Urban Development. Today, FHA administers over 30 programs that provide insurance on single-family homes, multifamily projects, mobile homes, residential condominiums, cooperatives, and housing for the elderly.

SMALL BUSINESS ADMINISTRATION (SBA)

The **Small Business Administration** was established in 1953. Today, the SBA provides financial and management assistance to small businesses and to victims of natural disasters. The SBA provides financial support through direct loans and guaranteed loans. The SBA also provides guaranteed loans to small-business investment companies (SBICs). These are privately owned and SBA-regulated organizations that supply venture capital and long-term financing to small businesses.

SBA-guaranteed loans, like GNMA securities, carry the full faith and credit guarantee of the federal government. As a result, they are considered free of default risk and can be bought and sold easily.

✓ Checkpoints

A3-11 Which government credit programs provide liquidity to private financial institutions?

A3-12 What do the FNMA and FHLMC have in common?

Impact of GSEs on Private Intermediaries

Recent concern over the growth of GSEs comes at a time when both commercial banks and thrifts are finding it difficult to earn reasonable profits. Also, they are being accused of engaging in high-risk activities, such as making loans to developing countries, participating in leveraged buyouts, and investing in commercial real estate and junk bonds. In addition, banks and thrifts are feeling the sting of higher capital standards, more intense examination scrutiny, and higher deposit insurance premiums.

If these fast-growing agencies have used their preferred, government-granted borrowing advantages; lower capitalization requirements; and securities and tax exemptions to undercut the commercial banks and thrifts in markets they once dominated, then it could be argued that this has contributed to greater risk-taking by these institutions and increased failure rates. Agency inroads into traditional bank and thrift markets may be one of the major reasons that banks and thrifts began lending into riskier markets where yields have not been held down by government activity. Lower yields on traditional activities may also account for the poor profitability of depository institutions in recent years and their increased failure rate. If this is so, it makes the issue of GSE growth an important one for our public policymakers.

How

it

Really

Works

CONGRESS CLIPS SALLIE MAE'S WINGS

Over the years, GSEs prospered, thanks to their government-granted competitive advantages. The most important of these advantages has been their preferred borrowing position in the capital markets related to their close relationship to the U.S. Treasury. They have also benefited from their monopoly or near-monopoly market positions in the markets they serve. The Student Loan Marketing Association is no exception. In just two decades, Sallie Mae grew to become the over $40 billion behemoth of the government student loan business, with earnings over $400 million in 1992.

In 1993, however, the government again proved that governments that give can also take away. The Congress passed a law requiring that by 1998, 60% of all student loans be made directly by the government instead of by commercial banks and other lenders. These lenders subsequently market them to Sallie Mae. The programmatic change will cut into over one-half of Sallie's market. In addition, Congress added a fee of 0.3% on all loans purchased by Sallie.

Congress's action sent Sallie Mae's stock price down about 30% and sent shivers through the managements and shareholders of Fannie Mae and Freddie Mac, which receive benefits similar to those of Sallie. It also elevated the conflict over whether the GSEs have gotten too big at the expense of private-sector competitors.

It also raises questions about the impact of new agencies that have been created in recent years. Congress has authorized the **Federal Agricultural Mortgage Corporation (Farmer Mac)**, a secondary market for farm loans; the **College Construction Loan**

Insurance Corporation (Connie Lee), a reinsurer of College academic facility bonds; and is also considering an agency to buy and package small-business loans. The latter would cut into commercial banks' so-called middle market for business loans, which has been a major area of investment emphasis for banks in recent years, and raises the question of whether banks would have any unique lending role left to play. This question has already been raised concerning thrift institutions, in which government agencies dominate the residential mortgage market—historically the thrift's principal market.

✓ Checkpoints

A3-13 How might GSEs adversely impact private intermediaries? Which groups are helped and hurt by the GESs?

A3-14 Which private financial institutions are most likely to be adversely impacted by the GSEs in terms of their portfolio management activities?

SUMMARY AND REVIEW

1. **Discuss the rationale for government credit programs.**

   Government rationalizes its involvement in the credit markets in order to: (1) reduce perceived market imperfections; (2) achieve national priorities; (3) assist disadvantaged groups; and (4) meet emergency needs.

2. **Describe the three primary types of government credit programs and discuss the special advantage of government sponsored enterprises**

   The federal government's credit programs can be classified into three primary groups: (1) direct loans; (2) loan guarantees; and (3) government sponsored enterprises. The largest of these programs are the GSEs. Their substantial growth and profitability are the result of advantages granted them by the federal government. These include the following: (1) they issue debts that are allowable investments for many intermediaries; (2) they have the implied guarantee of the federal government; (3) they are exempt from Securities and Exchange Commission registration; (4) they have regional or national monopolies; and (5) they are not subject to depository capital requirements.

3. **Explain the activities of private financial institutions with government credit programs.**

   Private financial institutions are involved with government credit programs in three ways. They originate loans purchased, insured, or guaranteed by government credit programs; service loans for government credit programs; and take advantage of government programs to obtain liquidity and long-term credit.

4. **Describe the primary federal lending program beneficiaries and the types of credit they make available.**

   At present, there are over 350 different government credit programs. Through federal credit programs, more generous credit is made available at lower cost to a wide range of borrowers, including homebuyers, farmers, small businesses, college students, rural electrical cooperatives, and exporters.

5.   **Explain the impact of GSEs on private intermediaries.**

The growth in the GSE programs has raised serious questions about the impact of these dominant programs on private-sector institutions. Their ability to raise funds at lower costs than most depositories make them the low-cost producer of credit for certain types of loans. They can undercut the private sector, create unfair competition, and contribute to failures.

CHAPTER 4

Regulation, Insurers, and Regulators of Financial Institutions

Learning Goals

After studying this chapter, you should be able to:

1. Explain the public good theory of regulation and list the primary goals of public policy in regulating financial markets and institutions.
2. Discuss the public policy debate over federal government deposit insurance programs.
3. Explain several theories that explain how the regulatory process really works and how regulation affects the management of financial firms.
4. Describe the relationships among the primary regulators and insurers of financial institutions.

If you plan to work in or with a financial firm, then you should understand how the regulatory implementation process can influence the performance of a financial institution just as much as the quality of the firm's management can.

Regulation is a basic component of the U.S. financial system. Since the crash of 1929 and subsequent Depression of the 1930s, regulation of the financial services industry has expanded in both scope and breadth. In the 1980s, regulators overhauled quite a bit of financial regulation and increased surveillance and monitoring of institutions—largely because of the thrift industry debacle and the failures of commercial banks and insurance companies but also because of scandal, fraud, and self-dealing in some sectors of the financial services business. These problems also prompted the legislators to increase penalties for such acts. Today, most regulating authorities have a greater assortment of effective tools and resources to implement regulation and to examine a financial firm's compliance.

This chapter raises a number of questions about the regulatory process as it relates to managing a financial firm. Why does government regulate the financial services industry? How does it implement and enforce regulation? What are the major regulatory agencies and insurance organizations; more specifically, how do they affect the industry? The appendix to this chapter expands upon the more sweeping regulatory and legislative improvements since the Depression, such as the **Financial Institutions Reform, Recovery, and Enforcement Act of 1989 (FIRREA) and the Federal Deposit Insurance Corporation Improvement Act (FDICIA) of 1991.**

Public Good Rationale for Regulation

One possible rationale for much of existing regulation of the financial services business is that it is for the public good. The **public good theory of regulation** helps us to understand how regulatory decisions are made on the premise that regulation of financial markets and institutions is justified when it corrects an alleged or proven deficiency in the competitive market process.

The **model of competitive markets** provides a framework for analyzing whether a market is indeed operating toward the public good. For example, the number of sellers in a market may be limited, as in a monopoly (one seller) or an oligopoly (few powerful sellers). The seller can pretty much control the transaction. Buyers may not understand information about the product due to its complexity. Consequently, societies impose regulations on the marketplace to eliminate any unfair advantage that one party—usually the seller—might have over the other in a transaction. A fair amount of this legislation provides customers with equal access to markets and information. The following section discusses some of these regulatory goals, their effects on the operation of financial institutions, and managerial implications.

1. *Increase competition:* Some regulation provides potential sellers with equal access to a market in order to encourage competition, which usually benefits the consumer through improved quality of service at a lower price. At one time, bank and thrift regulators could restrict the development of market monopolies by approving new branches of an institution only in markets not already concentrated by that institution. A **highly concentrated market** is a trade area with few institutions competing in it. In 1991, before the Bank of America merged with the Security Pacific Banks of California, managers of both institutions and regulators analyzed levels of financial concentration, determined which branches might have produced high levels of concentration in those markets after the merger, and then sold off the least strategically advantageous branches. This process reduced excessive concentration. In 1991, Salomon Brothers, Inc., the large investment banker, admitted violating Treasury auction trading rules. This admission raised doubts about the adequacy of competition in the primary Treasury security market and resulted in a major modification of the auction process so that more investors could participate.

2. *Reduce information asymmetries:* Claims of inadequate or misleading information account for a growing amount of consumer-oriented financial regulation—not necessarily because of underhanded activity but because financial contracts, like insurance policies, are becoming more complex and difficult

to interpret. And so public policymakers and consumer groups demand new regulations on disclosure and toward standardization of product and service descriptions, so as to provide consumers with equal access to information. Table 4.1 summarizes many of these major consumer protection laws that deal with information asymmetries and others dealing with discrimination.

T A B L E   4 . 1

Major Consumer Lending Protection Laws

Law	Effect on Financial Service Industry
Consumer Credit Protection Act	Creditors must state the cost of borrowing in a common language, to ensure easy comparisons of costs between lenders.
Real Estate Settlements and Procedures Act	Lenders must estimate certain costs related to closing on a home purchase and obtaining a mortgage.
Equal Credit Opportunity Act	Lenders must treat all credit applicants equally with respect to personal characteristics.
Community Reinvestment Act	Regulators consider local lending records of a depository before approving mergers and acquisitions. If records suggest discrimiation, then the depository may not win approval for restructuring.
Fair Credit Reporting Act	Lenders must follow set procedures for correcting mistakes on a credit report.
Fair Credit Billing Act	Creditors must promptly correct billing mistakes.
Electronic Fund Transfer Act	Lenders and other institutions servicing electronic payments must meet certain conditions regarding transfers.
Home Mortgage Disclosure Act	Lenders must maintain records on mortgage lending by census tract.
Truth-in-Savings Act	Depositories must disclose methodology used to access fees and pay interest on accounts.
Affordable Housing Act	Mortgage lenders must (a) allow borrowers to review calculations on their mortgages and (b) notify borrowers if their mortgages are sold.

There are a number of regulations concerning equal and fair access to information. The first major piece was the Consumer Credit Protection Act of 1968. This act required lenders to use a consistent methodology for quoting interest rates on loans, referred to as **truth-in-lending,** so that consumers can more easily compare interest rates offered by various institutions. Insurance companies must also provide standardized information about policies so that potential buyers can better understand and compare complicated deals according to their individual needs. Regulators also insist upon prompt settlement of insurance claims and truth in the marketing of insurance products serviced. Furthermore, publicly held corporations and other organizations selling securities to the public must comply with disclosure mandates (often through accounting practices and documentation) so that potential buyers as well as owners can more thoroughly analyze and compare the products available. Clearly, there are considerable administrative costs in capturing, analyzing, and disseminating such a volume of educational information and financial reports.

3. *Reduce potential for insider abuse and fraud:* Related to reducing information asymmetries is protecting investors from fraud and insider misuse of information. Most of our security laws and insider-trading restrictions work to ensure that a company's officers and directors do not buy and sell a company's stock or bonds using information to which only they, because of their position, have access. Information released by companies and their officers is also subject to disclosure regulations to ensure that it is factual and timely and to discourage insiders from giving misleading signals to unknowing buyers of the company's securities.

4. *Reduce prejudice or bias of supply:* Years ago, federal aviation regulations forced airlines to fly to cities that were not profitable locations. Similarly, the Federal Reserve System influences the payments system to ensure that all parts of the country have access to the check-clearing system, even if servicing remote areas is unprofitable. Another form of discrimination based on locality is **redlining** in mortgage lending, where a lender refuses to provide mortgages to customers who live in certain neighborhoods where property values are feared to decline. The term *redlining* originated when a lender got caught with a city map on which censored neighborhoods were outlined in red pencil.

In the 1960s, 1970s, and again in the 1990s, eliminating racial and sexual discrimination became a high social priority, with many laws passed toward achieving that goal. With respect to the financial markets, legislation focused on discriminatory practices of institutions lending to specific classes of consumers on the basis of race, sex, and sexual orientation.

Price may also be discriminatory. In some instances, access to markets is physically possible and necessary but price-prohibitive, as with insurance for those who live in flood planes or along fault lines. In such cases, the federal government has intervened and sometimes provided subsidies so that consumers can afford flood insurance and earthquake insurance. Another type of program is **life-line banking,** a mandate requiring depositories to offer a basic, low-cost checking account service to the poor.

5. *Encourage socially desirable credit allocation:* Regulators occasionally have altered the lending powers of financial institutions to encourage credit allocation toward what is socially desirable, defined by Congress and government bureaucrats through legislation and regulation. Owning a home might

POLITICAL CONTRIBUTIONS AND BOND DEALS

In the fall of 1993, pressure on investment banking firms grew so great that they had to take up a messy issue. It seems that the nation's major investment bankers, which underwrite municipal securities, had been making large political contributions to state and local public officials who have a say in selecting the investment banker to underwrite their securities. The state and municipal bond market is one of the largest and least regulated of all markets. The $1.2 trillion market issued well over 1 million bonds in 1992 by over 50,000 different issuing authorities. This activity represents significant underwriting fees for the investment bankers who vie for a piece of the action. Moreover, since most municipalities do not require competitive bidding for this business, it is tailor-made for nonprice competition and questionable payments to politicians.

Eventually, the Public Securities Association and the Municipal Securities Rulemaking Board, private organizations made up of municipal bond underwriters, developed proposals and rules prohibiting the contributions. Following the proposals, a majority of the large underwriting firms agreed to a moratorium on political contributions to potential customers.

In the wake of the investment bankers' action, attention turned to the legal firms that represent municipal bond issuers and the investment bank underwriters. Law firms involved in bond underwriting are also major contributors to politicians. Despite the pressure on the investment bankers, however, the lawyers maintained that there was no connection between their contributions and legal work needed by state and local governments.

Source: "The Trouble with Munis," *Business Week*, Sept. 6 1993, pp. 44–47.

Legal and Ethical Issues

STAMPING OUT REDLINING

For nearly 20 years, the federal government has been in the business of stamping out redlining in mortgage lending by analyzing an institution's lending data. The Department of Housing and Urban Development (HUD) works with groups who use testers—people hired to act as customers to determine if discrimination takes place, much like undercover officers in drug enforcement. Examiners from the Office of the Comptroller of the Currency (OCC) aggressively refer suspected discriminatory banks to the Justice Department, which can sue lenders considered guilty of redlining.

How do regulators prove the practice of redlining? Many experts view this question as an unusually murky one in the law. After all, the whole purpose of underwriting loans and establishing credit standards is to discriminate the low risks from the high and to have a choice in the level of risk that one wishes to bear. How would you respond to an examiner's accusation that your "sound" credit analysis is discriminatory?

Source: "Sniffing Out Unfair Lenders, *Buisness Week*, Oct. 11, 1993, p. 143.

Legal and Ethical Issues

*L*EGAL *and* *E*THICAL ISSUES

DO LAWSUITS REDUCE IPO SHARE PRICES?

One of the biggest threats to the managers and directors of a company's initial public offering (IPO) is the shareholder class-action suit. A number of law firms monitor company stock prices looking for companies that experience a large price drop. These are candidates for the shareholder class-action suit. The lawyers then develop a complaint, usually alleging that managers and directors withheld information or provided misinformation in the offering materials used in connection with marketing the IPO. This represents a classic case of a potential information asymmetry. The suits rarely go to a court, however. The lawyers, working on contigency-fee basis, like to settle out of court for their usual fee of 30–35% plus expenses.

The risk of lawsuits may create an interesting and perverse incentive. Issuers of IPO's, concerned about the lawsuit threat, have the incentive to sell the stock for below its true value, hoping it will rise in price once the secondary market develops. A rising price provides evidence that management, directors, and underwriters made no untrue statements or omissions in the registration statements.

Research on the subject seems to suggest that lawsuits are primarily focused on larger companies where settlements are potentially the largest. Small IPOs do not seem to attract the lawyers, even when shareholders are hurt from declining prices.

Source: "Class Acts," *Economist*, March 19, 1994, p. 95.

be considered socially desirable, based on the high percentage of assets that S&Ls are required to invest in home mortgages. Other attempts to increase the supply of home mortgage credit include the creation of the **Government National Mortgage Company** (Ginnie Mae) and the expansion of the **Federal National Mortgage Association** (Fannie Mae) in 1968 and the chartering of the **Federal Home Loan Mortgage Company** (Freddie Mac) in 1970. Education might also be considered socially desirable, based on the establishment of the **Student Loan Marketing Association** (Sallie Mae) to ensure an adequate supply of funds for student tuition at colleges, universities, and trade schools.

6. *Promote safety and soundness:* As with *public good* and *socially desirable*, regulation and legislation define how a financial firm is s*afe and sound*—not likely to fail. Over the years, proponents of government intervention have justified various regulating agencies and laws as means of ensuring the safety and soundness of individual financial intermediaries, to preserve the integrity of the financial system overall. Benston and Kaufman (1988) outlined some of the fears that regulations of commercial banks attempt to allay:

1. Costs of financial panics and threatened interruptions to the payment system related to commercial bank failure.

2. Possible local and regional economic disruptions caused by commercial bank failures in particular pockets of the country.

3. Loss of wealth of depositors, which is especially harsh for low- and moderate-income households.

4. Excessive risks involved in lending activities as a result of the commercial banking industry's ability to issue liquid deposits.

5. Potential excessive competition between banks and nonbanks.

6. Conflicts of interest between banking activities and securities issuance and commerce.

There are many examples of intervention to address these issues. During much of the period from the 1930s through the 1970s, regulatory agencies worked to maintain barriers to market entry, restrict branching activities, control interest rates on demand deposits and savings accounts, and limit the nonbank activities of bank holding companies. The **Glass-Steagall Act** of 1933 was passed to prohibit banks from underwriting corporate stocks and bonds, and the **McFadden Act** of 1927 was approved to prohibit interstate branching. More recently, FIRREA of 1989 and the FDICIA of 1991 were ratified to increase the capital requirements of commercial banks in response to the failure of the FSLIC and the increased number of commercial bank failures in the 1980s.

7. *Protect taxpayers from deposit insurance fund failures:* Should a regulatory body protect: (1) the depositor's funds in the institution, (2) the deposit insurance corporation's reserves, or (3) the institutions in distress? or all three? Since the answer may change as each governmental administration defines or redefines *safety and soundness,* managers of financial institutions should keep up with the predominant political views on regulation, so as to predict regulatory response to financial distress.

Since the 1930s, regulators have acted to protect each of the above groups at one time or another. Most consistently, regulation has safeguarded depositors, even during the recent failure of the FSLIC. Occasionally, it has preserved very large financial institutions and their shareholders, despite the failure or impending failure of the institution. For example, in 1984, the FDIC helped the Continental Bank of Illinois to avert failure and ended up owning stock in Continental; the Federal Reserve Bank of Chicago also pitched in to alleviate a more severe liquidity problem at the bank.[1]

8. *Support monetary policy goals:* The Great Depression of the 1930s left over 9,000 bank failures and resulted in a significant reduction in the nation's money supply, which many economists say contributed to the Depression's length and severity. If a smoothly functioning financial system is essential to the successful implementation of monetary policy, then a central bank would find its efforts to achieve targets for the growth of several monetary aggregates or for specific interest rate levels frustrated by bank failures and financial stress. The Federal Reserve wants the banking system to respond to a more stimulative monetary policy by increasing loans and investments in the economy.

---

[1]The assistance given Continental Bank was a government bailout success. The bank returned to financial stability, and the government was able to sell securities it received at a profit. The bank was purchased by BankAmerica Corporation, the large holding company, in 1994.

DUELING REGULATIONS?

As you may have noticed, regulation and the Fed's own goals are sometimes at odds. Many of the goals behind the safety-and-soundness rationales for regulation run counter to those toward the public good. Consequently, some laws were abolished during the period of deregulation in the 1980s. The most significant legal and regulatory changes to affect depositories was the elimination of interest rate ceilings on time and savings accounts and the expansion of transaction account powers to thrift institutions. But others continue to create conflict. Consider the following scenarios.

During the autumn of 1990, the Federal Reserve expressed concern over the tightening of commercial bank lending policies due to an increased number of problem loans and investments and reduced real estate values, and stiffened regulation of lending policies. These troubles put a strain on commercial bank financial solvency. Because of significantly toughened regulatory solvency requirements, bankers may have been too conservative in their lending policies. But tighter lending policies complicated the Federal Reserve's ability to pursue a more stimulative monetary policy and get the economy out of the 1990–1991 recession.

Federal regulators require that information in examination reports remain confidential, to avoid a potential run on a weak financial firm. But without adequate and timely disclosure of this information about financial position, how can unknowing investors make the best decision about purchasing uninsured investments in a potentially risky depository?

A government's striving toward integrity of the financial system may directly hamper individual firms from responding to increased competition from nonbanks, foreign banks, and other federal government agencies. If regulators continue to restrict the ability of regulated firms to respond to competitive market forces—let alone innovate so as to lead the market—then how can these firms remain safe and sound without further government protection?

Next, legislation that prohibits credit discrimination in order to provide equal access may have the opposite effect. For example, prohibiting a lender to use a valid factor to assess risk could lead to **adverse selection**, which occurs when high-risk cases are not differentiated: the loss experience of the loan pool increases so that the lender must raise rates across the board, driving the lower-risk groups out and making the loan pool even riskier. Do financial institutions assess risk so that some customers, regardless of their risk rating, can no longer borrow? Or must the intermediary face financial crisis and be bailed out?

Finally, the sheer cost of doing business under existing regulation increases the price of products and services. Financial institutions must incur administrative costs of reporting certain types of information, legal costs associated with individual and class-action lawsuits, and penalties of regulators who deny mergers or other requests if an intermediary is deemed deficient in its lending practices. What would further government protection cost a financial firm?

Since the answers to these questions change as each government administration defines or redefines *public good* and *safety and soundness,* managers of financial institutions should keep up with the predominant political views on regulation, so as to predict regulatory response.

COSTS OF REGULATION

The goals of regulation are fairly well understood today. However, as mentioned briefly above, there are extremely high costs associated with regulating the financial sector, the most obvious of which include:

1. Administrative costs of regulation both to financial firms and to customers, whether they be shareholders or consumers of a firm's financial products.
2. Misallocation of resources caused by financial regulation.
3. Inability of regulated firms to respond to new market opportunities and competition.

Again, regulation carries large administrative costs—personnel time, reporting costs, and costs of examination and supervision—which are not easy to estimate yet are quite significant and growing. Any senior manager of a regulated firm must understand how to analyze and control these costs through effective use of information systems and other financial management tools.

Much of the regulation discussed affects the investment options available to financial institutions. Those that constrain the asset investment options of intermediaries can increase the cost of capital to various borrowers and industries. And capital requirements and charter restrictions can favor some borrowers over others in ways that can negatively influence real economic growth or lead to excessive investment in less-productive areas. Many economists have argued that the United States has many regulatory and chartering provisions favoring residential real estate investments, signalling a "socially desirable" aim. But such investments may reduce capital available for plant and equipment investment. Managers might begin to see the value of governmental lobbyists on the behalf of the financial services sector and other industries of the economy.

Finally, regulation inhibits the ability of regulated institutions to respond to new markets and competitive threats. The most obvious the prohibition on savings and loans offering adjustable-rate mortgages, which contributed to many financial institution failures. Largely as a result of this restriction, savings and loans went into the high-interest rate period of the late 1970s and 1980s with a portfolio of fixed-rate mortgages and sharply rising deposit costs and became insolvent. The regulatory price constraints on deposit interest rates in effect through the early 1980s also added to the growth of money market mutual funds in the late 1970s; and this competition is still potent despite the absence of price ceilings.

✓ Checkpoints

4-1 What does the public good theory of regulation mean to a financial manager, and how does regulation define the *public good*?

4-2 What are several reasons for regulation? What are some examples currently in the news?

4-3   What are some instances where regulation tries to reduce imperfect information?

4-4   What is an imperfect market structure, and how does regulation seek to improve a marketplace?

4-5   How does prejudice relate to regulation?

4-6   Why do monetary authorities care about financial regulation?

Issues Related to Deposit Insurance Programs

The failure of the **Federal Savings and Loan Insurance Corporation (FSLIC)** in 1989 and the near insolvency of the Bank Insurance Fund (BIF) in 1991 highlight a number of issues that define public policy debate over how to operate a financially sound deposit insurance program.[2] Questions include the following:

1.   Does moral hazard undermine deposit insurance programs?

2.   What does the too-big-to-fail policy of protection really accomplish?

3.   What is the most appropriate method for levying deposit insurance premiums on insured institutions?

4.   How effective are competitive constraints and barriers to entry in reducing the probability of financial institution failure?

MORAL HAZARD AND DEPOSIT INSURANCE

The banking experience in the United States in the 1800s and the early 1930s prompted a perceived need for a deposit insurance program to promote safety and soundness in the financial system. The failure of the FSLIC has provided nearly conclusive evidence that the U.S. government will stand behind the safety of deposits in all insured commercial banks and thrifts. But this stability has its costs, one of which is the cost associated with moral hazard. A **moral hazard** exists when financial decision makers are willing to bear excessive risk because they know that any loss will be shifted to another party.

In the U.S. system of deposit insurance, three types of moral hazards exist. The first involves depositors who are unconcerned about depositing funds in weak institutions as long as the funds receive deposit insurance. Would customers open savings accounts if they believed that they could lose all their money? The second builds upon the first moral hazard but concerns managers and shareholders of weak depository institutions. The presence of deposit insurance eliminates the market's natural response to a firm that has risky assets and low capital. Normally, as a firm increases business risk and financial leverage, its cost of capital rises. Since depositors—the suppliers of capital to a financial firm—will con-

---

[2]The history of the financial soundness of deposit insurance programs in the United States is generally not comforting. There was the failure of the New York Safety Fund in the 1840s and the numerous more-recent failures of state-run deposit funds since 1985, in Ohio, Maryland, and Rhode Island. These failures dramatically focus attention on the difficulties of operating an actuarially sound government deposit insurance program.

tinue to supply funds as long as their money is protected, managers can incur as much risk as the regulators permit the firm to bear. The third hazard involves the regulators themselves. If they are evaluated by their bosses and constituents by the number of depository failures occuring during their tenure in office, then they have incentive to delay taking over institutions until a new government appointee takes office.

While the U.S. deposit insurance system is believed to have all but eliminated the potential for financial panic and significant disruption to the payment system, the taxpayer-financed bailout of the depositors of failed savings and loans and commercial banks in recent years has been substantial. Estimated cost per taxpayer will probably exceed $500. Problems of moral hazard suggest that a government seek new approaches to reduce these costs of safety and soundness to society.

TOO BIG TO FAIL

One result of the post-1930s regulatory administration of depository failures is known as the **too-big-to-fail (TBTF) policy,** where depository regulators support distressed large financial institutions in ways not available or offered to smaller institutions. Generally, this support includes providing special liquidity sources and guaranteeing deposits over the $100,000 insurance limit. Supporters of the TBTF policy contend that the failure of a very large bank could lead to a ripple effect throughout the financial system, affecting many other banks and international banking and disrupting monetary policy implementation, where failures of smaller banks would not. But these smaller firms consider the TBTF policy inequitable because it enables large banks to raise funds more easily than smaller ones can. Thus, to some extent, the policy encourages both moral hazard and misallocation of financial resources.

The rationale behind this attitude toward large institutions is similar to the general concern over the cost of bank failures. Kaufman (1989) stated his opinion in this way:

> TLTF [Too Large to Fail] is frequently used by bank regulators to avoid taking actions that could put them in conflict with powerful parties who would experience large dollar losses, such as uninsured depositors and other creditors, management, owners, and even large borrowers. In addition, the regulators frequently believe that such actions would be an admission of failure not only of the bank, but also of their own agency, which is charged with bank safety and evaluated by many on its ability to achieve this condition. In using TLTF, the regulators play on the widespread public fears of the contagiousness of bank failures, that is, on fears that individual bank failures may ignite a domino or chain reaction that would tumble other "healthy" banks nationwide, other financial institutions, and possibly even nonfinancial institutions and the aggregate macroeconomy.[3]

---

[3]George G. Kaufman, "Are Some Banks Too Large to Fail? Myth and Reality," Working Paper Series, Research Department, Federal Reserve Bank of Chicago, Aug. 1989.

Recent cases raise doubts about the fairness of the TBTF policy. The bailouts of the Continental Illinois National Bank in 1984, the American Savings and Loan Association of Stockton, California, in 1984, and the Bank of New England in 1991, protected large *uninsured* depositors and granted other benefits to creditors, owners, and management. Proponents point to the large disruptive withdrawals prior to these bailouts, withdrawals that could have sparked widespread panic. But there is no conclusive evidence that allowing these banks to fail, with the attendant loss to uninsured depositors and creditors, would be a serious economic problem either locally or nationally.

Analysts looking at the TBTF history conclude that uninsured creditors probably should bear some of the costs of failure, thus providing incentive for more-effective monitoring of these institutions and reducing moral hazard risks. In addition, others feel that regulators should intervene earlier to lessen the failure risk of large institutions. As a result, the FDICIA bill was passed in late 1991 to alter the TBTF policy in a significant way. The bill prohibits paying off uninsured depositors in the event of bank failure unless the Federal Reserve, FDIC, and the Treasury deem it essential to protect against the disruption of the financial system. Effective January 1, 1995, FDICIA also mandates early intervention by depository regulators for weakly capitalized institutions.

PROTECTING DEPOSIT INSURANCE FUND SOLVENCY

A major area of public debate in the 1990s is focusing on how best to avoid another failure of a deposit insurance institution. The FIRREA legislation of 1989 attacked the problem directly by permitting higher insurance premiums for both the **Savings Association Insurance Fund (SAIF)** and the **Bank Insurance Fund (BIF)**. Many consider this solution to be counterproductive, since higher deposit premiums will detract from the already weakened profitability of depositories; yet these premiums will still be used to make the insurance programs more fiscally sound. The FDICIA also allows the BIF to borrow from the Treasury, provided that insured banks repay the loans out of higher deposit premium fees.

Regulators complemented the potentially counterproductive effect of higher deposit premiums with capital adequacy requirements, establishing minimum levels of equity in each firm's capital structure and stronger examination and supervision standards—all reinforced by the FIRREA legislation. Regarding capital adequacy, financial intermediaries face compliance with a system of risk-based capital standards. The debate over insurance coverage has produced a large number of recommendations, many of which are covered by FDICIA (see Appendix 4A). These proposals involve:

1. **Risk-based insurance premiums,** where the riskiness of an institution's assets would affect the amount of premium paid. The FDICIA put this program into effect in July 1993.

2. **Co-insurance plans,** where a portion of the deposit insurance coverage would come from a private insurance company, because some believe that private firms can provide the necessary depository surveillance more cost-effectively and efficiently than the government can. The FDICIA

also permits the FDIC to implement a reinsurance coverage plan that, while not technically a co-insurance program, could make private resources available for deposit insurance.

3.   Lower deposit coverage, which would entail lowering the maximum deposit insurance coverage to below the current $100,000 per account or capping coverage on all of a household's accounts regardless of how many institutions the household invests in.

4.   Greater disclosure of the financial position of the insured institution. The FDICIA mandated independent audits for more institutions and greater disclosure of the market values of assets and liabilities and contingent assets and liabilities.

5.   Prohibiting use of brokered deposits, which are insured deposits distributed through security brokers. Financial depositories are able to grow excessively through brokered accounts. However, many failed thrifts used such accounts; and so the FDICIA restricted the use of brokered insured deposits by reserving this source of funding for the highest capitalized, least risky institutions.

6.   Early government intervention, made possible by the increased role of capital and other measures of commercial bank financial soundness set by the FDICIA as criteria for determining the need for further intervention. The act authorized bank regulators to establish a program of five capital levels that, combined with other criteria such as bank earnings, could be used to determine the level of regulatory oversight and intervention and to effect change in weak financial institutions.

CONSTRAINTS ON COMPETITION TO ENSURE FINANCIAL SOUNDNESS

Over the years, Congress and regulators of depositories have safeguarded the value of depository charters to reduce the chance of institutional failure. The most notable of these efforts to limit competition among financial institutions since the 1930s include the following:

1.   Prohibiting commercial banks from underwriting securities under the Glass-Steagall Act.[4]

2.   Prohibiting commercial banks from selling insurance.

3.   Prohibiting interstate banking through the McFadden Act.[5]

---

[4]During the 1990s, the Federal Reserve Board has authorized several bank holding companies to own and operate investment banking firms which underwrite and distribute corporate securities. The Federal Reserve requires that the activities of the investment bank be totally separate from those of the commercial bank(s) owned by the bank holding company.

[5]In the spring of 1994, the U.S. Congress passed legislation to overturn the prohibition against nationwide branching for federally chartered commercial banks. This will permit the many multiple-bank holding companies to operate their out-of-state banks as branches.

4. Controlling prices through such measures as Regulation Q to prevent depositories from taking excessive risks and paying excessive deposit rates.

5. Granting commercial banks a monopoly on transaction deposit services.

6. Controlling stock and bond brokerage rates.

Many academicians have noted that entry barriers and other constraints often lead to near substitutes, such as the growth of money market mutual funds as an alternative to savings accounts, out-of-state loan production offices, off-shore branches and affiliates, bank-like services provided by nonbank financial firms, and a host of technological systems that enable nationwide bank-type services, such as check cashing and so forth. With so many substitute market and product innovations, is there any institutional value in maintaining many of the remaining competitive restrictions listed above? Congress actively debated this question as it developed FDICIA in 1991 but rejected liberalizing or eliminating any of these enduring few. The concern remains that a flurry of competition could weaken commercial bank and insurance companies.

As the 1990s unfold, the debate will continue over whether higher capital requirements and stronger regulation, or else greater freedom to compete and profit by one's financial strategy, is ultimately the better financial protection for the U.S. deposit insurance system. In an effort to ensure that no bank fails, will governments develop a system in which banks cannot make a decent return for their shareholders?

✓ Checkpoints

4-7   What are the primary goals of public policy accomplished through financial regulation? Which are the most important to financial managers of intermediaries?

4-8   Why do issues of safety and soundness concern financial regulators so much?

4-9   How can regulation affect the allocation of credit?

4-10   Should financial regulators provide special financial assistance to the depositors, creditors, and shareholders of financial firms deemed too big to fail?

4-11   How have competitive constraints reduced the potential for deposit insurer loss, and what are some other recommendations for reducing such loss?

The Process of Regulation

Thus far, this chapter has looked at why regulation exists and how a society enforces its regulations, to some extent, by providing most financial institutions with incentives such as deposit insurance, business charters to alter or expand operations, or participation in federal government lending programs. But how does the regulatory process actually work? Congress has passed laws requiring recipient institutions to pursue public policy goals in exchange for such benefits. George Stigler's special interest theory and Edward Kane's dialectical theory of regulation provide some framework for answering this question.

STIGLER SPECIAL INTEREST THEORY

George Stigler's special interest theory of regulation stemmed from the public good theory and his observation that once the government acted to correct an alleged market deficiency, the regulatory body established to maintain ongoing supervision often became captured by the group it was set up to regulate. Stigler noted that the regulated group, more so than other groups, would study the regulator's activities and then position itself to present its case for change more frequently and persuasively. He also noted that many times the staff of the regulatory agency went to work for firms within the regulated industry; or, alternatively, individuals within the industry entered the regulator agency. Some observers allege that the pre-1989 recycling of talent from the FHLBB into the S&L industry and trade associations exascerbated the thrift crisis: the regulated industry obtained undue influence over its own regulation. Under such circumstances, how can an agency objectively defend and protect the public good?

KANE DIALECTICAL THEORY OF REGULATION

Kane viewed the regulatory process as a dialectical process wherein society identifies a market failure, such as those represented by the model of competitive markets, and then argues for regulation. The affected industry then responds by avoidance and financial innovation or presents counterarguments to weaken the impact of the regulation. This cycle perpetuates regulation and further response. Over the last few years, for example, depository institutions have coped with higher capital requirements by developing off-balance-sheet financing techniques designed to circumvent the new capital requirements. These innovations have spawned another round of modifications to the regulatory capital requirements.

REGULATORY PROCEDURES

Although each regulatory agency handles the logistics of regulation differently, the primary activities of each agency are similar. They typically conduct two types of examinations of the regulated firms: one for compliance and one for safety and soundness. Compliance examiners investigate how well the regulated firm performs the many duties associated with its socially mandated responsibilities, such as how truthful it is in its lending practices or how nondiscriminatory it is in real estate lending.

Examiners focusing on issues of safety and soundness analyze the institution as an operating concern and its risk of failure, with special attention to the firm's investment policies and procedures, the extent to which the board of directors monitors the actions of management, and the company's capital adequacy.

The examiners start with the various reports that firms must prepare and submit on a monthly, quarterly, or annual basis, according to agency specifications. Examiners also have access to all accounting data kept by the firm and its independent accountants. Privately held firms may be required to report information that publicly held companies are not. For publicly held firms, the examiners may compare the firm's market value relative to its book value and to that of competing firms, because market value is a very good indicator of possible failure.

For more telling measurements of capital supply and solvency, interest rate risk, and off-balance sheet risk pertinent to issues of safety and soundness, regulators have worked to go beyond accounting data and required reports. One important technique is the on-site review. During this review, examiners have access to all information in the firm, including accounting records, but also loan documentation, records of loan delinquency and loss experience, appraisals, and the correspondence and meeting minutes of management committees and the board of directors. The examining staff may meet with employees, managers, and board members as necessary.

If examiners deem conditions unsafe or unsound, then they interfere with the activities of the firm by issuing cease and desist orders, removing management, limiting growth of the firm, stopping dividend payments, or requesting additional capital to be held. The FIRREA and FDICIA increased the authority of the bank and savings and loan regulators and increased the penalties that regulators can assess to managers and directors of firms operating outside law and regulation. Regulators of life insurance companies also monitor insurance premium levels, because one obvious way to meet the solvency requirement is to maintain high insurance premiums.

REGULATORS' IMPACT ON FINANCIAL PERFORMANCE AND OPERATIONS

Why are managers of financial institutions so concerned about regulation? The preceding paragraph lists some of the more immediate consequences of not complying with regulation. But regulators of most financial institutions have broad and usually far-reaching authority that greatly influences long-term decision making and financial performance of regulated firms. Indeed, the shareholders of a regulated firm sometimes find that the regulatory environment in which the firm operates may have more to do with the firm's performance than the efforts of management. In some respects, regulation does for financial institutions what most financial managers must do in firms outside the financial services industry, in terms of setting performance goals and formulating business strategies. For example, regulators set the decision-making agenda for managers of financial institutions in the following ways, specifically by:

1. Defining the firm's equity requirements and other financial performance standards.
2. Designating through the firm's charter what transactions a manager can make with respect to allowable investments, liabilities, and so forth.

3. Determining the indirect and direct costs of examination and supervision.
4. Designating the nature or organization of business operations. For example, the Community Reinvestment Act affects the firm's cost structure.
5. Rejecting management, directors, and controlling shareholders.
6. Authorizing acquisitions and mergers, thereby controlling the competitive environment.
7. Restricting a host of business transactions.

Chapter 2 introduced the financial claim/function matrix as a decision-making tool for determining which claims and functions to perform as part of the firm's institutional strategy while still abiding by federal and state chartering laws and subsequent legislation.

✓ Checkpoints

4-12 How are the Stigler special interest theory of regulation and the Kane dialectical theory of regulation similar? How are they different?

4-13 What two primary activities do regulators perform in their regulatory duties?

4-14 How do regulators influence the short- and long-term activities of managers of regulated financial institutions?

Financial Institution Regulators and Insurers

The U.S. regulatory system is complex and pervasive. Even a firm without a specific overseeing agency will find itself complying with regulation as it conducts its business. For instance, mortgage banking lacks a specific regulator, but mortgage bankers must conform to regulatory requirements when originating mortgages to be insured by the FHA or servicing mortgages guaranteed by GNMA.

STRUCTURE OF THE REGULATORY SYSTEM

The web of financial institution regulation in the United States is really the product of political forces seeking to perserve: (1) the involvement of individual states in the regulatory and chartering process and (2) the specialization of financial institutions, such as savings and loans and credit unions, within the system. As a result, the U.S. regulatory and insurance system includes three deposit insurance funds, an insurance fund for assets held in brokerage accounts, and a guarantor for pension benefits. There are also insurance, commercial bank, and thrift regulators in all 50 states, five federal commercial bank and thrift regulatory groups, a regulator for pension funds, one for futures trading, and another for securities firms, with overlapping jurisdiction over all publicly held stock financial companies. Table 4.2 lists the regulated and insured financial institutions in the first column and then indicates all the regulatory and insurance agencies that oversee each of those firms in the second column.

TABLE 4.2

Major Regulatory and Insurance Agencies, Both Federal and State

Regulated Organization	Regulators and Insurers
Commericial banks	Federal Reserve System Federal Deposit Insurance Corporation (FDIC) Bank Insurance Fund (BIF) Comptroller of the Currency State banking commissions

Thrift institutions	Federal Deposit Insurance Corporation (FDIC)
	    (S&Ls, mutual savings banks, and credit
	    unions)
	Office of Thrift Supervision (OTS)
	Savings Association Insurance Fund (SAIF)
	State thrift regulators
	National Credit Union Administration (NCUA)
	National Credit Union Share Insurance Fund
	    (NCUSIF)

Life insurance companies	State insurance commissions
Private pension funds	Department of Labor Pension Benefit Guarantee Corporation (PBGC)
Security firms	Security and Exchange Commission (SEC) (investment bankers) Security Investor Protection Corporation (SIPC)
Commodity futures brokerage	Commodity Futures Trading Commission (CFTC)
Mutual funds	Security and Exchange Commission (SEC)

Mortgage bankers	Department of Housing and Urban
	    Development (HUD)
	Federal Housing Administration (FHA)
	Government National Mortgage Administration
	    (GNMA)
	Veterans Administration (VA)

Publicly held institutions	Security and Exchange Commission (SEC)

REGULATORY ARBITRAGE

One consequence of such complexity is choice: many financial firms can choose among regulators. This decision typically depends upon the comparative costs of compliance and examination, the degree of regulatory scrutiny, and the benefits such as deposit insurance derived from having a particular charter and regulating body. For example, in the United States, a commercial bank not organized as a bank holding company can apply for either a federal bank charter or a state bank charter. If the firm secures a federal charter, then it falls under the jurisdiction of the Office of the Comptroller of the Currency. If it gets a state charter, then the Federal Deposit Insurance Corporation oversees its activities. Credit unions, savings and loan associations, and savings banks can all choose between federal and state charters, depending on which would be more likely to support the firm's business strategy. This choice of regulator is referred to as *regulatory arbitrage.*

Internationally, commercial banks can avoid oppressive regulation in one country by establishing subsidiaries in countries with greater business freedoms as well as protections. The off-shore operations in the Grand Cayman Islands, for instance, are not subject to heavy taxation as those nearby in the United States. Conversely, the Bank of Credit and Commerce International (BCCI), a Luxembourg-chartered institution with Middle Eastern ownership, may not have received adequate regulatory oversight in that small country but operated in the United States where its deposits would be insured. In effect, it had the incentive to take greater risks than would U.S. firms but with equal coverage of funds.

Presently, the **Organization for Economic Cooperation and Development (OECD)** is trying to harmonize such regulatory differences among the economically advanced countries. The OECD established the Basel Committee on Banking Regulation and Supervisory Practices of the Bank for International Settlements, also known as the Basel Committee, to coordinate regulation of banks with international activities. Its first major contribution was the 1975 Basel Concordat, revised in 1983, with further agreement in 1987. Generally, the economically developed countries of the OECD agreed that: (1) foreign banks should be regulated, (2) regulatory responsibilities should be divided between a bank's home and host countries, and (3) there should be minimum capital requirements.

OFFICE OF THE COMPTROLLER OF THE CURRENCY

The **Office of the Comptroller of the Currency (OCC)** is the oldest bank regulator. Formed in 1863 and reporting to the U.S. Treasury department, the comptroller's office grants federal charters, supervises and examines all federally chartered commercial banks, and approves or prevents mergers and branching of national banks. National banks owned by holding companies are also subject to Federal Reserve regulation.

FEDERAL RESERVE SYSTEM

Created in 1913, the U.S. Federal Reserve System supervises commercial bank holding companies. It establishes reserve requirements for all depositories, oversees the nation's payment system, and promotes many of the consumer-oriented regulations that affect all depositories, such as provisions for truth in lending and home mortgage disclosure. The FDICIA in 1991 expanded the regulatory powers of the Fed over foreign banks operating in the United States.

_L_EGAL

and

_E_THICAL

ISSUES

BANK OF CREDIT AND COMMERCE INTERNATIONAL: MONEY LAUNDERING AND INTERNATIONAL INFLUENCE PEDDLING

Few financial scandals cross borders. Even fewer involve allegations of misdeeds and influence peddling in over 70 countries around the world. Newsworthy, then, is the case of the Bank of Credit and Commerce International (BCCI), a large bank holding company headquartered in Luxembourg with approximately $20 billion in assets and 400 branches worldwide. Formed in 1972, BCCI expanded out of its original market in the Middle East into eastern Asia, the Caribbean, Africa, and the subcontinent of Asia. It was accused in 1991 of illegally acquiring controlling interest in several U.S. financial institutions and of unrecorded deposits with the Bank of England.

Within a few weeks, allegations of money laundering and influence peddling worldwide began to circulate. Representatives of BCCI were accused of using political influence to obtain favorable concessions for banking activities in Zimbabwe, China, Hong Kong, and the United Arab Emirates, among others. In the United States, BCCI-controlled financial institutions were investigated for political influence peddling. An affiliate of BCCI was indicted for money laundering in Florida and pleaded guilty, leading to the closing of a number of BCCI offices in the United States. BCCI was also found to secretly control a U.S. bank run by two individuals with considerable political influence.

The BCCI experience raised major questions worldwide about the structure of examination and supervision needed to control financial institutions operating internationally. The FDICIA granted the Federal Reserve additional supervisory authority over foreign banks operating in the United States. The Federal Reserve has also called for the development of stronger international agreements for bank regulation and financial reporting.

Source: Rob Norton, "Lessons from BCCI," *Fortune*, Sept. 9, 1991, pp. 153–55.

FEDERAL DEPOSIT INSURANCE CORPORATION

Until the passage of FIRREA in 1989, the Federal Deposit Insurance Corporation, discussed earlier throughout this chapter, examined all banks and thrifts—primarily state-chartered mutual savings banks—covered by its insurance fund. Through FIRREA, Congress eliminated the **Federal Home Loan Bank Board (FHLBB)** and its separate insurance program, the Federal Savings and Loan Insurance Corporation (FSLIC), partly due to the FHLBB's role in the thrift debacle. Congress then expanded the FDIC's powers by setting up two new insurance funds—the Savings Association Insurance Fund—and the Bank Insurance Fund—and the Resolution Trust Corporation (RTC), all managed by the FDIC. Appendix 4A discusses the RTC's responsibilities more fully.

STATE BANKING AND THRIFT REGULATORS

Each state has an agency or group of agencies to regulate commercial bank and state-chartered thrifts. In most cases, however, states share the examination and supervision responsibilities with federal agencies. The Federal Reserve establishes reserve requirements for all state banks. State-chartered banks insured by the BIF are subject to FDIC regulation and examination. State-chartered banks owned by holding companies are regulated by the Federal Reserve. And state-chartered thrift institutions insured by the SAIF are subject to both federal and state regulation.

OFFICE OF THRIFT SUPERVISION

The **Office of Thrift Supervision (OTS)**, the youngest of the federal regulatory institutions, charters all federal savings and loans institutions and savings banks and supervises all SAIF-insured thrifts and thrift holding companies. Created by the FIRREA in 1989, the OTS replaces the FHLBB—but as a department within the U.S. Treasury like the OCC, not as an independent agency like the FHLBB. Given the expanded role and responsibilities of the FDIC, some question whether the OTS should remain a separate department or should exist at all.

NATIONAL CREDIT UNION ADMINISTRATION

The **National Credit Union Administration (NCUA)** is the principal regulatory agency for federally chartered and National Credit Union Share Insurance Fund (NCUSIF) insured credit unions. Approximately 60% of all credit unions have federal charters and are regulated by the NCUA. In addition, approximately 60% of the remaining state-chartered credit unions are members of the NCUSIF insurance fund and thus become subject to NCUA regulation and supervision.

DEPARTMENT OF LABOR

Private uninsured pension funds were largely unregulated until 1974, when Congress passed the **Employee Retirement Income Security Act (ERISA)**. ERISA established minimum vesting, funding, and fiduciary standards for private pension funds and created the Pension Benefit Guarantee Corporation (PBGC) to guarantee the benefits of insured and uninsured pension funds. The Department of Labor implements such ERISA provisions as the following:

1. Fiduciary standards covering asset managers, trustees, and advisors.
2. Vesting requirements and scheduling related to an employee's right to benefits.
3. Financial reporting and disclosure requirements for informing plan participants as well as the Department of Labor.
4. Portability provisions so that vested employees who change jobs can roll over their funds into a new plan or into a self-administered individual retirement account.
5. Funding standards that set minimum levels for adequate funding of current and past plan participants.
6. Plan termination insurance through the PBGC.

COMMODITY FUTURES TRADING COMMISSION

Established in 1974 to centralize the federal government's regulation and supervision of futures markets, the **Commodity Futures Trading Commission (CFTC)** monitors the futures markets for manipulative behavior in trading futures contracts. The CFTC also ensures that new contracts serve an economically justifiable purpose, enforces exchange rules, audits brokerage firms and clearing associations, and investigates alleged or suspected violations of laws and regulations.

SECURITIES AND EXCHANGE COMMISSION

Founded in 1934, the SEC acts as an independent bipartisan administrative agency with a broad agenda of administrative requirements and provisions:

- Requirements that public offerings of securities include an SEC-approved registration statement setting forth certain required information.
- Provisions against false and misleading disclosures by public institutions.
- Maintenance of reporting requirements of firms listed on particular national exchanges.
- Provisions governing the solicitation of proxies for holders of securities.
- Provisions governing the disclosure of information when control of a company is sought through a cash tender offer and for other stock acquisitions.

- Provisions that stockholders are provided information on insider trading activities.
- Requirements for the registration of security exchanges, security associations, brokers and dealers, and municipal security dealers.
- Provisions for regulation of options on any securities and security indices.

STATE INSURANCE COMMISSIONS

Insurance companies are not regulated by the federal government because of the McCarran-Ferguson Act of 1945. As a result of this legislation, the federal government exempted insurance companies from federal antitrust laws as long as they were regulated by the states. Publicly held companies must adhere to SEC requirements, and life companies involved in the investment of pension fund assets are subject to Department of Labor ERISA requirements.

Although insurance companies are regulated by their state of domicile, there is considerable coordination between the various state insurance commissions. These commissions have established the **National Association of Insurance Commissioners (NAIC)** to coordinate their actions and share information. In 1991, this body adopted a standard that limited the holdings of junk bonds to 20% of a life company's assets. The NAIC has also developed a new minimum standard from policy reserves based on the risk profile of each company.

Most states also provide protection of policyholders through state-run insurance guarantee funds. These are funded by the life companies that are licensed to sell policies in the state. Most of these funds, however, have limited resources in relation to the size of the companies whose policyholders they guarantee.

State insurance regulations define what kinds of assets an insurance company may invest in and also how each asset is to be treated in terms of valuation. They also establish the minimum level of reserves needed to meet the obligations of policyholders. The states also regulate the reporting and accounting methods used by insurance companies.

SECURITIES INVESTOR PROTECTION CORPORATION

Established by Congress in 1970, the **Securities Investor Protection Corporation (SIPC)** is not a regulator but insures most accounts separately in brokerage firms up to $500,000, including up to $100,000 in cash. Account owners can increase coverage using separate joint accounts and trust accounts. The resources of the SIPC come from a fund developed from assessments paid by member brokerage firms registered with the SEC; at year-end 1989, this fund approximated $400 million. The agency also has a line of credit of $500 million from a group of commercial banks and, as a last resort, a $1 billion line of credit with the U.S. Treasury. If a brokerage firm fails, the SIPC freezes all brokerage accounts and goes to court to have a trustee appointed. The trustee then tries to get another brokerage firm to assume the accounts. If such a firm cannot be found, then the trustee processes the claims individually.

DEPARTMENT OF HOUSING AND URBAN DEVELOPMENT

The **Department of Housing and Urban Development (HUD)** has some authority over financial institutions involved in the secondary mortgage market, such as savings and loans, commercial banks, and mortgage banking companies. HUD implements the FHA-insured mortgage programs, manages the GNMA, establishes minimum capital requirements for servicers of mortgages, sets certain standards for servicing FHA loans and loans guaranteed by GNMA.

PENSION BENEFIT GUARANTEE CORPORATION

Created by the Employee Retirement Income Act of 1974 and financed by premium payments levied against private pension plans, the **Pension Benefit Guarantee Corporation (PBGC)** insures employee assets in private pension funds. It is not a regulator of pension plan sponsors, a duty that belongs to the Department of Labor. The PBGC assures employees that a minimum level of their retirement payments can be made even if a pension plan sponsor goes bankrupt.

✓ Checkpoints

4-15 What problems are posed by there now being insurance programs for accounts held in security firms (the Security Investor Protection Corporation) and for pension obligations of individuals (the Pension Benefit Guarantee Corporation)? How do these problems compare to the problems experienced in our deposit insurance programs?

4-16 What are the primary regulators and insurers of depositories and nondepository institutions?

SUMMARY AND REVIEW

1. **Explain the public good theory of regulation and list the primary public policy goals of financial regulation.**

   The **public good theory of regulation** holds that regulation is justified whenever there are deficiencies in the competitive market process.

The primary public policy goals of financial regulation include the following:

1. **Achieving adequate competition** in our financial markets.
2. **Reducing imperfect information.**
3. **Eliminating prejudice** or bias in supply.
4. **Achieving equal access.**
5. **Improving implementation of monetary policy.**
6. **Pursuing socially desirable credit allocation.**
7. **Reducing potential for insider abuse** and fraud.
8. **Reducing potentially disruptive impacts of financial institution failures.**
9. **Protecting taxpayers** from deposit insurance fund failures.

2. **Explain the public policy issues raised by the offering of federal government deposit insurance programs.**

The deposit insurance system creates **three moral hazards.** First, **insured depositors are not concerned** about depositing in weak institutions. Second, management and **owners of insured firms are willing to maximize business and financial risks** on the basis that the cost of capital will not be affected by rising agency and distress costs. Third, **regulators attempt to delay closing failed institutions** until their successor is appointed to avoid being held responsible for the failure.

3. **Explain several theories that explain how the regulatory process really works and how regulation affects the management of financial firms.**

George Stigler and **Edward Kane** have developed two theories of how the regulatory process actually works. Stigler observes that after a time the regulator develops a symbiotic relationship with the organizations being regulated, resulting in the regulated industry achieving undo influence on the regulator's decisions. Kane sees regulation in financial services as a dialectical process in which regulations bring industry avoidance efforts and innovation to reduce the impact of the regulation. This is followed by another regulation, and so forth.

Regulators have very significant impacts on the management of financial institutions. The most important include the following:

1. Establishing **capital requirements.**
2. Implementing laws covering **asset, liability, and service powers.**
3. Affecting **operating costs** through examination and supervision.
4. Determining the **burden of compliance legislation.**
5. **Disapproving management, directors, and controlling shareholders.**
6. **Approving mergers, acquisitions, and consolidations.**

4. **Describe the relationships among the primary regulators and insurers of financial institutions.**

The primary depository financial institutions regulators are the **Comptroller of the Currency, Federal Reserve Board, FDIC, OTS, NCUA,** and **state bank and thrift regulators.** Nondepository regulators are the state insurance commissioners, **Department of Labor, SEC, HUD, and CFTC.** The federal government also sponsors insurance corporations that include **SAIF** and **BIF,** which are supervised by the FDIC, the **NCUSIF,** the **SIPC,** and **PBGC.** States also insure life insurance companies through state insurance guarantee funds.

The Financial Institutions Reform, Recovery, and Enforcement Act of 1989: A Case Study in Regulatory Retribution

The Financial Institutions Reform, Recovery, and Enforcement Act of 1989 was passed in response to growing evidence in the mid-1980s that there would be insufficient resources in the FSLIC to handle the costs of failed savings and loans. The events that led to the passage of the FIRREA provide an excellent example of the potential for regulation to create valuable financial institution charters and, in the case of the savings and loans, eliminate much of that value.

The legislation was passed in a highly charged emotional atmosphere. The eventual size of the FSLIC failure had grown, based on regulatory estimates, from approximately $10 billion in 1985 to over $50 billion in early 1989. By 1992, the estimates by the government's RTC had grown to as high as $100 billion.

Failure Due in Large Part to Early Economic Policies

Most of the failures were related to the substantial operating losses and erosion of capital that occurred in the late 1970s and early 1980s. These losses were due to the combined impact of tight monetary policy and resultant high interest rates, combined with the deregulation of interest rates on savings accounts. By the early 1980s, the tangible capital base of the industry was largely depleted.

The thrift industry prior to the late 1970s had performed very well. For most of the period from the 1950s through the 1970s, the thrifts were the fastest growing financial institutions. Their prosperity was primarily the result of a beneficial regulatory climate. The thrifts were allowed to leverage their capital resources much more than commercial banks due to a policy of regulatory forebearance. They had favorable access to low-cost credit advances from the FHLBs. Finally, when high interest rates threatened them in the 1960s, they were brought under savings rate controls, **Regulation Q,** to protect them from having to pay high interest rates on their deposits. Moreover, Regulation Q was administered so that thrifts could always pay higher interest rates than their competitors, the commercial banks.

Unfortunately, these price controls stopped being effective during the rapidly rising interest rates of the late 1970s, and the thrifts were caught in a deregulation atmosphere holding a large percentage of their assets in low-yielding fixed-rate mortgages. It was in this environment that the thrift debacle of the 1980s took place.

During the 1980s, many examples of inadequate regulatory supervision and lax behavior fueled the emotional nature of the Congressional debate concerning what to do to the thrifts. Everyone wanted to know who was responsible. Moreover, a few of the failures were related to fraud and incompetent behavior on the part of a number of flamboyant thrift executives, whose actions and life-styles were not considered appropriate in a tightly regulated industry that benefited from government guaranteed deposits.

Adding insult to injury, a number of representatives and senators were accused of applying pressure on federal regulators so that a number of the weak thrifts could be allowed to continue operating. Before the legislative process ran its course, virtually everyone connected with the business was singled out as a contributor to the costly bailout, as it was termed.

Finding the Scapegoat(s)

Industry representatives were accused of fraudulent and incompetent behavior. Regulators were accused of lax regulation and implementing forbearance policies that exacerbated the problem. Elected officials were accused of applying political pressure that served to prolong the improper activities of a few in the business. The thrift trade associations were accused of minimizing the severity of the problem and promoting policies that eventually increased the cost of the solution. Finally, the Reagan administration was accused of ignoring the problem until after the 1988 election.

The widespread media coverage of the events made it difficult for the legislative process to resolve this problem unemotionally. It became clear early in the deliberations that the causes of the crisis were too complicated for the average American to understand. The causes related to a number of regulatory and economic stabilization policies that were implemented over a period of several decades. It became difficult for the media to focus on these causes when the blame could be placed so easily and more colorfully on a few industry members, regulators, and politicians.

Congress Reregulates and Weakens the Thrift Charter

The process of resolving these problems resulted in a major reregulation of the S&Ls without much attention being given to the eventual implications of what narrowing the charter powers and authorities would mean to the industry and its insurer. Public opinion, shaped in large part by the press, convinced most elected officials that a balanced response was not called for, given the large and growing costs of liquidating a large portion of the industry. Consequently, the impact of FIRREA will be felt for many years. It will also contribute to the failure and poor financial performance of many additional thrifts into the foreseeable future.

FIRREA will have two types of impact on the formerly FSLIC-insured institutions. First, their asset powers will be greatly reduced, as they are forced to concentrate a greater percentage of their investment activities in residential real estate and mortgage investments. Second, the cost of their operations will be increased as the cost of deposit insurance premiums increases while the dividends on their holdings of FHLB stock are reduced. This will occur since a portion of the FHLB earnings will be used to fund low-income housing programs and help pay for the bailout. They will also face a substantial increase in their examination and supervision costs.

Major Provisions Impacting Thrifts

The major provisions of the FIRREA that impact thrifts relate to insurance of accounts, powers of thrifts, and regulatory structure.

INSURANCE OF ACCOUNTS

The act changed the insurance of accounts for both FSLIC-insured and FDIC-insured institutions by creating a new insurance fund for FSLIC-insured institutions. This new fund is called the Savings Association Insurance Fund. The SAIF is administered by the FDIC rather than the FHLBB, which was abolished by the act. The FDIC insurance fund is renamed the Bank Insurance Fund and continues to be administered by the FDIC.

Changes in the cost of the insurance for both SAIF- and BIF-insured institutions are of great importance. In 1994, the cost of deposit insurance premiums was 23 basis points (bp) per annum or more for both commercial banks and S&Ls. This was up from 12 bp for commercial banks and 20.8 bp for S&Ls in 1990.

POWERS OF THRIFTS

The asset investment powers of thrifts were substantially reduced in a number of ways by the legislation. This was accomplished by eliminating or reducing certain powers and by redefining the **qualified thrift lender test (QTLT)**. The QTLT defines the percentage of a thrift's assets that must be invested in specified types of qualifying assets.

The more restrictive the QTLT, the less flexibility the thrift has in its investment strategy. The following are some of the changes made to this asset test:

- Nonresidential real estate lending is to be limited to 400% of the institution's capital.

- High-yield bonds have been deleted from the 10% commercial business loan authority for federally chartered thrifts, and all existing bonds must be divested of within five years of enactment.
- Limits on loans to one borrower have been tightened to that which applies to national banks. Generally, this is 15% of unimpaired capital and surplus, and an additional 10% if it is secured by readily marketable collateral.
- The QTLT has been made more restrictive. Essentially, the new test includes the following as qualified assets:
    1. Loans and securities collateralized by residential mortgages.
    2. Obligations of the FSLIC and FDIC.
    3. A limit of 15% in a basket that includes personal, family, and educational purpose loans, 50% of loans made and sold within 90 days, and 200% of loans on low-income housing, churches, and nursing homes.

By July 1, 1991, a new QTLT will be in effect at 70% of assets in qualifying loans and investments. The impact of the new test will be to reduce the asset powers of thrifts.[1]

REGULATORY STRUCTURE

The FIRREA completely alters the regulatory structure relating to thrifts, since the FHLBB is eliminated. The board's historical activities were to insure the deposits of FSLIC-insured institutions, to promote the activities of thrifts, and to advance thrifts' funds through the FHLBs.

These three functions will now be performed by three new agencies. First, the new Office of Thrift Supervision will supervise, regulate, and charter federally chartered institutions. Next, a new Finance Board has been created to monitor the activities of the FHLBs. The act permits nonmember institutions to join the banks and obtain advances. Finally, the FDIC will be responsible for administering the SAIF and BIF.

Major Act Provisions Impacting Industry Structure

The FIRREA has a number of significant provisions that relate to the future structure of our nation's depositories. These provisions relate to the conversion of thrifts into banks and the acquisition of thrifts by banks.

CONVERSION OF THRIFTS INTO COMMERCIAL BANKS

The act does not permit conversions of institutions from the SAIF to the BIF before August 10, 1994, except under special circumstances. Conversions before this date can only occur if they involve a conversion of less than 35% of a member's assets or if the conversion assists a member in default, or in danger of default, and the loss to the insurance fund would be less through the conversion than through the default. Exit fees to the SAIF and entry fees into the BIF will be required if conversion takes place prior to 1997.

---

[1]The QTLT was made less restrictive in 1991 by the FDICIA. The QTLT percentage was lowered to 65%. See also Appendix 4B.

COMMERCIAL BANK ACQUISITIONS OF THRIFTS

At any time, a bank holding company can merge or consolidate a thrift subsidiary with a bank subsidiary if it receives approval, but certain asset and capital requirements must be met. SAIF deposits in a bank subsidiary will be subject to SAIF premiums.

The acquisition provisions suggest that public policy will encourage the acquisition of thrifts by banks while discouraging the acquisition of banks by thrifts. Later in the decade they also will permit the shifting of SAIF-insured thrifts into the BIF. Both of these provisions will work overtime to reduce the importance of the thrift industry as a factor in our financial system.

Resolution Trust Corporation

The **Resolution Trust Corporation (RTC)** was established by Congress in the fall of 1989. The purpose of this corporation is to manage and sell the assets of failed S&Ls insured by the former FSLIC. The RTC was also charged with managing the assets of the Federal Asset Disposition Association, which was established earlier to manage the sale of failed S&Ls. From its inception in August 1989 until May 1994, the RTC has assumed control of 743 institutions with assets at the time of takeover totaling $401.8 billion. By April 30, 1994, the assets of the institutions still controlled by the RTC had shrunk to $51.1 billion as a result of resolutions and asset sales and pay-offs. The RTC manages these institutions as conservatorships upon assuming control and then as receiverships when sale or liquidation occurs. The assets of these institutions consist primarily of cash, securities, and mortgages.

The RTC finances its operations primarily from public funds. Table A4.1 shows the sources and uses of funds from the RTC from its inception through April 30, 1994. The vast majority of these funds will be used to fund the losses sustained in the sale and liquidation of failed S&Ls.

The majority of the RTC's funds come from Treasury appropriations. The 12 FHLBs contributed $1.2 billion as a requirement under FIRREA. The RTC also borrows using the Federal Financing Bank (FFB) and has assumed the obligations of the REFCORP, which was a forerunner of the RTC.

TABLE A4.1

Resolution Trust Corporation Sources and Uses of Funds
Until April 30, 1994
(dollars in billions)

Sources:	
Initial Treasury appropriations	$ 18.8
Additional appropriations	40.7
FHLB contributions	1.2
REFCORP borrowings	30.1
FFB borrowings	27.4
Total external sources	$118.2
Recoveries from receiverships	103.8
Total sources	$222.0

continued

Table A4.1, continued

Uses:	
Resolutions and receivership funding	$199.9
Conservatorship advances	6.7
FFB interest	8.4
Other disbursements	−0.7
Total Uses	$214.3
Net Cash Available	$ 7.7

Source: *RTC Review* 5, no. 6 (June 1994).

It completed disposition of 710 institutions through April 1994. Most of these were through the purchase and assumption of the failed institutions' deposit liabilities and a certain amount of assets. The others were resolved by the RTC contracting with other institutions to pay off depositors or by paying off depositors directly. Commercial banks were the acquiring institutions in 70% of the cases.

Because of its sheer size, the RTC has been the subject of considerable criticism and public scrutiny. It is organized in an unusual manner. It has an Oversight Board made up of the Chairman of the Federal Reserve Board and Secretaries of the Treasury and HUD. The Chairman of the RTC is the Chairman of the FDIC. This cumbersome structure has resulted in frequent accusations that the RTC is excessively bureaucratic.

✓ Checkpoints

A4-1   What are the major provisions of FIRREA?

A4-2   What are some arguments for and against the opinion that FIRREA was really a bill designed to lead to the ultimate elimination of S&Ls?

A4-3   What kind of impact will the FIRREA provision requiring S&Ls to invest a higher percentage of assets in residential mortgages have on this industry given the growing dominance of mortgage government sponsored credit enterprises?

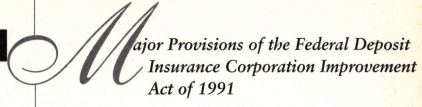

Major Provisions of the Federal Deposit Insurance Corporation Improvement Act of 1991

The Federal Deposit Insurance Corporation Improvement Act of 1991 (FDICIA) was passed in the wake of new revelations about potential large failures of commercial banks and inadequate BIF resources. Bank reform measures, such as allowing interstate banking, reducing Glass-Steagall restrictions, and permitting commercial banks to sell insurance, were all debated in 1991. The support for these reform proposals, however, gave way to growing concerns about the financial soundness of the BIF and the potential for another taxpayer bailout similar to the thrift debacle.

As a result, Congress passed a bill that rejected the reform proposals in favor of a narrow bill designed to increase financial resources for the FDIC and BIF and increase examination and supervisory authorities. The bill provides for the first Congressionally-mandated supervisory responses to financial institutions with low capital levels. Congress also used the bill to increase consumer disclosures and other protections.

Safety and Soundness Reforms

The FDICIA provided additional resources for the BIF to handle commercial bank failures. The line of credit of the FDIC on the Treasury was increased from $5 billion to $30 billion. Any loans taken down would have to be repaid over a 15-year period using assessment charges against BIF-insured institutions.

The FDICIA provided for supervisory reforms that required all insured depository institutions, with a few exceptions, to receive on-site examinations at least once a year. The act also required all institutions over $150 million in assets to provide their regulator with audited financial statements prepared by an independent accounting firm. Finally, the act required accounting reforms including the preparation of all financial statements consistent with Generally Accepted Accounting Principles, a method for valuing contingent assets and liabilities, and a disclosure requiring a market value accounting for the values of assets and liabilities.

Regulatory Powers for Dealing with Undercapitalized Depositories

Probably the most significant provisions of the FDICIA as it relates to the powers of depository regulators concerns the statute's requirements for regulators to deal with weakly capitalized insured institutions. Depository regulators classify depositories under the following five categories:

1. **Well capitalized:** An institution that significantly exceeds the required capital level for each capital standard.

2. **Adequately capitalized:** An institution that meets the required minimum level of capital for each capital standard.

3. **Undercapitalized:** An institution that fails to meet the required capital standards.

4. **Significantly undercapitalized:** An institution that is significantly below the required capital standards.

5. **Critically undercapitalized:** An institution that fails to meet the regulator's critical capital standard, which must be no less than 2% tangible equity and 65% of the permitted leverage limit (total assets divided by equity).

FDICIA requirements that depositories in the last three capital classifications must meet are discussed briefly in Table B4.2.

TABLE B4.2

Minimum Restrictions Imposed on Undercapitalized Depositories
by the FDICIA

Capital Classification	Permitted or Required Regulatory Actions or Restrictions
Undercapitalized and significantly undercapitalized	Must submit a capital restoration plan. Controlling companies of the depository must guarantee compliance with the plan or accept financial liability up to 5 percent of the insured's assets. Is prohibited from acquisitions, opening or purchasing new branches, and engaging in new businesses.

continued

Table B4.1, continued

Undercapitalized and failing to meet capital plan goals	May have to sell shares or obligations to raise capital.
	May be required to have their institution acquired or merged with another.
	May have transactions with affiliates restricted.
	May have directors and officers removed.
	May have deposits from correspondents restricted.
	May have distributions from holding companies restricted.
	May restrict level of deposit rates paid.
	May be required to divest or liquidate certain subsidiaries.
	May be restricted from paying bonuses or increasing salaries of executive officers.
Critically undercapitalized	Restrict interest payments on subordinated bonds.
	Appoint a conservator or receiver unless firm is meeting capital plan goals.
	Restrictions on other unusual transactions.
	Prohibitions of credit in highly leveraged transactions.
	Prohibitions on changes to charter, bylaws, and accounting methods.
	Prohibitions on paying excessive compensation and bonuses.
	Prohibitions on paying excessive deposit rates.

Other Major Regulatory and Institutional Powers Changes

The following are changes in major regulatory and institutional powers:

- *Too big to fail policy restrictions:* The FDICIA effectively eliminated the TBTF option that has been available to depository regulators and reduced the use of the Federal Reserve's discount window. As of January 1, 1995, the act prohibits the FDIC from protecting deposits above the maximum insurable amount and other creditors in which the deposit insurance fund would suffer a loss. The only exception would require agreement by the FDIC, the Federal Reserve, and the Treasury in consultation with the president.

- *Discount window restrictions:* The act also restricted the Federal Reserve from making discount window advances to undercapitalized institutions for more than 60 days in a 120-day period.

- *Brokered deposits restrictions:* Undercapitalized institutions are restricted from selling brokered deposits. Adequately capitalized institutions that do offer the deposits are prohibited from paying a rate higher than deposits of similar maturity in the institution's market area or a national rate for similar deposits.

- *Risk-based insurance assessments:* The FDICIA is authorized to establish a risk-based assessment system, which was implemented in July 1993.

- *State bank restrictions:* The act effectively restricts state-chartered banks from engaging in activities not permitted to nationally chartered banks. There are several exceptions.

- *Restrictions on real estate lending:* The act requires the regulatory agencies to adopt standards for real estate lending.
- *Periodic capital standards review:* The FDICIA sets up a schedule requiring periodic regulatory review of capital standards along with any modifications necessary to minimize loss to the insurance funds.

Savings and Loan Qualified Thrift Lender Test Expanded

The very restrictive QTLT standards that were implemented as a result of FIRREA were modified in the FDICIA. The percentage of qualifying assets was reduced from 70% to 65%; a greater percentage of consumer loans, stock in GSEs, and loans to churches, schools, hospitals, and nursing homes included as QTLT assets were allowed, and the percentage of assets invested in liquid assets, which are excludable from the asset base when calculating the QTLT, was increased. Overall, the modifications increased the portfolio diversification potential of S&Ls.

Depository Acquisitions of Institutions with Different Insurers

The FDICIA increases the ability of a BIF-insured institution to acquire an SAIF-insured institution, and vice versa. The resulting institution, rather than transferring insurance coverage to one insurer, will have deposits insured on a pro-rata basis by both insurers who will share coverage.

✓ Checkpoints

B4-4 What was the purpose of the FDICIA? What were the reform objectives when the FDICIA was first advocated, and what happened to them?

B4-5 How did the FDICIA respond to the recommendations for changing the deposit insurance programs?

CHAPTER 5

The Global Competition for Capital

Learning Goals

*After studying this
chapter, you should
be able to:*

1. Explain how the savings
   process contributes to
   capital formation.
2. Describe how the vari-
   ous economic units compete for capital.
3. Cite some factors affecting the movement of
   capital between coun-
   tries.
4. List some factors motivating foreign direct investment.
5. Explain how countries
   encourage capital in-
   flows.
6. Describe how security
   markets and financial
   institutions facilitate the
   global flow of capital.

While most careers today require an awareness of cultural diversity and international protocol, finance demands a keen eye
on competitive global markets. Communication and data processing technologies will continue propelling information-based
professions like finance across international boundaries with relative ease and rapidity. As walls collapse and economies open
for business, technological innovation will accelerate the movement of capital throughout the world.

The global dimension largely affects the outcome of two
closely related problems that financial managers must solve: (1)
Which of our investment opportunities will yield the highest expected return given an acceptable expected level of risk? and (2)
Where are the lowest cost sources of funds to be used to finance
investments? Managers of financial intermediaries can invest
and raise capital anywhere in the world, not just in the state or
country of their charter or headquarters.

This chapter will help you to appreciate the significance of international capital flows to a nation's business and economic
growth. You will look at the factors influencing global move-

ment among countries, which, in some cases, resembles the capital flow among the 50 states of the United States.

The Savings Process and U.S. Capital Stock

To consume or not to consume—that is the question. The answer in the United States is that a bias in favor of consumption exists, but the enormous size of the nation's economy has resulted in the United States holding the largest capital stock of any country in the world, a stock consisting primarily of individual savings. The process of saving begins when individuals make a straightforward consumption choice. Through some medium of exchange, a person with income can choose to consume now or later. Before deciding, the individual must consider all opportunities available to earn a profit on income during the period of delayed consumption and then weigh the later payoffs against the benefits of immediate consumption. An individual who can earn a high return on savings may postpone consumption to the future. The tradeoff between consumption today and consumption in the future is known as **time preference**.

REASONS FOR SAVING

If you asked classmates or colleagues, "Why do you save money?" you would no doubt get many different answers, especially from different age groups. People, like corporations, save for a variety of reasons:

1. To weather periods of financial distress—unemployment, illness, or other emergency—that affect household cash flows.
2. To amass funds for large purchases.
3. To even out cash flows over time.
4. To increase future income and consumption, usually by investing funds in those opportunities likely to increase future in-flows.

Typically, a worker's earnings start low at entry level, increase with experience throughout the worker's middle years, and then fall at retirement. Individuals and households can level the curve of this **life cycle income pattern** by borrowing in the early years, saving in the middle years, and consuming accumulated funds late in life.

METHODS OF SAVING

Both large corporations and small businesses make **direct investments** in assets that directly increase wealth. For example, the publisher of this textbook might invest in laptop computers for all sales representatives to increase sales productivity on the road, or a certified public accountant might buy a high-powered personal computer to increase productivity of the bookkeeping practice. Households as well as businesses also direct savings to intermediaries who can more shrewdly invest funds for profit in exchange for a financial asset against some portion of that expected income. This transaction constitutes an indirect investment, where the saver purchases a financial claim, such as deposit in a bank, which converts it into a business loan or mortgage against another individual or entity. You may have already recognized this process to be that of intermediation.

The *Flow of Funds Accounts,* produced by the Federal Reserve System and depicted in Table 5.1, overview how individuals hold their wealth.[1] As a country that provides for private ownership of housing, production facilities, land, and capital, a large percentage of households invest in financial assets.

TABLE 5.1

Assets of Households* Year-end 1993
(dollars in billions)

	$ Amount	Percent of Total
Tangible assets:		
Residential structures	$4,226	15.6%
Nonprofit plant and equipment	467	1.8
Consumer durables	2,338	8.6
Land	2,865	10.6
Total tangible assets	$9,905	36.5%
Financial assets:		
Deposits	$ 3,270	12.0
U. S. government securities	462	1.7
Tax-exempt securities	483	1.8
Corporate and foreign bonds	80	0.3
Mortgages	178	0.7
Open market paper	167	0.6
Mutual fund shares	1,084	4.0
Corporate equities	3,009	11.1
Life insurance reserves	489	1.8
Pension fund reserves	4,775	17.6
Personal trusts	659	2.4
Equity in personal businesses	2,221	8.2
Miscellaneous	353	1.3
Total financial assets	$17,230	63.5%
Total assets	$25,696	100%

*Includes personal trusts and nonprofit corporations

Source: *Balance Sheets for the U.S. Economy 1945–93*, Board of Governors of the Federal Reserve System, March 9, 1994, p. 25.

---

[1]The *Flow of Funds Accounts* are published quarterly by the Board of Governors of the Federal Reserve System. The reports include data on the net changes in financial assets and liabilities issued by and owned by the primary economic sectors—households, businesses, and governments—and by the primary financial institutions. In addition, data are provided which link the national income and product accounts published by the Bureau of Economic Analysis to changes in the supply of savings and to changes in the balance sheets for the primary economic sectors and institutions.

The data in Table 5.1 estimate asset holdings in residential housing, consumer durable goods such as automobiles and appliances, and real estate as well as in financial assets including those issued by financial institutions, corporations, and government units, and those held as reserves in life insurance companies and pension funds. Many households invest their reserves in debt instruments of corporations and corporate equities and in the assets of foreign countries, including tangible direct investments in businesses and indirect investments through foreign governments, businesses, and financial institutions. Table 5.2 further distills these major foreign assets.

TABLE 5.2

Foreign Assets Held by U.S. Investors
Year-End 1993
(in billions)

Asset Type:	Dollar Amount
Private deposits	$119
Credit market instruments:	
Corporate bonds	207
Bank loans	25
Commercial paper	67
Acceptance liabilities to banks	8
U.S. government loans	52
Trade debt	21
Direct investments	704
Total	$1,203

Source: *Flow of Funds Accounts, Fourth Quarter 1993*, Board of Governors of the Federal Reserve System, March 9, 1994, p. 84.

INDIVIDUAL ALLOCATION OF WEALTH AND SAVINGS

Both finance theory and practice suggest that a higher return of future income for any specified level of risk compels individuals to increase their savings, regardless of whether the form of savings is a direct or an indirect investment. A quick review: When allocating savings, individuals consider a number of financial factors:

- Expected returns on assets available for investment.
- Expected risk of receiving the returns anticipated.
- Ability to diversity risk across assets in an investment portfolio.
- Impact of taxation on returns from different types of assets.

Regarding the last factor, the U.S. federal tax laws encourage U.S. citizens to invest in certain types of assets, such as housing. For example, if you buy a home, then you benefit from housing services provided by the dwelling, which are not taxed, while at the same time interest paid on debt to buy the house is deductible against other income. Renters, on the other hand, must pay for shelter with after-tax income. Finally, it is possible to profit on your investment in housing if inflation appreciates its value: that is, you can sell your home for more than you paid for it—even beyond the rate of inflation. Other assets in which the government encourages investments are state and municipal bonds, Series E U.S. savings bonds, individual retirement accounts (IRAs), and life insurance policies with investment components. State and municipal bond interest is tax-free at the federal level of taxation. Interest on Series E savings bonds, income earned on IRAs, and income earned on reserves held in investment-type life insurance policies are all deferred until the funds are withdrawn from the investment.[2]

Assets held by U.S. households differ markedly from those held by households in the former Soviet states. Until recently, government units and bureaucrats owned and controlled most of these assets, including housing and real estate. The major political hurdle ahead of citizens of the former Soviet Union is **privatization;** transforming a centralized economy to private ownership.

✓ Checkpoints

5-1   Why do people save in general, and what would entice them to save even more?

5-2   Where do most U.S. citizens save their money, and in what form of asset?

5-3   What factors—and which decision makers—affect the allocation of people's savings?

The Competition for Capital

Since capital is a scarce asset, the competition for it is relentless and occurs on several playing fields: (1) between private and public sectors, (2) among countries and governmental jurisdictions, (3) among industries and firms, and (4) within each firm.

COMPETITION FOR CAPITAL BETWEEN THE PUBLIC AND PRIVATE SECTORS

Each country makes political as well as economic decisions about means of production: What industry should the public control for public good, and what

---

[2]Series E savings bonds are zero-coupon bonds sold to individuals by the U.S. government in small denominations. An individual retirement account (IRA) is a special tax-preferred retirement account created by employers for benefit of employees or used by employees to roll over pension reserves from a previous employer's pension fund. Life insurance policies with savings components include whole life, single-premium annuities and variable life policies. These allow for large investments to be made which earn interest that is not taxed until the reserves are withdrawn.

can the private sector manage effectively and toward the benefit of all the public? In socialist countries, the government owns and appoints officials to operate a large percentage of the economy's productive sectors. For example, in the Soviet Union, the government owned all productive land, factories, and equipment throughout the satellite republics. Differences also exist in developed countries concerning whether such businesses as airlines, railroads, telephone systems, and many other industries should be publicly or privately owned.3

Other governments establish a mix of public and private enterprise. In most capitalistic economies, governments control such productive sectors as air- and seaports, schools, postal services, highways, and sanitation. This public ownership may extend to certain industries such as railroads in most European countries, telephone systems in most South American countries, and commercial

How

it

Really

Works

GOVERNMENTS SELLING STATE-OWNED ENTERPRISES IN RECORD NUMBERS

Throughout the world, countries have been initiating programs to sell state-owned enterprises. The most obvious examples have been the former republics of the Soviet Union. In these new countries, tens of thousands of formerly state-owned enterprises have been sold to individuals, employees, management, and sometimes foreign investors. But privatization, as it is referred to, is really a worldwide phenomenon. It's not limited to formerly socialist states or developing countries.

Developed countries are also active in the process. France has plans to sell its major airline and commercial banks. Germany is selling a portion of its state-run telephone company. The United Kingdom is winding down over a decade of active privatization actions which included everything from airlines to autos. Now plans are underway to sell British Coal and British Rail. The U.S.'s privatization efforts are concentrated mainly at the state and local government level. Here everything from garbage delivery services to airports to public schools are involved.

Why so much interest in privatization? The reasons include: (1) the fact that many state-owned enterprises are money losers that revenue-strapped governments can no longer afford; (2) the tendency for state-owned enterprises to be subject to greater labor union pressures than private companies; (3) the tendency for state-owned enterprises to operate inefficiently (e.g., such as a poorly used bus route) due to political pressure; and (4) the belief that private owners will demand greater accountability in the investment of their capital.

Source: "Survey of International Finance," *The Economist,* April 27, 1991.

---

[3]One of the most far-reaching financial structural changes in the last decade has been the accelerated trend toward privatization of formerly government-owned enterprises. These privatization initiatives have not been limited to former republics of the Soviet Union, but are occurring with increased frequency in developing and developed countries.

banks, as in the privatization of formerly publicly owned commercial banks and telephone companies in Mexico.

The business of government in most countries is diverse: it provides health, education, retirement, and other services; builds and maintains public facilities, such as roads and waterways; and preserves the peace and safety of its citizens. Government-run activities require capital; and so the bureaucracy competes with its private constituents for capital in federal, state, and local arenas. Government raises capital through taxation and borrowing, or running budget deficits. From political campaigns to editorial pages, the questions recur: What goods and services should government really provide? How much of a nation's capital, in the form of taxes and savings, should flow to fund these government activities? Can the private sector do a better job at less cost per citizen? For the manager of financial institutions, other questions come to mind: To what extent will politics affect the use of this firm as an intermediary? How will politicians influence this firm's role in allocating capital?

COMPETITION FOR CAPITAL AMONG COUNTRIES AND GOVERNMENTAL JURISDICTIONS

The competition for capital among countries and other political jurisdictions is ardent. Most countries want to provide jobs and to increase income for their citizens; and most political platforms and campaign promises incorporate these two objectives. To attract businesses that will build plants and provide employment opportunities, government officials implement various strategies, including:

1.   Offering financing to new businesses through government lending and guarantee programs. (Such aid was provided by the state of Alabama in 1993 to entice the building of a German-owned Mercedes Benz plant in that state.)

2.   Altering their political system to provide greater stability, or reduce political risks, to the foreign investor. (Pressures to reform a country's political processes have been widely felt throughout the developed—Italy and Japan—and lesser-developed countries—China and Mexico.)

3.   Augmenting the infrastructure of roads, airports and sea ports, and telecommunications channels to encourage business investment in their countries. (Such investments have been integral to the development of countries such as Thailand, Taiwan, Indonesia, and many others.)

4.   Making their currency convertible into other foreign currencies. (Conversions to convertible currencies have been essential to the development of a number of republics of the former Soviet Union as well as to developing Asian countries.)

5.   Investing in the education of their labor force, which is a strong inducement for many potential employers. (Such policies have been used extensively in the developing countries of Asia.)

States and municipalities also compete rigorously for capital to attract job-producing capital. More jobs mean higher tax revenues, lower unemployment, and decreased payouts of social welfare. More jobs also translate into better services and improved living standards for citizens through education, recreation, and the infrastructure. To draw business facilities into their jurisdictions, some states and municipalities offer special benefits such as tax forgiveness, lower tax rates, low cost tax-exempt loans, and new roads and other services. Such benefits lower the initial financing costs for targeted firms. In 1994, the state of Virginia agreed to provide financing and infrastructure assistance to Disney Corporation to entice the development of a proposed U.S.-history theme park.

COMPETITION FOR CAPITAL AMONG FIRMS

Each firm also competes for capital, according to what investment opportunities exist for it relative to all other firms. If firms have high-earning investment opportunities for any given level of risk, they are in a better position to bid higher rates of return for savers to get the needed capital.

In the early 1990s, young biological technology (bio-tech) firms—each hoping to become another Genetec Corporation (one of the largest U.S. bio-tech firms, specializing in new drugs for health care and genetically-engineered products to improve food production)—convinced investors that they had great prospects for extremely high returns on invested capital. So high were these expectations that the high risks of these untested companies appeared acceptable. And so investors poured hundreds of millions of dollars into these companies as they went public and sold stock. Simultaneously, well-established auto manufacturers like General Motors Corporation struggled in the late 1980s to raise capital needed for competing in the world automobile market. Finally, even institutions within the financial services industry competed globally for investor capital.

Those firms that effectively and consistently manage their assets, as well as their client portfolios, will be able to attract capital and grow their business. Since the scrimmage for capital among firms and industries will continue, managers of financial intermediaries must be able to identify not only the firms that will consistently provide high returns on investments, but also the financial assets that will pay off.

COMPETITION FOR CAPITAL WITHIN THE FIRM

Within each business firm, business units may often scrimmage for short- and long-term capital. For example, the production and the sales departments of a typical manufacturing firm each may like to maintain large inventories: where the production group needs raw materials on hand to avoid process delays, the sales staff wants finished goods to fulfill customer orders on demand quickly. Sales representatives also want financial managers to initiate short-term financing policies that provide lenient sales terms and discounts, which increase accounts receivable on the firm's balance sheet. But both of these current assets are costly to finance. For long-term capital investments, production staff may need to update equipment, modernize facilities, and reengineer processes; sales may need additional offices; and accounting and legal staff may require new personal computers and database management software. Who gets the money? While each department must present its case through uniform presentation of data, the financial manager uses financial techniques to analyze each case and determine which asset investments will maximize the present value of the firm. Likewise, the manager of a financial institution uses similar financial tools in the asset-allocation decision-making process. These tools are the subjects of the Chapters 11 to 13 on credit risk, Chapters 17 to 18 on interest rate risk, and Chapters 20 to 21 covering management of liquidity and other assets.

Businesses compete for capital by pursuing profitable investment opportunities, those that provide a return greater than the cost of capital needed to fund the investment. Investments that earn the highest expected returns, given an acceptable level of risk, will get the capital.

✓ Checkpoints

5-4 What are some examples of the competition for capital among government jurisdictions, between firms, and within firms?

5-5 How does the return that a firm receives on one of its investments affect the flow of funds to that firm?

5-6 What are the social and political motivations behind incentives for capital allocation?

Land, Labor, and Capital

Classical economics uses the **doctrine of comparative advantage** to describe the movement of commodities from one country to another. These advantages relate to the relative distribution of land, labor, and capital among nations. Under this doctrine, for example, a country considered the relative lowest-cost producer of a particular commodity would try to specialize its production and export to other countries. If each country pursued a similar strategy, then the world would maximize use of available land, labor, and capital and would, in turn, improve worldwide living standards.

MOBILITY OF LABOR AND CAPITAL

However, with increased global movement of human and capital resources, labor and capital are not bound by citizenship or homeland. Indeed, large labor forces have flowed steadily from from less developed countries to Western Europe and the United States. Even more significant movements of capital occur between countries. And so land is the only factor of production to which the comparative advantage doctrine still applies; topographical, geographical, geological, and meteorological differences provide comparative advantages in raw material availability, manufacturing and distribution, real estate development, and food production. Countries blessed with large petroleum resources clearly win when selling oil and gas. Countries with special climatic advantages can produce products like bananas and pineapples more efficiently than others. Outside of these types of advantages, the movement of capital, and to a lesser extent labor, has essentially invalidated the doctrine of comparative advantage. This is why the global movement of capital is a more important topic today.

A **multinational corporation (MNC)** is a business firm that operates in more than one nation. An MNC, for example, can raise dollars in U.S. capital markets and exchange them for Greek drachma to pay for construction of a manufacturing plant in a suburb of Athens. Or a Japanese computer company can design a personal computer in the United States, buy parts from Taiwan, Korea, and Thailand, and then assemble the new machines in Mexico. Such firms clearly move a good bit of financial and human capital around the world.

INTERNATIONAL ✪ FOCUS

JAPAN'S CAPITAL MOVEMENT STRATEGY

Japan has been successfully implementing an Asian industrial strategy designed to insure its leadership in world exports. The region that Japan hopes to dominate is eastern Asia. In particular, Japan has been implementing specific investment strategies in the major developing countries in that region, including Hong Kong, Singapore, South Korea, and Taiwan (countries known as the Four Dragons, the most developed countries outside of Japan) and the lesser developed countries of Indonesia, Malaysia, the Philippines, and Thailand (the larger members of the Association of Southeast Asian Nations, ASEAN). The next group to come under Japan's wing are expected to be coastal China, India, Vietnam, and Bangladesh, the least developed of the group. If one were to measure labor costs and skills, they would generally find Japan on top, followed by the Four Dragons, then the ASEAN, and finally the least-developed group.

Japan's industrial strategy is simple. It is focusing investments for the most value-added products in Japan, followed by the Four Dragons. Value-added products are those that require considerable capital input and higher-skilled workers. Investments in the most labor-intensive products are being channeled into the countries with the lowest labor costs, the ASEAN and the least developed group of countries.

Over the last decade, Japan has moved more value-added products, such as automobiles, into plants in Four Dragon countries and lesser value-added products, like air conditioners and TVs, into the ASEAN countries. As the ASEAN countries develop and wage rates rise, the next group of countries, including China, India, Vietnam, and Bangladesh, can be expected to benefit from Japanese investments in the more labor-intensive industries. The favorable impact that these investments have on the receiving countries has caused them to accept growing Japanese dominance in the region.

This capital allocation strategy is being followed to a lesser extent by the United States with its North American Free Trade Agreement (NAFTA) with Mexico and Canada. Capital for labor-intensive production is moving to Mexico. Western European countries are looking for similar opportunities to move capital for labor-intensive production into eastern Europe and the former republics of the Soviet Union.

Source: Joseph Romm, "Japan's Flying Geese," *Forbes,* Nov. 23, 1992, pp. 108–12.

Key strategic decisions that financial managers of MNCs must make include determining where to operate, invest, and raise funds. The outcomes of these decisions may increase employment opportunities, wages, and the overall living standards in the chosen countries. Moreover, countries that can attract capital can develop more sophisticated output capabilities, educate the labor force, and transition into more knowledge-based production, which requires more capital investment. This industrial evolution explains, to some extent, why the capital stock per worker in highly developed countries like the United States, Japan, Germany, the United Kingdom, and other Western European countries is far greater than those ratios in developing nations. Since expert labor is in short supply, it is much more expensive and so companies channel their most sophisticated capital into economies with more skilled labor.

Capital is one of the most mobile means of production, more so when the definition of capital includes knowledge: with capital, flows enlightenment, so to speak. Moving capital among nations is a major job of financial managers at MNCs, and the task of efficient allocation involves financial analysts working in international commercial banks, investment banks, pension funds, life insurance companies, and mutual funds.

DISTRIBUTION OF CAPITAL AROUND THE WORLD AND ACROSS A NATION

How do finance professionals distribute capital globally? The process entails factors similar to those affecting the movement of capital among the various U.S. states:

- Comparative advantage of investment opportunities from city to city, state to state, or country to country.
- Differences in political and economic systems between countries and between states.
- Willingness of investors to bear risk.
- Necessity to diversify investment portfolio risk.
- Availability and cost of information concerning prospects in different countries, availability of requisite technology, and cost of cross-border transactions.

The following sections explore how each of these factors influences the capital investment decision.

Differences in Investment Opportunities

The comparative advantage of investment opportunities from city to city, state to state, or country to country is a key factor affecting the movement of investment capital. As we have come to expect, capital flows to those investments with the highest expected rates of return for a given level of risk.

But what factors increase the potential for higher return? One is low cost labor, an important stimulant for investing capital in most developing countries

SMOKESTACKS TO METERED PIPELINES

How

it

Really

Works

Eastern Europe's primary source of heat and electricity is the coal-fired heating and electricity plant. The result is that these countries are filled with smokestacks and generally dirty air. As independence has taken hold, there is growing interest in replacing these coal-fired plants with cleaner natural-gas-fueled plants.

To Daniel Industries, a major U.S. manufacturer of gas meters, the business opportunity caused by this change is a potential bonanza. Gas pipelines mean demand for thousands of gas meters. The question for Daniel was how best to supply these meters. The company considered export, manufacturing in the former West Germany, and manufacturing in the former East Germany.

The final decision was based on the relative cost and training of labor in the former East and West Germanies and on other costs of doing business. The company found that the former East German workers were well trained, having gone through apprentice programs similar to the former West German worker. Yet, German wages in the former East Germany were much lower, about one-half that in the former West Germany. In addition, land and buildings were much more expensive in the former West Germany. These factors, plus the political stability advantage of a new unified Germany, prompted Daniel to purchase the assets of Messtechnik Babelsberg, a measuring-instrument firm that was part of a former East German state-run enterprise. Daniel has invested heavily in the plant and substantially increased productivity. This capital investment allowed them to reduce employment from 600 to 60. Thus, profits were enhanced due to higher productivity and lower wage rates.

or moving capital between states. For years, politicians in high-wage, high-tax states such as New York and California have been working to slow the movement of businesses and jobs to close by but less-costly states such as New Jersey, Arizona, and Nevada. When deciding where to operate, financial managers must analyze the wage-rate differences for a given required skill and the cost of equipment. Table 5.3 reveals some noteworthy differences among average hourly compensation rates around the world as measured in U.S. dollars. If you ran a labor-intensive firm, then where in the world might you locate your business?

The availability of raw materials also sways capital movement decisions. After the dissolution of the Soviet Union, much joint-venture capital has flowed to the Republic of Russia in establishing cross-border partnerships in Russia's vast oil and gas reserves. Developers of the rich Russian Tengiz oil field, with its recoverable reserves of up to 9 billion barrels, expect to require $10 billion in investments over ten years.

Climate, a natural resource of sorts, also influences the movement of capital—in part because it affects the cultivation and production of other resources. For example, the climates of Hawaii and Florida account for the large and fast-growing tourist industries in those states, whereas southeastern and northwestern states support timber harvesting, attracting a high concentration of lumber and paper-product investments.

TABLE 5.3

Average Hourly Manufacturing Compensation in Selected Countries for 1991

Country Type and Country	Hourly Wage in Dollars
Developed economies:	
Britain	$19.42
Germany	22.17
Ireland	11.90
Japan	14.41
United States	15.45
Moderately developed economies:	
Singapore	4.38
Recently developing economies:	
China	0.26
India	0.39
Jamaica	1.61
Mexico	2.17
Thailand	0.68

Source: "Looking Ahead," *Fortune,* Dec. 14, 1992, p. 58.

While higher expected returns motivate capital flows, the flow of capital itself tends to keep actual returns roughly equal around the world. That is, the rapid flow of capital acts to reduce the potential for higher expected returns in any particular spot because the increased supply of capital, with equal demand, results in a new lower equilibrium price for capital, thereby reducing the potential returns from subsequent capital investment in that country. Over time, differentials in wage rates, land costs, and other factors of production tend to equalize as a result of changing supply/demand equilibrium. In effect, capital movement acts as a self-correcting mechanism.

Political and Economic Factors Affecting Capital Movement

Differences in political and economic systems among countries and states also affect capital allocation decisions. One difference is taxation structure. Each country or state determines the taxes levied on businesses within its borders. Taxes may be direct, such as income, value-added, or sales taxes, or they may be indirect, through laws and regulations that increase the costs and risks of doing business. Table 5.4 compares the United States to other major countries in terms of estimates for 1991 of the effective tax rate on income earned in each country and income earned through activities of a U.S.-based affiliate. For example, if a Swedish firm operates in Sweden, then Sweden taxes the company's income at an effective rate of 30%. But if that same firm sets up a U.S. affiliate to perform the same activity and generates the same profits before taxes, Sweden will tax the income at an effective tax rate of 48%. If you managed this Swedish firm, where would you prefer to operate? Considering the tax differential alone, you would probably opt to produce goods and services in Sweden!

TABLE 5.4

Effective* Tax Rates on Income Earned on U.S.-Located Affiliates, Compared to a Domestic Investment for January 1991

Domestic Country	Income on U.S. Affiliate	Income Earned Domestically
Australia	44%	43%
Belgium	43	24
Canada	53	49
France	46	23
Germany	46	23
Japan	56	49
Luxembourg	40	40
Netherlands	40	30
Sweden	48	30
Switzerland	38	25
United Kingdom	38	37
United States	N/A	44

*The effective tax rates include the taxes levied in all legal jurisdictions within the country (e.g. federal, state, and local governments in the United States).

Source: J. Steven Landfeld, Ann M. Lawson, and Douglas B. Weinberg, "Rates of Return on Direct Investment," *Survey of Current Business*, Aug. 1992, p. 84.

A country's or state's regulatory requirements and business laws beyond taxation can also affect capital movements. Pollution standards, the legal system's propensity to produce costly litigation, and worker protection legislation can expedite or impede the flow of foreign capital into a particular country.

Another aspect of a country's investment desirability is known as *political risk, country risk,* or *sovereign risk.* This risk is discussed more fully in Chapter 12. The likelihood of **expropriation,** or seizure by the host government of an investment owned by a company or citizen of another country, also influences the investment decision. During the Cold War era of the 1950s and 1960s, host governments sometimes seized many businesses owned by multinational firms and private individuals, and the owners often did not get a fair market price for their assets. In the 1980s and 1990s, the converse has occurred: privatization of government-owned enterprise has often rewarded potential buyers with the opportunity to buy underpriced assets. Some U.S. companies and investors hope that the collapse of the Soviet Union signals hope for someday recovering assets seized by other communist regimes, such as those in Fidel Castro's Cuba.

National governments can also influence capital allocation through trade policy. One item on the political agenda may involve tariff barriers and payment services.[4] **Tariffs** are taxes on goods and services that the importing firm must pay to the country's government. Governments use tariffs and other restrictions to discourage certain countries from importing and to protect domestic industries. For example, the 1993 passage of the North American Free Trade Agreement opened up Mexico's financial services industry to U.S. financial institutions as never before. As you might expect, countries that erect high trade barriers and restrictions may impede the flow of foreign capital in a variety of ways. A firm may circumvent a barrier to entry by opening a factory within the foreign country. Such a factory could implement the same competitive strategy, design, and technology used in its home market at costs lower than exporting from its home turf to foreign soil but with social benefits to the foreign base. For example, the United States instituted voluntary restraint export programs on Japanese auto imports; to access the U.S. market, the Japanese built auto plants right in the States, opening job opportunities to U.S. citizens. But the risk of foreign investment is the loss of valuable technologies to hostile host countries.

Risk Preferences

The willingness of investors to move capital outside their country involves risk preferences. The riskiness of the stock of available investments of developed countries may differ from that of less developed ones. If investments in developed countries are far less risky than those in developing countries and if developed countries' investors have greater risk tolerance, then they may invest in developing countries assuming they anticipate the required higher expected returns. Conversely, if a developing country's investors prefer less-risky opportunities, then they might commit capital to developed countries even though expected returns are less.[5] Risk preferences relate not just to location of asset but also to type of asset. For example, investors with a greater risk tolerance might pick direct investments in foreign businesses over foreign government bonds. On the other hand, investors with less risk tolerance might choose government bonds of the foreign country rather than stock in any of the country's businesses.

Investment Diversification

Foreign countries also provide the opportunity to diversify risk in an investment portfolio. An investor who can invest only in one country is at the mercy of that country's business cycle, taxation, and other regulatory policies. To some extent, investors can mitigate these risks through MNCs; but thousands of investment opportunities, especially to diversify such country risk, are not possible through MNCs.

---

[4]These other restrictions can take a variety of forms. Countries have used content restrictions to lessen imports by requiring that a certain percentage of a product's total content be locally manufactured. Another restriction might involve a government ownership limitation. Such a limitation would require that a foreign firm cannot own more than a minority of the stock of a firm operating in the host country.

[5]One irony of international capital movement is that developing countries with high expected returns on capital frequently experience a flight of capital if political risks are preceived as high by local residents. At various times in the 1980s, there were large flights of capital from Mexico and Hong Kong.

Risk diversification *within* the United States is also important, because certain types of investments are very susceptible to business cycles. That is, the sales and prices of certain products and assets fluctuate up and down with the economy. Commercial real estate is a prime example. Office buildings, apartments, shopping outlets, and strip malls cannot be relocated. If developers overbuild an area or demand drops due to economic recession, then vacancies increase, rent rates fall, and property values plummet. To diversify this risk, most real estate investors buy commercial real estate in several regional markets. Manufacturers of heavy equipment, such as bulldozers and heavy trucks, are susceptible to a similar business cycle. During periods of rapid economic growth, construction of new plants, offices, and warehouses is strong. Heavy construction equipment manufacturers' sales increase during these periods but drop during recessions. Other businesses, like commercial banks, may find the margins between the return on invested funds and cost of liabilities expand significantly in the last stages of an economic recession. This is one reason why common stocks of financial firms tend to lead the rest of the stock market out of a recessionary downturn.

INFORMATION AND TRANSACTION COSTS

Availability and cost of information, availability of requisite technology, and cost of cross-border transactions all affect the flow of funds to foreign investments. Search and information costs can be high. Interpreting information about the prospective foreign asset may require language translation, accounting adjustments to harmonize different procedures and disclosure requirements in each country. These factors, together with the difficulty of accurately forecasting the success of a foreign business selling products in foreign markets, makes gathering the data for decision making quite challenging indeed.

Transaction costs are another major factor affecting the ease and cost of making foreign investments. Deregulation of such things as brokerage commission rates in the United States and the United Kingdom, and the financial deregulation of capital flows in Japan, Taiwan, and other countries has decreased transaction costs overall, thus lowering barrier-to-entry costs for new competitors. Institutional investors have also helped to lower transaction costs by creating investment fund pools that fold investments of smaller denominations into larger investment portfolios.

International investment banks and commercial banks have also increased availability of information and reduced transaction costs by such innovations as the 24-hour-a-day trading room in large-scale security trading organizations. These security trading organizations, such as Morgan Stanley & Co. and Citicorp, maintain contact with market information and prices worldwide, using on-line real-time information systems that provide users with access to up-to-the-minute information. Today, a security investor in Frankfurt, Germany, can find out what the head of the Federal Reserve System said during a speech in Washington, D.C., just as quickly as anyone on Wall Street.

✓ Checkpoints

5-7   What is the doctrine of comparative advantage, and why is it relevant today?

5-8   What factors influence the movement of capital around the world?

The Foreign Direct Investment (FDI) Decision

Foreign direct investments are tangible assets acquired in another country. For example, an electrical components manufacturer based in Germany seeks global investment opportunities akin to its primary business. In making this foreign direct investment decision, the financial manager of the firm considers several factors, quite similar to determinants of interstate investing in the United States. Two major factors involve operational and nonoperational benefits. Among the operational considerations are the following:

- *Economies of scale:* **Economies of scale** exist when a firm can produce additional units at a cost below the average cost per unit. The cost of producing additional units is an out-of-pocket or variable cost; the fixed cost is already allocated to prior output. With an available excess manufacturing capacity, a firm can expand sales of goods to other markets, such as foreign countries. The German firm could choose to open sales offices in other western European countries to distribute excess product in those markets. However, as a marketing ploy, some firms dump the additional product into new markets. *Dumping* refers to selling goods at a price below their average cost to manufacture. The German firm could continue selling components in Germany at the standard unit cost of the normal batch but start selling the excess components in Italy for the lower cost achieved through economies of scale. This lower unit cost may substantially undercut the prices of Italian-based firms.

- *Use of technology:* Technology that increases operational efficiencies can motivate foreign expansion. To compete in a less technologically advanced country with prohibitive trade barriers, the German firm might decide to build its own plants in that country. The German-designed manufacturing processes in the new plants might give the firm a cost advantage over domestic firms.

- *Vertical integration:* **Vertical integration** occurs when a firm acts to align its raw materials with its ultimate sales to final customers. Such alignment prompts investment in foreign operations. The German firm may use a raw material, like petroleum, not found abundantly in Germany. To maintain a steady supply of petro, the German firm will make a direct foreign investment in a country like Russia, where the material is located.

- *Cost of labor and regulatory compliance:* Differences in labor costs and regulatory burden constitute reasons for foreign expansion. The German firm might open a plant in Hungary, where wage rates are lower and pollution requirements not so strict. Similarly, a U.S. firm might relocate operations from a heavily unionized northern state to a state with lower wages.

- *Successful competitive strategies:* Some companies develop and implement unique, successful strategies for domestic marketing and production; and these strategies may work equally well in foreign countries. Fast food, for example, worked in U.S. markets; and U.S. fast-food chains have successfully exported their eat-and-run concept beyond American borders. Just-in-time inventory management strategies came from Japan. Recently popular strategies—with such names as *total quality management, continuous improvement, statistical process control,* and *lean production*—require some reengineering of financial decision making but can provide a competitive advantage in foreign markets. The German electronics manufacturing company, for instance, could export its state-of-the-art retail distribution strategy to other countries.

WHAT COUNTRIES MUST DO TO ENCOURAGE CAPITAL FLOWS

The global demand for capital has skyrocketed in recent years due to worldwide political reform, privatization, and consequent desire to improve living standards. To attract the much-needed capital for change, countries like the former Soviet republics must significantly reform their financial systems in the following important ways:

- *Monetary controls:* Foreign investors prefer a governmental authority to control the value of a country's local currency; such control of the money supply helps to avoid hyperinflation.

- *Adequate payment services:* Rudimentary payment systems inhibit commercial and industrial development by forcing firms and individuals to use cash and bartering as primary payment mechanisms.

- *Convertible currency:* Investors need to know that they can liquidate assets or the profits from these assets and convert the value from one foreign currency to another or to their own. The former Soviet republics all suffered from the lack of covertible currencies at one time or another.

- *Legal protection of property rights:* Countries where the state owns most enterprises must redesign their legal systems and pass laws for protecting private ownership and transferring private property.

- *Financial markets, institutions, and financial assets:* Countries with developed financial markets and institutions can facilitate the movement of capital more efficiently than those with primitive systems. Innovation in creating financial assets also speeds capital movement by reducing risk and lowering transaction costs.

U.S. FOREIGN DIRECT INVESTMENT

The destruction of European and Japanese economies during World War II positioned the United States at the forefront of manufacturing so that U.S. firms could eventually expand sales offices and manufacturing capacity abroad. Throughout the Cold War, the United States became the leading foreign direct investor. During the 1980s, however, huge U.S. government deficits, rather than productive assets, have consumed a large percentage of the nation's capital; and so growth in foreign direct investment has slowed proportionately. Still, at year-end 1993, U.S. direct foreign investments totaled $703 billion. The vast majority of these investments were in the developed countries of Europe, the United Kingdom, Canada, and Japan. However, U.S. investors were picking up their pace of investment in Latin America and Asia.

The primary reason for U.S. direct investments is to gain access to foreign markets; that is, to sell goods to customers outside U.S. borders. Therefore, most capital goes to highly developed countries with affluent consumers. Approximately 80% of foreign investment capital of U.S. multinational companies goes to majority-owned affiliates of the MNCs. (*Majority-owned* means that the U.S. MNCs control over 50% of the affiliate stock.) Interestingly, U.S.-owned MNCs, despite their growth in assets and sales, are not increasing employment in foreign countries.

FOREIGN DIRECT INVESTMENT IN THE UNITED STATES

While the growth in U.S. foreign direct investment slowed in the 1980s, the foreign flow of capital into the United States rose rapidly, the inverse result of the substantial U.S. trade deficit. American consumers and businesses simply bought more in goods and services from other countries than foreigners purchased from the United States. If foreigners who receive U.S. dollars do not consume U.S. goods and services, then they must loan or invest this money in U.S. securities or direct investments, or else exchange the dollars with someone who *will* invest in U.S. securities or direct investments. In the 1980s, they did both.

At year-end 1993, foreign direct investment in the United States reached $520 billion. The vast majority of these investments were made by developed countries in Europe, and by the United Kingdom, Japan, and Canada.

Just as U.S. direct investments in foreign countries create jobs, so do direct foreign investments in America. Since foreign companies operating in the United States want to sell their goods and services to eager U.S. consumers, the employment opportunities and sales of foreign wholesale and retail firms have grown. The U.S. manufacturing market has opened to foreign competitors in the food, mining, and chemical businesses.

✓ Checkpoints

5-9   What do individual countries do to attract inflows of capital?

5-10   What are some of the operational reasons why firms invest in foreign countries?

5-11   What are some of the nonoperational reasons why firms invest in foreign countries?

5-12   How must a developing country reform its financial and political system to attract capital inflows?

5-13 Where has the United States invested most of its foreign capital, and why?

5-14 Who has invested heavily in the United States, and why?

Securities, Markets, and Institutions Facilitate Capital Flows

Securities move capital faster than foreign direct investments do, because securities enable investors to: (1) manage risk through risk sharing and pooling and (2) reduce transaction costs. Securities created for worldwide sale have helped institutional investors to diversify their investment portfolios internationally. Global integration of security markets has allowed commercial and investment banks to trade around the clock and around the world through offices located in New York, Tokyo, London, and other financially important cities. Table 5.5 provides evidence of the increased trading volume of U.S. equity securities by foreigners.

TABLE 5.5

Aggregate Foreign Purchases and Sales of U.S. Equity Securities
by Country of Origin: 1980–1993
(dollars in billions)

Country	1980	1985	1993	$ Change, 1980–1993
Canada	$12	$22	$76	$64
Total Europe	46	83	304	258
Total Asia	10	25	97	87
Latin America	7	26	141	134
Other	0	4	6	6
Total	$75	$159	$624	$549

Sources: Joseph A. Grundfest, "Internationalization of the World's Securities Markets," *Journal of Financial Services Research*, Dec. 1990, p. 353; and *Treasury Bulletin*, March 1994, pp. 111–12.

Financial markets—whether operating as **organized markets,** such as the New York Stock Exchange, or operated as **dealer markets,** such as the **over-the-counter market** operated by security dealers—facilitate the efficient flow of capital flows by reducing the costs of moving capital. They: (1) reduce information collection and processing costs by, for instance, providing data on current bid and ask prices and prices on recent transactions; (2) assist in finding buyers and sellers; and (3) reduce risk for market participants by promoting standardization of financial contracts and reducing the risk of the security settlement process. While the United States may currently have the best-developed financial markets in the world, other nations are quick to innovate.

NEW STOCK EXCHANGES NEED CONSULTING ADVICE

The number of newly formed stock exchanges has skyrocketed in recent years. Asia and eastern European countries are the homes of newly organized exchanges for their newly created private sectors. Many of these countries have no experience with capitalistic organizations like stock exchanges. As a result, the demand for technical assistance is booming.

Officials of these exchanges have many decisions to make. Should their new market be a floor-based auction system like the New York Stock Exchange or a computerized system like the National Association of Security Dealer's NASDAQ system? What regulatory system must be established to control such issues as security fraud and corruption? The question of standardized accounting systems is another issue that must be addressed by these newly formed exchanges. Some of the other issues are very basic questions, such as whether securities should be registered. Setting up systems for settlement and clearing are also high on the list of issues.

Some experts believe that, at present trends, China will be the world's largest economy by the year 2000. To accomplish this, the country's two stock exchanges, with their 1,500 listed stocks, will have to develop significantly to attract the foreign capital that will be needed to maintain that country's rapid growth.

Source: "Babysitting the World's Emerging Bourses," *Business Week*, Nov. 1, 1993, pp. 112–15.

FINANCIAL INSTITUTIONS' ROLE IN FACILITATING GLOBAL CAPITAL MOVEMENT

Financial institutions are the primary decision makers in moving capital around the world. Although MNCs choose ways to deploy their own capital, financial institutions determine how to invest the capital of depositors, mutual fund investors, pension beneficiaries, and the insured of life companies. These intermediaries look for the highest risk-adjusted rates of the return on capital throughout the world. If they relied solely upon domestic markets, then their liabilities might not be competitive with those issued by a competitor earning a higher risk-adjusted return in a foreign market.

Financial institutions contribute to the worldwide movement of capital by providing the functions described in Chapter 2: origination, servicing, brokerage, and portfolio management. The major competitors in the global financial services industry are large commercial banks, investment bankers, large insurance companies, pension funds, and specialized international mutual funds.

✓ Checkpoints

5-15 How do security markets facilitate the flow of capital around the world more than foreign direct investment?

5-16 What role do financial institutions play in worldwide capital movement?

148 MANAGEMENT OF FINANCIAL INSTITUTIONS

SUMMARY AND REVIEW

1. **Explain how the savings process contributes to capital formation.**

    Savings capital is created by the desire of individuals to acquire sufficient assets to make large purchases, protect themselves from financial emergencies and alter their pattern of consumption over their life and between generations. Savings can be encouraged if a higher return is provided on the investments available to savers.

2. **Describe how the various economic units compete for capital.**

    The **competition for capital** occurs at many levels. Within each country there is competition for capital between the **public and private sectors. Countries** compete for capital in order to provide employment opportunities and increase real wages. **Smaller political jurisdictions** also compete for capital in order to provide tax revenue and reduce some government transfer payments. **Firms** compete with each other for capital. Finally, each **division within individual firms** represents competing interests for capital which are allocated using financial capital budgeting techniques.

3. **Cite some factors affecting the movement of capital between countries.**

    The factors that affect capital allocation decisions around the world include: (1) **expected returns on investments**; (2) **tax structures**; (3) **desire for risk-reducing diversification**; (4) **cost of information and transaction costs**; and (5) **risk**.

4. **List some factors motivating foreign direct investment.**

    One major method of moving capital is **foreign direct investment**. Direct investment is motivated by **operational factors** including: (1) presence of economies of scale; (2) technology; (3) vertical integration; (4) cost differentials, and (5) competitive strategies; and **nonoperational factors**. Nonoperational factors include: (1) financial factors such as cost and availability, expected returns and risk and expected changes in exchange rates; (2) taxation; and (3) tariff and non-tariff trade barriers.

5. **Explain how countries encourage capital inflows.**

    Countries can do the following to **enhance their ability to attract capital**: (1) control their domestic money supply to avoid hyperinflation; (2) provide an efficient payment system; (3) provide for currency convertibility; (4) provide a system to insure property and contract rights; and (5) encourage the creation of financial markets, institutions, and assets.

6. **Describe how security markets and financial institutions facilitate the global flow of capital.**

    Financial securities contribute to the global movement of capital by **reducing risk through risk sharing and pooling** and by **reducing the cost of financial transactions**. Financial institutions contribute by providing origination, servicing, brokerage, and portfolio management services on a worldwide basis.

CHAPTER 6

Structural Changes in the Financial Services Industry

Learning Goals

After studying this chapter, you should be able to:

1. Identify several major trends in financial structure and provide examples of each from the popular business press.
2. Explain how government sponsored enterprise affects a nation's financial structure.
3. Characterize the major ingredients—technological, economic, governmental or political, and competitive—needed to alter financial structure.
4. Describe how capital as well as profitability affects financial structure.
5. Explain government policymakers' concern about changes in structure.

"What a debacle!" "Yet another failure!" and worse headlines appeared during the volatile 1980s and early 1990s to report the financial condition of U.S. financial intermediaries. The American system of specialized home lenders—the savings and loan associations—collapsed to a mere fraction of its pre-1980 size. Record commercial bank failures in the late 1980s accelerated industry consolidation in the 1990s. And several life insurance companies faced serious problems and even failed.

In contrast, other types of intermediaries have thrived and continue to perform well. The assets of mutual funds, investment banks, and finance companies, as well as government sponsored enterprises (GSEs are discussed fully in the Appendix to Chapter 3) have grown amidst those groaning thrift institutions and many commercial banks forced to retrench.

This chapter reviews the major financial trends, catalysts for structural change in the financial system, and modifications to the U.S. system from the 1960s through the early 1990s.

Financial Trends into the 1990s

A very stable period of gradual changes in inflation and interest rate levels in the 1950s and 1960s gave way to rising financial volatility in the late 1970s and 1980s. During the last 20 years, major advances in information processing and communication technology, and government deregulation of the competitive structure have reduced the costs of doing business for some financial institutions and increased market efficiencies. Where oligopoly of the depository market structure concerned regulators in the 1960s, overcapacity and excessive institutional failure top the policymakers' agenda today. New competitors have found loopholes into what were once highly regulated depository markets.

Understanding these change factors is essential to financial-institution managers involved in setting strategic plans or policies. Some of the most significant changes in financial structure within the last decade include:

1.   Shrinkage of mortgage-related thrifts.
2.   Consolidation of commercial banks.
3.   Accelerated growth of mutual funds.
4.   Continued expansion of pension funds.
5.   Expansion of government sponsored enterprises.
6.   Globalization of financial markets.

SHRINKAGE OF MORTGAGE-RELATED THRIFTS

The most wrenching change in the U.S. financial structure has been the shrinkage of the mortgage-related thrift institutions, the savings and loans and savings banks. Caught with a long-term fixed-rate mortgage portfolio in the early 1980s, just as open market interest rates were climbing to record post-World War II highs, the financial fortunes of the mortgage thrifts deteriorated rapidly. The National Commission on Financial Institution Reform, Recovery and Enforcement established by Congress to explain the thrift debacle emphasized in their July 1993 report that four principle causes created the debacle: (1) the presence of deposit insurance which allowed financially weak institutions to continue to attract deposits; (2) the interest rate spike from 1979 to 1982 and the resulting financial shock; (3) financial deregulation that permitted thrifts to make risky investments unrelated to residential real estate; and (4) relaxed capital requirements that permitted weak institutions to continue growing.[1] Of the four principles, commissioners viewed the presence of insurance as a necessary condition for the debacle while the other factors merely aggravated the situation.

Moving from the status of a protected industry to a competitive one has left thrifts a much smaller piece of the financial services industry. Table 6.1 shows the

---

[1]There have been hundreds of excellent books and academic articles written on the thrift debacle (many are included in the references to this chapter). Although the popular press has focused on government forbearance, fraud, and mismanagement, the consensus conclusion is that the deregulation of deposit rates in 1980, combined with record high interest rates in the late 1970s and early 1980s, left the savings and loans in such a weak earnings and capital position that few viable options existed after 1982 to return most of the firms to viability. It is also the case that expanded powers to invest in risky assets, especially commercial real estate and raw land, contributed to losses.

number of institutions and the total assets for all U.S. Savings Association Insurance Fund (SAIF) insured savings and loans and Bank Insurance Fund (BIF) insured savings banks at year-end 1988 and 1993. Mortgage-related thrifts probably will continue to lose market share for several reasons. First, they must compete against mortgage-related government sponsored enterprises which get special government treatment. Second, they are largely confined to the highly competitive residential mortgage market. And, third, they probably will remain takeover targets of commercial banks wishing to expand into new markets and penetrate existing markets.

TABLE 6.1

Number and Total Financial Assets of Mortgage-related Thrifts Year-End 1988 and December 31, 1993

	1988	1993	Change
Number of BIF savings banks	492	404	−88
Number SAIF savings and loans and savings banks	3,584	1,930	−1,654
Total financial assets (in billions)	$1,516	$1,001	−$515

Sources: Federal Deposit Insurance Corporation, Federal Reserve Board, and Office of Thrift Supervision.

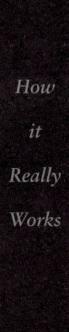

COMMISSION RECOMMENDS ELIMINATION OF MORTGAGE-RELATED THRIFTS AND BROADLY BASED DEPOSIT INSURANCE

The nation's financial structure would experience significant changes if the National Commission on Financial Institution Reform, Recovery and Enforcement got its way. Reporting its recommendations in July 1993, the commission advocated two significant changes to the country's financial system. First, it recommended eliminating mortgage-related thrifts as separately chartered and regulated entities. They would have the thrifts adopt commercial bank charters. This would permit the Office of Thrift Supervision to be eliminated, along with the Comptroller of the Currency, by having all regulatory and insurance activities assumed by the Federal Deposit Insurance Corporation.

The other significant recommendation would be to eliminate all deposit insurance except that which applies to narrowly defined, separately capitalized money market funds that invest only in short-term debt instruments. These entities could be owned by commercial banks and are referred to as *monetary service companies*. They would offer federally insured short-term deposits used for third-party transactions activated by checks and electronic transfers. The result would be elimination of "full faith and credit" government guarantees on all other deposits sold by financial institutions. The federally insured time deposits would be history.

Source: *Origins and Causes of the S&L Debacles: A Blueprint for Reform*, National Commission on Financial Institution Reform, Recovery and Enforcement (Washington, D.C.: U.S. Government Printing Office, July 1993).

How it Really Works

CONSOLIDATION OF COMMERCIAL BANKS

Many of the forces causing problems for the mortgage-related thrifts have also affected commercial banks. However, because the commercial banking system was more diversified and had significantly more capital and fewer fixed-rate mortgages, it fared better than the thrifts. Still, the industry has consolidated for three reasons: (1) to grow the average size of banks to improve their ability to diversify, (2) to reduce operating costs by eliminating redundant activities, and, probably most significant, (3) to increase market power by combining institutions that previously were competitors. Table 6..2 shows the result of this consolidation within the commercial banking system.

TABLE 6.2

Number, Total Financial Assets, and Average Size of BIF-Insured Commercial Banks Year-End 1988 and 1993

	1988	1993	Change
Number of commercial banks	13,123	10,957	–2,166
Total financial assets (in billions)	$3,131	$3,868	$737
Average size (in millions)	$239	$353	$114

Sources: Federal Deposit Insurance Corporation and Federal Reserve Board.

Although the financial health of the commercial banking system improved significantly in 1992, 1993, and 1994, the basic forces behind consolidation still push ahead. Most observers expect the number of banks to decrease steadily while the size of each increases. With interstate branching now a reality the trend toward consolidation may accelerate.

ACCELERATED GROWTH OF MUTUAL FUNDS

With the depository industry in turmoil, U.S. mutual funds rapidly expanded in size and variety of offerings. Early growth of these funds coincided with the period of interest rate control in the 1970s: during this period, mutual fund investments in money market instruments could pay higher yields than could banks and thrifts, which lost business as a result. In the early 1980s, mutual fund distributors targeted primarily the certificate of deposit, with taxable and tax-exempt bond funds among the fastest growing.

More individuals are choosing professionally managed and diversified equity mutual funds over direct investment in specific common stock; through mutual funds, individuals can access foreign security markets—typically difficult for individuals to get directly. Consequently, holdings of mutual funds by households have surged while holdings of deposits have plummeted. Table 6.3 compares the holdings of deposits and mutual funds by households, personal trusts, and non-profit organizations at year-end 1988 and 1993. The share of these two financial assets held in mutual fund shares increased by over 15% in only five years.

TABLE 6.3

Deposit and Mutual Fund Share Holdings of Households and Nonprofit Organizations Year-End 1988 and 1993
(dollars in billions)

Type of Asset	1988	Share	1993	Share
Deposits	$2,719	80.6%	$2,821	65.0%
Mutual fund shares	655	19.4	1,524	35.0

Source: *Flow of Funds Accounts, Fourth Quarter 1993,* Board of Governors of the Federal Reserve System, March 9, 1994.

The higher capital requirements imposed on banks and thrifts, plus the higher deposit rate premiums, will reduce the demand of depositories for these liabilities, reduce the rates that depositories will pay for them, and, in the end, increase the popularity of mutual funds. Moreover, many bank holding companies and thrifts are marketing their own proprietary mutual funds directly to their deposit customers along with those managed by others through captive brokers and dealers.

PENSION FUNDS CONTINUE EXPANSION

Pension funds have also been growing for two basic reasons: (1) the U.S. labor force has aged and "baby-boomers" have assimilated into the labor force; and (2) assets invested in major pension funds have become significantly more valuable during stock and bond market rallies in the early 1990s. Although many pensions of industrial companies remain underfunded, others have performed extremely well. Again, focusing on the 1988 to 1993 period, Table 6.4 points out that pension fund reserves are the single largest share of total financial assets of households, personal trusts, and nonprofit organizations. Also, the share of total financial assets increased significantly in the five-year period shown. The growth in pension fund assets has made this intermediary the U.S.'s largest source of long-term capital.

TABLE 6.4

Pension Fund Reserves' Share of Total Financial Assets of Households, Personal Trusts, and Nonprofit Organizations Year-End 1988 and 1993
(dollars in billions)

Asset type	1988	Share	1993	Share
Pension fund reserves	$2,755	22.3%	$4,776	27.7%
Total financial assets	$12,356	100%	$17,230	100%

Source: *Flow of Funds Accounts, Fourth Quarter 1993,* Board of Governors of the Federal Reserve System, March 9, 1994.

EXPANSION OF GOVERNMENT SPONSORED ENTERPRISES

During the last decade, the government has supported a large number of borrowers, so that now government sponsored enterprises represent the largest federal credit program. Even though many of these federally funded firms have largely converted to private ownership, their initial government sponsorship gives them special status in the credit markets. The most recent GSEs have sprung up as privately-owned corporations with substantial government conferred advantages. These benefits, alluded to in the above discussion of GSE advantage over the thrift industry, include various combinations of the following:

1. The ability to issue stock and debt securities that federally regulated financial institutions can hold but that private companies are prohibited from issuing.

2. An implied guarantee from the federal government, referred to as *agency status,* which allows these agencies to borrow at interest rates below even the best-rated private borrowers.

3. Exemption from Securities and Exchange Commission registration requirements.

4. National or regional monopolies in credit-granting activities.

5. Regulatory net worth or capital requirements lower than those imposed on comparable private institutions.

Taking these overwhelming advantages over private-sector competitors, GSEs account for most of the rapid growth in government credit programs. Table 6.5, which shows the total assets plus the securities guaranteed by each of the privately owned GSEs including the Federal Home Loan Banks (FHLBs), the Federal National Mortgage Association (FNMA), the Federal Home Loan Mortgage Corporation (FHLMC), the Student Loan Marketing Association (SLMA), and the Farm Credit Banks (FCBs), provides dramatic evidence of this growth—especially in the mortgage-related GSEs.

TABLE 6.5

Total Assets Plus Guaranteed Securities of the GSEs
Year-End 1988 and 1993
(in billions)

Enterprise	1988	1993
FHLBs	$136	$ 142
FNMA	116	696
FHLMC	298	492
SLMA	29	53
FCBs	55	53
Total	$634	$1,436

Sources: Tables 1.44 and 1.54, *Federal Reserve Bulletin,* Board of Governors of the Federal Reserve System, March 1994.

As discussed in the appendix to Chapter 3, many of these GSEs undercut costs of competitors and offer lower cost loans in markets where commercial banks and thrifts once dominated, perhaps prompting these depositories to lend in riskier markets and increase their exposure to failure.

GLOBALIZATION OF FINANCIAL MARKETS

Since capital now flows rapidly across borders to find higher risk-adjusted rates of return, internationally based commercial and investment banks have re-tooled operations. With access to international debt and equity markets, pension funds and individuals have redesigned their investment strategies. Investors must be able to analyze a whole set of new investment alternatives to increase their portfolio returns for given levels of risk. Such analysis requires the ability not just to access information worldwide on economic, industry, and firm events but also to understand the issues involved in foreign financial markets.

✓ Checkpoints

6-1 How have major financial trends affected commercial banks, mortgage-related thrifts, mutual funds, pension funds, and government sponsored enterprises?

6-2 Which trends do you think will continue to influence your work in the business world, and why?

Catalysts for Change

Catalysts for change in the financial service industry are both powerful and fast acting. Managers of financial institutions must be able to spot the presence of these catalysts in order to manage their effects. Over the last 10 to 15 years, four general catalysts, all interdependent, have influenced trends in the financial services industry. They are: (1) technology, (2) economics, (3) politics, and (4) competition.

TECHNOLOGY AS CATALYST FOR CHANGE

Financial institutions are in the information business: they process data and communicate financial information in their underwriting, servicing, brokerage, and portfolio management functions. Any upgrade in computer technology can alter the cost structure of this processing and communicating. Less-costly computer power significantly reduces the cost of gathering and disseminating information: just by moving from a once state-of-the-art mainframe computer to many personal computers, an institution can decrease data processing expenses and decentralize communication activities, making information user friendly, so to speak. Some firms, by incorporating technology into their strategic plans, have designed and are managing highly specialized computer software systems to handle large-volume activities.

Any change in communications technology can increase market efficiency by increasing and linking the number of buyers and sellers and by moving information faster throughout the marketplace. Institutions with archaic systems cannot serve customers at greater distances from their offices. Only the most up-to-date firms—those that can distribute and service product worldwide—compete successfully in the bank credit card market, for example. Also, late-breaking financial news from highly placed government sources can travel across global communications systems producing more instantaneous market adjustments.

The positive and negative effects of both data processing and communication technology on financial intermediaries are difficult to assess. Very small firms benefit from lower costs of data processing and communication capabilities without large administration and bureaucracy costs, but firms specializing in large-scale activities might benefit from economies of scale or scope of technological advances. With so much information available to all investors for analysis and decision making, investors may turn from retail broker expertise to a discount brokerage house. In general, though, global access to communication systems may decrease the profitability of the brokerage function. In terms of technology, innovative intermediaries will dominate and expand business while less-efficient providers will struggle even harder to compete.

ECONOMICS AS CATALYST FOR CHANGE

The financial institutions in the United States were largely structured in the 1930s to meet the need for relatively stable inflation and interest rates. During the Depression, customers called upon the nation's savings and loan associations to invest short-term time and savings deposits in long-term fixed-rate mortgages. In the 1970s, intermediaries abandoned this policy as rising inflation destabilized interest rates. Other macroeconomic events have contributed to the performance of U.S. financial institutions during the last several decades.

October 1979 Federal Reserve Policy Change

In October 1979, Federal Reserve Chairman Paul Volcker shocked the financial markets by reporting that the Federal Reserve open-market committee would be focusing more on the rate of growth of the monetary aggregates and less on the absolute level of interest rates. Experts immediately (and correctly) interpreted this statement to mean that interest rates could go to levels unsurpassed in previous cycles. In the late 1970s and early 1980s interest rates did reach new highs. The prime commercial bank lending rate finally peaked at a record 21.5% in the early 1980s.

The decision to abandon the policy to control the level of interest rates and focus on monetary aggregate growth left the thrift institutions, with their large portfolios of fixed-rate mortgages, unable to cope. Regulation Q, interest rate controls which had been used since the 1930s' Depression to control deposit costs at commercial banks and thrifts, became an even less useful tool for providing stability and actually became a destabilizing tool for controlling bank and

S&L deposit interest rates.[2] The inflation of the 1970s combined with the Fed's new policy strategy to essentially bankrupt the S&Ls by the mid-1980s—or much earlier if solvency had been measured by determining the liquidation value of the firms.

These economic policies also had a profound effect on life insurance companies. Life companies financed a large percentage of their assets with policy reserves of whole life insurance policies. Many of these policies had an option permitting policyholders to borrow the amount of the policy reserves at low interest rates[3]—an option that many exercised during the late 1970s and 1980s, making it necessary for life companies to sell high-yielding market rate assets and replace them with low-yielding policy loans. This situation also soured many potential purchasers of life insurance policies on the investment merits of whole life policies. Instead, many chose term policies. Life companies responded by developing and marketing policies such as annuities and selling liabilities such as guaranteed investment contracts with higher investment yields to build their liability bases. These liabilities, however, carried much higher interest rates which cut into insurance company profit margins.

Oil Price Cycle

The rise and fall of oil prices in the 1973 to 1985 period caused significant financial institution stress. Some developing countries, such as Mexico and Venezuela, and states such as Texas, Oklahoma, and Louisiana, were able to borrow against the large oil reserves they had safely in the ground. As the price of this collateral rose, the collateral supported even higher lending levels. However, once the value of the collateral fell with the decline in oil prices, so did the ability of the borrowers to repay their debt. The result was that commercial banks and thrifts took heavy losses on loans made in states and countries that based their development and growth on the oil and gas business.

POLITICS AS CATALYST FOR CHANGE

The U.S. financial system of the 1930s was characterized by governmentally established barriers between the various financial firms. The Glass-Steagall Act, for example, forbade commercial banks from underwriting and distributing se-

---

[2]Technically, Regulation Q was first applied only to commercial banks in 1930s. These interest rate controls, administered by the Federal Reserve Board, were expanded by Congress in 1966 to apply to savings and loans associations insured by the former Federal Savings and Loan Insurance Corporation and to state-chartered savings banks insured by the former Federal Deposit Insurance Corporation insurance fund. Open market interest rates exceeded the ceiling by such an extent in the late 1970s that Congress finally abandoned the controls in 1980.

[3]Most whole life policies written in the 1950s and 1960s contained a financial clause allowing the owner of the policy to borrow up to the entire amount of cash values built up in the policy. The interest rate on the loan was set when the policy was written, usually 4–5%. When open market interest rates rose far above those levels in the late 1970s, many policy owners exercised the option to borrow their cash values.

curities. Other laws denied S&Ls the authority to make business loans or offer demand accounts until the 1980s.

As competitive conditions increased and interest rates became more volatile, the government system of protection, price controls, and competitive compartmentalizing became unworkable and impossible to sustain. Unfortunately, deregulation came too slowly and was poorly executed.

Regulation Q and Delayed Deregulation

The history of S&Ls is one of government regulation and protection. A product of the 1930s, the modern S&L was envisioned as a narrowly defined home-lending intermediary. In return for operating with very narrow asset and liability powers, the government granted the S&L industry a few benefits, such as its own supportive regulatory system, insurance corporation, and lending agencies; tax advantages; and, eventually under Regulation Q, the permission to pay a higher interest rate on deposits than commercial banks could and to operate with lower capital requirements than commercial banks. Unfortunately, the social costs of maintaining this system in the face of rapidly rising interest rates in the late 1970s and early 1980s became evident. These institutions could no longer be expected to borrow short and lend long. First, the saving public began to campaign politically for higher rates on deposits. Second, the disintermediation from depositories into direct investments and money market funds proved the ceilings were no longer effective.

Popular opinion cried out for deregulating thrifts and expanding their powers to resemble those of commercial banks. Government officials dismantled Regulation Q in two stages: (1) the passage of the Depository Institutions Deregulation and Monetary Control Act in 1980, and (2) the Garn-St. Germain Depository Institutions Act of 1982. Unfortunately, interest rates reached such high levels in the early 1980s that the operating losses of thrifts all but wiped out their equity. New lending markets opened by this legislation did not help decrease interest rate risk or produce higher operating income for many years. The elimination of Regulation Q and the expansion of thrift powers came much too late to save the industry.

Loss of Commercial Banking Monopoly in the Payment System

The deregulation of the early 1980s allowed savings and loans, mutual savings banks, and credit unions to offer consumer interest-bearing transaction accounts, the mainstay of commercial banking business. Providing payment services was a major franchise value embedded in the commercial bank charter, devalued in amazingly short time. Increased competition prompted thrifts to price their new services more aggressively for commerical bank market share, but competition failed to reduce a bank's cost of providing payment services. In 1980, Congress passed the Monetary Control Act, which required the Federal Reserve to price its payment services to cover direct and indirect costs. The act also allowed thrifts into the credit and debit card market, again reducing the profit potential for commercial banks.

Inadequate Regulation and Supervision

Inadequate regulation and supervision of the deposit insurance corporations galvanized losses in the 1980s and 1990s. Instead of increasing capital requirements for S&Ls in the early 1980s, regulators lowered them, allowing S&Ls to enter new markets with inexperienced personnel and control systems without monitoring the novice activity.

Overall, the financial institution regulators were ill-equipped for the financial turmoil of the 1980s. As discussed in Chapter 4, the moral hazard issues related to deposit insurance and regulation are difficult to solve. Indeed, public policy-makers likely have overreacted on the side of conservatism, evident in FIRREA and FDICIA demands for higher capital and reduced risk-taking authority. These policies will challenge all but a substantially reduced segment of these businesses to achieve adequate profitability.

DID FIRREA AND FDICIA UNDULY HURT SMALL BUSINESS?

Commercial banks are the largest single source of credit for small businesses. Moreover, small businesses have been the major source of jobs and increased output of goods and services during the last decade. Consequently, anything that hampers the ability of small businesses to attract capital is a national concern.

Many observers have argued that the combination of provisions in 1989's FIRREA and 1991's FDICIA, combined with more conservative examinations, has made lending to small businesses riskier for boards of directors and managers of commercial banks concerned about officer and director negligence claims made by government supervisory agencies should a loan default. Thousands of officers and directors of failed financial institutions have been sued for negligence by the FDIC and RTC in recent years. Accordingly, many say that the only sure way to avoid this fate is to make only "cream-puff" loans.

In order to open up lending, the four depository regulatory agencies in early 1993 developed the Joint Interagency Policy Statement on Credit Availability. It was designed to encourage more lending to small business. The recommendations in the statement act to reduce documentation and encourage lending based more on a borrower's "character" and "reputation" than solely on collateral and other harder criteria. Depositories with strong capital can also make character loans (see Chapter 12) without concern that examiners will criticize them for inadequate documentation. The policy statement also reduced certain appraisal requirements for real estate loans made to some businesses. Whether any of this improved the plight of small businesses is questionable. What it does seem to suggest is that examination philosophy is important in determining the cost of capital to borrowers.

Source: Katherine A. Samolyk and Rebecca Wetmore Humes, "Does Small Business Need a Financial Fix?" *Economic Commentary*, Federal Reserve Bank of Cleveland, May 15, 1993.

How

it

Really

Works

Expanded Deposit Insurance Coverage and Moral Hazard

In 1980, Congress increased deposit insurance coverage from $40,000 per account in any institution to $100,000, thus exacerbating the moral hazard problem for the depository regulators. Depositories could raise large volumes of deposits from depositors who could care less about the financial soundness of the institutions, resulting in the creation of excess insured deposits.

These excess insured deposits tended to be invested in higher-yielding, riskier assets as a result of the declining profit margins in traditional lending markets. Not surprisingly, decision makers used brokered insured deposits to fund many of the higher-risk loans and investments, growing institutions very quickly without developing a consumer franchise.

The National Commission Financial Institution Reform, Recovery and Enforcement concluded in 1993 that our nation's deposit insurance program should be radically reformed. The Commission suggested that financial firms could offer insured low-interest-paying checking and demand deposits as long as they invested proceeds from the sale of these accounts into safe and marketable U.S. government and low-credit-risk corporate short-term securities. Firms could sell other deposits that would not carry government insurance.

Constraints on Interstate Branching and Consolidation

Most observers of financial institution structure would say that the United States in the early 1990s has excess capacity in its financial system, including more commercial banks and thrifts per capita than any industrialized country in the world—five to ten times as many depositories on a per capita basis as countries like Japan, Germany, France, and Great Britain. Despite this widely held view, the federal government did little to improve the climate for commercial bank mergers and consolidations and commercial bank acquisitions of thrifts until the early 1990s.[4] Indeed, the FIRREA—mainly for political reasons—did little to induce commercial banks to acquire S&Ls. The thrifts have spent many political dollars over the years to maintain a separate system of home finance institutions despite years of evidence that the system has not been working. Moreover, state banking regulators have been slow to offer up their regulatory turf to interstate banks. As a result, the pace of consolidation has been slow, exacerbating the overcapacity in the system.

1986 Tax Reform Act

Changes in tax legislation can significantly alter financial performance of different sectors of the economy. For example, the Tax Reform Act of 1986 reduced marginal tax rates and also eliminated a wide variety of deductions and tax preferences for individuals and corporations. For financial institutions, the act also changed marginal tax rates and a good deal more: it reduced many of the tax preferences for investors in real estate by eliminating capital gains treatment for real estate and disallowing depreciation losses against income for "passive in-

---

[4]At the time of this writing, the Congressional committees in the House and Senate have passed a nationwide branch banking law. The Clinton administration has also endorsed merging the regulatory duties of the Federal Reserve Board, Federal Deposit Insurance Corporation, Office of the Comptroller of the Currency, and Office of Thrift Supervision.

vestors." For many investors, the after-tax cash return on real estate fell, followed by the market value of many real estate projects. Real estate lenders foreclosed on many of these projects.

The act also affected the desirability of financial intermediaries to invest in state and municipal bonds. As discussed in Chapter 14, the act put an end to the deductibility of bank interest expense for tax-exempt securities purchased after 1986. This reduced the profitability of an asset that was an important component of the portfolio of commercial banks and S&Ls.

COMPETITION AS CATALYST FOR CHANGE

Throughout the last several decades, the overall structure of U.S. financial institutions has become more competitive through innovations like the money market mutual fund. The money and capital markets have become more accessible to U.S. companies financing themselves outside of the commercial banking system. The globalization and deregulation of the financial system have also increased competition.

Money and Capital Market Access to High-quality Borrowers

The entry of many of our nation's highest-grade borrowers into our money and capital markets has been a major challenge for our nation's commercial banks. These borrowers had been a primary source of loans and deposits for banks. The growth of commercial paper and medium-term notes made the high-grade borrower a less frequent commercial bank customer. Moreover, the availability of the direct issuance of securities has reduced pricing of commercial bank credit. Today, only a few of the less creditworthy customers have to pay the prime rate for funds. Most other borrowers are able to price their bank loans off of rates in the money markets. This has acted to exacerbate the profit squeeze on banks. Less than 30% of all bank customers pay the prime rate or higher for their bank credit according to surveys of the Federal Reserve Board.

Capital Market Access for Lower-quality Credits

Just as the money and capital markets have provided viable alternatives to commercial banks for the high-grade borrower, the emergence of the high-yield security (junk bond) market has provided an alternative source of funding for the low-grade borrower. The junk bond market has become a viable funding alternative for many growing businesses. This has also taken a toll on the nation's commercial banks by allowing another important class of borrowers to avoid the commercial bank and use the investment banker to obtain funds. Fast-growing pension funds and life insurance companies have provided ample funds for the public and privately placed bond market.

Growth in Foreign Banking Activities

As discussed in Chapter 3, the last decade has witnessed a major increase in the activities of foreign banks operating in the United States and elsewhere. While the European banks have continued to increase their historically strong international activities, the rise of the Japanese banks has been the most notable. The

Japanese banks, spurred by a strong market capitalization of their securities, large trade surpluses, and a high national savings rate, have had to look beyond their borders for investment opportunities. All this has added to the competitive structure confronting U.S. banks.

Competition from Investment Banks and Discount Brokers

Commercial bank holding companies offer brokerage services, and the large retail investment banking firms offer integrated accounts that provide transaction services, credit services, and a host of investment alternatives. The lines between the two types of institutions began to blur many years ago, resulting in a further increase in overall capacity to provide financial services without a commensurate increase in demand.

Nonbank Financial Competition

Competition has also come from nonbank competitors. Captive finance companies have taken a large and growing share of the secured auto loan and leasing markets. At the same time, Sears, American Express, General Motors, Ford, AT&T and many others have been the most visible new major entrants into the consumer credit card market. Another major source of competition has been finance companies' affiliation with large manufacturing companies that have been able to secure strong credit ratings. These firms have become more successful partly because, since deregulation, banks and thrifts have lost their source of low-cost consumer deposits. Overall, this new competition has acted to exacerbate the overcapacity in the financing industry.

✓ Checkpoints

6-3 Why should a manager of a financial institution keep on top of technological advances in information processing and communication?

6-4 What economic events altered the structure of the financial service industry, and how have they affected financial institutions?

6-5 How has government action helped and hurt certain financial institutions?

6-6 Why has competition increased steadily in the financial service industry?

Overcapacity: An Industry Curse

The factors so far discussed in this chapter point to one undeniable conclusion. The United States in the early 1990s has more financial service production capacity than there is demand. Normally, market forces of merger, consolidation, and failure would correct such a market disequilibrium, but that has not happened until recently in the United States for several reasons:

1.   The government allowed many depositories to remain in business and indeed expand their insured deposit liabilities when profit prospects were poor and capital for many inadequate.

2. The government regulatory agencies did not follow the market-cleansing process for many failed thrifts and banks of allowing the failed institutions to be liquidated and removed from the market.

3. During the 1980s, the insurance corporations granted insurance to a large number of newly chartered banks and savings and loans. Many were chartered under liberal state chartering laws, but the insurance of accounts came from the federal government. This added more unneeded capacity.

4. The rising cost of deposit insurance has made it more difficult for U.S. banks to be international competitors since the rising deposit insurance premiums and the need to hold reserves in zero earning accounts in Federal Reserve Banks further holds profit margins down.

5. The government has created and fostered major new competitors for commercial banks and thrifts in the form of GSEs. As more and more potential bank and thrift loans became GSE assets or GSE guaranteed securities, the potential market for good earning assets shrunk. The agencies also had the further disruptive impact of decreasing market yields on the assets available for thrift and bank investment.

IMPACT ASSESSMENT, 1990 TO 2000

Each of the agents of change discussed has had a significant impact on the financial structure of the nation. Unfortunately, it would be very difficult, if not impossible, to quantify the financial impact of each. What is important is the impact of these catalysts on the overall profitability and capital levels of financial institutions. This will be significantly affected by the actions of government financial policymakers.

Profits and Capital

The regulatory and Congressional actions of the late 1980s and 1990s have been partially counterproductive. FIRREA raised the operating costs of thrifts, decreased profit opportunities, increased capital requirements, and increased examination and enforcement costs. Regulators have also increased commercial banks' deposit insurance fees and capital requirements. To meet both higher deposit insurance fees and capital requirements, a firm must have a profitable charter value and positive future prospects.

The basic problem is that it took the lowest levels of short-term interest rates in over 20 years in 1992 to 1994 to produce decent commercial bank profits during these years. The sharp reduction in the number of competitors will help increase franchise values for the remaining institutions. However, the low interest rate levels are not a permanent condition. Consequently, deregulation of liability pricing, expansion of competition in the payment system, and the explosive growth of GSEs are some of the primary reasons why profit and capital pressures will likely continue. The spread between asset yields and liability costs is likely to decline after the cyclically induced record spreads of the early 1990s. Moreover, fee income, while increasing as fast as intermediaries are able, continues to be eaten up by increased operating costs, partly as a result of government regulatory system changes and, of course, problem loans.

Policy Options

Our financial structure could best be characterized as oligopolistic in many geographic markets from the Depression through the 1970s. Since then, technology, deregulation, globalization of financial markets, GSE competition, and the breakdown of institutional barriers have lessened the franchise value of insured depositories. Adding to the burden are higher capital requirements, deposit insurance premiums, and additional social regulations. Franchise value must be restored in order to reduce the chance of failure and improve the industry's prospects for attracting capital. This is likely to be a long-term effort that will continue into the next decade.

There is, of course, a risk that the process will swing too far toward concentration of market power. Shareholders in depositories should not be beneficiaries

---

How it Really Works

UNITED STATES SLOW TO CONSOLIDATE

Despite the increased consolidation in the U.S. financial system occurring over the last decade, the United States still has smaller financial institutions than any other major economic power. The table below provides a listing of several major countries with the number of commercial banks and specialized savings institutions (such as savings and loans, savings banks, postal savings institutions, etc.) that are among the world's 25 largest institutions, measured by total assets, as of year-end 1992.

TABLE 6.6

Number of the World's 25 Largest Commercial Banks, Savings Institutions, and Insurance Companies by Country

Country	Commercial Banks	Savings Institutions	Insurance Companies
France	4	0	0
Germany	1	3	1
Japan	16	0	11
Netherlands	1	1	0
United Kingdom	2	9	2
United States	1	5	9
Other	0	7	2

The table makes clear that even though the U.S. economy is the world's largest, it does not have the largest financial institutions. The insurance industry is the most concentrated of the three shown. The other financial industries would appear to be ripe for continued consolidation.

Source: "Fortune's Global Service 500," *Fortune*, Aug. 23, 1993.

of governmentally induced efforts to concentrate markets. This outcome must be watched carefully by regulators. However, at this point—and probably for many years into the future—the problem of excessive concentration seems unlikely to come to fruition.

Financial experts have been concerned that since the United States has smaller institutions than other countries do, it will be less able to compete in world markets. To date, there is little evidence to back this up.

Another recommendation of the National Commission of Financial Institution Reform, Recovery and Enforcement would reduce the risk of loss to the government by radically reducing federal deposit insurance coverage. The commission would also consolidate the commercial bank and mortgage-related thrift systems into one, thereby reducing the government's liability and letting private market forces dominate the system.

✓ Checkpoints

6-7   Why is profitability and capital adequacy so important in determining winners and losers in the financial industry?

6-8   How do you think government actions involving thrifts and commercial banks since 1989 are likely to affect their structure?

6-9   To what extent should the federal government worry about undue concentration in the provision of financial services? Do you think it is a problem today?

6-10   If the structure of our markets is such that competition is too severe, what can Congress and the regulators do to improve conditions? What changes are now taking place?

6-11   The mergers of BankAmerica/Security Pacific, Chemical/Manufacturers Hanover, and NCNB/C&S/Sovran are important transactions. What do they seem to tell us about the future of commercial banking in the United States?

SUMMARY AND REVIEW

1.   **Identify several major trends in financial structure and provide examples of each from the popular business press.**

Several of the major financial trends of the 1990s include: (1) the **shrinkage of mortgage-related thrifts;** (2) the **consolidation of commercial banks;** (3) the **accelerated growth of mutual funds;** (4) the **continued expansion of pension funds;** (5) the **continued expansion of government sponsored enterprises;** and (6) the **globalization of financial markets.**

2.   **Explain how a government sponsored enterprise affects a nation's financial structure.**

GSEs have been granted unique charters by the federal government to provide credit to specified borrowers such as farmers, homebuyers, and students. These organizations were granted **favorable security provisions, spe-**

cial borrowing advantages, and **usually monopoly market positions.** These organizations are among the fastest-growing government credit programs. One impact of these programs has been that they **compete unfairly with private-sector lenders.**

3. **Characterize the major ingredients—technological, economic, governmental or political, and competitive—needed to alter financial structure.**

    The primary agents of change impacting the financial services industry in the last decade are **technological agents of change, economic agents of change, governmental agents of change,** and **competitive agents of change.** Technological changes in data processing and communication have allowed financial institutions to expand markets and enter new markets, creating more competition. Economic policies of the last decade have resulted in greater amplitude and volatility of interest rates, creating significant problems for financial firms that carry significant interest rate risk, such as savings and loans and life insurance companies. Sharp fluctuations in the value of certain resources, such as oil, have also led to significant credit problems. Government legislative and regulatory responses to the changing competitive conditions in the financial services business have been largely detrimental. Deregulation of the nation's S&Ls came after many were insolvent. Regulatory forebearance policies exacerbated the size of the losses of the resulting failures. Until recently, governmental policies have discouraged consolidation and, therefore, contributed to overcapacity in the financial depository business. Competition from less-regulated financial institutions has resulted in a loss of market share and reduced profit margins at insured depositories. The globalization of financial markets and the economic resurgence of Western Europe and Japan have also increased competitive pressures on U.S. financial institutions.

4. **Describe how capital as well as profitability affects financial structure.**

    Ultimately, those financial institutions that are profitable and able to raise capital at the lowest cost will prevail in a competitive marketplace. Government policies can substantially affect profitability and the ability to raise capital by changing **powers and authorities, regulatory burden, cost of such benefits as deposit insurance,** and **examination and supervision practices.** In the late 1980s and early 1990s, most of these factors have made it more difficult for depositories to compete against nondepositories.

5. **Explain government policymakers' concern about changes in structure.**

    Government regulations in the form of **capital requirements, deposit insurance premium costs,** and **social regulation cost** affect the value of a depository's franchise as an ongoing concern. Excessively costly regulation and restricting the free market outcome of greater concentration could weaken the controlled institutions relative to others. Regulators must constantly balance the desire to provide adequate competition with the need to maintain strong and profitable firms.

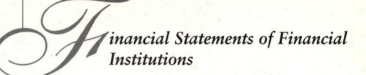

CHAPTER 7

Financial Statements of Financial Institutions

Learning Goals

After studying this chapter, you should be able to:

1. Explain the basic components of the stockholders' report.
2. Describe the format, features, and functions of the income statement, balance sheet, retained earnings statement, and cash flow statement.
3. Describe the special financial provisions in the financial statements that insurance companies create.
4. Show how to interpret footnotes to the basic financial statements of a financial firm.

Like nonfinancial firms, every financial institution keeps standardized records and generates reports of its activities for regulators, creditors, owners, and managers. In terms of uses and users, there are many parallels between the financial statements of financial institutions and those of other corporations in the United States. Regulators—federal and state depository regulators, insurance regulators, and securities commissions—enforce the proper and accurate disclosure of corporate financial data for compliance with law. Creditors use financial data to evaluate the firm's ability to meet scheduled debt payments. Owners and security analysts use these reports to assess the firm's financial condition and in deciding whether to own its stock. Managers use them to gauge regulatory compliance, creditor and owner satisfaction, and the firm's performance.

As a potential consumer of these reports, you must understand exactly how these financial statements differ from those of commercial and industrial firms. For example, financial firms do not report sales and cost of goods sold, but rather interest income and expense. This chapter covers such differences.

The Stockholders' Annual Report

The financial firm's primary vehicle for communicating to its owners is the stockholders' annual report. This report, usually supplemented by quarterly reports, provides the primary operating and financial analyses of the firm's previous year's performance. The report consists of management operating and financial discussions, primary financial statements, financial ratios, comparisons, analysis, and footnotes amplifying details not obvious or evident in the basic financial reports.

The guidelines used to prepare and maintain financial records and reports include the **generally accepted accounting principles (GAAP)** as well as the **regulatory accounting principles (RAP)**. As you learned in your accounting course work, only the Financial Accounting Standards Board (FASB) determines the GAAP. In contrast, whatever regulatory agency supervises a particular financial firm establishes the RAP. Over the years, financial records maintained under GAAP and RAP have become more comparable. In years past, for example, there were major differences between RAP and GAAP for thrift institutions, which resulted in the overstatement of the true financial solvency of savings and loan associations and contributed to the thrift debacle of the 1980s. Those differences have been largely eliminated. Insurance companies also experience differences between RAP—which in insurance company terminology is called *statutory accounting*—and GAAP, differences that relate primarily to how assets are valued and policy sales costs amortized.

FINANCIAL STATEMENTS

The **Securities and Exchange Commission (SEC)** requires all publicly owned financial institutions to prepare and file: (1) a statement of income, (2) a balance sheet, (3) a statement of shareholders' equity, and (4) a statement of cash flows. While the SEC monitors only publicly held firms, most other firms provide similar data to their regulators under RAP. The annual corporate report must contain these statements for at least the three most recent years of operation (two years for balance sheets). Historical summaries of key operating statistics and ratios for the past five to ten years are also commonly included with the financial statements.

✓ Checkpoints

7-1   Who sets and who follows GAAP? Who establishes and who abides by RAP?

7-2   What will you find in the key financial statements and the stockholders' report of publicly held financial corporations? What role does the SEC play in reporting this information?

Basic Financial Statements

This section goes through the four required corporate financial statements and some important additional supplemental reports of a hypothetical depository financial firm. Although the example focuses on a depository, you will find similar interest and expense items in the statements of a finance company or an investment banking firm.

STATEMENT OF INCOME

The **statement of income** provides a financial summary of the firm's operating results during a specified period. The statements of income for most firms cover a one-year period ending at a specified date, ordinarily December 31 of the calendar year. In addition, monthly statements are typically prepared for use by management, and quarterly statements must be made available to the stockholders of publicly held corporations.

Table 7.1 presents 1st National Corporation's income statement for the year ended December 31, 1995. The statement begins with **interest income**—the total dollar amount of interest earned on the firm's financial assets during the period—from which the **interest expense** is deducted. The resulting **net interest income** of $10,500,000 represents the amount remaining to satisfy operating, financial, and tax costs after covering the cost of the firm's financial liabilities. The **provision for credit losses** of $1,000 is deducted from net interest income. The resulting **net interest income after provision for credit losses** of $9,500,000 represents the profit earned from the portfolio management function of the firm; but it still does not consider administrative, sales, and tax costs. Next comes **noninterest income**, income sources that do not represent interest or dividends earned on the firm's financial assets and through origination, servicing, and brokerage functions. From this is subtracted **noninterest expenses**, all the general and administrative costs of running the firm. The resulting number is the firm's **net income before taxes**. From this federal, state, and local taxes are subtracted, leaving **net after-tax income**.

Dividing earnings available for common stockholders by the number of shares of common stock outstanding results in **earnings per share (EPS)**. EPS represents the amount earned during the period on each outstanding share of common

---

TABLE 7.1

1st National Corporation Statement of Income ($000) for the Year Ended December 31, 1995

Interest income	$40,500
Interest expense	30,000
Net interest income	$10,500
Less: Provision of credit losses	1,000
Net interest income after provisions for credit losses	$ 9,500
Noninterest income	6,500
Less: noninterest expense	8,500
Net income before taxes	7,500
Taxes	1,500
Net after-tax income	$ 6,000
Less: Preferred stock dividends	100
Earnings available for common stockholders	$ 5,900
Earnings per share (EPS)*	$ 5.90

*Calculated by dividing the earnings available for common stockholders by the number of shares of common stock outstanding ($5,900,000 ÷ 1,000,000 shares = $5.90 per share).

stock. In 1995 1st National Corporation earned $5,900,000 for its common stockholders, which represents $5.90 for each outstanding share.

SOURCES OF FINANCIAL INSTITUTION INCOME AND EXPENSE

The sources of financial institution income related to the primary functions of financial intermediaries—origination, servicing, brokerage, and portfolio management—but you may have noticed that the income statement shown above does not itemize these sources by function. The following section further classifies these sources by focusing on interest and noninterest sources of income and expense.

How it Really Works

DID LIBERAL ACCOUNTING PRACTICES CONTRIBUTE TO THE THRIFT DEBACLE?

Many analysts of the thrift debacle believe that questionable accounting methodologies allowed by the former savings and loan regulator, the Federal Home Loan Bank Board, contributed to the size of the thrift debacle. Most of these unusual accounting practices went under the heading *regulatory accounting principles (RAP)*. This means the practice was allowed for purposes of providing financial statements for the regulator (RAP), but they would not necessarily qualify under GAAP.

The first practice allowed S&Ls to issue "income certificates," which were purchased by the former deposit insurer, the Federal Savings and Loan Insurance Corporation. These were counted as capital under RAP, yet they were nothing more than debt of the issuing S&L. Another questionable practice was allowing S&Ls to sell below-market-rate mortgage loans at a loss for tax purposes without immediately recognizing the loss on the income statement. The loss was permitted to be amortized over the contractual life of the loans.

Probably the worst practice, acceptable under RAP, related to "goodwill." When one S&L acquired another using an accounting method called *purchase asset accounting*, the assets and liabilities of the acquired institution would be marked to current market value (see Chapter 17). This typically resulted in liabilities exceeding assets by 5–10%. The difference was added to assets of the consolidated institution in an account called *goodwill*. This nonearning asset could be written off against future income over up to a 40-year period. If the assets, primarily mortgages, were subsequently sold at more than their marked-down value, the firm could recognize the profit without eliminating the goodwill. The result: one weak institution experiencing operating losses could buy another and the acquired assets would be written down in value. If interest rates subsequently fell, the assets could then be sold at a profit which could be registered even though the sales price might still be below the initial book value.

All these practices have been eliminated. However, these experiences show the potential impact of accounting methodology.

Interest Sources of Income and Expense

For most intermediaries, interest income is the most important source of income—usually 75% or more of total income for depositories and finance companies. Financial firms earn interest on the loans and investments held in their portfolios strictly for investment purposes (where the management expects to hold the asset until maturity) or for sale purposes (where the management expects the asset to be sold before maturity; for example, trading portfolios and assets such as mortgages sold in the secondary market). The interest income on all these assets appears in the interest income line on the financial statement.

Interest expense includes all the interest paid on all the financial liabilities of the firm. Table 7.3 shows that these liabilities consist of deposits, short-term bor-

---

TABLE 7.2

Typical Balance Sheets for Financial Assets for Major Intermediaries
(in billions)

Type of Financial Institution

Asset Classification	Commercial Banks	Thrifts: S&Ls, Savings Banks, and Credit Unions	Life Insurance Companies	Finance Companies	Property and Casualty Insurance Companies
Short-term assets:					
Cash and due from banks	$ 73	$ 50	$ 32	$ 12	$ 38
U.S. government and agencies	336	226	N/A	N/A	N/A
Short-term corporate	67				
Negotiable CDs		31			
Investment securities:					
U.S. and agency bonds	N/A	N/A	282		151
Tax-exempt bonds	97	2	11		134
Corporate bonds	41	80	653		98
Loans and leases:					
Consumer loans	362	141	72*	122	
Mortgage loans and securities	1,120	675	247	68	5
Business loans and leases	576	9		296	
Equities and real estate:					
Corporate equities			191		73
Real estate		11			
Miscellaneous	232	200	107	24	109
Total	$2,904	$1,308	$1,595	$522	$570

*Policy loans.

rowings, and long-term debt. The difference between interest income and interest expense is known as the **net interest margin.** The net interest margin is also reported after subtracting the provision for credit losses from the net interest income earned during any specified period.

Even though it might be convenient to think about a financial firm's net interest income as the return on its portfolio management activities, interest income and expense do not account for all sources of income and expense related to portfolio management. Capital gains and losses associated with the sale of financial assets are not included in net interest income, nor are certain fees earned on loan commitments and for financial guarantees even though the portfolio management activities of the firm generate them. Finally, the operating costs associated with portfolio management activities are not classified by the type of function they support.

Noninterest Income and Expenses

The other primary sources of income and expense relate primarily to the origination, servicing, and brokerage activities of financial firms and those portfolio management activities just discussed. Exhibit 7.1 highlights the major income and expense items included in noninterest income and expense.

EXHIBIT 7.1

Major Noninterest Income and Expense Items

Noninterest Income	Noninterest Expenses

Noninterest Income

Servicing function sources:
- Service charges on deposit accounts
- Servicing fees earned on loans sold
- Credit card transaction and servicing fees
- Data processing services sold to others

Origination function sources:
- Loan origination fees
- Security underwriting fees
- Loan syndication fees

Brokerage function sources:
- Security brokerage commissions
- Insurance sales commissions

Portfolio management function sources:
- Loan commitment fees
- Third-party guarantee fees
- Trading gains and losses
- Gain or loss on sale of assets

Noninterest Expenses
- Salaries and benefits
- Occupancy costs
- Equipment rentals, depreciation, and maintenance
- Advertising and promotion
- Communication and data processing
- Deposit insurance premiums and examination costs

BALANCE SHEET

The **balance sheet** presents a summary statement of the firm's financial position at a given point in time. The statement balances the firm's assets against its financing, which can be either debt or equity. Tables 7.2 and 7.3 provide representative balance sheets for the major stock financial intermediaries. The amounts in each of the asset and liability classes are proportionate to each institution's size relative to others.

A more refined discussion of a financial firm's balance sheet is provided for the hypothetical 1st National Corporation, whose balance sheets on December 31 of 1995 and 1994—showing a variety of asset, liability, and equity accounts—are presented in Table 7.4. A major difference between financial firms and commercial and industrial firms is that the vast majority of the assets and liabilities of financial firms are represented by financial assets. Only a small percentage of

---

TABLE 7.3

Typical Balance Sheet of Financial Liabilities for Major Intermediaries
(in billions)

Type of Financial Institution

Liability Classification	Commercial Banks	Thrifts: S&Ls, Savings Banks, and Credit Unions	Life Insurance Companies	Finance Companies	Property and Causalty Insurance Companies
Short-term liabilities:					
Checkable deposits	$ 700	$ 20			
Small time and savings	1,370	1,075			
Negotiable CDs	216	N/A			
Fed funds and repos	234	19			
Commercial paper				$156	
Bank loans				38	
Long-term liabilities:					
Federal Home Loan Bank advances	6	73			
Corporate bonds	47	6		195	
Policyholder reserves			$436		439
Pension fund reserves			957		
Miscellaneous	50	36	12	65	1
Equity capital	281	89	190	68	130
Total	$2,904	$1,318	$1,595	$522	$570

Sources: Data in these tables are adapted from data in the *Flow of Funds Accounts* of the Board of Governors of the Federal Reserve System and *The FDIC Quarterly Banking Profile* published by the Federal Deposit Insurance Corporation. They are meant to provide useful indications of the relative difference between the various intermediaries.

the total assets of financial firms is invested in land, buildings, equipment, and other nonfinancial assets.

A few points about 1st National Corporation's balance sheets need to be highlighted. As is customary, the assets are listed beginning with the most liquid and ending with the least liquid. Liquid assets, therefore, precede fixed assets. *Cash and cash equivalents* represent very liquid short-term investments, such as deposits in other banks, federal funds, and reverse repurchase agreements. *Total financial investments in securities held for trading and investment* are the next-most liquid. These investments include government and agency debt, mortgage-backed securities, and corporate debt. The next investment category is *loans;* for most depository institutions, these include business loans, mortgages, consumer installment loans, credit card receivables, and leases. Following total loans is a debit item called *allowance for credit losses.* This amount is subtracted from total loans to arrive at net loans and leases. The allowance for credit losses represents previously established loan loss provisions that have been taken against net income in previous periods. However, because the asset is still on the books of the institution, the precise loss has not yet been established. This will not occur until the firm sells the loan or collateral underlying the loan or writes off the loan as uncollectable. *Net premises and equipment* represents the difference between gross fixed assets and *accumulated depreciation,* the total expense recorded for the depreciation of fixed assets.

The liabilities and equity accounts are also listed on the balance sheet from short-term to long-term. For a depository institution, the most *current liabilities* are usually deposits including transaction accounts, interest-bearing savings, and certificates of deposit. Large depository institutions and finance companies also borrow in the money and capital markets using negotiable CDs, commercial paper, and bonds. *Long-term debt* represents debt for which payment is not due in the current year. *Stockholders' equity* represents the owners' claims on the firm and consists of preferred and common stock. The *preferred stock* entry shows the historic proceeds from the sale of preferred stock ($1,000,000 for 1st National Corporation). Next, the amount paid in by the original purchasers of common stock is shown by two entries: common stock and paid-in capital surplus on common stock. The *common stock* entry is the **par value** of common stock, an arbitrarily assigned per-share value used primarily for accounting purposes. *Paid-in capital surplus* represents the amount of proceeds in excess of the par value received from the original sale of common stock. The sum of the common stock and paid-in capital surplus divided by the number of shares outstanding represents the original price per share received by the firm on a single issue of common stock. 1st National Corporation therefore received $4 per share [($1,000,000 par + $3,000,000 paid-in capital surplus) ÷ 1,000,000 shares] from the sale of its common stock. Finally, *retained earnings* represents the cumulative total of all earnings retained and reinvested in the firm since its inception.

1st National Corporation's balance sheets in Table 7.4 show that the firm's total assets increased from $554,350,000 in 1994 to $565,400,000 in 1995. The increase was due primarily to the increase in financial assets. The asset increase in turn appears to have been financed primarily by an increase of its deposits and

---

TABLE 7.4

1st National Corporation
Balance Sheets ($000)

	December 31	
	1995	1994
Assets:		
Cash and due from banks	$ 25,000	$ 24,500
Interest-bearing deposits in banks	60	55
Interest and other accounts receivable	13,000	13,000
Federal funds and reverse repurchase	4,940	3,445
Total cash and cash equivalents	43,000	41,000
Trading account securities	150	140
Investment securities	10,000	10,200
Mortgage-backed securities	20,350	20,100
Total investment and mortgage-backed securities	30,500	30,440
Student loans	400	350
Mortgages	30,500	30,300
Commercial loans	370,000	365,000
Consumer installment loans	25,000	22,000
Credit card receivables	20,000	18,000
Leases	45,000	46,000
Less: Allowance for credit losses	(10,000)	(9,500)
Total loans and leases	480,900	472,150
Net premises and equipment	11,000	10,900
Total assets	$565,400	$554,350
Liabilities and stockholders' equity:		
Noninterest-bearing deposits	$ 80,000	$ 78,000
Interest-bearing deposits	350,000	345,000
Total deposits	430,000	423,000
Short-term borrowings	80,400	76,450
Interest and other accounts payable	10,000	10,000
Long-term debt	8,000	8,000
Total liabilities	$528,400	$517,450
Stockholders' equity		
Preferred stock	$ 1,000	$ 1,000
Common stock—$1.00 par, 1,000,000 shares outstanding in 1995 and 1994	1,000	1,000
Paid-in capital surplus	3,000	3,000
Retained earnings	32,000	31,900
Total stockholders' equity	$ 37,000	$ 36,900
Total liabilities and stockholders' equity	$565,400	$554,350

short-term borrowings. Better insight into these changes can be derived from the statement of cash flows, which will be discussed shortly.

STATEMENT OF RETAINED EARNINGS

The **statement of retained earnings** reconciles the net income earned during a given year and any cash dividends paid, with the change in retained earnings between the start and end of that year. Table 7.5 presents this statement for 1st National Corporation for the year ended December 31, 1995. A review of the statement shows that the company began the year with $31,900,000 in retained earnings and had net profits after taxes of $6,000,000, from which it paid a total of $5,900,000 in dividends, resulting in year-end retained earnings of $32,000,000. Thus, the net increase for 1st National Corporation was $100,000 ($6,000,000 net profits after taxes minus $5,900,000 in dividends) during 1995.

TABLE 7.5

1st National Corporation
Statement of Retained Earnings ($000)
Year Ended December 31, 1995

Retained earnings balance (January 1, 1995)		$31,900
Plus: Net profits after taxes (for 1995)		6,000
Less: Cash dividends (paid during 1995)		
Preferred stock	($100)	
Common stock	(5,800)	(5,900)
Retained earnings balance (December 31, 1995)		$32,000

PUBLIC ACCOUNTANTS ATTACKED BY REGULATORS

How it Really Works

Many of the country's major accounting firms have had to pay a big price for providing accounting services to savings and loans. The Resolution Trust Corporation, in its capacity as receiver of failed S&Ls, accused many public accounting firms of negligent accounting practices resulting in false and misleading financial statements. These statements allegedly were used to mislead depositors, regulators, and security purchasers. The biggest case involved a suit against the "Big Six" accounting firm of Ernst and Young, which was settled out-of-court for $400 million. Most of the other large accounting firms were also sued as a result of their audits of savings and loans.

STATEMENT OF CASH FLOWS

The **statement of cash flows** summarizes the cash flows over any specified period. The statement, sometimes called a *sources and uses of funds statement,* helps analysts to understand changes in the firm's asset, liability, and capital structures. Table 7.6 depicts 1st National Corporation's statement of cash flows for the year ended December 31, 1995. Preparing this statement requires some understanding of the various aspects of depreciation.

✓ Checkpoint

7-3   What basic information will you find in:
   a.   The statement of income?
   b.   The balance sheet?
   c.   The statement of retained earnings?

Analyzing a Financial Firm's Cash Flow

The cash flow statement summarizes the firm's cash flow over a given period of time. It captures historic cash flow and serves as a statement (or normative model) for forecasting future cash flows. The following section describes the cash flow through the firm and the classification of sources and uses of funds.

THE FIRM'S SOURCES AND USES OF FUNDS

A firm's cash flows can be divided into cash flow from (1): operating activities, (2) investment activities, and (3) financing activities. The *operating activity cash flows* are cash flows—inflows and outflows—directly related to origination and sale of the financial firm's assets and to operating costs such as general and administrative expenses, sales of loans related to secondary market activities, security trading activities, interest received and paid, taxes, and sales of operating assets and repossessed or foreclosed collateral. *Investment activity cash flows* are cash flows associated with purchase and sale of both operating fixed assets and financial investments. Clearly, purchase transactions would result in cash outflows whereas sales transactions would generate cash inflows. The *financing activity cash flows* result from debt and equity financing transactions. Borrowing and repaying either short-term debt (deposits and short-term borrowing) or long-term debt would result in a corresponding cash inflow or outflow. Similarly, the sale of common or preferred stock would result in a cash inflow whereas the repurchase of stock or payment of cash dividends would result in a financing outflow. Summarizing the firm's operating, investment, and financing activity cash flows during a given period helps to account for changes in the firm's cash position from the beginning to the end of the period chosen.

TABLE 7.6

1st National Corporation
Cash Flow Statement ($000)
Year Ended December 31, 1995

Cash flows from operating activities:	
Net income	$ 6,000
Noncash items included in net income, including:	150
Depreciation and amortization of equipment	
Amortization of intangibles	
Provision for credit losses	
Noncash accounting adjustments	
Gains on sale of loans and securities	(230)
Purchases of trading account securities	(16,000)
Proceeds from sale of trading portfolio	16,050
Origination of loans held for sale	(120,000)
Proceeds of loans sold	115,000
Interest and other accounts receivable	1,200
Interest and other accounts payable	(2,300)
Deferred income taxes	200
Net cash flows from operating activities	$ 70
Cash flows from investing activities:	
Proceeds from maturing and paydowns of investment securities	75,000
Proceeds from sale of loans and investment securities	52,000
Net change in loans and investment securities held	(137,000)
Purchase of premises and equipment, net	(3,000)
Proceeds from repossessed and foreclosed collateral	9,000
Net sale (purchase) of subsidiaries, ignoring cash	(1,000)
Net cash flows from investment activities	($ 5,000)
Cash flows from financing activities:	
Deposits, net	$ 7,000
Short-term borrowing	62,250
Long-term debt borrowing	—
Issuance of preferred stock	—
Redemption of preferred stock	—
Issuance of common stock	—
Purchase of common stock	—
Net cash flows from financing activities	$ 69,250

The development of the cash flow statement requires information from both the balance sheet and income statement. In order to provide a complete statement, the development of the statement also requires flow data on asset purchases, asset sales, deposit withdrawals, maturing liabilities, and prepayment of assets which are not available from either the income or balance sheet statements.

Consequently, the statement shown in Table 7.6 cannot be created using the information in Tables 7.1 and 7.4 alone.

PRIMARY CLASSIFICATION OF A FINANCIAL FIRM'S SOURCES AND USES OF CASH

Financial firms differ from nonfinancial firms in that they typically process very large amounts of cash inflows and outflows relative to their total asset base. The cash flow statement summarizes these sources and uses of cash during a given period. Table 7.7 provides basic sources and uses of cash for 1st National Corporation. This statement is organized by categorizing cash flows by operating, investing, and financing activities.

A couple of notes on the classification scheme in Table 7.7: Noncash charges are considered cash inflows, or sources of cash. For financial firms, these noncash charges include such items as depreciation and amortization, accrued expenses and liabilities, provisions for credit losses, and writedown of intangible assets such as goodwill. Second, since the lines between operating, investment, and financing activity cash flows are somewhat ambiguous, these items require careful consideration.

TABLE 7.7

Primary Sources and Uses of Cash

Sources	Uses
Cash Flow from Operating Activities	
Sales of trading account securities	Purchase of trading account securities
Sales of loans in secondary market	Origination of loans to be sold in the secondary market
Net income after taxes	Net loss after taxes
Gains on sale of securities and loans	Losses on sale of securities and loans
Noncash expenses: depreciation and amortization, provision for credit losses, and writedown of intangibles	
Cash Flow from Investing Activities	
Repayments of principal on loans and investments	Origination of loans
Sales of loans and participations	
Sales of investment securities	Purchase of investment securities
Proceeds of sales of repossessed and foreclosed loan collateral and premises and equipment	Purchases of premises and equipment
Sale of subsidiaries (net of cash sold)	Purchase of subsidiaries (net of cash received)

Sources	Uses
Cash Flow from Financing Activities	
Deposits originated	Deposits withdraw
Short-term borrowings	Short-term borrowings repaid
Long-term borrowings	Long-term borrowings repaid
Preferred stock issued	Preferred stock redeemed
Common stock issued	Common stock purchased
Increase in any liability	Decrease in any liability
Net profits after taxes	Net loss
Depreciation and other non-cash charges	Dividends paid
Sale of common and preferred stock	Repurchase or retirement of stock

Use of the Cash Flow Statement

Managing cash is a very important activity for financial intermediaries. The cash flow statement provides the basic structure for being able to identify all sources and uses of cash. The process of liquidity management presented in Chapter 16 describes this process in greater detail. The primary reasons that cash management is so important relate to the following aspects of financial intermediaries:

- Depository intermediaries must hold reserves to meet Federal Reserve Regulation D reserve requirements. To manage the level of reserves optimally, very precise cash flow statements are necessary.
- Financial institutions are subject to very large cash inflows and outflows which require considerable planning ahead to insure they take place as required but do not at the same time tie up a large amount of funds unnecessarily in nonearning cash assets.

Financial depositories have many liabilities which can be retired on demand (transaction accounts and certificates of deposit). This results in considerable uncertainty over how much and when withdrawals will occur and, therefore, puts a premium on good cash flow analysis.

✓ Checkpoints

7-4   How does cash flow through the firm in terms of:
  a. Operating activities?
  b. Investment activities?
  c. Financing activities?

7-5   What are the sources and uses of cash for financial firms, and how important are noncash items?

7-6   How do financial managers and other interested parties intrepret and use the statement of cash flows to make decisions, especially for performing pro-forma cash flow projections?

Special Aspects of Financial Statements of Insurance Companies

The primary difference between the basic financial statements of insurance companies and those of depositories, finance companies, and investment bankers stems from the fact that insurance companies—both life insurance and property and casualty companies—derive most of their revenue from insurance premiums and most of their expenses from benefits paid.

This difference manifests itself in the income statement as a revenue line item for *insurance premiums earned* and an expense line item for *benefits paid to policyholders*. The difference shows up on the balance sheet as *insurance company liabilities to policyholders*. This item represents liabilities of the insurance company required to meet future insurance claims against it. The difference also shows up on the cash flow statement as a source of cash called "increase in insurance company liabilities to policyholders."

Another item that affects the cash flow statement is *policy acquisition costs*. One of the most difficult aspects of insurance company accounting to assess deals with the amortization of policy acquisition costs. For many insurance companies, the costs of attracting a new insurance customer, underwriting the risk, compensating a salesperson, and issuing the policy are very high. For many types of life insurance policies, these costs exceed the amount of the first year's premium.

Under GAAP, insurance companies are expected to amortize policy acquisition costs over the expected life of each type of policy the company writes, leading to unexpected decreases in income if policies do not last as long as expected. Under that circumstance, the firm would have to report the unamortized expenses related to policies written in early years which were redeemed early or not renewed as expected. In normal times for a growing company, however, the actual cash expense of policy acquisition costs tends to be higher than the amortization amount used in the income statement. This requires that the cash flow statement include a line item called *policy acquisition costs deferred*, shown as a use of cash since cash was expended and not taken as an expense against that period's revenue.

✓ Checkpoints

7-7   What are the principal differences between the income statements, balance sheets, and cash flow statements of depositories and insurance companies?

7-8   What difficulty can arise in the amortization of insurance company policy acquisition costs?

Footnotes: Important Financial Statement Information

Many analysts find the most important information in the footnotes to the financial statements relating to the following:

1. Significant accounting policies and changes to them.
2. Specific information on the allowance for credit losses and asset quality.
3. Important litigation, regulation, or legislation that may affect the firm's performance.
4. Special analyses of interest rate risk exposure.
5. Market value accounting statements for certain assets.
6. Contingent liabilities and other off-balance sheet items.
7. Employee benefit and stock incentive programs.

Each of these deserves attention since each involves major risks—risks concerning asset quality, interest rate, off-balance sheet activities, litigation, regulation, and legislation—that financial institution creditors and shareholders face.

SIGNIFICANT ACCOUNTING POLICIES

Over the years, GAAP has developed into a highly refined set of standards. Nevertheless, management, working with public accounting firms, still has a fair amount of discretion in applying GAAP to a firm's operations. Under the heading *significant accounting policies,* this footnote provides a description of each of these policies and changes that may have been made to them in recent periods. Some of the most important policies for financial institutions deal with amortization of intangibles such as goodwill, loan loss provisions, recognition of gains and losses for various transactions, and foreign currency translations. Analysts must carefully analyze this footnote when assessing corporate performance and comparing one firm to another.

CREDIT LOSSES AND ASSET QUALITY

For intermediaries with large portfolio management functions, assessing asset credit quality is both important and difficult because it demands such discretion. Determining appropriate allowances for credit losses for loans to developing countries, real estate development, commercial mortgages, and loans to highly leveraged firms is not an exact science; and so financial firm managers may apply different policies to different firms. Although regulators have forced greater uniformity, differences in loan loss provisioning policies exist between firms with similar charters and between firms with different charters, such as between commercial banks and insurance companies.

IMPORTANT LITIGATION, REGULATION, OR LEGISLATION

Early chapters have described just how highly regulated financial institutions are, with charters subject to substantial federal and state legislative modification and to regulator action. Any change could seriously alter the operations and performance of these institutions. New laws and regulations may require discontinuance of a firm's current activities; sanctions may reprove a firm that has not met a particular regulatory requirement; and resulting litigation may tie up valuable firm resources and impede positive performance.

INTEREST RATE RISK EXPOSURE

Depository institutions are particularly vulnerable to risks related to changes in market interest rates. These changes can cause substantial fluctuations in a firm's net income and, in the extreme, cause insolvency—as was the case of many savings and loans in the 1980s. As a result, most depositories provide additional analyses of their exposure to interest rate risk; more complete discussion of interest rate measurement appears in Chapter 17.

MARKET VALUE ACCOUNTING STATEMENTS

According to GAAP, financial firms use to report at historic cost. But FASB issued new guidelines requiring firms to value certain assets at **market value,** or to mark the asset value to market. Chapter 17 on interest rate management covers this **mark-to-market technique.** For a bond, a rise in market interest rates can result in a sharp decline in the bond's market value. Until recently, managers could ignore this loss of value if they planned to hold the bond to maturity. Now, firms must report on differences between historic value and fair market value for their investment securities; and some do so through financial statement footnotes.

CONTINGENT LIABILITIES AND OTHER OFF-BALANCE SHEET ITEMS

Financial firms engage in many transactions not shown on the balance sheet. A commitment to grant a loan to a customer obligates the firm but this **contin-**

MORTGAGE SERVICING: ON OR OFF THE BALANCE SHEET?

How it Really Works

Your firm is a major servicer of mortgage loans. Until recently, when your firm originated a mortgage, sold it in the secondary market, and then serviced it, the value of this servicing contract did not show up on the balance sheet. Even though your firm incurred the costs of origination, it did not reflect the servicing contract asset. However, if the same firm bought a servicing contract from another firm at 1.5% of the loan's principal value, the balance sheet would account this amount as an asset.

Major originator/servicers of mortgages argue that their servicing contracts should be counted as assets, which would strengthen their balance sheet by increasing reported income and net worth. In 1992, the Financial Accounting Standards Board finally agreed with the industry and ruled that intermediaries could include a portion of the value of the servicing contracts produced in current income to offset the cost of originating mortgages.

Source: Jim Carlton, "Mortgage Bankers Seek FASB Change to Boost Profits," *The Wall Street Journal*, Nov. 23, 1993, p. B3.

gent liability does not appear on the balance sheet. Similarly, commitments to buy and sell securities, conduct foreign exchange and other assets called *options, futures,* and *swaps* do not show up on the balance sheet and are called **off-balance sheet transactions.** A quick look at this text's index will indicate where this book discusses many such off-balance sheet activities. Because these transactions involve risk, firms discuss their risk exposures in financial statement footnotes.

EMPLOYEE BENEFIT AND STOCK INCENTIVE PROGRAMS.

Employee benefit and stock incentive plans vary significantly from firm to firm and are sufficiently complex to merit considerable descriptions and analysis. As a result, most firms recapitulate the major features of employee benefit and stock incentive programs in financial statement footnotes.

✓ Checkpoints

7-9 Why should financial analysts carefully assess the footnotes to a firm's financial statements? What should they be looking for, and what might they find?

7-10 Which types of financial institution risks should managers describe in the financial statement footnotes?

SUMMARY AND REVIEW

1. **Explain how to interpret the basic components of the stockholders' report.**

   The **annual stockholders' report** of a publicly traded corporation includes, in addition to the letter to stockholders and various subjective and factual information, four key financial statements: (1) **the income statement,** (2) **the balance sheet,** (3) **the statement of retained earnings,** and (4) **the cash flow statement.**

2. **Describe the format, features, and functions of the income statement, balance sheet, retained earnings statement, and cash flow statement.**

   The **income statement** summarizes operating results during the period of concern. The **balance sheet** summarizes the firm's financial position at a given point in time. The **statement of retained earnings** reconciles income and cash dividends with retained earnings for the period. The cash flow of a firm over a given period of time can be summarized in the **cash flow statement.** The firm's cash flows can be broken into operating flows, investment flows, and financing flows. Interpretation of the statement of cash flows involves evaluation of both the major categories of cash flow and the individual items of cash inflow and outflow.

3. **Describe the special financial provisions in the financial statements that insurance companies create.**

   Insurance companies' largest income and expense items relate to the sale of insurance policies. This creates income statement revenue called *insurance premiums earned* and an expense item called *policyholder benefits.* On the balance sheet, premiums held by the company for insurance coverage not yet earned create a liability called *liability to policyholders.* The cash flow statement of insurance companies is affected by changes in liabilities to policyholders due to the fact that policy acquisition costs are amortized.

4. **Show how to interpret footnotes to the basic financial statements of a financial firm.**

   Considerable additional important information concerning the past and future performance of firm are found in footnotes to the financial statements. Of particular interest to analysts of financial firms are additional reports on: (1) significant accounting policies; (2) credit losses and asset quality; (3) important litigation, regulation, and legislation; (4) interest rate risk exposure; (5) market value accounting statements; (6) contingent liabilities and other off-balance sheet items; and (7) employee benefit and stock incentive programs.

PROBLEMS	PREPARING THE INCOME STATEMENT

7-1

Use the proper items from the alphabetical list below to prepare Victory Savings Bank's income statement for the year ended December 31, 1995.

Item	December 31, 1995 (dollars in thousands)
Cash and due from banks	$12,000
Deposits	17,500
Interest expense	900
Interest Income	1,215
Loans and leases	18,098
Net income after-taxes	____*
Net income before taxes	____*
Net interest income	____*
Net interest income after provision for credit losses	____*
Noninterest expense	225
Noninterest income	195
Preferred stock	1,000
Premises and equipment	2,090
Provision for credit losses	30
Taxes	45

*To be computed.

PROBLEMS	BALANCE SHEET PREPARATION

7-2

Use the proper items from the alphabetical list below to prepare Victory Savings Bank's balance sheet for the year ended December 31, 1995.

Item	December 31, 1995 (dollars in thousands)
Allowance for credit losses	$ (200)
Cash and due from banks	500
Commercial loans	7,400
Common stock	20
Consumer installment loans	500
Credit card receivables	100
Depreciation expense	12
Federal funds and reverse repurchase	100
Interest-bearing deposits	7,000

continued

Item (cont.)	December 31, 1995 (dollars in thousands)
Interest-bearing deposits in banks	12
Investment securities	200
Leases	900
Long-term debt	100
Mortgage-backed securities	410
Mortgages	610
Net premises and equipment	220
Noninterest-bearing deposits	1,315
Noninterest expense	5
Noninterest income	4
Paid-in capital surplus	60
Preferred stock	20
Retained earnings	640
Short-term borrowings	1,608
Student loans	8
Taxes	3
Total assets	*
Total cash and cash equivalents	*
Total deposits	*
Total liabilities	*
Total investment and mortgage-backed securities	*
Total loans and leases	*
Total stockholders' equity	740
Total liabilities and stockholders' equity	*
Trading account securities	3

*To be computed.

CLASSIFYING SOURCES AND USES   PROBLEMS

7-3

Classify each of the following balance sheet and income statement items as a *source* or a *use* of funds.

Item	Change ($)	Item	Change ($)
Cash and due from banks	+100	Interest-bearing deposits	-800
Consumer loans	+120	Net income before tax	+60
Short-term borrowing	+500	Depreciation	+100
Long-term debt	+100	Preferred stock issued	+10
Leases	+80	Cash dividends paid	+60
Premises and equipment	+12	Taxes	+25

PROJECT 7.1

FOOTNOTES TO FINANCIAL STATEMENTS

7-1

Obtain a copy of a financial institution annual shareholder report. Review the footnotes to this report and describe some of the important issues found in them.

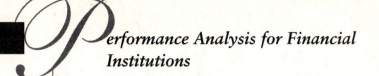

CHAPTER 8

Performance Analysis for Financial Institutions

Learning Goals

After studying this chapter, you should be able to:

1. Describe time-series, cross-sectional, combined, and common-size techniques for presenting and analyzing financial data.
2. Describe the primary areas of financial ratio analysis.
3. Describe some of the most important financial ratios used by property and casualty companies, life insurance companies, and pension funds and the sources of financial data.

How well is the firm doing compared to past performance? Is it on track with its business forecasts? Is its business strategy working as planned? How does it compare to similar firms in its market or in different markets? Is it complying with government capital adequacy requirements? How liquid are its assets? How efficient are its operating systems? In what areas can its management improve performance?

Financial ratios are used by management and directors, current and prospective shareholders, creditors, and regulators to assess financial strength and operating performance of financial firms. Management and directors are concerned with all phases of firm performance. Creditors and regulators, on the other hand, are primarily concerned with financial strength by focusing chiefly on capital adequacy and loan quality. Prospective and current shareholders are primarily concerned with firm profitability risk, and operating efficiency.

Conducting a thorough performance analysis develops a database of consistent and meaningful operating statistics to answer these questions—not just about nonfinancial companies but also about financial institutions. Much of what you've learned in prerequisite accounting and corporate finance courses will help you to master performance analysis of financial firms.

Since performance analyses usually involve the major familiar areas of operations, this chapter overviews the general measurement tools—financial ratios, that is—applicable to all financial firms, and then highlights a few ratios especially relevant to nondepository institutions such as life insurance companies, finance companies, property and casualty companies, and pension funds. After looking at some particular examples from the financial reports of publicly traded companies, you should have a better sense of how the tools and the decision criteria used in analyzing these firms differ from each other.[1]

Types of Ratio Comparisons

As with nonfinancial firms, there are several types of ratio comparisons that financial analysts, owners, managers, and regulators use to analyze performance, specifically the time-series analysis, cross-sectional analysis, and a combined analysis shown in common-size statements. Here's a quick review.

TIME-SERIES ANALYSIS

Time-series analysis looks at the financial performance of a firm over time. By comparing present to past performance through ratio analysis, we can detect improving or deteriorating performance. However, decision makers must identify whether any change over time follows a business cycle or economic condition, signals an important emerging trend, flags a serious managerial or operational flaw, or simply confirms the expected outcome of the firm's business strategy. The key point to remember is that any change—or the lack of change when change was planned—merits further investigation in order to project future performance and plan necessary courses of action.

Table 8.1 depicts a hypothetical time-series analysis of the return on equity (ROE) of First Federal. Table 8.1 shows that the ROE of First Federal has been volatile and trending down over the period covered by the analysis.

TABLE 8.1

Time-series Analysis Percent Return on Beginning-of-the-Year Equity
First Federal Savings Quarterly 1995–1996

	1995				1996			
Institution	I	II	III	IV	I	II	III	IV
First Federal	−0.2%	12.2%	9.0%	8.0%	12.4%	5.6%	8.0%	6.5%

---

[1]Financial firms with publicly traded stock typically make available financial data in the form of annual reports which are issued about three months after the firm's fiscal year, quarterly reports issued about one month after the quarterly reporting period, and reports required by the Security and Exchange Commission called *10-K reports* which are made available to stockholders upon request to a company's secretary. Larger firms also provide statistical supplements to their annual reports which provide additional data used for analysis.

CROSS-SECTIONAL ANALYSIS

Cross-sectional analysis compares the financial performance of one financial institution with that of others at a given point in time. This analysis of financial ratios enables decision makers to compare different branch operations of a single firm, different competitors within a certain market, or different types of firms within the financial services industry. Studying differences in performance against the market leader often enables financial managers to identify major operational differences, thereby getting new ideas for ultimately improving the underperformer's efficiency. Analyzing deviations in performance from the industry norm gets managers closer to potential problems as well as opportunities. This form of ratio comparison provides a snapshot of the institution's financial ratios in comparison to a peer group of one or more competitors. Table 8.2 provides a cross-sectional financial ratio analysis of a hypothetical commercial bank and several of its competitors.

Table 8.2 shows that the Briggs Bank does not compare well on a financial performance basis with its primary competitors. The bank's profitability as measured by return on equity is below the competition, as is its capital position measured by net worth to total assets; and its expenses are higher for the period.

TABLE 8.2

Cross-sectional Financial Ratio Analysis of Briggs Bank and Two Competitors

Financial Ratio	Institution Name		
	Briggs Bank	First National Bank	State Bank
Net worth to total assets	6.70%	7.30%	8.10%
Return on equity	8.50%	11.20%	12.50%
Operating expenses to average assets	4.02%	3.40%	3.24%

COMBINED ANALYSIS

A particularly effective approach to ratio analysis is to combine time-series and cross-sectional analyses in a combined analysis. The combined analysis enables analysts to compare financial ratios over time and with competitors or peer groups. Table 8.3 shows the return on equity for First Federal and its peer group over a period of time and indicates that First Federal has experienced lower and more volatile returns on equity than its peer group for the period shown.

TABLE 8.3

Time-series Analysis Percent Return on Beginning-of-the-Year Equity
First Federal Savings and Peer Group Quarterly 1995–1996

Institution	1995				1996			
	I	II	III	IV	I	II	III	IV
First Federal	-0.2%	12.2%	9.0%	8.0%	12.4%	5.6%	8.0%	6.5%
Peer Group	12.3%	14.5%	10.9%	11.8%	14.5%	8.7%	10.0%	12.3%

Common-Size Statements

Common-size statements combine the results of time-series analysis and cross-sectional analysis. The common-size statement depicts percentages of total assets using data from the balance sheet and total revenue using data from the income statement. Analysts typically use these statements to contrast a firm's financial results over time or with its market group, to identify trends in the industry or to pinpoint specific shortcomings or strengths of the firm compared to the norm. Common-size financial statements also help to simplify comparisons between institutions with differences in asset size. Tables 8.4a and 8.4b provide examples of a common-size income statement and a balance sheet for a hypothetical commercial bank.[2]

TABLE 8.4a

Common-Size Income Statement and Supplemental Data
(dollars in millions)

	Year					
	1996		1995		1994	
Item	Actual Revenue	% of Total	Actual Revenue	% of Total	Actual Revenue	% of Total
Total income	$410	100.0%	$380	100.0%	$337	100.0%
Interest income	375	91.5	350	92.1	310	92.0
Interest expense	280	68.3	260	68.4	220	65.3
Net interest margin	95	23.2	90	23.7	90	26.7
Noninterest income	35	8.5	30	7.9	27	8.0
Noninterest expense	87	21.2	80	21.1	72	21.4
Provision for credit losses	12	2.9	10	2.6	10	3.0
Net operating income before tax	31	7.6	30	7.9	35	10.4
Taxes	9	2.2	8	2.1	9	2.7
Net income after taxes	$22	5.4%	$22	5.8%	24	7.1%
Shares outstanding (000s)	2,000		1,900		1,900	
Earnings per share	11.00		11.58		12.63	
Dividend per share	8.00		7.80		7.80	

---

[2]Caution: Common-size statements permit simple comparisons of firms that are not practically comparable; that is, users would not benefit by comparing them. Comparing a $10 million asset bank to a $1 billion asset bank provides little insight since the functions and activities of these two banks differ greatly. The same is true when using industry aggregate data, which large firms may dominate to the extent of distorting comparisons of smaller firms to industry averages. The results may be misleading.

TABLE 8.4b

Common-Size Balance Sheet and Supplemental Data
(dollars in millions)

	1996		1995		1994	
Item	Actual Revenue	% of Total	Actual Revenue	% of Total	Actual Revenue	% of Total
Assets:						
Cash and due from banks	$ 182	7.0%	$ 173	7.2%	$ 163	7.1%
Investment securities	416	16.0	360	15.0	322	14.0
Federal funds and reverse repos	312	12.0	240	10.0	207	9.0
Loans	1,661	63.9	1,598	66.6	1,580	68.7
Premises and equipment	29	1.1	29	1.2	28	1.2
Total assets	$2,600	100%	$2,400	100%	$2,300	100%
Liabilities:						
Core Deposits	$1,872	72.0	$1,680	70.0	$1,564	68.0
Negotiable CDs	78	3.0	96	4.0	138	6.0
Short-term borrowings, fed funds, and repos	234	9.0	240	10.0	276	12.0
Long-term debt	104	4.0	96	4.0	69	3.0
Other liabilities	65	2.5	72	3.0	57	2.5
Total liabilities						
Preferred stock	0	0.0	0	0.0	0	0.0
Common stock	247	9.5	216	9.0	196	8.5
Total net worth	247	9.5	216	9.0	196	8.5
Total liabilities and net worth	$2,600	100%	$2,400	100%	$2,300	100%
Book value per share (in dollars)	$123.50		$113.68		$103.16	
Market value per share of common stock (in dollars)	$140.00		$155.00		$165.50	
Supplemental Data						
Off-balance-sheet commitments:						
Commitments to extend credit	$1,234		$1,129		$1,075	
Standby letters of credit and foreign office guarantees	204		197		209	
Other letters of credit	20		89		10	
Total commitments	$1,458		$1,415		$1,294	
Net loan charge-offs	$13.5		$12.9		$11.0	

LIMITATIONS OF RATIO AND FINANCIAL ANALYSIS

Judgment and experience are essential prerequisites for performing financial ratio analyses. It is important for the analyst to understand how the business being analyzed operates. There are a number of limitations in the development and use of ratio and financial analysis. A few of the most important are discussed below.

Financial Ratios Are Not All Created Equal

A review of the annual reports of financial companies will demonstrate the considerable use of financial ratios. Comparing these ratios among several firms will reveal frustrating differences in the exact way they are computed—differences that are sometimes very subtle and hard to detect and which can produce significant differences when comparing ratios among firms. For example, return on equity is frequently computed as: (1) after-tax net income divided by beginning-of-the-year net worth or (2) after-tax net income divided by average net worth over the period under review. These differences can easily lead to inaccurate analyses when comparing firms.

Users of Financial Ratios Are Not Created Equal

Financial ratios are used by actual and potential shareholders, creditors, and regulators. Each of these groups may evaluate the same ratios differently. This is because they have different perspectives and concerns. Creditors and regulators will normally give high overall ratings to institutions with high capital ratios, high loan quality, and low financial leverage. Shareholders, on the other hand, may view these same qualities as signs that management is not maximizing returns on the firm's capital resources. The perspective of the reviewer should be considered when using financial analyses.

Financial Firms Are Not All Created Equal

A major limitation of financial ratio comparisons of two or more institutions is the differences in functions and activities performed by the firms. As discussed in Chapter 2, the financial functions performed by financial firms are usually very different from one another. This is even more of a problem today with the lowering of regulatory constraints on the powers and authorities between different types of financial institutions.

These differences in functions performed by financial firms translate into significant differences in revenues and capital and labor inputs, which in turn significantly affects the financial ratios produced. This is true for firms of nearly equal size as well. For example, a firm with large loan servicing activities for loans sold to others will experience higher operating expenses as well as non-interest income, all else held constant, without comparably larger assets than a firm of equal size that does not service loans for others.

Equally difficult for the analyst is the evaluation of large, well-diversified financial firms. Citicorp, as the U.S.'s largest bank holding company, has so many different subsidiaries and performs so many financial functions that it has units that are comparable to investment banking, thrift institutions, mortgage banking, brokerage, and insurance, as well as many foreign operations. Unless it is possible to obtain financial data on each of the major functional units, it is very difficult to assess performance using aggregate data.

Another problem in comparing like institutions relates to the impact of foreign exchange for financial firms with international dealings. The Financial Standards Accounting Board's Statement Number 52 requires the firms dealing with foreign currency to reflect changes in the value of foreign currency in their financial statements. This foreign exchange accounting adjustment will also make financial ratios comparisons more difficult.[3]

✓ Checkpoints

8-1   How does time-series analysis differ from cross-sectional data analysis? When would you want to use one over the other, or a combined analysis?

8-2   How do common-size financial statements differ from the typical income statement and balance sheet for a financial firm? When would you want to use them?

8-3   What are the limitations of using ratios in identifying problems? What other sources of information must managers use when interpreting ratios?

Types of Financial Ratios

A thorough performance analysis considers several aspects of a firm, among them the firm's profitability and its financial and operating risks, including capital adequacy, funding risk, asset credit quality, interest rate risk position, off-balance sheet risk, operating efficiency, and liquidity.

Profitability ratios measure return. Capital adequacy ratios measure financial leverage (the magnitude of risk and return introduced through fixed-cost financing such as debt or preferred stock) and can signal potential financial distress. The greater the financial leverage, the greater the financial risks, and consequently, the closer the regulatory scrutiny. Operating risk ratios measure the levels of interest rate risk, and credit risk, and operating expenses that the firm carries. Funding risk ratios call attention to an institution's risk in borrowing money which depends on the sensitivity or reliability of each funding source to the firm's financial situation. Off-balance sheet risk ratios measure the degree to which an institution extends its financial commitments, engages in swaps and forward transactions in security and foreign exchange trading, and conducts any other business transactions affecting credit, interest rate, and liquidity risks not shown on the balance sheet. The following section walks you through each group of tools measuring the aforementioned aspects of all financial firms.

---

[3]Foreign currency transactions are covered by FASB-52. which establishes accounting and reporting standards for translation of foreign currency financial statements and foreign currency transactions. FASB-52 attempts to preserve the financial results and relationships expressed in the foreign currency by converting the financial statements denominated in a currency different from the reporting currency into the reporting currency using appropriate foreign exchange rates.

PROFITABILITY ANALYSIS: MEASURES OF FINANCIAL PERFORMANCE

The most common measures of financial institution performance are measures of profitability. These measures are used to evaluate how well management is investing the firm's total capital and raising funds. Profitability is generally most important to the firm's shareholders. However, profits serve as a cushion against adverse conditions such as losses on loans or losses caused by unexpected changes in interest rates. Consequently, creditors and regulators concerned about failure also look to profits to protect their interests. Profitability measures have one serious drawback: they ignore the firm's risk. Therefore, relying on profit analysis alone will not provide an adequate evaluation of a firm's overall performance.

Profits depend on three primary structural aspects of financial institutions: financial leverage, net interest margin, and nonportfolio income sources. Regulation also impacts profitability. In comparing profitability across different types of financial institutions, differences in regulation must be taken into account. Therefore, when interpreting profitability ratios, financial decision makers must consider other measures of operation, such as overall portfolio performance, capital adequacy, and the interest rate and credit risks that the institution carries.

The two most telling measures of general financial performance are net income to beginning-year equity, **Return on equity (ROE)**, and net income to average assets, **Return on assets (ROA)**. Virtually all shareholder-owned financial intermediaries use the ROE ratio. Depositories, finance companies, and life insurance companies find the ROA measure particularly meaningful.

A major source of income for depository firms, which is typically reported as a special line item on their income statement, is noninterest income. The sources of noninterest income relate to origination, brokerage, and servicing and are the subject of Chapter 23. One measure of how successful a firm is at generating revenue apart from the firm's asset portfolio is the ratio of *noninterest income to average assets*. In recent years, many financial institutions have put considerable effort into generating higher levels of noninterest income.

Return on Average Assets and Beginning-Year Equity
1996–1995

Return on average assets:
Equation: Net income$_t$ ÷ [(Total assets$_{12/31/96}$ + Total assets$_{12/31/95}$) ÷ 2]
Computation: Tables 8.4a and 8.4b: 1996: $22 mil. ÷ $2,500 mil. = .88%

Return on beginning-of-the-year equity:
Equation: Net income$_{1996}$ ÷ Shareholders' common stock equity$_{12/31/95}$
Computation: Tables 8.4a and 8.4b: 1996: $22 mil. ÷ $216 mil. = 10.2%

	1996	1995
Actual return on average assets	.88%	.94%
Actual return on beginning-of-the-year equity	10.2 %	11.2 %

continued

Noninterest Income to Average Assets 1996–1995

Equation: Noninterest income$_{1996}$ ÷ [(Total assets$_{12/31/96}$ + Total assets$_{12/31/95}$) ÷ 2]
Computation: Table 8.3: 1996: \$35 mil. ÷ [(\$2,600 mil. + \$2,400) ÷ 2] = 1.40%

	1996	1995
Actual noninterest income to average assets	1.40%	1.28%

The primary measure of the profitability of the portfolio management function of intermediaries is the **net interest margin.** The net interest margin measures the difference between the total interest income earned on the institution's earning assets and the interest expense on its interest-costing liabilities. The net interest margin for period t is shown in Equation 8.1.

Net interest margin$_t$ = Interest income – Interest expense$_t$

A number of factors influence the net interest margin—factors that are important to understand when comparing the net interest margin of several intermediaries and when analyzing the trend in the net interest margin for a single institution over time. The primary factor affecting the net interest margin is the quantities of assets and liabilities of a firm. Size impacts the net interest margin in a significant way. As a result, the net interest margin is not very useful when comparing the portfolio management activities of different-sized institutions or in reviewing trends of a single institution that is growing or shrinking. To overcome this deficiency, the net interest margin is scaled by the total dollar amount of earning assets and interest-paying liabilities. The result is the **net interest spread,** which is expressed as a percentage interest rate as shown in Equation 8.2.

Net interest spread$_t$ = [Interest income$_t$/Average earning assets$_t$] – [Interest expenses$_t$/Average interest–paying liabilities$_t$]

A problem with the net interest spread is that the dollar amount of earning assets and liabilities is rarely equal. Thus, firms with unequal dollar amounts of interest-earning assets and interest-paying liabilities or a high level of nonperforming assets experience quite different net interest spreads. In order to eliminate the distortion caused by unequal dollar amounts of assets and liabilities, the net interest margin is frequently computed by taking the interest income and interest expense and dividing them by the average assets of the firm. This produces the *net interest margin to average assets* shown in Equation 8.3.

Net interest spread to average assets$_t$ = [Interest income$_t$ – Interest expense$_t$]/Average assets$_t$

The net interest margin, net interest spread, and net interest spread to average assets for 1996 computed using the data in Tables 8.4a and 8.4b are shown in Table 8.5.

Management's selection of a portfolio strategy influences many factors that impact the net interest spread and net interest spread to average assets.

Paramount in importance is the willingness of management to take interest rate and credit risk. Also of major importance is the selection of funding sources used by the firm. The relationship between the dollar amount of earning assets versus liabilities is a factor that impacts the net interest margin. It is worthwhile to review in greater depth how these factors influence net interest spread and net interest margin to average assets.

TABLE 8.5

Net Interest Margin, Net Interest Spread, and Net Interest Spread to Average Assets
1996
(dollars in millions)

Item	1996
Average interest-earning assets (a)	$2,471
Interest income (b)	375
Interest income to average earning assets % (c)	15.18%
Average interest-paying liabilities (d)	$2,200
Interest cost (e)	280
Interest cost to average interest-paying liabilities (f)	12.73%
Net interest margin (g) = (b − e)	$ 95
Net interest spread (i) = (c − f)	2.45%
Net interest spread to average total assets (h) = (g/$2,500)	3.80%

CAPITAL ADEQUACY: MEASURES OF FINANCIAL LEVERAGE

Capital adequacy relates to the firm's overall use of financial leverage. Generally, firms with high financial leverage will experience more volatile earnings behavior. As you might expect, regulated financial firms with high financial leverage may find themselves under a sharp regulatory eye, with sanctions on permissible activities and diminished flexibility in implementing business strategies.[4]

The adequacy of a firm's capital depends on many variables. A financial firm is likely to have more capital, everything else held constant, if it:

1. Holds a high percentage of risky assets.
2. Maintains a large unmatched interest rate risk position.
3. Uses a high percentage of wholesale funding sources.

---

[4] Capital requirements are discussed extensively in Chapter 22. The capital requirements for commercial banks and thrifts have been made nearly uniform. Capital is measured as Tier 1 capital composed of tangible equity including common stock; retained earnings and perpetual preferred stock; and supplemental capital made up of subordinated debt, loan-loss reserves, intermediate-term preferred stock, and some other minor items. Financial depositories subject to these capital requirements must maintain a Tier 1 capital ratio of 4% and 8% for total capital, respectively, of total risk-weighted assets.

4. Holds a high concentration of assets in a few markets.

The *net worth to total assets ratio* tells us about the firm's overall financial leverage relative to those assets held on the balance sheet. The higher the ratio, the lower the financial risk of the company. The reciprocal of the net worth to total assets ratio is the **equity multiplier (EM)**. The EM measures the degree of financial leverage of a financial firm. The greater is a financial firm's debt relative to equity, the higher its EM.

Net Worth to Total Assets and Equity Multiplier
Year-End 1996, 1995, and 1994

Net worth to total assets:
Equation: (Total shareholder's equity and preferred stock)$_{12/31/96}$
 ÷ Total assets$_{12/31/96}$
Computation: Table 8.4b: 1996: $247 mil. ÷ $2,600 mil. = 9.5%

Equity multiplier:
Equation: Total assets$_{12/31/96}$ ÷ (Total shareholder's equity and
 preferred stock)$_{12/31/96}$
Computation: Table 8.4b: 1996: $2,600 mil. ÷ $247 mil. = 10.53×

	1996	1995	1994
Actual net worth to total assets	9.5 %	9.0 %	8.5 %
Actual equity multiplier	10.53×	10.90×	11.76×

Shareholders are very sensitive to the overall performance and future prospects of a company. But what about those sources of capital—a large, venerable loan servicing unit or, in contrast, a rising volume of loan commitments—that do not appear on the firm's balance sheet but affect performance positively or negatively? The capital adequacy ratio, *market value of common stock equity to book value of equity per share*, helps to highlight the relationship between the firm's market value of assets and liabilities and the corresponding book value. A sharp plummet in the market value of a firm's common stock caused by a deterioration in asset quality might signal financial distress, whereas the long-term ongoing revenue from a large loan servicing unit would add value beyond its accounting worth to the firm.

Market Value of Common Stock Equity to Book Value Per Share
Year-End 1996–1994

Equation: Market value per share$_{12/31/96}$ ÷ Book value per share$_{12/31/96}$
Computation: Table 8.4b: 1996: $140.0 mil. ÷ $123.5 mil. = 113%

	1996	1995	1994
Actual market value of common stock equity to value per share	113.0%	73.3%	62.3%

ASSET CREDIT QUALITY: MEASURES OF CREDIT RISK

Asset credit quality refers to the credit risks embodied in the institution's asset portfolio. An institution with a high percentage of U.S. government Treasury and agency securities, and other high-quality, short-term securities has exposed itself less to credit risk than a firm heavily engaged in construction lending for building shopping centers.

The credit assets listed below are usually considered risky. If you plan to work within a financial institution, then you might want to learn more about how each of these loans might be an especially precarious investment for your firm:

1.   Consumer loans, generally excluding single-family first mortgages.
2.   Commercial and industrial loans (loans to business).
3.   Income property mortgages.
4.   Foreign loans.
5.   Merger/acquisition, real estate development, and construction loans.

Another criterion in measuring credit quality is the performance of loans on the books, specifically the loan loss experience and delinquency rates of various loan portfolios. One measure of such credit risk is the *net loan charge-offs to average net loans* (including leases) ratio, which signals the extent to which the firm has written off losses on loans and leases. Typically, the net loan charge-offs (or credit losses) are divided by average net loans and leases to form a ratio that you can compare reasonably to those of any other financial institution.

Net Loan Charge-offs to Average Net Loans 1996–1995

Equation: Net loan charge-offs$_{1996}$ ÷ (Total loans and leases$_{12/31/96}$ + Total loans and leases$_{12/31/95}$) ÷ 2)

Computation: Tables 8.4a and 8.4b: 1996: $13.5 mil. ÷ [($2,400 mil. + $2,600 mil.) ÷ 2] = .54%

	1996	1995
Actual net charge-offs to average loans	0.54%	0.55%

Analysis of allowances for credit losses on total loans also provides more information about credit risk. The current-period credit loss provision indicates the extent to which financial firms use profits to establish reserves against anticipated future losses on loans and leases. The loan loss provision is based on an assessment of the quality of the firms' asset portfolios. Each type of asset portfolio is evaluated using statistics on delinquency, repossession, foreclosure, and asset disposition to determine the potential loss that the firm can expect to sustain given the deterioration in the quality of the distressed loans. Managers typically set up such reserves to cover losses that they did not expect to charge off until future periods. These loss provisions are somewhat subjective and therefore are reviewed carefully by accounting firms and regulatory agencies.

The customary way to express the relationship of credit loss provisions to total loans (including leases) is by the ratio *loan loss provision to average loans*.

Loan Loss Provision to Average Total Loans
Year-End Balances, 1996–1995

Equation: Loan loss provision$_{1996}$ ÷ (Total loans and leases$_{12/31/96}$ ÷ Total loans and leases $_{12/31/95}$) ÷ 2]

Computation: Tables 8.4a and 8.4b: 1996: $12 mil. ÷ [($1,598 mil. + $1,661 mil.) ÷ 2] = 0.74%

	1996	1995
Actual loan loss provision to average loans	0.74	0.629%

Delinquency ratios also provide timely information about the credit quality of specific asset categories like mortgage loans, credit cards, and auto loans held by the firm. Credit managers can compare the measures to delinquency ratios of other financial firms as well as industry statistics, not just to rate the quality of financial assets but also to see how effectively the firm's overall loan-servicing policies are working.

INTEREST RATE RISK POSITION: MEASURES OF INTEREST RATE RISK EXPOSURE

Interest rate risk is today one of the most sophisticated areas of analysis within well-run financial firms. **Interest rate risk** is the risk that a change in interest rates will cause the market value of a firm's assets to move closer to the market value of the firm's liabilities and thereby reduce the firm's equity. The greater the firm's exposure to such an occurrence, the greater its interest rate risk.

Several measures of identifying the interest rate risk position of the firm are discussed fully in Chapter 18. The most common measure, which is frequently reported in a footnote to the financial statements of depository institutions, is periodic GAP. Below is a hypothetical schedule for the institution shown in Tables 8.4a and 8.4b. Since there is insufficient data in Tables 8.4a and 8.4b to develop this schedule, the timing of the cash flows of the firm's financial assets and liabilities are estimated. The computation of this schedule is the subject of Chapter 17.

Periodic GAP Buckets for Various Periods
(in billions)

Period t, $t+1$	0–30 Days	31–90 Days	91–365 Days	0–365 Days	Over 365 Days
Earning assets	$0.65	$0.35	$0.15	$1.15	$1.40
Sources of funds	$0.64	$0.36	$0.18	$1.18	$1.44
GAP$_{t, t+1}$	$0.01	–$0.01	–$0.03	–$0.03	$0.04
GAP$_{t, t+1}$ to total earning assets$_t$	1.5%	–2.9%	–20.0%	–2.6%	2.9%

Another assessment of a firm's interest rate position, *market value to the book value* of the firm's securities, shows whether the firm has off-balance sheet assets and liabilities, and/or a potential gain or loss on its holdings of securities based on their current market value. For example, a large portfolio of securities which

COMMERCIAL BANK PERFORMANCE TURNAROUND IN 1992

In most June and July issues of the *Federal Reserve Bulletin* in recent years, the Fed has published comprehensive performance data on profits and balance sheet data on the U.S.'s commercial bank system. The 1992 data were revealing since they chronicled an unprecedented turnaround in commercial bank performance. Financial ratios were taken from an article published in July 1993 covering 1992 and 1991 performance.

	1992	1991
Return on average equity	12.80%	7.86%
Return on average assets	.92	.52
Net charge-offs to average loans	1.29	1.58
Net interest margin	3.90	3.61
Noninterest income to average assets	1.95	1.81
Operating expense to average assets	3.87	3.74

The data reveal a striking improvement in overall profitability. The main causes for the turnaround were related to: (1) the sharp increase in the net interest margin as declining open market interest rates allowed banks to reduce deposit rates faster than loan rates; (2) a substantial decrease in loan charge-offs as credit quality improved due in part to the economic recovery and less new lending; and (3) an increase in noninterest income that was greater than the increase in bank noninterest expenses.

Behind these numbers are a couple of other factors. The failure of thousands of commercial banks and thrifts reduced competition for the surviving institutions. The Fed also reduced reserve requirements in late 1991 which helped earnings. Finally, the very low short-term interest rates in 1992 and sharply upward-sloping term structure made generating profits much easier. Although this improved pattern continued in 1994, it will be several years before the true long-term condition of banks can be established.

Source: Allan D. Brunner and William B. English, "Profits and Balance Sheet Developments at U.S. Commercial Banks in 1992," *Federal Reserve Bulletin*, July 1993, pp 651–73.

How it Really Works

have unrealized gains or losses may reflect potential profits or losses that are not revealed by the firm's profitability measures. These schedules also reflect any impact that sharp increases or decreases in open market interest rates may have had on the firm. For that reason among others, the U.S. accounting profession is now mandating, through FASB Number 115, that all financial firms report this comparison of market to book value in their financial statements. Because these data are now normally provided in an optional footnote,[5] Table 8.4b does not include them.

---

[5]FASB Statement 115, which became effective on January 1, 1994, provides that a firm account for certain investments in debt and equity at their current market value if the firm's management anticipates that the asset will be sold before maturity. The financial assets so classified are marked to

Mark-to-Market of Investment Securities Portfolio
December 31, 1996
(in millions)

Security	Book Value	Market Value
U.S. Treasury	$ 14	$ 15
Other U.S. government	123	120
State and municipal	210	200
Other bonds, notes, and debentures	56	52
Federal Reserve Bank and other securities	185	184
Total	$588	$571

FUNDING RISKS: MEASURES OF OVERALL LIQUIDITY

Funding risks refer to an institution's risk in maintaining liquidity. A firm can borrow funds from retail sources such as local branches of commercial banks and thrifts or from wholesale sources such as institutionally sold negotiable certificates of deposit, brokered-insured deposits, and other capital market pools of, say, commercial paper. Studies show that retail deposits, also called *core deposits,* will be less price flexible, or, interest elastic, and therefore more stable, than deposits attracted from wholesale distribution channels. The same is true for insurance policies sold to individuals as opposed to those sold to corporate clients by life insurance companies. In general, then, retail funding risk will be lower than wholesale risk and higher if the institution relies more on nonretail deposits.

Two measures of funding risk are comparisons of *core deposit sources to total funding sources,* and *brokered deposits and other deposits over $100,000 to total deposits.* The balance sheet for 1996 in Table 8.4b provides the needed data to assemble the statement below, which users might find as a footnote to financial statements of commercial banks.

Core Deposits to Total Funding Sources, 1996
(in millions)

Core deposits	$1,872
Noncore deposits	78
Short-term borrowings	234
Acceptances outstanding	0
Senior long-term debt	104
Other liabilities	65
Subordinated debt	0
Total	$2,353

Equation: Core deposits$_{12/31/96}$ ÷ Total funding sources$_{12/31/96}$
Computation: Table 8.4b: 1996: $1,872 ÷ $2,353 = 79.6\%$

Actual core deposits to total funding sources (12/31/96)   79.6%

their current market value and any difference between that value and its book value is added or substracted from the firm's equity as a separate component of the equity account on the balance sheet. These adjustments do not immediately affect current income.

OFF-BALANCE SHEET RISK MEASURES

Today, many of the risks of financial institutions do not show up on the balance sheet. Why? Because financial firms engage in a wide variety of activities that current reporting requirements do not cover. That doesn't mean that managers of financial firms should ignore these activities. On the contrary, institutions may have commitments outstanding that could increase both credit and interest rate exposure.

Some of the most common off-balance sheet exposures include **loan commitments**, involving obligations of lending firms to originate loans on demand of a borrower; **standby letters of credit**, involving obligations of lending firms to provide a back-up source of financing to a firm selling commercial paper; and **loans sold with recourse**, which involve the sale of a loan to another institution with the provision that the seller will repurchase it if the buyer proves that the asset did not perform as contracted.

One measure of off-balance sheet risk is the ratio, *loan commitments and standby letters of credit to total assets*. Using data from the statement on on-balance sheet commitments in Table 8.4b, a statement such as the one below is commonly shown as a footnote to financial statements of commercial banks.

Commitments Outstanding Year-End 1996 and 1995
(in millions)

	1996	1995
Commitments to extend credit	$1,234	$1,129
Standby letters of credit and foreign office guarantees	204	197
Other letters of credit	20	89
Loans sold with recourse	0	0
Total	$1,458	$1,415

Equation: (Total commitments$_{12/31/96}$ + Standby letters$_{12/31/96}$ + Other letters of credit$_{12/31/96}$ + Loans sold with recourse$_{12/31/96}$) ÷ Total assets$_{12/31/96}$
Computation: $1,458 ÷ $2,600 = 56.1%

	1996	1995
Actual commitments as percent of total assets	56.1%	59.0%

OPERATING EFFICIENCY: MEASURES OF
INTERMEDIATION PROCESSING

Since financial institutions can perform a variety of financial functions and deal with different types of financial claims, comparing the operating efficiency of firms is no easy task. Each financial firm operates in different markets with vastly different retail and wholesale asset and liability strategies. Each varies the functions it performs on each of the financial claims it chooses to originate, service, broker, or invest, and pursues different strategies for originating, servicing, and brokering new claims. While higher interest rate margins may offset the operating cost differences and yield higher profits, one firm may appear to operate less efficiently than its competitors. For example, a commercial bank with a high percentage of assets in a credit card activity will generally experience higher operating expenses as a ratio of average assets compared to a bank with a lower level of assets in credit card receivables. Still, the bank with the higher credit card receivables may well have a much higher interest rate margin and greater overall profitability. Operating expenses and noninterest income, rather than total assets, may reflect the effectiveness of these strategic differences. As a result, the most common measures of operating efficiency signal the need for further investigation of performance efficiency or incompetence.

Operating expenses (noninterest expenses) to average assets is the most frequently used measure of operating efficiency. The resulting ratio tends to be higher for highly diversified firms such as large commercial banks than for specialized firms such as thrifts, because the diversified firms have more expenses related to origination and servicing for their many different types of financial assets and liabilities. Also, firms that originate and service assets for others tend to have higher operating expenses to average assets ratios, because the cost of servicing is included in the ratio's numerator and the loans serviced are not shown in the firm's average assets.

Operating (Noninterest) Expenses to Average Assets 1996–1995

Equation: Noninterest expense$_{1996}$ ÷ [(Total assets$_{12/31/96}$ + Total assets$_{12/31/95}$) ÷ 2]

Computation: Tables 8.4a and 8.4b 1996: \$87 mil. ÷ [(\$2,600 mil. + \$2,400 mil.) ÷ 2] = 3.48%

	1996	1995
Operating (noninterest) expenses to average assets	3.48%	3.40%

✓ Checkpoints

8-4 What aspects of financial firms do financial ratios help managers to analyze?

8-5 Why is measuring capital adequacy important, and what ratios accomplish that?

8-6 What are limitations of the measures of operating efficiency?

8-7 Are measures of interest rate risk suitable for all financial depository institutions? Why or why not?

8-8 What financial ratios measure funding risk, and what do they indicate?

Additional Performance Measures for Nondepository Firms

Performance measures for nondepository institutions—finance companies, property and casualty companies, insurance companies, and pension funds—have the same objective as those for depositories. The major categories of performance and risk—such as capital adequacy, profitability, asset quality, interest rate risk, funding risk, and operating efficiency—are all still relevant. Consequently, many of the tools already covered help in measuring the performance of these nondepository institutions, but some categories differ significantly. For example, property and casualty insurance companies accept the risks of health and accident costs, fire, and other hazard liabilities, as well as personal liability. Life insurance companies accept mortality risk, as do pension funds. Due to differences in the nature of these risks, asset and liability structures, and operations between these two broad categories, financial decision makers need some additional performance measures and alternative decision criteria for nondepositories. The following section adds to the manager's toolbox of performance measures particularly suitable for analyzing nondepository institutions.

FINANCE COMPANIES

Since finance companies operate much like depository institutions, the analyst can use many of the same performance measures in financial analysis. The main difference lies in choice of peer group, if any. The added measures relate primarily to the high concentration of **consumer receivables** (consumer loans) on some of the finance companies' books for those companies specializing in consumer finance.

For the finance company, an added measure of credit risk is the ratio, *direct cash loans to gross receivables;* another measure of operating efficiency is the ratio, *operating expenses to average net receivables,* ignoring loan losses.

PROPERTY AND CASUALTY COMPANIES

Many of the performance measures for depositories, such as return on equity, operating expenses to average assets, interest rate periodic and duration GAPs, and market value of equity to book value of equity—are the same for property and casualty companies (P&Cs). But P&Cs must account for the special risks related to the hazards insured and intensified by changes in laws, social forces, and the weather—all very difficult to forecast with confidence! The sharply rising costs of health care, legal civil liability, and repair of damaged goods expose P&Cs to enormous risks in their basic business.

The three most important special financial ratios for P&C companies relate to casualty risk: they are the underwriting loss, expense, and combined ratios. These ratios provide measures for the performance of the firm's property and casualty risk management function and operating efficiency. The **underwriting ratio** indicates the relationship of property and casualty losses sustained by the P&C to the premium earned during a specified period and thus reflects the adequacy of premium rates and/or the ability of the company to control for excessively risky customers. The **expense ratio** is a measure of operating and administrative efficiency. P&C companies strive to have very low expense ratios. The **combined ratio** provides the most comprehensive measure of the company's overall success in covering its operating costs and property and casualty losses without relying on investment income sources. The best way to understand these ratios is to look at Table 8.6, which provides an abbreviated income statement for a property and casualty insurance company.

TABLE 8.6

Income Statement and Selected Ratios for a Property and Casualty Insurance Company
1996 and 1995
(dollars in millions)

Item	1996	1995
Net premiums earned	$500	$450
Less: Losses paid and reserves added for future losses	325	290
Expenses for:		
Policy acquisition and underwriting	170	155
Loss adjustment	65	60
Underwriting loss	–60	–55
Net investment income	72	65
Net profit before taxes	$ 12	$ 10
Taxes	5	4
Net profit after taxes	$ 7	$ 6
Operating Ratios (percent of total)		
Underwriting loss ratio:		
Loss and loss adjustment expenses to premiums and other insurance income/premium and other insurance income	77.2%	74.3%
[1996: ($325 + $65) ÷ $500]		
Expense ratio:		
Commissions and other expenses/premium and other insurance income	35.1%	37.0%
[1996: ($170 ÷ $500)]		
Combined ratio:		
Loss ratio + expense ratio	112.3%	111.3%
[1996: (77.2% + 35.1%)]		

LIFE INSURANCE COMPANIES

Life insurance companies also use many of the same profitability, operating efficiency, and capital adequacy ratios that depository institutions do. These measures include return on equity, capital to total assets, market value of equity to book value of equity, operating expenses to average assets, and net interest spread. But the life insurance business has changed significantly in the last 20 years: policy purchasers are more sophisticated in purchasing insurance contracts, and many now favor term insurance over whole life, and investment insurance products such as universal life, variable life, annuities, and variable universal life policies. As a result, life companies have much more interest-sensitive liabilities than in previous times and compete for new products on the basis of cost for the term policies and on the basis of yields on annuity products. Another product offered by the life company is the **guaranteed investment contract (GIC)**, an obligation to pay an agreed-upon return to the purchaser. Life companies sell GICs to administrators of pension funds and employee tax-sheltered retirement programs, such as 401k programs, needing a safe, high-yielding investment.

Funding risk ratios specially designed to measure the percentage of a life company's total policy and contract reserves relate to the less interest-sensitive whole life policies, compared to more interest-rate sensitive policies. The other group of ratios relates to the sensitivity of the insurance company's customers to changing economic and competitive circumstances. The ratio of *policy lapses to total policies* is very important, since a high ratio of lapsed policies is very costly to insurance companies. This is because insurance companies have large policy acquisition and marketing costs to put new business on the books. These ratios will be computed using the abbreviated balance sheet of a life insurance company shown in Table 8.7.

TABLE 8.7

Balance Sheet for Life Insurance Company
1996 and 1995
(dollars in millions)

Item	1996	1995
Assets:		
Cash	20	15
Investments:		
Bonds and notes	$15,000	$14,000
Preferred stock	50	50
Common stock	300	215
Policy loans	360	340
Mortgages	525	620
Short-term investments	150	275
Investment real estate	140	110
Other investments	50	50
Deferred policy acquisition costs	1,625	1,550
Property and equipment	100	95
Accounts receivable	375	420
Other	1,000	800
Total assets	$19,645	$18,445
Liabilities and net worth:		
Life insurance reserves (future policy benefits)	$ 6,500	$ 5,800
Other policyholders' deposit funds	10,400	9,800
Guaranteed investment contracts	950	725
Other liabilities	145	670
Shareholders' equity	1,650	1,450
Total liabilities and net worth	$19,645	$18,445

Policy loans are also undesirable to insurance companies, since they represent financial options held by the insured. Policy loans tend to get taken out only when market interest rates exceed the policy loan rate. This works to the insurance company's disadvantage, since it must sell high-earning assets to fund the policy loans.

Policy Life Insurance Reserves to Total
Life Policy Reserves and Policy Deposit Account Balances
December 31, 1996, and 1995
(dollars in millions)

	1996	1995
Life insurance reserves	$6,500	$5,800
Policyholder deposit accounts	$10,400	$9,800
Total reserves and deposit accounts	$16,900	$15,600
Ratio of life reserves to		
total reserves and deposit accounts		
(1996: $6,500 ÷ $16,900 = 38.5%)	38.5%	37.2%

Policy Loans to Life Insurance Policy Reserves
December 31, 1996, and 1995
(dollars in millions)

	1996	1995
Policy loans	$360	$340
Life policy benefit reserves	$6,500	$5,800
Ratio of policy loans to benefit reserves		
(1996: $350 ÷ $6,500 = 5.54%)	5.54%	5.86%

PENSION FUNDS

A primary financial ratio of concern to the pension fund manager is the relationship between the fund's *market value of assets and its actuarially determined liabilities*. Using this performance ratio, the manager and benefit recipients can determine whether a pension fund is underfunded or overfunded.

Pension Fund Market Value to Projected Benefit Obligation
December 31, 1994–1996
(dollars in millions)

	1996	1995	1994
Pension benefit obligations	$3,579	$3,624	$3,047
Plan assets at fair value	$3,504	$3,769	$3,138
Ratio of asset value to			
benefit obligation	−2.1%*	4.0%	3.0%
Funding	Underfunded	Overfunded	Overfunded

*This is calculated as [($3,504 − $3,579) ÷ $3,579 = −2.1%].

FINDING FINANCIAL DATA

Data used for analyses of financial firms is quite easy to obtain for regulated commercial banks and most thrifts but more difficult to get for life insurance companies and other intermediaries. Typically, a firm's data comes from its published financial reports, such as its annual report, quarterly reports, and 10k filings. A number of private data collection firms publish comparative data for commercial banks and thrifts. These include Sheshunoff and Co. and SNL Securities, L.P. Insurance data are available from A. M. Best Company, Standard & Poor's Corporation, and Moody's Investors Services. Considerable help for publicly traded companies is available from security analysts.

Data for commercial banks, S&Ls, and SBs are available from regulators at the FDIC, OTS, and the Board of Governors of the Federal Reserve System. Performance measures for peer groups are available in the annual report, *Uniform Bank Performance,* published by the Federal Financial Institution Examination Council and in the report, *Statistics on Banking,* published annually by the FDIC.

The less-regulated firms require that the analyst use data filed with the Securities and Exchange Commission for publicly traded companies or from the many computer databanks that provide access to these data.

The best approach, however, is to use the company's financial reports and those of a small group of companies who compete with the firm.

✓ Checkpoints

8-9 What special ratios do property and casualty companies use?

8-10 Why should the trustees of a pension fund worry about the overfunding or underfunding measure of pension fund performance?

8-11 Why might the credit quality of a financial institution be difficult to ascertain?

8-12 Where do financial analysts obtain data for financial analyses of most financial institutions?

SUMMARY AND REVIEW

1. **Describe time-series, cross-sectional, combined, and common-size techniques for presenting and analyzing financial data.**

   Time-series analysis refers to the exposition of financial data with comparisons at discrete periods over time. Typically, a firm is compared to itself at different points in time using one or more ratios. *Cross-sectional analysis* refers to comparisons of financial data at one point in time compared with similar data of another company or peer group. *Combined analysis* refers to comparisons using both time-series and cross-sectional data. **Common-size financial statements** present financial statements that are standardized by dividing total assets for the balance sheet and total revenue for income statements.

2. **Describe the primary areas of financial ratio analysis.**

Profitability measures are used to assess the firm's profitability in relation to shareholders' equity and levels of earning assets and liabilities. Portfolio performance is measured using such measures and ratios as the **net interest margin, net interest spread,** and **net interest spread to average assets. Noninterest income** is also an important focus of profitability analysis. **Capital adequacy** or **financial leverage ratios** are used to determine the degree of financial risk of the institution. A number of these ratios are also used to compare a financial institution's capital position to that required by its regulator. **Interest rate risk measures** are used to assess the extent to which the firm has a mismatch between the cash flow and repricing characteristics of its assets and its liabilities. These ratios are designed to measure the potential that interest rate volatility will adversely impact the firm's profitability and equity values. **Credit risk data** are used to assess the quality of the firm's assets in terms of credit risk exposure. **Operating efficiency ratios** are used to determine the relative efficiency of the financial firm in relation to some measure of activity. **Funding risk measures** relate to how the financial firm generates its liabilities. Financial liabilities are typically attracted through retail and wholesale distribution channels. It is assumed that in most cases retail-generated liabilities will be less interest elastic and more stable. Several financial ratios are designed to measure the relative use of each of these funding strategies. **Off-balance sheet risks** are measured using supplemental data that show the extent to which the firm incurs interest rate risks, liquidity risks, and credit risks related to financial transactions that are not reflected on the current balance sheet. The primary sources of financial data are the firm's balance sheet, income statement, and supporting financial exhibits.

3. **Describe some of the most important financial ratios used by property and casualty companies, life insurance companies, and pension funds and the sources of financial data.**

Property and casualty companies focus on underwriting **loss, expense** and **combined ratios,** life companies focus on ratios of **policyholder reserves** and ratios related to **policy loans,** while pension funds focus on the relationship between **benefit obligations and plan assets.**

CASE 8.1

PERFORMANCE EVALUATION: FIRST INDEPENDENT BANK OF BOISE

Introduction

The First Independent Bank of Boise was founded in 1918. It was owned by the Brown family until 1954, when the bank was sold in a secondary public offering. Currently, the majority of the bank is owned by local Boise residents.

William Bradford is now the chairman of the board and chief executive officer. He recently came back from a meeting in which a group of bank executives were discussing the performance of their respective institutions. They talked about capitalization, profitability, high credit risk assets, and a host of other subjects. What disturbed Mr. Bradford was that these other executives had the ability to compare a variety of financial ratios with one other. Several of the banks belonged to an informal peer group that shared this type of financial information among themselves. Mr. Bradford belonged to no such group.

Mr. Bradford came back from the meeting convinced that his bank was deficient in establishing a system for reporting and monitoring the financial position of his bank and in comparing his bank's performance to other similar banks. Mr. Bradford wanted to develop a system that would be updated quarterly or annually depending on the ratio's importance.

The first thing that Mr. Bradford did was ask Bob Fine, the financial officer of the bank, to assemble the bank's latest balance sheets for 1995 and 1996 and its 1996 income statement. These are shown in Tables C8.1 and C8.2.

PROBLEM

With the information obtained from Mr. Fine, it was determined that you should develop a sources and uses of funds statement for the year 1996 using Exhibit C8.1.

TABLE C8.1

First Independent Bank of Boise
Balance Sheet December 31, 1995–1996
(dollars in thousands)

	1995	1996
Assets:		
Cash and due from banks	$ 12,300	$ 11,690
U.S. Treasury securities	13,500	12,460
Agency securities	21,900	20,876
Short-term deposits, reserve repos, and federal funds sold	24,675	25,765
Municipal bonds	40,000	38,000
Mortgage pass-through securities	12,000	14,000
Loans*		
Residential first mortgage loans	34,509	38,990
Business loans	35,097	47,087
Consumer loans	12,765	23,456
Plant and equipment	7,879	8,543
Foreclosed and repossessed assets	3,453	5,765
Other assets	1,234	2,543
Total assets	$219,312	$249,175

Liabilities and Net Worth:

Demand deposits	$ 42,900	$ 45,789
Money market deposits	12,097	13,490
Savings deposits	54,070	47,768
Consumer certificates of deposit	81,647	90,097
Large-denomination CDs	8,098	22,601
Repurchase agreements	0	5,980
Other liabilities	1,000	2,620
Stockholders' equity		
(1,200,000 shares outstanding)	19,500	20,830
Total liabilities and Shareholders' equity	$219,312	$249,175

*Loan commitments outstanding at December 31, 1996 were $12.0 million.

TABLE C8.2

First Independent Bank of Boise
Income Statement 1996
(dollars in millions)

Income	
Interest and fees on loans	$12.030
Interest on investments	7.975
Other income	2.750
Total interest income	$22.755
Interest expense	
Interest on consumer deposits	$ 9.750
Interest on other	1.530
Borrowed funds	.400
Total interest expense	$11.680
Fee and noninterest income	$ 4.400
Noninterest expense	
Salaries and employee benefits	$ 5.320
Net occupancy expenses	.800
Furniture and equipment	.920
Other operating expenses	3.890
Total noninterest expense	$10.930
Provision for loan losses	$ 1.315
Income before taxes	$ 3.230
Income tax expenses	1.100
Income before security transactions	2.130
Security gains (and losses)	0
Net income	$ 2.130

This year is considered important because that was when the bank under-
took a much more aggressive strategy. In particular, the company decided to
increase its market share of the loan market while decreasing investments. It

EXHIBIT C8.1

Sources and Uses Statement for 1996

	Sources	Uses
Cash and due from banks	_____	_____
U.S. Treasury securities	_____	_____
Agency securities	_____	_____
Municipal bonds	_____	_____
Mortgage pass-through	_____	_____
Short term deposits, reverse repos, and federal funds	_____	_____
Loans	_____	_____
Plant and equipment	_____	_____
Foreclosed and repossessed assets	_____	_____
Other assets	_____	_____
Demand deposits	_____	_____
Money market deposits	_____	_____
Savings deposits	_____	_____
Consumer certificates of deposit	_____	_____
Large-denomination CDs	_____	_____
Repurchase agreements	_____	_____
Other liabilities	_____	_____
Retained earnings	_____	_____
Dividends paid	_____	_____
Total	_____	_____

also chose to increase its reliance on wholesale funding sources. Mr. Bradford was interested in seeing how this affected the sources and uses of funds statement. Another aspect of the business strategy was to continue to originate mortgages for sale to the secondary market mortgage credit agencies. Over the years, the bank has built up a very large mortgage-servicing portfolio. This has been designed to increase the fee income of the bank. The bank now services over $600 million in mortgages for other investors. Mr. Bradford expects that this activity should improve the fee income of the bank.

Mr. Fine indicated that he was concerned that the new strategy to increase loans and decrease security investments had increased the credit risk exposure of the bank. Mr. Fine stated that risk assets were defined to be all loans, except residential first mortgages, plus foreclosed and repossessed assets. He also disclosed the need for additional space, since the bank now had grown to 125 employees. He further indicated that the company paid a cash dividend of $800,000 in 1996. The price of First Independent stock as listed over the counter was last traded at $14.875 per share.

Mr. Bradford also supplied you with Exhibit C8.2, a schedule of important financial ratios of a group of five similar banks whose management he met with

EXHIBIT C8.2

First Independent and Peer Group Ratios for 1996

	First Independent	Peer Group
Capital adequacy:		
Equity to total assets	_____	8.10 %
Market value of equity to book value of equity	_____	1.05x
Asset quality:		
Loan loss provision to average net loans	_____	0.85 %
Foreclosed and repossessed loans to net worth	_____	10.52 %
Operating efficiency:		
Operating expenses to average assets	_____	3.35 %
Profitability:		
Net income to beginning equity (ROE)	_____	8.75 %
Net income to average assets	_____	0.81 %
Interest income to average assets	_____	9.42 %
Interest expense to average assets	_____	4.75 %
Interest expense to average interest-paying liabilities	_____	5.02 %
Noninterest income to average assets	_____	0.92 %
Funding risks:		
Wholesale funding sources to total funding sources	_____	1.44 %
Brokered and other large CDs to total deposits	_____	1.11 %
Off-balance sheet risks:		
Loan commitments to total assets	_____	3.20 %

at the meeting. These will provide you with a peer group to compare with First Independent Bank.

Questions

1. Using the information supplied above, develop a sources and uses of funds statement using Exhibit C8.1. Discuss how you would respond to Mr. Bradford's statement that the company tried in 1996 to increase its loan port-

folio at the expense of investments and that it relied more on wholesale, as compared to retail, funding sources. Do you agree or disagree?

2. Mr. Bradford would like you to determine the ratios listed in Exhibit C8.2 on peer group ratios. He is concerned about how his bank compares in terms of these ratios. He would like you to comment on each of the ratios shown.

Do you feel that First Independent Bank is correct in its effort to increase its loan market share using wholesale funding sources? Use financial ratios to support your answer. What other ideas do you have for the bank to improve its financial position?

What do you think about the strategy to originate and sell loans in the secondary market? Does it seem to be working for the bank? Use financial ratios to support your answer.

CASE 8.2

PERFORMANCE EVALUATION: MARITIME NATIONAL BANK

Marcus opened the envelope and took out the contents. It was the recently issued annual report of Maritime National Bank. Marcus, a financial analyst for Britain Investments, was in charge of doing financial analyses of financial institutions. Britain Investments is a large investment company that manages money for institutional investors as well as a group of mutual funds. Total assets under management were $16.8 billion at year-end 1996.

Marcus had already assembled comparative financial data which would be used to evaluate Maritime. The financial statements Marcus was most interested in were the balance sheet, income statements, statement of loan losses, and statement of off-balance sheet risks.

PROBLEMS

Marcus asked you to prepare the following:

- Common-size balance sheet.
- Common-size income statement.
- Comparisons of Maritime to industry average common-sized income statement.
- Primary financial ratios.
- Comparisons of financial ratios for Maritime to industry averages.

After completing these statements and ratios, Marcus asked you to prepare a review of Maritime's performance.

Maritime National Bank
Consolidated Balance Sheet 1996 and 1995
(in millions)

	1996	1995
Assets:		
Cash and due from banks	$ 894	$ 1,337
Interest-paying deposits in banks	1,201	500
Federal funds sold and securities		
purchased subject to repurchase agreement	386	616
Total cash and cash equivalents	2,481	2,453
Trading account assets	45	61
Investment securities	954	1,076
Loans	12,579	13,190
Less: Allowance for loan losses	408	402
Net loans	12,171	12,788
Customer's acceptance liability	228	230
Other real estate owned	296	250
Other assets	375	349
Total assets	$16,843	$17,474
Liabilities and shareholders' equity:		
Deposits in domestic offices:		
Demand	$ 4,634	$ 4,057
Savings, time, interest bearing and large	7,744	8,447
Total domestic deposits	12,378	12,504
Deposits in foreign offices	476	656
Total deposits	12,854	13,160
Federal funds purchases and securities		
sold under repurchase agreements	764	813
Commercial paper	533	585
Other borrowed funds	634	1,065
Other liabilities	526	453
Subordinated capital notes	430	322
Total liabilities	$15,740	$16,399
Shareholders' equity		
Common stock: $5 par value, authorized		
40,000,000 shares, issued 32,401,614 and		
32,316,955 outstanding as of December 31,		
1996, and 1995, respectively	162	162
Surplus	568	587
Retained earnings	373	328
Total shareholders' equity	1,103	1,075
Total liabilities and shareholders' equity	$16,844	$17,474

Maritime National Bank
Income Statement 1996 and 1995
(dollars in millions)

	1996	1995	1996 Industry Average % of Total
Total revenue: Interest and noninterest	$1,380	$1,629	100.0%
Interest income:			
Loans	$1,038	$1,292	72.2
Investment securities—taxable	61	80	8.4
Investment securities—tax-exempt	17	21	2.2
Other interest	41	40	2.0
Total interest income	1,157	1,432	84.8
Interest expense:			
Deposits in domestic offices	292	466	20.0
Deposits in foreign offices	26	44	.5
Federal funds and securities sold under repurchase agreements	24	52	.7
Commercial paper	23	41	.5
Other borrowed funds	31	50	2.0
Subordinated capital notes	23	24	.5
Total interest expense	420	677	24.2
Net interest income:	737	756	60.6
Provision for loan losses	156	200	8.1
Net interest income after provision for loan losses	582	556	52.5
Noninterest income:			
Service charges on deposit accounts	79	64	8.7
Credit card merchant fees	26	23	3.0
Trust fees	34	34	3.5
Foreign exchange and services	34	30	1.1
Other fees	49	46	4.0
Total noninterest income	223	197	20.3
Noninterest expense:			
Salaries and employee benefits	317	326	21.4
Net occupancy	61	62	3.4
Equipment	32	33	2.0
Other real estate owned and joint ventures	39	15	1.5
Other	196	183	16.0
Total noninterest expense	645	617	44.3
Securities gains and (losses)	6	3	0
Income before income taxes	165	139	28.5
Income tax expense	63	45	11.4
Net income	$102	$93	17.1%
Weighted number of shares	32,401,614	32,316,955	

Maritime National Bank
Summary of Off-Balance Sheet Risk
December 31, 1996, and 1995
(dollars in millions)

	1996	1995
Contractual amounts:		
Commitments to extend credit	$5,517	$5,455
Standby letters of credit	1,440	1,413
Other letters of credit	151	236
Foreign exchange		
Commitments to sell	274	365
Commitments to purchase	265	356
At notional amounts:		
Interest rate swap agreements	780	427
Interest rate cap agreements		
Purchased	437	299
Sold	437	331
Interest rate floor agreements		
Purchased	22	81
Sold	22	81

Maritime National Bank
Statement of Changes to Allowance for Loan Losses
1996 and 1995
(in millions)

	1996	1995
Balance, beginning of year	$402	$320
Loans charged off	(188)	(146)
Loan loss recoveries	38	28
Total net loans charged off	(150)	(118)
Provision for loan losses	156	200
Balance, end of year	$408	$402

Industry Averages for Several Important Financial Ratios: 1996

1. Net income to average assets .92%
2. Net income to equity 14.76%
3. Net worth to total assets 8.90%
4. Market value of common stock to book value 1.78x

continued

Table, continued

5.	Net charge-offs to average net loans	.45%
6.	Credit loss provisions to average total loans	1.23%
7.	Gap buckets, one-year periodic GAP	2.10%
8.	Operating expenses to average assets	3.65%
9.	Noninterest income to average assets	1.56%

CHAPTER 9

*P*lanning for Financial Institutions

Learning Goals

After studying this chapter, you should be able to:

1. Describe the overall planning process, including reasons for, and timing of, the process.
2. Distinguish among financial firms' strategic plans, operating and financial plans, and action plans.
3. Discuss the strategic planning process, including the purpose of external and internal situation analyses and the strategic statement.
4. Explain how financial firms prepare and use operating and financial plans, and identify who provides input into these plans and who implements them.
5. Explain how financial firms devise and use action plans, and identify who contributes feedback and who carries them out.
6. Provide current examples of the theories of financial innovation.

Over the last 20 years, deregulation of financial institutions, accelerated financial innovation, globalization of markets, and increased competition for capital all have complicated the financial services industry. How do managers of financial firms move their businesses beyond survival and regulatory compliance toward market leadership? The answer sounds deceptively simple: through careful planning. This chapter walks you through the planning process within the financial institution so that you can better appreciate the need for strategic, insightful, and comprehensive plans.

Overview of the Planning Process

Planning is an activity that not only sets a firm's goals but also ascertains the human, physical, and capital resources needed to accomplish them. Planning takes place throughout an organization because all personnel must understand their specific roles and responsibilities in achieving these goals. Furthermore, all efforts toward goal achievement require some financial incentive and support. The following section considers the planning process by studying three broad questions: What is planning in terms of the financial intermediary? Why should a financial firm plan? When should planning occur?

WHAT IS PLANNING TO A FINANCIAL INTERMEDIARY?

Financial intermediaries exist to facilitate the allocation of scarce capital resources primarily by bringing those who have capital together with those who need capital. In the dynamic international arena—with growing global markets, innovative products, and new players every day—there are many ways to move these resources quickly around the world. Therefore, planning within a financial firm is first and foremost about how to deploy scarce resources most effectively: How will we facilitate capital movement? What actions and measures do we need to take, and how can we most efficiently accomplish them?

There are several types of plans, from the very general to the very specialized. Exhibit 9.1 organizes these types of plans into a hierarchy, with strategic planning at the top, action planning at the bottom, and operating and financial planning in between.

For most corporations, the operating and the financial plans need not be separate and are typically integrated in practice. However, since so many parties scrutinize the performance and the soundness of a financial intermediary, this chapter distinguishes operating from financial objectives so that readers can fully appreciate the importance of the financial plan to the firm's managers.

The planning process results in a set of pro forma financial statements and an extensive budget, which managers must present to the firm's board of directors for approval. Upon board approval, the statements and budget serve as a game plan to guide the firm's activities and to measure its success. The board, upon accepting these plans, might use the pro forma financial reports to establish managerial compensation packages and employee incentive programs to motivate the firm's managers and staff toward goal achievement. Such packages and programs would constitute agency costs, as discussed in Chapter 1.

WHY DO FINANCIAL FIRMS PLAN?

As in nonfinancial firms, shareholders expect a firm's management and directors to outline their plans so that they—the shareholders—can decide whether they want to invest more capital in the firm, hold fast, or sell their claims of ownership. Creditors look at a firm's plan to assess the likelihood of repayment when

EXHIBIT 9.1

Planning Hierarchy

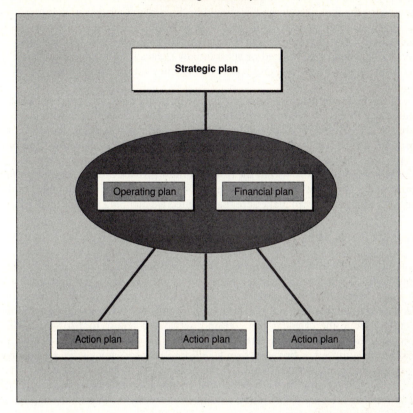

Strategic plan

Operating plan

Financial plan

Action plan

Action plan

Action plan

expected. Regulators monitor a firm's plan to flag the possibility of financial failure. Clearly, the outcome of the planning process can signal something to the marketplace about a firm's financial fortitude or frailty. A plan may call for incurring greater risks than an owner or creditor is willing to bear or than a regulator is willing to deem as safe and sound, thus raising the firm's cost of capital, lowering its market value, or subjecting it to further regulatory restriction. Or it may not be aggressive, forward-looking, or innovative enough to survive in the global competition for capital. As important as these interests in planning may be, the most critical need for a firm's plans lies within the firm. Planning directs resources toward an expected or desired outcome. Each employee ultimately must understand how his or her work contributes to the firm's objectives.

WHO PLANS?

If planning is to be meaningful, it must involve the total commitment of senior management. In too many organizations, planning is a perfunctory activity designed to produce a document that occupies shelf space and not much else. Some organizations spend significant resources using consultants and other professional "planners" with little to show for the effort. A plan must direct the resources of the firm. If it doesn't, it should be discarded. One reason that some organizations avoid specificity in planning is because managers don't want to deliver bad news. Invariably, the process of allocating resources will identify activities that will be eliminated or substantially reduced. This message is hard for some managers to deliver, and consequently, they refrain from specifying such changes.

In the planning process, managers do the planning and planners should facilitate the process. While some organizations are large enough to have planning groups, the planning staff should not be the doing the planning but should act to provide needed resources and analyses and should act to transcribe the decisions made. The planning staff should also assist in making sure needed resources are forthcoming from those within the firm that must provide them. However, in the final analysis, it is each manager's responsibility to plan and it is the board of director's responsibility to make sure that an effective planning process takes place.

WHEN SHOULD FINANCIAL FIRMS PLAN?

One might expect planning to occur according to schedule, at some point during the fiscal year or the calendar year. But, as previous chapters illustrated, the financial services industry is globally dynamic and subject to changes in available technology, competitive and regulatory environments, and financial innovation. And so, while the calendar can certainly serve as a handy tool for measuring progress, *events,* rather than dates, should drive the planning cycle as shown in Exhibit 9.2. Indeed, a financial firm's ability to respond quickly, in a proactive rather reactive manner, will keep the firm's competitors on the defensive. What types of events might affect a firm's plans? Exhibit 9.3 describes a few scenarios. These events are organized around a number of events to be discussed in greater depth later in the chapter.

The accounts in Exhibit 9.3 can and do occur without notice, and all merit revision of some kind to a firm's plans, regardless of calendar date. What might call for formal planning revisions? If a situation is dire enough, a firm's in-house management team may spring back to the drawing board or the board of directors may demand a new written plan of attack. Regulators may require revised plans for monitoring a firm's financial health during distressed times. Potential buyers of a financial institution's securities in the public market may ask the underwriter to explain its business strategy. Shareholders may challenge the management team and board of directors during the annual shareholder's meeting; and, similarly, security analysts, institutional investors, and members of the financial press may pose difficult questions about business policies and strategies. Deep understanding of the planning process and the issues involved as well as keen awareness of the need for replanning, prepare managers of financial firms to respond quickly and confidently.

✓ Checkpoints

9-1　What three types of plans do financial firms create and use?

EXHIBIT 9.2

Events Leading to Plan Revisions

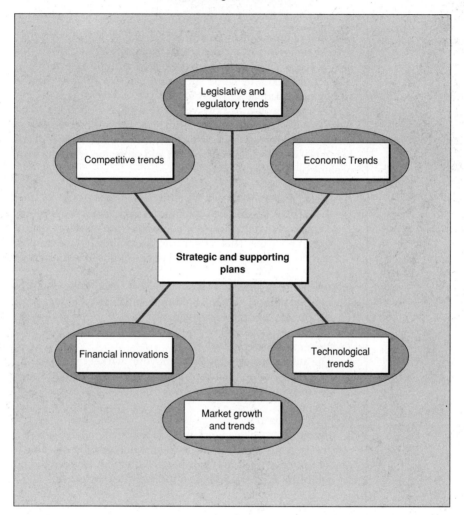

9-2 Why do financial firms plan, and what do they accomplish during the planning process?

9-3 When should a firm schedule its planning? What is the appropriate planning cycle?

The Strategic Planning Process

Strategic planning is the most difficult of all planning. It attempts to answer the most basic questions: Why does this financial organization exist? Whose interests does it serve? Whose needs does it fulfill? Who are its competitors? What do its

EXHIBIT 9.3

Events Calling for Plan Revisions

When should a firm reconsider its plans? This exhibit describes several newsworthy incidents that have actually occurred over the last 15 years. These events are organized around six external events. The actions taken by some successful firms to address these events will be described later in the chapter.

You might consider how you would have responded to each of these events if you managed a financial firm. Which events call for minor adjustments and which warrant major plan overhauls? Exhibits 9.4 –9.9 will revisit this list and report on what the managers of some of these firms actually did.

Economic Trends:
1. A sharp decline in fixed-rate mortgage rates prompts your customers to refinance their adjustable-rate mortgages into fixed-rate loans. This refinancing boom alters your loan portfolio and decreases your production of new adjustable mortgages.

Legislative and Regulatory Trends:
2. The Fed authorizes bank holding companies to underwrite and distribute corporate securities.

Technological Trends:
3. The automated clearing house in your market creates the technology to transact pre-authorized payments and to accept payroll checks electronically.

Financial Innovations:
4. Investment bankers working with mortgage-related government sponsored enterprises create collateralized mortgage obligations which make fixed-rate mortgages more popular even though your firm is committed to adjustable-rate mortgages.

Market Growth and Trends:
5. Mutual funds attract a large and growing amount of funds from your institution's savings and time deposits. Mutual fund management and distribution companies are also offering bank-type credit cards and other financial services.

Competitive Trends:
6. Your strongest local market competitor fails.

owners intend it to be? What are its basic values and philosophies? What are its lasting goals? Where is the firm today relative to those goals? What are its strategic advantages and competitive weaknesses in achieving these goals? There are many ways to answer these big-picture questions within a strategic plan. The complexity of the plan depends on the intricacy of the organization and its long-term goals.

Although strategic planning is not universally supported, it is still necessary for organizations to give some definition to its long-run product and service package, target customer base, and techniques for successfully reaching the target customer. Shareholders and directors want to have some understanding about the expected returns and risks related to the company's strategy. These people can't assess these returns and risks if the company's strategic plan reads vaguely, "to compete successfully in the financial services industry." This statement is too general. What functions will the firm perform? Who will be the target customers? What competitive techniques will be used to give the firm a competitive advantage? This broad strategy doesn't answer any of those questions.

For established firms, developing a strategic plan typically involves an accurate appraisal of past performance, the reasons for its successes and failures, as well as a realistic forecast of future performance. General Electric Credit Corporation has emphasized its financial strength and risk assessment and management skills to compete successfully. This large and diversified finance company likes to acquire large asset portfolios from other intermediaries where there are few, if any, other bidding organizations. Being the only bidder gives the seller few choices and puts GECC is a strong bargaining position.[1] For new firms, developing a strategy usually requires extensive economic and market analysis identifying domestic and global market needs and financial opportunities, and some evidence to support how the firm's founders intend it to meet these needs. The founders of a new bank need to supply ample evidence that the market they plan to serve is either underserved now or will be shortly due to excellent growth prospects. Both prospective shareholders and regulators responsible for granting a charter want to see evidence of market need and future success for the new venture. The process typically involves several steps:

1. Assess the current economic and regulatory environment, business opportunities, technological and market or government barriers. This is the job of senior management, who must stay attuned to the most sweeping changes affecting the business.

2. Assess the current situation within the existing company, its strengths and weaknesses against its competitors. The firm's financial manager should be most attuned to the firm's financial performance and operating strengths and weaknesses.

3. Identify those opportunities that the firm can reasonably exploit and those it should either avoid or watch closely for future planning. Those closest to the customers should be in the best position to assess customer needs and business. The front-line employees talk to customers every day.

4. Develop the strategic statement of direction that summarizes product lines, markets, and operations. Senior management must now synthesize this information and analyze it to create a useful strategic plan.

---

[1]In economics, a single buyer is known as *monopsony*.

ASSESSING THE EXTERNAL ENVIRONMENT

For new and established firms alike, assessing the external environment is a key step forward in the strategic planning process. This assessment usually involves broad to narrow analysis of trends: a careful study of global economic trends, current and expected legislative and regulatory trends in the key financial centers of the world, technological trends, effects of the competition's recent financial innovations, market growth trends and potential, and the competitive environment. The changes identified in Exhibit 9.3 will be restated in this section along with a discussion of how some successful firms actually responded to the changes presented.

Economic Trends

International, domestic, regional, and local economic trends all influence the potential profitability of financial institutions. For example, if the World Bank releases a study forecasting that a certain country will soon enter a period of "tight money," meaning that fewer funds will be available to lend under restrictive monetary policies, then financial firms should rethink plans to launch a new loan product. Areas such as Denver in the early 1980s and most other large urban centers by the late 1980s, suffering from overbuilding, can face up to ten years or more of declining property values and low construction.

EXHIBIT 9.4

Responding to Economic Trends

Economic Trend: A sharp decline in fixed-rate mortgage rates prompts your customers to refinance their adjustable-rate mortgages into fixed-rate loans. This refinancing boom alters your loan portfolio and decreases your production of new adjustable mortgages.

Successful Response: A number of large, specialized mortgage thrifts responded to this trend using a secondary marketing and servicing strategy. To profit from the increase in demand for fixed-rate mortgages, these firms originated fixed-rate mortgages, sold them to government sponsored mortgage enterprises, and retained the servicing business.

Legislative and Regulatory Trends

Few industries are as sensitive to changes in legislation and regulation as the financial services industry is. Regulators have much to say about financial products and services provided, the markets served, the capital required, and the information disclosed. Regulation is dialectical: over long periods of time, the reach and the grasp of the regulatory hand extends and intensifies, and then retracts and relaxes. As Chapter 4 discussed, financial managers took advantage of deregulation in the early 1980s, only to adjust to reregulation in the late 1980s and early 1990s, and now anticipate movement toward deregulation through the mid-1990s into the twenty-first century. Such trends help managers to establish time frames for their strategic plans.

EXHIBIT 9.5

Responding to Legislative and Regulatory Trends

Legislative and Regulatory Trends: The Fed authorizes bank companies to underwrite and distribute corporate securities.

Successful Response: A small number of very large bank holding companies responded to this opportunity by applying to the Fed for permission to establish a bank holding company investment bank subsidiary to underwrite and distribute corporate securities. These were primarily large money center banks with many pre-established large corporate customer relationships.

Technological Trends

Available and affordable technology is a key factor in determining the types of products and services that financial firms plan to offer. Computer hardware and software innovations have significantly improved the design flexibility and efficiency in the offering of financial services. Once tied to a large mainframe computer, financial firms (like many corporations outside the financial services industry) depended upon expensive software modifications and upgrades to introduce new products or else used software provided by a service bureau. This was very evident in data processing systems used to support demand deposits accounting and processing systems. Moreover, the advent of powerful mid-sized and personal computers with fast data processing capabilities, user-friendly data analysis, and decision-making software vastly improved financial managers' efficiency and quality of planning. Consider the following management techniques and products made available due to new technology:

- Computerized credit-scoring techniques.
- Computerized customer account relationship, profitability, and cross-selling databases and analyses.
- Trading services available 24 hours a day.
- Hybrid securities to alter cash flows of existing securities.

Financial Innovations

Financial innovation can create whole new markets and make other products and services obsolete. Outside or even within the firm, financial innovation is not a purely random event. Certain conditions—especially changes in tax laws and financial regulations—lend themselves to increased innovation; and managers must anticipate these conditions, if external, or else build them into the internal environment. A more extensive discussion of innovation is provided later in this chapter.

EXHIBIT 9.6

Responding to Technological Trends

Technological Trends: The automated clearing house in your market creates the technology to transact pre-authorized payments and to accept payroll checks electronically.

Successful Response: A large number of financial depositories offering transaction account services jumped quickly to offer services to provide direct deposit of payroll checks and other periodic payments such as social security and other retirement checks as well as services to pay reoccurring bills such as mortgage payments and utility bills. These firms found that they could lock in customers more effectively by making these services available while at the same time increasing the inconvenience for these customers to change account relationships.

EXHIBIT 9.7

Responding to Financial Innovation

Financial Innovations: Investment bankers working with mortgage-related government sponsored enterprises create collateralized mortgage obligations which make fixed-rate mortgages more popular even though your firm is committed to adjustable-rate mortgages.

Successful Response: Depositories with large investments in adjustable-rate home mortgages have responded to the increased competition coming from government sponsored mortgage enterprises by pursuing two strategies. One strategy is to originate and invest in mortgages that do not meet the underwriting criteria of the government enterprises. This permits the depositories to charge a premium over the generally lower government sponsored enterprise induced mortgage rates. Another strategy emphasized jumbo mortgage loan origination and investment. These are home mortgages the dollar amount of which is too large to qualify for purchase by the government sponsored enterprises. By avoiding direct competition with the government enterprises, these firms are able to earn a higher return on the mortgages they invest in.

Market Growth and Trends

Most financial firms operate in a relatively small geographic market. The few exceptions, such as international and large regional banks, are national financial service providers. Even these firms must be attuned to local market trends in the many markets in which they do business. Consequently, managers should analyze and monitor local and regional economic trends more closely than national or global patterns. For example, in the 1950s and 1960s, many central cities like New York, Boston, Washington, D.C., and Philadelphia aged; household owners packed up and moved their belongings—and their wealth—to the suburbs. Banks and thrifts had to follow their customers or else find new business. Regional economic developments might suggest a particular business strategy. For instance, a market that experiences a sharp increase in existing home values might be ripe for a second mortgage program; and a financial institution might initiate a new program or heavily promote an existing service or product line. Conversely, a financial firm operating in a market of declining property values might want to postpone or discontinue its second mortgage line.

EXHIBIT 9.8

Responding to Market Growth and Trends

Market Growth and Trends: Mutual funds attract a large and growing amount of funds from your institution's savings and time deposits. Mutual fund management and distribution companies are also offering bank-type credit cards and other financial services.

Successful Response: A large number of depository holding companies established broker/dealer and insurance agency subsidiaries to offer their customers mutual funds, investment-type insurance policies, and securities. Although set up primarily as a defensive measure, these subsidiaries provided profitable products to be offered as an alternative for customers seeking investments to replace maturing certificates of deposit.

Competitive Trends

The nature and intensity of competition are crucial variables in the external environment. Competitors affect pricing, risk, and, therefore, actual and potential profitability of each product and service offered. As with the airline industry, deregulation of financial services, combined with financial innovation, has intensified competition between depository and nondepository firms. Each financial intermediary has faced new competitors on what was once its home turf. The competitive analysis determines whether a firm or its competition has special advantages that could allow it to exploit and eventually dominate the market. Nondepository firms, for example, have a lesser regulatory burden, lower costs of compliance, and less-stringent capital and disclosure requirements. However, depositories have access to insured deposits as a sources of funds.

EXHIBIT 9.9

Responding to Competitive Trends

Competitive Trends: Your strongest local market competitor fails.

Successful Response: In recent years, many depository institutions responded to failures by aggressively expanding market share or moving into new markets. Buying branch offices of weak or failed institutions operating in a market in which a surviving firm had a respectable market share enabled many institutions to obtain a commanding market share. Branch systems of weak and failed institutions also provided a great opportunity for stronger firms to expand into new markets without the high cost of opening a new office and building market share from scratch.

ASSESSING THE CURRENT SITUATION WITHIN THE FIRM

The firm's self-assessment may be one of the most difficult aspects of strategic planning. Every organization likes to believe that what it does, it does very well, that its systems are most efficient, its managers are true leaders in the industry, and its employees among the most productive and highly paid. Obviously, this cannot be true for the thousands of financial firms. Some ultimately fail and others disappoint their shareholders and customers alike.

A good place to begin assessing the current position of the firm is to describe the firm's functions using the financial function/matrix discussed in Chapter 2. A matrix for assets and liabilities for the hypothetical Wilson County Bank is shown in Exhibits 9.10 and 9.11. The exhibits show an "X" for each financial claim the firm originates, services, brokers, or holds in portfolio at the present time. A "P" has been inserted for all the new financial claims and functions the firm is planning to offer in the next three years. As the exhibits indicate, Wilson County Bank is planning a major expansion. It hopes to offer origination, servicing, and investment capabilities for income-property mortgages and leases on the asset side of the balance sheet and FHLB borrowings, repos, negotiable certificates of deposit and asset-backed security capabilities on the liability side of the balance sheet. Only brokerage between third parties is shown.

The assessment of the current situation calls for a good, hard, and extremely candid look in the mirror. It requires a review of the firm's financial position, operating, and capital resources; product lines and services; operational strengths and weaknesses against the competition; customer satisfaction; and managerial talents and shortcomings. All of these are discussed below.

Financial Position and Resources

Chapter 8 explained some analytical techniques for conducting a review of the firm's financial situation, the most important of which are measures of capital re-

EXHIBIT 9.10

Wilson County Bank Financial Claim/Function Matrix for Assets

Type of Claim	Origination	Servicing	Brokerage	Portfolio Management
Government:				
United States			X	X
Agency				X
State and municipal				X
Business:				
Income-property mortgages	P	P		P
Leases	P	P		P
Loans	X	X		X
Household:				
Installment	X	X		X
Credit card				
Residential mortgages	X	X	X	X

sources, profitability, and risk. This review helps managers to isolate the strong from the weak links in the firm's current operating plan and to estimate whether existing capital will be adequate to fund new activities.

The assessment involves a financial review. Table 9.1 provides several financial ratios for Wilson Country Bank and its peer group.[2]

The financial comparisons in Table 9.1 indicate that Wilson County Bank is performing below par. Its profitability is well below the peer group. The reasons appear to be lack of investment capability and low noninterest income.

Products and Services

The firm must assess the profitability of its current product line, claim by claim. Distinguishing the fruitless products and services from successful ones not only helps managers to identify their vulnerabilities and areas of firm expertise but also guides them in exploring new markets or developing new products. It is not at all uncommon for financial institutions to add to their product and service mix to meet actual and perceived competitive threats and customer needs. Many of these products and services remain as part of the product offering of these institutions even though demand waned or new products have been developed. A review of these products with an eye toward eliminating those that cannot be effectively supported is an important aspect of the planning process.

---

[2]Chapter 8 provides a discussion of the ratios discussed here.

EXHIBIT 9.11

Wilson County Bank Financial Claim/Function Matrix for Liabilities

Type of Claim	Origination	Servicing	Brokerage	Portfolio Management
Transaction accounts:				
Demand deposits	X	X		X
NOW accounts	X	X		X
Money market demand accounts	X	X		X
Time and savings deposits:				
Passbook accounts	X	X		X
Certificates of deposit	X	X		X
Capital market funding sources:				
Collateralized debt				
FHLB advances	P	P		P
Repos	P	P		P
Asset-backed securities	P	P		P
Unsecured debt				
Negotiable CDs	P	P		P
Bankers' acceptances				

Operational Strengths and Weaknesses

Financial firms depend on computer hardware and software to deliver their products and services successfully. The quality and reliability of these information processing capabilities significantly affect product quality, design, cost, servicing, and customer satisfaction. An assessment of the firm's operational capabilities is extremely important in an overall assessment of strengths and weaknesses.

Customer Evaluation of the Firm's Products

As any marketing manager or sales representative knows, today's consumers are savvy enough at both household and corporate levels to recognize that they have a choice among products, services, and companies. Rivalry is fierce. To keep on top of customer needs and ahead of the competition, many businesses poll their customers regularly. To survive, financial firms should do the same; and managers should plan to obtain independent customer feedback on the firm's strengths and weaknesses. Usually, the marketing professionals gather these data through telephone and mail surveys, focus group discussions, questionnaires, and other techniques or hire an independent market research firm for the job.

TABLE 9.1

Comparison of Financial Ratios for Wilson County Bank and Peer Group December 31, 1995

Ratio	Wilson County Bank	Peer Group	Assessment of Wilson Performance
Net interest margin	3.45%	4.12%	Lower than peer group due to limited lending opportunities in local market
Noninterest income to average assets	0.56%	1.23%	Very low noninterest income. Firm provides few services and charges low fees
Noninterest expenses to average assets	2.67%	3.15%	Low expenses due to limited product line and few fee-generating services
Loan loss provisions to average assets	0.18%	0.98%	Low losses due to low level of risk assets
Return on average assets	0.34%	0.97%	Very low due to limited lending and low noninterest income sources

Human Resource Capabilities

Any strategic plan for a firm in such a service-driven industry would be grossly incomplete without reference to the required human resources to implement the plan successfully. Job assessments and employee appraisals that focus on knowledge, experience, skills, and potential all help to identify personnel hiring, training, or downsizing needs—all of which require funding. Managers may find such assessments especially helpful when designing new positions for areas of asset growth or transformation.

Generally, if a financial firm is serving its market efficiently and profiting by a particular product or service, customers—and shareholders—will speak up. Of course, the converse is true. Managers should consider the feedback on these activities as guides for learning from or building upon the firm's strengths and improving upon or else cutting its loss-makers. In the financial services industry nowadays, firms that spread themselves too thinly, perhaps promising more than they know how to deliver efficiently, may quickly find themselves in financial distress and under close regulatory eye. The financial landscape is replete with failed depository institutions that created commercial real estate lending departments in the 1980s, only to find they had inexperienced personnel to assess risk and insufficient assets to properly diversify the risk they took on.

THE STRATEGIC STATEMENT

The strategic statement is simply a formal written description of a firm's long-term vision. It captures the firm's answer to the questions posed earlier: Why does this financial organization exist? Whose interests does it serve? What does it hope to achieve, and how? Generally, such a statement affirms the company's product, market, and operational goals. There is no formula: these statements can come in many lengths, forms, and structures, so long as they effectively communicate the broad mission of the firm to its employees, shareholders, creditors, consumers, regulators, competitors, and other constituents in the community at large.

A small neighborhood commercial bank like our hypothetical Wilson County Bank might develop a strategic plan consisting of only the few short statements found in Exhibit 9.12.

EXHIBIT 9.12

Strategic Plan for Wilson County Bank

> The mission of Wilson County Bank is to achieve above industry average profitability by providing financial services to consumers and businesses within Northwest Wilson County. Our primary competitive strategy will be to provide the most basic competitively priced financial services with a competitively higher level of customer service. Both household and small business customers will be able to differentiate our bank by its high level of service and the strong support we provide in delivering our quality products and services.

Despite its brevity, Exhibit 9.12 actually says a lot about this bank. It clarifies the firm's financial goal of higher-than-industry profitability, which industry indexes will help to measure. It defines the bank's geographic market, Northwest Wilson County, specifically serving household consumers and local proprietors. It explains its product strategy of staying with basic products and its marketing strategy of noticeably bolstering its customer service, priced near the competition, with strong product support.

✓ Checkpoints

9-4 What can managers learn from and accomplish through the strategic planning process?

9-5 Why do managers analyze both external and internal situations, conduct financial analyses, and prepare a strategic statement?

Operating and Financial Planning

Once the firm has developed its strategic plan—an overall vision of the company—it can focus on devising operating and financial plans. The operating and financial plans further specify the objectives a firm must accomplish toward fulfilling the firm's vision, or at least making significant progress to that end, for a stated period of time. Operating plans establish the firm's nonfinancial objec-

EXAMPLES OF STRATEGIC STATEMENTS

Occasionally, annual reports of public companies include statements that serve as strategic statements. Below are excerpts from three actual firms: Norwest Corporation, a large midwest-based bank holding company with over $50 billion in assets and offices throughout the United States and Canada; Charles Schwab Corporation, the nation's largest discount brokerage firm; and Dean Witter, Discover & Co., a nationwide broker/dealer and issuer of the proprietary Discover credit card.

NORWEST CORPORATION*

We seek to:
- Create an environment in which diversity is valued, teamwork is emphasized and where employees care and are committed to doing their best while having fun.
- Promote the long term success of our customers and communities.
- Be our customer's first choice for service and solutions.
- Create stockholder value through strong, consistent growth in our businesses and their profitability.
- Be the best in financial services.

THE CHARLES SCHWAB CORPORATION†

Schwab's focus has been, and will continue to be, on serving the needs of investors by providing high-quality, low-cost brokerage and other financial services. I believe that as financial information becomes more widely distributed, more individuals will conclude that they can do a better job of meeting their financial needs if they take personal control of their investment decisions.

Based on this belief, our Company will continue to invest in expanding the range of our products and services, increasing the size and capabilities of our branch network and computer systems, and improving the quality of our service to our customers.

DEAN WITTER DISCOVER & CO.‡

Strategic Focus

All Dean Witter, Discover & Co. credit services and securities activities are focused on the nationwide marketing and delivery of quality products and services primarily to the individual consumer. The company's strategic approach to both businesses emphasizes a low cost structure and innovative products and services that deliver value to our customers.

*Source: *Norwest Corporation Annual Report 1992*, Norwest Corporation, 1993, inside front cover.

†Source: *The Charles Schwab Corporation 1992 Annual Report*, The Charles Schwab Corporation, 1993, Statement of Charles Schwab, inside front cover.

‡Source: *Dean Witter Discover & Co. 1992 Corporate Profile*, Dean Witter Discover & Co, 1993, p. 4.

How it Really Works

tives, related to products and services, operations, technologies and systems, human resources, and plant and equipment. The financial plan, which must complement the operating plan, maps out the financial objectives in a set of pro forma financial statements, to be measured by specified ratios such as capital adequacy ratios, profitability targets, market share goals, and market indicators such as stock price. Actual financial statements and reports filed with regulatory agencies will provide documentation of achievement. Financial and operating plans are usually the responsibility of senior management. They represent the condensation of the top-down and bottom-up planning process.

OPERATING PLAN

The operating plan should support the strategic plan. It establishes broad objectives that, if accomplished successfully, will bring the firm one step closer to achieving its long-term strategic vision. Senior management and board members usually set the primary objectives in the operating plan and then invite heads of operating departments to recommend how their units might be able to carry out these objectives or otherwise contribute to the strategic plan. The larger and more complex the organization, the more active the departments will be in the process. Extremely large regional and international organizations must necessarily delegate the planning responsibilities to the operating departments and subsidiaries. The biggest problem for large corporations is providing standardized approaches to comparing investment projects across corporate boundaries.[3] With an initial list of objectives, managers can move forward to estimate, through the pro forma balance sheet, amounts of financial operating resources needed to tackle the list. Some firms approach this process from the top down; that is, senior management ultimately sets the goals and scales back the unrealistic or self-serving contributions of its staff. Other firms manage from the bottom up, by starting with what the customers want, asking their staff how to meet customer needs, and then harmonizing these ideas with shareholder expectations.

Again, the business of intermediation is to facilitate market efficiency; managers and regulators can use the operating plan to assess the operational effectiveness of the firm, to diagnose maladies in the system, and to prescribe effective treatment. Management might use comparative data from peer groups or, if the firm is a commercial bank or thrift, data such as the Federal Reserve Board's Functional Cost Analysis to assess the operational efficiency and cost structure of its product areas. Functional cost data are collected annually by the Fed, covering approximately 600 banks. These reports provide a breakdown of cost allocations for various products and services produced by the commercial banks in the sample.[4]

---

[3]The customary approach to comparing projects throughout the company is to use net present value or internal rate of return criteria. These criteria can be used just as effectively for financial firms.

[4]There is considerable debate over whether functional cost data are representative of the wide range of different-sized banks. A fairly small number of surveyed banks are large banks which may provide underrepresentation. There is also a continuing argument of the definition of the correct output of a bank. The discussion in Chapter 2 suggests that the functions of financial institutions should be categorized into origination, servicing, brokerage, and portfolio management. This is not done in the functional cost data, which may be a limitation.

FINANCIAL PLAN

Developed simultaneously with the operating plan, the financial plan covers three areas:

1. An operating expense budget that itemizes staffing and other expenses to be monitored and controlled.
2. A forecast of origination or underwriting, servicing, brokerage, and portfolio management activities in terms of revenues, costs, equity investment, staffing, and other resources.
3. A profit plan that incorporates the assumptions of the operating plan and simulates pro forma income statements.

As in corporate finance, most financial organizations develop an annual operating budget under the assumption that most activities will continue—that by and large the firm is an ongoing entity. Periodically, the firm adjusts this annual budget to reflect growth, new and discontinued products, and any other changes occurring over the previous period.

Exhibit 9.13 show some operating objectives of Wilson County Bank.

EXHIBIT 9.13

Selective Operating Objectives of Wilson County Bank

- Develop a credit overdraft program for our checking accounts and implement by July 1.
- Open a new branch near Highway 65 and River Road.
- Reduce length of customer lines during lunch hour in branches to less than a five-minute waiting time.
- Solicit homeowners in Northwest Wilson County for second mortgages.
- Develop a program to sell at least $30 million of first mortgages to government sponsored enterprises.

CONTROL

The operating and financial plans, once completed, represent the primary control device of the firm for tracking actual performance throughout the period. By continually comparing actual to expected performance throughout the year, managers can make midcourse adjustments. This flexibility is critical if some economic, technological, regulatory, or market condition changes occur without warning or anticipation. However, plans that are too vague or too easily revised are impossible to use as control tools. In order to be useful for control, these reports must hold individuals accountable.

These plans also allow firms to establish performance guidelines in the form of:

- *Operating efficiency standards,* such as servicing a set number of loans per staff member in a given amount of time.
- *Marketing standards,* such as setting a minimum market share for certain products, given a market size estimate.
- *Pricing standards,* such as holding the commission price level to a lower third of competition.
- *Customer service standards,* such as answering telephone calls before three rings 99% of the time.

Sometimes major plan revisions are necessary. Predicting interest rates is a task fraught with danger. And since the demand for many financial institution loan and investment products is affected by interest rate levels, a forecast error can result in unreasonable goals. Changes in exogenous factors such as interest rates may provide justification to modify control targets and individual appraisal targets.

✓ Checkpoints

9-6 What elements would you expect to find in an operating plan, and whose input would you expect to see?

9-7 In what three ways might you use a financial plan?

9-8 How might the operating and financial plans help you control your firm's activities and manage your employees more effectively?

Action Plans

The next level of planning—**action planning**—specifies activities that must be performed to accomplish the firm's operating and financial plans and assigns responsibility for performing them. Well-developed action plans are specific, create accountability, establish deadlines or budgets when appropriate, and usually motivate achievement with some type of incentive. They specify what, why, who, by when, and for how much: What is the task? Why is it important? Which business unit, department, team, or person will do it? What is the deadline for or the cost of completion? Planning without knowing what, why, who, when, and at what cost is a futile exercise. The action plans truly determine whether the operating and financial plans are realistic or merely wishful.

For a great sense of ownership and commitment to the strategic statement, operating units must contribute to the planning process by indicating what they will need in order to accomplish the established objectives. Managers should be asking their direct reports questions like: Are systems set up to perform the task? Do they have the financial and human resources necessary? Is the timing realistic? Whose cooperation do they need? Whose work will be affected by the outcome?

The action plans provide another tool for control, provided that they are specific enough in deadline or outcome of completion to determine whether they have been accomplished. If plans prove to be ineffective or inoperable, then managers must quickly ask why. Also, managers can use the major documented actions to assess employee and unit performance and to award executive compensation and employee bonuses.

The key to having staff members develop useful action plans is to provide them with an in-depth understanding of the firm's strategic plan and operating and financial goals. Without a clear understanding of these goals, action plans will be inconsistent with them or will be inconsistent with those of other units within the firm. Developing action plans also provides an excellent means to flush out overlapping organizational responsibilities. It is not at all uncommon for two individuals or organizational units to plan to address the same customer need.

Exhibit 9.14 provides a few action plans for Wilson Country Bank.

EXHIBIT 9.14

Selective Action Plans for Wilson County Bank

- Retail banking department will design and implement a checking overdraft program by May 15.
- The branch supervisor will develop a part-time teller program to reduce customer lines at lunch hour in those branches that require it by the end of March.
- The mortgage lending department will design and mail a direct-mail second mortgage piece to homeowners in Northwest Wilson County in September.

✓ Checkpoints

9-9 How do action plans differ from operating plans, and who contributes to an action plan?

9-10 How can managers use action plans to motivate and monitor employee and team performance?

Financial Innovation: Theory and Practice

By now, readers should have an excellent sense of how volatile the financial services industry has been in the last three decades and how dynamic it continues to be, in part because of exciting financial innovation. Professionals have dreamed up countless new types of financial claims, distribution systems, information processing systems, and risk management techniques, all of which can complicate—or facilitate—the planning process, depending on how savvy the firm's management is. Understanding how financial innovation affects planning and the course of one's plans calls for three basic questions:

1. Is a particular financial innovation planned or random?
2. How does it involve technology?

3.   How can a firm profit by it or anticipate it?

Which forces give rise to a financial innovation, or alternatively, is the innovation simply a product of spontaneous random behavior? Managers may logically assume that the events motivating innovative behavior can also determine which conditions are ripe for profitable innovation.

How does financial innovation relate to technological improvement? Clearly, technology improves money and capital market efficiency: information systems link financial institutions throughout the world, facilitating the flows of capital and information, improving tools for data analysis and management, and opening markets to new competitors. Increased market efficiency allows financial institutions to participate more actively in dynamic portfolio management strategies by lowering transaction costs.

How can a firm use financial innovation to its advantage? Potential managers should keep in mind that innovation means change, and change is always risky: it can diminish fortunes of established institutions and open opportunities for others. Planning must take recent and potential innovations into account. The introduction of personal computers with modem capabilities has forced many brokerage firms to develop computer-based security trading and security information services.

THEORIES OF FINANCIAL INNOVATION

There have been a number of excellent studies on the subject of financial innovation over the years. The basic premise of this research is that innovation tends to take place most frequently during periods of rapid change in technology, regulation, taxation, and price volatility. This section looks at many of the theories developed in the last several decades.

Silber's Constraint Theory of Innovation

William Silber (1975) attributes financial innovation to attempts by profit-maximizing firms to reduce the impact of various types of constraints that have the impact of reducing profitability. Silber's theory is one of the most general of the theories and is, therefore, consistent with each of the others that follow. Silber postulates that financial institutions, as profit-maximizing organizations, will attempt to innovate to increase business opportunities or reduce costs. This may involve innovation in order to circumvent constraints that restrict the operations or market opportunities of the firm. Under this theory, the old law prohibiting the thrifts from offering transaction accounts provided the incentive for them to innovate. The result was the development of negotiable order of withdrawal accounts in 1978.

Kane's Market, Technology, and Political Theory of Innovation

Edward Kane (1984) sees financial innovation as an institutional response to financial costs created by changes in technology, market needs, and the political sphere, particularly laws and regulations. Kane refers to the interactive process of regulation that follows institutional avoidance and innovation as a dialectical process. This dialectical process works in a manner similar to Kane's dialectical regulatory theory discussed in Chapter 4. Regulations create institutional responses designed to avoid the impact of regulation which, in turn, provides the seeds of a new round of regulation. Kane's contribution includes technology and market needs.

Miller's Regulation and Taxation Theory of Innovation

Merton Miller (1986) states that major innovations in the last 20 years have been almost exclusively the result of changes in tax laws and regulatory changes. He attributes the development of many new financial claims to attempts to alter the amount and timing of taxable income. He also notes that many innovations have resulted from regulatory barriers and the desire of financial firms to avoid the impact of regulatory constraints. Certainly every change in the tax law is a major event for tax lawyers, accountants, and investment bankers, who try to profit from finding profitable ways to reduce the tax burden. The 1986 Tax Reform Act virtually eliminated the tax-shelter limited partnership business.[5]

Merton's Market Efficiency Theory of Innovation

Robert Merton (1990) also provides a valuable rationale for financial innovation. His theory is based on the notion that financial innovation is motivated by forces designed to increase market efficiency and improve social welfare. Financial innovation, as it is used in this context, must provide true economic benefits.

Merton gives three motivations for producing innovation: (1) the creation of financial claims that allow for risk sharing, risk pooling, and hedging, as well as new financial structures that allow for transferring resources over time; (2) the improvement of economic efficiency and liquidity; and (3) the reduction of agency costs. The last is a result of unequal information between two parties to a transaction and imperfect information about a firm's performance and prospects. Like Silber's, Merton's theory of market efficiency is very general. Security innovations such as asset-backed bonds have been used for risk sharing and pooling.

TECHNOLOGY AND FINANCIAL INNOVATION

Technological advances in information processing have created many obvious innovations in the financial services business. Since financial institutions are information processing companies, they have been impacted more than many other types of business by technological progress in data processing and telecommunication. The following are some of the more important innovations prompted by technology.

Automated Tellers and Home Banking/Brokerage

The advent of inexpensive computers has made it possible to deliver financial transactions and information services to many new locations, including the

---

[5]Prior to the Tax Reform Act of 1986, limited partnerships investing in real estate, oil and gas exploration, and energy savings equipment such as windmills and solar cells were popular among high marginal tax investors who could write off investment tax credits and accelerated depreciation against wage and salary income. This spawned the creation of thousands of limited partnerships for these types of investments. Among other things, the 1986 act eliminated the ability of investors to write off the losses against wage and salary income.

CENTRUST SAVINGS BANK: PATENTS ON FINANCIAL PRODUCTS

How

it

Really

Works

Innovation in the financial services business has been routine during the last 20 years. New hybrid and derivative financial products have been developed that have sometimes created great profits for the innovating firm. However, as many innovators have found out, their innovation lasts about as long as it takes for the ink to dry on the newly issued prospectus. A successful new product is quickly replicated by a multitude of competitors. Until the case of *College Savings Bank* (plaintiff) *vs. Centrust Savings Bank* (defendant), it was unheard of for the innovator of a financial product to protect itself with a patent by applying the concept of "intellectual property."

In 1988, College Savings Bank applied for several patents on a CollegeSure Certificate of Deposit. The CollegeSure CD is an adjustable-rate CD that pays interest tied to an index of college costs. College claimed that Centrust infringed on the idea. The suit was settled with the agreement that Centrust would pay license fees for using certain features of the CollegeSure CD. A number of years earlier, Merrill Lynch & Company won a settlement concerning its innovative CMA account, an account that consolidated security transactions and holdings with a transaction account and credit card. Merrill's legal action against several competing firms offering similar products eventually led to Merrill receiving license fees.

The issue of whether a financial product can be patented is still unresolved. Some believe that, like computer software itself, if a financial product relies on specialized computer hardware or software, it can be protected.

home. ATMs are found in airports, shopping centers, colleges and universities, and grocery stores. Today, many of these systems are tied together into regional and national network systems. These ATM networks will permit essentially nationwide 24-hour-a-day access to information and transaction capability.

The home personal computer coupled to a modem permits access to both depository and brokerage account information. These systems also are used to provide access to a wide variety of financial information services that permit security analysis such as historical price information to permit price charting.

Consolidated Statements

The ability to merge information from a number of data files and the increased speed and reduced costs of mainframe computers have led to the development of consolidated statement accounts. These accounts bring together financial information on credit, security, and transaction accounts into one statement. The Merrill Lynch "Cash Management Account" was one of the first and most popular of the consolidated statements.[6]

---

[6]The cash management account allows customers to place securities, money market funds, credit cards, check-writing capability, and other assets is a single account which provides a single combined statement. Most other large, full-service broker/dealers have been providing similar accounts for many years.

Improved data processing and communication technology have impacted all financial institutions. Some institutions, particularly depositories, have found that the technologically driven lower costs of performing transactions have greatly increased competition among firms in providing the demand deposit and other transaction services.

Technology has also greatly expanded the geographic boundaries serviced by financial institutions. Customers no longer have to be near the financial institution they do business with. Mortgage servicing firms now service mortgage loans nationwide, for example.

REGULATION AND FINANCIAL INNOVATION

Probably the single most important stimulant to financial innovation in the last several decades has been financial regulation. The structure of our financial system remained relatively unchanged from the Depression until the mid-1960s. That system was a product of extensive legislation passed in the 1930s. As the economy began to experience the inflation of the 1960s, increased interest rate volatility combined with technology to trigger major financial innovation. This volatility provided the impetus for financial institutions to find ways to reduce the adverse impact of the many controls and restrictions built into our 1930s financial structure.

The recent move to higher capital requirements for depositories has been the impetus for significant innovation in changing the credit risk characteristics of financial claims. One example of this type of financial engineering involves recent developments in the creation of new asset-backed securities.

New Collateralized Securities

One new claim initially created to avoid the imposition of capital requirements was the senior-subordinated security. The rationale behind these securities was to permit a financial institution to use the assets on its books as collateral for a multirisk class of securities. During the 1980s, this structure was used to create billions of dollars of mortgage securities on both home mortgages and apartment mortgages sold to institutional investors. Subsequently, the regulators tightened up on capital requirements for these subordinated securities.

The creation of these credit risk partitioned securities and the regulatory response to them is a excellent example of Kane's dialectical theory of financial innovation. First a new regulation is issued, constituting the higher capital requirement. This causes the innovative response, such as the senior-subordinated security. The regulator then realizes that the new capital regulation has been circumvented and is forced to modify the regulation to bring about its desired goal.

Money Market Mutual Funds

Although taken for granted today, the money market mutual fund was not a significant competitor to depositories until the mid-1970s, when market interest rates rose to levels far above the interest rates that federal regulators permitted banks and thrifts to pay on deposits. The Regulation Q interest rate ceilings imposed on depositories at that time provided the impetus for this innovation.

Negotiable Orders of Withdrawal

The negotiable order of withdrawal (NOW) account was the innovation of a state-chartered savings bank in New England. Like the money market mutual fund, the NOW account innovation was stimulated by commercial banks not paying interest on demand deposits and thrifts not offering demand deposit services.

Foreign Currency Futures

The growth in foreign trade and the increased volatility in exchange rates created the climate for a formal market in foreign exchange futures. Prior to the establishment of this new market, only large money center banks handled foreign exchange transactions.

Interest Rate Swaps

Interest rate volatility also played an important role in stimulating the development of the interest rate swap market. Here, financial institutions and other firms alter their exposure to changing interest rates by agreeing to pay the other institution's interest rate obligation on a specified amount of debt. Interest rate swaps were given a major boost by the regulators of thrift institutions. In the early 1980s, these regulators wanted thrifts to reduce their interest rate risk. One quick way to do that was by using an interest rate swap.

Collateralized Mortgage Obligations

Collateralized mortgage obligations (CMOs) are securities collateralized by mortgages or mortgage pass-through securities. These securities partition the cash flows from the underlying mortgages. Because fixed-rate mortgages have long maturities and prepayment uncertainty, many investors are not interested in these securities. CMOs create a series of securities that appeal to particular investors, such as S&Ls, that require shorter-term assets to meet regulatory requirements.

In addition to regulation, CMO development requires significant computer simulation. These simulations required advances in computer technology, which occurred at a rapid rate in the 1980s.

TAXES AND FINANCIAL INNOVATION

Changes in the tax law have always been a major stimulant of financial innovation. Financial products such as those created by real estate investment trusts, limited partnerships, real estate mortgage investment conduits, and mutual funds are the result of specific sections of the tax code. The mortgage pass-through security is also a creature of the tax code that created a tax entity called a **grantor trust,** and more recently, the **real estate mortgage investment conduit.** The growth of the single premium life insurance policy in recent years is the result of the favorable tax treatment it obtains under the tax code.

Zero-Coupon Bonds

One of the early stimulants to the growth of **zero-coupon bonds** was the tax law in Japan. In the early 1980s, many American companies and federal agencies created zero-coupon bonds to be sold in Japan, since the Japanese at the time gave these bonds favorable tax treatment.

Tax-Exempt Revenue Bonds

Ambiguity in the federal tax law regarding what is an appropriate use of funds from a tax-exempt state or municipal bond became the stimulant for considerable innovation in state and municipal finance in the 1970s and 1980s. Many government units created tax-exempt bonds, collateralized by mortgages on factories, shopping centers, and homes, for borrowers who never had the benefit of being financed at tax-free interest rates. The tax law was subsequently changed in the early 1980s to restrict the use of tax-exempt financing for the benefit of private-sector households and businesses. This was another example of a dialectical process.

NEW PRODUCTS AND INNOVATION

Probably the simplest innovations to consider relate to new products. Each new product—be it a computer, recreational vehicle, or newest imported auto—must establish its collateral value for a loan market to develop. Many times the manufacturer or distributor becomes the first organization to extend credit, when the collateral has no established secondary market and resale value cannot be readily established. Innovative lenders, however, will consider these new products and for a sufficient reward will extend credit on them.

✓ Checkpoints

9-11 How do Silber, Kane, Miller, and Merton differ in their theories on financial innovation? Can you distinguish these theories by providing examples?

9-12 How might a change in the federal tax law motivate financial innovation? Can you cite a few recent cases?

9-13 How might a change in a financial regulation stimulate financial innovation? Again, what instances have you seen lately?

SUMMARY AND REVIEW

1. **Describe the overall planning process, including reasons for, and timing of, the process.**

   The planning process consists of a hierarchy with a strategic plan on top, operating and financial plans in between, and specific action plans on the bottom. The planning process is management's responsibility and typically involves staff throughout the organization. Operating and financial plans usually are performed on an annual cycle. However, major events within and external to the firm should affect the planning cycle.

2. **Distinguish among financial firms' strategic plans, operating and financial plans, and action plans.**

Strategic planning normally results in the development of a strategic statement or long-term vision for the firm. Operating and financial plans consist of achievable objectives which can be accomplished within the timeframe of the plan. These plans provide a near-term road map for the firm as well as a control devise. The action plan is a detailed set of activities that spells out what, who, and when for each action item. These plans provide a detailed blueprint for what is to happen.

3. **Discuss the strategic planning process, including the purpose of external and internal situation analyses and the strategic statement.**

The strategic planning process includes an internal review of where the firm stands today, including its strengths and weaknesses. It also includes a major review of the external environment, including competition, the legislative and regulatory situation, technological trends, and economic trends and innovations. These analyses serve to shape the opportunities and obstacles facing the firm. This analysis provides a framework for the development of the strategic statement, which normally provides the firm's overall product and service, market, customer, and operating philosophies.

4. **Explain how financial firms prepare and use operating and financial plans, and identify who provides input into these plans and who implements them.**

Operating and financial plans are developed simultaneously as a means of specifying the near-term objectives to be accomplished by the firm during the planning period. The operating plan typically involves objectives concerning products and services, markets, and operational issues. The associated financial plan provides the pro forma income statement, balance sheet, and financial ratios that are contemplated by successful accomplishment of the operating plan. These are used to guide the firm and provide a means of control by measuring actual results against the pro forma objectives.

5. **Explain how financial firms devise and use action plans, and identify who contributes feedback and who carries them out.**

Action plans are prepared with primary input from the operating units. The initial objectives spelled out in the operating plan must be considered in terms of achievability, resource requirements, coordination needs, and timing. The operating units can provide this input and produce a specific list of action items spelling out what, who, and when. These plans are used to establish accountability and provide input into incentive compensation and employee performance review programs used by many firms.

6. **Provide current examples of the theories of financial innovation.**

The primary theories of financial innovation suggest that it is fostered by changes in operating constraints such as regulation, taxation, technology, and opportunities to improve market efficiency. Innovation is a very important aspect of the planning process. Financial innovations can result in some products becoming obsolete. Alternatively, new products are able to create opportunities for new firms.

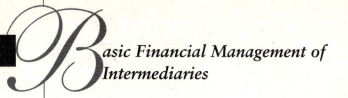

CHAPTER 10

Basic Financial Management of Intermediaries

Learning Goals

After studying this chapter, you should be able to:

1. List the primary financial management duties of managers of financial institutions.
2. Explain how to determine the optimal capital structure for a financial intermediary and define financial and business risks.
3. Describe and define the sources of financial institution revenue and expenses.
4. Describe some of the possible objectives of mutual institutions other than maximizing long-term profits.

Financial intermediaries generate revenue from their portfolio management, servicing, origination, and brokerage activities. Each intermediary selects from the financial claim/function matrix the functions it wants to perform and endeavors to profit from these activities. This chapter reviews the basic principles of financial management for financial intermediaries.

Although certain portions of this chapter are relevant to a firm with insured deposits, most of the issues relate to all intermediaries. Thus, references are made to depositories, issuers of government-insured liabilities, and the all-inclusive intermediaries. The chapter also provides a section on the objectives of mutual financial institutions.

Primary Financial Management Duties

The duties and responsibilities of managers of financial institutions now require greater sophistication and training than before, when liquidity management duties were more important. In today's secular profit squeeze, the declining spread between yield on assets and cost of liabilities, rising interest rate risk related to a substantial increase in asset price volatility, and the profit squeeze related to deregulation and increased competition have combined to complicate management duties.

These changes have necessitated an upgrading of the financial tools used in the field. Several of the more important financial duties and responsibilities include:

1. Valuation of financial claims.
2. Measurement and management of credit and interest rate risk.
3. Pricing of loans and liabilities.
4. Determining the optimal capital structure.

VALUATION OF FINANCIAL CLAIMS

As you might expect, financial firm managers must be able to value the financial claims that they originate, service, broker, and manage in their portfolios. The primary valuation tools rely upon (1) present value theory and (2) options pricing theory, which prerequisite courses in finance covered. Chapters 15 and 16 of this book review these theories in the context of the financial intermediary. The job of the financial analyst is to determine the attributes of the financial claim, to develop a cash flow statement for it, and then to identify any embedded options. The financial firm manager uses present value techniques and options pricing models for managing interest rate risk, trading loans and securities, and designing and pricing new types of loans and liabilities.

CREDIT RISK MANAGEMENT

Directed by a credit officer, the firm's credit unit manages the firm's exposure to *credit risk*, the probability of loss of interest and principal on a financial firm's debt assets. Typically independent of the asset origination or servicing groups, the credit unit may report indirectly to the board of directors to ensure an independent and impartial analysis of the credit situation. Overall business plans for the firm specify how this group manages the credit function; planning includes creating policies and procedures for underwriting loans in the origination units, analyzing the financial position of guarantors and issuers of securities held by the firm, creating policies and procedures for servicing assets, monitoring the credit experience of the institution's asset portfolios, and participating in the establishment of proper loan loss reserves. Readers who are interested in careers within credit operations should pay special attention to the strategies, tools, and techniques detailed in Chapters 11 and 12. Exhibit 10.1 depicts the roles of a typical credit office.

BROKER OBTAINS LARGE BID-ASK SPREAD

The need to know the true value of financial assets was evident in the case of Commerce Savings Association of San Antonio, Texas. In 1987, it purchased $45 million in three issues of mortgage securities from Kidder, Peabody Group, Inc., a large investment banking firm. Commerce must not have known their true value. According to a legal challenge, Kidder had sold one issue to Commerce for $28.3 million which it had purchased earlier in the day from another institution for $22 million. The profit markup of 29% exceeded the regulatory guidelines which restrict such profit markups to 5%.

Ultimately the thrift failed and the Resolution Trust Corporation, which took it over, received $3.7 million from Kidder in a lawsuit settlement. Somehow the management at Commerce did not know enough about the value of their proposed purchase to avoid overpaying by $6.3 million. That's a major valuation error!

Source: "Kidder Bond Traders Came under Fire Well before Jett," *The Wall Street Journal*, May 6, 1994, pp. C1.

*L*EGAL *and* *E*THICAL ISSUES

To accomplish credit management duties and responsibilities, the firm must understand financial analysis, servicing, loan documentation, loan covenants, and environmental analysis. It must also maintain sound records on the credit performance of its portfolios of risky assets, because any changes in underwriting, product design, servicing effectiveness, and laws and regulations can significantly alter its loan loss experience.

EXHIBIT 10.1
Functions of Credit Office

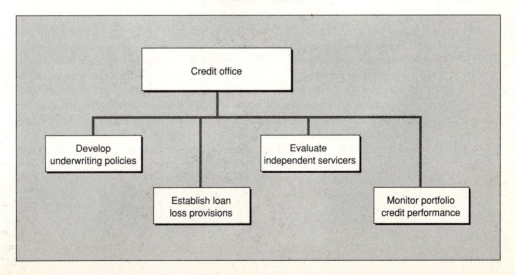

INTEREST RATE RISK MANAGEMENT

The portfolio management unit usually assumes the responsibilities for managing *interest rate risk,* the potential effects of fluctuation in market interest rates on a firm's asset and liability values and income stream. In many financial depository institutions, a group such as an *asset/liability committee* (ALCO) usually prices assets and liabilities, develops the optimum asset and liability structures, manages the interest rate risk of the firm, and oversees the management of liquidity. Exhibit 10.2 shows the roles of a typical ALCO.

EXHIBIT 10.2

Functions of Asset/Liability Committee

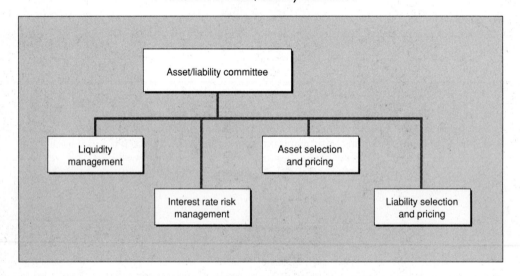

Managing interest rate risk, a sophisticated task with all the new risk management tools available, necessarily involves using mathematical models to capture the complexity of today's financial claims. Readers who are interested in risk management positions within a financial intermediary should pay attention to coverage of these risk management models—periodic GAP, duration, mark-to-market, and income simulation—in Chapter 17. Risk managers use each of these tools to measure the exposure of the financial intermediary to the effects on the firm's equity and income resulting from changes in open market interest rates.

Altering the financial institution's interest rate risk position necessarily involves a risk/return tradeoff. Reducing the interest rate position of the firm will almost always lower the earnings of the firm in the short run. Risk managers must develop a strategy that provides acceptable earnings to the firm's shareholders without risking potential insolvency or creating unacceptable volatility in the income stream of the institution.

PRICING LOANS AND LIABILITIES AND SELECTING DISTRIBUTION CHANNELS

The portfolio management group determines the profitability of loans and investments by identifying the lowest-cost funding alternatives and, at the same time, targeting potential asset acquisitions that would provide expected returns equaling or exceeding the intermediary's cost of capital. The ALCO may also assume some responsibility for these duties, the subject of Chapters 20 through 22. Whether a loan stays in the portfolio or goes to the secondary market, the firm must know to price it in the context of all the firm's costs, including debt, capital, servicing, origination, and credit.

To reduce transaction costs, financial firms also seek the least costly distribution channel for their products. Retail-based firms develop a franchise value related to their ability to market new products or cross-sell existing customers. Existing customers are normally less price-sensitive compared to the wholesale market or to potential new customers. Thus, the firm must develop new profit measurement tools to maximize the value of its retail franchise. Chapter 24 describes distribution issues further.

Pricing also requires the firm to evaluate the cost of selling its liabilities using a variety of different distribution channels. Is it more cost effective, for example, for a bank to raise funds with six-month maturities through its retail branches, negotiable certificates of deposits, or brokered deposits? The answer will change over time as competitive pressures in local markets change.

✓ Checkpoints

10-1 What activities do intermediaries perform to make a profit?

10-2 What are the primary financial duties of management in intermediaries?

10-3 Who manages credit risk, and what does the job require?

10-4 Who manages interest rate risk, and what does the job entail?

Capital Structure and Financial Leverage

A primary issue for any business is determining its **optimal capital structure.** This is no less important an issue for financial intermediaries. However, the job is made more complicated for intermediaries that are subject to minimum capital requirements.

One obvious difference between financial depositories and commercial and industrial businesses is the financial firm's high degree of **financial leverage,** the extent to which it uses debt in its capital structure. Financial leverage is measured by the firm's debt, D, to total assets, A, ratio D/A. Financial depository intermediaries usually have debt that consists of 90–95% of its capital structure. Other financial firms also typically have higher degrees of financial leverage than commercial and industrial firms.

A depository's ability to issue government-insured deposits has significant implications for its use of financial leverage. These firms are able to utilize financial leverage to a much greater extent than other businesses. Indeed, as we will see, the depository has a tremendous temptation to leverage itself. Consequently, a government regulator's requirement to hold capital may be a necessary, but not sufficient, constraint to control the excessive leveraging of insured depository institutions.

A financial firm's optimal capital structure can be thought of as a function of several business-risk variables over which management has control. The firm's management probably would pursue a lower level of financial leverage:

1. The greater its use of wholesale funding sources.
2. The greater its use of uninsured and uncollateralized funds sources.
3. The higher its asset portfolio credit risk.
4. The higher its portfolio interest rate risk.
5. The lower its diversification of asset portfolio risk.

A simple way to see how financial leverage works is to compute a financial firm's equity multiplier *(EM)*. The firm's *EM* is computed by dividing the firm's total assets by its net worth *(NW)*. The *EM*, like the *D/A*, is a measure of financial leverage. A financial firm with $250,000,000 in assets and $15,000,000 in equity would have an equity multiplier of

$$EM = \$250,000,000/\$15,000,000 = 16.67$$

There is a mathematical relationship between the financial firm's **return on assets *(ROA)*,** net income divided by total assets, and its **return on equity, *(ROE)*,** net income divided by total net worth. This relationship is expressed as

$$ROE = ROA \times EM$$

Return on equity = Return on assets $\times$ Equity multiplier

Achieving both a high *ROE* and low *EM* is difficult, because financial leverage tends to improve the return on equity. For financial firms, especially insured depositories, the cost of debt is significantly less than the cost of equity. Therefore, managers may be tempted to increase *ROE* by increasing *EM*. Of course, a higher *EM* also implies greater financial risk.

FINANCIAL LEVERAGE

As a firm replaces debt for equity, its financial risk increases. As financial risk increases, the direct and indirect costs of debt go up. The tendency for creditors of the financial firm to impose greater costs on the firm that uses a higher percentage of debt in its financial structure relates back to agency problems in the form of *agency costs,* monitoring and surveillance, restrictive covenants in loan agreements, and higher interest rates on loans. A highly leveraged firm also has a higher probability of experiencing bankruptcy which creates distress costs. Distress costs are estimated as the present value of the costs of bankruptcy times the probability of bankruptcy; and distress costs also increase, everything else constant, with the rise in financial leverage.

The tendency of distress and agency costs to increase debt costs is short circuited when the firm can issue government-insured deposits. In this case, the buyer of the deposits is more concerned about the government's commitment to insure the obligations of the deposit funds than the viability of the individual firm that issues the deposits. The tendency for depositors to be unconcerned about the strength of the institution in which they have their money is known as *moral hazard*. Because depository firms do not face significantly higher debt costs and other agency costs as financial leverage increases, they have a strong incentive to replace shareholder capital with government guaranteed debt.

The extent to which financial depositories leverage themselves also depends on whether they use uninsured or uncollateralized borrowings, such as commercial paper, large negotiable certificates of deposit, or Fed funds liabilities. The more uninsured debt in the capital structure, the more monitoring by private investors and the higher the agency costs. In other words, the uninsured investor does not present the same moral hazard problem as the insured depositor.

The other constraint on leverage is the government regulatory system. Government regulators can increase agency costs of the firm. They do this by putting limits on the holdings of risky assets by intermediaries and by limiting the extent of financial leverage through the establishment of minimum capital requirements. For a financial firm with inadequate capital, the government can impose a host of restrictions on growth, lending, asset composition, and mergers and acquisitions that have a direct bearing on the business's future financial performance. This represents significant financial agency costs.

In 1989 and 1991, the passage of FIRREA and the FDICIA gave depository regulators sharply expanded supervisory powers to deal with institutions deemed undercapitalized. The FDICIA actually prescribed a list of **prompt corrective actions** that regulators must take against financial institutions with capital levels below the higher classification. These include the power to carry out the following actions.

1. Require shrinkage of assets.
2. Prohibit lending.
3. Implement conservatorship.
4. Eliminate specific lending and investment activities.
5. Force a merger.
6. Change the composition of management or directors.

Exhibit 10.3 describes the very difficult job of finding the optimal capital structure for a firm. It applies equally well to an insured depository as it does to a manufacturing firm. The graph has the market value of the firm's equity, V, on the vertical axis and the debt-to-asset ratio, D/A, the horizontal axis. The line $Ve-V$, without regulatory agency costs, shows that if the management of a financial

EXHIBIT 10.3

Optimal Capital Structure for an Intermediary

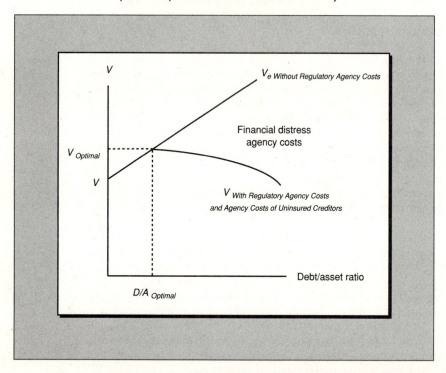

firm wants to maximize the equity value of the firm it will continue to replace equity with debt until it has virtually no equity in its capital structure. Two strong motivations for doing this are the tax deductibility of interest on debt and the low cost of deposits raised with the help of deposit insurance. In fact, the firm is motivated to continue to replace equity with debt until one of two events occurs. In the first event, the regulator will intervene and require more equity by establishing minimum capital requirements and threatening adverse regulatory sanctions, one form of agency costs. The second possible event would be for private investors in the firms using uninsured liabilities to demand higher interest rates and additional costly debt covenants, other forms of agency costs.

In addition, as financial leverage increases, the probability of bankruptcy increases. Distress costs also motivate management to limit the degree of financial leverage. Considering Exhibit 10.3, the firm will be motivated to increase its D/A ratio by moving along the upward sloping line until sufficient agency and distress costs cause it to bend down. The highest point, $V_{optimal,}$ is where the optimal D/A for the firm is found and where the firm experiences its lowest weighted average cost of capital.

In practice, both higher agency and distress costs occur as D/A increases. Were it not for these two costs, we would expect that insured financial intermediaries would leverage almost to the point of replacing all their capital with debt. Indeed, one can easily argue that between 1981 and 1988, the FHLBB allowed savings and loans to do just that, since many had no tangible net worth. Without a strictly enforced capital constraint, the institutions kept increasing their asset base with insured deposits without facing either agency monitoring costs from depositors or their regulator.

It is easy to see why this is the case if we look at Exhibit 10.4. This graph shows the cost of equity and insured deposits (debt) to an insured depository that is not subject to a capital constraint by its regulator. On the vertical axis is the cost of equity and debt. On the horizontal axis is the firm's *D/A* ratio. Because the insured firm does not face meaningful agency and distress costs that increase the cost of raising deposits, the firm can lower its weighted cost of capital as its *D/A* ratio increases. This is true even though the higher financial risk of the firm increases its equity cost. The lack of significant agency costs results in only very slowly rising debt costs. As a result, the weighted average cost of capital keeps falling as the *D/A* ratio increases. A lower weighted average cost of capital permits the firm to increase profits by increasing its size and taking on more investments whose yields exceed the firm's weighted cost of capital.

EXHIBIT 10.4

Cost of Equity, Debt, and Weighted Cost of Capital

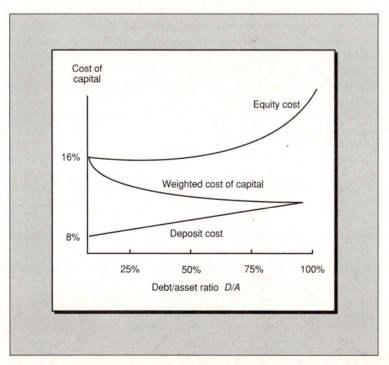

DEPOSITORY CAPITAL REQUIREMENTS

The tendency for government-insured depositories to accept excessive financial leverage puts considerable pressure on regulators to enforce minimum capital requirements that reduce the probability of failure. In the United States, commercial banks and thrifts are subject to essentially equivalent capital requirements. Over the last decade, capital requirements have been changing in response to the large number of thrift and commercial bank failures. Commercial banks have been subject to a capital requirement based on their leverage ratio, LR. A bank's LR is a simple aggregate measure of capital computed by dividing the firm's core capital defined as common and perpetual preferred stock equity and certain equity accounts of consolidated subsidiaries and shown in Equation 10.1:

$$LR = Core\ capital_t \div Total\ assets_t \qquad [10.1]$$

Under this definition the firm is well capitalized if $LR \geq 5\%$, adequately capitalized if $5\% \geq LR \geq 4\%$, undercapitalized if $4\% \geq LR \geq 3\%$, significantly undercapitalized if $3\% \geq LR \geq 2\%$, and critically undercapitalized if $2\% \geq LR$.

Since January 1, 1993, the commercial bank and thrift regulators have focused on a system of capital requirements based on the riskiness of the firm's assets. An additional capital requirement used by commercial bank, savings bank, and savings and loan regulators is known as **risk-based capital requirements**. The Federal Reserve of New York and the Federal Reserve Board in the 1950s employed such a system, which was called the ABC formulas. Over time, the formulas became very complex and the system fell into disuse, being replaced in the 1960s and 1970s by the CAMEL ratings. CAMEL stands for capital, assets, management, earnings, and liquidity and is used by the Fed, FDIC, Comptroller of the Currency, and National Credit Union Administration.[1] This approach to examination and supervision is still in use today. It is important since the risk-based capital requirements are tied to the CAMEL ratings in a few instances. The highest CAMEL rating is 1 and the lowest is 5. Only about 20% of all the commercial banks in the nation receive the highest rating. The CAMEL rating is a regulatory rating system and does not necessarily conform to shareholder objectives.

The reasons for the latest effort to develop a risk-based system include:

- A simple capital to asset ratio, or its reciprocal, the equity multiplier EM, was not sensitive to the broadening of on- and off-balance sheet risk exposures.
- Overall capital to assets ratios were declining for the banking system in the 1970s and 1980s.
- Regulators wanted to provide consistency with the international risk-based Basel systems.
- There was concern over the deregulation of deposit rates on bank costs and profitability.

---

[1]The Office of Thrift Supervision used a similar system called *MACRO*.

- Bank activities expanded into new, more risky activities, including securities and real estate development.

- Banks were allowed to include loss reserves as capital, which may have diminished the value of the capital account.

The risk-based system establishes minimal capital levels based on the types of assets held by the firm, its off-balance-sheet risks and counterparty risk related to off-balance-sheet derivative contracts.[2] Under the initial risk-based system developed under the auspices of the Bank for International Settlements and known as the **Basel Agreement,** capital is measured in two ways, Tier I capital, called *core capital,* and Tier II capital, called *supplemental capital.* Table 10.1 defines the eligible capital sources under these two definitions.

T A B L E   1 0 . 1

Eligible Sources of Tier I and Tier II Capital

Capital Definition	Acceptable Sources
Tier I (core capital)	
	Common stock tangible equity*
	Perpetual preferred stock and qualified (25% Tier I ≥), mandatory convertible debt
	Minority interest in equity of consolidated subsidiaries
Tier II (Supplemental capital)	
	Nonspecific loan loss reserves up to 1.25% of risk-adjusted assets
	Perpetual preferred and mandatory convertible debt not included in Tier I capital
	Long-term subordinated debt (must be ≤ Tier I capital, and it phases down in last five years of maturity)
	Nonperpetual preferred stock (treated as long-term subordinated debt)

*Tangible equity is total equity less good-will.

The risk-based capital requirement is a two-part evaluation based on the percentage of the firm's total Tier I plus Tier II capital to total weighted risk assets and the other based on Tier I capital. Risk weighted assets are discussed fully in Chapter 21. They include on-balance sheet financial assets, off-balance sheet con-

---

[2]The risk-based system also recognizes risk of counterparty noncompliance to off-balance sheet futures, options, forward, swaps, caps, and other derivatives involving financial assets and currencies. This counterparty risk is discussed in Chapter 18. Regulators have developed a set of conversion factors to determine loss exposure based on the notional principal involved in the contracts. The system of risk-based capital discussed here was fully implemented on January 1, 1993. The risk-based system also includes interest rate risk. This regulation was not finalized at this time. However, a discussion of it in proposed form is included in Chapter 18.

tingent and guarantee contracts, and off-balance sheet derivative futures, options, and swap contracts. Under this system, the total risk-based capital ratio is defined by Equation 10.2 and the Tier I capital ratio by Equation 10.3. Under this requirement, the *total risk-based capital ratio* must be ≥ 8% and the *core capital ratio* ≥ 4%.

$$Total\ risk\text{-}based\ capital\ ratio =$$

$$(Tier\ I + Tier\ II)_t \div Risk\text{-}adjusted\ assets_t \qquad [10.2]$$

$$Core\ (Tier\ I)\ capital\ ratio = Tier\ I_t \div Risk\text{-}adjusted\ assets_t \qquad [10.3]$$

The risk-based capital standard involves the establishment of a risk weight for each asset on the balance sheet, a conversion factor for all off-balance sheet risk positions, and a minimum capital requirement, currently 8%. The risk weights determine the percentage of the minimum capital requirement that must be held against the book value of particular assets. A single family mortgage with a risk weight of 50% would be required to have a capital reserve of (50% × 8% =) 4%. The total capital requirement for the institution is determined by calculating the capital required under the standard for all on- and off-balance sheet assets and risk exposures and adding them up. Off-balance sheet risk exposures include, but are not limited to, the following:

1. Credit guarantees.
2. Standby letters of credit.
3. Forward currency transactions.
4. Interest rate and currency swaps.
5. Unused loan commitments over one year.
6. Assets sold with recourse.
7. Forward commitments to purchase assets.

INTERNATIONAL ◙ FOCUS

BASEL COMMITTEE RESPONDS TO NEW BANK RISKS

The Basel committee is a group of central bank regulators from the world's richest nations. In 1988, the committee developed a set of risk-based capital standards for commercial banks involved in international banking. These standards, which were fully implemented in 1992, focus primarily on the credit quality of commercial bank assets and tend to ignore several other important risks.

The committee in 1992 went to work on two other risks, interest rate risk and trading, or positioning, risk. Interest rate risks, discussed in Chapter 17, relate to the potential that sharp changes in interest rates will reduce the value of bank assets more than liabilities, while positioning risk deals with unhedged commitments to buy and sell foreign currencies and securities. The Basel group is concerned that the rapid growth in commercial bank trading is not being addressed by the capital standards.

An illustration of the proposed risk-based risk weights for a sampling of assets for commercial banks and thrifts regulated by the OTS is shown in Table 10.2. These regulatory-based capital standards provide the minimum capital requirements for a depository. They establish the maximum leverage of the firm's equity, based on the regulator's estimates of an asset's riskiness.

TABLE 10.2

Risk-Based Capital Requirement Risk Weights for Commercial Banks and Thrifts Regulated by the Office of Thrift Supervision

Investment Type	Risk Weight
Banks	
Category 1:	
Cash	
U.S. Treasury securities	
U.S. agency securities (full faith and credit-backed) including GNMA-backed mortgage securities	0%
Category 2:	
U.S. government sponsored agency securities (not full faith and credit) including FNMA-, FHLMC-backed mortgage securities; CMOs backed by GNMA, FNMA, or FHLMC collateral (other than residual or stripped securities)	
State and municipal general obligation bonds	
Claims collateralized by U.S. Treasury agency and government sponsored agency securities	20%
Category 3:	
One- to four-family residential mortgage loans meeting typical secondary market tests	
CMOs backed by qualifying residential mortgages (other than residuals or stripped securities)	
State and municipal revenue bonds	50%
Category 4:	
All other assets not specifically covered elsewhere, including multifamily residential mortgages, other income property loans, unsecured commercial loans, and Third-World debt	100%
Off-balance Sheet exposures:	
Unused portion of loan commitments with less than one year original maturity and unconditionally cancellable loan commitments	0%
Commercial letters of credit and self-liquidating, trade related contingencies	20%
Transaction-related contingencies such as letters of credit backing nonfinancial performance, unused loan commitments, and revolving underwriting facilities, note issuance facilities, etc.	50%
Direct credit substitutes such as standby letters of credit and loans sold on recourse	100%

continued

Table 10.2, continued

Investment Type	Risk Weight
Thrifts	
Category 1:	
Cash and Federal Reserve Bank balances	
U.S. Treasury securities	
U.S. agency securities (excluding GNMA-backed mortgage securities)	0%
Category 2:	
GNMA-, FNMA-, and FHLMC-backed mortgage securities and collateralized CMOs	
All secondary mortgage market (SMMEA)-qualified "mortgage related" securities, including IOs and POs except residuals	
State and municipal general obligations	
Claims collateralized by the U.S. Treasury and government sponsored enterprises	20%
Category 3:	
One- to four-family residential mortgages	
Non-SMMEA mortgage-related securities backed by qualified residential mortgages	
State and municipal revenue bonds	50%
Category 4:	
All assets not specifically covered elsewhere including residential construction loans, multifamily residential loans, income property loans, and other secured or unsecured loans	100%
Category 5:	
Goodwill and other intangibles	
Category 6:	
Real estate acquired by foreclosure	200%
Equity securities	
Real estate held for development	
Investment in subsidiaries	
Category 7:	
High loan-to-value ratio and nonresidential construction loans	300%

DEMONSTRATION PROBLEM

CALCULATING A DEPOSITORY'S MINIMUM RISK-BASED CAPITAL REQUIREMENT

Situation

Windmill State Bank's December 31, 1996 balance sheet of financial assets is shown in Table 10.3. It also has $5 million in standby letters of credit outstanding and $2 million of loans sold with recourse. You have been asked to determine its risk-based reserve requirement.

TABLE 10.3

Windmill State Bank Balance Sheet of Financial Assets
December 31, 1996
(dollars in millions)

Asset Classification	Amount
Cash and Fed balances	$ 5
U.S. Treasury securities	15
State and municipal general obligation bonds	5
One-to-four family first mortgages	60
Consumer loans	15
Commercial and industrial loans	32
Total financial assets	$132

Result

Using the data in Table 10.3 for each of the on- and off-balance sheet items in Windmill State Bank Table 10.4 is produced showing the risk-based capital requirement for each on- and off-balance sheet risk category.

TABLE 10.4

Risk-based Capital Requirement for Windmill State Bank
December 31, 1996

Asset Classification	Amount	Regulatory Reserve Requirement	Risk Weight	Regulatory Reserve Requirement
Cash and Fed balances	$ 5,000,000	8%	0%	$ 0
U.S. Treasury securities	15,000,000	8	0	0
State and municipal general obligation bonds	5,000,000	8	20	80,000
One- to four family first mortgages	60,000,000	8	50	2,400,000
Consumer loans	15,000,000	8	100	1,200,000
Commercial and industrial loans	32,000,000	8	100	2,560,000
Total financial assets	$132,000,000			6,240,000
Standby letters of credit	5,000,000	8	100	400,000
Loans sold with recourse	2,000,000	8	100	160,000
Total on- and off-balance-sheet	$139,000,000			$6,800,000

Windmill's risk-based capital requirement is shown to be $6,800,000.

To understand fully the system of capital requirements, it is necessary to combine them with a group of regulatory provisions passed in the FDICIA in which Congress specified a set of prompt corrective actions the regulators must take against depositories deemed to have inadequate capital. Table 10.5 is a effort to summarize each of the reserve requirements and the most important prompt corrective actions called for in each capital classification.

TABLE 10.5

Capital Categories under the Prompt Corrective Action System

Capital category	Total (Tier I and Tier II) Risk-based Ratio	Core (Tier I) Risk-based Ratio	Leverage Ratio	Summary of Selective Restrictive Actions
Well capitalized	≥10%	≥6%	≥5%	None
Adequately capitalized	≥8%	≥4%	≥4%*	Requires approval to offer brokered deposits
Undercapitalized	<8%	<4%	<4%*	Asset growth restrictions; capital plan; approval for branching, new activities
Significantly undercapitalized	<6%	<3%	<3%	All the above; restrictions on compensation, interest on deposits, and affiliate transactions
Critically undercapitalized			<2%	All the above; restrict interest on debt; placed in receivership in 90 days

*May be 1% lower for CAMEL highest-rated institutions.

Source: Federal Reserve Board of Governors.

Although we have been discussing depository institutions in this section, we could just as easily have been referring to other intermediaries. Insurance companies must meet capital requirements imposed by state insurance commissions. Investment bankers must meet minimum capital requirements imposed by the Securities and Exchange Commission. Finance companies, on the other hand, finance their operations with privately issued debt. The investors in finance company debt impose very real agency costs on these institutions since they realize that there is no deposit insurance corporation to cover losses in the event of financial distress.

HOW FINANCIAL INSTITUTIONS RESPOND TO CAPITAL REQUIREMENTS

Regulatorily set capital requirements are only effective if they act to reduce the probability of bankruptcy. However, any set of regulatory requirements is bound to lead to perverse responses by the regulated industry. As discussed in Chapter 4, if the result of the requirements is to restrict the profit opportunities of the regulated industry, then the industry can be expected to be creative in getting around the requirements so it can avail itself of profitable opportunities. Some ways in which a capital-regulated industry can be expected to lessen the adverse impact of the requirements include the following:

Reallocate Portfolio to Assets Improperly Risk-weighted

Some financial firms wishing to increase reported income will seek out assets that are actually riskier than suggested by the arbitrary risk weights selected by the regulators. While residential mortgages have a risk weight of 50%, it is possible to invest in mortgages on higher-risk high-valued property or to high-risk borrowers and earn higher yields. Similarly, a portfolio of commercial and industrial loans to high-risk borrowers can earn a higher yield with no greater capital.

Reallocate Portfolio to Reduce Capital Requirements

It is possible to perform certain "window dressing" transactions to achieve a lower required capital requirement to coincide with the measurement of the capital requirements.

Ignore Risk-reducing Diversification Opportunities

Financial intermediaries must reduce credit risk by holding large enough portfolios to take advantage of diversification opportunities, especially for potentially high-risk assets such as corporate and commercial real estate loans. The fact that these loans are given high risk weight may cause firms to hold a lower quantity of these loans than is optimal for diversification.

Increase Operating Cost Risk

In recent years many regulated depositories have pursued noninterest income generating activities which involve sometimes large investments in information processing capital investments and large staffs of people, resulting in increased operating cost risks for these firms. Since the risk-based capital requirements ignore operating cost risk, depositories can be expected to focus on these noninterest income sources even at the expense of increasing overall business risk. A small commercial bank, for example, could employ hundreds or even thousands of people in a large mortgage origination and servicing operation and still be subject to very low risk-based capital requirements.

RELATIVE CAPITAL POSITIONS OF THE MAJOR FINANCIAL INSTITUTIONS

Deposit insurance has a profound impact on the ability of these financial firms to leverage their capital base. The presence of deposit insurance effectively eliminates agency costs imposed by creditors purchasing insured deposits. As a result, the minimum capitalization of deposit firms must be determined by regulators. Consider the differences in the equity-to-total-assets ratios for commercial banks, securities brokers and dealers,[3] life insurance companies,[4] property and casualty insurance companies[5] and business and personal finance companies. Table 10.6 provides data from 1980 to 1989 for publicly-traded companies and updated ratios where available through 1993.[6] These data show the commercial banks with the lowest equity-to-assets ratios and the property and casualty and securities firms with the highest. In all cases, the nondepositories have at least twice as much capital as the commercial banks. The data also show the trend toward lower capital ratios for life companies and, to a lesser degree, finance companies.

BUSINESS RISKS

The optimal capital structure is also related to the riskiness, or volatility, of the firm's income stream. Financial firms with a high degree of interest rate risk will experience larger fluctuations in income than firms that have small interest rate risk exposure. Similarly, financial firms with large portfolios of risky assets or high concentrations of assets that are not well diversified will experience larger income fluctuations.

Private investors and government regulators are concerned with these portfolio characteristics when buying debt or insuring deposits. These risks are termed

---

[3]Securities brokers and dealers have capital requirements set by the Security and Exchange Commission. The basic approach is to require these firms to calculate the market value their assets and liabilities each day. Based on this mark-to-market approach, these firms must maintain a market value of equity $\geq 2\%$ of total assets. Mark-to-market is covered in Chapter 17. The procedure used by securities broker dealers in calculating this ratio involves reducing the value of certain assets from current market value by sometimes large percentages (e.g., 40%) to reflect the potentially large market fluctuations.

[4]State regulators of life insurance companies have proposed a system of risk-based capital requirements. This system proposed by the National Association of Insurance Commissioners (NAIC) classifies risk of the life insurance business into asset risk, insurance risk (mortality risk), interest rate risk, and business risk.

[5]Property and casualty companies have capital requirements established by state insurance commissions. The most common limitation is to set a maximum ratio of insurance premiums earned as a percentage of capital. The most common maximum level is 300%. That is, a property and casualty company must limit premiums earned to three times its capital base. As discussed in Chapter 7, the investment income of property and casualty companies is its first line of defense against losses stemming from poor risk underwriting.

[6]By comparison, the capital ratio of FDIC-insured savings banks and savings and loans has increased from 5.36% in 1990 to 7.85% at year-end 1993. The chief reason for the increase is the fact that a large percentage of the industry failed and was assumed by the Resolution Trust Corporation.

TABLE 10.6

Median Equity to Total Assets Ratios*
Major Types of Publicly Traded Intermediaries
(by percentage)

Year	Large National Bank Holding Company	Securities Brokers and Dealers	Life Insurance	Property and Casualty Insurance	Business Finance Company	Personal Finance Company
1980	5.60	19.51	19.71	23.12	19.53	14.85
1981	5.67	24.49	21.06	24.20	20.42	14.71
1982	5.70	17.89	20.69	24.42	22.28	15.32
1983	5.72	28.92	19.92	23.08	20.42	14.22
1984	5.83	21.63	18.26	20.48	19.66	12.66
1985	5.94	19.94	15.44	16.85	19.16	12.34
1986	6.01	18.04	14.62	22.98	20.73	12.51
1987	6.03	23.41	13.40	21.91	17.04	14.26
1988	6.21	26.41	12.67	20.51	16.07	13.49
1989	6.27	19.69	12.37	22.29	13.76	13.30
1990	6.17†					11.82‡
1991	6.49†					11.55‡
1992	7.20†					11.98‡
1993	7.75†					11.92‡

*Data were taken from Standard & Poor's Compustat Service, Inc. Nonbank institutions with redeemable preferred stock have had the stock figures removed from their capital accounts so asset totals will be consistent.

†Source: For all commercial banks. Federal Deposit Insurance Corporation, *The FDIC Quarterly Banking Profile,* fourth quarter 1993, p. 3.

‡Source: For domestic finance companies. Board of Governors of the Federal Reserve System, *Federal Reserve Bulletin,* April 1994, p. A36.

Source: Department of the Treasury, *Modernizing the Financial System: Recommendations for Safer, More Competitive Banks,* Feb. 1991, Section II, p. II–5.

business risks. Intermediaries assume many types of business risks including the following:

1. Credit risks of the institution's asset portfolio and off-balance sheet obligations and guarantees.

2. Interest rate risk including off-balance sheet exposures.

3. Liquidity risks.

4. Funding risks related to the mix of funding sources between more-interest-rate elastic wholesale versus less-interest-rate-elastic retail funding sources.

5. Operating cost risks relating to maintaining costly origination and servicing organizations.

Because of business risks, deposit insurers and regulators must be concerned with each of these five sources of financial distress. If regulators simply established capital requirements in the form of maximum *D/A* ratios, financial firms would be motivated to take large business risks. This is because their insured deposit sources of funds are unaffected as to availability and cost by these risks. Consequently, regulators also look at these risks in their examination and supervision activities.

✓ Checkpoints

10-5 How do insured depositories differ from other financial firms with respect to agency and distress costs?

10-6 How has the FIRREA of 1989 and FDICIA of 1991 increased financial agency cost at insured intermediaries?

10-7 Explain the system of depository capital requirements including the minimum leverage ratio, total and core risk-based capital ratios, and the system of prompt corrective actions.

10-8 Why did many S&Ls essentially replace all their equity with debt in the 1980s?

Intermediary Profitability

Chapter 2 described the functional structure of intermediaries as origination, servicing, brokerage, and portfolio management. To the extent that these functions represent the primary activities of intermediaries, it would seem as though the income statement of these firms should be categorized using the same functional organization. Unfortunately, under generally accepted accounting principles, the income statements of intermediaries are not organized in this manner.

This doesn't mean, however, that a conceptual redesign of the income statement can't be developed for management control and reporting purposes using the functional breakdown from Chapter 2. This is done by unbundling the various functions of the intermediary and demonstrating how each of these functions generates its own revenues and costs. Equation 10.4 defines the intermediary's total profit.

$$\textit{Total profit before tax (TP)} = NOI + NSI + NBI + NPI \qquad [10.4]$$

where:

$$NOI = \textit{net origination income}$$

$$NSI = \textit{net servicing income}$$

$$NBI = \textit{net brokerage income}$$

$$NPI = \textit{net portfolio income}$$

NET ORIGINATION INCOME

The loan origination unit's function is to work with the investor(s) of the assets it originates to create desirable loans profitably. The origination manager must originate assets with specific risk and return parameters to meet the needs of the portfolio manager or a secondary market purchaser. The origination unit's revenue can be thought of as being derived from contractual agreements with the portfolio management function or secondary market investors. If assets can be originated at a cost lower than the agreed upon contractual fee, the difference is profit.

The origination unit also sells its underwriting and investment expertise. One example of this revenue is from the firm selling whole loans, securities, or loan participations or syndications to third-party investors at higher prices than were originated.

The unit's origination income statement will look like Equation 10.5:

$$NOI = Ro - Co \qquad\qquad [10.5]$$

where:

$Ro = \Sigma_i^n = 1\ (A_iF_i) = $ *Origination revenue for asset i times fee i for n claims originated*

$A_i = $ *Asset i represented in dollars*

$F_i = $ *Fee i represented as a percent of* A_i

$Co = $ *Costs of origination*

An example of *NOI* would be a mortgage originating unit of a commercial bank that originates \$42 million of loans in a year and receives a 1% origination fee that is determined by management as an internal transfer price. However, the fee is based on market considerations since the portfolio manager can always buy assets from the secondary market which would involve the implicit payment of an origination fee. If the unit's cost of operations were \$400,000 per year, the unit's profit would be (\$42,000,000 × .01 − \$400,000 =) \$20,000.

NET SERVICING INCOME

The servicing units also act as contract agents for the portfolio manager and any outside institutions that invest in assets serviced by it. All claims must be serviced. Consequently, the intermediary must determine who will service each claim it holds in portfolio. Servicing can be done by the firm itself or contractually by a third party. Chapter 14 discussed the fact that one factor making up the yield on a loan or investment is the cost of servicing. This servicing cost is the revenue stream to the servicing unit.

A commercial bank syndicating a commercial term loan would have to obtain a price from the servicing unit for the servicing activities it performs for outside investors. If the servicing unit is particularly efficient, it will be able to service at a price below the contract price. This creates profit for the servicing unit.

The income statement of the servicing unit is seen as Equation 10.6:

$$NSI = \Sigma_i^n = 1 \ (Rs_i - Cs_i) \tag{10.6}$$

where:

$i = Servicing \ for \ firm \ i$

$n = Number \ of \ firms \ serviced \ for$

$Rs_i = Revenue \ from \ servicing \ fees \ paid \ by \ the \ portfolio$
$\qquad and \ outside \ investors, \ i$

$Cs_i = Servicing \ costs \ for \ servicing \ for \ i$

An example would be a commercial bank that has sold loan syndications on $80 million of loans. It services the loans for a fee of 0.25% of the principal balance per annum. If it costs the servicing unit $170,000 per year in operating costs, its profit from servicing would be ($80,000,000 × 0.0025 − $170,000 =) $30,000.

NET BROKERAGE INCOME

Brokerage income from third-party brokerage is easy to measure. This revenue is simply the difference between what the brokerage function is able to obtain as a commission, defined to be the difference between the price received by the seller, and the price paid by the buyer.

The broker's income statement would look like Equation 10.7:

$$NBI = Rb - Cb \tag{10.7}$$

where:

$Rb = \Sigma_i^n = 1 \ (Ps_i - Pb_i)$

$n = Number \ of \ brokerage \ transactions$

$Pb_i = Price \ of \ claim \ i \ bought \ from \ a \ third \ party$

$Ps_i = Price \ of \ claim \ i \ sold \ to \ a \ third \ party$

$Cb = Cost \ of \ operating \ the \ brokerage \ unit$

An example would be a discount security brokerage that sells 10,000,000 shares of stock per year at an average commission rate of .30 per share. If this firm had a cost of $2,900,000 per annum, its profit would be (10,000,000 × $.30 − $2,900,000 =) $100,000.

NET PORTFOLIO INCOME

Portfolio income is measured solely on the performance of the portfolio in terms of net interest margin on loans and securities held in portfolio and the gain or loss on loans and securities sold. The portfolio manager must manage interest rate risk, credit risk, mortality risk, and liquidity. The contribution of the portfolio manager is normally measured by the net interest margin. However, fees paid for origination, servicing, and brokerage are subtracted from the portfolio's income.

The portfolio management unit's income statement would be as shown in Equation 10.8:

$$NPI = R_p - I_p - C_p - L_a - R_o - R_s \qquad [10.8]$$

where:

R_p = *Portfolio income from interest and gain and loss on sale of assets*

I_p = *Portfolio interest paid on liabilities and cost of capital to support assets held*

C_p = *Cost of portfolio management services*

L_a = *Loan losses*

R_o = *Fees charged by origination unit for their services*

R_s = *Fees charged by servicing unit for their services*

An example would be a savings bank with interest income and gain on sale of securities of $120,000,000 in 1993. Its interest costs are $115,000,000 per annum. The firm pays its own or an unrelated origination unit 1.5% of the loans that are put in the firm's portfolio. In 1993, $30,000,000 were originated for the portfolio. The servicing unit services $90,000,000 of loans for the portfolio. It has negotiated a fee, or internal transfer price, of 0.20% of the principal dollar amount of loans serviced. The institution suffers loan losses of $65,000 during the year. The cost of operating the portfolio management unit is $234,000. This savings bank's income statement would look like Table 10.7.

A review of any intermediary's income statement would reveal that the interest margin from the portfolio and fees generated from origination, brokerage, and servicing are all major components. The revenues and costs shown here are accounted for differently under GAAP because in most intermediaries the functions are integrated for accounting purposes. Most firms do not have the system designed to measure the appropriate data. More firms are developing this ability, however. Consequently, this conceptual framework is important for developing management information and incentive systems.

| TABLE 10.7 |

Savings Bank Income Statement

Interest income (R_p)	$120,000,000
Interest expense (I_p)	115,000,000
Net interest margin	$ 5,000,000
Loan loss provisions (L_a)	65,000
Net interest margin after loan loss provision	$ 4,935,000
Expenses of portfolio management unit (C_p)	−234,000
Less cost of origination (.015 × $30,000,000) (R_o)	−450,000
Cost of servicing (.002 × $90,000,000) (R_s)	−180,000
Net portfolio income (pre-tax)	$ 4,071,000

PORTFOLIO AND NONINTEREST INCOME

As we have seen, intermediaries generate income from the origination, servicing, brokerage, and portfolio management activities they engage in. These are usually classified as net interest income and noninterest income. The interest and capital gains income generated by an intermediary's portfolio after the liability costs have been subtracted is called *net interest income*. Depositories also generate noninterest income which is sometimes called *fee income*. In recent years, noninterest income has become a faster growing percentage of total income for many intermediaries. This income relates to the origination, servicing, and brokerage functions of intermediaries. Table 10.8 shows the importance of portfolio interest and noninterest income for all commercial banks in 1993, illustrating the relative importance of both interest income measured as the net interest spread (4.41%) and noninterest income to earning assets (2.37%) to the overall profitability of commercial banks (1.21% of average assets).

Because some of these firms are major participants in the nation's payment system, they generate fee income by providing demand deposit, credit card and debit card, telephone and wire transfer, and computer funds transfer services. These fee-based services are all related to the role of depositories as payment service providers. Mortgage loan servicing and student loan servicing are major sources of servicing income for loans sold to government sponsored enterprises in the secondary markets. Large depositories also syndicate large loans that are sold to other financial firms for which servicing income is earned.

Brokerage produces income through the brokerage of securities, foreign exchange, and other financial claims for individuals and institutional customers.

Intermediaries also generate fee income from their origination and portfolio management activities. Examples of these are loan modification fees, appraisal fees, letters of credit, and document preparation fees.

TABLE 10.8

Income and Expenses of Commercial Banks, 1993
(as a percent of earning and average assets)*

Interest income (taxable equivalent)	7.75%[†]
Interest expense	3.34[†]
Net interest spread	4.41[†]
Noninterest income	2.37[†]
Loss provision	.80[‡]
Noninterest expenses	4.41[†]
Before tax income	1.33[§]
Tax	.36[§]
Net Income	1.21%[‖]

*The FDIC reports these data as percents of earning assets, average assets, or as a percent of loans and leases. Therefore, these line items are not strictly comparable.

[†]percent of earning assets

[‡]percent of net loans and leases

[§]computed

[‖]percent of average assets

Source: Federal Deposit Insurance Corporation, *The FDIC Quarterly Banking Profile,* fourth quarter 1993.

FACTORS AFFECTING PORTFOLIO INCOME

Portfolio income is affected by management's decisions concerning the risk and return profile of the firm's assets measured by credit and interest rate risks, its funding strategy, and holdings of tax-exempt securities. These factors are discussed more fully below.

Credit Risk

The willingness of the institution to accept credit risk is a major factor influencing the net interest spread. Risky assets have a credit risk premium built into their yield. If properly underwritten, the loss experience will be less than the risk premium and the firm will earn a higher profit. Whether this is the case or not, the net interest spread will tend to be higher for those intermediaries that invest in riskier assets.

Nonperforming Assets

Credit risk not only affects the portfolio's current return on earning assets, it also has a delayed impact on the firm's performance in the form of nonperforming assets.[7] A financial firm that accepts high credit risk normally will have a high

---

[7]Although a financial firm's loss reserves *should* cover future losses on its assets in a mature portfolio experiencing little growth, that is rarely the case. Many credit risks are related to the economy's business cycle or regional cycles. They cannot be anticipated by management even in a mature portfolio that is not growing.

net interest spread. However, it will also tend to have a higher percentage of non-performing assets. These are assets that no longer accrue interest income because of their delinquent status. Such firms may experience the apparent anomaly of a relative high net interest spread and a relatively low net interest margin.

Interest Rate Risk

The interest rate risk position of the intermediary will also influence the net interest spread. The acceptance of higher interest rate risk does not necessarily mean a higher net interest spread, however. An intermediary holding long-term, fixed-rate assets funded with short-term, floating-rate liabilities experiences a higher net interest spread when the term structure of interest rates is upward sloping and a lower net interest spread when the term structure is flat or downward sloping.

For many decades, the thrift industry profited by taking large interest rate risks by investing in fixed-rate mortgages with short-term liabilities. During the 1950s and most of the 1960s, this turned out to be profitable, since the term structure was generally upward sloping. The reverse occurred in the early 1980s.

Funding Sources

The retail deposits of financial depositories usually cost less than the whole-sale funding sources of these firms. Deposits attracted from retail customers may pay a lower interest rate, but there are hidden servicing costs, such as the cost of providing convenience through costly branches and other services. However, these operating costs do not influence the net interest spread. Consequently, depositories that rely more on retail funds will typically experience a higher net interest spread.

Another funding factor that impacts the net interest spread is the percentage of lower interest cost transaction accounts the depository has in its liability structure. A depository with a high percentage of demand deposits and other low-interest-paying transaction accounts to total liabilities will, if everything else is unchanged, have a lower interest cost. Again, as in the case of the retail deposits, a high percentage of demand deposits may produce a higher net interest spread. However, because of the higher cost of servicing transaction accounts, the full cost of these liabilities will not be reflected in the net interest spread.

Tax-Exempt Securities

Some depositories hold large investments in tax-exempt securities. These are held by institutions with high taxable income and high marginal tax rates. If a depository holds tax-exempt securities, it will appear to have a lower net interest spread due to the lower interest return on these assets. In order to compare these firms with others that do not hold tax-exempt securities, it is customary to use the taxable equivalent yield on the tax-exempt bonds in determining the net interest spread. The result is referred to as the taxable equivalent net interest spread.

✓ Checkpoints

10-9 What are the sources of income and expenses of intermediaries?

10-10 How can the sources of income and expenses of intermediaries be quantitatively defined? Why don't intermediaries report their income and expenses according to these formulas?

10-11 What are the business risks of an intermediary?

10-12 What factors impact on an intermediary's portfolio income?

10-13 Financial firms that hold tax-exempt securities as investments cannot directly compare the yield on their assets to firms that hold no tax-exempt securities. What should be done to allow such comparisons?

Objectives of Mutual Institutions

Many savings and loans, insurance companies, savings banks, and all credit unions are mutual institutions. They are owned by their members, which may include depositors, borrowers, and policyowners. Over the years, researchers have explored the question of whether mutual institutions behave similarly to stock-owned institutions or whether they seem to be responsive to objectives other than profit maximization. These differences are important when comparing the financial performance of stock and mutual institutions and when trying to understand their decision-making framework. Some researchers have concluded that a number of objectives may be more important to mutual institutions than to stock-owned institutions.

GROWTH

Some researchers maintain that profit is not the primary objective of a mutual, insisting instead that maximizing the satisfaction of as many customers as possible is their objective. The assumption is that a potential customer who is not satisfied will not become a client. The objectives of mutual institutions would then be to maximize satisfaction by maximizing growth in assets or in number of customers. Put simply, maximizing growth will maximize satisfaction.

MANAGEMENT INCOME

There is another reason to consider growth in assets to be a major objective of mutual institutions. This relates to the often-observed fact that the managers of mutual institutions tend to be compensated based on the size of the institution they manage, providing a major motivation for mutuals to become larger.

MANAGEMENT'S NONPECUNIARY REWARDS

The mutual savings and loan business was jokingly characterized in the 1960s and 1970s as the 3, 6, 3 business. This means that the savings and loan would borrow at 3%, lend at 6%, and the senior management would be on the golf course at 3 p.m. *Nonpecuniary* means nonmonetary. Less job stress and more leisure time would be the objective of management here. The point is that the mutual institution has less incentive to be a profit-maximizing firm when a lower level of performance is acceptable. Some have held that the expenses of mutual institutions also tend to be higher since mutual managers have less reason to produce profits for shareholders. These firms may have a tendency to provide higher management and employee perks than profit-maximizing firms.

How

it

Really

Works

CONVERTING FROM MUTUAL TO STOCK FORM OF ORGANIZATION

The primary limitation of the mutual form of organization is the inability to raise additional capital. This limitation has resulted in the development of several methods of conversion of mutual institutions into stock form. The most popular is used by mutual savings and loans and savings banks. Under a complicated formula, these firms may sell newly issued common stock to existing depositors, management, and the general public. The depositors are given a preemptive right to purchase the stock in relation to their deposits as of a specified date. Stock not all subscribed by the depositors can then be purchased by management and the public through a public offering.

One interesting aspect of the conversion is that the new stockholders are putting all the new capital in the firm and are also receiving the value of the existing capital base. Critics have argued that this is too good a deal for the new stockholders. Regulators in 1994 began to concern themselves that corporate insiders were purchasing a large percentage of the stock of converting institutions at low prices. They denied several conversion plans on the basis that the appraised value of the proposed stock sales price was inadequate.

Despite the closer scrutiny by regulators, conversions of mutual savings banks and savings and loans have occurred frequently. In 1993, 111 institutions were converted; As of April 22, 44 institutions had been converted in 1994.

Source: Steven Lipin, "FDIC Bars Plan for Conversion by Mutual Bank," *The Wall Street Journal*, May 6, 1994, p. A2.

RISK MINIMIZATION

Others feel that risk minimization is a strong objective of mutual institutions, as compared to stock-owned companies. Since the management and board of directors or trustees of mutual institutions are not rewarded based on profits and return on equity, they have less incentive to take potentially profitable business risks. Risk of failure is of greater concern because failure means loss of employment. Taking risks that result in higher returns does not benefit the mutual management group as much as those operating stock institutions. This one-sided aspect of the risk-return tradeoff for mutual managers could make them more risk averse.

MEETING THE COMPETITION

Some believe that market competition will influence how mutual institutions behave. Mutual institutions do not operate in a vacuum; rather, they are influenced by competitors who are frequently stock-owned institutions. Consequently, when competition is strong, mutuals are forced by competitive market forces to behave more like stock institutions. Since stock institutions impact pricing, marketing, and the cost of inputs such as employees, mutual institutions have to emulate stock companies to survive.

CONTROL

Many believe that one advantage of mutual firms is that the board of directors and senior management maintain control of the organization. When depositors open accounts in mutual savings and loans, they typically sign proxies that name a person close to the existing board and management to vote at the firm's annual meeting. Many state-chartered savings banks have self-perpetuating boards of trustees that name their own successors. Mutual life companies also have essentially self-perpetuating boards. These practices create effective control by the group currently in authority. With control comes the ability to set salaries and other benefits for the management and board. Such effective control also stifles criticism from the outside.

There are important differences in the motivation and behavior of the management and directors of mutuals as compared to stock institutions. Unfortunately, motivation is not easy to quantify and measure. Nor is the number of hours management spend on the golf course easy to measure given available data. Nevertheless, it is important to consider alternative objectives of mutual institutions when evaluating them.

✓ Checkpoint

10-14 What are several objectives that might be adopted by mutual institutions?

SUMMARY AND REVIEW

1. **List the primary financial management duties of managers of financial institutions.**

   The primary duties of financial managers are **valuation** of financial claims, **interest rate risk management, credit risk management, pricing** of loans and liabilities, and determining the **optimal capital structure.**

2. **Explain how to determine the optimal capital structure for a financial intermediary and define financial and business risks.**

The optimal capital structure for an intermediary depends on the impact of **agency** and **distress** costs on the cost of debt and equity at intermediaries. Intermediaries with insured deposits face regulations that establish minimum capital levels. Regulators also influence the extent to which insured depositories can accept business risks.

Financial risk is a term that describes the increased probability of financial distress as a firm increases its debt-to-assets ratio. *Financial leverage* relates to the return on stockholders' equity in the following relationship:

$$\textit{Return on equity} = \textit{Return on assets} \times \textit{equity multiplier}$$

$$ROE = ROA \times EM$$

Financial leverage of regulated financial institutions is limited by regulatory capital requirements. Commercial banks and thrifts are subject to very complicated capital requirments including minimum **leverage ratios, total and core risk-based capital requirements,** and **prompt corrective measures** for institutions unable to meet the requirements.

Business risk relates to the extent to which a financial firm accepts risks that are unrelated to capital structure. For financial firms, these business risks include the following: (1) **credit risks** related to asset quality; (2) **interest rate risk;** (3) **liquidity risk** related to available funding sources; (4) **funding risks** related to the mix of retail and wholesale liabilities; and (5) degree of **operating leverage** relating to the operating costs of origination and servicing units.

3. **Describe and define the sources of financial institution revenue and expenses.**

The primary sources of income and expenses of financial intermediaries relate to the **origination, servicing, brokerage,** and **portfolio management** functions of these firms.

4. **Describe some of the possible objectives of mutual institutions other than maximizing long-term profits.**

Mutual financial institutions are motivated by objectives different from those of shareholder-owned institutions. Objectives that are thought to motivate mutual financial institutions include the following:

1. Growth.
2. Management income.
3. Management's nonpecuniary rewards.
4. Risk minimization.
5. Meeting the competition.
6. Maintaining management and director control.

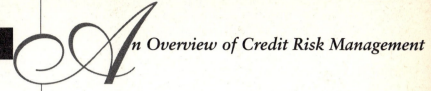

CHAPTER 11 *An Overview of Credit Risk Management*

Learning Goals

After studying this chapter, you should be able to:

1. Describe the major trends that have spurred credit losses of intermediaries over the last few decades.
2. Characterize the primary types of credit risk.
3. Explain why diversification is important in managing credit risk and how to diversify by law of large numbers and by portfolio structure.
4. Describe the primary techniques that managers use to measure and control credit risk in lending transactions.
5. Describe off-balance sheet credit risk and major sources of such risk.

What do you do when you starting losing your largest and most reliable customers? That's the question that managers at financial institutions found themselves asking each other as their most creditworthy corporate accounts learned how to go directly to the financial markets to raise and invest corporate capital. Less-solvent firms discovered the high-yield bond market. And, rather than maintain bank deposit balances, corporate and household money managers found retail and wholesale money market mutual funds to hold their idle capital. Thrifts watched the federal credit agencies gain dominance in the residential mortgage market.

Issuing credit became a riskier business. To increase returns on loan accounts, financial institutions had to bear more risk, the likelihood that borrowers would default on their loans. In response to the thrift debacle and savings and loan crisis of the 1980s, academic analysis has focused more on interest rate risks than on credit risk analysis and provided techniques for managing interest rate risk. Few methodologies exist for managing credit risk in a such a dynamic, competitive industry, and yet this skill is vital to financial firm managers today. All the more reason to study the following material carefully!

This chapter quickly reviews why credit risk has increased and will continue to do so. It then identifies the types of credit risk, explains the rationales behind loan portfolio diversification, demonstrates two techniques for diversifying such assets, identifies the primary methods for controlling credit risk, and reviews off-balance sheet sources of credit risk.

Recent Trends in Debt Market Credit Risk

Over the last few decades, the business of global intermediation has suffered from an international debt crisis, credit problems related to the thrift debacle, bank and insurance company failures, plummeting global commercial real estate markets, and losses during a highly leveraged loan and junk bond era. Loss of actual principal on which interest is paid accounts for only a portion of the total loss figure on a defaulted loan, which may include any of the following elements:

1. Accrued but uncollected interest that the borrower still owes the intermediary.
2. Transaction costs of documenting, analyzing, and restructuring the loan, and of repossessing and selling the collateral—all involving legal and managerial expenses
3. Cost of legal action.
4. Opportunity cost of the lag time from when the loan stops accruing interest to when the principal is recovered.

Since customers can recognize and take advantage of more lucrative financial opportunities, financial institutions are finding higher yielding assets, or creating altogether new markets, with much financial growth and increased activity in the following:

- Third world country lending by financial intermediaries around the world.
- Acquisition, development, and construction lending by thrifts and commercial banks.
- High-yield bonds investing by thrifts and insurance companies.
- Leveraged buyout and corporate acquisition lending and financing by commercial banks.
- Liberalized terms on consumer loans, like the five-year automobile financing, by commercial banks and finance companies.
- Limited documentation on residential real estate loans designed to reduce loan underwriting costs.
- Off-balance sheet credit exposures through interest rate and currency swaps, loan commitments, recourse sales, and asset securitization.

The tendency of financial institutions to pursue these types of transactions has increased the activities of loan workout departments in both industry and government. There's a need for finance professionals with credit risk management skills.

Students who can demonstrate mastery of credit risk analysis techniques may find themselves to be more marketable candidates for the positions of credit officer, loan underwriter, institutional credit analyst, loan servicer, and loan monitor.

✓ Checkpoints

11-1 Why did financial institutions increase their credit risk exposure in the 1970s and 1980s?

11-2 How have these institutions adapted to dynamic market conditions?

A Primer on Credit Risk

Credit risk is the possibility that the actual returns on a loan or debt investment may differ from what the lender expected, the difference of which usually constitutes a financial loss. According to Donaldson (1989), lenders face several major types of credit risk exposures: pure credit risk, underwriting risk, settlement risk, documentation risk, operating risk, event risk, and political risk. The following section quickly overviews each type.

PURE CREDIT RISK

Pure credit risk is the chance that the borrower may not live up to the terms and conditions of the loan agreement as expected, resulting in a financial loss to the lender. The amount of pure credit risk in any lending transaction depends on how the lender structures the claim, incorporating provisions for collateral, guarantees, sound documentation, covenants, and other lender safeguards to minimize such risk exposure. A borrower in financial distress may need a loan restructuring. Loan restructurings were necessary for virtually all the large commercial real estate developers of the 1980s, including the well-known Donald Trump.

UNDERWRITING RISK

Underwriting risk is the probability of loss that the loan underwriter assumes between the points of origination and sale of a financial claim in the secondary market. For example, investment bankers hold securities for their own account prior to distribution. Commercial banks lend money, only to sell a loan participation to other banks. Mortgage lenders originate mortgages to sell in the secondary market. In each instance, the claim originator accepts an element of credit risk, the possibility that the seller's claim may not meet the buyer's credit standards. Mortgage lenders that originate loans in the secondary market to sell to the government sponsored mortgage enterprises call the loans that are not acceptable due to poor underwriting *lame loans.*[1]

---

[1] A lame loan does not mean that it can never be sold. Usually, after a reasonable period in which the borrower has performed as required, the loan can be sold as a "seasoned" loan. However, the lender must finance the loan and accept both credit and interest rate risk during the seasoning period.

SETTLEMENT RISK

Settlement risk is the chance of a counterparty's unwillingness or inability to complete the transaction. For instance, if the transaction involves price volatility of an underlying claim, then any change in price may represent a loss for the counterparty, who may renege on the purchase or sale commitment. If settlement does not occur, then the broker or dealer may experience a loss. Investment banking firms and commercial banks that service huge trading portfolios of securities, foreign exchange, or other secondary market instruments usually bear the greatest settlement risks.

DOCUMENTATION RISK

Documentation risk is the chance that a financial claim may be a poorly drawn legal document or a poorly structured loan agreement. The documentation to each financial claim often involves many provisions, covenants, and descriptions—sometimes buried in the infamous fine print at the bottom of a page—to monitor and resolve disputes if a borrower defaults on the committment. Since the legal profession often drafts these contracts for other lawyers and judges, the financial intermediary's personnel responsible for fulfilling the terms of the agreement may not understand or properly comply, thus exposing the financial firm to risk and increasing transaction costs. Consequently, many firms standardize their contracts and educate staff as needed. Similarly, there have been many efforts to standardize legal documents industrywide for the consumer's benefit. For example, the secondary market government sponsored mortgage enterprises have spent millions of dollars developing standardized mortgage contracts, servicing contracts, and other documents to facilitate the sale and servicing of mortgages. Despite these efforts, documentation risk is inherent in the lending and security origination processes.

OPERATING RISK

Operating risk relates to a loan originator's inability to carry out the terms of the loan, perhaps due to inadequate training, capacity, or systems. A lender may get involved in a transaction that it simply is not set up to handle or the competition for loans may be so fierce that originators cannot complete the necessary tasks for properly and carefully originating the loans. For example, in 1986 and again in 1993, sharp declines in mortgage rates prompted borrowers to refinance their home mortgages. Many lenders could not process these loans within the timeframes promised or expected, and many found themselves burdened more by lawsuits and bad press.

Both documentation and operating risks increased with additional credit legislation and regulation such as the truth-in-lending, equal credit opportunity, and home mortgage disclosure acts, all of which increased the complexity—and therefore the cost—of each transaction.

EVENT RISK

Event risk is the chance of unexpected changes in ownership, control, capital structure, or business activity of a firm that alters its credit rating. For example, a leveraged buyout or a major equity repurchase program frequently exposes the senior holders of high-grade debt to risk. Or, an established firm's acquisition of a relatively new, potentially risky business can downgrade the acquiring firm's debt rating and subject the firm's debt holders to loss.

In the 1980s, several firms purchased savings and loan associations which suffered later in the decade. The creditors of these firms suffered since riskiness of the parent firm increased significantly due to the addition of the S&L. An acquisition is an event that frequently adds to creditor risk.

COUNTRY RISK

As in most business transactions, political risk has several dimensions, one of which is called *country risk,* or *sovereign risk,* the chance of a country's or a government's honoring its debt commitments and those of private companies in its jurisdiction. Chapter 12 explains how to manage country risk.

Recent investments in republics of the former Soviet Union represent significant country risks. Some investors in Russia complain that bureaucrats are constantly changing rules for doing business and implementing costly new taxes and fees.

Another type of country risk involves the international differences in government regulation, legislation, and supervision of the financial services industry. The Bank of Commerce and Credit International (BCCI) scandal is a perfect example. BCCI, an international bank chartered in Luxembourg but operating in over 70 countries carried out alleged illegal activities by taking advantage of differences in supervisory practices.

In light of the increasingly fierce global competition for capital, and control of the international allocation process, all financial institutions will need employees who can manage international credit risk exposures, work effectively with foreign institutions' personnel, and keep up with regulatory changes, domestic or otherwise, that affect the profitability of international transactions with foreign firms or within other countries.

✓ Checkpoints

11-3   What are the differences among pure credit risk, underwriting risk, and settlement risk?

11-4   What are some similarities and differences between event risk and political risk? How might a change in a country's leadership increase credit risk in a transaction? What have you read or heard recently in the news that might serve as examples of these risks?

11-5   How might the volume of transactions in the origination of a particular type of loan impact operating risk?

Techniques for Managing Credit Risk

Given the number of macroeconomic, industrial, international, legal, and ethical factors influencing the outcome of each loan transaction, analysts and academicians alike have struggled to develop really powerful models for predicting the effects of these forces on the debt market. The various types of credit risk simply do not make for highly analytical tools and methodologies. But, like the investor and the corporate financier, the financial firm manager strives to create an efficient portfolio of loans, one that minimizes credit risk so as to reduce the return volatility. Developing such a portfolio involves the process of asset diversification.

This portion of the chapter focuses on some basic, but important techniques for managing and controlling credit risk through diversification

DIVERSIFICATION OF CREDIT RISK

The failure of many financial institutions in the 1980s and early 1990s demonstrated the hazards of undiversified asset portfolios. There are two ways to diversify a portfolio of debt assets: (1) take a statisically large sample of assets representing all types of accounts, borrowers, and geographical areas, so that, as the number of loans increases, the actual return will approach the likely return, according to the law of large numbers and (2) use statistical measures to select combinations of loan assets for underwriting and servicing so that the positive return on one loan offsets the loss on another, according to modern portfolio theory.[2]

DIVERSIFICATION BY LAW OF LARGE NUMBERS

The first type of diversification applies to investments made in a particular type of risky asset. It involves the probability that a specific lender's credit loss experience on a portfolio of particular loans will deviate from the actual loss experience for the population of loans from which they are drawn. Diversification by the **law of large numbers** means that as the number of loans increases, the more closely the actual return will approach the probable return.

Extended Example

A financial institution would like to develop a loan program for automobile lending. After analyzing this market, management decides to offer credit to potential buyers who cannot meet the higher credit standards of captive auto finance companies such as General Motors' GMAC. Upon determining the underwriting requirements, the institution estimates that the likely credit loss experience on such a program would be an expected average three percent (3%) repossession rate. Management also expects the losses, which include the loss from the sale of repossessed cars and holding costs, to be 60% of the loan bal-

---

[2]Harry Markowitz wrote a pioneering monograph entitled *Portfolio Selection—Efficient Diversification of Investments* (New Haven, Conn.: Yale University Press), 1959.

ance at time of repossession. Given the prices that the bank can charge in the current loan market, management agrees to accept the loss experience and move forward with the program.

The decision to make is, how big must this program be, so that the resulting portfolio of loans is large enough to produce the expected loss rate of the population with a high degree of confidence? The bank has only $40 million in assets and can devote only $2 million to the new program. Since the average loan in the market is about $12,000, the bank could make around 167 loans ($2 million/$12,000 = 166 2/3) Considering this limit, bank officials worry that the program may not yield an adequate number of loans to reach the 3% repossession rate. A staff analyst turns to statistical sampling for the optimal number of loans. The distribution of the mean loss percentage for the sample of loans the bank originates from the population of auto loans is a **binomial distribution**.[3] The analyst considers each loan made to be a draw from a distribution of loans that had three bad loans from every hundred loans in a population of loans underwritten according to the selection criteria. The standard error of sample means from a binomial distribution taken from a population with a known loss parameter, b, is shown in Equation 11.1.

$$\text{Standard Error, SE: } (b = .03) = \sqrt{b\ g/n} \qquad [11.1]$$

Where:

n = The number of loans

b = The percentage of bad or repossessed loans in the population, and

g = The percentage of good loans in the population.

Clearly, $b = (1 - g)$. Exhibit 11.1 shows how the standard error of the mean of a sample repossession rate b changes as n increases.

In this example, the lender set 4% as the maximum loss rate acceptable to commence with the program. It also wants to be extremely confident that their loss percentage will be less than or equal to 4%.

Exhibit 11.1 shows that the bank must sample over 300 loans to get a standard error of the sample loans originated from the population to be 3% (+/–) one standard error of 0.98%, which occurs with 84% degree of confidence. The degree of confidence is based on the statistical postulate that the mean of samples taken from a binomial distribution will approximate a normal distribution if n is large. The standard error of the sample will fall within one standard error (1 SE) of the population mean with 84% degree of confidence, 97.7% within two standard errors (2 SEs), and 99.9% within three standard errors (3 SEs). However, managers focus on the probability that the loss percentage is above the mean, the area under the standard normal distribution above the mean. This is known in probability theory as a *single-tailed test*. For one standard error (SE), the area under the single tail is [1.00 – ((1.00 – .841)/2) =] 92%; for two standard errors,

---

[3]The binomial distribution is a theoretical for the random error of a variable that takes on discrete values. In our case, the variables represent p and q which are proportions adding to 1.

EXHIBIT 11.1

Standard Error of Sample with Repossession Rate of Population of 3% as
n Increases from 25 to Infinity ($g = .97$, $b = .03$)

Standard Error of the Sample Mean

n	$\sqrt{b\ g/n}$
25	.0341
50	.0241
100	.0171
300	.0098
400	.0085
500	.0076
750	.0062
1,000	.0054
Infinity	.0000

the area under the single tail is $[1.00 - ((1.00 - .977)/2) =]$ 98.85%; and for three standard errors, $[1.00 - ((1.00 - .999)/2) =]$ 99.99%. Using the one-tail test, we could achieve 98.85% degree of confidence at $[2(SEs)/2 \cong .01)]$ with approximately 300 loans. The next decision is, can the bank underwrite and service 300 automobilie loans worth $3.6 million ($300 \times \$12,000$) when it has budgeted only $2 million for the program? It probably cannot.

This example highlights how small lending programs have difficulty diversifying risk effectively through the law of large numbers.[4] Under this methodology, management might reject the program. This example also shows how many institutions might not do well by diversifying their portfolios across many different types of assets. Most financial institutions too small to accumulate a portfolio that represents the population from which it is drawn, specialize in a few lending programs in which they can achieve an adequate number of loans. By necessity, this strategy fails to diversify the loan portfolio adequately; and so many of these small firms in the United States hold a high percentage of their portfolio in very riskless assets, such as U.S. government and agency securities.

DEMONSTRATION PROBLEM

DETERMINING THE SIZE OF A LOAN PORTFOLIO TO ACHIEVE LAW OF LARGE NUMBERS DIVERSIFICATION

Situation

In recent years, financial institutions of all types have suffered substantial losses on loans on commercial real estate, loans that are usually fairly large. It is determined that to provide adequate diversification the institution should

---

[4]Another problem that credit managers must deal with is the fact each institution's underwriting criteria differ to some extent. That means that the population loss percentage will not be accurate for each institution. The population probabilities are typically drawn from industrywide data sources which may represent more or less conservative underwriting than the firm uses.

hold a portfolio located in at least five distinct metropolitan areas in at least three geographical regions of the country. If the loss experience is 1.5% on commercial loans, then what is the number of loans needed to diversify in each market in order to reduce the standard error to 1% or less with 98.85% confidence (2 SE for a one-tail test). This will provide sufficient confidence to management that the loss rate on the loans in each region will be less than 2.5% (1.5% + 1.0%).

Results

Using Equation 11.1 you can solve for the number of loans needed using Equation 11.2. To achieve 98.85% confidence, it is necessary to solve for n such that 2 SE is less than or equal to (.01/2 =).005.

$$\sqrt{(b\ g/n)} = \sqrt{(.015 \times .985/n)} = .005 \qquad [11.2]$$

$$.014775/n = .005^2$$

$$.014775/.000025 = n$$

$$n = 591$$

In this example, it would take a portfolio of 591 loans to achieve the confidence level required. This would require a portfolio of $591 million in each market, if the average loan size was only $1 million. Such diversification would be very hard to achieve for all but the very largest institutions. This example again serves to highlight one reason so many financial intermediaries experienced large losses on commercial loan portfolios. They had portfolios that were not large enough to provide law of large numbers diversification, not to mention being inadequately diversified geographically. This is true even for institutions that underwrote these loans in a very professional manner.

PORTFOLIO DIVERSIFICATION

Although many investment experts and scholars have contributed much to modern portfolio theory, which applies statistical measures—expected returns, standard deviations of returns, and correlation between returns—to create a portfolio, the theories of Markowitz remain the basis for the diversification of portfolio assets. This type of portfolio diversification concerns the variance in the return on the firm's entire asset portfolio when it consists of different combinations of assets: investments should be evaluated on the basis of two dimensions, expected return on the ith asset, $E(r_i)$, and the expected volatility of return, measured by the standard deviation of return, $E(SD_i)$. Markowitz showed that two or more investments whose returns are not perfectly correlated can be combined to produce a portfolio whose risk, as measured by expected standard deviation of the *expected return on the portfolio, $E(SD_p)$*, is lower for a *given expected portfolio return, $E(r_p)$*. Simply put, diversification can produce a more optimal result for the risk-adverse investor, a higher return for any specific degree of risk.

The key to this result relates to the covariation of returns of the various assets comprising the portfolio. The financial firm manager's objective is to define what Markowitz referred to as the *efficient frontier*, comprised of a unique set of portfolios with the highest expected return, $E(r_p)$, for any given level of risk, $E(SD_p)$—the optimum achievable trade-off between risk and return.

Extended Example

An institution would like to invest in home mortgages (Exhibit 11.2). Its management considers a portfolio consisting of two assets: the first is a three-year adjustable rate mortgage *(a)* tied to the three-year Treasury with a spread of 2.25%; the second is a government sponsored mortgage enterprise guaranteed mortgage pass-through security collateralized by 15-year fixed-rate mortgages *(f)*. The ARM is a mortgage whose interest rate adjusts every three years to a rate 2.25% above the prevailing 3-year Treasury note rate. The 15-year fixed-rate mortgage is a fully amortizing loan. Exhibit 11.2 shows the monthly annualized returns on these two assets computed by dividing the interest return plus change in market price during the month by the beginning period price. The exhibit also shows the values for the difference between the monthly return and the mean, or, in this case, the $E(r_a)$ and $E(r_f)$, and the standard deviations and covariance between the two assets. (For simplicity, readers should assume that the returns for 1995 are a good estimate of future expected returns and standard deviations.)

EXHIBIT 11.2

Computation of Returns, $E(r_{af})$, Standard Deviations, $E(SD_{af})$, and Covariance of Returns, Cov_{af}, for a Three-Year Adjustable-Rate Mortgage (a) and 15-Year Fixed-Rate Pass-Through (f): 1995

Month/ Year	ARM return r_a%	Pass-through return r_f%	ARM $(r_a-E(r_a)\%)^2$	Pass-through $(r_f-E(r_f)\%)^2$	$(r_a-E(r_a))\times (r_f-E(r_f))$
Jan. 1995	6.5	9.5	1.577	0.766	-1.2578
Feb. 1995	7.8	6.5	0.002	4.516	.2922
March 1995	9.3	7.5	2.384	1.266	-1.5328
April 1995	7.0	10.9	0.571	5.176	-2.1328
May 1995	7.0	10.5	0.571	3.516	-1.7578
June 1995	7.25	9.5	0.256	0.766	-.6016
July 1995	7.02	9.5	0.541	0.766	-.8028
Aug. 1995	8.1	6.5	0.118	4.516	-.3453
Sept. 1995	8.6	7.5	0.713	1.266	-.7453
Oct. 1995	7.2	6.6	0.309	4.101	1.4934
Nov. 1995	8.4	9.5	0.415	0.766	.4047
Dec. 1995	8.9	9.5	1.309	0.766	.8422
Average	7.7558	8.625	*Sum* = 8.766	28.187	-6.143

$SD_a = 8.7675/12 = 0.731$
$SD_f = 28.1825/12 = 2.349$
$Cov_{af} = -6.1437/12 = -0.5120$

To diversify the portfolio most efficiently, managers study how the covariance between the two assets affects the overall portfolio standard deviation. Equation 11.3 is the formula derived by Markowitz for calculating the portfolio standard deviation.[5]

Portfolio standard deviation =

$$SD_p = \sqrt{[\Sigma_{i=1}^n W_i^2 SD_i^2 + \Sigma_{i=1}^n \Sigma_{j=1}^n W_i W_j Cov_{ij}]} \qquad [11.3]$$

$$i \neq j$$

where:

W_i = *The weight in percent of asset i in the portfolio*

SD_i = *Standard deviation of asset i return*

SD_p = *Standard deviation of portfolio return*

Cov_{ij} = *Covariance between returns on assets i and j*

n = *Number of assets*

Equation 11.4 shows the derivation of the standard deviation of a portfolio with 20 percent ARMs and 80 percent fixed-rate mortgages using the data in Table 11.1.

$$SD_{af} = \sqrt{[.20^2 \times 0.731^2 + .80^2 \times 2.349^2 + 2 \times (.20 \times .80 \times -0.512)]}$$
$$= 1.841\% \qquad [11.4]$$

Table 11.1 summarizes the results of calculating the expected portfolio return and portfolio standard deviation for different weightings (W_i) of the two assets. In our two-asset example, $W_a = 1.00 - W_f$. Exhibit 11.3 also provides the weighted average returns and portfolio standard deviations for several combinations of fixed and three-year Treasury-based adjustable-rate mortgages (ARMs). Three-year ARMs combined with fixed-rate mortgages yields a higher return with a lower standard deviation than does a portfolio of just 3-year ARMs. More specifically, then the portfolio consists of 80%, 3-year ARMs and 20%, 15-year pass-through securities, the expected portfolio return exceeds the 100 %ARM portfolio with a lower standard deviation of expected return. Exhibit 11.4 graphs these two portfolios.

In recent years, some of the largest U.S. commercial banks have begun to develop asset portfolio diversification strategies based on this risk/return framework. A word of caution to the financial firm manager: like technical analysis of

---

[5]The equation is also frequently presented by replacing Cov_{ij} in Equation 11.3 with $(r_{ij} \times SD_i \times SD_j)$ where r_{ij} is the correlation coefficient between the returns on assets i and j. In Equation 11.3 $r_{af} = Cov_{af}/(SD_a \times SD_f) = -0.04266$

stock investments, statistical approaches to building loan portfolios rely upon historical data to determine expected risk and return.

TABLE 11.1

Portfolio Expected Returns, $E(r_{af})$, and Standard Deviation, $E(SD_{af})$, for Different Portfolio Weighting of Assets: Three-year ARM Weight = W_a and Fixed-rate Weight = W_f

Portfolio	W_a ARM Weighting	W_f Fixed-rate Weighting	$E(r_{af})\%$ Return	$E(SD_{af})\%$ Standard Deviation
1	1.00	0.0	7.756	0.731
2	0.80	0.20	7.930	0.637
3	0.60	0.40	8.104	0.910
4	0.40	0.60	8.277	1.350
5	0.20	0.80	8.451	1.841
6	0.00	1.00	8.625	2.349

EXHIBIT 11.3

Efficient Frontier for Commercial Banks and Thrifts

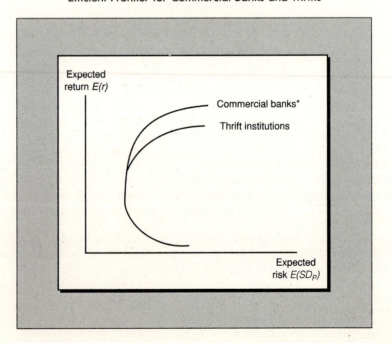

EXHIBIT 11.4

Risk-Return Frontier (Fixed- and Adjustable-rate Mortgage Portfolio)

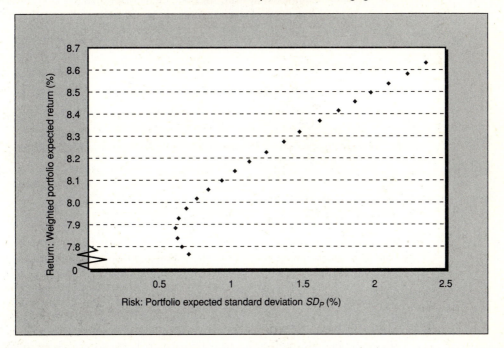

COMPARISON OF THE LAW OF LARGE NUMBERS AND MODERN PORTFOLIO THEORY APPROACHES TO DIVERSIFICATION

As mentioned earlier, few financial institutions are large enough and experienced enough to implement both the law of large numbers and modern portfolio theory in diversifying portfolio risks. Management must usually find some trade-off between the two methods. When size is the limitation, most smaller institutions determine the few markets in which they can achieve substantial activity to benefit from a large number of loans and then invest the rest of the portfolio in relatively risk free assets. For example, a small commercial bank might choose U.S. government and agency securities, a small insurance company might go for high-grade bonds, and a small thrift might select government sponsored enterprise guaranteed assets like mortgage securities.

When experience in a new market might be a limitation, firms assess the underwriting and servicing talent needed for effective diversification. For instance, prudent managers diversify their loan portfolios by geographic location, but implementation depends upon the availability of mortgage loan underwriters and origination experts with local experience.

Many of the institutions in the U.S. financial system are small and cannot diversify their assets in an effective way. Exhibit 11.3 shows a hypothetical efficient frontier for diversified commercial banks and less-diversified intermediaries like thrift institutions. Commercial banks have charters that grant them greater investment opportunities and, thus, greater potential for effective diversification. Other charters, like those of thrift institutions, restrict the ability to diversify by limiting the institution to such assets as mortgages and consumer loans.

✓ Checkpoints

11-6 How does a manager control risk using the law of large numbers?

11-7 How can diversification reduce a firm's overall credit risk according to modern portfolio theory?

11-8 Why do smaller financial intermediaries have trouble diversifying credit risk, and what can they do?

Techniques for Controlling Credit Risk

The primary role of the credit group and credit underwriters within the financial firm is to control credit risk. While all lending and investment businesses expect some losses, those financial firms which minimize actual losses compared to anticpated or even industrywide expected losses—and yet achieve their goals for return—may very well outperform the competition. How can the credit group contribute to this success? The tools available are several and can be used before, during, and after the transaction. Essentially, there are tools of selection, such as the credit analysis; tools of documentation such as the covenant; and strategies for risk sharing, such as the loan participation. The following section overviews these tools and possible strategies so that readers can understand how to devise an overall credit risk management plan. Later chapters flesh out the details so that readers can actually apply these tools on the job.

CONTROLLING CREDIT RISK THROUGH COLLATERAL

At one time, lenders granted loans primarily upon the borrower's ability to offer and maintain collateral, the market value of which determined the likelihood of repayment. But, during the 1980s, financial institutions experienced the largest credit losses since the Great Depression. Even though loans were secured by collateral valued at amounts well in excess of the loan principal, lenders sustained losses due to the volatility of collateral values and to the structures of the loans relative to the collateral values.

Volatility of Collateral Value

In the 1980s and early 1990s, S&Ls, commercial banks, and life insurance companies lost big on loans collateralized by commercial real estate, valued using pro-forma estimates of future rent levels and space absorption. (The cycle of market values in commercial real estate is measured in half decade periods, if not longer. The length of this cycle challenges the lender's ability to assess the credit risks assumed.) Mathematically, the appraised values were generally accurate given the assumptions; the assumptions, however, proved to be dangerously erroneous. The national rate of office vacancies shot up from 5% in 1980 to nearly 20% by 1990; rent levels, adjusted for inflation, fell from the early 1980s through the early 1990s. As builders added new buildings to the market and developers used a variety of lenders, the forecasts of rent levels and space absorption became increasingly warped. The long lead time between building concept and occupancy only skewed the estimates more, as did the 1990–91 recession. Because collateral values endure long, volatile market cycles, lenders can at best diversify risk through the portfolio selection process.

Structure of the Loan

The other important feature of asset-based lending relates to the structure of a loan relative to the collateral's value. An automobile provides good collateral for many auto lenders, but it depreciates in value. As as result, lenders must decide how to structure loans and leases to account for collateral depreciation. In the mid-1980s, the five-year installment auto loan and lease became very popular, but this length of time decreased the market resale value of used cars at a faster rate than did the principal balance on the loans used to finance them. The lower the down payment required and the longer the amortization period, the greater the credit risk assumed by the lender. Large defaults and repossessions prompted many lenders to revise their loan structures for higher down payments and shorter terms.

CONTROLLING CREDIT RISK THROUGH THE CREDIT ANALYSIS

As mentioned, lenders granted loans primarily upon the borrower's ability to offer and maintain collateral, the market value of which determined the likelihood of repayment. Clearly, there are limits to using collateral as a safeguard against loss. More financial firms today grant loans according to the borrower's ability to generate sufficient cash flow from operations to satisfy the terms of the loan agreement. The loan decision rests more upon the value of the firm as a going concern—that a loan is most likely to be repaid from company earnings than from the liquidation of the firm's assets and working capital. In highly leveraged acquisition and buyout financings, however, lenders may issue loans and bonds to the ongoing firm even though it lacks adequate cash flows from operations because it can still sell such assets as subsidiaries, real estate, or operating divisions to repay its debt.

Financial firms also grant loans for longer terms than before; these longer maturing loans are called **term loans,** which expose the lender to a much higher degree of risk than do shorter-term loans. To many lenders, pro forma estimates of earnings before interest and taxes (EBIT) are synonymous with credit analysis.

Here is the more complete definition: **credit analysis** is the process of determining the probability that a potential borrower can and will fulfill the obligations of a loan agreement or other debt claim. During this extensive inquiry, credit analysts conduct

1. *Audits & due diligence:* The acts of verifying the accuracy of information—deposit balances, collateral values, financial statements, and so forth—which the potential borrower supplies, not just to screen for potential fraud but also to understand more about how the company arrives at the information it uses for decision making and reporting purposes.

2. *Cash flow analysis:* The process of identifying sources and uses of cash and then forecasting future cash flows.

3. *Financial analysis:* The process of assessing financial soundness by reviewing financial ratios and other financial measures of performance.

4. *Behavioral analysis:* The process of assessing the management, organization structure, and actions of management.

5. *Credit scoring for consumer loans:* A statistical approach to assessing credit risk by assigning point values to various criteria thought to be associated with credit risk.

DUE DILIGENCE, FRAUD, AND CREDIT RISK

While basic human error, systems failure, and miscommunication can account for some of the misreporting or misrepresentation of financial data, fraud, a deliberate deception perpetrated to obtain an advantage, is still a risk during the lending and investing process. For example, loan applicants may stretch the truth—or blatantly falsify information—on their income, employment, tax returns, credit reports, deposits held in institutions, appraisals, financing outstanding, and a host of other relevant underwriting data factoring into the lending decision. They may provide business pro-formas that lack relevant data or are knowingly too optimistic. Loan brokers may double-sell (sell to two buyers) a loan contract that they service; and borrowers may pledge assets as collateral to more than one lender.

How can lenders distinguish honest mistakes from instances of fraud? Usually, they require potential borrowers to obtain independent audits of statements from trusted accounting firms. And they develop due diligence procedures including calling accountants, lawyers, customers, lenders, and others who have personal experience with the prospective borrower to improve detection and reduce the severity of fraud.

Once audits and due diligent processes have verified the integrity of the financial data, then the credit analyst can move on to the more thorough analysis of it. (After all, why would a firm want to waste its human and technological resources on studying bogus data?)

Cash Flow Analysis

Since cash flow statements supply important pieces of data, credit analysts should consider factors of risk assumed by the firm in the cash flow analysis, to identify and forecast the operating cash flows of the potential borrower. The major cash flow risks, and related what-if scenarios to study, include the following:

- *Production:* How does production affect cash flow? What if the firm loses access to raw materials, suppliers, technology, fuel, or other vital ingredients interrupting production of goods or services?

- *Marketing:* How do market conditions affect cash flow? What is the market for the product? Who are the competitors? What substitutes exist? How elastic is the price of the product or service? Who are the customers? What if there are new entries into the market? What if a few major customers go out of business?

- *Personnel:* How do availabililty, cost, and harmony of the work force affect cash flows? What if there is a labor union strike? What if new technology emerges to displace hundreds of workers?

- *Finance:* How vulnerable is the firm to sharp rises in the cost of credit? How much credit risk does the firm itself carry? What are its rates of accounts receivable and delinquency on its liabilities?

- *Domestic and international transactions:* How subject is the firm to increased domestic and international competition? How effective are its overseas operations? What if there are changes in trade restrictions and other trade policies?

- *Government:* How much does the government influence or regulate this business? Is the firm complying with all environmental and safety codes and antitrust laws? What if the government passes a new consumer protection law, increases industry safety standards, or downsizes its military operations?

Financial Analysis: Altman's Z Score

Once credit analysts have a richer understanding of the firm's business and its cash flows, they can delve more deeply into all the financial statements of the firm, ask more relevant questions, and interpret their findings with greater insight. In 1968, Edward Altman[6] took an empirical approach to determining a firm's creditworthiness. He conducted a **discriminate analysis** of financial ratios, a test to discriminate irrelevant ratios from those that help predict financial distress leading to bankruptcy. Altman isolated the following five variables:

1. Working capital divided by total assets, X_1.
2. Retained earnings divided by total assets, X_2.
3. Earnings before interest and taxes divided by total assets, X_3.
4. Market value of equity divided by book value of total debt, X_4.
5. Sales divided by total assets, X_5.

---

[6]A good summary and update of Altman's work is found in E. I. Altman, "Managing the Commercial Lending Process," in *Handbook of Banking Strategy,* eds. R. C. Aspinwall and R. A. Eisenbeis (New York: John Wiley), 1985, pp. 473–510. Another good reference is C. G. Turvey, "Credit Scoring for Agricultural Loans: A Review with Applications," *Agricultural Finance Review* 51 (1991), pp. 43–54.

He then estimated a discriminate function—a linear probability model using historical data to explain the probability of default for a group of defaulted and current loans—by running the empirical test using a large population of good and bad business loans. This test provides weights for each of the significant variables. The discriminate function using the above variables might look like Equation 11.4.

$$Z = 1.3X_1 + 2.1X_2 + 2.8X_3 + 1.2X_4 + .9X_5 \qquad [11.4]$$

A credit analyst can input data from the prospective borrower into Equation 11.4 to calculate the borrower's credit score, called a *Z score,* a measure of the probability of distress for a firm. If the subject prospective borrower has $X_1 = .20$; $X_2 = .25$; $X_3 = .8$; $X_4 = .8$; and $X_5 = .5$, then the borrower's Z score would appear as Equation 11.5.

$$Z = 1.3(.2) + 2.1 (.25) + 2.8 (.8) + 1.2 (.8) + .9 (.5) = 4.435 \qquad [11.5]$$

Discriminate models like Altman's provides a score that separates potentially good loans from weak ones. If the financial institution designated the cut-off or "passing" score to 2.83 in this case, then the credit analyst would consider the subject loan as a good loan since the firm's Z score exceeds the cutoff or switch point of 2.83. While financial firm managers use Altman's work in underwriting loans and in other commercial business lending decisions, the Z score may not help to predict the financial distress and failure of small businesses because Altman studied larger firms in his sample.[7]

Limitions of Financial Analysis

Financial analysis using discriminate analysis has several limitations. First of all, discriminate models tell much about the firm but only at a given point in time. Analysts who use Altman's Z score, for example, must expect the variables and Z values to change over time and anticpate any new factors that might contribute to future default. In fact, Altman and others later added several other variables to the Z score, including stability of earnings, equity divided by total assets, and total assets of the firm. Also, discriminate analysis separates loans into two categories, like the pass-or-fail grading system. But since the probability of default is a continuous variable, not a discrete one, any scoring system merely provides a benchmark for the lending decision. Finally, there are many behaviorial indicators of financial distress and failure that discriminate analysis does not incorporate. The following section describes a more subjective approach to credit analysis.

---

[7]Altman's linear discriminate model has motivated many researchers to extend his work. In addition to discriminate models, logit models (which constrain the cumulative probability of default to range between zero and one given a logistic distribution of loan default) and probit models (which are similar to logit models but assume the probability of default is a normal distribution) are some of the most common extensions of the methodology.

Behaviorial Aspects of Credit Analysis: Argenti's Analysis

In 1976, John Argenti went beyond the financial statements and looked more subjectively at the organizational structure, behavior, and information systems of failed companies his study attributed financial distress and failures to several causes such as:

1. Weak management, evidenced in one-man rule, nonparticipative board of directors, unbalanced top management, shallow management, weak finance function, and combined chairman/chief executive

2. Inadequate information for decision making.

3. Failure to respond to change.

4. Excessive growth or overtrading.

5. Launch of a big project.

6. Excessive financial leverage.

7. Creative accounting techniques, the use of accounting conventions that inflate revenue and decrease costs of the firms, and the use many times of systematically distorted assumptions, to arrive at the audited financial statements of the firm.

Credit Analysis of Consumer Loans: Credit Scoring

Consumer loans include collateralized loans such as installment loans for automobiles or student loans, and uncollateralized loans such as credit card accounts and other lines of credit. Extensive statistical studies of consumer credit loans have identified some factors that help to differentiate between performing and defaulted loans, including borrower age, marital status, income, status as homeowner or renter, job stability, credit record, occupation, and number of dependents. Chapter 12 details some techniques for consumer credit analysis.

Many large consumer lenders have developed **credit scoring** systems for screening potential borrowers. A credit score is like a Z score for the consumer market, a measure of the creditworthiness of the potential borrower. Lenders usually score consumers by inputting data supplied by the applicant and credit agencies into computer models. Computerized credit scoring techniques also enable lenders to set preapproved credit lines and to compile mailing lists for direct mail credit card campaigns.

CONTROLLING CREDIT RISK WITH LOAN COVENANTS

Originators of financial claims can use several tools for altering the risk characteristics of specific financial claims, specifically to reduce the probability of losses. One tool is the **loan covenant,** a term under the debt contract that spells out the borrower's obligations regarding financial performance, establishes standards of business conduct, and mitigates agency issues by, for example, constraining the actions of management and directors.

Lenders and investors can protect their interests by using covenants when creating financial claims. For instance, in collateralized loan contracts, a firm can specify a quick delivery date of the collateral if the loan defaults. Or it can insist upon proper use and maintenance of collateral, so as not to devalue the collateral through negligence before repossession or foreclosure on the defaulted loan.

These covenants are generally developed by the staff involved in loan origination and drafted by a financial firm's legal counsel. Although loan covenants are written by the legal staff, they are a crucial part of the risk and return parameters of the lending decision. Because covenants are designed to reduce the probability of principal loss, it is important that the financial organization's loan origination, servicing, and portfolio management groups understand and participate in the drafting of the covenants. The origination unit must be involved because they are responsible for negotiating the contract and documenting the transaction. The servicing unit must be involved since they will be responsible for monitoring the transaction to determine whether any events take place that could trigger a violation of a covenant provision. The portfolio manager is interested in the covenants because they will affect the forecast of the probability of loss and will, therefore, affect the pricing of the loan.

The three lists in the pages that follow contain sample covenants found in the most common forms of debt contracts. Those covenants associated with investment-grade debt reflect how large the losses have been on such loans. And those covenants restricting business activities, sales of assets, and changes in ownership and control reveal how severe losses have been on high-yield bonds and how sensitive such debt is to event risk.

Typical Covenants Found in Consumer Durable Loans for Car, Boat, or Recreational Vehicle

- *Collateral:* The collateral covered shall include all accessories and parts now and any replacements in the future. The borrower must be the owner of the collateral and the collateral must be free of any lien, security interest, and/or encumbrance.

- *Sale or transfer:* The borrower will not sell, contract to sell, or dispose of the collateral, or any interest therein, without prior consent of the lender.

- *Location:* The borrower will not remove the collateral from the state for more than three days without the express written consent of the lender.

- *Protection of collateral:* The borrower will keep the collateral in good condition and will not use the collateral illegally or improperly.

- *Insurance:* The borrower will insure the collateral with companies acceptable to the lender against such casualties and such amounts as the lender shall require with a standard clause in favor of the lender.

- *Premiums, taxes, and license fees:* The borrower will pay promptly all insurance premiums, taxes, license fees, and other charges affecting the collateral.

- *Decrease in value of the collateral:* If the collateral has materially decreased in value, the borrower will provide enough additional collateral to satisfy the lender. Otherwise the loan amount will be reduced.

- *Lender may declare security and take possession of property:* Upon the occurrence of default, the lender may declare all obligations secured immediately due and payable or seize collaterals and sell them.

While these lists may suggest ways for knowledgeable lenders to alter credit risk characteristics, borrowers can still take action to neutralize these contractual protections. Ultimately, when a dispute arises, either a court of law or a bankruptcy judge rules on the case. Since the legal process is often costly and time consuming, financial firm managers can better spend talent, time, and effort on assessing and controlling credit risk and monitoring outstanding loans and investments.

Typical Covenants in a Municipal Revenue Bond on an Electric-Generating Facility

The bonds are payable solely out of the **net operating revenue** (gross operating revenue less operating and maintenance expense).

- *Electric rates:* The city must establish rates and collect charges in an amount sufficient to service the bonds, after operation and maintenance expenses.
- *Reserve account:* The city must maintain a reserve account in an amount equal to the maximum amount of **annual debt service** (principal plus interest) on the bonds.
- *Insurance and other issues:* The city must maintain adequate insurance on the electric system, maintain and enforce valid regulations for payment of bills, not invest proceeds of bonds in a way that makes taxable bonds, and pay and discharge all lawful claims.

Typical Covenants in Noninvestment-Grade Corporate Bonds

- *Minimum net worth:* The company must maintain a *minimum net worth,* which forces it to manage its affairs properly and protect bondholder interests.
- *Limitation of restricted payments:* If the company's net worth falls below a specified amount, or if a condition of default exists respecting the note, then the company cannot issue restricted payments like stock dividends, stock repurchases, and company advances.
- *Limitation on additional indebtedness:* The company cannot incur more debt unless its fixed charge coverage ratio falls within some predetermined range for a certain period of time preceding the desired date of indebtedness.
- *Restrictions on dividends:* As long as any notes are outstanding, the company cannot pay a dividend or make any other distribution on its capital stock.
- *Restrictions on affiliate transactions:* The company cannot participate in unusual transactions such as sale, purchase, lease, or loan by affiliates or subsidiaries, unless it shows the transaction to be in its best interest.

- *Limitation on redemption of junior debt:* The company cannot purchase or redeem any junior debt unless it concurrently redeems some multiple of senior notes or unless its capital base exceeds a predetermined amount.

- *Limitation on conduct of business:* The company cannot engage in any business other than those predetermined.

- *Limitation on ranking of future indebtedness:* The company cannot incur any debt that lowers the rank of current notes.

- *Restriction on merger, consolidation, or sale of assets:* The company may merge with another company if default is avoided and net worth, maintained

- *Effects of certain takeover:* If there is a takeover attempt, then noteholders have option to ask for redemption of notes.

- *Right of holder to require purchase upon change of control:* The noteholders retain the right to require the repurchase of their notes upon a change of control.

CONTROLLING LARGE LOAN CREDIT RISK: RISK-SHARING

The methods discussed so far have relied on statistical techniques for diversification that assume each of the loans or investments are of nearly equal size. In reality, the sizes of loans and investments vary significantly, quite a challenge to the credit-risk manager who faces a special credit risk such as the failure of several large loans in the firm's portfolio. Long recognizing this possibility, regulators restrict the size of loans that commercial banks and S&Ls can issue to one borrower. The limit for nationally chartered banks and S&Ls is 15% of unimpaired capital and surplus and an additional 10%, if the loan is secured by readily marketable collateral. In the 1980s and 1990s, there was no limit on the number of loans collateralized by real estate that an S&L could issue to one borrow, and the result was a crisis.

Large loans present special risk problems for intermediaries. A lending institution can manage excess loss exposure by selling **participations.** A participation is a loan originated by one institution in which a portion of a loan contract is sold to another lending institution. For years, commercial banks have cultivated relationships with loan correspondents who invest in a portion of the large loans. In a participation, the originating institution retains a portion of the loan in its portfolio, say 15%, and sells the remainder to one or more correspondent institutions. The originating firm also services the loan. In exchange, the originating firm earns a portion of the yield as a servicing fee to augment its income and cover the costs of origination and servicing. Chapter 21 shows how to conduct a profit analysis of this type of transaction. A related transaction is a **syndication,** in which several institutions work together as a group to originate a loan and retain a portion for investment.

Insurance companies are also confronted with similar large scale risk positions. They have developed a technique called **reinsurance,** which permits an insurance company to sell the excess coverage beyond the risk tolerance of the com-

LOAN SALES: A MAJOR ACTIVITY FOR BANKS

About one-third of all commercial banks engage in loan sales. Throughout the 1980s loan sales grew rapidly, reaching over $250 billion in 1989. Since then the general slowdown in lending at banks has reduced the pace of loan sales to around $100 billion in 1993. The high levels of the 1980s were the result of the longest peacetime economic expansion and the high level of mergers, acquisitions, and financial restructurings.

Loan sales are structured in three ways. Participations involve the originating bank selling an interest in the loan. The originating bank, however, holds the borrower's note and services the loan. An assignment involves transfer of the borrower-lender relationship from the originating bank to another bank. In an assignment, the loan buyer obtains the ability to directly relate to the borrower in the event of default. The originating bank may still have obligation to the borrower and perform some servicing activities such as holding collateral. Finally, a **novation** is a complete transfer of the loan to the buyer. The originating bank is out of the picture.

The growth in loan sales is also further evidence of the blurring of the wall between commercial and investment banking. A loan sale is much like a security sale. The originating bank must prepare documents to transfer all or part of a loan and develop a distribution capability to identify prospective buyers of loans.

Source: Joseph G. Haubrich and James B. Thomson. "The Evolving Loan Sales Market," *Economic Commentary*, Federal Reserve Bank of Cleveland, July 15, 1993.

How it Really Works

pany to one or more companies that can properly diversify the risk. Some insurance firms, called *reinsurers,* specialize in assuming a portion of the risk from large exposures. A reinsurer might, for example, assist in insuring a very large oil refinery against fire or providing a $10 million life insurance policy on a key person in a corporation, for example.

✓ Checkpoints

11-9 What are the major factors that must be considered in a cash flow analysis of a company.

11-10 What is Altman's Z score designed to do?

11-11 What were Argenti's findings regarding failed companies? How did his analysis differ from the Altman approach?

11-12 What is a loan or security covenant?

11-13 What types of covenants would you expect to find in a consumer loan collateralized by a durable good such as an automobile?

11-14 What types of covenants would you expect to be written into a loan agreement on a corporate loan or corporate bond to a less than investment-grade borrower?

11-15 What is loan participation and syndication? Why are they used?

11-16 What is reinsurance and what is it used for?

Off-Balance Sheet Transactions and Risks

The recent proliferation of financial innovation has enabled financial institutions to initiate and participate in transactions that legally side-step the formal reporting rules for financial firms. These off-balance sheet transactions (OBSTs), transactions that need not appear on the institution's balance sheet, help firms in bypassing capital requirements, maximizing origination and servicing capabilities, and diluting undiversified risk. However, off-balance sheet activity still exposes the financial institution to liquidity risk, credit risk, foreign exchange risk, and interest rate risk. And so, in dialectic response, regulators of depository institutions have developed risk-based capital requirements for off-balance sheet transactions as well. There are several types of off-balance sheet transactions and related risks:

Type of Off-Balance Sheet Transaction	Risks Involved
1. Loan commitments	1. Liquidity, credit and interest rate risk
2. Foreign exchange trading in the forward markets	2. Foreign exchange and credit risk
3. Interest rate and currency swaps	3. Credit and interest rate risk
4. Subordinated securities created from senior-subordinated security structures	4. Credit risk
5. Sales of higher quality assets in portfolios	5. Increased credit risk to remaining portfolio
6. Sales of assets with recourse	6. Credit risk

Exhibit 11.6 breaks down the primary off-balance sheet activity of commercial banks from 1984 to 1990, the growth of which has been significant. The following section elaborates upon the above table of transactions and related risks.

LOAN COMMITMENTS: COMMERCIAL LINES OF CREDIT, BANKER'S ACCEPTANCES, AND FINANCIAL GUARANTEES

Most financial institutions that originate financial claims issue loan commitments potentially involving interest rate risk, credit risk, and liquidity risk. Through a line of credit for a customer, the institution accepts: (1) interest rate risk if the loan involves a fixed rate and the rate is set before the loan is closed, (2) credit risk if unforeseen events lower the borrower's credit standing, or (3) liquidity risk if the customer draws down the line at an inopportune time. **Adverse self-selection** occurs in the loan commitment process when the least creditworthy customers are most likely to draw down oustanding loan commitments.

EXHIBIT 11.6

Bank Off-Balance Sheet Activity: 1984 and 1990

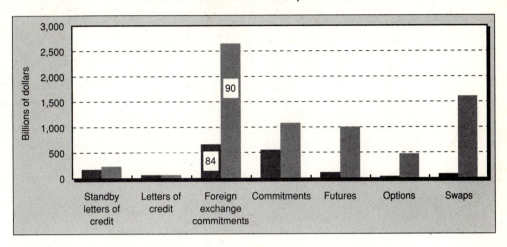

Commercial banks are major issuers of **standby letters of credit,** agreements that obligate the commercial bank to honor a claim brought against its customer in the event the customer defaults. Standby letters involve considerable credit risk for the issuing institutions because commercial customers use them to guarantee commerical paper, bonds, and notes as well as performance under such service-oriented contracts as construction. Businesses also pay banks for standby letters to obtain credit at a lower cost, since the investor will assess the creditworthiness of the bank, the ultimate credit behind the transaction.

FOREIGN EXCHANGE TRANSACTIONS

Large commercial banks and investment bankers actively trade in the foreign exchange markets as brokers and traders. Trading involves taking a position in the forward markets for foreign currencies and accepting considerable foreign exchange risk not reflected on the balance sheet. In such a transaction, the trader actually invests in foreign currency with the hope that it can be sold at a higher price in a few minutes, hours, or days.

INTEREST RATE AND CURRENCY SWAPS

A number of commercial banks and other financial institutions arrange interest rate and currency swaps, transactions that typically put the intermediary where it, by definition, belongs—between two other parties. Interest rate swaps are financial contracts that involve two parties who agree to pay each other interest on a specified amount of principal while currency swaps involve agreements to exchange currencies with an agreed-upon repayment schedule. Financial intermediaries are active in writing swap agreements. These contracts are discussed fully in Chapter 16. The intermediary may issue a fixed rate or variable-rate swap to one party and then issue an offsetting, or partially offsetting, swap to another firm. If the firm cannot complete the offsetting swaps, then the intermediary must accept credit risk and interest rate risk simultaneously.

SENIOR-SUBORDINATED SECURITIES

As securitization has become more popular, the financial restructuring of credit risk has resulted in the creation of the senior-subordinated security. This innovation is discussed in Chapter 15. It involves creating at least two classes of securities collateralized by the pool of assets. The senior class is of higher quality, since it suffers no credit losses until the subordinated class's principal has been eliminated through credit losses. The risk of these securities is highest for the subordinated holder. In some cases, the issuer of the security finds it difficult to sell the subordinated class and leaves it on the balance sheet. This gives the appearance of a higher capital ratio, even though the risk of the entire issue is concentrated in the subordinated security.

LOAN SALES AND ASSET-BACKED FINANCING

Many financial institutions are involved in loan sales and asset-backed financings designed to increase origination and servicing activity. Frequently, however, financial institutions find it easiest to sell or securitize those assets of least credit risk. This serves to increase the overall credit risk exposure of the firm. One reason selling risky assets is so difficult is that the underwriting of these assets is costly and time-consuming. In addition, with an asset-backed security, the rating agencies will require loans of a uniform high quality in order for the security to meet a specified rating.

LOANS SOLD WITH RECOURSE

Occasionally financial institutions sell loans with recourse. This means that the seller agrees to repurchase the loan if it goes into default. The result is that the selling institution bears all the credit risk on these assets even though they are off-balance sheet.

The increased number of financial institution failures in recent years has heightened the attention paid by regulators and analysts to the nature of the risks accepted by institutions that are not reflected on their balance sheets. Today, the disclosure of these transactions is mandatory. However, disclosure is usually in a footnote to the financial statements.

✓ Checkpoints

11-17 In what common types of transactions do financial institutions engage that are not shown on the balance sheet?

11-18 What kinds of risks are posed by three types of off-balance sheet transactions?

SUMMARY AND REVIEW

1. **Describe the major trends that have spurred credit losses of intermediaries over the last few decades.**

    The reasons financial intermediaries still experience large credit losses is due in part to **business cycles,** the presence of **fraud,** and the unpredictable nature of **collateral values.** Making matters more difficult is the fact that the value of collateral that supports so many loans has long price cycles that are difficult, if not impossible, to predict.

2. **Characterize the primary types of credit risk.**

    There are many different types of credit risks. The primary sources of credit risk include: **pure credit risk (nonperformance of debt provisions), underwriting risk (debt which does not meet buyers standards), settlement risk (nonperformance of debt transfer), documentation risk (legal or performance weaknesses of debt contract), operating risk (problems caused by poor execution), political risk (losses caused by government action),** and **event risk (borrower actions that increase risk).**

3. **Explain why diversification is important in managing credit risk and how to diversify by law of large numbers and by portfolio structure.**

    Two primary techniques used to control credit risk include diversification and the **law of large numbers** and portfolio diversification. The law of large numbers diversification refers to the probability that a lender's credit experience will approach that of the population from which the loans are drawn. **Portfolio diversification** deals with combining assets with different expected returns and standard deviations of return to obtain the highest expected return for any given level of expected risk.

    Under the law of large numbers diversification, risk can be reduced by establishing a loan portfolio with a sufficient number of loans so that the expected credit losses fall within an acceptable level around the population's loss percentage. The binomial distribution was shown to be one method for determining the minimum size of the portfolio needed to achieve such confidence. The equation for the standard deviation of the mean of a sample taken from the binomial distribution is:

    $$\text{Standard error of sample mean} = \sqrt{(b\,g/n)}$$

    Portfolio diversification was shown to be effective if the firm develops a diversification of assets strategy. This strategy is accomplished by selecting assets having sufficient covariance with one another so that the portfolio expected return is maximized for any level of expected portfolio return variance.

4. **Describe the primary techniques that managers use to measure and control credit risks in lending transactions.**

Credit analysis is the primary method of reducing the credit risk on a single loan request. It relies most heavily on cash flow analysis for business. **Credit scoring,** using a variety of different individual factors, is used in analyzing consumer loans.

Altman's Z score and **Argenti's analysis** of factors that are related to failed companies were found to be helpful in identifying financial ratios and other factors that influence the probability of bankruptcy.

Loan covenants are an important technique used by lenders to reduce the credit risk on a wide variety of loans. Large loans are a special area of credit concern. Credit exposures from large loans or large insurance coverage on a single risk exposure can be effectively reduced through loan **participation sales, syndications,** and **reinsurance.** Regulators are also concerned about loans to one borrower and frequently establish limits on such loans.

Collateral is used increasingly by financial institutions to lower credit risks. However, collateral price volatility continues to produce significant credit losses at financial institutions.

5. **Identify off-balance sheet credit risk and major sources of such risk.**

Financial institutions carry considerable credit risks off their balance sheets. The primary **off-balance sheet transactions** involving sometimes significant credit risks include **loan commitments, foreign exchange trading, interest rate and currency swaps, subordinated securities, asset-backed financing,** and **asset sales with recourse.** OBSTs have grown significantly in recent years.

SELF-TEST PROBLEM | **LAW OF LARGE NUMBERS DIVERSIFICATION**

11-1

Williams Bank wants to begin a regional credit card program for college students. It expects to open 4,000 accounts with an average credit balance of $500 each.

The national delinquency rate on student credit cards is 11%. The relationship between delinquency rate and credit losses as a percent of credit balance is shown in the following chart:

Delinquency Rate %	Credit Loss %
10%	4.0%
11	4.5
12	5.0
13	6.0
14	7.0
15	9.0

Williams is pricing the loans anticipating a 12% delinquency rate and 5% loss rate.

Will 4,000 cards ensure that William's delinquency rate will be at or below 12 percent with 99.9% confidence (3 SE)? If not, how many cards does Williams need to issue?

Answer on page 308.

LAW OF LARGE NUMBERS DIVERSIFICATION	PROBLEM

11-1

Safety National Bank will originate auto loans. It plans to originate 1,000 loans at $14,000 average loan size for a total of $14,000,000. The delinquency rate on loans similar to the ones Safety plans to originate is 6%.

What is the highest delinquency rate Safety can expect with 99.9% degree of confidence?

LAW OF LARGE NUMBERS DIVERSIFICATION	PROBLEM

11-2

Nashville Bank is considering a regional recreational-vehicle financing program. It has $30 million available for this program. The average loan size is $22,000, and the industry statistics indicate the loans have an 8% delinquency rate. Nashville wants to know how large a program in dollars it will need to be 99.9% certain of experiencing a delinquency rate no larger than 9.5%

DISCRIMINATE ANALYSIS OF DEFAULT RISK	PROBLEM

11-3

You have been asked to evaluate a prospective loan customer with the following financial date. Use the discriminate function in Equation 11.4 to determine whether the loan is potentially strong or weak. The company has 3 million shares outstanding with a market value of $45 per share. The Z score switch point is 2.81.

Income Statement
(in millions)

Sales	$456
Cost of goods sold	376
Gross profit margin	80
Operating expenses	15
Interest expense	10
Net profit before taxes	55
Taxes	20
Net profit after taxes	$ 35

Balance Sheet
(in millions)

Assets		Liabilities and Net Worth	
Cash	$ 15	Accounts payable	$150
Accounts receivable	85	Bonds	100
Inventory	120	Net worth	170
Plant and equipment	200		
Total assets	$420	Total liabilities and net worth	$420

SELF-TEST PROBLEM SOLUTION	LAW OF LARGE NUMBERS DIVERSIFICATION

11-1

Solution

The objective is to determine the *n* such that 3 SE is less than or equal to 1%. The target delinquency rate is 1% ≥ 3 SE: 1SE = .33%

$$.0033 = \sqrt{[(.11 \times .89) \times n]} = \sqrt{(.097900 \times n)} = .0033$$

$$.0033^2 = .000010890 = .097900 \times n$$

$$n = .097900/.000010890 = 8,990 \ cards$$

William's goal of 4,000 cards is too low.

PROJECT 11.1

COVENANTS

One of the most important functions of professional financial experts is the origination of financial claims. Financial claims represent legal contracts evidencing ownership of a stream of income or assets under the control of a third party. All debt and equity are evidenced by a contract. Debt contracts are usually quite complicated.

It is not unusual for consumers who borrow money for a car or home purchase to sign a complicated contract without paying close attention to all the provisions. For a business, the contractual provisions are particularly important, since they normally constrain the activities of management and shareholders. These constraints are known as *covenants*. Covenants are contractual provisions that must be upheld by the borrower in order to meet the terms of the contract.

Obtain a legal note or prospectus of a debt, such as an offering statement that provides a discussion of the covenants. The following is a list of notes that could be used.

Auto Loan
Recreational vehicle loan
Boat loan
Mortgage loan—residential property
Mortgage loan—apartment
Mortgage loan—commercial office building
Construction loan agreement
Corporate bond indenture (high or low grade)
Municipal bond indenture
Mobile home loan
Collateralized debt

PROJECT 11.2

After obtaining a copy of the loan agreement or offering material, analyze it and identify the covenants in the contract. Describe each covenant and explain why you think it was included in the contract.

CHAPTER 12

Evaluation of Loan and Investment Credit Risk

Learning Goals

After studying this chapter, you should be able to:

1. Describe the credit policy process including the importance of diversification, developing underwriting guidelines, setting approval limits, and establishing credit analysis procedures.
2. Explain the major types of loans and investments held by intermediaries, including loans and investments of business, consumers, and international borrowers.
3. Explain the primary credit risk factors summarized by the Cs of credit.
4. Describe the major types of information needed to analyze business, real estate, and consumer loans and securities.
5. Describe country risk and explain several methods to measure it.

Financial intermediaries must determine the process for selecting loans and investments. This job involves the board of directors, senior management, and virtually everyone involved in the lending and servicing functions. This chapter explains the basic credit policy process, the primary types of loans and investments originated or purchased by intermediaries, and the important information and method of analysis of the credit risk of these assets.

The Credit Policy Process

Every financial intermediary must develop policies and procedures for its lending and investment function to control the level of credit risk, grant operating authority to decision makers, and determine the process for selecting loans and investments. The federal depository regulators provide guidance to examiners who must review the credit policies of commercial banks. For example, the most important five attributes of a strong policy according to the Federal Deposit Insurance Corporation (FDIC) include the following:

1.   A statement describing the firm's goal for loan composition (type, location, size, quality etc.).
2.   A statement describing underwriting criteria for each loan class.
3.   Guidelines for assessing, reviewing, and monitoring collateral.
4.   Establishment of credit approval limits decision authority.
5.   A plan for detecting and resolving problem loans.

The remainder of this section discusses some of the most important elements of the credit policy processes. Attribute 5 in the above list is discussed in Chapter 13.

LOAN COMPOSITION: DIVERSIFYING THE PORTFOLIO

As mentioned in the last chapter, diversification of risk is the most important method to control credit risk. A major goal in setting credit risk policies is ensuring proper diversification of risk, not just through asset composition of the portfolio but also through measurements of results toward the planned objective. Chapter 11 introduced readers to *diversification,* the process of minimizing the variability of a financial firm's earnings stream by investing in different assets with return characteristics that demonstrate low levels of correlation with one another.

The purpose of diversification is to minimize a financial institution's exposure to **unsystematic risk,** credit risk unique to the investment, related to a specific industry, geographic location, or firm. Diversification across many industries, geographic locations, and firms minimizes exposure to unsystematic risk. But diversification will not reduce **systematic risk,** the market risk affecting all assets, such as unexpected inflation and recessions. Properly diversified, the expected returns on assets should be relatively unrelated and should not all move together in reaction to a given event. Thus, returns over time will demonstrate lower variance.

The asset portfolios of most financial intermediaries consist of business, real estate, and consumer loans and investments. Each of these types of assets is subject to certain types of unsystematic risk which can be reduced through diversification. Table 12.1 shows the primary unsystematic risk types that dominate each of these assets. These risk types should be the basis for monitoring the diversification of each loan and investment portfolio classification.

This system of determining the most important types of unsystematic risk for each loan and investment classification can be more refined than that shown

TABLE 12.1

Primary Type of Unsystematic Risk by Loan and Investment Classification

Loan or Investment Class	Unsystematic Risk Type
Business loans and corporate securities	Industry type
Residential real estate mortgages and securities	Location
Income-property mortgages and securities	Location and property type
Consumer loans and securities	Location and collateral type

here. It is possible to diversify by more than one factor. This is the case for income-property mortgages shown in the table. The risk of income-property loans is affected by location and property type. Office buildings may fare worse than warehouses in a geographically weak market, for example.

Using this risk classification system, the financial firm can provide reports to management, directors, and regulators, if necessary, showing the degree of diversification for each loan and investment classification. Consider a portfolio of corporate bonds and business loans. Since industry type has been determined to be the most important source of unsystematic risk, the financial institution with a portfolio of these assets might produce an analysis such as the one shown in Exhibit 12.1.

EXHIBIT 12.1

Industry Breakdown for Business Loans and Corporate Debt Securities

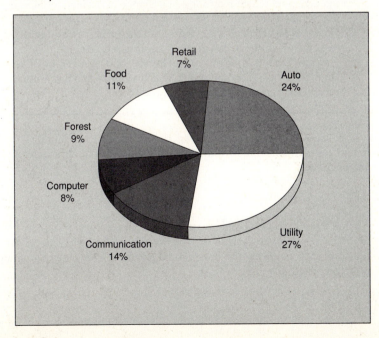

Retail 7%
Food 11%
Auto 24%
Forest 9%
Computer 8%
Utility 27%
Communication 14%

A similar chart would be developed for real estate loans by geographic area and for income-property mortgages by property type. These data would then be monitored carefully to insure that proper diversification was taking place.

SETTING UNDERWRITING GUIDELINES

Once a credit risk diversification strategy has been developed, it is necessary to develop policies and procedures for assessing the risk of each asset originated or purchased. These are known as *underwriting guidelines*. A set of underwriting guidelines for an unsecured business loan might look like those shown in Exhibit 12.2.

EXHIBIT 12.2

Underwriting Guidelines for Business Loans

1. Determine external critical business success factors (e.g., price, quality, labor harmony, weather, etc.).
2. Determine internal critical business success factors (e.g., management talent, research success, owner-manager dependence etc.).
3. Establish benchmarks.
   A. *Operating environment:* Discuss the internal and external factors identified above that are now impacting the business favorably or unfavorably.
   B. *Management behavior:* Explain any unusual actions of management which may suggest a change in business prospects. (e.g., change in accountants, unavailability for meetings, etc.)
   C. *Nonfinancial factors:* Factors that affect the firm's performance. (e.g., key customers, contract bid success rate, etc.)
   D. *Financial factors:* Analysis of pro forma balance sheet, income statement, cash flow statement, and inventory and accounts receivable turnover for the next three years.

The firm should develop underwriting guidelines such as those shown in Exhibit 12.2 for each loan and investment classification that it anticipates adding to its balance sheet.

CREDIT ANALYSIS

A major activity of the loan and investment selection process shown as Item D in Exhibit 12.2 relates to analysis of financial factors of the firm. The primary financial information obtained and duties to be performed for the credit analysis process include the following:

- Past financial statements.
- Pro forma balance sheets, income and cash flow statements.

- Financial ratio analysis.
- Quality of collateral offered.

The credit analysis typically includes comparative financial information. There are many reliable sources of financial comparative information organized by industry classification. Exhibit 12.3 provides a list of commonly available sources of financial information for businesses, consumers, and state and local governments.

EXHIBIT 12.3

Sources of Comparative Financial Information

Business loans and investments:
  Annual Statement Studies (Robert Morris and Associates)
  Business Ratings and Key Business Ratios (Dun & Bradstreet)
    Bond Ratings (Moody's Investor's Services, Standard & Poor's
    Corporation, and Fitch Investment Services)
  Industrial Manual and Banking and Finance Manual (Moody's
    Investor Services, Inc.)
  Industry Survey's (Standard & Poor's)
  Troy's Almanac of Business and Industrial Ratios
  Quarterly Financial Report for U.S. Manufacturing Corporations
    (Federal Trade Commission and Security and
    Exchange Commission)
Consumer loans:
  Credit bureaus
State and local governments:
  Government Manual (Moody's Investor Services, Inc.)

In addition to the many sources of comparative financial information shown, most large companies have their debt rated by one of the nation's bond rating services. These ratings are discussed later in this chapter. Dun & Bradstreet (D&B) provides credit ratings for thousands of smaller firms. Robert Morris Associates (RMA), and Leo Troy (Troy), are major sources of comparative financial ratio information organized by industry classification. The sources of information vary. RMA data come from commercial banks which supply financial information on their customers. Troy collects data from the Internal Revenue Service. D&B maintains financial reports on over 1 million corporations, partnerships, and sole proprietorships organized by Standard Industrial Classification, SIC code.

CREDIT APPROVAL LIMITS

Financial firms typically delegate loan and investment decisions to individuals and committees. It is common for a loan officer to meet with a potential borrower and develop a loan package that includes information called for in the firm's underwriting guidelines. This package, with the loan or investment officer's recommendation, is then circulated to members of a loan committee who must assess the creditworthiness of the potential borrower and approve or reject the application. Depending on the size of the loan, the level of delegation may eventually reach a committee of the board of directors, which decides on the merits of large loan or investment requests.

In a commercial bank or thrift institution, a junior loan officer might be given the authority to approve loans of up to $200,000. A senior loan officer might be able to approve loans to $500,000 or more. Above those levels, it is typically necessary to seek approval from a loan committee made up of senior management and other loan officers. This committee reviews the loan underwriting material developed by the loan officer assigned to the potential customer. Loan committees usually meet regularly since loan applications are developed continually in active organizations.

✓ Checkpoints

12-1 What are the most important issues to be included in a financial firm's credit policy?

12-2 Why is diversification important in controlling credit risk? What is the difference between systematic and unsystematic risk?

12-3 What is the importance of underwriting guidelines, credit analysis, and credit authorizations in the typical credit policy?

Primary Credit Factors—The Cs of Credit

One of the easiest systems for classifying the primary credit parameters is through the use of the "Cs" of credit. These factors number from three to seven depending on whose list is used—ours includes six. This list presents the major factors that affect credit risk in a convenient—and, we hope, easy to remember—manner. A short description of each C follows.

CHARACTER

The *character* of the borrower is the first factor and the most difficult to assess. Character is the quality of a borrower that indicates his or her intent to live up to the loan agreement or bond indenture. Traits such as integrity, honesty, responsibility, strong purpose, and truthfulness characterize good borrowers.

How does an analyst determine character? Generally it is done by talking to others who have had dealings with the prospective borrower. **Due diligence** is a process of inquiry used by the credit analyst to determine from other lenders, customers, suppliers, accountants, lawyers, and other references information on the borrower's character. Due diligence also covers such research as reviewing the quality of collateral offered, any contracts involved in the transaction, environmental risks, and a host of other factors that impact on a loan or investment's risk.

BRINGING BACK CHARACTER

A large number of savings and loan and commercial bank failures in the late 1980s and early 1990s caused the U.S. Congress and depository regulators to tighten up substantially on documentation, appraisals, and procedures used by depositories to make loans to businesses and real estate developers. This led to charges by many small businesses that a credit crunch had developed in 1991 which was slowing economic growth. The charge was that loans required excessive documentation for even well-established customers with excellent "character."

By 1993, the president and major depository regulators responded by making it easier for strong depositories to make loans based more on "character" and less on other more-quantitative lending factors. The regulators defined *character* as a borrower's proven track record in repaying debt over time.

How it Really Works

CAPACITY

Capacity deals primarily with the legality of the loan or investment. Loans and investments involve actions of officers and directors of businesses, officials of governments, and individuals. These individuals make representations and warrants about their authority to sign documents and meet the obligations called for in the loan or security documents.

The credit analyst must be sure to determine that the people executing loan agreements and security documents do have the legal standing and authority to execute the documents. This may require resolutions passed by the firm's board of directors, partnership agreements for businesses or proof of residency or age for consumer loans.

CAPITAL

Capital refers to the financial ability to pay; it is a shorthand description of the results of financial analysis into the creditworthiness of the prospective borrower. Capital deals with an assessment of the borrower's financial leverage, operating leverage, and pro forma cash flow.

Loans and investments are paid off through internally generated cash, sale of assets, or new debt and equity fund-raising activities. The credit analyst must be assured that the borrower has a viable plan involving one of these three approaches to pay off the debt.

CONDITIONS

Conditions is a catchall for all the environmental factors that can affect the ability of a borrower to repay debt. For businesses, it includes assessment of industry trends, competition, the labor situation, technology trends, pricing, raw material availability, and other factors that are generally beyond the control of the business. For an individual, conditions includes such issues as job stability and local market conditions that affect property values on home mortgages.

COLLATERAL

Collateral specifically looks to the value of assets that can be used to repay a loan if internally generated cash or new financing is not available. Collateral has become an increasingly important factor in debt analysis. Typically, a lender or investor will attempt to obtain rights to certain assets in the event of default. These are called *collateralized borrowings*. Some of the most common types of collateral are residential property, income-producing property, land, inventory, accounts receivable, and large capital equipment such as airplanes.

CONTROL

Control deals with the operating effectiveness of the information systems used by the borrower to manage the business. Not all borrowers have good internal financial and operating systems. This can lead to unexpected problems with meeting cash flow requirements. The lender and investor must be assured that the firm's accounting system is effective, that the firm meets all regulatory and other legal requirements, and that its management information systems are adequate to manage it effectively.

✓ Checkpoints

12-4 What is meant by each of the Cs of credit?
- **a.** Character?
- **b.** Capacity?
- **c.** Capital?
- **d.** Conditions?
- **e.** Collateral?
- **f.** Control?

12-5 What actions would you take to evaluate each of the credit Cs listed in Question 12-4 for a business or consumer loan?

Evaluating Business Loans and Investments

Each loan or investment necessitates collecting specialized information unique to that type of loan. Business debt analysis relies heavily on an evaluation of management's capability and track record, current and past financial performance, and an evaluation of future prospects. The process begins with a loan request or security proposal. Then the issue of character is reviewed. Finally, financial analysis is performed on past, current, and pro forma statements.

THE INITIAL REQUEST

The borrowing decision for any business begins with a proposal which discusses the purpose, amount, and timing for a borrowing. Whether the borrower is interested in short-term working capital loans or long-term bond financing, it is necessary for management and directors to formalize the borrower's needs in the form of a loan request or security offering material.

The primary purpose of this information is to allow lenders and investors to evaluate the legitimacy of a borrowing request. The range of borrowing justifications is wide. The most common purposes include:

- Increasing working capital for inventory and accounts receivable expansion.
- Making capital investments.
- Refinancing existing debt.
- Increasing financial leverage.
- Making acquisitions.

Most commercial bank loans made to businesses are for working capital purposes. However, commercial banks also have been active in making higher-risk loans used to increase a firm's financial leverage or make acquisitions. Larger firms can basically ignore commercial banks by issuing commercial paper and bonds sold in the money and capital markets.

MANAGEMENT AND OPERATIONS

A critical aspect of a business analysis involves assessing the firm's management and operations. The management and directors of a business firm are essential to its success or failure. Assessing management is a difficult assignment, which involves reviewing information on the experience, past track record, and professional credentials of the senior officers and key directors and obtaining first-hand information by talking directly to people who have done business with the firm. It is also very important to know what type of financial investment the officers and directors have in the firm in order to determine whether these people have a major financial stake in the success of the company.

This analysis also includes a review of the firm's operations which involves understanding the product or service, competitors, reliance on technology, raw material, labor, and industry trends. To aid in this analysis, it is usually useful to talk to customers, suppliers, and others involved in the industry.

This review process also requires an assessment of the extent to which the firm has honored past debts by reviewing past loans your organization has made to the firm or by talking to other lenders and investors that have provided debt capital. The key is to determine whether the firm has a history of always living up to its financial obligations.

FINANCIAL ANALYSIS

Financial analysis is the process of assessing the operating and financial performance of a firm over time, compared to itself and at specified points in time compared to industry competitors. Comparing financial performance measures over time is called *time series analysis,* and comparisons at one point in time are referred to as *cross-sectional analysis.* Typically, both forms of analysis are used in financial ratio analysis.

Financial ratios are commonly used to assess financial performance of business firms, allowing firms of different sizes to be compared on a standard basis. The primary factors investigated with financial ratios include the firm's:

- Liquidity.
- Working capital and asset turnover.
- Capital structure (financial leverage).
- Profitability.

The best way to review the use of financial ratios is with an example. Exhibit 12.4 provides recent balance sheets and income statements for Academic Software Inc. (ASI). This hypothetical firm was started five years ago to develop and market specialized software to colleges and universities and to professors and students. It has grown rapidly. Colleges and universities are notoriously slow in paying bills, which has led to a sharp rise in accounts receivable at ASI. Moreover, bookstores typically overpurchase and then return unsold goods, which has tended to inflate the inventory at ASI. Both these problems have caused the need for additional working capital. To assess the loan request, a financial ratio analysis will be completed for the most current year, 19xy, and the previous year, 19xx.

LIQUIDITY ANALYSIS

There are two ratios and one other measure commonly used to analyze liquidity of business firms. These are the measure for **net working capital** and the **quick** and **current** liquidity **ratios**. Maintaining adequate liquidity is essential to the firm's ability to meet normal and unexpected obligations. For ASI, this measure and ratios for 19xy and 19xx are:

Net working capital (NWC) = *Current assets – Current liabilities*

19xy: NWC = $1,560 – $1,203 = $357

19xx: NWC = $1,260 – $919 = $341

Quick ratio = *Cash and marketable securities ÷ Current liabilities*

19xy: ($250 + $160) ÷ $1,203 = .34×

19xx: ($190 + $150) ÷ $919 = .37×

Current ratio = *Current assets ÷ Current liabilities*

19xy: $1,560 ÷ $1,203 = 1.30×

19xx: $1,540 ÷ $919 = 1.68×

WORKING CAPITAL AND ASSET TURNOVER ANALYSIS

There are a number of ratios used to measure whether the firm is productively using its assets. It is not good for a firm to make investments in idle assets. Firms generally want sales and goods in process inventory to move quickly through the firm, since it is costly to finance it. The same is true of fixed assets. Investments in idle plant or rarely used equipment are costly. Some of the more common ratios used to measure turnover for ASI are:

Inventory turnover = *Cost of goods sold ÷ Inventory*

19xy: $1,700 ÷ $450 = 3.78×

19xx: $1,350 ÷ $370 = 3.65×

Average collection period = *Accounts receivable ÷ (Annual sales ÷ 360)*

19xy: $700 ÷ ($5,070 ÷ 360) = 49.7 days

19xx: $370 ÷ ($4,120 ÷ 360) = 32.3 days

Average payment period = *Accounts payable ÷ (Annual purchases ÷ 360)*
(assuming ASI's purchases are 60% of cost of goods sold)

19xy: $560 ÷ [(.60 × $1,700)÷ 360] = 197.7 days

19xx: $540 ÷ [(.60 × $1,350) ÷ 360] = 240 days

Fixed asset turnover = *Sales ÷ Net fixed assets*

19xy: $5,070 ÷ $1,740 = 2.91×

19xx: $4,120 ÷ $1,540 = 2.67×

Total asset turnover = *Sales ÷ Total assets*

19xy: $5,070 ÷ $3,300 = 1.54×

19xx: $4,120 ÷ $2,800 = 1.47×

EXHIBIT 12.4

Balance Sheets and Income Statements for Academic Software, Inc. (000's)
19xx and 19xy Actual

Balance Sheets

Assets:	19xy	19xx
Current assets		
Cash	$ 250	$ 190
Marketable securities	160	150
Accounts receivable	700	550
Inventories	450	370
Total current assets	$ 1,560	$ 1,260
Gross fixed assets (at cost)*		
Land and buildings	$ 580	$ 470
Machinery and equipment	850	800
Furniture and fixtures	700	670
Vehicles	400	300
Other (includes financial leases)	17	90
Total gross fixed assets (at cost)	$ 2,700	$ 2,330
Less: Accumulated depreciation	960	790
Net fixed assets	$ 1,740	$ 1,540
Total assets	$ 3,300	$ 2,800
Liabilities and stockholders' equity:		
Current liabilities		
Accounts payable	$ 560	$ 540
Notes payable	473	259
Accruals	170	120
Total current liabilites	$ 1,203	$ 919
Long-term debts (includes financial leases)+	$ 350	$ 350
Total liabilities	$ 1,553	$ 1,269
Stockholders' equity		
Preferred stock—cumulative 7%, $100 par,		
1,000 shares authorized and issued	$ 100	$ 100
Common stock—$1.00 par, 500,000 shares		
authorized, shares issued and outstanding		
in 19xy: 90,000; in 19xx: 85,000	90	85
Paid-in capital in excess of par on		
common stock	267	246
Retained earnings	1,290	1,100
Total stockholders' equity	$ 1,747	$ 1,531
Total liabilities and stockholders' equity	$ 3,300	$ 2,800

*In 19xy, the firm has a six-year financial lease requiring annual beginning-of-year payments of $50,000. Four years of the lease have yet to run.

+ Annual principal repayments on a portion of the firm's total outstanding debt amount to $52,000 in 19xx and 19xy.

continued

Exhibit 12.4, continued

Income Statements

	For the Years Ended December 31	
	19xy	*19xx*
Sales revenue	$ 5,070	$ 4,120
Less: Cost of goods sold	1,700	1,350
Gross profits	$ 3,370	$ 2,770
Less: Operating expenses		
Selling expense	$ 1,800	$ 1,650
General and administrative expenses	950	850
Lease expense	50	50
Depreciation expense	170	160
Total operating expense	$ 2,970	$ 2,710
Operating profits	$ 400	$ 60
Less: Interest expense	46	35
Net profits before taxes	$ 354	$ 25
Less: Taxes (rate = 30%)	106	8
Net profit after taxes	$ 248	$ 17
Less: Preferred stock dividends	7	7
Less: Common stock dividends	51	0
Earnings available for retained earnings	$ 190	$ 10

CAPITAL STRUCTURE (FINANCIAL LEVERAGE) ANALYSIS

The amount of debt used to finance the assets of a corporation is important for two reasons. First, the more debt in the capital structure, the less cushion for the firm to experience operating losses without defaulting on the debt. Second, the greater the amount of debt, the greater the ongoing obligation to service the interest and principal repayments. These two features are measured by a number of financial ratios, which for ASI are:

Debt ratio = *Total liabilities ÷ Total assets*

19xy: $1,553 ÷ $3,300 = 47.1%

19xx: $1,269 ÷ $2,800 = 45.3%

Debt-equity ratio = *Long-term debt ÷ Stockholders' equity*

19xy: $350 ÷ $1,747 = 20.0%

19xx: $350 ÷ $1,531 = 22.9%

Times interest earned ratio = *Earnings before interest and taxes ÷ Interest*

19xy: $400 ÷ $46 = 8.70x

19xx: $60 ÷ $35 = 1.71x

PROFITABILITY ANALYSIS

There are many ways to analyze profitability. One is to relate it to the quantity of sales to determine the profit generated on products and services sold. Another is to relate it to the investment that stockholders alone or stockholders and creditors together have in the firm. Several of the more important of these ratios for ASI are:

Gross profit margin = *(Sales − Cost of goods sold) ÷ Sales*

19xy: ($5,070 − $1,700) ÷ $5,070 = 66.5%

19xx: ($4,120 − $1,350) ÷ $4,120 = 67.2%

Net profit margin = *Net profits after taxes ÷ Sales*

19xy: $248 ÷ $5,070 = 4.9%

19xx: $17 ÷ $4,120 = 0.4%

Return on assets (ROA) = *Net profits after taxes ÷ Total assets*

19xy: $248 ÷ $3,300 = 7.5%

19xx: $17 ÷ $2,800 = 0.6%

Return on equity (ROE) = *Net profits after taxes ÷ Stockholders' equity*

19xy: $248 ÷ $1,747 = 14.2%

19xx: $17 ÷ $1,531 = 1.1%

TIME SERIES AND CROSS-SECTIONAL ANALYSIS ON ASI

Now that all the data and ratios have been assembled and calculated, it is time to analyze what they mean. This is done using time series and cross-sectional comparisons. Only two years of data for ASI are shown here, even though three to five years would typically be called for. For comparisons, industry data from a source such as Robert Morris Associates could be used, but we have used hypothetical data. The data are analyzed by reviewing changes in the condition of the firm from 19xx to 19xy and by comparing it to the industry median figures covering 19xy. A short assessment is also provided in Exhibit 12.5.

EXHIBIT 12.5

Ratio Analysis for ASI

Ratio Type	19xx	19xy	Industry	Comment
Liquidity Ratios				
Net working capital	$341	$357	$234	Strong
Quick ratio	.37x	.34x	1.23x	Very weak
Current ratio	1.68x	1.30x	1.56x	Average to weak
Working Capital and Asset Turnover				
Inventory turnover	3.65x	3.78x	4.56x	Weak
Average collection period	32.3 days	49.7 days	28 days	Weak and worsening
Average payment period	240 days	197.7 days	65 days	High
Fixed asset turnover	2.67x	2.91x	2.78x	Average
Total asset turnover	1.54x	1.47x	2.10x	Below average
Capital Structure				
Debt ratio	45.3%	47.1%	37.8%	Above average
Debt-equity ratio	22.9%	20.0%	15.8%	Above average
Times interest earned	1.71x	8.70x	4.56x	Volatile but now adequate
Profitability				
Gross profit margin	67.2%	66.5%	45.5%	Very high
Net profit margin	0.4%	4.9%	6.7%	Volatile and low
Return on assets	0.6%	7.5%	12.9%	Volatile and low
Return on equity	1.1%	14.2%	18.1%	Volatile and low

A review of the two years of ratios for ASI and comparison with its peer group indicate some serious problems: both the quick and current ratios show ASI is in need of liquid assets; its inventory and accounts receivable ratios are both much higher than those of its competitors. These factors account for the loan request for more working capital for inventory and accounts receivable expansion. However, the ratios could suggest that poor management policies may be the cause. The debt ratios also indicate that ASI has much higher financial leverage than its peer group. High-tech companies usually have low debt in their capital structure because of the high risk and volatility of the business. These low ASI liquidity turnover and debt ratios and high financial leverage ratios do not support the request for a loan to finance additional working capital.

The profit ratios at ASI are also of concern. Although 19xy is much better than 19xx, the high volatility and weak comparison to its peer group represent a red flag. If a loan were to be considered, the lender should demand that inventory return policies be reevaluated along with accounts receivable collection policies.

The lender could also collateralize the loan with accounts receivable and inventory, if it is sufficiently marketable. Otherwise, ASI should consider additional equity financing.

There are many other issues to be reviewed which are typically shown in the footnotes to financial statements. Some of the most important include:

- Litigation exposure.
- Changes in accounting policies.
- Contingent liabilities.
- Pension obligations.

These factors must be included in any assessment of the firm.

The Cash Flow Statement

It takes cash to pay interest on loans and repay principal. As a result, the cash flow statement is a key to the analysis of a firm planning to issue debt. Commercial bank regulators require that cash flow statements be prepared for loan customers, and Security and Exchange Commission reporting requirements for public companies require cash flow statements in stockholder financial statements. One unfortunate fact in preparing cash flow statements using the readily available income statement and balance sheets is that not all the information on cash receipts and expenditures is shown in these statements. You must be satisfied with using net changes in balance sheet balances to determine the sources and uses of cash. Flow data are not available. The basic sources and uses of cash are shown below:

Sources of Cash	Uses of Cash
Increases in liabilities	Increases in noncash assets
Decreases in noncash assets	Decreases in liabilities
New issues of equity	Purchases of redemption of equity
Cash revenues	Cash expenses
	Cash taxes paid
	Cash dividends paid

Exhibit 12.6 provides a cash flow statement for ASI for 19xy, using the statements in Exhibit 12.4 and a hypothetical pro forma for the next year 19xz.

The pro forma 19xz cash flow statement for ASI reveals that the company is expecting to be very dependent on proceeds from borrowings and accounts payable to meet its cash needs for the year. The company is also anticipating another average profit performance, which is a risky proposition given the firm's historical profit volatility. Moreover, the firm is contemplating eliminating its cash dividend on common stock to help meet its cash needs. Again the data seem to support the need for new policies to reduce the growth in accounts receivable and inventories and the need to collateralize any loan made to the firm.

EXHIBIT 12.6

Cash Flow Statement for ASI for 19xy and Pro forma for 19xz (000's)

	Year Ended 19xy	Pro Forma for Year Ended 19xz
Cash Provided by (used for) Operating Activities		
Net income	$ 248	$ 300
Noncash items included in income:		
Depreciation	170	190
Change in certain assets and liabilities		
Accounts receivable	(150)	(200)
Inventories	(80)	(120)
Other current assets		
Accruals	50	25
Net cash provided by operating activities	$ 238	$ 195
Cash Required by (used for) Investing Activities		
Additions to property, plant and equipment	$ (370)	$ (350)
Net cash required for investing activities	$ (370)	$ (350)
Cash Provided by (used for) Financing Activities		
Proceeds from borrowings and accounts payable	$ 234	$ 200
Issuance of long-term debt	0	0
Reduction in total debt	0	0
Net change in total debt	$ 234	$ 200
Payment of cash dividends	(58)	(7)
Sale of common stock	26	0
Sale of preferred stock	0	0
Net cash required for financing activities	$ (32)	$ (7)
Net increase (decrease) in cash	70	38
Cash and marketable securities at beginning of year	340	302
Cash and marketable securities at end of year	$ 410	$ 340

✓ Checkpoints

12-6 What information is important in the prospective borrower's initial financing request?

12-7 What types of information are needed, and what is the objective of the prospective lender's analysis of the firm's management and operational performance?

12-8 What are the most important financial ratios used to analyze a nonfinancial firm's liquidity, asset turnover, capital structure, and profitability? What is the role of the cash flow statement in credit analysis?

Evaluating Mortgage Loans and Securities

Mortgages represent the largest quantity of nongovernmental borrowing. The vast majority of mortgage debt is used to finance residential housing. However, mortgages and mortgage securities are used to finance income properties, such as apartments, office buildings, warehouses, hotels, and shopping centers.

The analysis of prospective mortgage borrowers relies principally on two criteria. First, the value of the property must be established. Since real property is the collateral for a mortgage loan, a critical factor in the mortgage lending decision is the proper establishment of value.[1] Secondly, the ability of the borrower to make the principal and interest payments of the mortgage, called *debt service,* must be established. Debt service for a home buyer relies on the sources of income of the owner-occupants. Debt service for the owner of income property relies principally on the rent and other income derived from the property, less its operating expenses.

ESTABLISHING COLLATERAL VALUE—THE APPRAISAL

The huge real estate losses sustained by savings and loans and commercial banks in the late 1980s and early 1990s have provided considerable evidence about the difficulty in establishing true value for real estate. They also established the extreme volatility in real estate values. Most of these properties had appraisals done by professional appraisers using proper appraisal techniques. Even so, changes in market conditions resulted in losses of 30–50% or more.

The appraisal process relies on three approaches to establishing value. These are the (1) **market comparable approach**; (2) **replacement**, or **cost, approach**; and (3) the **income approach**. Although a full discussion of appraisal is beyond the scope of this book, a short discussion will serve to explain the differences.

Market Comparable Approach

This approach requires finding prices of similar properties that have recently been sold and comparing the subject property to them by making price adjustments up and down for such factors as location, amenities, size, and condition. This approach is almost exclusively used in residential property appraisal.

Replacement Approach

This approach attempts to establish the cost of replicating the subject property at today's construction costs. The main deficiency in this approach is that land value is a high percentage of the value of many properties. Land value must rely on market conditions, which makes it a mixture of the market comparable approach and cost approach. Another problem is that many expensive improvements may have little value to a prospective buyer.

---

[1]Equity in real estate is also the collateral used for home equity lines of credit or second mortgages. It is not uncommon for a second mortgage lender to finance the difference between the principal of the first mortgage and up to 90% to 95% of the property's market value.

Income Approach

This approach, used primarily for income-property lending, relies on standard discounted cash-flow models of the revenue and costs derived from owning the subject property. It is particularly suited for apartments, office buildings, shopping centers, and all other property where market rents and property operating costs are identifiable.

The poor real estate lending experiences of the 1980s have caused lenders to be much more conservative in the amount of loan they will provide in relation to property or owner income. This ratio, called the *loan-to-value-ratio (LTVR)* is a major criterion in both residential and income-property lending. The *LTVR* is computed by taking

$$LTVR = Loan\ amount \div Accepted\ property\ valuation$$

Needless to say, the higher the *LTVR*, the riskier lenders consider the loan to be. In residential loans, which rely more on *LTVR* levels than income-property loans, a *LTVR* of 70–80% is common. *LTVRs* above 90% usually require the lender to obtain additional credit protection such as mortgage insurance from a third-party insurer.

WHEN THE LOSS IS MORE THAN THE PRINCIPAL

Commercial real estate lenders have lost more than loan principal on bad real estate loans in recent years. The problem stems from the cost of environmental cleanup laws. Property found to be environmentally unsafe may involve cleanup costs greater than the owner can afford. The solution: let the property go into default and have some deep-pockets bank foreclose. Then the Environmental Protection Agency can force the bank to pay the cost of cleanup. The bank faces not only the loss of loan principal, but an additional unknown loss of an environmental cleanup that may exceed its capital base.

All this has had a dampening effect on the willingness of banks to lend. The American Bankers Association, the primary U.S. commercial bank lobbyist, found in a survey that nearly 90% of U.S. banks have altered lending policies to avoid the potential for environmental surprises. Some businesses, such as printers, dry cleaners, gas service stations, and users of paint, have found themselves "greenlined" by lenders unwilling to lend to them because of the added risk of cleanup costs. A similar liability is spreading to Britain and the European continent making this an international lending issue. The Basel committee of central bankers, which formulated worldwide capital rules, already faces problems of how to measure capital of banks with contingent environmental cleanup liabilities.

Source: "Where Bankers Fear to Tread," *The Economist*, May 21, 1994, pp. 85–86.

How it Really Works

DEBT SERVICE

Debt service is the other major factor in the mortgage lending decision. Mortgage payments are covered by the income of the borrower in the case of residential properties or by the net operating income of the property in the case of income properties.

For residential properties, lenders typically limit the ratio of a borrower's gross income from salaries, wages, some bonuses, and investment income to approximately 25% of the property's monthly mortgage payment principal (P) and interest (I) payments, real estate taxes (T), and property insurance (I), (PITI). This ratio is referred to as the debt-to-income ratio. A similar ratio, including additional obligations of the borrower for installment loans and other periodic obligations, might be allowed to rise to 33% of gross income. These ratios are defined as:

Debt-to-income without installment debt = PITI ÷ Borrower's monthly gross income

Debt-to-income with installment debt = (PITI + Monthly installment and other payments) ÷ Borrower's monthly gross income

For income properties, establishing the acceptable debt service level is generally more difficult. It involves a financial analysis of the revenue and costs of operating the subject property using pro forma data similar to the analysis of an operating nonfinancial business shown earlier. The basic analysis requires establishing the property's pro forma net operating income (NOI) using data such as this:

(a)	Gross monthly operating income	$30,554
(b)	Less: 5% vacancy	1,528
(c)	Actual monthly income	29,026
(d)	Less: Operating monthly expenses	12,485
	Less: Monthly repair and maintenance	2,300
(e)	Net monthly operating income (NOI)	$14,241

From these data, the lender can calculate a ratio called the **debt coverage ratio (DCR)** which establishes the relationship between the monthly mortgage debt service and the property's net monthly operating income. If the owner of this property requested a loan with a $12,500 monthly principal and interest payment (PI), the DCR would be:

$$DCR = NOI \div PI = \$14,241 \div \$12,500 = 1.1393$$

A ratio of 1.14 might be acceptable for a quality apartment in a desirable neighborhood, but it would be considered very low for a motel. The lender would consider both the LTVR and DCR in the lending decision. Within ranges, there may be a tradeoff of a higher acceptable DCR for a property with a low LTVR.

It should be fairly clear by now that real estate mortgage lending is conceptually similar to lending to businesses. The borrower (character), property (operating entity), financial attributes (financial ratios), and cash flow issues apply equally to decisions regarding the credit risk of each type of loan.

✓ Checkpoints

12-9 What are the two primary factors used to underwrite the credit risk of real estate loans?

12-10 What is the role of the appraisal process in originating real estate loans? What are the three basic approaches to real estate appraisal?

12-11 How are *LTVR* and *DCR* used in the evaluation of credit risk for mortgage loans?

Evaluating Unsecured and Secured Consumer Loans

In addition to home mortgages, consumers are significant borrowers of consumer credit. Consumer loans are typically divided into unsecured and secured loans. The most common form of unsecured loans are credit card receivables, debt consolidation loans, and transaction account overdraft accounts. Secured consumer loans include loans for automobiles, mobile homes (which are considered personal property in most states), recreational vehicles and boats, second mortgages, and loans secured by appliances. Like the mortgage loan, a consumer loan involves the analysis of collateral value if it is a secured loan and ability to meet debt-service requirements. Consider the two factors explained in the next section.

COLLATERAL VALUE AND LOAN STRUCTURE

The collateral for secured consumer loans is almost always an asset with declining market value over time. A loan collateralized by a new automobile with a small down payment would generally have insufficient collateral value after the car has been driven from the dealer. The relationship between the market value of the collateral over time and the unpaid balance of a loan is the key to determining such loan attributes as down payment and term-to-maturity. One easy way to lower the risk of secured loans is to increase the size of the down payment. For most durable goods used as collateral, a large enough down payment will insure that at all times the market value of the collateral will exceed the unpaid balance on the loan. Another approach to reduce risk is to shorten the maturity on the loan. A short maturity for an installment loan means faster principal reduction, also decreasing risk.

Competition among lenders has led to fairly large changes in the types of loan terms offered on secured consumer loans. Car loans, which rarely went beyond 36 months in the 1970s, reached 60 months in the late 1980s. Down payment requirements have also changed over time as economic conditions changed and competition among lenders tightened or eased.

Another technique that has become more popular in recent years is to relate the terms of the loan offered to the creditworthiness of the borrower. Strong borrowers (using credit scoring techniques to be discussed next) would be offered lower interest rates, lower down payments, and/or longer terms-to-maturity. Lower-quality loans would usually also be charged a higher interest rate, require higher down payments, and shorter terms-to-maturity than loans to more credit-worthy borrowers.

CREDIT SCORING

Credit scoring is used to assess the debt-carrying capacity and character of the consumer borrow. Credit scoring systems are also beginning to be used for home-mortgage lending evaluations. Unsecured loans rely primarily on credit scoring techniques to make credit decisions. These systems may be statistical, judgmental, or a combination of the two. The approach of statistical credit scoring is to determine quantitative relationships between easily substantiated factors that describe the borrower. All evaluation approaches must avoid using factors that discriminate on the basis of gender, race, religion, or national origin, since discrimination based on these factors is illegal. Exhibit 12.7 provides a hypothetical list of factors and a point system assigned to each factor. The point system is based on statistical procedures such as multiple regression and discriminate analysis, which relate the factors to historical experience with good and bad loans.

In this example, the lender has determined that the cutoff for loan acceptance is 32 points. This borrower with 38 points would qualify. A borrower with less than 32 points might try to obtain someone to cosign the loan which would make the cosigner equally liable to meet the obligation. This reduces the credit risk of the lender.

How

it

Really

Works

MERCURY FINANCE CO. FINDS NICHE

Mercury Finance is a consumer loan company that specializes in lending to borrowers who are typically turned down by traditional lenders. Military personnel, first-time borrowers, and borrowers with poor credit records do not necessarily mean high credit losses. Lending on used cars and trucks is another specialty. Making a profit out of high-risk borrowers is not a problem if you price the credit to cover higher-than-average credit losses.

Mercury's average loan in 1983 earned about 21% at a time when their cost of money was 6.5%. Most traditional consumer lenders use cut-and-dried consumer credit scoring methodologies which give little room for judgment. Mercury spends time looking behind the credit record of the new customer.

The strategy has clearly paid off for Mercury so far. The eight-year-old firm hit $775 million in assets in June 1993. Over the four years ending in 1982, the company earned a average return on equity of 38%.

EXHIBIT 12.7

Credit Scoring System

	Credit Score (borrower rating noted by *)	Cumulative Score
Gross Annual Income		
< $15,000	1	
$15,000–$30,000	5 *	5
> $30,000	12	
Consumer Loan Payments to Gross Income Including Loan Request		
< 20%	12 *	17
20%–35%	5	
> 35%	1	
Number of Credit Cards		
0	1	
1–3	7 *	24
> 3	5	
Credit History		
No derogatory comments	12	
No record	3	
Slow on payments	0 *	24
Age		
< 30 years	1 *	25
≥ 30 years	5	
Residence		
Rent	1 *	26
Homeowner < 2 years	5	
Homeowner ≥ 2 years	12	
Job Situation		
< 3 years	1	
≥ 3 years	12 *	38
Retired	10	
Total		**38**

Using data on collateral valuation over time and credit scoring techniques, it is possible to both design consumer loan programs with different levels of risk and control credit risk for loan programs established.

✓ Checkpoints

12-12 How can you use information on the market value of collateral offered for a secured consumer loan to design loan terms that adjust for risk?

12-13 How can credit scoring techniques be used to assist in the credit decision?

Country Risk

Investing in securities and lending in foreign countries presents an additional level of risk. This risk is known as *country,* or *sovereign, risk. Country risk* relates to the potential of foreign governments to take actions that result in the violation of investment and loan terms and covenants. Such actions may involve obligations of private companies that are otherwise creditworthy. Consequently, country risk must be evaluated separately and apart from normal credit risk concerns. This section will consider the ways in which countries can affect the creditworthiness of loans and securities issued by private and government units within their borders. Various models and measures of evaluating country risk will be presented.

SOVEREIGN GOVERNMENTS AND INVESTOR SAFETY

Governments have significant influence on the ability of government and private organizations within their jurisdictions to meet their debt obligations. Basically, they can take three actions that will adversely affect investors in loans and securities of businesses and government units within their jurisdiction. These include:

- *Expropriation:* Expropriation is the seizure by a government unit of the assets of private firms and individuals. Owners of debt and equity in these firms or of real assets such as real estate simply lose the value of these assets.

- *Repudiation:* Repudiation is the cancellation of all outstanding debt obligations of specified government and private units within a country. It may involve only government borrowing units or may include private issuers of debt. Owners having an equity position in certain assets may be left unaffected. Repudiation has been used infrequently since the World War II. The most recent repudiation of debt occurred in 1964 in North Korea.

- *Debt rescheduling:* Debt rescheduling is the modification of debt contractual terms on outstanding securities and loans. These modifications include moratoriums on scheduled payments of interest and principal, reductions in scheduled interest rates, and delays in scheduled payments of principal and interest.

U.S. international commercial bankers have learned a lot about country risk during the last decade. Commercial banks lending in eastern European countries of the former Soviet Union and in certain Latin American countries have faced significant losses on credit extended in these countries during the 1980s. This experience underscored the importance of country risk for financial institutions.

Adding to the importance of this topic is the accelerated globalization of financial markets during the last decade. Today, most large institutional investors have included foreign securities in their investment portfolios. At the end of 1993, approximately 12% of the market value of all publicly owned equities in the world were from developing countries, where country risk is the greatest. This means that a significant percentage of debt and equity is exposed to country risk.

MEASURING COUNTRY RISK

Evaluating the risk of a potential adverse action by a foreign government is at best a difficult proposition. Still, governments—like business firms and individuals—have limited resources. When these resources are insufficient to meet foreign financial obligations, there is always a chance the government will renege on these obligations. Consequently, it is necessary to identify those factors that contribute to or are associated with a country's reneging on financial obligations.

There are several methods available for evaluating country risk. These include:

- Published country-risk indices.
- Proprietary credit scoring models.
- Market pricing indices.

Over the years, a number of organizations have developed and published indices of county risk. These are based on economic data and professional opinion. Proprietary models are statistical credit scoring models used by large international lenders and investors which are typically far more sophisticated than the published indices. Market pricing indices are based on data indicating the secondary market value of foreign debt or securities.

Published Country-Risk Indices

Several organizations have developed indices of country risk based on a number of financial factors. One such index has been developed by *Euromoney,* an international financial publication. The *Euromoney Index* is an index ranking from 0 (highest country risk) to 100 (lowest country risk). It is based on nine factors, which are rated from 1 to 10. These ratings are subjective since they include such factors as: (1) economic performance; (2) political performance (double-weighted); (3) debt indicators; (4) access to bank lending; (5) access to short-term finance; (6) access to capital markets; (7) access to and discount on forfeiting; (8) credit ratings; and (9) debt in default or rescheduled.

The financial publication, *Institutional Investor,* has also developed an index of credit risk. The *Institutional Investor Index* is based on twice-yearly surveys of commercial bank lending officers. These officers provide the magazine with subjective ratings of the country-risk exposure of countries based on a 0 (highest country risk) to 100 (lowest country risk) scoring system.

The financial publication *The Economist* has a sister unit called *Economist Intelligence Unit,* which produces a country-risk rating. This rating system ranges from a low risk rating of 0 to the highest risk rating of 100. This quarterly rating system is based on economic and political risk factors such as economic performance, fiscal budget position, inflation rate, and policitical stability.

Proprietary Credit Scoring Models

Major international lenders and investors typically develop their own proprietary country-risk scoring systems. This process involves determining a set of economic, financial, and behavioral characteristics that are associated with country risk. These are then used in a discriminate statistical analysis to produce a Z score. The methodology is the same as the Altman Z score methodology discussed in Chapter 11. Other statistical methods have been deployed as well. The variables used in these models are generally based on macroeconomic measures of performance of the foreign economies. Several of the more common variables used include: (1) debt service ratio (Principal and interest payments on foreign debt ÷ Exports); (2) the import ratio (Total imports ÷ Gross domestic product); and (3) money supply growth rate (Money supply in period ÷ Beginning period money supply). As many as 30 or more variables might be used in a statistical analysis of this type.

The single biggest problem with these statistical models is that they do not make it possible to incorporate political risks that relate to country risk. Changes in the political power structure of a country may be the largest country risk. Consequently, statistical models of country risk must be augmented by additional analysis of a more subjective nature.

Market Pricing Indices

With volume of loans to developing countries (LDC debt) having reached over $250 billion, the market participants have created a secondary market in LDC debt. This trading activity makes it possible to track the bid and ask prices for LDC debt. These data typically are maintained by large international commercial banks and investment bankers. On a particular week, the debt of Zaire might be selling for 23% of par value while Brazil is 85%. Changes in these prices provide a market indicator of increasing or decreasing country risk.

✓ Checkpoints

12-14 What is country risk, and what actions of governments create it?

12-15 What approaches do analysts have available to assess country risk?

SUMMARY AND REVIEW

1. **Describe the credit policy process including the importance of diversification, developing underwriting guidelines, setting approval limits, and establishing credit analysis procedures.**

    The process used to create a credit policy to control the level of credit within a financial institution involves strategies, policies, and procedures. Developing a **portfolio strategy** which attempts to minimize risk while providing a high return on assets is the first duty. Then policies and procedures must be developed. Each type of loan added to the portfolio must have **underwriting guidelines** and **procedures for analyzing credit risk** established for each prospective borrower. Finally, the board of directors must establish **approval limits** for decision makers within the firm.

2. **Explain the major types of loans and investments held by intermediaries, including loans and investments of business, consumers, and international borrowers.**

The major types of loans and securities used by businesses to borrow money include secured and unsecured bank loans, commercial paper, and corporate bonds. Mortgages are used to finance residential and income properties. Governments borrow using a variety of secured and unsecured bonds.

3. **Explain the primary credit risk factors summarized by the Cs of credit.**

    The primary factors to be considered in evaluating the credit risk of prospective borrower are described by the Cs of credit. **Character** involves the willingness of a borrower to repay. **Capacity** deals with the legality and documentation of the loan. **Capital** relates to the financial ability to pay. **Conditions** involve the impact of environmental factors on the ability to repay a loan. **Collateral** describes the value of assets that may be available to the creditor in the event of default. **Control** relates to the operating effectiveness of the borrower and the ability to control ongoing operations.

4. **Describe the major types of information needed to analyze business, real estate, and consumer loans and securities.**

    Business loan credit risk is analyzed by reviewing the **purpose** of the proceeds of the loan, management and operational **effectiveness,** and **financial capability.** Mortgages are evaluated based on the **value of the real estate** financed and the ability of the borrower to meet **debt service** payments. Consumer loans primarily rely on the ability of the borrower to meet debt service requirements and collateral value.

5. **Describe country risk and explain several methods to measure it.**

    Country risk is the risk that a sovereign government will take actions that result in creditors of that country failing to meet their obligations to debtors. Measures of country risk include **published country risk indices, proprietary credit scoring models,** and **market pricing indices.**

CREDIT SCORING   **PROBLEM**

You are being trained for the consumer credit loan underwriting function. The following information about a potential borrower has been given to you.

Name: Melissa Mortax
Age: 25
Residence: Apartment, 2 years
Current installment loan payments: $0
Loan payment for this request: $234
Job: Sales representative, 1.5 years
Monthly income: $1,500 annually
Number of credit cards: 0
Credit history: No record

Using the credit scoring system represented by Exhibit 12.7, complete a preliminary credit scoring of this applicant. The lender's minimum score for acceptance of a loan is 28 points.

CASE 12.1

BUSINESS LOAN EVALUATION: IMPEDE INC.

Impede Inc. is a recently incorporated company that designs and manufactures highly specialized computer chips for manufacturers of machinery, space systems, and specialized audio components. The firm was started three years ago by two engineers and a recent business school graduate. The firm has built a business with annual sales in the last year, 19xy, of $1.67 million. The firm was unprofitable in its first two years but earned $56,000 in 19xy.

The industry in which Impede competes is competitive, but not nearly as much so as the high-volume segment that produces customized chips for the computer, auto, and communications industries. Therefore, Impede's profit margins are high and it has developed fairly strong relationships with about 15 customers. One customer accounts for 35% of the company's sales.

The small management team at Impede has concluded that by expanding its sales force and increasing its manufacturing and design capabilities it can expand rapidly in the years ahead. The budget for this expansion is reflected in Exhibit C12.1. It shows basic financial information for the two previous years, 19xx and 19xy, and the pro forma for next year, 19xz.

As a loan officer, you have been asked to take the exhibit home overnight to do a quick review of the financials as provided. You won't be able to assess management, operations, and industry at this time. Based on these data, what can you say about the desirability of this firm obtaining a loan from your employer? Impede is interested in a term loan of two years maturity. The only collateral available is accounts receivable and some specialized machinery with combined market values equal to 75% of the loan request.

Based on these facts, comment on the financial ratios presented and make preliminary recommendations for a loan to Impede Inc.

CASE 12.2

GROUNDTRACK, INC.

Martin woke up at 3 A.M. in a cold sweat. He had trouble falling asleep and was again bothered by the events of the previous day. Martin Parks was one of six loan officers of the Bay National Bank of San Palo. Bay was created 12 years ago by a number of prominent business people and investors who felt San Palo needed a local business bank that would provide quality business banking services and loans to small- and middle-market firms. Martin joined Bay four years ago. He had worked as a trainee at a large regional bank and had one year of experience as an assistant loan officer following the training program. The opportunity to have de-

EXHIBIT C12.1

Ratio Analysis for Impede, Inc., for 19xx and 19xy
and Industry Comparisons for 19xy

Ratio Type	19xx	19xy	Industry 19xy	19xz Pro Forma	Your Comment
Liquidity Ratios					
Net working capital	$123	$154	$234	$176	
Quick ratio	.75x	.56x	1.10x	.86x	
Current ratio	1.12x	1.22x	2.56x	1.30x	
Working Capital and Asset Turnover					
Inventory turnover	7.68x	8.98x	5.55x	8.90x	
Average collection period	45 days	44 days	62 days	42 days	
Average payment period	72 days	77 days	98 days	90 days	
Fixed asset turnover	5.49x	6.54x	3.45x	4.40x	
Total asset turnover	3.45x	3.87x	2.44x	3.09x	
Capital Structure					
Debt ratio	23%	32%	28%	45%	
Debt-equity ratio	10%	12%	12%	25%	
Times interest earned	−2.30x	.80x	3.45x	1.12x	
Profitability					
Gross profit margin	45%	52%	41%	47%	
Net profit margin	−12%	2.0%	15%	8%	
Return on assets	−2%	.5%	11%	2%	
Return on equity	−10%	5%	17%	7%	

cision-making responsibilities and direct customer contact caused him to jump at the chance to join Bay.

The last four years flew by. Attracting deposits at Bay proved easier than expected. Lots of smaller firms hoping to establish alternative banking relationships liked the idea of a local bank with local decision making. Many larger firms were willing to keep fully insured $100,000 accounts because they liked the idea of a local bank to support local businesses. This meant that Bay's loan officers had plenty of funds to lend. Their challenge was to find sound businesses to lend to. During the first two years of Bay's existence, every weak business tried to establish a relationship with the bank. Many newly formed businesses and entrepreneurs were also attracted, thinking that the bank's loan committee would make riskier loans to build its portfolio. To some extent, Bay did have to consider some of these riskier firms. Attracting businesses with existing loan and account relationships was not easy. It was this reality that contributed to the granting of a loan to Groundtrack Inc.

Groundtrack Inc. is a six-year-old company manufacturing all-terrain three- and four-wheel vehicles (ATVs). Bob Ramon, the founder of Groundtrack Inc., is a flamboyant young executive and entrepreneur. Prior to forming Groundtrack, Bob was a very successful commercial real estate broker. Bob enjoyed outdoor activities of all types, including skydiving and motorcycles. The three- and four-wheel ATVs were a natural extension of Bob's interest in outdoor adventure. Bob teamed up with Bill Marion, a car repair shop owner, to design and manufacturer a new three-wheel design. They started in Bill's shop, and early success led to the firm incorporating and moving to a 42,000-square-foot manufacturing facility north of San Palo. In 1992, after only four years of operation, Groundtrack Inc. reached sales of 450 units and $2.7 million.

Business was continuing to expand when the Federal Safety Commission and several state agencies began to investigate injuries and deaths related to three-wheel ATVs. It was alleged that the three-wheelers were inherently unstable. Groundtrack Inc. was affected significantly by the charges. They found themselves, along with several other manufacturers, facing a class action suit brought against them on behalf of all purchasers of the alleged unsafe vehicles. Groundtrack Inc.'s product liability and directors'- and officers'-liability insurance carrier settled the case out of court two years later. In the meantime, Groundtrack stopped selling three-wheel vehicles and began selling its newly designed four-wheel ATV. However, the publicity cut into sales, and the cost of lawyers and the loss stemming from the lawsuit of the high deductible amount on their insurance policies cost the firm $265,000 over a two-year period. Another impact of the lawsuit was to increase the cost of product-liability insurance so much that the firm's officers and directors decided to drop the coverage and self-insure.

Despite these problems, Groundtrack Inc. was able to sell stock to several business associates and friends of Bob Ramon. Bob and Bill still controlled 55% of the common stock. However, the new stockholders led to the addition of two new board members. The Board of Directors is shown in Exhibit C12.2.

William Pursell's interest in Groundtrack was motivated by his belief that his investment banking firm would likely have an opportunity to underwrite an initial public offering (IPO) for Groundtrack. Earnest Lamp's law firm represented Groundtrack

---

EXHIBIT C12.2

Groundtrack Inc. Board of Directors

Board Members	Age	Stock Held
Robert Ramon, Chairman of the Board, Chief Executive Officer, and President of Groundtrack	38	345,000
Bill Marion, Chief Operating Officer of Groundtrack	43	123,000
Mary Ramon, Director, wife of Robert Ramon	34	12,000
William Pursell, Director, President of San Palo Banking Co. (regional investment banking firm)	56	98,000
Earnest Lamp, Director, Partner in the law firm of Marshall, Jackson, and Clinton	61	45,000

and Earnest believed Groundtrack would produce additional business as well as being a good investment when the IPO took place.

Martin Parks got out of bed to think though the events of the previous day. Martin had lunch with Bob Ramon to discuss business affairs. Martin had made an appointment with Ramon over five weeks ago, but for one reason or another, Ramon had to reschedule on three occasions. It was a very short and not very productive lunch. Bob Ramon seemed to be preoccupied. He indicated a desire to extend and increase Groundtrack's $350,000 line of credit by $150,000. Bob told Martin that the litigation, bad publicity, and recent economic slowdown were creating a temporary cash flow problem but that foreign sales were improving since several foreign distributorships were brought on. Moreover, several foreign governments were buying the ATVs to use for guarding borders. Several sales totaling 30 units had taken place in the last six months. Martin made no commitment and stressed to Bob that Groundtrack's financials would have to be reviewed. He also pointed out to Bob that the credit analysts at the bank had not received the financials which were due three weeks earlier. Bob's excuse was that Groundtrack was not satisfied with the cost of its accounting firm and had to make a change. This would delay the completion of the financials by another two weeks. Bob did provide Martin with several unaudited statements, which are shown in Tables C12.1 and C12.2.

TABLE C12.1

Groundtrack, Inc.
Balance Sheet for December 31, 1995, and June 30, 1996
(dollars in thousands) (unaudited)

Assets:	12-31-95	6-30-96
Cash and demand deposits	$ 86,000	$ 12,000
Accounts receivables	546,000	665,000
Inventory	456,000	512,000
Total current assets	$1,088,000	$1,189,000
Equipment	435,000	440,000
Less depreciation	230,000	250,000
Net equipment	205,000	190,000
Design and engineering for new ATV	120,000	120,000
Total assets	$1,413,000	$1,499,000
Liabilities and net worth:		
Accounts payable	$ 376,000	$ 543,000
Bank loans	290,000	350,000
Total current liabilities	$ 666,000	$ 893,000
Common stock and paid-in capital	100,000	100,000
Retained earnings	547,000	506,000
Total stockholder's equity	$ 647,000	$ 606,000
Total liabilities and net worth	$1,413,000	$1,499,000

TABLE C 1.2.2

Groundtrack, Inc. Income Statement
First Half 1995 and 1996
(unaudited)

	First Half 1996	First Half 1995
Sales revenue	$2,560	$2,879
Less: Cost of goods sold	1,152	1,382
Gross profits	$1,408	$1,497
Less: Operating expenses		
Selling expense	810	851
General and administration expenses	510	505
Depreciation expense	34	32
Operating profit	54	109
Interest expense	149	90
Net profits before taxes	$ (95)	$ 19
Less: Taxes paid (refund), i.e., rate 36%	(34)	7
Net profit after taxes	$ (61)	$ 12

Martin reached for his working folder on Groundtrack, in which he kept some key operating numbers and ratios for the firm. Some of these data are shown in Table C12.3.

TABLE C 1 2.3

Key Operating Statistics and Ratios for Groundtrack 1992–1995
(dollars in millions)

Statistic or Ratio	1992	1993	1994	1995
Unit sales of ATVs	450	740	490	520
Gross sales	$2.70	$4.80	$3.50	$4.40
Sales of repair parts	$.3	$.5	$.6	$.8
Net working capital	$.350	$.497	$.512	$.422
Current ratio	1.62	2.10	1.89	1.63
Inventory turnover	5.60x	6.00x	5.70x	5.05x
Average collection period (days)	36.2	38.0	46.3	28.5
Total asset turnover	4.20x	5.21x	3.89x	4.07x
Debt ratio (%)	42.0	44.0	42.8	47.1
Times interest earned	2.97x	3.31x	2.24x	1.21x*

*Annualized from semiannual data.

Martin reviewed the loan agreement. Bay Bank had no obligation to extend additional credit to Groundtrack. The loan note had a number of covenants that could be of interest, several of which dealt with the requirement that the firm maintain certain financial ratios. These included a semiannual requirement that the firm's current ratio remain above 1.50x, its times interest earned exceed 1.20x (this can be missed once during each annual period), net working capital a minimum of $100,000, and that the debt ratio remain below 50.0. The bank had the option to call the note due and payable within 60 days if any two of these ratios fell below the required levels. The loan would be collateralized by all the firm's accounts receivable, and much of the inventory would be used as collateral by the firm's suppliers.

Martin looked at the financial information Bob Ramon supplied and began to sweat again. He would have to prepare a report for Bay's loan committee in two days and make a recommendation to senior management at that time.

PROBLEMS

1. What factors of importance should Martin discuss in his credit report?
2. How well did Groundtrack live up to its credit covenants based on the June 30, 1996, unaudited statements?
3. What options do you suggest Martin review?
4. What option should Martin recommend to Bay's credit committee?

APPENDIX 12A

Primary Debt Financial Assets

Learning Goals

After studying this appendix, you should be able to:

1. Describe the basic provisions of debt contracts and the relative amount and types of primary debt outstanding.

2. Explain the use of debt by businesses and the primary types of debt issued by nonfinancial businesses.

3. Discuss the basic types of real estate debt outstanding.

4. Describe the primary types of consumer, state and local, and foreign debt outstanding.

Financial debt includes both loans and securities issued by businesses, consumers and government units. This appendix provides descriptions of the primary types of debt issued. The analyst must understand the attributes of each type of debt in order to properly evaluate its risk.[1] The distinction between a loan and a security is a moot one when the credit risk of the investment is the issue. Credit analysis for assessing the creditworthiness of loans and securities involve the same set of factors. Since the structure of debt is important to credit analysis, it is necessary to understand the characteristics of primary debt issued.

---

[1]U.S. government issued debt is not discussed in this appendix since credit issues are not typically an issue for investors in this debt.

Attributes of and Volume of Primary Debt

Loans and security debt have several basic characteristics. Generally the debt contract includes some or all of the following provisions:

1. A provision indicating the amount of interest to be received by the holder or how that amount is to be determined.

2. A provision stating the amount of principal to be paid at a date of maturity or a stipulated schedule for principal repayments.

3. A provision that gives the borrower the option to repay the asset on or after a specified date, but before maturity, with or without a fee for prepayment.

4. A series of provisions, called covenants, that may require the borrower to fulfill certain conditions concerning its financial stability or the condition of collateral, if any.

Ordinarily, the borrower or issuer of the asset will negotiate the provisions to be found in a financial asset with a lender such as a commercial bank. In the case of publicly issued securities, this is done on behalf of the investors by an investment banker acting as an underwriter. In practice, the underwriter discusses the provisions with the borrower and prospective investors as the contract is being drawn up to insure that the securities will be sold.

Businesses, consumers, and governments had $12.7 trillion of financial debt outstanding at year-end 1993. Exhibit A12.1 shows the volume of outstanding financial assets, by sector from year-end 1981 through year-end 1993. The financial assets shown here consist only of *primary financial debt*. That is debt issued by the capital deficit unit or user of the capital.

EXHIBIT A12.1

Primary Financial Debt by Sector: 1981 and 1993 (dollars in billions)

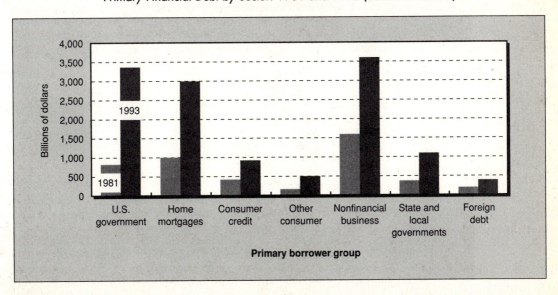

Source: *Flow of Funds Accounts, Fourth Quarter 1993,* Board of Governors of the Federal Reserve System, Washington, DC, March 9, 1994.

The volume of financial debt assets grew by a compound rate of 9.3% from 1981 to 1992. The fastest growth was registered in the obligations of the U.S. government, and the slowest growth was in the obligations of foreign borrowers. Consumer debt for home mortgages grew rapidly during the decade. Debt of state and local governments also grew rapidly.

✓ Checkpoints

A12-1 What are the major provisions found in a financial debt asset?

A12-2 What are the relative volumes of the major debt classifications?

Business Debt

The primary debt of nonfinancial businesses falls into two basic classifications, loans and securities. The primary loan and security classifications are shown in Exhibit A12.2 along with the percentage of the total $4,550 billion outstanding as of December 31, 1993. Nonfinancial businesses involved in commercial and industrial activities obtain credit directly from suppliers called *trade debt*. Other borrowings are accomplished through financial institutions such as bank loans and through direct borrowing in the money and capital markets. The business sector uses the money and capital markets to raise funds through corporate bonds, commercial paper, and industrial development bonds. Some debt, such as mortgages and bank loans, are issued to financial institutions.

BUSINESS LOAN DEBT

Businesses finance their short-term financial needs with a variety of funding sources. This section describes the most common types of business loans. Businesses can borrow from their suppliers in the form of trade debt or from financial institutions such as commercial banks and finance companies. Each of these will be described.

Trade Debt

Trade debt is a major source of unsecured short-term financing from business firms. Such accounts result from transactions in which merchandise or services are purchased but no formal note is signed to show the purchaser's liability to the seller. The purchaser, by accepting merchandise, in effect agrees to pay the supplier the amount required in accordance with the terms of the sale. The credit terms extended in such transactions are normally stated on the supplier's invoice.

Short-term Unsecured Loans

Financial institutions are a major source of unsecured short-term loans for business. **Unsecured short-term loans** are negotiated and result from deliberate actions taken by the financial manager of the business. The major type of loan made by banks to businesses is the short-term self-liquidating loan. Self-liquidating loans are intended merely to carry the firm through seasonal peaks in financing needs, mainly buildups of accounts receivable and inventory. As receivables and inventories are converted into cash, the funds needed to retire these loans will automatically be gener-

EXHIBIT A12.2

Primary Debt Issued by Nonfinancial Businesses
Dec. 31, 1993 (dollars in billions)

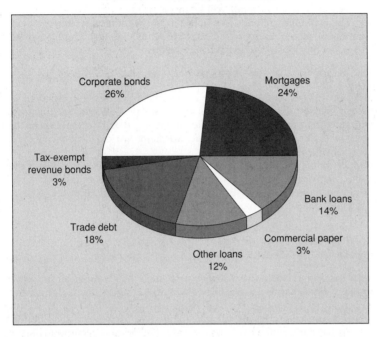

Corporate bonds 26%

Mortgages 24%

Tax-exempt revenue bonds 3%

Bank loans 14%

Trade debt 18%

Commercial paper 3%

Other loans 12%

Source: *Balance Sheets for the U.S. Economy 1945–93,* Board of Governors of the Federal Reserve System, March 9, 1994.

ated. In other words, the use to which the borrowed money is put provides the mechanism through which the loan is repaid (hence the term *self-liquidating*). Banks lend unsecured short-term funds in three basic ways: through single-payment notes, lines of credit, and revolving credit agreements.

A **single-payment note** can be obtained from a commercial bank by a creditworthy business borrower. This type of loan is usually a simple transaction made when a borrower needs additional funds for a short period. The resulting financial asset is a note, signed by the borrower, stating the terms of the loan, which include the length of the loan (the maturity date) and the interest rate charged. This type of short-term note generally has a maturity of 30 days to nine months or more. The interest charged on the note is generally tied in some fashion to the **prime rate of interest,** an administered floating rate charged by commercial banks or to a market rate index. The prime rate is discussed in detail in Chapter 21. A note may have either a fixed or floating rate.

A **line of credit** is an agreement between a financial institution and a business specifying the amount of unsecured short-term borrowing the lender will make available to the firm over a given period of time. A line of credit agreement is typically made for a period of one year and often places certain constraints on the borrower. A line of credit is not a guaranteed loan but indicates that if the lender has sufficient funds available it will allow the borrower to owe it up to a certain amount of money. The amount of a line of credit is the maximum amount the firm can owe the bank at any point in time.

A **revolving credit agreement** is nothing more than a guaranteed line of credit—guaranteed in the sense that the lender making the arrangement assures the borrower that a specified amount of funds will be made available regardless of the scarcity of money. The guarantee of funds availability is not without cost: borrowers must pay a commitment fee to obtain the guaranteed funds availability. This fee typically is assessed against the unused portion of the agreement.

Secured Short-term Loans

Businesses use accounts receivable assets and inventory as **collateral** to secure short-term loans. Financial institutions prefer to have collateral securing short-term loans granted to businesses. This collateral serves to reduce the risk on the loan. Commercial banks and finance companies are major sources of financing for both accounts receivable and inventory.

Another source of funds involves selling accounts receivable to a specialist. This is known as *factoring*. A **factor** is a financial institution that purchases accounts receivable from businesses for cash. It profits by purchasing the receivable at a discount from the book value of the receivable.

BUSINESS SECURITY DEBT

In the last several decades, a higher percentage of nonfinancial businesses have been able to finance through the sale of securities. In part this is due to the advantages of securities as compared to bank loans—advantages that include price and generally fewer restrictions. More recently, the market for bonds issued by financially weak firms has cut into the bank loan market. The primary securities issued by nonfinancial businesses are discussed below.

Commercial Paper

Commercial paper is a short-term money market debt financial asset issued by financial and nonfinancial businesses. Commercial paper may be unsecured or secured by assets. Larger business firms with strong credit ratings are the largest users of commercial paper. They prefer issuing their debt directly in the money market as opposed to borrowing from financial institutions, which may involve more paper work, less flexibility, and higher costs.

Secured, Collateralized, or Asset-backed Debt Securities

Financial securities supported by assets have been an integral part of the financial markets for years. A home mortgage is a financial asset in which residential real estate serves as collateral. These types of debt have a variety of names including *secured, collateralized,* or *asset-backed debt. Collateral* is the asset that is transferred to the investor if the borrower defaults under the obligation.

Another whole class of financial assets supported by other financial assets used as collateral are asset-backed debt. These assets pool other financial assets as collateral. A mortgage-backed security is a good example of a asset-backed financial asset. In this case, the collateral is a pool of mortgages on homes or apartments. This represents a new set of collateralized financial assets that pool other financial assets as collateral. Today, **mortgage-backed securities** represent the largest class of asset-backed debt, with over $1 trillion of these securities outstanding. The asset-backed security can be used to finance a wide variety of different financial assets, such as auto loans and credit card receivables.

Corporate Bonds

Corporate bonds—financial assets representing an obligation of a corporation—come in several different forms. The basic classifications include collateralized (secured) or uncollateralized (unsecured), senior or subordinated (junior), callable or noncallable, and convertible bonds.

Collateralized Corporate Bonds Collateralized bonds are issued with assets that transfer to the bondholder in the event of default and represent a form of asset-backed security. They are considered secured bonds. Corporations use a variety of assets as collateral for a bond issue. Collateral may consist of fixed assets or intangible assets, such as stock of a subsidiary. If the stock of a subsidiary is used as collateral, the bond is known as a *collateral trust bond.* These bonds include provisions that protect the investor in the case of default, such as transferring the voting rights of the subsidiary to the **trustee** for the bondholder, and periodically establishing the value of the subsidiary stock to insure it exceeds principal value. The trustee is typically a commercial bank that ensures that the issuer of the bond lives up to the collateral agreement.

Mortgage bonds are issued by corporations with substantial investments in property, such as public utilities. Collateral in this case may be a power plant.

When a corporation uses equipment such as airplanes, railroad cars, or trucks as collateral, the bond is known as an *equipment trust certificate.* With this type of certificate, a trustee for the bondholders retains title to the equipment and leases it to the corporation. The amount of equipment trust certificates issued is less than the value of the equipment. The remaining amount is paid by the corporation to the trustee to cover the cost of purchasing the equipment.

Unsecured Bonds, or Debentures Corporations issue bonds that carry no collateral, known as *debentures.* These are unsecured obligations of the issuer. If the company fails, the holder of a debenture is considered a general creditor of the company with no claim against the value of specific assets. As a result, in a bankruptcy, the unsecured creditor will ordinarily lose some or all of the money invested.

Subordinated Debentures Corporations that are heavy borrowers will occasionally issue obligations that are of higher credit risk than even an unsecured debenture. These are called *subordinated debentures* because preference as to payment in bankruptcy is below that of secured lenders and general creditors.

Convertible Debentures One way for corporations to increase the demand for their unsecured debt and to provide for future growth of equity is to issue bonds that can be converted into a specified number of shares of common stock in the company. Such bonds are known as *convertible debentures,* and the right to convert the bond into stock is called the *conversion privilege.*

Other Bond Provisions Corporate bonds may carry a number of other provisions to improve their appeal to investors or to the issuing corporation. The **call provision** is designed to improve the flexibility of the issuer by allowing the issuer the option to prepay, or call, the bond on or after a specified date and at a specified price.

A **sinking fund provision** improves a bond's investment appeal by requiring the issuer to periodically retire a specified percentage of the issue. This may be done by the issuer giving the bond trustee enough funds to redeem a percentage of the bonds chosen randomly or by delivering bonds purchased in the secondary market.

Serial bonds are designed so that a specified principal amount of the bond's par value comes due on predetermined dates during the life of the issue. These bonds are typically used when the collateral value is likely to decline over time, such as in the case of equipment trust certificates.

Industrial Development Bonds Industrial development bonds (IDB) are used by state, county, or city government economic development agencies. These agencies must meet requirements of the Internal Revenue Service that insure that the purpose of the agency is to stimulate economic development and job growth. The agency issues tax-exempt revenue bonds to finance industrial plants or other business facilities. The business then leases the facility from the agency and pays enough to cover the bond's interest and principal. The bond is also collateralized by the industrial development. Obviously, the advantage of the IDB is that it allows the corporation to finance at a federally tax-exempt interest rate.

Bond Ratings

The riskiness of publicly traded bond issues is assessed by independent organizations such as Moody's and Standard & Poor's. Moody's has 9 ratings; Standard & Poor's 12. These organizations derive their ratings by using financial ratio and cash flow analyses. Table A12.1 summarizes the ratings. There is normally an inverse relationship between the quality or rating of a bond and the rate of return it must provide bondholders. High-quality (high-rated) bonds provide lower returns than lower-quality (low-rated) bonds. This relationship reflects the risk-return trade-off of the lender. When considering bond financing, the financial professional must therefore be concerned with the expected ratings of the firm's bond issue since these ratings can significantly affect the saleability and cost of capital to the company.

Ratings in the highest four classifications are considered investment-grade ratings. Certain investors are constrained by law and regulation to invest only in **investment-grade** bonds. Ratings below the top four classes are known as **noninvestment-grade** ratings. These bonds are also called *junk bonds* because of the low rating. Below-investment-grade bonds became controversial in the 1980s due to their use in financing **hostile takeovers,** and **financial restructurings,** as well as the investment in them by life insurance companies and savings and loans.[2] This controversy led to the adoption of the expression *junk bond*. Prior to the 1980s, to obtain a below-investment-grade rating, the bond issuer had to experience deteriorating financial health. This would cause their bonds to be downgraded to the lower below-investment grade. These bonds are called *fallen angels.* The primary new issue market was developed and became very active in the 1980s.

The rating organizations constantly review the ratings of companies. They usually alert bondholders by publicly indicating that they are reviewing a company for a possible upgrade or downgrade in the company's rating. Usually, investors anticipate the actions of the rating organizations by bidding up or down the price of the bond even before a rating change takes place.

---

[2]Junk bond investment restrictions have been placed on insured depository institutions through the Financial Institutions Reform, Recovery and Enforcement Act of 1989 and by insurance regulators in the early 1990s. The result is that depositories have no authority to purchase junk bonds and life companies have less authority. The result is that households, primarily through mutual funds and pension funds, hold a higher percentage of these bonds.

TABLE A12.1

Moody's and Standard & Poor's Bond Ratings

Moody's	Interpretation	Standard & Poor's	Interpretation
Investment-grade Ratings			
Aaa	Prime quality	AAA	Bank investment quality
Aa	High grade	AA	
A	Upper medium grade	A	
Baa	Medium grade	BBB	Lowest investment grade
Noninvestment-grade ratings (junk bonds)			
Ba	Lower medium grade	BB	Speculative
B	Speculative	B	
Caa	From very speculative to	CCC	
Ca	Near default	CC	
C	Lowest grade	C	Income bond
		DDD	In default: rating based on
		DD	estimated liquidation
		D	value

Source: Moody's Investors Services, Inc., and Standard & Poor's Corporation.

Guaranteed Financial Loans and Securities

There are a wide variety of financial assets which are issued with financial guarantees. The purpose of **financial guarantees** is to lower the risk of default and thereby lower the financing cost of the issuer. Financial guarantees come in three types. First are guarantees represented by additional equity capital invested into the issuer. Additional equity, all other things held constant, will reduce the risk of default and thereby provide additional guarantee that the debt security issuer will fulfill all obligations under the debt contract. For a firm's securities, the amount of equity in relation to debt is called the *capital structure* of the firm. Second, a guarantee can be obtained from a financially strong private third party which is willing to guarantee performance of the contract terms on debt issued by another entity. Strong commercial banks guarantee commercial paper issued by private corporations. This effectively substitutes the creditworthiness of the issuer with that of the commercial bank. Strong corporations also guarantee the debt of weaker subsidiaries. There are a number of private insurance firms that guarantee the debt of municipal bond issuers. Finally, a debt issuer can obtain a guarantee from the U.S. government or agency of the government. The largest of these programs is federal deposit insurance. Deposit insurance programs allow commercial banks and other depositories to issue debt that is effectively government guaranteed. The Federal government has programs to guarantee student loans, mortgages, business loans, and mobile home loans.

✓ Checkpoints

A12-3 What are the features of the most popular types of unsecured short-term debt businesses use?

DERIVATIVES POSE SPECIAL CREDIT PROBLEMS

How

it

Really

Works

In the world of risk management, financial derivatives pose new management problems. Derivatives are financial contracts that are based on the price of some other financial claim. Futures, forward cash contracts, options, and swaps are the most common. The growth in the volume of these contracts outstanding and the increased complexity of many of the new derivatives offered has made it difficult for credit analysts concerned about the risk profile of firms with large derivative holdings and obligations.

Some derivative contracts can lose considerable value, which could cause a firm to default. Forward cash transactions and swaps are particularly susceptible to price fluctuations that can create losses not offset by such requirements as margin. To limit this exposure, some parties to forward cash and swap transactions are requiring their counterparties to put up collateral to cover losses on outstanding positions. Others require a "netting agreement," which requires that all the swap contracts with a particular counterparty be closed out in the event of default on one contract.

Another problem with many derivative contracts is valuation. Many derivative contracts do not actively trade, so there is no established market to value the contract. This means it is necessary to use complicated computer valuation models to establish value. These are not perfect, however, making valuation uncertain.

Another problem is the fact that the laws establishing the obligations of the parties to derivative contracts have not been tested. Worse is the fact that some laws regarding derivatives differ from country to country. This could mean that one party to a derivative contract may be unable to use the court to get the counterparty to live up to the obligations of the contract.

Source: Sean Becketti, "Are Derivatives Too Risky for Banks?" *Economic Review*, Federal Reserve Bank of Kansas City, third quarter 1993, pp. 27–42.

A12-4 What are bond ratings? What are they used for, and which organizations issue them?

Real Estate Debt

Real estate provides the collateral for a significant amount of financial debt. The largest category of real estate debt is home mortgages issued by households. These assets have become more complex in recent years due to the increase in the number of different types of mortgages issued. Mortgages are also used to finance income-producing real estate such as apartments, office buildings, and shopping centers. The following are several of the more important mortgages available.

FIXED-RATE MORTGAGES (FRMS)

Fixed-rate mortgages (FRMs) have been the more prevalent type of mortgages issued to finance homes. The typical FRM is a fixed-payment loan with a maturity from 15 to 30 years. Typically, too, it is a fully **amortizing loan,** meaning that it combines interest and principal payments into equal periodic (monthly) payments in such as way that the principal is completely paid off at the end of the loan's term to maturity.

Borrowers can repay most FRMs at any time without a prepayment penalty. This **prepayment option,** also referred to as a *call option,* makes the fixed-rate mortgage very appealing to borrowers but less attractive to lenders and investors. Mortgage borrowers commonly refinance a high-rate FRM during periods of low interest rates. Because the rates available to a holder of a prepaid mortgage are lower during such periods, the FRM is said to have high prepayment or reinvestment risk to the holder.

ADJUSTABLE-RATE MORTGAGES (ARMS)

Adjustable-rate mortgages (ARMs) became far more common in the 1980s. ARMs come in a wide variety of different forms. One common feature is an interest rate that floats in relation to an index. The index may be for a specific security or an index of interest rates. For example, the index may reflect the one-year Treasury bill rate or the average cost of funds at savings and loan associations.

INCOME-PROPERTY MORTGAGES

Income property is very commonly used as collateral for borrowing, because it provides its own revenue to repay principal and interest payments used to finance it. Income property includes residential real estate, including apartments and nonowner-occupied housing. It also includes nonresidential property such as office buildings, warehouses, retail centers, and factories. Some projects are so large that they involve mixed-use developments of residential and nonresidential uses.

Income property is financed with a mortgage. Typically, income-property mortgages are held by long-term lenders such as insurance companies and pension funds. Sometimes short-term interim financing is used until a long-term lender can be found. These mortgages are frequently made by commercial banks. Sometimes very large projects or groups of properties such as gambling casinos and warehouses are financed through bonds collateralized by mortgages.

✓ Checkpoints

A12-5 What are the primary types of mortgages debt outstanding?

A12-6 How do fixed-rate and adjustable-rate mortgages differ?

Household Consumer Debt and Debt of State and Local Governments, and Foreigners

Households, state and local governments, and foreigners are large issuers of debt. Households use consumer debt for the purchase of nondurable goods and to finance income shortfalls. State and local governments use debt primarily to finance long-lived capital investments as well as to meet cash flow needs between tax receipts. Foreigners issue debt in the United States primarily to finance U.S.-based operations and investment.

CONSUMER INSTALLMENT AND CREDIT CARD LOANS

Consumer loans are used to purchase durable and nondurable goods and services. Some of these loans are secured by durable goods such as automobiles, mobile homes, recreational vehicles, and boats.[3] Others are unsecured. The most common unsecured consumer loans are credit card receivables. These cards are issued by financial institutions and retailers. At year-end 1993, households had $858 billion consumer debt outstanding.[4]

DEBT ASSETS ISSUED BY STATE AND LOCAL GOVERNMENTS

State and local governments are major issuers of primary financial debt. Two of the more important reasons for issuing debt are to obtain funds for operating fund needs prior to tax collections and to provide funds for long-term capital expenditures or financial deficits. At year-end 1993, state and local governments had $1,057 billion in bonds outstanding. The two basic types of state and local government bonds are *general obligation* and *revenue* bonds.

General Obligation Bonds (GOs)

General obligation bonds (GOs) are debt instruments issued by municipalities—states, counties, cities, towns, and districts—that are secured by the issuer's general taxing authority. Most of these bonds are used to finance long-lived, or capital, assets such as roads, jails, sewage treatment facilities, parks, and the like.

Municipalities also issue short-term GO securities to bridge the gap between the time funds are needed and when they will actually be received. Government entities can receive funds through taxes, grants such as federal government grants, fees charged for municipal services, and bond issuances. Short-term borrowings, of one year or less, issued in anticipation of receiving revenues, are known an *tax, revenue, grant,* and *bond anticipation notes*—TANs, RANs, GANs, and BANs.

Revenue Bonds

Revenue bonds are issued by state and local governments to finance public projects and private enterprises that generate specific revenues, such as airports, college

---

[3]Second mortgages are classified as either real estate debt or consumer debt depending on the source.

[4]Of the $858 billion in consumer loans, $807 billion is installment debt. The balance is noninstallment single-payment debt.

facilities, schools, industrial plants, hospitals, sports complexes, sewer and water facilities, and public power plants. The important feature of a revenue bond is that
principal and interest on the bond are paid only when revenues are sufficient to meet
those payments. When revenues are not enough, the municipality need not use other
available funds or raise taxes to meet these payments. Thus, revenue bonds are usually riskier investments than general obligation bonds.

Up to this point in the chapter, only assets issued by domestic individuals and organizations have been considered. As our financial markets have become more global,
it has become necessary for financial market analysts to learn about financial assets
issued by internationally based issuers.

INTERNATIONAL ISSUERS OF DEBT

Foreign governments and agencies, as well as foreign private corporations, issue
assets that are purchased by investors in the United States. These assets are issued
both in foreign currency denominations and in U.S. dollars. Foreigners also issue a
variety of private assets held by U.S. investors. These include bonds, trade credit, and
other assets. At year-end 1993, foreigners had $363 billion of debt outstanding in the
United States.

✓ Checkpoint

A12-7 What are the basic types of consumer, state and local government, and foreign debt issued?

SUMMARY AND REVIEW

1. **Describe the basic provisions of debt contracts and the relative amount and
   types of primary debt outstanding.**

   Debt contracts include provisions related to **interest, principal, maturity of
   principal payments,** and **covenants.** The major types of debt issued by non-
   U.S. government issuers include nonfinancial business debt, real estate debt,
   consumer debt, state and local government debt, and foreign debt.

2. **Explain the use of debt by businesses and the primary types of debt issued
   by nonfinancial businesses.**

   Nonfinancial businesses issue debt that is used primarily to finance capital
   expenditures and meet working capital needs. Business issues debt in the
   form of loans and securities. The primary loan debt is **trade debt** and **business loans.** The primary security debt issued includes secured and unsecured
   bonds and commercial paper.

3. **Discuss the basic types of real estate debt outstanding.**

   Real estate debt is used to finance homes and income-producing properties
   such as apartments, office buildings, retail developments, hotels and motels,
   factories, and warehouses.

4. **Describe the primary types of consumer, state and local, and foreign debt outstanding.**

Consumer loans include **installment loan** and **credit card debt.** State and local governments issue **general obligations** and secured debt.

CHAPTER 13

Managing Problem Loans and Investments

Learning Goals

After studying this chapter, you should be able to:

1. Discuss the risk and return trade-off in lending and investment.
2. Explain what factors contribute to a problem loan.
3. Describe the problem-loan management process with emphasis on loan monitoring, protecting collateral, repossessing and foreclosing collateral, obtaining judgments, and handling bankruptcies.
4. Explain the process for establishing loan loss reserves.

What happens when competitive lending pressures force a financial institution to find new markets? If screened, structured, and serviced carefully, such claims may prove profitable. But, over the last decade, lending commitments have more than burdened the balance sheets of depositories and strained the resources of deposit insurance agencies, financial regulators, and the U.S. financial system in general. To reduce the losses suffered by the average American taxpayer, Congress established the Resolution Trust Corporation (RTC) in 1989 to manage and liquidate the assets of failed thrifts at as high a value as possible; and the RTC fast became the largest single depository of problem loans.

Perhaps worse than this increase in nonperforming loans is the misallocation of significant investment dollars within the global economy. Clearly, when it comes to loan contracts, the process of intermediation has gone slightly awry. This chapter quickly reviews how loans can become problematic for financial intermediaries and how financial firms can effectively manage the problem-loan portfolio.

The Risk-Return Trade-off in Lending

What is the trade off between the *risk* that the loan will enter default and result in a loss, and the *return* that the institution will receive in fees and interest income? The answer to this question, through analysis of the risk-return trade-off, is the crux of all investment decisions: the yield on risky assets must incorporate expected credit losses. If the risk of default is high, then the return should be commensurately high. Inevitably, investors expect to lose on loans and investments excepting those relatively risk-free vehicles. As with any portfolio of assets, the management challenge is to insure that the experienced losses are less than or equal to those expected when the firm acquired and priced the assets; and managers can achieve this stability through careful origination and servicing of individual assets and strategic portfolio diversification and management.

What types of credit losses do investors expect? Large portfolios of personal credit card receivables typically experience losses of 3% to 5% annually. This loss rate may seem very high; but for a well-managed credit card portfolio, it can still be extremely profitable. From 1985 to 1990, the loan loss rate at large commercial banks ranged anywhere from 2.57% to 3.29%; but the banks thrived by charging a going rate of 18% to 20% on the outstanding credit line, as well as substantial annual membership and transaction fees.

Loans on leveraged buyout transactions may also be considered highly risky. But managers must weigh this risk against the return of a fee of 1% to 2% or more of the loan balance up front and an earned interest rate tied at 1.5% to 2.0% above prime. The typical quality business loan would unlikely earn as much as the prime rate.

Despite the potential profitability of riskier loans, the large portfolio losses tied to real estate, foreign lending, and leveraged corporation transactions, not to mention the decline in overall bank profit margins, confirm the need for finely tuned credit management skills among financial firm professionals. Since building and managing a portfolio of known problem loans is challenging in itself, you can imagine how formidable a task is managing a loan portfolio that has become unexpectedly problematic over time. The rest of this chapter deals with those cases in which an intermediary's screening process did not or could not anticipate the risk of default, so that the firm's management must take alternative measures to manage what has become shaky credit.

✓ Checkpoints

13-1 What is the trade-off between risk and return, relative to loans and investments?

13-2 What is the lender's objective in dealing with credit risks inherent in the lending process?

Factors Leading to Loan Default

What makes a loan go bad? Since the viability of a loan relates to cash flow, a loan may enter default when unforeseen events interrupt or inhibit the sources of the borrower's cash flow. Sometimes, the cash value of the underlying collateral drops to the point where selling it will not repay the debt. For example, some intermediaries make leveraged buyout loans because they expect a firm's management to divide it into several operating units, to be sold at a certain multiple of cash flow. If conditions such as a new technology used by a competitor alters either the valuation multiple or the underlying cash flows of the target firm, then its debt is a possibility for default.

The two types of risk that can increase the likelihood of loan loss include operating risk factors and financial risk factors. Operating risks, those that involve the general ongoing activities of the borrower, include:

1. General economic conditions at global, national, and regional levels.
2. Technological obsolescence.
3. Competitive forces in domestic and foreign markets.
4. Management skills and experience.
5. Market need for a firm's product or service.

Financial risks include:

1. Excessive use of debt in the firm's capital structure.
2. Excessive reliance on price-sensitive wholesale funding sources.
3. Use of short-term debt to finance long-term assets.

TYPES OF PROBLEM LOANS

With such pressure on depository interest rate margins during the 1970s and 1980s, many lenders expanded their loan operations to new markets, sometimes extending credit on more lenient terms. However, this aggressive lending posture resulted in four types of problem loans, the signs of which today's financial firm practitioner must be able to recognize quickly in order to manage the situation effectively.

Loans to Developing Countries

The first major type resulted from the expansion of U.S. banks into the foreign lending markets, particularly to those developing countries eager to grow their economies in the late 1960s and 1970s. Facing increased domestic competition, many U.S. money centers as well as large regional banks opened up loan processing offices in foreign countries to obtain a share of the fast growing foreign-lending business. But the economic shocks of rising and falling oil prices adversely affected the cash flows and the performance of these borrowers so that many could not fulfill the terms of their loans despite government support. The loans to developing countries (LDC) marked the first wave of significant large loan problems experience by many large U.S. banks.

Loans Based on Collateral Prices

The second type of loan problem involved real estate in the oil producing states. Just as developing countries used their oil reserves to support large loans,

ACQUISITION, DEVELOPMENT, AND CONSTRUCTION LENDING

How

it

Really

Works

There is no area of lending that resulted in greater losses to savings and loans and commercial banks in the early 1990s than acquisition, development, and construction (ADC) loans. ADC loans were particularly risky because many of the developments had equity value well below the loan amount. Developers would come to a lender with the option on some land and propose a retail, commercial, or residential development based on a pro forma statement that assumed a rate of property sales or rate of leasing of the completed project. This pro forma also assumed a sales or lease price. These pro formas were particularly appealing given the favorable treatment of real estate under the 1981 tax act, conditions which were reversed by the 1986 tax act.

Based on such a pro forma, the land would be revalued upward as if it were developed property. This was always well above the value that the developer had purchased or optioned the land for. Adding to the incentive to lend was that fact that most lenders would charge a large origination fee, sometimes as high as 10% to 12% of the loan amount, and book this amount as current profit. These fees were usually added to the loan amount.

Unfortunately, the success or failure of the development might take 24 to 36 months to ascertain. In the meantime, other lenders were financing competitive developments, which would soon lead to oversupply in the target market. The result of all this activity was billions of dollars in losses for financial institutions and eventually the taxpayer. Depository regulators have tightened up on underwriting standards for ADC loans. Today a developer must put substantial "real" equity into a project loan.

The following table shows the extreme differences in the riskiness of different types of real estate loans held by commercial banks on December 31, 1992. These data show the percent of loans in each category past-due 90 days or more and those loans on a nonaccrual status (that means no longer accruing interest).

Percent of Noncurrent Secured Real Estate Loans at All Insured Commercial Banks, December 31, 1992

Category of Loan	Percent Noncurrent
Construction and development	13.99%
Commercial real estate	5.21
Multifamily residential real estate	4.77
One- to Four-family residential	1.43
Home equity lines of credit	0.72

Source: Federal Deposit Insurance Corporation, *FDIC Quarterly Banking Profile*, fourth quarter 1992, p. 4.

so did borrowers from oil- and oil-shale-producing states such as Texas, Colorado, Oklahoma, and Louisiana. These states benefited from the sharp run-up in oil prices, to borrow directly or indirectly against this increased oil value as collateral for large real estate developments and other investments. As the value of the oil resource decreased, the collateral value backing these loans fell drastically. Continental Bank and Trust of Chicago, an aggressive energy lender like many real estate and energy lending banks and thrifts in Texas and Oklahoma, suffered greatly and verged on failure. Continental, unlike many of the smaller local depositories, survived because it worked out a government-financed bailout.

Loans on Speculative Real Estate

The third wave of troubled lending again related to real estate, but more to real estate speculation based on favorable local economic trends rather than to commodity prices such as oil. In the late 1980s throughout the New England states, and in cities such as New York, the technology-driven economy began to slow down, as did the growth of the financial services industry; both resulted in substantial loan losses on residential and commercial real estate. Even real estate developer Donald Trump lost big on real estate devaluations. California endured similar losses as it entered a severe recession in the early 1990s.

Loans to Excessively Leveraged Companies

The fourth type of problem loan occurred in conjunction with the excessive financial leveraging of the 1980s. Stock repurchase programs, hostile and friendly leveraged buyouts, corporate takeovers, and management buyouts sharply increased overall corporate financial leverage, evidenced by the explosion of the high-yield bond market and the proliferation of highly leveraged corporate loans by commercial banks. Such leveraging increases the instability in the reliability of cash flows; therefore, intermediaries should consider such possibilities when making the loan decision.

✓ Checkpoints

13-3   What factors contribute to increased problem loans and investments?

13-4   What were some characteristics of the four types of loan losses affecting financial institutions over the last several decades?

Problem Loan Management

What do you do when you barely pass—or even fail—an examination? You might study longer and more thoroughly for the next test. Similarly, given the disappointing increase in problem loans, managers of financial firms have increased their time and attention to learning about and keeping track of sour credits. What was once a not-very-glamorous area of expertise is fast becoming a much demanded specialty in financial institutions: problem loan workout. With demand comes reward: some loan workout practitioners can take an equity interest in a problem loan so that if the loan's value increases, they get some or all of the upside. Investment limited partnerships specializing in defaulted commercial loans of banks and thrifts may buy defaulted high-yield bonds with hopes to realize the loan value despite the borrower's protracted period in Chapter 11 bankruptcy.

So what does problem loan management involve from a financial institution's perspective? The management process includes the following activities:

1. Monitoring loan portfolio and identifying problem loans.
2. Protecting collateral rights and value.
3. Repossessing collateral and foreclosing on loan.
4. Obtaining and collecting a judgment.
5. Declaring bankruptcy.

MONITORING LOAN PORTFOLIO AND IDENTIFYING PROBLEM LOANS

In terms of our claim/function matrix, the staff responsible for determining whether a loan is performing against the agreed-upon terms and conditions (specifically whether the borrower is meeting all the loan covenants found in the agreement) is servicing the claim. In doing so, the lending institution can discover problem loans in a variety of ways. The borrower may simply and blatantly default or notify the lender of pending difficulties. Or the borrower's financial reports may signal financial deterioration of the core business. Internal audits may also disclose possible loan violations or fraud. Death of an owner-manager (as in the case of Robert Maxwell, media mogul and head of Maxwell Enterprise), filing for bankruptcy by the borrower's main customer, or some other major event may put the loan at greater risk.

The loan servicing function must incorporate effective policies and procedures to identify and quickly handle deteriorating credit. To perform this function,

SMALL BUSINESS ADMINISTRATION LOAN PROGRAM HIT BY FRAUD

The Small Business Administration, an agency of the federal government, has several loan guarantee programs designed to encourage financial institutions to make loans to small and medium-sized businesses. The guarantees range from 70% to 90% of the loan's principal. Many small businesses used the program in the early 1990s as many commercial banks tightened their lending credit standards in response to more rigorous capital requirements and examinations. Another result of the increase in SBA-guarantee program use was the increase in loan fraud. One common practice had loan brokers put together loan packages with the necessary financial information for prospective borrowers. Some of these packages contained fraudulent tax statements that inflated the prospective borrowing business's income and profits. The loan broker reaped huge loan fees for loans successfully guaranteed by the SBA. The SBA and the bank investing in the bad loans took the losses.

Source: John R. Emshwiller, "Fraud in SBA Loans May Be Widespread," *The Wall Street Journal*, April 15, 1994, p. B2.

managers at the planning stage must develop delinquency and problem loan tracking reports, late notice of payment notifications, periodic reviews of financial statements, collateral inventorying, and analyses of borrower information that may impact on the borrower.

As alluded to earlier, the most common problem loan is one simply in default, which occurs when the loan payment is past due or when the borrower fails to meet a specified term or condition of the loan contract or a covenant in the loan or security agreement. At one time or another, you may have missed a credit card or student loan payment, putting your own account into default. Once a loan goes into default, the credit management team can initiate a number of defensive activities to minimize loss to the institution. Credit managers start by asking: What are the prospects of repayment? What can we do to improve our prospects? Can we work with the customer to identify problems leading to default and possible strategies for solving them? If not, what steps can we take immediately to ensure the best possible recovery?

If working with the borrower's current management is feasible, then the intermediary may develop a loan modification that supports the borrower in implementing a recovery plan. Such a loan modification may involve substantially altered terms and conditions and loan covenants, or it might rely on additional new collateral, if any is available. In exchange, the borrower may receive an extended loan repayment period, or possibly even additional funds if needed, to keep the firm viable and to forestall—if not prevent—bankruptcy.

Since a lender will almost always profit by responding to a problem loan earlier rather than later, the lending institution must develop adequate loan servicing and monitoring capabilities.

PROTECTING COLLATERAL RIGHTS AND VALUE

Loans backed by collateral are less risky only to the extent that the collateral retains value and can be legally and readily identified, recovered, and if necessary, sold. Making sure that collateral meets each of these conditions is not as straightforward as it might seem. In a problem-loan situation, all stockholders and creditors look to collateral as the primary asset for raising cash and paying the firm's obligation.

The implications for the servicing function in developing an appropriate collateral strategy are several: servicing will require assessments of: (1) collateral documentation to ensure that the collateral meets the legal standard, (2) periodic valuation of the collateral, (3) the location and, if applicable, the physical inventory and condition of the collateral, and (4) actions to repossess or foreclose on collateral.

REPOSSESSING COLLATERAL AND FORECLOSING ON LOAN

When a secured lender is reasonably certain that a workout will not result in repayment, the lender must consider the process of repossession or foreclosure of the collateral underlying the loan—not at all a straightforward process and often complicated by a bankruptcy filing. If the borrower believes that repossession or foreclosure will further endanger the firm's recovery, then the firm will probably go the bankruptcy route. If the lender can repossess or foreclose without the threat or actuality of a bankruptcy filing, then the lender should initiate all the necessary legal steps under the laws of the state and then determine how to realize the highest value for the collateral. Not surprisingly, if the collateral value exceeded the loan principal, then the borrower probably already sold it to avoid default and repossession or foreclosure. Thus, repossession and foreclosure are unlikely to make the lender whole in most cases.

Another problem with repossession and foreclosure is that a secured lender must still consider the rights of other creditors who will operate in their own best financial interests despite the lender's being secured. An unsecured lender may decide that the borrower's bankruptcy filing provides the greatest chance of recovery, whereas the secured lender may want to sell the collateral as quickly as possible to achieve maximum recovery.

In recent years, financial institutions with large portfolios of foreclosed real estate properties have used bulk sales to dispose of the assets. A **bulk sale** is the sale of defaulted loans or repossessed or foreclosed assets in large portfolios.

For example, institutions lacking sufficient expertise to manage a wide variety of different types of real estate in different geographic areas may team up with real estate professionals; or those in real estate may join institutional investors to buy large portfolios of real estate and defaulted loans secured by real estate, with hopes of using their real estate management and development skills to profit.

OBTAINING AND COLLECTING A JUDGMENT

In the case of unsecured loans or loans with insufficient collateral, an intermediary must make a legal claim to collect any outstanding loan principal and interest by obtaining a judgment against the borrower identifying the amount owed and the borrower's other obligations to the creditor.

Seeking a judgment is easy; collecting on it is another matter. Usually a judgment will spur the borrower into action, such as filing bankruptcy or attempting to shift assets to entities protected from court action. Many of these techniques are illegal in themselves and can be challenged in court. However, such challenges take time and money. Sometimes, the judgment will get the borrower to pay or at least be willing to negotiate a workout.

Another approach to collecting a judgment is to use court-approved collection techniques such as:

- *Levy and public sale,* a seizure of the borrower's property used to settle the debt, where the property is sold at a public auction with the proceeds used to pay the judgment.
- *Garnishment,* the process whereby a creditor gets a third-party (such as an employer) that owes the borrower (the employee) funds (wages or salary) to pay the creditor. As the parethentical examples might suggest, garnishment of wages is the most common form.

- *Receivership,* the process whereby a court-appointed receiver controls the borrower's assets so that they are not removed or their value impaired.

DECLARING BANKRUPTCY

Despite everyone's best efforts, resorting to bankruptcy is the inevitable course for many businesses and individuals. Bankruptcy is a long, costly, and technically difficult course for most businesses to follow, as the cases of Trans World Airlines or U.S. Gypsum Corp. Yet, it provides certain protections for the stockholders and creditors, so that bankruptcy may come about at the request of the individual or business or involuntarily as a result of a petition by the creditors.

U.S. bankruptcy laws protect the rights of creditors without unduly harming the debtor. The three main chapters of the bankruptcy laws are 7, 11, and 13. Individuals can file a petition for straight bankruptcy under Chapter 7 or seek relief under Chapters 11 and 13. Most individual bankruptcies involve voluntary petitions. A sole proprietor with a small business might seek a reorganization of debt under Chapter 13, through negotiation of a court-approved plan for the repayment of debt. An individual with a business whose value would be destroyed by liquidation might seek relief under Chapter 11, to keep the business going while a court-approved reorganization plan is developed. Corporate businesses seeking protection from creditors most often use Chapter 11.

LENDER LIABILITY

Legal and Ethical Issues

A loan officer reviewed the proposed development with a developer planning to renovate a hotel at a well-known Colorado mountain ski resort. The loan officer wrote the borrower describing the loan review process at his institution. The lender's letter to the borrower clearly stated that the request must go before a loan review committee before a firm commitment could be drawn up. The loan review committee denied the loan. The borrower sued the lender and the lender lost the case before a jury for several million dollars. Welcome to the world of lender liability!

The legal precedent of lender liability became a popular source of lawsuits against lenders in the 1980s. Behind the legal theory is the notion that lenders can mislead borrowers into making financial commitments, spending time and money on the project, or taking risks on the basis of representations made by the lender. Alternatively, a lender that calls a loan due and payable under a provision of the loan agreement may force a lender into bankruptcy or cause severe losses. In either of these cases, the borrower can make a legal claim against the lender for the loss.

Lender liability has made the process of originating new loans and servicing outstanding loans all the more risky. Now a lender can lose money on loans it doesn't even originate.

How

it

Really

Works

TWA REORGANIZATION TAKES 18 MONTHS

Trans World Airlines filed for bankruptcy protection on January 31, 1992. Its debt load was approximately $1.6 billion, after experiencing two years of huge operating losses. Nearly 18 months later, on August 11, 1993, TWA received court approval to emerge from bankruptcy protection. During its bankruptcy protection period, the airline was able to reduce its long-term debt to nearly $1 billion.

　　The reorganization plan will produce a firm owned 55% by creditors and 45% by employees. To obtain their 45%, the employees offered to take $600 million in wage and benefit concessions. The employees' unions will also be heavily represented on the board of directors with 4 of 15 seats.

Source: Robert L. Rose, "TWA's Plan to Reorganize Wins Approval," *The Wall Street Journal,* Aug. 12, 1993, p. A3.

　　In 1978, Congress revised the U.S. bankruptcy law significantly, to increase the asset exemptions applicable to bankruptcy. This liberalization, combined with the growth in consumer credit, has sharply increased the number of bankruptcies per capita. Exhibit 13.1 shows the number of bankruptcies from 1980 to 1992. The number is fast approaching 1 million bankruptcy filings per year.[1] This increase in bankruptcy also relates to the increased percentage of debt to disposable personal income. Exhibit 13.2 shows the ratios of total, home mortgage, and consumer debt to total personal income from 1980 to 1993.

　　Once in bankruptcy, all parties lose considerable control, since a court-appointed judge will become the major decision maker. Even the most secure lenders will be subject to considerable loss of control and rights to their collateral. Bankruptcy proceedings can take a long time, jeopardizing the value of collateral or the business's franchise value. Also, decisions of bankruptcy proceedings may adversely affect the value of the remaining entity. In virtually all cases, however, bankruptcy results in a substantial increase in legal expenses, reduces the value for stockholders and creditors alike, and increases the intermediary's transaction costs. The legal aspects of bankruptcy for businesses and individuals contain many features, important to any loan recovery strategy. Students seeking careers in the financial services industry would be wise to take additional courses in business law, a subject that is beyond the scope of this book.

✓ Checkpoints

13-5　What are some activities associated with problem-loan management?

13-6　How can intermediaries monitor loans so as to discover potential problems, and which groups within the financial institution are typically involved in this activity?

---

[1]Research on bankruptcies indicates that personal bankruptcies are related to such events as unexpected medical expenses, divorce, or unexpected job loss.

EXHIBIT 13.1

Personal Bankruptcies, 1960–1992

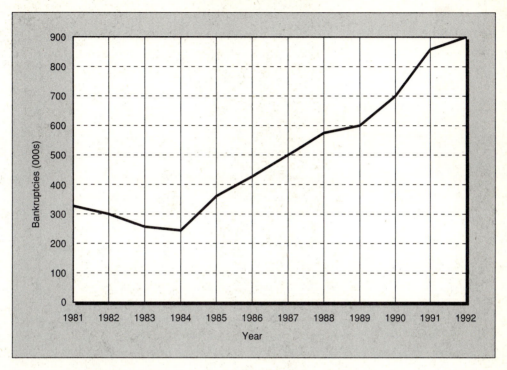

Source: American Bankruptcy Institute.

13-7   How does a financial institution protect collateral, and how does it implement the repossession and foreclosure processes?

13-8   What are some remedies used in the process of obtaining a judgment against a defaulted borrower?

13-9   How do bankruptcy laws protect and frustrate creditors?

Loan Loss Provisions, Charge-offs, and Recoveries

Problem loans take their toll on the income statement and can lead to lender insolvency. Financial institutions must anticipate the possibility of losses on loans in a number of ways, through loan loss provisions, charge-offs, and recoveries.

   Loan loss provisions set aside by intermediary policy or government regulation to cover estimated potential loan losses—are established based on individual asset performance or specific performance of designated portfolios of homogeneous assets. A **charge-off** is simply the amount taken against the firm's loan loss reserve which represents the actual, as opposed to estimated, loss from a bad loan or investment once the final disposition of the asset is determined.

EXHIBIT 13.2

Household Debt as a Percent of Personal Income, 1982–1993

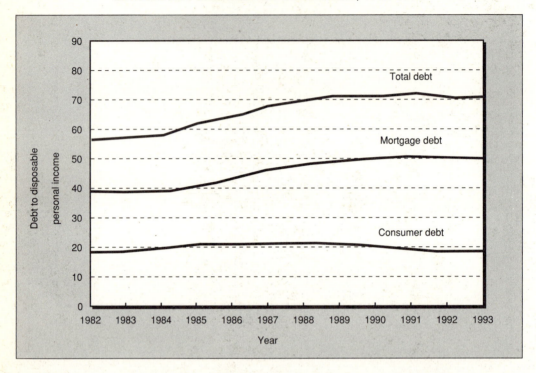

Source: *Flow of Funds Accounts, First Quarter 1994*, Board of Governors of the Federal Reserve System, Washington, DC, June 19, 1994.

What is the right amount of a loan loss provision? Commercial banks and thrifts use a loan classification system required by their examiners; this system places loans and investments into three classifications—substandard, doubtful, and loss—defined in Exhibit 13.3. The definitions of these assets are somewhat subjective. As a result, the management of financial institutions, their independent auditors, and regulators frequently differ on how to classify a particular loan and on how much of a loss reserve to establish. Many financial institutions have been forced to establish additional loan loss provisions and reserves after the completion of an examination.

For individual assets, such as commercial business loans or real estate loans, the performance of each loan is considered. GAAP, regulatory standards, and the institution's loss reserving policies will influence how the firms establish loan loss provisions and reserves and take charge-offs and recoveries. Loan loss provisions and reserves are established prior to the actual recording of a loss and serve to reduce current income for GAAP accounting purposes. A charge-off occurs when the final amount of the loss is known, at which time it can be used to reduce income for tax purposes. A **recovery** occurs when the amount of the loss is less than

EXHIBIT 13.3

Regulatory Asset Classification System

Substandard assets: A substandard asset is inadequately protected by current sound worth and paying capacity of the obligator or the collateral pledge, if any.

Doubtful assets: An asset classified as doubtful has all the weakness inherent in a substandard asset, with the added characteristic that the weakness makes collection in full or liquidation highly improbable.

Loss assets: Assets classified as a loss are considered uncollectible and of such little value that their continuance as bankable assets is not warranted.

Source: *Commercial Bank Examination Manual,* Board of Governors of the Federal Reserve System, 1989.

that which was established in the loan loss provision reserve. Table 13.1 shows loan charge-offs by medium-sized and large commercial banks from 1986 to 1992 for several types of credit, including large losses on loans to foreign governments, businesses, and depositories and the rising loss experienced in real estate lending.

For individual assets, a default of 90 to 120 days will almost always trigger a loss provision. Other mediating factors may influence the extent of the write-down, however. For large homogeneous portfolios, the loss provision may be based on historical loss experience in the portfolio. For example, a portfolio of credit card receivables in which underwriting standards has remained largely unchanged may have experienced a historical loss of 3% per annum. The institution may then choose to use that experience in establishing a loss reserve of 3% of the outstanding receivables in this portfolio, adjusted to reflect the net of actual charge-offs and recoveries.

TABLE 13.1

Loan Charge-offs at Medium-sized and Large Commercial Banks
1985–1992
(percent of average loans)

Type of Loan	1986	1987	1988	1989	1990	1991	1992
Commercial and industrial	1.14	0.96	0.95	0.93	1.31	1.82	1.45
Consumer	1.58	1.58	1.52	1.63	1.86	2.67	2.60
Real estate	0.38	0.47	0.42	0.52	0.92	1.28	1.41

Source: "Bank Profits and Balance Sheet Developments," *Federal Reserve Bulletin,* July 1993, p. 658.

The basic process for establishing loan loss reserves is shown as follows in Exhibit 13.4. First, the institution determines which loans are uncollectible. These loans are taken off the balance sheet, and the loss is written off against the previously established loan loss reserve. This balance is known as *current loan charge-offs* (Step 1, line b). Second, any recoveries are determined. **Recoveries** represent revenues received by the firm from sale of collateral or unexpected loan collections on loans which has previously been charged off (Step 2, line c). These are subtracted from the loan loss reserve to determine the *net charge-offs* (Step 3, line d). The loan loss reserve which reflects the net charge-offs is calculated (Step 4, line e). The bank then determines loss provisions for loans that have been identified during the current period for which losses are expected to be taken. These loss estimates for the current period are known as *loan loss provisions* (Step 5, line f). If a loan that was not identified as a loss earlier were to be charged off during the period, it would require an additional loan loss provision at that point. Finally, the end-of-period loan loss reserve is determined by adding the current period's loan loss provision (Step 6, line g).

EXHIBIT 13.4

Loan Loss Financial Reporting Example
(dollars in millions)

Steps	Amount	
Beginning period loan loss reserve	$ 234.00	(a)
1. Determine current period charge-offs	$ 23.40	(b)
2. Determine loan recoveries	$ 3.20	(c)
3. Determine net charge-offs (b−c)	$ 20.20	(d)
4. Subtract d from last period's loan loss reserve balance Balance (a−d)	$ 213.80	(e)
5. Determine current provisions for loan losses	$ 25.00	(f)
6. Determine end-of-period loan loss reserve balance (e+f)	$ 238.80	(g)

Despite specific loan loss provisioning policies required by regulators and accountants, a number of academics have studied bank behavior in setting up loan loss reserves, to determine whether factors other than the discovery of problem loans influence the timing of these provisions. Several analysts have concluded that bank managers attempt to use the timing of loss reserves to smooth earnings.

GAAP and regulatory policies regarding loan loss provisions have become more consistent over time, but they are not always perfectly so. In recent years, however, regulators have pressured accounting firms to adopt very conservative loan loss provisioning policies. As already mentioned, loss reserves may not represent a tax deductible expense, creating another inconsistency in the accounting for loan losses.

SHAREHOLDER CLASS-ACTION LAWSUITS

The sharp rise in problem loans during the 1980s and early 1990s has contributed to a growing legal specialty, the shareholder class-action lawsuit. Many financial institutions announced large additions to loss reserves that have surprised investors, leading to sharp declines in share prices. Law firms specializing in shareholder class-action lawsuits represent classes of shareholders who purchased the stock prior to the announcement and suffered a financial loss due to the stock price decline.

A typical suit alleges that management and directors knew about the losses before they were announced or engaged in unwise lending programs, causing the large losses. In either case, the suits typically call for damages of many millions of dollars. Most of these cases are settled out of court, resulting in large settlements and legal fees.

LEGAL and ETHICAL ISSUES

The large problem loan portfolios built up in the 1980s have raised numerous questions about procedures for setting up adequate loss reserves. Regulators have taken a leading role in this debate, since loss reserves provide another cushion before the capital of the institution is impaired. In the last decade, real estate appraisal practices were subject to regulations from the former thrift regulatory agency, the FHLBB. These regulators felt that appraisals provided overly inflated valuations of problem loans. There has also been controversy over what commercial bank regulatory agencies have been calling adequate reserving for loans to developing countries.

Loan loss reserving policies are very important issues for financial institution management, directors, accountants, and line managers. For publicly traded institutions, proper security disclosure practices also rely on these policies. Many institutions have faced stockholder class-action lawsuits due to large accounting adjustments covering losses on problem loans. Consequently, senior management and directors today spend considerable time reviewing the problem loan area and the adequacy of loss reserves.

✓ Checkpoints

13-10 What are the differences among loan loss reserves, loan loss provisions, net charge-offs, and recoveries?

13-11 How do financial firm managers determine or set loan loss provisions?

SUMMARY AND REVIEW

1. **Discuss the risk and return trade-off in lending and investment.**

   Taking losses on loans and investments is an inevitable part of investing. The objective is to be adequately compensated for the losses that are forthcoming.

2. **Explain what factors contribute to a problem loan.**

A problem loan is one that is not paying interest or repaying principal on a timely basis and in which the debtor may have inadequate cash flow to pay the claim. Some of the causes of problem loans include: (1) **general economic conditions** at both the national and regional levels; (2) **technological obsolescence;** (3) **competitive forces** at both the domestic and foreign levels; (4) **management capabilities;** (5) specific aspects of the **product and its marketability** in the case of a loan to a product-producing company.

3. **Describe the problem-loan management process with emphasis on loan monitoring, protecting collateral, repossessing and foreclosing collateral, obtaining judgments, and handling bankruptcies.**

The problem-loan management process involves establishing a systematic process for **monitoring the performance of borrowers** under loan and security agreements; **identifying, inventorying, and protecting the value of,** and **seizing collateral; developing and implementing procedures to repossess and foreclose** on collateral in a way that will retain its value and sell the assets for the highest value; **obtaining court-approved judgments** against defaulted borrowers and **collecting on the judgments;** and **working through the bankruptcy process** to improve the probability of repayment.

4. **Explain the process for establishing loan loss reserves.**

The loan loss provisioning process involves determining **current period charge-offs, recoveries,** and **loan loss provisions.** The remainder of current charge-offs less recoveries—**net charge-offs**—are subtracted from the beginning period loan loss reserves. From this is subtracted **current loan loss provisions** to determine end-of-period **loss reserves.**

PROBLEM   **LOAN LOSS RESERVING**

13-1

The Elmwood Bank had a loss reserve at year-end of $23 million. The firm's net loan charge-offs for the most recent period were $2 million. Answer the following questions.

a. If Elmwood's loan loss provisions for the most recent period were $5 million, what was the firm's beginning-of-period loss reserves?
b. If Elmwood's recoveries for the most recent period were $1 million, what was the firm's loan charge-offs for the most recent period?

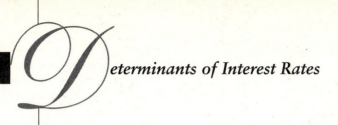

CHAPTER 14

Determinants of Interest Rates

Learning Goals

After studying this chapter, you should be able to:

1. Explain the real interest rate and what impacts it, and describe the factors that affect the supply and demand of loanable funds.
2. Discuss the impact of inflation expectations on interest rates and define the Fisher Effect.
3. Explain the term structure of interest rates and describe the expectations, segmentation, and liquidity preference theories of the term structure.
4. Explain the implied forward rate and how to compute it.
5. Describe the concept of the risk-free interest rate.
6. Discuss the factors that affect the interest rate on specific financial assets.
7. Explain and know how to compute the tax equivalent yield.

Every public announcement, press conference, or news release related to change in the interest rate generally prompts lenders and creditors alike to action in the global reallocation of funds. Such shifts in the United States often ripple the flows of capital movement around the world, and all types of intermediaries can either take advantage of this movement or suffer from it. To anticipate the opportunities as well as the consequences, financial firm managers should understand: (1) the economic forces behind interest rate fluctuation with the business cycle; (2) the determinants of the supply and demand for loanable funds; (3) the effects of inflation; (4) the relationship between interest rate levels and the maturity of a financial debt asset, referred to in practice as the *term structure of interest rates;* (5) the determinants of interest rate levels related specifically to the types of financial claims; and (6) the concept of a risk-free rate. This chapter provides practical managerial insights into all these topics.

Interest Rate Fluctuation

Finance professionals study the causes of interest rate changes because they frequently rely on forecasts of interest rates in making borrowing and investment decisions. Interest rate forecasts help to determine the optimal timing and maturity of a loan or investment.

THE REAL RATE OF INTEREST

Some people are induced to save today if they can consume more tomorrow. Their ability to increase future consumption is based on the return they receive on their savings. *Interest rates* represent the return an individual saver receives for forgoing consumption today. Conversely, interest rates are the prices that borrowing economic units pay for the privilege of consuming today. During any specified time period, the suppliers and borrowers of savings create a market for loanable funds. A simplified example: if there were only one market for loanable funds, where all savers and borrowers met to bargain for available loanable funds, then many of the market participants would determine how much to save and borrow based on the price eventually set in this market.

What actually factors into the price? One variable is the available investment opportunities of the borrowers. For instance, if a small undeveloped country like Rwanda just discovered a huge oil reserve, it would demand great savings to invest in oil exploration, drilling, and building a distribution system. Because of the large oil reserve, oil investors would expect to earn a very high return on their investment and would offer to pay a high interest rate for loanable funds. Such a situation would not only induce the citizens of the country to save more but also attract increased foreign savings. Table 14.1 provides a schedule of investment opportunities in this undeveloped country and the rates of return that these opportunities are expected to earn.

TABLE 14.1

Investment Opportunity Schedule for Undeveloped Country

Investment Description	Amount ($)	Expected Return on Investment
Oil exploration equipment	$15,000,000	28%
Oil pipeline	6,500,000	18
Office building	5,000,000	14
Apartment building	3,000,000	12
Single-family houses	2,000,000	10
Farm machinery	1,500,000	8

This **investment opportunity schedule (IOS)** is effectively the demand schedule for loanable funds for the country. There are similar schedules produced internally by management for each business and by international investment analysts for each country around the world.

Loosely speaking, the investment opportunities and the propensity of consumers to consume now or later interact to define the real interest rate. The real rate of interest—this relationship between the productivity, or demand for savings and the supply of loanable funds—is not the interest rate observed in the real world with inflation. The interest rates actually experienced in the financial markets are **nominal interest rates,** composed of the real interest rate and a premium for market inflation expectations and influenced by additional factors discussed later in this chapter.

The **equilibrium real rate of interest** is simply the intersection of the demand curve for loanable funds of borrowers and the supply curve of loanable funds of savers. Exhibit 14.1 shows the upward-sloping supply curve *S* and downward-sloping demand curve *D*. *D* is the investment opportunity schedule for the small

EXHIBIT 14.1

The Real Rate of Interest Supply and Demand for Loanable Funds

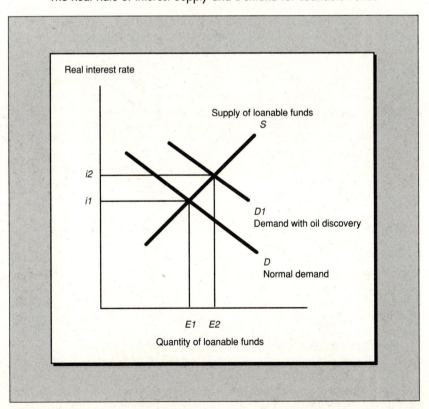

undeveloped country, which appears as a straight line, excluding the oil equipment and pipeline investments. Equilibrium would include a supply and demand of loanable funds of *E1* and real interest rate of *i1*.

The exhibit also shows a demand curve *D1*, an additional curve designed for some sensitivity analysis, to show what could happen in the small country after finding new oil reserves. Investment opportunities would increase, shifting the demand curve out to *D1*. The result would be to expand demand of loanable funds to *E2*, resulting in a higher real rate of *i2*. Obviously, all this activity represents potential ventures for the financial intermediary; and managers should monitor such change with a keen eye toward seizing opportunities, protecting existing business, and revisiting strategic plans.

SUPPLY AND DEMAND FOR LOANABLE FUNDS BY SECTOR

The supply and demand of loanable funds within a particular country change according to the capital allocation decisions of households (individuals and families), businesses, government at all levels, and central banks. Countries also import and export their savings. Why do interest rates fluctuate over the course of the business cycle? To answer this question, financial managers must keep in mind the supply and demand sides of the market for loanable funds.

During short time periods, each sector of the economy is capable of being a saver or a borrower. In the United States, the household sector is the primary capital surplus unit, because individuals hold the vast majority of the wealth. Yet many younger householders are borrowers: first-time homebuyers, purchasers of other durable goods such as cars and appliances, students who take on debt to obtain their college education. Many more households are savers, through contractual savings such as pension funds and life insurance policies or through depository accounts and institutional investments such as mutual fund shares.

Governments, on the other hand, tend to be capital deficit units, partially because many government units do not produce balance sheets as a measurement tool; often, they simply measure receipts and expenditures as if all resources were for immediate consumption.

The international sector has, over time, moved from being a capital deficit to a capital surplus unit. The U.S. balance of trade is a driving factor here: when the United States experiences a balance of trade surplus, it sells more goods and services to foreign countries than it purchases, thereby increasing its holdings of foreign currencies subsequently allocated to foreign investments. In the last decade, however, the United States has balanced trade deficits. Japan, other Pacific Basin countries, and Western Europe have sold more goods and services to the United States than it has sold in return. As a result, foreign countries, particularly Japan, have been investing huge amounts of capital in the United States.

The business sector is also a capital deficit sector, although individual businesses may periodically save. Businesses generate savings through retained earnings. However, as a group, they use all retained earnings plus additional borrowings for investments in plant and equipment and working capital, such as accounts receivable and inventory.

In summary, the business and government sectors have traditionally been net demanders of loanable funds, while the household and foreign sectors have been net suppliers.

INCOME AND INTEREST RATE IMPACT ON SUPPLY AND DEMAND FOR FUNDS

Changes in the net loanable funds position of these sectors of the economy—the difference between the sector's gross borrowing and gross lending—depend on two primary economic variables: total aggregate income, approximated by a measure such as gross domestic product, and the level of interest rates.

Periods of rapid income growth accompany economic recoveries and mature economic expansions, providing businesses with unusually rich investment opportunities. The business sector also tends to increase accounts receivable financing and hold higher inventories during expansions, to become more of a net demander of funds during periods of economic expansion than during periods of slow income growth such as recessions.

The government sector, on the other hand, tends to develop spending plans well in advance of known tax receipts, often increasing expenditures when income growth is slowest, as for unemployment insurance. As you might expect, during periods of rapid income growth tax receipts rise more rapidly than expenditures. The opposite occurs when income growth slows—that is, tax receipts fall and expenditures rise. This financial pattern makes the government sector **countercyclical** to the rest of business: it borrows more during periods of slow income growth and less during rapid income expansions.

The household sector is not easy to characterize in terms of its net demand and supply of funds in relation to income. Overall, the household sector's net contribution of savings is relatively stable, in part because a large percentage of savings is contractual by nature. Again, **contractual savings** include reserves in pension funds and life companies. Nevertheless, households tend to borrow for houses and durable goods during the early and middle stages of an economic recovery.

Income changes affect the international sector's net demand or supply of savings. If income growth is rapid, U.S. consumers purchase more goods and services from foreign countries, which worsens the balance of trade because imports rise faster than exports. During rapid growth, foreign investors build up holdings of U.S. dollars; those not spent for U.S. goods and services are invested in real assets and financial claims of the United States, increasing the overall supply of loanable funds.

In sum, the business, government, and international sectors experience the most significant swings in their net demand and supply for funds in relation to changes in aggregate income. During periods of rapid income growth, the business sector's net demand rises while the government and international sectors reduce demand (or increase supply). Overall, during economic booms, the strong net demand for funds from households and businesses tends to more than offset the lesser net demands from governments and the international sector. The result is higher interest rates. These changes are reversed during recessions, causing interest rates to fall.

INTEREST RATE IMPACT ON SUPPLY AND DEMAND FOR FUNDS

The interest rate is the clearing price for establishing equilibrium in the demand and supply of loanable funds: if all other factors remain constant, a higher interest rate will result in an increased supply of savings offered and a reduced amount demanded. An important question that a strategist at a financial firm might ask is "To what extent do changes in interest rates affect the amount supplied or demanded?" How will these changes require some revisions in the firm's long-term goals? The answer may lie in analysis of **interest rate elasticity,** the relationship of the supply offered and demand for loanable funds to changes in interest rates. Elasticity is defined as the %Δ in demand for loanable funds for a 1% Δ in the interest rate.[1] Supply or demand is interest rate *elastic* when the quantities supplied and demanded change significantly for small changes in the interest rate level. Demand or supply is interest rate *inelastic* when the changes in quantities demanded and supplied change little for a given change in interest rate levels. Exhibit 14.2 presents two supply and two demand schedules, including both elastic and inelastic schedules.

EXHIBIT 14.2

Interest Rate Elastic and Inelastic Supply and Demand Schedules

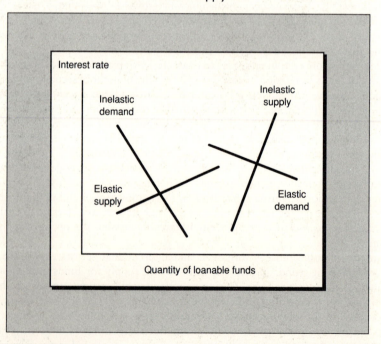

[1]Since elasticity is computed for a 1% Δ at each point along the supply and demand curve, the calculated elasticity will change at different points along the supply and demand curves. The focus of this discussion is on the elasticity at the point of intersection of the supply and demand curves.

The elasticity of the demand and supply of loanable funds relative to interest rates differs for each sector of the economy. Borrowing businesses, younger net borrowing households, and foreign investors are all quite sensitive to changes in interest rates. Thus, the business sector's and younger households' demand schedules and the foreign sector's supply schedules would be interest elastic. Government demand and most other household savers' supply schedules tend to be relatively inelastic.

DEMAND AND SUPPLY OF LOANABLE FUNDS AND THE BUSINESS CYCLE

If you like challenges, then you might try summarizing the effects of income and interest rate fluctuations on the supply and demand for loanable funds in four economic sectors simultaneously. This is known as the *loanable funds theory of interest* rates. To simplify this task, managers can characterize each sector as a net supplier or net demander of loanable funds. A net supplier sector lends more than it borrows. A net demander sector borrows more than it lends. Table 14.2 characterizes the normal position of each of the sectors during a period of weak economic income growth (recession) and a period of rapid economic expansion (boom).

TABLE 14.2

Change in Loanable Funds Position by Sector during Expansions and Recessions

Sector	Recession	Expansion—Boom
Household	Net supply strong	Net supply weak
Business	Net demand weak	Net demand strong
Government	Net demand high	Net demand weak
International	Net supply weak	Net supply strong

As you examine the information in Table 14.2, can you determine whether the aggregate quantity of loanable funds is higher or lower during recessions or booms? Probably not. This ambiguity lies in the fact that the household sector is by far the largest net supplier of funds and the business sector the largest net user. As a general observation, the shifts in net supply and demand in the business and household sectors tend to swamp the changes in the government and international sectors. Consequently, as Table 14.2 shows, during recessions the household supply is high and business demand weak, whereas during booms the reverse is likely. Exhibit 14.3 depicts these conditions, with the aggregate demand and supply schedules for loanable funds during an economic boom and recession. The boom shows a much higher demand schedule, *DB*, with only slightly stronger supply schedule, *SB*. During the recession, demand, *DR*, is relatively weak and supply, *SR*, only slightly less so.

A main feature to note in Exhibit 14.3 is the change in interest rates from *iB* during recession to *iR* during boom. As the economy moves from a recessionary

EXHIBIT 14.3

Aggregate Supply and Demand for Loanable Funds during Economic Recessions and Booms

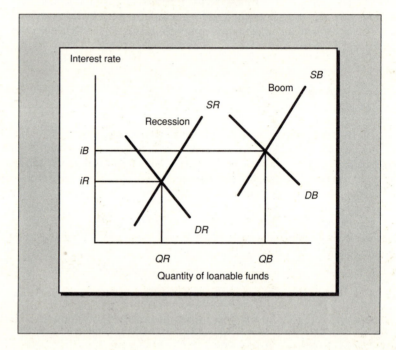

period of weak income growth to economic expansion, interest rates tends to rise regardless of Federal Reserve policy or inflation. Exhibit 14.4 shows the fluctuations in interest rates from 1965 to 1993. The boxed areas represent periods of recession. As the graph indicates, interest rates tend to peak near the beginning of each recession and fall during recession periods.

FEDERAL RESERVE'S IMPACT ON INTEREST RATES

The Federal Reserve has powerful mechanisms and considerable authority over the level of interest rates. Its primary management tool is its **open market operations,** with which it purchases or sells securities such as Treasury securities. When the Fed buys securities, it adds to the supply of loanable funds. The sellers of these securities can reinvest in other loans and investments. When the Fed sells securities, the opposite occurs.

Exhibit 14.5 shows how the aggregate supply and demand for loanable funds schedules reflect a **stimulative monetary policy,** where the Fed tries to increase the supply of loanable funds and to reduce interest rate levels, thus stimulating economic activity. To incite further growth, the Fed also can reduce the level of the **discount rate,** the rate charged by its district banks to their members for short-term loans. The action of changing the discount rate signals the Fed's anticipa-

EXHIBIT 14.4

Interest Rate Fluctuations and the Business Cycle, 1965–1993

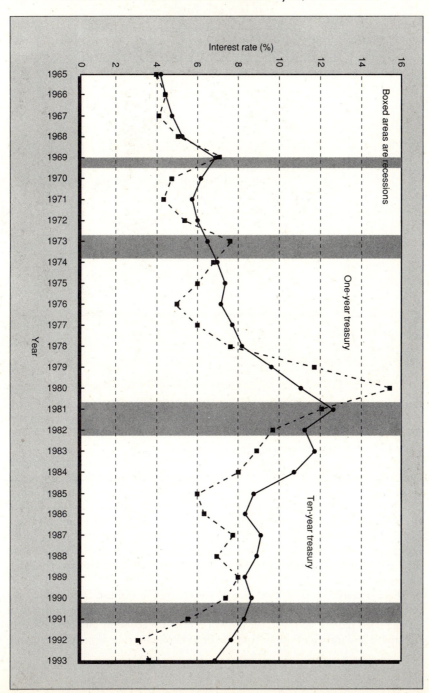

EXHIBIT 14.5

Federal Reserve Open Market Operations Used to Increase the Supply
of Loanable Funds

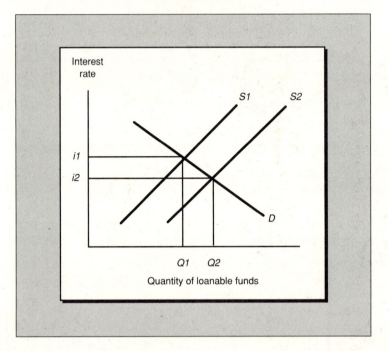

tion and support of the level of market interest rates. To free up funds for lending, the Fed can also reduce the level of **reserve requirements,** those required
funds held in Federal Reserve banks and vault cash held by depository institutions as a percentage of certain types of deposits.

Exhibit 14.5 depicts what happens when the Fed purchases securities, thus
adding to the supply of loanable funds. The supply schedule which had been *S1*
shifts to *S2*. The result is an increase of loanable funds, from *Q1* to *Q2*, and a
decrease in interest rates from *i1* to *i2*. If the Fed sold securities, increased the discount rate, and raised reserve requirement, then it would be pursuing a **restrictive monetary policy.** Managers of financial institutions should be aware of the
political biases of those elected and appointed monetary policymakers, so as to
anticipate periods of restrictive or stimulative plans as they might affect the availability of loanable funds.

There is considerable debate over how effective the Fed can be in influencing
changes in interest rates except over very short-term periods. The transmission of
an increased money supply to the growth rate of the economy and price changes
is variable and difficult to predict. If the Fed increases the money supply and sup-

pliers and demanders of funds view this act as inflationary, then interest rates could rise due to rising inflationary expectations.[2]

The Fed acts upon many factors, the most important being the level of aggregate employment and inflation: when the economy has slack resources and high unemployment, the Fed tends to foster stimulative open market policies; during periods of low unemployment and rising inflation, it promotes more restrictive policies. Exhibit 14.4 indicated earlier that interest rates tend to rise during expansions and booms and to fall during recessions, but this visual representation does not show the big picture. From 1974 to 1981, interest rates rose significantly during this economic expansion, as expected. However, during the expansion from 1982 to 1990, rates generally fell, inconsistent with our previous analysis. Consequently, financial firm managers should analyze movements for context but look further to isolate other variables influencing interest rates.

✓ Checkpoints

14-1 Why should managers of financial institutions monitor interest rate fluctuation?

14-2 Why do interest rates fluctuate?

14-3 What is the loanable funds theory of interest rates?

14-4 In terms of the demand for loanable funds, what is the difference between an elastic and an inelastic supply and demand curve?

14-5 How does the Federal Reserve affect interest rates?

Determinants of Market Interest Rates

By now, you should have some sense of the relationships between interest rates, supply and demand of loanable funds, and the business cycle (or fluctuation of aggregate output). But how are interest rates determined? Why did long-term interest rates rise during the economic expansion of the 1970s and fall during the expansion of the 1980s? Are the terms to maturity of interest rates the same for all financial debt assets? The answers to these questions start with a look at the relationship of inflation to interest rates, how interest rates vary in terms of maturity, and other shocks to the level of interests rates specific to each financial asset.

INFLATION AND INTEREST RATES: THE FISHER EFFECT

The sharp rise in interest rates in the 1970s and decline in the 1980s suggests other factors are involved. As mentioned earlier, the interest rates observed in the money and capital markets are nominal interest rates, rates that are in actuality

---

[2]The discussion of the changes in Fed open market operations on the real economy, inflation, inflation expectations, and interest rates is oversimplifed. In reality, there are long and variable time lags between changes in Fed open market actions and changes in real output and inflation.

higher than the real interest rate. One factor adding to this disparity is the rate of inflation. In the 1970s, inflation rose to double-digit rates by late in the decade. The early 1980s experienced high inflation until about the middle of the decade, and the decline in inflation and inflationary expectations occurred during an economic expansion.

Irving Fisher, in his 1930 book *The Theory of Interest,* developed the theory for real and nominal interest rates. He concluded that the primary cause of the difference between nominal and real interest rates was **inflation expectations,** a relationship referred to as the *Fisher Effect.* Inflation expectations affect both prospective borrowers and lenders. For example, a business planning its inventory levels or a household contemplating a home purchase will buy sooner if it expects prices to rise. If it expects prices to climb considerably, then it may purchase excess inventory or a larger house than first contemplated. Therefore, rising inflation expectations cause households and businesses to consume earlier and borrow more.

Conversely, a prospective saver who anticipates higher inflation will be less likely to lend funds if the interest rate is near the expected rate of inflation. Postponing consumption would yield no benefit if the principal and interest received on the investment would purchase less than could be purchased with today's dollars.

To summarize, borrowers will pay a higher interest rate if they expect an increase in inflation, and savers will demand a higher interest rate if they anticipate a decline in the dollar's purchasing power. The relationship between the nominal interest rate r_n and the real interest rate r_i is approximated by the Equation 14.1:

$$\textit{Nominal interest rate } (r_n) \cong$$
$$\textit{Real interest rate } (r_i) +$$
$$\textit{Expected change in price } E(\Delta \textit{ in } P)$$

$$r_n \cong r_i + E(\Delta \textit{ in } P) \qquad\qquad [14.1]$$

The equilibrium nominal rate of interest will be approximately equal to the real rate of interest plus an incremental interest return that is approximated by the expected percentage change in the general price level.[3]

Interest rates are related to the actual rate of inflation, but the relationship is not perfect and accurately gauging expected inflation is nearly impossible. The actual rate of inflation may be unexpectedly higher or lower than that which the level of nominal interest rates reflects. Moreover, changes in nominal interest rates may result from changes in real interest rates, due to the supply and demand factors discussed earlier. Most economists, however, believe that the real rate of interest is relatively stable, ranging from 2% to 4%, while the $E(\Delta P)$ is far more volatile.

---

[3]We have focused on expected inflation as opposed to actual price increases. Actual price increases can be separated from expected price increases. When prices actually rise, the money holdings of users of money fall in real terms. To restore lost purchasing power, they demand additional money balances, causing interest rates to rise. The price level effect and inflation expectations effect are combined here to simplify the discussion.

So far, our investigation into interest rates has focused on fluctuations in interest rates with similar maturities. Now we look at how the maturity of a bond or other debt instrument might alter its interest rate.

THE TERM STRUCTURE OF INTEREST RATES

The relationship between interest rates on debt securities that differ only with respect to maturity is known as the ***term structure of interest rates.*** Finance professionals study the term structure because they must often decide between short- or long-term borrowings or investments. Understanding why the shape of the term structure changes provides financial firm managers a basis to make these decisions.

The term structure can be graphically represented by a **yield curve,** a graph of the bond yields on a specified date and for a specified type of bond. The bonds must differ only as to maturity. Normally, the yield curve for Treasury zero-coupon bonds is used because of the large number of issues of varying maturities. Yield curves for Treasury bonds as of March 30, 1994, and April 3, 1993, are shown in Exhibit 14.6.

Over time, the yield curve takes on a wide variety of shapes. Exhibit 14.4 indicates that most times the 1-year rate is well below the 30-year rate. This is referred to as an *upward-sloping* or *normal yield curve.* In 1969, the 1-year and 30-year rates were approximately equal, depicted by a *flat yield curve.* Occasionally, as in 1974 and 1980, the 1-year rate is above the 30-year rate, shown by a *downward-sloping yield curve.*

There are three useful theories for explaining the shape of the yield curve:

1. Expectation theory.
2. Market segmentation theory.
3. Liquidity preference theory.

Each theory provides useful insights, not be considered mutually exclusive.

Expectations Theory

The basis for the **expectations theory** is the simple notion that borrowers and savers have choices to make with respect to the maturity of their loans and investments. A borrower needing funds for two years can borrow for two years or alternatively borrow for one year and then borrow again for the next year. A saver with a five-year time horizon can buy a three-year bond and reinvest the proceeds in a two-year bond or alternatively buy a five-year bond. How borrowers and savers make these choices according to the expectation theory is a function of their expectations about the future level of interest rates.

A simple example will help you to understand the theory. You have just received $5,000 and are planning to use it, and any income derived from investing it, as a down payment on a car in two years. You can invest in: (1) a one-year Treasury bond yielding 6.00%, the balance to be reinvested in another one-year Treasury bond at the prevailing rate one year from now; or (2) a two-year

EXHIBIT 14.6

Term Structure of Interest Rates

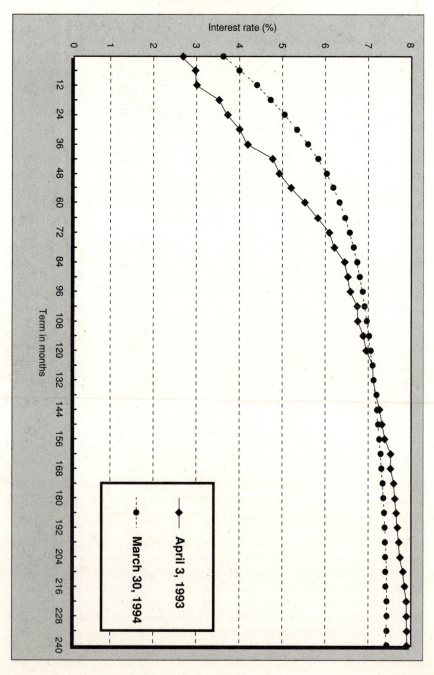

Treasury bond yielding 6.25%. To decide, you form an expectation of what you think one-year rates will be one year hence. Assuming reinvestment of interest payments, you can calculate the two-year investment's worth:

$$(1 + .0625)^2 \times \$5,000 = \$5,644.53$$

The one-year investment, followed by the reinvestment, would only be worthwhile if the one-year rate one year hence were equal to or greater than *xx* in Equation 14.2 below:

$$(1 + .060)\ (1 + xx)\ \$5,000 = \$5,644.53$$

$$1 + xx = 1.065006$$

$$xx = .065006 = 6.5006\% \qquad [14.2]$$

The 6.5006 percent is called the *forward rate* on a one-year bond.[4] If you believed the forward one-year rate would rise above the 6.5006%, then you would probably buy the one-year bond and reinvest. If not, then the two-year rate would make the better choice.

The expectations theory carries this type of trade-off to a market equilibrium. Savers and borrows constantly consider these maturity trade-offs and regard the different maturities as close substitutes for one another. If there is a change in market expectations, so that more market participants feel that the one-year rate, one year hence will be 7% instead of 6.5006%, then the market equilibrium rates will change. With 7% forward-rate expectations for the one-year rate one year hence, borrowers would be inclined to borrow for two years and savers would be inclined to lend for one year and then reinvest, effectively lowering one-year rates (due to greater supply and lower demand) and raising two-year rates. This shift in rates would occur until the market's expected equality between the two-year investment return and the sequential one-year investments were equal once again.

The expectations theory rests on a simple premise, that long-term interest rates represent the market participant's expectations for future short-term rates. As our example indicated, provided that the one-year rate is known, the two-year rate represents the market's expectation for the forward one-year rate, one year hence.

The expectations theory plausibly explains any yield curve.[5] Exhibit 14.7 shows the three hypothetical term structures. The upward-sloping term structure would exist when the market participants expect short-term interest rates to rise, usually at the end of a recession, or when the demand for loanable funds and in-

---

[4]The forward rate is not related to expectations. In theory, if borrowing and lending could take place at a rate reflected in the term structure then it is possible to create forward loans. For example, if one wanted to borrow for 2 years, 10 years from now, it would require borrowing at the existing 12-year rate and lending at the existing 10-year rate. The result would be a 2-year loan beginning 10 years from now.

[5]The expectations theory attempts to explain the actual forward rates that exist.

EXHIBIT 14.7

Three Term Structures: Expectations Hypothesis

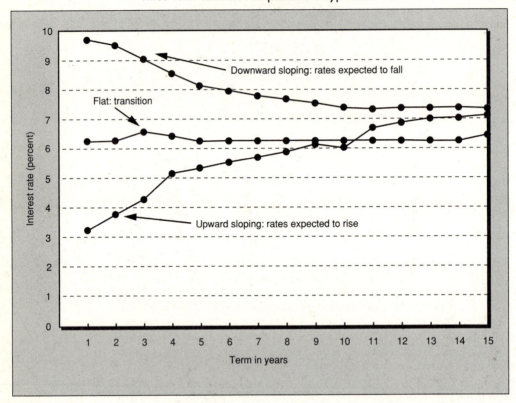

flation are rising, early in an economic recovery. The downward-sloping term structure exists usually when the economy is booming, credit demand is strong, and inflation is high—all prompting the Federal Reserve to adopt a restrictive monetary policy. During such a period, the market participants typically expect an economic downturn. Downward-sloping term structures are rare; but when they have occurred, economic slowdowns usually follow. The flat term structure occurs during transitions between the other two more pronounced curves.

Forward Interest Rate

Financial firm managers can calculate the actual forward interest rate for any forward period by using Equation 14.3:

$$(1 + r_1)^n (1 + r_2)^{t-n} = (1 + r_3)^t \qquad [14.3]$$

where:

t = Period of longer investment

n = Period of shorter investment

t – n = Period of reinvestment investment

r_1 *= Rate on an investment of term n*

r_2 *= Rate on an investment of term t – n*

r_3 *= Rate on an investment of term t*

n < t

In this equation, the *r(s)* represent interest rates for selected periods, *n, t* and *t – n*. Consider the following example. The current rate for a four-year bond, r_3, is 7% with *t* = 4. The current rate on a three-year bond, r_2, is 6.8% with *t – n* = 3 and *n* = 1. Using Equation 14.3, we have:

$$(1 + r_1)^n (1 + r_2)^{t-n} = (1 + r_3)^t$$

$$(1 + r_1)^1 (1 + .068)^3 = (1 + .070)^4$$

$$(1 + r_1) (1.2182) = (1.3108)$$

$$r_1 = (1.3108/1.2182) = 1.0760 - 1.00$$

$$r_1 = .0760 = 7.60\%$$

Although the forward rate is easy to calculate, the market equilibrium forward rates based on expectations theory have not been found to be accurate. However, these rates do provide a method for making investment decisions by comparing your forecast rate to that implied by the term structure. For example, if the forecast forward rate for one-year debt claims three years from now exceeds 7.6%, then investing for three years at 6.8% and then for one year at the expected higher forecast rate would be a wise plan.

COMPUTING IMPLIED THE FORWARD RATE   **DEMONSTRATION PROBLEM**

Situation

The interest rate on a three-year Treasury note is 10% and on a one-year note 8%. Under the expectations theory, what is the implied forward rate on a two-year Treasury note one year from now?

Result

You must solve for the implied forward two-year rate, r_2, one year from now. We assume that the returns from investing for three years will be comparable to investing for one year and then reinvesting the proceeds at the expected forward two-year rate:

$$n = 1$$

$$t = 3$$

$$t - n = 2$$

$$(1 + r_1)^n (1 + r_2)^{t-n} = (1 + r_3)^t$$

$$(1 + .08)^1 (1 + r_2)^2 = (1 + .10)^3$$

$$(1 + .08) (1 + r_2)^2 = 1.3310$$

$$(1 + r_2)^2 = 1.3310/1.08 = 1.2324$$

$$(1 + r_2) = \sqrt{1.2324} = 1.110$$

$$r_2 = 1.110 - 1.00 = .1100 = 11.00\%.$$

The 11% implied forward rate indicates that the two-year rate one year from now must be 11% or higher to provide the same return or higher as the three year investment. Since your forecast is for a two-year rate of 10.5%, it is appropriate to make the three-year investment.

Segmentation Theory

The validity of the aforementioned expectations theory depends critically on the *substitutability* of investments and loans by lenders and savers; that is, it applies when and because there are comparable alternatives or substitute investments available. In contrast, the segmentation theory assumes that investors consider the substitution of maturities too risky. For example, if each maturity class of securities trades in its own distinct market, then short-, intermediate-, and long-term bond rates would be determined by the unique supply and demand schedules for each of these markets. Segmentation means that the supply and demand for bonds of different maturities are independent of each other. That is, the supply and demand for two-year bonds is independent of the supply and demand for four-year bonds. This notion of market separation is called the **segmentation theory**. A crucial assumption of the segmentation theory is that once the savers and borrowers have chosen the best maturities for their loans and investments, an intermediary probably cannot entice them into other maturities by higher levels of interest rates in markets for longer and shorter maturity assets.

The segmentation theory also helps to explain each type of yield curve shape. An upward-sloping term structure results from weak demand and/or strong supply of short-term loanable funds, with commensurately strong demand and/or weak supply of long-term loanable funds. The downward-sloping yield curve results from the opposite conditions. Exhibit 14.8 depicts the segmentation theory for short-, intermediate-, and long-term bonds, where a unique set of supply and demand schedules, independent of one another, determines each rate.

One rationale behind the segmentation theory is that borrowers and savers want to match the maturities of their assets and liabilities. This matching process

TILTING THE YIELD CURVE

During 1991 to 1993, economists at the U.S. Treasury and Federal Reserve Board held discussions concerning a plan to revise Treasury debt-financing operations. Throughout the 1990 to 1991 recession and the subsequent slow recovery, the level of long-term interest rates was considered to be too high as compared to the very low levels of short-term rates. These high long-term rates were felt to be inhibiting economic growth by restraining business capital spending and housing construction. Some financial professionals concluded that long-term interest rates would fall if the Treasury reduced the volume of long-term bonds issued and did most of its financing in short-term maturities. Others argued that the Treasury's interest costs would be reduced by borrowing at the lower short-term rates. Reducing the supply of long-term bonds was expected to increase their price and lower their yield.

Such a program was attempted years earlier and was called "Operation Twist." This meant twisting the yield curve to a less upward slope. Enough government officials were persuaded by the arguments that the Treasury reduced the volume of long-term bond sales in 1993.

For such a program to work, the segmentation theory must have some validity. Yet, there remains little available empirical evidence that such a program could produce the desired results.

How

it

Really

Works

avoids the risk that interest rates change significantly to upset the financial plans of the saver or borrower. If a household planning for retirement wanted to build a specified sum of funds to have during retirement, it could eliminate risk by buying long-term bonds that would mature when the household needed to consume the funds. If the household bought short-term bonds, and reinvested periodically, it would bear the risk of falling interest rates and decreased returns on the investment. Consequently, the household would invest in long-term assets because it had long-term financial needs. Savers who invest for consumption just a few years in the future, on the other hand, would invest in bonds of short maturities.

Efforts to prove the segmentation theory have been largely unsuccessful. As a result, practitioners use the segmentation hypothesis to explain pricing differences in yields between markets, such as those for tax-exempt and taxable bonds.

Liquidity Preference Theory

The **liquidity preference theory** rests on the premise that long-term bond prices are more volatile than short-term bond prices. Short-term investments reduce the risk that unanticipated interest rate movements will produce losses to investors. The additional price volatility of long-term bonds produces additional risk for investors. Since investors are risk adverse, they must be compensated for accepting it. Thus, liquidity preference holds that the liquidity premium rises as the maturity of bonds increases. Savers must be compensated to lend long by the amount of the liquidity premium.

EXHIBIT 14.8

Term Structure: Segmentation Hypothesis

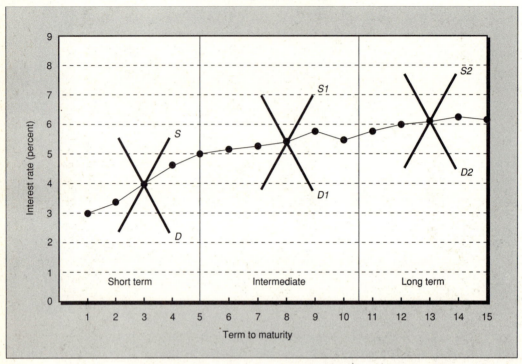

Exhibit 14.9 shows the expectations theory yield curve with a liquidity premium built into it. This steeper upward-sloping yield curve results from the rising liquidity premium.

A majority of economists prefer to combine the expectations theory and liquidity preference, because considerable empirical evidence supports the existence of a liquidity premium.

✓ Checkpoints

14-6 How do inflation expectations influence the level of interest rates? What is the Fisher Effect? What is the relationship between the nominal interest rate and the rate of expected inflation?

14-7 How do interest rates tend to behave during periods of recession, economic booms, and high or rising inflation?

14-8 What is the term structure of interest rates?

14-9 How does the expectations theory of the term structure differ from and relate to the liquidity preference theory and to the segmentation theory?

EXHIBIT 14.9

Term Structure: Expectations Plus Liquidity Premium

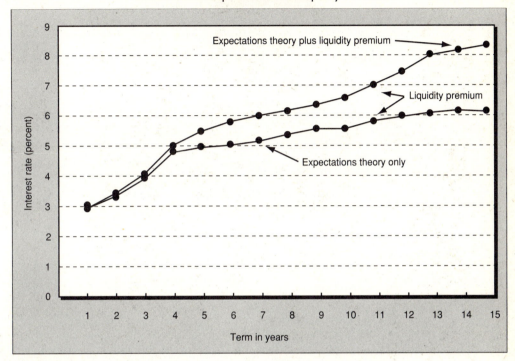

14-10 What does this expression mean: "We can't test the empirical validity of the expectations theory because we can't measure expectations"? Do you agree with it?

14-11 If you observe an upward-sloping term structure, what would the proponents of the expectations theory expect to be the course of future short-term interest rates? What about a downward-sloping term structure?

Specific Risk and Cost Factors Affecting Interest Rates

Table 14.3 lists interest rates on different types of debt securities, as of April 20, 1993, including a sample of different debt instruments with maturities of around ten years. The table shows the U.S. government debt, the Commonwealth Edition corporate debt, and a Federal National Mortgage Association mortgage pass-through security, a bond collateralized by a pool of home mortgages, so that you can see the large differences in their market interest rates. Specific factors provide the basis for how financial professionals price different types of loans.

| TABLE 14.3 |

Interest Rates on Several Financial Assets
April 20, 1993

Debt Instrument	Year	Yield
Treasury bond 8.25%	2005	5.39%
Commonwealth Edison 8.75%	2005	8.40
Federal National Mortgage Association mortgage pass-through 8% coupon mortgages		6.43

Source: *The Wall Street Journal*, April 20, 1993.

There are a number of factors influencing the differences in these rates:

1.   Credit or default risk.
2.   Marketability risk.
3.   Call or prepayment risk.
4.   Servicing costs.
5.   Exchange rate risk.
6.   Taxability.

THE RISK-FREE RATE

The concept of an interest rate that provides a return on investment without risk is an important building block for many financial theories. The **risk-free interest rate,** R_F, is considered to be a long-term interest rate on a bond that has no credit risk and is highly marketable. That means the bond cannot default for any reason and can be bought and sold with negligible transaction costs. For practical applications, the rate of interest on a long-term U.S. Treasury bond provides a good proxy for the risk-free rate. The risk-free rate is a nominal interest rate. Consequently, it will change whenever the real interest rate changes and whenever inflation expectations change.

The importance of the risk-free rate concept is related to the basic financial theory that investors demand a higher return on risky assets as compared to riskless assets. In this context, the risk-free rate represents the lowest return on an investment that an investor should be willing to accept. It will be discussed further in Chapters 10 and 17. If the investor's investment portfolio were to have an expected return below the risk-free rate, then the investor would not be optimizing.

The factors discussed below represent additional returns that investors must earn on investments in order to absorb the specific costs and risks related to each financial asset and still achieve the risk-free rate.

CREDIT OR DEFAULT RISK

Financial claims involve the potential for loss to investors. The primary reason for loss on many claims is a default on the part of the borrower. **Credit** or **default**

risk involves the potential that a saver will receive less principal and interest on the financial claim than the contract specifies.

Credit risk requires making estimates of the potential for loss. This probability is then converted into an interest rate premium, the *credit or default risk premium (crp)*, and added to the saver's required nominal yield. Typically, the Treasury security is considered to be credit risk free.

Table 14.3 shows that the yield on the Commonwealth Edison bond maturing in 2005 is 8.40% versus 5.39% on the Treasury bond maturing in the same year. A large percentage of this 3.01% spread can be related to the higher credit risk of the Commonwealth Edison bond.

MARKETABILITY RISK

Marketability risk deals with the degree of difficulty in being able to convert a financial claim into cash at or near its most recent transaction price. This conversion assumes, of course, that no new information has occurred to change the fundamental value of the financial asset. One of the best ways to understand marketability risk and quantify it is to obtain the bid and ask prices for a particular financial claim. The **bid price** is the price that a willing buyer offers to purchase the claim. The **ask price** is the price a willing seller offers to sell. Most security dealers and organized exchanges quote bid and ask prices. Savers who purchase investments with poor marketability expect to be compensated for the lack of marketability, representing an additional interest spread referred to as the *marketability risk premium (mrp)*.

CALL OR PREPAYMENT RISK

Some financial claims offer the borrower the right to call or repay the principal debt prior to maturity. On financial assets like bonds, these provisions are referred to as *call provisions*. On financial assets such as home mortgages and installment auto loans they are called *prepayment provisions*. These provisions are *options:* the borrower has the option to call or prepay the debt.

The investor in a financial claim that is callable or subject to prepayment accepts risk. The risk is that if interest rates fall, the borrower will call the bond or prepay the mortgage. The investor receiving the cash finds that he or she cannot reinvest it at an interest rate as high as the rate on the prepaid debt. This risk is called *call or prepayment risk*. The compensation that investors demand in order to accept this risk is an additional interest spread referred to as the *call option premium (cop)*.

SERVICING COST

Some financial claims are difficult to service. This means that the process of collecting interest and principal payments, providing accurate records, or monitoring the ongoing credit position of the borrower involves considerable operating costs. Certainly it makes sense that the cost of servicing $10 million of small auto loans is higher than the cost of servicing the same dollar amount of Treasury bonds. The auto loans would involve collecting payments and accounting for 800 to 1,200 different loans. The Treasury bond involves receiving two interest payments per year.

Lenders must be compensated for the costs of servicing. This cost is imbedded into the interest rate charged, and is referred to as the *servicing cost (sc)*.

NOMINAL INTEREST RATES ON TAXABLE DEBT

For the vast majority of taxable debt, finance practitioners estimate the order of magnitude of the factors discussed above to understand the level of nominal interest rates for specific domestic financial debt assets. Equation 14.4 facilitates this estimation; it shows the risk-free rate of interest and the amount of additional yield each of the factors above is estimated to be worth for both borrowers and investors which must be added to the risk-free rate to create a market nominal interest rate for debt claims of type i for a term of t, r_i^t. In this equation, the risk-free rate for Treasury securities is the base rate. For many financial assets, the appropriate rate is the weighted cost of capital for the financial institution making the loan.

$$r_i^t = R_F^t + crp + mrp + cop + sc \qquad [14.4]$$

Nominal interest rate on claim i of term t = Risk-free rate of term t (R_F^t)
+ Credit risk premium (crp) + Marketability risk premium (mrp)
+ Call risk premium (cop) + Servicing costs (sc).

DEMONSTRATION PROBLEM | **NOMINAL INTEREST RATE ON SPECIFIC TYPE OF DEBT**

Situation

Consider the yield on an auto loan that has an interest rate of 10.25% in the marketplace. A comparable maturity Treasury rate is 8%. Auto loans include an expected credit loss premium of 0.50% per annum. They also cost 1.25% per annum to service. The loans carry a 0.2% marketability premium. Since these can be prepaid by the borrower before maturity, they also carry a call or prepayment premium. What is this prepayment premium?

Result

Using Equation 14.4 we have:

$$10.25\% = 8.00\% + 0.50\% + 0.20\% + 1.25\% + X$$

$$X = cop = 0.35\%$$

This loan carries a premium yield of 0.35% to compensate for the borrower having an option to prepay the loan before maturity. This option is potentially costly to the lender, so lenders demand a higher yield.

EXCHANGE RATE RISK

As financial markets go global, there has been a huge growth in the borrowing and investing in foreign denominated financial claims. A U.S. company establishing a manufacturing facility in Belgium might issue bonds denominated in Belgian francs rather than U.S. dollars. Investors also have available to them many investments that are denominated in foreign currencies. These transactions involve **foreign exchange rate risk.** This risk relates to the potential that the rate of exchange between the domestic currency and foreign-denominated currency will change as a result of any number of factors. The primary risk for the borrower is that the value of the borrowed currency rises in relation to the domestic currency, resulting in an unexpected cost on the international loan, since the loan would have to be repaid in the foreign currency which has risen in value relative to the domestic currency. Changes in exchange rates cannot be predicted with confidence. Nevertheless, professionals of multinational organizations must make forecasts about changes in exchange rates in order to make borrowing and investment decisions and pricing decisions for goods bought and sold in foreign markets. This potential change in currency values must be reflected in these decisions. Consider the interest rate relationship in Equation 14.5.

$$r_{tc} = r_f + [(FX_d^{t+1}/_f - FX_d^t/_f) / FX_d^t/_f] \qquad [14.5]$$

Foreign total borrowing cost = Foreign interest rate +
Percent change in domestic currency price for one unit of foreign currency

r_{tc} = *Total cost, expressed as an interest rate, of foreign borrowing*

r_f = *Interest rate on foreign financial debt borrowing*

$FX_d^t/_f$ = *One foreign exchange unit priced in terms of the domestic currency at time t (e.g., $.57 = 1 German mark)*

FOREIGN EXCHANGE IMPACT ON BORROWING COST	DEMONSTRATION PROBLEM

Situation

A U.S. company considers issuing a one-year bond denominated in German marks, DM. The domestic United States annual interest rate, r_d, is 3.5%. The German annual interest rate, r_f, is 5.0%. The marks borrowed will be immediately converted to dollars and used in the United States. The price of one

DM priced in terms of U.S. dollars is expected to go from the current .59 US$/DM to .57 US$/DM in one year. The firm would like to know the cost of borrowing in Germany.

Results

To answer this, it is necessary to determine the expected change in the value of the German mark. This is represented by the percent change of:

$$[(.57 \ \$/DM - .59\$/DM) \ / \ .59\$/DM] = -3.39\%.$$

Since the U.S. dollar is expected to increase in value by 3.39%, the U.S. borrower will have to factor in the decreased currency cost of repaying at period $t + 1$ in German marks that are 3.39% less valuable in relation to U.S. dollars. This 3.39% reduced cost of borrowing German marks brings the true cost of borrowing to:

$$\textit{German interest rate + Increased (decreased) value of marks in}$$
$$\textit{relation to the \$ = Total cost of German loan}$$

$$5.00\% - 3.39\% = 1.61\%$$

Since this 1.61% is far below the U.S. borrowing rate of 3.50%, it would pay to borrow in the German market.

Although accurately forecasting future exchange rates is not really possible, actual forward exchange rates in different countries do reflect differences in interest rates between countries. These forward exchange rates are not good forecasts of the future, however; there is exchange rate risk for borrowers and investors and buyers and sellers alike.

TAXABILITY

The final factor influencing the changes in interest rates is taxability. Financial asset income is typically subject to taxation both by federal and state governments. Since the value of a financial asset is based on its anticipated cash flow, taxation acts to alter those cash flows.

Not all income generated by financial assets is taxed equally, however. A notable exception is income on U.S. government securities which is not subject to state income tax. Most state and local municipal bond interest is not subject to federal income tax. Other financial assets allow investors to defer taxation. Savings held in pension funds and as insurance policy reserves provide for income tax deferrals at the state and federal levels of government.

With the Tax Reform Act of 1986, the number of tax-preferenced investments has been sharply reduced. State and local municipal bond tax preferences have largely survived tax reform. These securities are notable because they are exempt from federal income tax and frequently state income tax also, for taxpayers living in the same state in which the bond is issued.

Because they are exempt from taxes, municipal bonds pay lower interest rates than taxable securities of comparable risk and term. The relationship between the yields on a tax-exempt bond and taxable bond is known as the *taxable equivalent yield (TEY)*. This yield allows comparison of yields between tax-exempt and taxable securities.

To use this yield, you must know the taxpayer's marginal federal *(MFR)* and marginal state tax rates *(MSR)*. The state tax rate only comes into play if the municipal bond is tax exempt in the state of issuance and the taxpayer is from that state. The taxable equivalent yield can be computed using Equation 14.6:

$$TEY = Tax\text{-}exempt\ rate\ (TER)\ /\ [1 - (Marginal\ federal\ rate\ (MFR) +$$
$$Marginal\ state\ rate\ (MSR))]$$

$$TEY = TER\ /\ [1 - (MFR + MSR)] \hspace{2cm} [14.6]$$

CALCULATING THE TAXABLE EQUIVALENT YIELD   **DEMONSTRATION PROBLEM**

Situation

A municipal security has a tax-exempt rate *(TER)* of 7.05%. The investor from the state issuing the bond would have a federal marginal tax rate of 34% and a state marginal tax rate of 6%. What is the bond's taxable equivalent yield?

Results

In this case, the *TEY* can be found using Equation 14.5:

$$TEY = 7.05\% \ /\ [1 - (.34 + .06)]$$

$$= 11.75\%$$

Thus, a taxable security would have to yield 11.75% to provide an after-tax return equal to the return on a tax-exempt security yielding 7.05% for an investor in the 40% combined marginal federal and state income tax bracket.

The Tax Reform Act of 1986 had a significant impact on the demand for municipal bonds by large federal taxpaying intermediaries, such as commercial banks and insurance companies. The act mandated that by 1987 intermediaries would lose the ability to take the interest paid on debt sold to finance tax-exempt bond purchases as an expense for federal tax purposes. A commercial bank with a cost of funds *(COF)* of 4.00% is considering purchasing a 7.05% yielding tax-exempt bond. To determine the taxable equivalent rate using the same federal and tax rates as above, we would use Equation 14.7:

$$TEY = [TER - (COF \times MFR)]/[1 - (MFR + MSR)]$$

$$TEY = [7.05\% - (4.00\% \times .34)]/[1 - (.34 + .06)]$$

$$TEY = 9.48\% \hspace{2cm} [14.7]$$

Understandably, now tax-exempt bonds have lost a lot of their appeal for many intermediaries that had been major investors.

REINVESTMENT RISK

The **reinvestment risk** applies generally to all investments that generate cash flows for the investor prior to the maturity of the investment. When the **yield to maturity** is computed on investments, the calculation process assumes that all cash flows are reinvested at the yield computed. The **internal rate of return** *(IRR)* calculation found in any textbook on business finance shows that one of the limitations of the internal rate of return calculation for investments is the assumption that all the cash flows received before the end of the investment period are reinvested at the *IRR*.

The reinvestment problem creates reinvestment risk for investors. This is the risk that the cash flows received before the maturity of the investment cannot be reinvested at the yield to maturity of the investment. To see clearly how reinvestment risk works, we consider the following types of investments. Each of these investments has a yield to maturity of 6%, yet they have different cash flows.

1. *Installment loan:* two equal payments received at end of each period.
2. *Interest-paying bond:* annual interest payments received at the end of each of next two years and principal due at end of the second year.
3. *Discounted bond:* all principal and interest due at maturity at the end of two years.

The cash flow for these three investments, each having a yield of 6%, is shown in Table 14.4.

Note that each of the investments has a different net cash flow. This is because we have not yet reinvested the early cash flows. In Table 14.5, we will reinvest the early cash flows at the 6% yield of the investments.

Our reinvestment assumption results in the net cash flows becoming equal, proving that as long as we can reinvest early cash flows at the investment's yield to maturity, each of these investments with a 6% yield will produce the same net

---

TABLE 14.4

Cash Flows
6% Interest Rate
No Reinvestment of Cash Flows

Date	Installment Cash Flow (dollars)	Interest Bond Cash Flow	Discounted Bond Cash Flow
Jan. 1, 1993	$–1,000.00	$–1,000.00	$–1,000.00
Jan. 1, 1994	545.44	60.00	—
Jan. 1, 1995	545.44	1,060.00	1,123.60
Total	$ 90.88	$ 120.00	$ 123.60

cash flow for the investor. What would happen if the reinvestment rate were not 6%, but rather 4%? Table 14.6 depicts the result of this reinvestment assumption on the net cash flows of our three investments.

With this lower reinvestment rate, the three investments result in significantly different net cash flows. The differences that result from changes in the reinvestment rate represent reinvestment risk. Loan portfolio managers can eliminate this risk by purchasing discounted securities, such as the discounted bond shown in Table 14.6.

✓ Checkpoints

14-12 What are some of the specific factors that affect the interest rate on any specific debt instrument?

14-13 Two bonds both have ten-year maturities and neither is callable. The yield on one is 6.50% and the other 7.12%. What accounts for the difference?

14-14 How does taxation affect the yield on various bonds.

14-15 If your firm is considering borrowing in a local currency of a foreign country, what factors should it consider?

14-16 What is reinvestment risk? What types of investments have high reinvestment risk and which have low risk?

TABLE 14.5

Cash Flows
6% Coupon Rate
Reinvestment of Cash Flows at 6%

Date	Cash Flow (dollars)	Reinvestment at 6%	Cash Flow + Reinvestment Interest
Installment Loan			
Jan. 1, 1993	$-1,000.00		$-1,000.00
Jan. 1, 1994	545.44	$(1. + .06)^1$	578.17
Jan. 1, 1995	545.44		545.44
Total			$ 123.61
Interest-paying Bond			
Jan. 1, 1993	-1,000.00		-1,000.00
Jan. 1, 1994	60.00	$(1 + .06)^1$	62.40
Jan. 1, 1995	1,060.00		1,060.00
Total			$ 123.60
Discounted			
Jan. 1, 1993	-1,000.00		-1,000.00
Jan. 1, 1994	0.00	$(1. + .06)^1$	0.00
Jan. 1, 1995	1,123.60		1,123.60
Total			$ 123.60

TABLE 14.6			

Cash Flows
6% Coupon Rate
Reinvestment of Cash Flows at 4%

Date	Cash Flow (dollars)	Reinvestment at 4%	Cash Flow + Reinvestment Interest
Installment Loan			
Jan. 1, 1993	$-1,000.00		$-1,000.00
Jan. 1, 1994	545.44	$(1. + .04)^1$	567.26
Jan. 1, 1995	545.44		545.44
Total			$ 112.70
Interest-paying Bond			
Jan. 1, 1993	-1,000.00		-1,000.00
Jan. 1, 1994	60.00	$(1 + .04)^1$	62.40
Jan. 1, 1995	1,060.00		1,060.00
Total			$ 122.40
Discounted			
Jan. 1, 1993	-1,000.00		-1,000.00
Jan. 1, 1994	0.00	$(1. + .04)^1$	0.00
Jan. 1, 1995	1,123.60		1,123.60
Total			$ 123.60

SUMMARY AND REVIEW

1. **Explain the real interest rate and what impacts it, and describe the factors that affect the supply and demand of loanable funds.**

   The **real interest rate** is the rate that equates the next most desirable investment opportunity to marginal interest return demanded from the marginal saver. Increased investment opportunities tend to increase the real rate of interest—the rate of interest without consideration of inflation.

   The **loanable funds theory** holds that interest rates are determined by the demand and supply of funds from the business, household, government, and foreign sectors of the economy and by actions of the Federal Reserve. Typically, during booming economic conditions, the relative demand for funds rises in the business and household sectors and falls in the government and international sectors. During economic recessions, the reverse tends to occur.

2. **Discuss the impact of inflation expectations on interest rates and define the Fisher Effect.**

   Inflation expectations are known to be a major influence on the level of interest rates. Expectations of rising inflation cause businesses to build inventory and households to consume now, while causing investors to refrain from lending without being compensated for the expected loss in purchasing power. This is known as the *Fisher Effect.* This theory holds that:

Nominal interest rate = Real interest rate + Expected inflation

3. **Explain the term structure of interest rates and describe the expectations, segmentation, and liquidity preference theories of the term structure.**

   The **term structure of interest rates** shows the level of interest rates for different maturities. The most powerful explanation of the term structure is the **expectations theory.** The expectations theory holds that long-term interest rates represent the market's expectation of what future short-term interest rates will be. The **market segmentation** theory holds that the relative demand for and supply of securities in different maturity ranges account for the changing shape of the term structure. The **liquidity preference** theory is based on the notion that investors are risk adverse and therefore prefer short-term investments with less interest rate risk than long-term investments. This theory holds that the term structure has a more pronounced upward slope than would be reflected if only the expectations theory yield curve were shown.

4. **Explain the implied forward rate and know how to compute it.**

   The **implied forward rate** is the market's expectation of future interest rates as reflected by the expectations theory and the prevailing term structure. It is possible to calculate the forward interest rate for any forward period using the equation:

   $$(1 + r_1)^n (1 + r_2)^{t-n} = (1 + r_3)^t$$

   In this equation the r(s) represent interest rates for selected periods.

5. **Describe the concept of the risk-free interest rate.**

   The **risk-free interest rate** is an important financial concept denoting a return from an investment that involves no risk.

6. **Discuss the factors that affect the interest rate on specific financial assets.**

   There are financial asset-specific factors influencing the structure of interest rates. These factors include: (1) **credit or default risk,** or the likelihood that the borrower will not pay in full and on time; (2) **marketability,** or the ease of selling the debt; (3) **call or prepayment risk,** the risk that the borrower will repay before maturity if interest rates fall; (4) **servicing costs,** the costs relating to insuring that the debt performs according to its contractual terms; (5) **exchange rate risk,** the risk that attaches to debts repayable in a currency other than the one you own; and (6) **tax treatment.**

7. **Explain and know how to calculate the tax equivalent yield.**

   Tax-exempt securities are very popular investments for individuals with high marginal tax rates. The investor in a tax-exempt bond is interested in comparing the yield on a tax-exempt bond with a taxable bond. This requires using the before-tax equivalent yield (*TEY*). The equation for the *TEY* is

$$TEY = TER \div [1 - (MFR + MSR)]$$

where *TER* is the tax-exempt yield, *MFR* is the marginal federal tax rate, and *MSR* is the marginal state tax rate.

An intermediary must adjust the equation to eliminate the tax deduction for interest. This adjustment results in the following equation:

$$TEY = [TER - (COF \times MFR)]/[1 - (MFR + MSR)]$$

where *COF* is the cost of deposits or debt used to finance the tax-exempt bonds.

SELF-TEST PROBLEMS | **FORWARD RATE**

ST-14-1

Suppose the yield on a 20-year Treasury note is 7% and on a 19-year note 6.95%. What is the forward rate on a 1-year Treasury note 19 years from now? (Assume annual interest payments.)

Answers found on page 405.

FOREIGN BORROWING INVESTMENT RETURN

ST-14-2

A U.S. investor considers purchasing a three-year bond denominated in Japanese yen, Y. The domestic U.S. one-year interest rate r_d, is 4.5%. The Japanese one-year interest rate, r_f, is 4.0%. The dollars will be immediately converted into yen and used to purchase the Japanese investment if that is shown to be the best investment. The price of one Y priced in terms of the U.S. $1 is expected to go from .0095 US$/Y at point t to .0096 US$/Y at point $t + 1$. The firm would like to know the expected return of investing in Japan.

TAX EQUIVALENT YIELD

ST-14-3

Bob Jones is considering purchasing a corporate bond maturing in five years. The yield to maturity is 7.40%. A security broker has told him that a tax-free bond of comparable risk and maturity can be bought to yield 4.80% for out-of-state bonds and 4.40% for bonds issued locally. Bob's state income tax marginal rate is 8.00%. His federal income tax marginal rate is 34%. Which security should Bob buy and why?

TAX EQUIVALENT YIELD

ST-14-4

Maryland and Southern Bank (MSB) is considering replacing some short-term agency securities in its liquidity portfolio with some short-term municipals. The bank is earning 6.75% on agency securities. The yield on the municipals of local issuers is 5.40%. MSB estimates its cost of funds at 4.00%. MSB's combined federal and state marginal tax rate is 40%. Its marginal federal tax rate is 34%. Should MSB make the swap?

FORWARD RATES   PROBLEMS

14-1

If the interest rate on a three-year Treasury is 9.5% and on the one-year Treasury 7.5%, what is the forward rate on two-year Treasuries one year from now? Assume annual interest payments. Show your work.

FORWARD RATES

14-2

The yields on Treasury securities over the next 24 months are:

6-month	5.55%
12-month	6.00
18-month	6.25
24-month	7.40

You have been asked to develop a forecast on the future 6-month Treasury rate using the expectations theory as your guide. Based on the above information, what do you calculate future 6-month Treasury bill rates to be 6, 12, and 18 months into the future?

FORWARD RATES

14-3

You are going to invest funds for five years. An attractive three-year investment will provide an annual yield of 6%. A five-year investment is available at 7%. You believe that interest rates will be increasing. In three years, you expect that you can earn 8% on a two-year investment. Should you invest for five years at 7% or three years at 6% with a reinvestment for two years?

SPECFIC FACTORS AFFECTING RISKY DEBT RATES

14-4

The yield on a ten-year Treasury is 8.5%. The yield on a conventional fixed-rate mortgage is 9.55%. The credit risk premium on the mortgage is expected to be 0.15% and the marketability premium 0.20%. The mortgage also requires the investor to pay 0.10% to service the payments on the loan. What accounts for the remaining yield differential between the two debt instruments?

FOREIGN BORROWING COST

14-5

Your firm is considering financing in the United Kingdom. The rate that would be required on a six-month bond would be 7% in pounds. The U.S. financing alternative would cost 9%. The U.K. pound (pd) is expected to change in value from $1.70/pd to $1.75/pd. Should the firm finance in the United Kingdom?

FOREIGN BORROWING COST

14-6

The interest rate for a one-year loan in France is 6%. A comparable one-year loan in the United States would cost 8%. The exchange rate between U.S. dollars and French francs is $.18 per French franc (ff). What exchange rate would have to prevail in one year to make the borrower indifferent between financing in the United States or France?

TAX EQUIVALENT YIELD

14-7

An investor is considering a federal tax-exempt state bond that is also exempt from state taxation. The yield is 7.30%. The investor's federal and state marginal tax rates are 36% and 7% respectively. What is the taxable equivalent yield on this investment (*TEY*)?

TAX EQUIVALENT YIELD

14-8

David wants to invest in a ten-year security. He has two choices: (1) a taxable bond yielding 8% or (2) a federal and state tax-exempt municipal bond with the same credit risk yielding 4.90%. David's marginal tax rates are 35% federal and 6% state. Which security should he purchase and why?

TAX EQUIVALENT YIELD FOR INTERMEDIARY

14-9

Bergen Bank is considering replacing some taxable securities with municipal bonds. As a financial analyst, would you recommend the security swap in either of the following situations? Answer yes or no and supply calculations to support your answers.

1. The bank earns 7.3% on the securities held. They can be sold at no gain or loss. The municipal securities of equivalent risk would earn 5.5%. The

bank's cost of funds is 4.5%. The bank's marginal federal and state tax rates are 36% and 5% respectively.

2. The same conditions as above are true except the bank can earn 6% on the municipal bonds.

TAX EQUIVALENT YIELD FOR INTERMEDIARY

14-10

Sanwan Bank has a cost of funds of 3.80%. It is contemplating investing in a tax-exempt bond. The marginal federal tax rate for the bank is 36% and the state marginal rate is 7%. Considering the impact of the 1986 Tax Reform Act, compute the taxable equivalent yield (*TEY*) on a municpal bond exempt from state taxes yielding 7.30%.

SOLUTIONS	SELF-TEST PROBLEM

ST-14-1

Solution:

It is necessary to solve for the two-year rate *(r)* expected to prevail one year from now assuming that their is no arbitrage profit opportunity.

$$n = 19$$

$$t = 20$$

$$t - n = 1$$

$$(1 + .0695)^{19} (1 + r_2)^1 = (1 + .07)^{20}$$

$$(1 + r_2)^1 = (1 + .07)^{20} / (1 + .0695)^{19}$$

$$1 + r_2 = 3.86968/3.58455 = 1.07954 - 1.0 = .07954$$

$$r_2 = 7.954\%$$

ST-14-2

Solution:

To answer this, it is necessary to determine the expected change in the value of the Japanese yen. This is represented by the percent change of:

$$[(.0096 \text{ \$/Y} - .0095 \text{ \$/Y}) / .0095 \text{ \$/Y}] = +1.053\%$$

Since the Japanese yen is expected to increase in value by 1.053%, the Japanese security investor will have to factor in the increased currency appreciation derived from holding a Japanese yen-denominated investment. This 1.053% increases the return of the Japanese investment and brings its total return to:

Japanese interest rate + Increased (– decreased) value of yen in relation to the \$ = Total return on Japanese bond

$$4.00\% + 1.053\% = 5.063\%.$$

Since this is $(5.063 - 4.500 =) .563\%$ above the U.S.'s bond rate of 4.50%, it would pay to invest in the Japanese bond market.

ST-14-3

Solution:
The objective here is to calculate the before-tax equivalent yields on the tax exempt bonds and compare them to the taxable corporate bond. The equation used to do this is tax equivalent yield, *TEY*, equals tax exempt rate, *TER*, divided by unity minus the sum of the taxpayers marginal federal, *MFR*, and state tax, *MSR*, rates.

$$TEY = TER / [1 - (MFR + MSR)]$$

For the out-of-state tax exempt bond, the state tax rate does not apply, so we have:

$$TEY = 4.80\% / [1 - (.34)] = 7.27\%$$

For the in-state tax exempt bond, the state tax rate applies, so we have:

$$TEY = 4.40\% / [1 - (.34 + .08)] = 7.59\%$$

Bob should buy the tax-exempt bond issued in his home state since it is exempt from state as well as federal income tax and therefore has a higher *TEY*. This assumes the interest on this bond is exempt from the minimum preference tax.

ST-14-4

Solution:
The objective is to calculate the before-tax yield equivalent on the tax-exempt bonds giving consideration that the interest cost on the funds used to buy the bonds is a non-deductible expense for federal income tax purposes. We use the equation below for this computation:

$$TEY = \{TER - [(COF \times MFR)/ (1 - MFR - MSR)]\}$$

$$TEY = [5.40\% - (4.00\% \times .34)] / [(1 - .34 - .06)]$$

$$TEY = [5.40\% - 1.36\%] / .60 = 6.73\%.$$

It is not in the best interests of MSB to make the swap. It is obtaining a higher yield on the agency securities.

CHAPTER 15

Valuation of Financial Claims

Learning Goals

After studying this chapter, you should be able to:

1. Explain and know how to use the basic valuation equations for determining present value, future value, compounding, yield to maturity, and equivalent annual yield.
2. Explain and know how to calculate the values of discounted bonds such as T-bills and zero-coupon bonds, perpetuities, and interest paying bonds with and without call provisions.
3. Describe a coupon-stripped Treasury security and explain how it is valued.
4. Explain why fixed-rate mortgages are so difficult to value and describe some of the approaches used to value them.
5. Describe the process of stripping fixed-rate mortgage securities into interest-only and principal-only securities and explain the difficulty in valuing them.
6. Explain the theory behind the creation of collateralized mortgage obligations (CMOs) and describe how they are formed.
7. Explain the theory behind the creation of senior-subordinated securities and describe how and why they are formed.

"What is it worth?" may very well be the most asked question throughout your study of finance. Since financial institutions originate and purchase financial claims, the most successful managers at financial institutions are adept at valuation techniques. The ability to determine value relates closely to structuring and pricing claims and ascertaining whether an investment is worth more or less than its market value.

To prepare you for valuing claims within the financial services industry, this chapter provides you with three sections: (1) present value theory, with a quick review of the tools for calculating present value, future value, yields, and compounded interest; (2) valuation techniques and yield formulas for the most common types of financial debt instruments; and (3) valuation techniques for fixed-rate mortgages and a number of the hybrid financial claims, including the popular Treasury strips, interest-only and principal-only securities derived from mortgage securities, servicing strips, collateralized mortgage obligations, and senior-subordinated securities.

The Basics of Present and Future Values, Yields, and Compounded Interest

Present value theory enables us to calculate values and yields for a series of cash flows. By now in your study of finance, you should have a financial calculator to compute the basic calculations in this section and the next.

PRESENT VALUE THEORY

Present value theory helps to value assets under certainty. In prerequisite financial management courses, you learned how corporations apply the tools derived from this theory to make capital budgeting decisions. The real estate industry also uses present value techniques to value commercial real estate; and financial analysts in and outside the corporate world apply present value theory to value bonds and stocks.

Those working in a financial intermediary can follow present value methodology to find today's value for a future stream of known cash flows to be received or paid, and to determine the yield on a financial claim when the cash flows on the claim and today's value are known.

Present value calculations involve the following four variables:

- r, the discount rate or base rate.
- Cf_t, the cash flows.
- PV, the present value.
- t, the number of annual periods over which the investment is outstanding.

Equation 15.1 shows a financial claim with a simple future cash flow.

$$PV = CF_t/(1 + r)^t \qquad [15.1]$$

In this equation, present value, PV, is the *present* value measured in today's dollars of receiving a future cash flow, CF_t, at time period t. This future cash flow is referred to as **future value,** denoted by FV. The future cash flow is at a discount rate r for t periods. The interest is expressed as percent and hundredths of 1%, which are known as **basis points.** One basis point equals 0.01% or 0.0001 in decimal form.

DEMONSTRATION PROBLEM   **CALCULATING A FUTURE VALUE**

Situation

You have opened a $2,000 savings account on which a bank promises to pay a 9% annual return for two years. In two years what will it be worth?

Result

Using Equation 15.1, you solve for CF_2, which is the future value when $r = .09$, and $t = 2$.

$$PV \times (1 + .09)^2 = CF_2 = FV$$

$$\$2,000 \times (1 + .09)^2 = \$2,376.20$$

In this case, the amount of money we expect to receive in two years is the future value $2,376.20.

The factors $1/(1 + r)^n$ and $(1 + r)^n$ are programmed into financial calculators and are available in the financial tables found in the back of this book. $1/(1 + r)^n$ is known as $PVIF_{r,n}$ and $(1 + r)^n$ is known as $FVIF_{r,n}$.

Many investments involve periodic cash flows. Cash flows occurring at equal intervals of time are called *annuities*. An ordinary annuity is a series of periodic cash flows of equal dollar amount that occur at the end of a finite number of periods. Equation 15.2 represents the present value of an ordinary annuity.

$$PV = CF \left[(1 - (1 + r)^{-n}) / r \right] \qquad [15.2]$$

CALCULATING THE PRESENT VALUE OF AN ANNUITY	DEMONSTRATION PROBLEM

Situation

You have just taken out a term loan. This type of loan requires a periodic constant payment. A term loan has a $314 annual payment, CF, due at the end of each of the next five years, n. You have been asked to calculate the present value of these payments discounted at a rate of 9%, r.

Result

Using Equation 15.2 to solve for PV with $CF = \$314$ and $r = .09$ you have

$$PV = \$314 \left[(1 - (1 + .09)^{-5}) / .09 \right]$$

$$PV = \$314 \left[(1.0 - .6499314) / .09 \right]$$

$$PV = \$314 \,(3.8897) = \$1,221.37$$

The factor $[(1 - (1 + r)^{-n})/r]$, known as $PVIFA_{r,n}$, is also programmed into financial calculators and is available in financial tables found in the back of the book. Using tables: $PV = \$314 \times (PVIFA_{9.00,5})$

$$PV = \$314 \times 3.890 = \$1,221.40$$

COMPOUNDED INTEREST

Compounded interest is interest paid or accrued within a one-year period, and compounding allows investors to reallocate their interest to earn additional amounts within the year. The *number of interest payments or accruals, m,* is the number of compounding periods per year. Modifying Equation 15.2 produces Equation 15.3 to depict a situation in which the bank compounds interest *m* periods per year:

$$PV \times [1 + (r/m)]^{tm} = FV \qquad\qquad [15.3]$$

DEMONSTRATION PROBLEM	FUTURE VALUES WITH COMPOUNDING OF INTEREST

Situation

Using the same example future value problem solved above, assume that you can earn 9%, *r*, compounded monthly, *m* = 12. What would the future value be for a $2,000 investment at the end of two years, *t* = 2?

Result

In this equation derived from 15.3, *m* is 12 for monthly compounding.

$$\$2,000 \, [1 + (.09/12)]^{2 \times 12} = \$2,392.83$$

The variable *m* would be 4 for quarterly payments and 2 for semiannual compounding. By compounding monthly instead of annually, we have increased our future cash flow by $16.63 ($2,392.83 − 2,376.20).

STIFF COMPETITION IN THE SAVINGS CERTIFICATE COMPOUNDING MARKET

"Would you like a free toaster with your interest?" That's the ubiquitous question that institutions asked to attract savers without violating rate-control Regulation Q. Regulation Q set the maximum interest rates on savings accounts that insured commercial banks and thrift institutions could pay to customers. It resulted from the Great Depression of the 1930s to regulate commercial banks and was extended in the 1960s to govern savings and loans and savings banks. The ceilings were eliminated in 1980.

Another means of innovating around Regulation Q was to offer more frequent compounding of interest on accounts, so that the saver would earn a higher interest return for any specific interest rate ceiling. Several variables determine the amount earning interest: the initial deposit, *PV*; the number of compounding periods, *m*; the annual interest rate or base rate, *r*; and the number of years, *t*. In compounding, the intermediary applies an interest rate called the *periodic rate,* the determinant time period between compounding, *r/m*. Here, *m* is the number of compounding periods within a year, and *mn* is the number of periods. Equation 15.4 shows the future value:

$$FV = PV\,(1 + r/m)^{mn} \qquad [15.4]$$

Table 15.1 provides an example of the future value of a $1,000 savings account after one year using five different compounding frequencies.

TABLE 15.1

Future Value of $1,000 Savings Account Using Different Compounding Frequencies
(base interest rate 5.00%)

Compounding Frequency	Future Value of $1,000 Investment in One Year
Semiannually	$1,050.625
Quarterly	1,050.945
Daily 360 days	1,051.267
Daily 365 days	1,051.268
365/360 (360-day factor applied 365 days)	1,051.998

The following equation summarizes the future value calculation for the 365/360:

$$FV = \$1,000 \times (1 + (.05/360)^{365}$$

This equation applies the interest factor for a 360-day year ($r/360$), and compounds for 365 periods, a practice referred to as "compounding 365 over 360" or "365/360."

If an intermediary wanted to offer an infinite number of compounding periods, the service of **continuous or infinite compounding,** then the following expression would apply:

$$[1 + (r/m)]^{mt} \text{ approaches } e^{rt} \text{ as } m \to \infty$$

where e is the number 2.71828 ..., r is the annual interest rate, and m is the number of yearly periods or fraction thereof. Many financial calculators have a function to calculate this expression. Compounding the 5% account for one year using an infinite number of periods yields the following:

$$e^{rt} = e^{.05(1)} = 1.05127$$

Notably, the amount of 1.05127 is higher than daily compounding, but lower than the 365/360.

YIELD TO MATURITY

Derived from the present value equation, the *yield to maturity* on a financial claim is the annualized interest rate, r, that equates the future cash flows to the present value, given a specified compounding approach. The interest rate on an investment is quoted in terms of a specified number of compounding periods, m. Bonds paying interest twice a year feature yields calculated by semiannual compounding, $m = 2$. The yield of a mortgage that requires payment 12 times per year is calculated using monthly compounding, $m = 12$. In computing the yield on the bond, the generalized present value Equation 15.5 works well:

$$PV = \{\Sigma_{n=1}^{t} \, CF_n/[1 + (r/m)]^{nm}\} + Par\ value/[1 + (r/m)]^{t} \qquad [15.5]$$

DEMONSTRATION PROBLEM

PRESENT VALUE OF A COUPON BOND

Situation

A bond pays interest semiannually at the base rate of 9% per annum. For a bond, it is customary to refer to the base rate as the *coupon rate*. The **par value** of the bond is $25,000. The par value is the amount upon which interest is paid. A broker states on April 15, 1993, that the bond can be purchased at a price of 98.25. That means we can buy the bond for 98.25% of its par value. The bond is said to be selling at a **discount** from its par value. If the bond were selling at a price above 100, or above 100% of its par value, it would be selling at a **premium**. You have been asked to estimate the value of this bond.

Result

Using the coupon rate to calculate the actual interest cash flows, you determine them to be $(.09/2 \times \$25,000 =)$ $1,125.00 per six-month period. The principal will be repaid on April 15, 1998. The number of compounding periods, m, is 2. The par value of the bond is $25,000.

Solving the problem using Equation 15.5 above results in:

$$\$24,562.50 = \Sigma_{n=1}^{10} \, \$1,125/[1 + (r/2)]^{n} + \$25,000/[1 + (r/2)]^{10}$$

The yield to maturity, r, is 9.45%.

DEMONSTRATION PROBLEM

YIELD TO MATURITY ON A CERTIFICATE OF DEPOSIT

Situation

Broader Bank offers a certificate of deposit that pays a 10% yield to maturity compounded quarterly. The managers of First Bank want to set a yield to maturity on their comparable maturity account that produces the same future value. However, First Bank compounds interest monthly. What yield to maturity should First Bank select?

Result

Yield to maturity at Broader Bank =

$$r = .10$$

$$(1 + r/4)^4 = 1.1038 = Future\ value$$

$$Yield\ to\ maturity\ at\ First\ Bank = (1 + r/12)^{12} = 1.1038$$

$$1 + r/12 = 1.0082638$$

$$r/12 = .0082638$$

$$r = .09917$$

The yield to maturity for First Bank's certificate should be set at $r = 9.917\%$.

EQUIVALENT ANNUAL YIELD

Because the yield to maturity is expressed for different compounding periods, comparing the yields to maturity on investments of different compounding schedules is like comparing apples to oranges. To make more meaningul comparisons, practitioners use the **equivalent annual yield** *(EAY)*, an annual interest rate computed without compounding which shows what an investment must earn to match its future value when compounding is used. The *EAY* facilitates the comparison of interest rates on a variety of financial claims with differing compounding periods, as shown in Equation 15.6:

$$(1 + EAY)^1 = (1 + r/m)^m$$

$$EAY = (1 + r/m)^m - 1) \qquad [15.6]$$

EQUIVALENT ANNUAL YIELD **DEMONSTRATION PROBLEM**

Situation

Libor Bank pays 9% yield to maturity compounded quarterly on its certificates of deposit. The manager of Marion Bank wants to offer a certificate that provides the same *EAY* as Libor Bank. However, Marion's certificate will be compounded monthly. What yield to maturity, *r*, must the bank offer?

Result

Find the *EAY* on Libor's certificate. It is computed in the equation

$$EAY = (1 + r/m)^m - 1.0$$

$$= (1 + .09/4)^4 - 1.0$$

$$= (1.0225)^4 - 1.0 = 9.31\%$$

Marion's certificate will have the same *EAY* of 9.31%. The yield to maturity, *r*, that will produce that *EAY* with monthly compounding is

$$0.0931 = [1 + (r/12)]^{12} - 1.0$$

$$[1 + (r/12)] = (1.0931)^{(1/12)}$$

$$r/12 = .0074$$

$$r = .0893 = 8.93\%$$

The *EAY* for an investment with a yield to maturity, *r*, of 9.45 compounded semiannually would be

$$(1 + EAY)^1 = (1 + .0945/2)^2$$

$$EAY = 9.67326$$

The *EAY* of 9.67326% will result in the same future value as a yield to maturity of 9.45% with semiannual compounding. The quantity called effective yield that is advertised by financial depositories for certificates of deposit is the *EAY*. The effective annual yield is sometimes referred to as the simple interest equivalent yield.

CASH FLOWS

Determining the present value of any particular investment is easier than predicting the behavior of an investment's cash flows. That's why financial managers endeavor to create cash flow schedules, perhaps the most difficult but necessary first step in any worthwhile valuation analysis. The **cash flow schedule** identifies the timing and the magnitude or amount of each cash inflow and outflow related to an investment. If you cannot determine cash flows, then you cannot continue your asset valuation.

Let's look at a simple two-year bond: specifically, a $10,000 investment in a bond with a par value of $10,000 pays interest twice a year at the rate of 8% per annum, or $400 every six months. At the time of bond maturity, the investor also receives the original investment back. Table 15.2 depicts the investment's cash flows.

TABLE 15.2

Cash Flow Schedule

Date	Inflows	Outflows	Description
Feb. 1, 1993		$10,000	Investment
Aug. 1, 1993	$ 400		Interest
Feb. 1, 1994	400		Interest
Aug. 1, 1994	400		Interest
Feb. 1, 1995	10,400		Interest and principal

Analysts can use this form of cash flow schedule for any present value problem; students can prepare such a table to see for themselves how the cash flows of an investment behave.

✓ Checkpoints

15-1 How does present value differ from and relate to future value, and how does the compounding process affect each of these values?

15-2 Why do analysts develop cash flow schedules when conducting present value analysis?

Valuation and Yields for Common Debt Claims

This section reviews the yield and valuation formula for the more common money market financial claims and bonds; the next section will introduce the concept of mortgage prepayment and then discuss the valuation and yield of fixed-rate mortgage claims and other innovative hybrid mortgage securities.

DISCOUNTED TREASURY SECURITIES

The most actively traded debt securities are **Treasury bills,** or T-bills, issued by the U.S. Treasury in original maturities of 91 days (13 weeks), 182 days (26 weeks), and 364 days (52 weeks). They do not pay periodic interest but are issued at a discount from par value and redeemed at par, so that the difference between the discount price and par is the gain or income on the investment.

The Treasury department frequently sells T-bills through an auction system open to most institutional investors. Before 1991, the Treasury used a group of 40 large commercial banks and investment banking firms, known as *primary dealers,* to conduct this auction; but the number of market irregularities warranted a more competitive system.

The Federal Reserve of New York reports the purchases and sales of U.S. government securities by the primary dealers. In 1990, the average daily volume of trading in outstanding T-bills was approximately $30 billion per day. Trading among this group in all types of Treasury securities was about $100 billion per day. In early 1994, the volume of T-bills outstanding was approximately $715 billion.

COMPUTING THE EFFECTIVE ANNUAL YIELD ON A DISCOUNTED BOND	DEMONSTRATION PROBLEM

Situaton

Martha is selling a discount T-bill to a dealer. The dealer's bid a percentage of the bill's par value. Thus a bid for a certain dollar amount of bills might be 97.787 on 182-day bills. This bid is a discount from the bill's par value of 100. Martha must calculate the yield on this discounted security.

Result

To compute the yield on this discounted security, Martha uses the same present value methodology used in the example of the five-year bond. The equation for a $1 million par value bid on T-bills would be:

$$\$977,870 = \$1,000,000 / [(1 + (r/(364/182)))]^{(182/182)}$$

In this example, r = 4.526%. This is known as the *effective annual yield* on the 182-day bills. Since this yield is actually earned for only six months, when quoting an annual yield the assumption is made that the $1 million received at maturity can be reinvested for an additional six months at the same yield.

BANK DISCOUNT AND COUPON EQUIVALENT YIELDS ON T-BILLS

Now that you have mastered the present value approach to calculating yields, we must throw you a curve. Back in the days before computers, government bond traders used a simple approach to calculating yields known as the *bank discount yield (BDY)*. This method of quoting yields on short-term securities is still around today.

The calculation involves Equation 15.7.

$$BDY = [[(Par\ value) - (Discounted\ price)]/(Par\ value)] \times [(360)/(Days\ til\ maturity)] \qquad [15.7]$$

DEMONSTRATION PROBLEM — **CALCULATING THE BANK DISCOUNT YIELD ON A DISCOUNT BOND**

Situation

Martha must determine the bank discount yield on the bond used in the previous demonstration problem.

Result

Martha uses Equation 15.7 above. The bank discount yield on a T-bill of 91 days, purchased at a price of 98.789, would be:

$$BDY = [(100 - 98.789)/100] \times (360/91)$$

$$= .0479 = 4.79\%$$

The coupon equivalent yield, *CEY*, is also quoted for T-bills. This calculation is similar to the *BDY*, except that it recognizes that the T-bill is purchased at a discount. Consequently the discounted price, rather than the par value, is used in the denominator of the equation. The calculation appears in Equation 15.8:

$$CEY = [(Par\ value - Discounted\ price)/Discounted\ price] \times (365/91) \qquad [15.8]$$

CALCULATING THE COUPON EQUIVALENT YIELD ON A DISCOUNT BOND

Situation

Martha must now calculate the coupon equivalent yield on the T-bill described in the previous two demonstration problems.

Result

She will use Equation 15.8. Using a 365-day year, she finds the coupon equivalent yield on the above T-bill is:

$$[(100 - 98.789)/98.789] \times (365/91) = 4.91685\%$$

Since the bank discount yield has a downward bias and underestimates the yield compared to the effective yield, practitioners usually do not use it to compare yields on T-bills with those of other investments. However, the financial press typically quotes the *BDY* with the results of Treasury bill auctions, as shown in Exhibit 15.1. And some secondary market transactions in T-bills can incorporate the *BDY*.

EXHIBIT 15.1

Report of Treasury Bill Auction, August 23, 1991

In early trading yesterday, the yield on three-month bills fell as low as 4.89%, but recovered before the bill auction. Here are details of yesterday's bill auction.

Rates are determined by the difference between the purchase price and face value. Thus, higher bidding narrows the investor's return while lower bidding widens it. The percentage rates are calculated on a 360-day year, while the coupon equivalent yield is based on a 366-day year.

	13-Week	**26-Week**
Applications	$29,124,050,000	$32,545,805,000
Accepted bids	$10,417,080,000	$10,400,915,000
Accepted at low price	83%	16%
Accepted noncompetitively	$1,585,595,000	$1,248,235,000
Average price (Rate)	98.683 (5.17%)	97.356 (5.23%)
High price (Rate)	98.706 (5.12%)	97.361 (5.22%)
Low price (Rate)	98.691 (5.18%)	97.351 (5.24%)
Coupon equivalent	5.33%	5.46%
CUSIP number	93279WWW0	9327794YA6

Both issues are dated Aug. 22, 1991. The 13-week bills mature Nov. 21, 1991, and the 26-week bills mature Feb. 28, 1992.

Source: *The Wall Street Journal.* Reprinted by permission of *The Wall Street Journal,* 1991. Dow Jones and Company, Inc. All Rights Reserved Worldwide.

Exhibit 15.1, the results of a T-bill auction, indicates that there were applications to buy (bids offered) of $29,124,050,000 for 13-week bills, of which $10,417,080,000 were accepted. Of the bids accepted, 83% were accepted at the low price of 98.691. T-bills equaling $1,585,595,000 were sold on a noncompetitive basis. These are bids made to the Federal Reserve Banks by small investors who purchase less than $1 million and are willing to pay the average bid price of 98.693. In this auction, the *BDY* is calculated using a 360-day year as follows:

$$BDY = [(100 - 98.693)/100.00] \times (360/91) = 5.17\%$$

The *CEY* in this auction is calculated using a 366-day leap year as follows:

$$CEY = [(100 - 98.693) / 98.693] \times (366/91) = 5.33\%$$

YIELD TO MATURITY TO A CALL

Equation 15.9 serves as a generalized tool for calculating the yield to maturity on a normal coupon bond assuming semiannual compounding, *m*. The only difference between this equation and Equation 15.5 (discussed earlier for calculating the yield-to-maturity on a bond) is that in 15.9, *Prin* can represent the call price of a bond:

$$PV = \{\Sigma_{n=1}^{mt} [CF_n/(1 + (r/m))^n\} + Prin/(1 + (r/m))^{mt} \qquad [15.9]$$

where:

$$PV = Value\ of\ bond$$

$$CF_n = Interest\ payments$$

$$Prin = Principal/call\ price$$

$$m = Compounding\ periods$$

$$n = Period\ of\ cash\ flow$$

$$t = Number\ of\ years\ until\ maturity$$

Some bond claims include a provision that allows the borrower to settle the bond before its stated maturity. Such a provision is an embedded option, more commonly termed a *call option*, which gives the borrower (the issuer of the bond) the right but not the obligation to pay bondholders after a specified date and at a specified price. The following demonstration problem illustrates a callable bond, a bond containing a call option.

CALCULATING YIELD TO MATURITY ON A CALLABLE BOND ·DEMONSTRATION PROBLEM

Situation

ACM Corporation issued a ten-year bond at a coupon rate of 8.75%. It has a call option that permits the company to redeem the bond at the end of five years at a price of 102.5% of par. It is purchased at $9,850 in the open market after it has been outstanding exactly two years. This means there are three years until the call. Juan has been asked to calculate the yield to maturity and yield to maturity to the call on this bond.

Result

Using Equation 15.9, Juan calculates the yield to maturity to be:

$$\$9,850 = \{\Sigma_{n=1}^{16} [\$437.50/(1 + (r/2))^n]\} + \$10,000/(1 + (r/2))^{16}$$

$$= 9.017\%.$$

Using tables:

$$\$9,850 \doteq \$437.50 \ (PVIFA_{4.50,16}) + \$10,000 \ (PVIF_{4.50,16})$$

$$r \cong 9.00\%$$

Then he calculates the the yield to maturity to the call to be:

$$\$9,850 = \{\Sigma_{n=1}^{6} \$437.50/[(1 + (r/2))]^n\} + \$10,250/[(1 + (r/2))^6$$

$$r = 10.076\%$$

Using tables:

$$\$9,850 = \$437.50 \ (PVIFA_{5.00,6}) + \$10,250 \ (PVIF_{5.00,6})$$

$$r \cong 10.00\%$$

Practitioners use the yield-to-call to analyze the effect of the call provision on the investment results. The investor knows that the borrower will call the bond only if the borrower profits by such action, usually if: (1) interest rates fall sharply, prompting the issuer to call the bond and borrow in the open market at the lower prevailing rate or (2) the borrower's credit rating improves substantially, for borrowing at a lower rate. The call effectively denies the investor benefits of the full expected increase in the bond's value if one or both of these events occurs.

REPURCHASE AGREEMENTS AND REVERSE REPURCHASE AGREEMENTS

Government security dealers and financial institutions frequently need to borrow for short periods of time. Since they often carry large inventories of government, agency, and agency mortgage-backed securities—all assets with high marketability and virtually no credit risk—they have good collateral for a loan, via a *repurchase agreement,* or *repo.* The repurchase agreement market, where the borrowing institution agrees to sell its securities at a specified price and to repurchase these securities on a specified date and at a specified price, has grown into a multibillion-dollar marketplace. A repurchase taking place in one day is an **overnight repo;** one that occurs over more than one day is a **term repo.**

Other financial institutions may find themselves with excess cash to invest for short periods of time. These firms look for safe short-term investments—frequently as short as one day—and purchase securities listed under a repurchase agreement through what is known as a *reverse repurchase agreement,* or *reverse repo.*

The repo rate *(RR)* is based on a 360-day period; Equation 15.10 depicts it as follows:

$$RR = [(Repurchase\ price - Sales\ price)/Repurchase\ price] \times [360/(Days\ till\ maturity)] \qquad [15.10]$$

DEMONSTRATION PROBLEM   **CALCULATING THE REPO RATE**

Situation

Your firm is involved in a typical repo transaction involving a large investment banking firm dealing in government securities, selling $5 million par value of U.S. agency bonds to a medium-sized bank at a price of $4,998,990. The investment bank then agrees to repurchase the bonds at $5,000,000 the next day. You have been asked to calculate the repo rate on this transaction.

Result

You use equation 15.10 to obtain:

$$RR = [(\$5,000,000 - \$4,998,990)/\$5,000,000] \times (360/1)$$

$$= .07272 = 7.272\%.$$

PERPETUITIES: PREFERRED STOCK AND CONSOLS

One type of security less common in the United States is the **perpetuity,** a security that pays a fixed amount of periodic interest or dividend payments *(CF),* but never returns the principal. Two examples of perpetuities are the **preferred stock** sold in the United States and the **consol** sold in the United Kingdom.

To determine the value (*PV*) of the perpetuity, you must know the fixed-payment interest or dividend cash flows (*CF*) and the market base rate (*r*).

The valuation equation for the consol is as follows:

$$PV = \Sigma_{n=1}^{\infty}\ CF/(1 + r)^n$$

This equation, fortunately, reduces algebraically to Equation 15.11:

$$PV = CF/r \qquad\qquad [15.11]$$

Notably, the period between the cash flows must be the same as the period used for the rate, *r*. If cash flows occur quarterly, then *r* must be a quarterly periodic rate.

CALCULATING THE VALUE OF A PERPETUITY **DEMONSTRATION PROBLEM**

Situation

Your firm purchased a perpetuity paying an interest payment of $50 per semi-annual period. The market's annual discount rate, *r*, for similar bonds is 8%. Your manager asks you to determine the value of the bond just purchased.

Result

The first measure that you must take is the market discount rate, which is comparable in terms of number of periods to the frequency of the interest payments. In this example it is 2. The semiannual market discount rate would then be *r*/2 = .04. Using Equation 15.11 we have:

$$\$50/.04 = \$1,250$$

ZERO-COUPON BONDS

The zero-coupon bond is just a longer maturity version of a discounted T-bill. This security usually has a maturity of several years to 30 years or more, suitable for investors who do not want the reinvestment risk associated with interest-paying bonds. The equation used to compute the yield on a zero-coupon bond is the same as that used for a discount bond:

$$PV = Par\ value/[1 + r/m)]^{mn} \qquad\qquad [15.12]$$

COMPUTING THE YIELD TO MATURITY ON A ZERO-COUPON BOND **DEMONSTRATION PROBLEM**

Situation

Your colleague asked you to compute the yield to maturity on a zero-coupon bond, assuming semiannual compounding, for a bond of $1 million par value maturing in nine years six months (19 periods), purchased at a price of 47% of par value.

Result

You have decided to use equation 15.12 to calculate the yield-to-maturity, r.

$$\$470,000 = \$1,000,000/[1 + (r/2)]^{19}$$

$$r = 8.108\%$$

✓ Checkpoints

15-3　What would be a good example of a discounted security?

15-4　What are some examples of perpetuities, and how do they differ from regular securities?

15-5　What is a zero-coupon bond, and what advantages does it afford an investor?

Valuation and Yields on Fixed-rate Mortgages and Hybrid Financial Claims

Financial engineering describes the process of deriving financial claims from other financial assets, generally by altering the cash flows or credit risk exposure on new claims. Engineering hybrid financial claims has been a major area of innovation in the 1980s. Financial engineers create hybrid claims by altering the credit and/or cash flow characteristics of an existing claim or group of claims.

The process of creating these new claims relies upon: (1) large volumes of more or less homogeneous securities such as U.S. T-bonds, agency, and government sponsored enterprise mortgage-backed claims, and (2) low-cost computer power for economic simulations and complex pricing models, to analyze a multitude of asset valuations in various economic settings. These new claims rely on a significant analysis of varying cash flows, which only computers can accomplish.

STRIPPED TREASURIES

One example of a hybrid security is the **stripped Treasury security,** or **strip-T,** in which the cash flows of the outstanding Treasury security flow into two or more hybrid securities. One of these classes of the Treasury security rests upon interest cash flows, and the other class uses the principal. Thus, an outstanding Treasury security has its interest payments and principal payments stripped in the creation process.

In 1982, Salomon Brothers came forth with their certificates of accrual on treasury securities, known as *CATS*. At about the same time, Merrill Lynch created their treasury income growth receipts, known as *TIGRs.*

STRIP-TS MADE EASY

Treasury officials have not always facilitated stripped Treasuries. In the 1970s, a secondary market developed as security dealers stripped Treasuries motivated by tax advantages for customers. An investor could sell stripped coupons at a small fraction of their face value and claim the difference as a loss for tax purposes. The Tax Equity and Fiscal Responsibility Act of 1982 put an end to that technique. It also ended the Treasury's objection to coupon stripping.

In 1983 another problem for Treasury "strippers" developed. The Treasury began issuing all new securities in book-entry form. This meant doing away with bearer notes and bonds with physical coupons attached, and registering owners in a computer system. Physical stripping was thus made impossible. Investment bankers responded with marketable "receipts" which evidenced ownership in a book-entry strip. These were then sold.

In 1985, the Treasury finally introduced a program called Separate Trading of Registered Interest and Principal of Securities (STRIPS) which allowed holders of all U.S. Government securities with maturities over ten years to exchange the security for separated components, strips.

How

it

Really

Works

These new securities are principal-only zero-coupon bonds, created through the process of **coupon stripping**. Table 15.3 is an example of a Treasury security whose cash flows are diverted by coupon stripping.

TABLE 15.3

Cash Flows from Treasury Securities $1,000,000 Par Value 7.5% Coupon Rate Five-Year Maturity

Date	Interest Cash Flows	Principal Cash Flows
June 30, 1995	$37,500	
Dec. 31, 1995	"	
"	"	
"	"	
"	"	
Dec. 31, 1999	37,500	
Dec. 31, 1999		$1,000,000

Engineers can create 11 securities from these two sets of cash flows. The first ten of these represent zero-coupon bonds with $37,500 semiannual interest payments representing the principal of the security. The other is created by using the $1,000,000 principal payment as the principal for the zero coupon. In order to determine the market value of each of these securities, we must discount each of the stripped security's cash flows by the relevant discount rates, r_t. The variable t denotes the time period. The market value of each of these 11 securities is shown by the following equations. The market discount rate for each is r_t.

$$\textit{Value of interest only}_{1} = \$37,500/(1 + (r_1))^1$$

$$\textit{Value of interest only}_{2} = \$37,500/(1 + (r_2))^2$$

..

..

..

$$\textit{Value of interest only}_{10} = \$37,500/(1 + (r_{10}))^{10}$$

$$\textit{Value of principal only}_{11} = \$1,000,000/(1 + (r_{10}))^{10}$$

In this example, creating the hybrid securities would be worthwhile only if they could be sold for a total value higher than the price of the Treasury notes. This sale can easily occur if the term structure of interest rates is upward sloping, so that the shorter term strips of a stripped Treasury will be discounted by the market using a discount rate that is lower than the longer-term strips. Referring to the equation, r_1 would be less than r_{10}, permitting the issuer to obtain a higher price for the shorter-term strips and a lower price for the longer strips. The result would be that the entire valuation of all the strips would be higher than the Treasury security trading as a whole. These prices would also have to be high enough to cover the costs of issuance, safekeeping, and distribution. Exhibit 15.2 shows the yield on several hypothetical Treasury stripped securities.

EXHIBIT 15.2

Reading the Financial Page Yields on Stripped Treasuries November 15, 1996
(typical listing)

Maturity	Type	Bid	Ask	Ask Change	Ask Yield
May 1995	i	70–12	70–15	+2	10.28%
Nov. 1996	p	65–14	65–17	+3	10.85

This table shows a typical listing of Treasury stripped coupon securities outstanding and their yields. The i stands for interest and p for principal. The investor can expect a higher volume of strips from the principal. This could also provide higher marketability. The prices are quoted as a percentage of par in thirty-secondths of 100%. The change is shown in thirty-secondths. The yields are based on a semiannual compounding assumption. The May 1995 security is assumed to mature on the fifteenth of the month. Its yield to maturity over seven semiannual periods would be:

$$\text{Ask yield: } r = 100.00 \, [1 \, / \, (1+r/2)^7]$$
$$70.46875 = 100.00 \, [1/(1 + r/2)^7]$$
$$\text{Ask yield: } r = 10.28\%$$

Table 15.4 shows the market value of the cash flows for the five-year, 7.5% coupon Treasury if it is discounted at the prevailing zero-coupon market interest rates, rn. In this table, the market value of each of the cash flows stripped from the Treasury security and discounted at the market yields for zeros is $1,008,005, a good example of how the sum of the parts is worth more than the whole. If the Treasury security can be acquired for $1,000,000 and stripped so that it can be sold for $1,008,005, then there is a potential profit for creating these hybrid securities and distributing them. In this respect, coupon stripping is like a leveraged buyout of a company—the various subsidiaries are sold at higher individual prices than they are worth bundled together.

TABLE 15.4

Market Values of Coupon and Principal Payments Discounted at Market Zero-Coupon Rates

Date of Cash Flow	Cash Flow (CF_n)	Zero Market Rate (r)	Period (n)	Discounted Value $(CF_n/(1 + r/2)^n)$
June 30, 1995	$ 37,500	4.75%	1	$ 36,630
Dec. 31, 1995	37,500	5.00	2	35,693
June 30, 1996	37,500	5.25	3	34,695
Dec. 31, 1996	37,500	5.50	4	33,644
June 30, 1997	37,500	5.75	5	32,545
Dec. 31, 1997	37,500	6.00	6	31,406
June 30, 1998	37,500	6.75	7	29,725
Dec. 31, 1998	37,500	7.00	8	28,478
June 30, 1999	37,500	7.25	9	27,218
Dec. 31, 1999	37,500	7.50	10	25,951
Dec. 31, 1999	1,000,000	7.50	10	692,020
Total				$1,008,005

So far, you have studied investments with easy-to-estimate cash flows. Now the chapter turns to mortgages—financial claims with difficult-to-estimate cash flows. If you plan to work in a financial intermediary, then you really should spend some time analyzing the nature of fixed-rate mortgages, for two reasons: (1) mortgages represent the largest type of financial claim, with mortgage debt exceeding $4.2 trillion by year-end 1993, well above the total Treasury debt; and (2) practitioners are more frequently using mortgages to create many of the popular hybrid securities. If you can value fixed-rate mortgages, then you should be able to grapple with valuation of these hybrid claims.

FIXED-RATE MORTGAGES AND MORTGAGE-BACKED SECURITIES

The standard fixed-rate mortgage (FRM) is one of the most difficult of all securities to value. Why? It looks just like a normal annuity. The principal and interest are returned in a specified constant payment every month for the term of

RECONSTITUTING HYBRIDS

How it Really Works

In October 1993, Salomon Brothers was in the market to buy zero-coupon bonds from institutions and individuals. These zeros had been created by Salomon Brothers years earlier from stripping Treasury long-term bonds. Their objective was to use the zeros to recreate the original bonds, a transaction known as a *reconstitution*. The reason for this transaction was a temporary shortage of long-term Treasuries caused by some investment bankers having sold Treasury securities short (selling bonds they did not own hoping to purchase them later at a lower price), anticipating that Treasury bond prices would fall. Prices didn't fall, and the dealers were left with the need to buy bonds to cover their short sales. Other dealers owning bonds decided not to sell, causing prices to rise further.

In stepped Salomon to relieve the short supply. By buying the zeros, Salomon hoped to reconstitute up to $10 billion of Treasury bonds. Imagine profits from stripping the bonds apart and then putting them back together—nice work if you can get it! In May 1987, the Treasury first permitted strip reconstitution allowing the components of a stripped Treasury to be exchanged for the original coupon bond.

the loan. The one major difference is a provision in the mortgage contract that allows the borrower to prepay the mortgage at any time. One reason for doing so is to refinance the property, which is profitable following a period of sharp declines in interest rates. The borrower could pay off the existing higher-rate mortgage and refinance into a mortgage at a lower prevailing mortgage rate.

The standard mortgage contains a prepayment option. Many studies have been conducted in an attempt to understand the patterns of prepayment that can be expected on a single mortgage or portfolio of mortgages. Present value theory requires the ability to specify the cash flows from any particular investment before calculating the yield. Herein lies the problem with the fixed-rate mortgage: it involves a prepayment option that can be exercised at any time, and that makes specifying the cash flows pretty tough. The following are some reasons for prepayment: (1) scheduled amortization of the principal on a mortgage (a known cash flow); (2) prepayment of all or part of the principal due to partial or total refinance; and (3) default. Reasons 2 and 3 are impossible to predict perfectly.

Inability to specify the cash flows with precision has forced mortgage market participants to use a number of assumed prepayment patterns for FRMs. It is critical to remember that these are nothing more than assumptions about how the cash flows on a mortgage or pool of mortgages will behave. These assumptions about the pattern of cash flows may have been based on a significant amount of theoretical and empirical analysis, but they remain assumptions.

Let's start our investigation of mortgages with a simple example, a mortgage that does not prepay for any reason, including default. The demonstration problem shows how to calculate the yield on a standard FRM.

Situation

An FRM is assumed to experience no prepayment or default during its life. The FRM has a principal value of $100,000 and a monthly payment of $1,058. Joan has been asked to calculate this mortgage's yield to maturity.

Results

To determine the yield to maturity, use the standard present value equation with a discount rate, or yield to maturity, r, assuming monthly compounding, $m = 12$, for a stream of equal monthly payments. Notice that the computation for determining the yield on an FRM is simply an ordinary annuity. The yield to maturity for a $100,000 mortgage with a monthly payment of $1,058 for 30 years, $n = 30$, is shown as

$$\$100{,}000 = \sum_{n=1}^{30 \times 12} \$1{,}058/[1 + (r/12)]^n$$

$$r = .1238 = 12.38\%$$

Using tables:

$$\$100{,}000 = \$1{,}058 \; (PVIFA_{1.00,360})$$

$$r \cong 12.00\%$$

PREPAYMENT ASSUMPTIONS AND MORTGAGE YIELDS

The first attempt to simulate a more realistic cash flow for a mortgage was the adoption of the 10- and 12-year loan life assumption. This assumption held that a mortgage would repay according to its scheduled amortization until a specified date after 10 or 12 years, when it would prepay in full.

To see how this affects the yield on a mortgage, let's take three different mortgages. One is a 9.50% coupon rate mortgage that does not prepay but rather amortizes according to its normal amortization schedule. The others will have the same monthly payments and term, but will prepay at the end of 10 or 12 years. We will also assume that the mortgage can trade in a secondary market and be purchased at prices of 100% of par, 99% of par, or 101% of par. We can determine their yields using the previous equation, but we must modify the *PV* using 99% to 101% of par and use only 120 periods in the case of a 10-year loan life and 144 periods in the case of a 12-year loan life. The 120th and 144th cash flow will be the unpaid principal on the mortgage at that time. Table 15.5 shows the impact of these prepayment assumptions.

| TABLE 15.5 |

Yield on a 30-Year, 9.50% Coupon FRM, Assuming 10- and 12-year Prepayment Purchase Prices of 99%, 100%, and 101% of Par

Mortgage Prepayment Assumption	Purchase Price (% of par)		
	99	100	101
No prepayment	9.62%	9.50%	9.39%
Prepay after 10 years	9.66	9.50	9.34
Prepay after 12 years	9.65	9.50	9.36

The table clearly shows that the cash flow assumption about prepayment has a very significant impact on yield. Whenever a mortgage is purchased at a price other than par, the prepayment of other-than-normal amortization of principal will affect the yield of the investment. Fast prepayment will increase (decrease) the yield on an FRM purchased at a discount (premium) from its par value. Slow prepayment will decrease (increase) the yield on an FRM purchased at a premium (discount) from par value. This is why so much effort has gone into trying to simulate the mortgage cash flows.

The next major breakthrough in the effort to estimate mortgage cash flow involved the use of information about how FHA mortgages actually prepaid. This new level of sophistication was driven by the rapid growth in mortgage pass-through securities issued by the Government National Mortgage Association (GNMA) and Federal Home Loan Mortgage Corporation (FHLMC). These securities contained pools of mortgages, which made the assumption of a prepayment on a specified date even more unrealistic. Also driving the change was the improvement in computer power.

The Federal Housing Administration (FHA) had been collecting data on the number of mortgages that prepay or default in each year following the year of origination. After 25 years, it has filled out an entire prepayment schedule, which is updated each year as another year's experience is added. The schedule allows computer-model builders to develop models incorporating the FHA prepayment experience on mortgage loan life, or *mortality,* as it has become known.

You can assume faster or slower prepayment by taking a percentage of the FHA prepayment experience. Alternative prepayment rates were first used by mortgage analysts who realized that mortgages prepay faster in certain parts of the country than in others.

Different prepayment assumptions are also used to simulate faster or slower prepayment pools of mortgages that have coupon rates above or below the current market mortgage rate. A mortgage pool can be expected to prepay rapidly if it contains mortgages that have coupon rates above the current market rate. This induces homeowners to refinance. The opposite can be expected if market rates are above the coupon rate on the mortgage.

Two other approaches to estimating cash flows on FRM pools are the **constant prepayment rate (CPR)** and the **Public Security Association standard prepayment model (PSA).** The CPR assumes that mortgages will prepay by some predetermined fixed percentage each month based on the existing principal outstanding, after the previous month's prepayment. The PSA approach uses a more complicated assumption in which the prepayment percentage starts low (at an annualized 0.2% [e.g., 0.2/12] of the mortgage principal in month one) in the early years of the mortgage's life and increases each month (by an annualized 0.2% [e.g., .02/12] per month) until it reaches an annualized 6% (e.g., 6.00/12, or 0.5% per month in Month 30). Obviously, as with the FHA case, this approach can be sped up or slowed down by taking a percentage of the PSA prepayment assumption.

BONUS INCENTIVES AND POOR CONTROLS PROVE COSTLY

In one of its few embarassments, General Electric Corporation (GE) reported first-quarter 1994 pre-tax profit $350 million lower than expected, due to a reversal of previously booked earnings. The adjustment related to the alleged activities of the former head of the government trading activities of Kidder Peabody Group, Inc., a GE-owned investment banking subsidiary. According to reports, huge government hybrid bond positions were being rolled into forward contracts. These transactions were made to appear to produce profits of $10–$20 million per month for Kidder. They also produced multimillion-dollar bonuses for the department head.

The losses raised a number of important issues for GE. First, how did such large transactions escape the review of both internal and external auditors? Second, how did they escape being identified by the firm's risk management systems and review, or by associate traders and supervisors? Finally, it raises the issue of how much of an employee's total compensation should be in incentive bonuses, bonuses that apparently help motivate dishonest behavior.

Sources: "How Will Welch Deal with Kidder Scandal? Problems Keep Coming," *The Wall Street Journal*, May 3, 1994, pp. A1–A6; "Why Didn't Kidder Catch On?" *Business Week*, May 2, 1994, p. 121.

Legal and Ethical ISSUES

The embedded prepayment option in the standard FRM causes the relationship between the market value of the mortgage and open market mortgage rates to be asymmetric; that is, if interest rates go down, a growing number of mortgages can be expected to prepay, due to higher home sales and refinance stimulated by the declining rates. As a result, investors in mortgages and mortgage pools do not experience as much of a gain in market value as they do when the mortgages are not callable. Exhibit 15.3 shows how we might expect the market value of a pool of 10% mortgages to change in value as open market interest rates on new mortgages rise and fall.

Exhibit 15.4 shows the hypothetical cash flows for a pool of mortgages experiencing prepayment due to refinance and payoffs from normal home sales. The graph shows how the cash flows from a pool of mortgages would be expected to behave without a dramatic rise or fall in open market interest rates.

To limit the impact of early prepayment, some mortgage lenders have incorporated a prepayment penalty in their mortgage contracts. This clause requires the borrower to pay an additional charge if the loan is repaid early. The prepayment penalty is the equivalent to a call premium on a corporate bond.

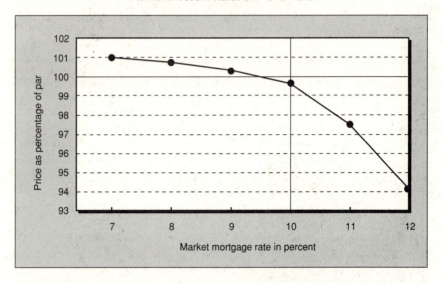

EXHIBIT 15.3

Market Value of 10% Coupon Mortgage Pool at
Market Discount Rates of 7% to 12%

Prepayment penalties are very common on mortgages made on office buildings and other commercial real estate but rare on home mortgages.

The asymmetric relationship between market value and changes in market interest rates makes the FRM a risky investment from a cash flow perspective. As a result, investors expect to be compensated for the additional risk relating to the embedded option in mortgage loans.

Even though pass-through securities of the GNMA have the full faith and credit guarantee of the U.S. government, the rates on GNMA securities typically range from 75 to 150 basis points over comparable maturity Treasury securities. The premium yield is the return for accepting the risk of early prepayment, as discussed in Chapter 2. If economic conditions stimulate prepayment, then the extra yield associated with the option premium is lost—lost because the prepayment assumption about cash flows was incorrect.

Exhibit 15.5 shows how the financial press quotes yields on a hypothetical selection of mortgage-backed securities. The table shows one item of information that has not yet been discussed. This is the **weighted-average life (WAL),** based on a specified prepayment assumption, any of those already discussed, or a proprietary estimate of a security dealer, which calculates the expected average length of time each dollar of principal is expected to be outstanding. Typically, the high-coupon securities are expected to have a very short weighted-average life due to expected fast prepayment. Conversely, the low-coupon securities have a longer expected weighted-average life, because borrowers are more likely to prepay a mortgage that has a high-coupon rate. The weighted-average life is calculated by adding the monthly expected principal cash flows and weighting them by the period in which they are expected to occur and dividing this sum by the

EXHIBIT 15.4

Cash Flows for Hypothetical Mortgage Pool
(pool principal: $1 million)

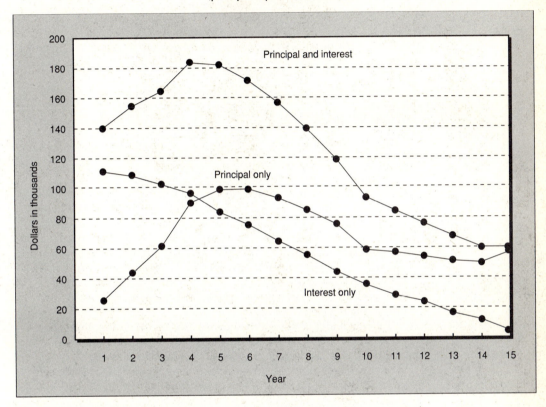

total principal: $WAL = (\Sigma_{i=1,n}$ Period $\times$ Expected principal cash flow) / Total principal outstanding. Let's consider the *WAL* calculation using annual cash flows for a mortgage pass-through security with five years remaining.

Period (in years)	Expected Principal Cash Flow	Period × Expected Principal Cash Flow
(a)	(b)	(a × b)
1	$ 14,000	$ 14,000
2	21,000	42,000
3	32,000	96,000
4	25,000	100,000
5	10,000	50,000
Total	$102,000	$302,000

WAL = $302,000 / $102,000 = 2.96 years

EXHIBIT 15.5

Reading the Financial Page
Yields on a Hypothetical Selection of Mortgage Securities
(typical listing)

Issuer	Coupon Rate	Remaining Life	Weighted-Average Life	Price	Yield	Change in Yield
GNMA						
(30-year)	8.5%	27.5	8.6	98–05	8.89%	+.12
FNMA						
(30-year)	8.5	25.8	9.8	99–12	8.61	+.11
FHLMC						
(15-year)	7.75	11.6	7.8	97–23	7.86	+.09

This table gives typical information on several mortgage-backed pass-through securities. These are securities issued by the GNMA, FNMA and the FHLMC. The original maturity shown for the mortgages in the pool is either 30 or 15 years. The coupon rate on the security is shown. The coupon rate on the actual mortgages in the pool will be above that of the security. This is because the servicer of the mortgage will obtain about 25 basis points to service and the agency will obtain 15 to 25 basis points to guarantee the mortgages. The remaining life is the number of years from now until the last payment is received on the mortgages, if prepayment does not take place.

The remainder of the information is based on the assumptions about prepayment. These assumptions usually vary between investment banking firms. The weighted-average life is calculated based on the prepayment assumptions. These assumptions are also used to calculate yield. Prices are quoted in percent of par and thirty-secondths of 100%.

INTEREST-ONLY AND PRINCIPAL-ONLY STRIPS ON MORTGAGE SECURITIES

In much the same way we altered the cash flow on a Treasury bond to create a class of zero-coupon bonds, it is possible to create **interest-only (IO)** and **principal-only (PO) strips** on mortgage securities. The IO is a security that receives all interest on all mortgages in the pool. The PO receives all of the principal. Calculating yields or market values on interest-only and principal-only strips requires a cash flow assumption used by the FHA, CPR, PSA or other prepayment approaches. From this, the cash flows are simulated, and a present-value equation is formulated to solve for market value or yield.

These mortgage hybrid securities tend to alter the prepayment risk associated with investments in standard FRMs. Consider the IO security first. For the investor in the interest-only security, a decline in open market interest rates that leads to the early repayment of principal will also reduce the amount of interest payments received over the life of the security. Thus the interest-only security is a better investment performer in a period of rising interest rates than it is in a pe-

ARMs AND INTEREST RATE MATH

Adjustable-rate mortgages (ARMs) are among the most complicated financial claims. They use a variety of indices, maximum and minimum rates, adjustment periods, and other complicating provisions. Since the mid-1980s, ARM lenders have been audited by private firms seeking to determine whether the lender has correctly computed interest and principal for the ARM programs they offered.

As it turned out, many lenders were incorrectly calculating interest charged. Problems included incorrect interest calculation, use of the wrong index, rounding errors, and payment-date discrepancies. Not all the errors hurt the borrowers, however. Clearly, many lenders have people writing computer programs that don't understand the ARM programs or don't know the math well enough.

Not to be left out, Congress in 1990 passed the Cranston-Gonzalez Affordable Housing Act which requires that when consumers complain to a lender about a potential error in their mortgage, the lender must acknowledge the letter within 20 days and address any problem within 60 days.

*L*EGAL *and* *E*THICAL ISSUES

riod of declining rates. When interest rates rise, the amount of interest payments on the IO are higher. The principal-only security behaves just the opposite. If interest rates fall, investors will receive their cash flows much earlier than expected. Since the principal-only security is purchased at a deep discount, the earlier repayment of principal will provide a higher yield on the security.

Table 15.6 shows the direction of the change in the market value of an IO and PO from changes in open market interest rates. Two factors cause these changes in market value: the first relates to the change in discount rates resulting from changes in open market rates. The second relates to changes in the cash flows of the two claims as a result of changing prepayment experience. The table shows that the impact of a rise in open market rates will decrease the value of a PO unambiguously. The higher discount rate decreases its value, as does the slowdown in cash flows. The change in the value of the IO, on the other hand, is ambiguous. The higher discount rate lowers value while the slowdown in prepayment causes the cash flows on the IO to increase. The IO could very well increase in overall value from a rise in interest rates. If so, it is the only debt security with this attribute. The opposite conditions prevail for a fall in open market interest rates. The unusual property of the IO has made it popular with investors who want to earn interest on a financial claim that has limited interest rate risk exposure.

SERVICING INCOME CONTRACTS (STRIPS)

Now that you understand the valuation of the interest-only strip, it is easy to understand a servicing income contract and its valuation. A **servicing income contract** is a contract granted to a loan servicing company for collecting payments, handling bookkeeping, and other responsibilities. The largest volume of

---
TABLE 15.6

Expected Market Value Changes of IOs and POs Due to Changes in
Open Market Interest Rates

	Type of Claim			
	IO	PO	IO	PO
Interest Rate Environment	Change in Value Due to Change in Market Interest Rate		Change in Value Due to Change in Prepayment Cash Flows	
Rising market interest rates	−	−	+	−
Declining market interest rates	+	+	−	+

servicing relates to servicing on home mortgages sold to the major government mortgage credit agencies.

The servicing organizations obtain a specified percentage fee on the outstanding balance of the loans serviced. Mortgage servicers attempt to earn at least 25 basis points (.25%) on standard FRMs, 37.5 basis points (.375%) on variable-rate mortgages, and 44 basis points (.44%) on FHA-insured or Veterans Administration (VA) guaranteed mortgages pooled into GNMA securities.

The calculation of the value of the servicing contract is handled the same way as the calculation for the interest-only strip. After all, a servicing income stream is exactly equivalent to an interest-only strip. Servicing income is a fixed percentage of the outstanding principal of the loans serviced.

In determining the value of a servicing strip, all the costs and revenues associated with servicing must be incorporated into the analysis. In the case of a home mortgage, the servicer has to cover the direct costs of servicing it. In addition to a fee, the servicer may obtain benefits such as interest income on property insurance and tax impounds, if any. The servicer may receive profits from insurance sales and other products sold to the homebuyer, and interest on the funds received and invested during the interim period prior to remitting to the investor.

Once a cash flow statement is completed and a prepayment assumption incorporated into the analysis, the discounted cash flow algorithm can be used to determine the value of the servicing contract. Like the interest-only mortgage strip, the servicing mortgage income contract will decrease significantly in value if interest rates fall. In that case, the mortgages will repay early and the servicing income stream will end early. This occurred in a significant way in the summer of 1992 when open market interest rates fell rapidly and by a large amount. The result was a nationwide refinancing of many high-rate FRMs. Consequently, the decline in interest rates wiped out the value of many financial institutions' servicing portfolios.

The same methodology can be used to establish value on all other types of servicing. Third-party servicing is done in large volume today on auto loans, credit card receivables, and commercial business loans. The valuation of servicing income contracts is very important since servicing is actively bought and sold. Mortgage banking companies are active as both buyers and sellers of mortgage servicing contracts. There is also active buying and selling among thrifts, commercial banks, and the Resolution Trust Corporation, which is charged with liquidating the assets of failed thrifts. Some of the assets it is liquidating are servicing contracts.

COLLATERALIZED MORTGAGE OBLIGATIONS AND REAL ESTATE MORTGAGE INVESTMENT CONDUITS

In 1983, a significant hybrid security was issued—the **collateralized mortgage obligation (CMO)**. The CMO reduces one of the more disagreeable aspects of home mortgages, namely cash flow uncertainty. The concept is to repackage the cash flows from a pool of mortgages or mortgage pass-through securities into several newly created hybrid securities. These newly created securities have more appeal to investors because they have more predictable cash flows. They also have expected maturities that differ significantly from the mortgage itself. The Tax Reform Act of 1986 provided for the creation of a new tax entity called the *real estate mortgage investment conduit* or **REMIC**. This conduit allows CMO-type securities to be offered through a REMIC trust and allows the issuer to develop a multiclass CMO structure off the firm's balance sheet. The added flexibility created by the REMIC legislation has caused the REMIC to largely supersede the CMO struture. However, the press and most analysts refer to CMOs and REMICs interchangably.

As discussed, a mortgage is like a series of monthly loans, each with a small amount of principal and interest due monthly in the early years and the reverse in late years. Viewed in this manner, it is easier to see how we can divide these cash flows to create a new class of securities. CMOs have three or more classes. A typical four-class CMO is discussed. The first is the short-term class called Class 1, with an expected maturity of 2 to 4 years. The second is Class 2, with an expected maturity of 4 to 8 years. Class 3 has an expected maturity of 8 to 12 years. The last class is the Z class. It is a residual class that receives cash flows only after all the other classes are paid off.

The CMO simply diverts all the cash flows on the mortgages so that the first three classes receive interest payments at a specified rate of interest and all principal repayments are used to pay off each class sequentially. Class Z then receives all remaining cash flows. This structure is easier to understand when you review Exhibit 15.6. This graph shows the principal payments on each class. Note that classes 2, 3, and Z receive no principal cash flows until the previous class is totally paid off.

The classes of the CMO, or *tranches,* as they are frequently called, make the new mortgage securities more appealing investments. The creation of these classes reduces the liquidity premium embedded into the term structure of interest rates discussed in Chapter 14. Investors looking for shorter-term and intermediate-term investments can consider the first two tranches. These are typically priced near the prevailing market interest rates on two-year and five-year Treasury notes. If the term structure of interest rates is upward sloping, the shorter and intermediate-term tranches will have a yield that is below the coupon rates on the mortgages used as collateral to create the CMO. This lower rate on the short-term tranches sold creates much of the incentive for investment dealers and others to create CMOs in the first place. The return on the CMO to the issuer also includes float income. CMOs pay interest and principal semiannually, while the issuer receives a monthly cash flow that can be invested until paid out. The interest the issuer earns on that cash is called *float income*. The excess cash flows associated with a CMO are known as the *CMO residual*. These residuals can be bought and sold just like the other CMO classes. You can create a nearly infinite variety of CMO structures. For each one, however, you will need to make a prepayment assumption—such as an FHA, CPR, or PSA prepayment assumption—to help you determine the relative size of each tranche. The investor must remember that while the CMO tranches have reduced cash flow uncertainty, they have not totally removed it. Thus, you can never know in advance the true yield on a CMO.

The financial press frequently quotes interest rates on CMOs as a spread over a specified maturity Treasury security. These CMOs have experienced yields approximately 110 to 120 basis points above the Treasury yield for a maturity closest to the weighted-average life of the CMO.

✓ Checkpoints

15-6 What is the motivates the creation of stripped Treasury securities?

15-7 How does a prepayment option embedded in a fixed-rate mortgage affect the value of the mortgage as rates rise and fall? How does this effect compare to a noncallable long-term fixed-rate bond?

15-8 What prevents accurately forecasting the principal prepayments on a pool of fixed-rate mortgages, and how can we get around this obstacle?

How

it

Really

Works

COMMERCIAL BANKS BECOME CMOS' LARGEST INVESTOR

The CMO structure allows issuers to design a bond to meet the needs of many investors. Investment bankers have worked hard to meet the needs for commercial banks for shorter-term investments that are similar in cash flow and interest-rate-sensitivity to commercial bank deposits. By 1993, some large commercial banks had upwards of 20% of their assets in CMOs, evidencing success in meeting commercial bank needs.

The trick has been to design CMO tranches that meet the strict requirements of bank regulators. In order for CMOs to qualify for lower equity requirements, they must meet several tests dealing with the CMOs' volatility of price and weighted-average life for given changes in open market interest rates. CMOs that are too volatile will not meet the regulatory tests.

The impact of these regulations has led to significant differences in the value of specific CMO tranches. A CMO that meets the regulatory test may trade at a price only .20% above a comparable Treasury. One that doesn't meet the test may trade at an expected yield 2.00% to 3.50% above the comparable maturity Treasury.

15-9 What is an interest-only and principal-only mortgage pass-through security, and which of these is most similar to a mortgage servicing contract?

15-10 How is a loan servicing contract is similar to an interest-only stripped security.

15-11 What is the objective of one who issues a collateralized mortgage obligation?

EXHIBIT 15.6

Principal Cash Flows for Collateralized Mortgage Obligation
(Typical Four-Class Series)
(15-year fixed-rate mortgages)

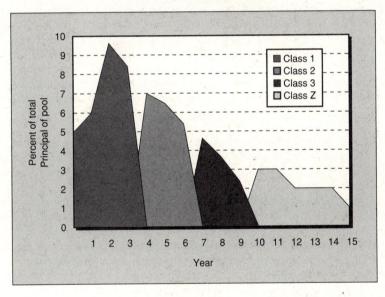

EVERYTHING BUT THE KITCHEN SINK

What do you do with classes of CMOs that are hard to sell? Answer: create a "kitchen-sinker." That's right—it's possible to take hybrid securities like various classes of CMOs and use them as collateral to create a new class of hybrids. The so-called kitchen-sinkers, named for their having everything in them but a kitchen sink, are one of the lastest hybrids.

Talk about a valution nightmare! If it's hard to value a regular CMO class security, imagine what it's like to combine a bunch of classes into a new hybrid with the combined cash flows of a group of CMO classes. Buyer beware!

How

it

Really

Works

Senior-Subordinated Securities

The creation of hybrid securities has not been limited to redistributing cash flows. Securities that redistribute the credit risk on the collateral underlying the security are also common today. An example of this is the senior-subordinated security structure.

A senior-subordinated class of securities is created by forming a pool of loans or securities. These securities or loans may be represented as mortgages or bonds. From this pool two or more new securities are issued using the loans or securities as collateral. A two-class senior-subordinated structure is comprised of senior and junior securities. The senior class is the lower-risk class. The junior, or subordinated, class has much higher risk, since this class will absorb the credit losses before the senior class is affected.

Let's consider an example starting with a pool of home mortgages totaling $50 million. Two securities are issued from this pool according to criteria provided by the credit rating services. The amount of the principal of the two securities depends on the credit quality of the collateral as evaluated by the rating services. Based on the quality of the collateral, we may assume that the rating organization will grant a AA rating to the senior class if at least 8% of the issue is made up of the subordinated class and no more than 92% is made up of the senior class.

In the case of the subordinated class, any loss of principal as a result of default and foreclosure on the mortgages in the pool will be charged against that class before the senior class is affected. In other words, the pool could experience foreclosure losses of principal of up to 8% of principal, or $4 million, before the senior class suffers any loss of principal.

The time for using the senior-subordinated structure is when the originator of the collateral believes that the credit quality of the assets is higher than perceived by potential investors. This structure allows the issuer to sell a portion of the perceived risky assets at an investment-grade rating of AA or higher, for example, and realize a higher price that is attributed to a high credit quality rating. The issuer may choose to hold or sell the subordinated portion of the transaction. In any case, for there to be a profit on the transaction, the weighted cost of the senior and subordinated securities must be less than the coupon yield on the collateral. That spread must also cover the cost of issuance, servicing, and administration.

DEMONSTRATION PROBLEM

DETERMINING COST OF A SENIOR-SUBORDINATED FINANCING

Situation

Western Beach Bank is contemplating becoming the issuer of a senior-subordinated security using home mortgages yielding 9.875%. The firm is able to issue a AA-rated security at a yield of 9.125%, which represents 92% of the pool. It must retain at least 25 basis points of the interest return on the mortgages to cover the cost of servicing the mortgages. It also learns of a potential buyer of the subordinated class that expects a yield of 10.50% on the remaining 8% of the pool. The cost of issuance and administration is 7 basis points per annum. Marlyn Parks has been asked to determine the weighted-average cost of this financing.

Result

Marlyn has developed the following table, which shows the weighted cost of this senior-subordinated structure to the issuer. The weighted cost for each factor is derived from multiplying the weight percent (Column 2) by the interest rate and costs expressed as interest rates (Column 3).

In the table, the total interest cost of financing with this structure is 9.555%, or 32 basis points (.32%) below the 9.875% coupon yield on the mortgages. This will likely make this a very profitable transaction. Senior-subordinated securities have become very popular for intermediaries that want to decrease the volume of assets on their balance sheets. This financing structure allows the firm to sell a large percentage of the pool and remove it from the balance sheet. As discussed earlier, the prepayment options embedded in a fixed-rate mortgage make its cash flows uncertain.

Example of Senior-Subordinated Structure for $50 Million in Home Mortgages
(dollars in millions)

Security and Cost Factors	Amount (1)	Weight Percent (2)	Interest Rate and Cost Expressed as an Interest Rate (3)	Weighted Cost (%) (2 × 3)
Senior class	$ 46	92%	9.125%	8.395%
Subordinated class	4	8	10.50	.84
Servicing cost	50	100	.25	.25
Administration and issuance	50	100	.07	.07
Total weighted cost				9.555%

✓ Checkpoint

15-12 How would you use a senior-subordinated security designed to alter the credit-risk characteristics of a pool of risky assets?

SUMMARY AND REVIEW

1. Explain and know how to use the basic valuation equations for determining present value, future value, compounding, yield to maturity, and equivalent annual yield.

   The following is a basic valuation equation for determining the **present value** on a cash flow or series of cash flows discounted at an interest rate of *r*:

$$PV = \Sigma^t_{n=1} CF_n / (1 + r)^n$$

This same equation is also used to determine the **future value** of a cash flow earning an interest rate of r.

$$FV = PV \, (1 + r)^n$$

Compounding is incorporated into this structure by calculating a periodic rate r/m where m is the number of **compounding** periods within a year. We then have the following PV equation:

$$FV = PV \, (1 + r/m)^{mn}$$

2. **Explain and know how to calculate the values of discounted bonds such as T-bills and zero-coupon bonds, perpetuities, and interest paying bonds with and without call provisions.**

   Discounted securities such as Treasury bills and zero-coupon bonds are valued using the simple PV formula. **Zero-coupon bonds** assume semiannual compounding so that their yield on a discounted security that pays no interest can be compared to bonds that pay interest. A perpetual interest or dividend-paying financial claim, such as perpetual preferred stock or British consol, can be valued by using the following expression:

   $$PV = CF \, / \, r$$

   The value of a $1,000 par value bond is determined by using the present value equation with a semiannual compounding assumption. If the bond has a call provision, then we modify the equation by replacing the par value of $1,000 with the call price and replacing the number of periods, tm, with the number of periods to the call.

   $$PV = \{\Sigma_{n=1}^{tm} \, CF_n \, [1 + (r/m)]^n\} + \$1,000 \, [1 + (r/2)]^{tm} \quad m = 2.$$

3. **Describe a coupon-stripped Treasury security and explain how it is valued.**

   The cash flows on any debt instrument can be stripped into as many securities as there are cash flows in the original security. A **coupon-stripped Treasury security** is a group of newly formed securities created by stripping a Treasury bond into each of its interest payments and its principal payment. The valuation of the various stripped Treasury securities is determined by using the equation for a zero-interest bond and the relevant discount rate. The discount rate will likely be different for each portion of the stripped Treasury since each strip has a different maturity.

4. **Explain why fixed-rate mortgages are so difficult to value and describe some of the approaches used to value them.**

   Fixed-rate mortgages are some of the most difficult debt securities to value, because they have an **embedded call option**. Normally, an FRM would be valued as an ordinary annuity with equal monthly payments. Unfortunately, the assumption that a mortgage will remain outstanding for its full term is a poor assumption to make. As a result, it is necessary to make alternative assumptions about cash flows on mortgages resulting from early prepayment. Some of the alternative assumptions discussed include **FHA mortality experience, Public Security Association** standard prepayment model (**PSA**), and the **constant prepayment model (CPR)**. Each of these approaches is designed to accurately simulate the cash flows on a pool of homogeneous mortgages.

5. **Describe the process of stripping fixed-rate mortgage securities into interest-only and principal-only securities and explain the difficulty in valuing them.**

   Mortgage securities can also be stripped like Treasury securities. **Interest-only** and **principal-only** securities have been developed by stripping the interest payments (IO) on a mortgage security from the principal payments (PO) and creating two new securities. Because of the prepayment option embedded in mortgages, the IOs and POs are very difficult to value. They require developing sophisticated cash flow models using the FHA, PSA, or CPR mortgage prepayment model structure or some alternative proprietary structure.

6. **Explain the theory behind the creation of collateralized mortgage obligations (CMOs) and describe how they are formed.**

   Modifying the timing of cash flows is also the theory behind the **collateralized mortgage obligation (CMO)** and the real estate mortgage investment conduit (REMIC). Here the technique is to divert the cash flows into sequential **classes** or **tranches** of securities. The shorter-term tranches receive principal cash flows while the longer-term tranches receive only interest, until the short-term tranches are paid off.

7. **Explain the theory behind the creation of senior-subordinated securities and describe how and why they are formed.**

   Just as we can dissect a security's cash flows, we can also modify its credit risk. One method is the **senior-subordinated security**. A pool of homogenous loans or securities is used to create two or more new securities. The senior securities that have been created have lower credit risk because they do not suffer a loss unless the junior or subordinated security is wiped out due to credit losses. The purpose for creating the senior-subordinated security is to be able to sell the senior portion at an interest rate less than the market yield on the underlying collateral, thus permitting the firm to get the assets off the balance sheet. It also earns an interest spread, which is computed to be the difference between the yield on the collateral and the yield on the securities sold, adjusted for the cost of issuance.

FUTURE VALUE AND COMPOUNDING	SELF-TEST PROBLEMS

ST-15-1

You have been offered the following two accounts from two competitors. Account 1 is a one-year certificate with a base rate of 7% compounded semiannually. Account 2 is a one-year certificate paying 6.9% compounded daily using a 365-day year.

Assuming you plan to hold the account to maturity, which would you select? Answer on page 447.

COMPOUNDING OF INTEREST

ST-15-2

Boston Mutual Savings Bank invests primarily in mortgages. It finances them with deposits. The weighted yield to maturity on its $150 million mortgage portfolio is 9.20% using monthly compounding. The weighted yield to maturity on its deposits is 6.90% using 360-day compounding. The firm earns interest monthly on the mortgages but pays interest daily on its deposits. It uses a 360-day year to compute interest on deposits.

Determine the net dollar interest margin for the 31-day month of January 1995 and the 28-day month of February 1995. Assume that there are no changes in interest rates or assets and liabilities.

Answer on page 448.

FUTURE VALUE AND COMPOUNDING

ST-15-3

A canvass of several commercial banks revealed the following account options for a $10,000 deposit. A two-year account could be secured at 1st Bank at a rate of 6.75% yield to maturity compounded quarterly. Barley Bank offered a two year 6.70% yield to maturity account compounded daily using a 360-day periodic rate factor for 365 days.

Which account would you take assuming they would be held to maturity? Answer on page 448.

MORTGAGE YIELD AND VALUATION

ST-15-4

Barton Investment Co. purchased a first mortgage on an apartment building on February 15, 1997. At the time, mortgages of comparable risk were yielding 11.0%. The mortgage Barton purchased, however, had a coupon of 12.00% and a yield to maturity of 11.5%. Barton paid a price of $10,222,750. The monthly payment on the mortgage is $110,108.61 per month. Unlike the other mortgages available on the market, however, the one Barton purchased had no prepayment penalty.

After nine months, Barton received a notice from the borrower that the loan would be paid off at the end of three months. At that time, the unamortized balance will be $9,885,623.74.

What was Barton's yield for the one year it held the mortgage? Answer on page 448.

YIELD ON A NON-CALLABLE BOND AND PREFERRED STOCK

ST-15-5

Steve Smith has been asked to value two securities using two different market discount rates. Security 1 is a 20-year noncallable bond paying an 8% annual interest rate with semiannual payments. Security 2 is a perpetual preferred stock paying an 8.25% annual dividend which is also paid semiannually.

Steve has been asked to value these at discount rates of 9% and 10%. Since you work for Steve, he asked you to solve the problems.

Answer on page 449.

TREASURY STRIP

ST-15-6

A three-year Treasury bond is being considered as collateral for a Treasury strip. The security is selling for a price of 99% of par and has a coupon rate of 9%. The strip will occur on the date of the next interest payment, January 1, 1996. The market yields on comparable zero-coupon Treasuries are shown below:

Market Yield on Treasury Zeros

Maturity	Annual Yield
6 months	6.10%
1 year	7.10
1.5 years	7.20
2 years	7.70
2.5 years	7.90
3 years	7.95

The cost of creating the strip is $14,000 per million. Would you advise going ahead and creating the strip if you could sell the strips securities at the yields shown above?

Answer on page 449.

SENIOR-SUBORDINATE STRUCTURE

ST-15-7

You work for an investment banker and are considering the formation of a senior-subordinate structure from a pool of $185 million in home mortgages. The pool is yielding an average 10.125%. From past experience, you know that total administrative costs on such an issue are about 33 basis points per annum on the outstanding principal.

a. If you put 92% of the pool into the senior class and the remaining 8% into the subordinate class, and the subordinate class can be sold at a premium of 275 basis points above the base yield of the pool, what is the maximum yield you can sell the senior class for and still break even?

b. A bond rating service tells you that your senior security can be up to 94% of the pool and still earn a AA rating. Similar securities are currently yielding 9.80%. However, the smaller subordinate class will command a 300 basis point premium. Should you proceed with the securitization?
Answer on page 450.

PROBLEMS | **COMPOUNDING AND FUTURE VALUE**

15-1

Which of the following would you rather have: (1) a savings account that pays 6.1% interest compounded semiannually or (2) a savings account that pays 6% compounded daily on a 365-day basis? Assume you invest $20,000 for one year.

YIELD TO MATURITY

15-2

Broader Bank offers a certificate of deposit that pays a 10% yield to maturity compounded quarterly. The managers of First Bank want to set a yield to maturity on their comparable maturity account that produces the same future value. First Bank compounds interest monthly. What yield to maturity should First Bank select?

BOND VALUATION

15-3

The Tyler Company has a bond outstanding that pays interest at the rate of 11% or $55 per semiannual period for each $1,000 of par value. The bond matures in exactly ten years. What is the market value of this bond if market interest rates for similar risky bonds are (1) 8%, (2) 11%, and (3) 12%?

EFFECTIVE ANNUAL YIELD

15-4

Libor Bank pays 9% yield to maturity, compounded quarterly, on its certificates of deposit. The manager of Marion Bank wants to offer a certificate that provides the same effective annual rate as Libor Bank. However, Marion's certificate will be compounded monthly. What yield to maturity must the bank offer?

YIELD TO THE CALL

15-5

It has been exactly two years since Majestic Corporation issued a 30-year bond. The bond pays a semiannual coupon at a 12% annual interest rate.

When it was issued, it had a five-year call provision that provided for a call at 110% of par any time after five years from the date of issue. Determine the present yield to maturity and yield to call, assuming the bond is selling at 112% of par.

FUTURE VALUE AND TAXATION

15-6

You have $1,000 to invest. Your marginal tax rate is 40%. Your savings options include:

1.   A savings account paying 8.5 % compounded semiannually.
2.   A savings account paying 8.35% compounded monthly.
3.   A tax exempt bond paying 5.1% paying interest quarterly.

What will your $1,000 be worth after one year for each alternative, with consideration to taxes?

PERPETUAL PREFERRED YIELD

15-7

A perpetual preferred stock is paying 7.75% in dividends semiannually. What is the value of this stock if market yields on comparable preferreds are 8%?

REPO RATE

15-8

Mainland Investment has agreed to a repurchase agreement with a local commercial bank. Mainland will sell to the bank $10 million par value of Treasury bonds at a price of $9,995,980. Mainland has agreed to buy them back at par in two days. What is the repo rate based on a 360-day year for this transaction?

EFFECTIVE ANNUAL YIELD AND BANK DISCOUNT YIELD

15-9

A security dealer bids on a new issue Treasury bill at auction. The bid price was 98.7% for the 182-day bills. What was the bank discount yield and the effect annually yield (assume semianual compounding) on this transaction? Use a 364-day year.

REPO RATE

15-10

An investment banker has agreed to sell to Pacific Bank $10 million par value of government securities at $9,995,899. The investment banker will repurchase the securities at par in three days. What is the repo rate (RR) and effective yield? Assume daily compounding.

TREASURY STRIP

15-11

A four-year Treasury bond is being considered as collateral for a coupon strip. It has a coupon of 9% with semiannual interest payments. The security is selling at par. The following table shows the market yield on comparable zero-coupon Treasury securities.

Current Yields on Zero-coupon Treasuries

Maturity (years)	Yield(%)
0.5	6.80
1.0	7.20
1.5	7.30
2.0	7.80
2.5	7.90
3.0	8.00
3.5	8.20
4.0	8.50

The cost of creating the strip is $13,000 per million. Would you advise going ahead and creating the strip if you could sell it at the yields shown in the previous table?

TREASURY STRIP

15-12

Fitzgerald Investment Bank, Inc., would like to create and distribute to its customers a Treasury strip on a two-year remaining maturity bond. The date of the transaction will be the next interest payment date of July 1, 1996. The coupon rate on the bond is 8.50%. The following table shows the yields on the strips to be sold.

Market Yields on Zero Coupons to Be Sold

Maturity	Annual Yield
Jan. 1, 1997	6.25%
July 1, 1997	7.25
Jan. 1, 1998	8.30
July 1, 1998	8.40

The cost of creating the strip is $20,000 per million of Treasury principal. What is the maximum price Fitzgerald can pay for the Treasury bonds to break even on the transaction?

SENIOR-SUBORDINATED SECURITIES

15-13

Lumbard Bank has a pool of $100 million in credit card receivables, yielding an average of 17.5%. It forms a senior security class for 90% of the value of the pool and a subordinate class for the remaining 10%. Consider the following problems:

1. The senior security can be sold to yield 15.75% and the subordinated class can be sold to yield 25%. If the total administrative costs for the issuance are 37.5 basis points per annum, what net yield spread will the bank realize from the securitization?

2. How would you as the bank's portfolio manager justify such a securitization to your board of directors?

SENIOR-SUBORDINATED SECURITIES

15-14

A pool of second mortgages yields 9%. For an administrative cost of 31.5 basis points per annum on the outstanding principal, a senior-subordinated structure can be formed with the senior class yielding 8.50% and the subordinated class yielding 10.35%. What is the maximum size the senior class can be as a percentage of the total pool without losing money on the securitization?

SOLUTIONS	SELF-TEST PROBLEMS

ST-15-1

Solution:
The objective is to calculate the future value, *FV*, of a specific amount of funds, *PV*, placed in each account for one year, giving consideration to the compounding approach used for each.

$$FV = PV\ (1 + r/m)^m$$

Account 1:

$$FV = \$1.00\ (1 + .07/2)^2 = \$1.071225 \text{ @ } 7.00\% \text{ compounded semiannually.}$$

Account 2:

$$FV = \$1.00\ (1 + .0690/365)^{365} = \$1.071429 \text{ @ } 6.90\% \text{ compounded} \\ \textit{daily for 365 days.}$$

The account yielding the highest present value is the one paying 6.90% compounded daily for 365 days.

ST-15-2

Solution:
The solution to this problem is simply to compute the interest income on the mortgages and interest expense on the deposits. The deposit interest cost will be more in the 31-day month than in the 28-day month.

$$Interest\ on\ mortgages = \$150,000,000 \times (.0920/12)$$

$$= \$1,150,000$$

Interest on deposits

$$31\text{-}day\ month = \$150,000,000 \times [(1.0 + .0690/360)^{31} - 1]$$

$$= \$893,815.53$$

$$28\text{-}day\ month = \$150,000,000 \times [(1.0 + .0690/360)^{28} - 1]$$

$$= \$807,085.01$$

Interest costs drop by $86,730.52 and the net interest margin rises from $256,184.47 in January to $342,914.99 in February.

ST-15-3

Solution:
The objective is to calculate the future value, FV, of depositing a fixed sum, PV, in each account for two years using the compounding method for each.

$$FV = \$10,000\ (1 + .0675/4)^8 = \$11,432.48$$

$$FV = \$10,000\ (1 + .0670/360)^{365 \times 2} = \$11,455.08$$

The account with 365/360 offers the higher return.

ST-15-4

Solution:
The objective is to calculate the yield for a present value equation made up of a cash outflow at time $t = 0$ of $-\$10,222,750$, followed by 12 cash inflows for periods $t = 1,12$ of the monthly payment, PMT, of $110,108.61, and a final payment at $t = 12$ of $9,885,623.74.

This can be done with a HP 12C calculator. The input includes:

g END f FIN
12: *n*
10,222,750: *PV*
$9,885,623.74: *FV*
110,108.61: *PMT*
Answer: .8144 = *i*
Annual rate: *i* × 12 = 9.7724 %

ST-15-5

Solution:
The objective is to determine the present value of the two securities using discount rates of 9% and 10%.

The noncallable bond must be done using a calculator such as the HP 12C. The input for this calculation include:

Assume current date: Jan. 1, 1990
9.00 and 10.00: *i*
8.00: *PMT*
g M.DY
1.011990 ENTER
1.012010
fPRICE

Solution:
@ 9.00% discount: 90.799201 % of par
@ 10.00% discount: 82.8409 % of par
The solution for the perpetuity uses only the equation

$$PV = PMT/r$$

$$PMT = \$82.50/2 = \$41.25 \ paid \ semiannually$$

$$r = 9.00\%/2 = .0450 \ and \ 10.00\%/2 = .05$$

Solution:
@ 9.00% *PV* = $41.25/ .0450 = 91.67 % of par
@ 10.00% *PV* = $41.25/ .05 = 82.50% of par

ST-15-6

Solution:
The objective is to determine the cash flows from the Treasury security and discount them at the yields shown in the table to determine the price that the firm will receive on the zero-coupon strips. This will be compared to the purchase price of the security less the cost of creating the strip. We use a $1,000 par value security in the example. The value of the strips is shown below:

Date of Cash Flow	Amount	Annual Yield	n	Periodic Rate	PV Factor	Present Value
July 1, 1996	$45	6.10%	1	.0305	1.0305	$ 43.67
Jan. 1, 1997	45	7.10	2	.0355	1.0723	41.96
July 1, 1997	45	7.20	3	.0360	1.1119	40.47
Jan. 1, 1998	45	7.70	4	.0385	1.1631	38.69
July 1, 1998	45	7.90	5	.0395	1.2137	37.08
Jan. 1, 1999	1,000 + 45	7.95	6	.0398	1.2639	826.81
Total						$1,028.68

One million will sell for $1,028,680. The cost of the bonds is $990,000, and the cost of completing the transaction is $14,000, for a total cost of $1,004,000. The firm should go ahead since it will experience a profit per million dollars of bonds of

$$($1,028,680 - $1,004,000) = $24,680.$$

ST-15-7

Solution to a:

$$\text{Yield on subordinate class} = 10.125\% + 2.75\% = 12.875\%$$

$$\text{Weighted cost of subordinate class} = 12.875\% \times 0.08 = 1.030\%$$

Now solve for weighted cost of senior class:

Pool yield	10.125%
Less weighted cost of subordinate	1.030%
Less administrative costs	0.330%
Weighted cost of senior class	8.765%

Now solve for yield of senior class:

Yield = 8.765 / 0.92 =	9.5272%

Solution to b:

$$\text{Yield on subordinate class} = 10.125\% + 3.00\% = 13.125\%$$

$$\text{Senior } 9.8\% \times 0.94 = 9.212\% \text{ weighted cost}$$

$$\text{Subordinate } 13.125\% \times 0.06 = 0.788\% \text{ weighted cost}$$

$$\text{Administrative costs} = 0.330\%$$

$$\text{Total costs } 10.330\%$$

Since total costs are more than 10.125% yield on the pool, you should not proceed with the securitization.

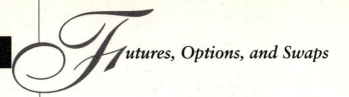

CHAPTER 16

Futures, Options, and Swaps

Learning Goals

After studying this chapter, you should be able to:

1. Describe a futures contract and the types of futures positions.
2. Discuss the factors that influence the value of a futures contract.
3. Discuss the role of margin in the futures market and how to calculate changes in required margin.
4. Describe options and the types of options.
5. Discuss the factors that impact the value of options and the direction of those impacts, and explain the Black-Scholes model and how it is used to value options.
6. Describe interest rate and currency swaps and explain how they are used.

If you keep on top of the financial news, then you know how acclaimed—or criticized—the often-used class of financial assets known as *derivative sercurities* have been over the last few years. These financial contracts derive their value from the value of underlying financial assets such as the value of a stock option being dependent on the value of the stock on which it is written. This chapter covers three of the most important of these contracts: futures, options, and swaps. The financial manager within an intermediary must be able to originate, service, and manage these claims so as to control the inherent price risks of all business transactions. Such management skills are especially valuable not just to financial institutions trading financial assets as their primary business, but also to commercial and industrial firms engaging in long-term financing and foreign exchange.

Functions of Futures, Options, and Swap Contracts

Financial assets are created to provide for risk sharing and to reduce the cost of transactions. Futures, options, and swaps are created for these same reasons. The primary role of these contracts is to provide an efficient method of sharing risks. Economic units facing price risks are among those that can be reduced using futures, options, and swap contracts. The process of reducing these risks is known as *hedging.* Other economic participants, known as *speculators,* profit from buying or selling assets expected to rise or drop in price.

Market participants use these contracts to shift price risks from a hedger to a speculator or to another hedger. Futures and options contracts also provide a more efficient method to speculate on changes in prices of financial assets. These contracts allow an investor to benefit from a favorable change in the price of an underlying financial asset without having to put up all the capital necessary to own it.

Although financial futures contracts were initially designed to hedge the price risk of agricultural commodities, futures and options contracts in financial assets represent the greatest use of the organized futures and options markets. The primary use of these contracts is to hedge the price risk associated with future purchases or sales of financial assets. Some of the most common uses of futures, options, and swap contracts include:

- Hedging the cost of future financing.
- Protect the price of a financial asset to be sold in the future.
- Reducing income volatility created by interest rate changes.
- Hedging a commitment to lend money in the future.
- Hedging the risk of changes in foreign exchange rates.

✓ Checkpoints

16-1   What is a derivative financial asset, and what are some examples?

16-2   Why would you use derivatives?

Financial Futures Contracts

The futures market in financial assets began relatively recently. In 1975, the Chicago Board of Trade (CBOT) developed a futures contract in Government National Mortgage Association pass-through securities. Several weeks later, the International Monetary Market (IMM) developed the Treasury bill contract, and two years later CBOT developed the Treasury bond contract. Table 16.1 shows the most active contracts and the exchange where each trades.

TABLE 16.1

Most Active Financial Futures Contracts
and the Exchanges Where They Trade: January 1993

Contract	Exchange
Treasury bill	IMM
Treasury note	CBOT
Treasury bond	CBOT
Five-year Treasury notes	CBOT
Libor one month	IMM

WHAT IS A FINANCIAL FUTURES CONTRACT?

A **financial futures contract** is a legal agreement between the buyer or seller and an organized exchange or its clearing house. The exchange or clearing house will insure delivery (to the buyer) or accept delivery (from a seller) of an agreed-upon quantity and quality of the asset at a specified time and place. Since futures contracts are derivative assets, delivery of the underlying asset is not expected to take place, although it is possible.[1] Rather, the buyer or seller of the contract is simply accepting the price risk inherent in the specific asset upon which the futures contract is written.

U.S. bond futures contracts are the most actively traded. Table 16.1 shows the trading information on the Treasury bond futures contract as it could be found in the financial press.

VALUATION OF FINANCIAL FUTURES CONTRACTS

Financial futures contract prices are directly related to the prices of the cash market financial asset on which they are written. The reason for this relationship is that future contracts typically allow the cash-market financial claim on which it is written to be delivered by the seller of the contract. Consequently, the contract acts as a proxy for the cash-market financial claim. This in turn accounts for the fact that the price of the futures contract will track in a predictable way the price of the cash-market financial claim on which it is written. This relationship is so important that if it were not strong, there would be an opportunity to earn a profit from buying or selling in the cash market and offsetting the position in the futures market and earning a riskless profit. Market forces work to eliminate this source of riskless profit, called *arbitrage.* Pure arbitrage involves holding a portfolio of financial assets that cost nothing to hold and produce a riskless profit. Consequently, arbitrage works to insure a predictable relationship between the cash and futures prices.

---

[1]Approximately 1%–5% percent of futures contracts experience actual delivery. There are also a few contracts such as stock index futures that are settled in cash, not the stocks in the S&P indices. Cash settlement is desirable when the costs of delivery are large, such as in the case of the S&P 500 stocks.

EXHIBIT 16.1

Reading the Financial Page
Treasury Bond Futures Contract
(typical listing)

Treasury bonds $100,000; 32nds of 100%
Chicago Board of Trade

Expiration	Open	High	Low	Settle	Change	Yield	Change	Open Interest
June	98–04	99–00	98–01	98–05	+7	8.12	–.07	175,000
Sept.	97–18	97–30	97–16	97–19	+6	8.23	–.06	45,000
Dec.	96–12	96–29	96–10	96–14	+7	8.30	–.06	32,000

Estimated volume: 300,000
Yesterday's volume: 250,000
Open interest: 320,000

The asset in this futures contract is a Treasury bond of $100,000 in principal value. The prices are quoted the same as the bond itself, in thirty-seconds of 100%. Thus the quote of 98–05 as the settle price for the June contract means that the contract price of the $100,000 in principal bonds is 98 5/32 or 98.15625 x $100,000 = $98,156.25. Each 1/32 is worth $31.25.

The columns include the month in which the various contracts expire, prices for the open trade, high for the day, low for the day, and the closing trade or settle price. Also shown is the price change from the settle price of the previous trading day. The bonds' yields to maturity are also shown computed from the settle price and the change in yield from the previous trading day. The open interest is the number of contracts outstanding for each month. The current trading volume is estimated and also given for the previous day. The open interest at the bottom represents all outstanding contracts in all expiration months. The Treasury bond contract requires initial margin of $2,500 per contract and maintenance margin of $2,000.

In the case of futures contracts, the relationship of the futures contract price and the spot cash price of the financial asset is known as the *cost of carry model,* shown in Equation 16.1.

$$\text{Futures contract price = Spot cash market price +}$$
$$\text{Cost of carry of the cash asset – Return on holding cash asset}\quad[16.1]$$

The relationship is easy to understand if you consider the following demonstration problem concerning a Treasury bond.

RELATING FUTURES AND CASH PRICES	DEMONSTRATION PROBLEM

Situation

Consider a T-bond yielding 10% that can be financed with debt borrowed at the six-month interest rate of 6%. There is a futures contract for this bond expiring in six months. What is the relationship between the cash and futures price of the T-bond?

Result

Because the bond can be financed at a profit over the short holding period of the futures contract, it will be worth more in the cash market than the futures market. Consequently, the futures price will be less than the spot market price by the amount of the difference between the cost of carry and the interest return on holding the bond—in this case at an annualized 4% (10% – 6%). If the difference between the futures price and the spot price were less than this difference, it would pay to buy the bond in the cash market, finance it with six-month debt, and sell a futures contract to deliver the bond six months in the future. This low-risk transaction would be replicated until the cash-market price of the bond was bid up and the futures price bid down, closing the gap once again to 4% annualized.

The difference between the spot, or cash, price less the futures price is known as *basis*.[2] As a futures contract approaches expiration, the basis will converge to zero. The process that results in a zero basis is called *convergence*. If the basis did not converge to zero, a profitable arbitrage could occur. If the spot price were above the future price on the deliverable asset at the deliverable location of the contract's expiration date, the holder of a long futures contract would demand delivery and sell it profitably in the cash market. If this opportunity existed, it would cause investors to buy futures contracts, demand delivery, and sell the deliverable in the cash market—a process that effectively eliminates the arbitrage profit by increasing futures prices and lowering cash prices. Convergence occurs because at the expiration of a futures contract, the cost of carry and return on holding the financial asset approaches zero in Equation 16.1. Spot and futures prices converge at expiration, as shown in Exhibit 16.1. It shows an example of *positive* and *negative* basis and convergence.

HEDGING WITH FUTURES

The theory behind the development of financial futures relates to an activity called *hedging*. Hedging is a process whereby the buyer or seller of a specified financial asset wishes to reduce the price risk inherent in holding a cash-market po-

---

[2]Occasionally *basis* is defined as the futures price minus the cash price. As a result, references to basis should be checked to determine the definition being used.

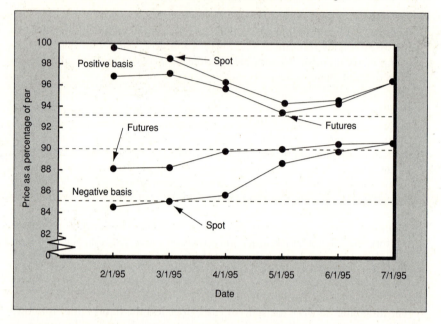

EXHIBIT 16.2

Convergence of Spot and Futures Prices (Positive and Negative Basis)

sition. Agricultural commodity futures are probably the best examples. In futures terms, a wheat farmer is said to be *long* wheat. Anyone who owns the commodity or a financial asset or has committed to buy it is considered long. The grain mill will purchase the wheat from the farmer after harvest and sell flour to a baker. Since the grain mill has already contracted with the baker to supply a specified quantity of flour at a specified price and time, the grain mill is said to be *short.*

In this classic example, both the farmer and the mill are at great risk. The farmer is uncertain whether the price of wheat at harvest time will cover the cost of seed, fertilizer, fuel, and capital costs. The mill operator, on the other hand, is uncertain about the cost of buying wheat in the future in order to profitably honor the contract with the baker. Both the farmer and the mill have accepted price risk.

If the farmer knows the mill operator, he could reduce his price risk by contracting before harvest to have the farmer supply a certain quantity of wheat of a particular quality at an agreed-upon price. This transaction would be known as a *forward cash-market transaction.*

The farmer might not know the mill operator, however; or he may be unsure that, if prices go down, the mill operator will honor the contract, forcing a legal dispute. The farmer's next option might be to sell (go short) a futures contract in wheat for delivery around harvest time. Similarly, the mill operator could buy (go long) a futures contract to take delivery of wheat around harvest time. In the futures market, the clearing house of the exchange assumes the credit risk of both the buyer and seller. Both futures contracts would be bought back, or covered, at the time of the cash-market transaction. If wheat prices fall, the farmer would experience a loss on the wheat harvested but a gain on the short futures contract. The mill operator would experience a favorable decline in the price of wheat, offsetting the loss on the futures contract. From this example, it is clear that a futures hedge can reduce the impact of price fluctuations. However, the hedger must give up a possible gain from a favorable change in prices in order to eliminate the loss from an unfavorable change.

HEDGING WITH A FINANCIAL FUTURES CONTRACT　　　**DEMONSTRATION PROBLEM**

Situation

You are a financial professional of a firm that will be selling $50 million in long-term corporate bonds in March, six months from now. You are concerned that interest rates will rise. If they do, the price you obtain for the bonds will be lower.

　One way to hedge this situation is to sell a futures contract in T-bonds. If interest rates rise, the firm will get less for the bonds it sells but will be able to repurchase its futures position at an offsetting lower price.*

Data Input
Spot price of 8% coupon corporate bonds　　　　　　100 0/32
March price of T-bond futures contracts　　　　　　101 0/32

Establishing Hedge Transaction
Sell $50,000,000 in T-bond futures at 101 0/32

Data Input
Market rates rise from 8% to 8.5% in six months.
Price received on 8% coupon corporate bonds:　　　95 8/32
Market price of T-bond contract:　　　　　　　　96 16/32

Result

Loss from cash sale of bonds: ($50,000,000 × 100%) –
($50,000,000 × 95.25%)

= $–2,375,000

Gain on futures position: ($50,000,000 × 101%) – ($50,000,000 × 96.50%)

= $2,250,000

*This example ignores transaction costs, which are a significant factor when undertaking some hedging programs.

Gain or (loss) after consideration of hedge:

$$\$2,250,000 - \$2,375,000 = -\$125,000$$

This hedge served to reduce the loss for the corporation. It was not a perfect hedge since the gain on the futures position did not perfectly offset the loss.

In hedging price risk for large portfolios of price sensitive assets, hedging can be performed in two ways. One method, a **micro-hedge,** involves assigning an off-setting futures position against each asset with unwanted price risk. A **macro-hedge,** on the other hand, aggregates the price risk of a portfolio of assets that possess unwanted price risk. This portfolio is then hedged in aggregate with one type of offsetting futures position.[3]

MECHANICS OF THE FUTURES MARKET

Some of the mechanics of using the futures market can be complicated. One of these aspects is margin.

MARGIN

Margin requirements relate to the amount of cash or Treasury securities that the hedging firm must hold with the member brokerage firm in relation to the equity value of the futures contracts outstanding. The opening of a contract requires the firm to put up an amount called *initial margin.*

After this, the amount of margin to be held with the futures brokerage dealer is determined by the value of the futures contract and the positive or negative equity which is computed as the difference between the value of the price of the futures contract at the time it was executed and the current price of buying it back in the market. The process of establishing this value is called *mark-to-market.* This means that everyday profits or losses are added to or deducted from the equity held in the futures trader's margin account. Any profits earned can be withdrawn daily by the trader and spent or invested. Losses are taken from the equity in the margin account. If losses are large, they may cause the equity position in the account to fall below a minimum required level of the exchange (**maintanence margin**) on which the futures contract in traded. At this point the trader gets a margin call. The trader can then add additional margin to bring the equity balance to the original initial margin level or the broker will close out the futures position. Required increases to the margin account, called *variation margin,* bring the margin account back up to its established initial margin requirement.

---

[3]One problem with macro-hedges is that accounting firms require the hedged assets to be identified in order to determine whether the hedge is effective. If the hedge is not effective—that is, does not offset a high percentage of the price change of the cash position—then gains and losses on the hedge must be taken immediately.

OPTIONS AND FUTURES MARKETS: ILLEGAL TRADING

In 1984 and again in 1989, the Chicago Board of Trade was shaken by allegations of illegal futures trading. The largest and most publicized allegations occurred in 1989 when over 40 members of the CBOT were indicted for illegal trading. These indictments were the culmination of approximately two years of investigations into trading practices by the FBI.

The alleged violations are very technical in nature. This is because the CBOT runs under a trading system called the **open outcry system.** Under this system, transactions are executed using hand and voice signals. As a result, there are poor records of transactions that take place and an even poorer audit trail for anyone seeking to substantiate specific trades.

Because of this system, the potential for abuse is high. The allegations included claims that traders executed orders off the exchange at prearranged prices with other traders. It was also alleged that traders were trading ahead of customer's orders and profited from this knowledge in their personal trades. Some brokers were also accused of arranging to have other brokers take the other side of a customer's order to deny profits to other traders.

One result of the allegations was technological reform at the CBOT. At a cost of several million dollars, the CBOT installed a system to keep track of trade orders. However, the system does not automatically match orders and thus does not eliminate the probability that many of the alleged violations will occur again. The CBOT experience called attention to the mechanics of how markets actually work. It also created more pressure to develop computerized trading systems with better audit procedures that lessen the chance of manipulation.

Legal and Ethical ISSUES

For example, the initial margin on the T-bond contract shown in Exhibit 16.2 is $2,500 and the maintenance margin is $2,000. This means that if the holder of the contract suffers a loss of more than $500, he or she must add additional margin to bring it back to the initial level of $2,500. A loss of less than $500 is acceptable.

COMPUTING MARGIN REQUIREMENTS

DEMONSTRATION PROBLEM

Situation

Morrison Manufacturing Co. took a futures position in Japanese yen. The company sold $4,000,000 in machines to a Japanese firm and will be paid in yen in three months at the current price of yen of $.008/yen. The firm is said to be long yen. The firm's financial officer is concerned that the value of the yen will fall relative to the dollar. Consequently, the firm sold yen futures contracts.

The yen futures contract on the IMM is written for 12,500,000 yen. The spot price of yen is $.008/yen. To hedge the $4 million requires ($4,000,000 / .$008 =) 500,000,000 yen or (500,000,000 yen / 12,500,000 yen per contract =) 40 contracts.

The next day after the contracts were sold, the value of the contract rose as high as $.0081/ yen and closed at $.00805/yen. The margin required is based on the difference between the price the contract was initially sold compared to the current value. What is the change in Morrison's margin position?

Result

The rise in the value of the dollar price of yen means that the cost of buying the futures contact back will cost more than the price at which it sold. This creates the need for additional margin.

The amount of additional margin is equal to:

$$(\$.00805/yen \times 40\ contracts \times 12,500,000\ yen/contract) - (\$.008/yen \times 40\ contracts \times 12,500,000\ yen/contract) = \$4,025,000 - \$4,000,000 = \$25,000$$

✓ Checkpoints

16-3 What are the key provisions in a futures contract, and what economic functions does a futures contract provide?

16-4 What is the role of margin in a futures contract?

16-5 What is convergence, in terms of futures and spot prices, and why must convergence occur?

16-6 What situations may require you to hedge?

Options

Options are frequently difficult to identify because they are embedded in an asset or are taken for granted in a transaction that otherwise seems straightforward. Also, options are difficult to value. This section looks at many types of options found in financial asset transactions common to financial management.

Options are the financial equivalent to a zero sum game. This is a game in which the gain of the winner is equal to the loss of the loser. There are two parties to every option transaction. The **option writer** must deliver or purchase the financial asset at a predetermined price. The agreed-upon price is called the *exercise*, or *strike*, **price**. As a practical matter, this only occurs when the market price of the optioned asset creates a profit for the party holding the option. The gain to the holder of the option is equal to the loss of the writer. So, why would anyone write an option? The answer is to earn an **option premium.** This is an amount of money that the owner of the option pays the writer to offer the option. The option writer receives the premium for risking an economic loss.

Options are classified in a number of different ways. First, options are classified on the basis of whether the agreement is to buy or sell. A **put option** is a contract that gives the owner the right, but not the obligation, to sell a financial asset at a predetermined price on or before a predetermined date. Call options were discussed in Chapters 14 and 15. A call option provides the owner with the right, but not the obligation, to buy a financial asset from the writer at a predetermined price on or before a predetermined date. **European options** provide that the purchase or sale occur on the last date of the option period or *exercise date*. An **American option,** on the other hand, provides the owner with the right to buy or sell on the exercise date and any time before the exercise date. Options are marketable if they are traded on organized exchanges. These options are typically sold before expiration. Others are not marketable and must be exercised by the owner if it is profitable to do so.

COMMON OPTIONS FOUND IN BUSINESS

Options are common features in many financial transactions and assets. Options are traded on organized exchanges. They are also commonly found in financial transactions of many types. Options traded on organized exchanges include:

- Puts and calls on individual common stocks.
- Puts and calls on stock indices such as the S&P 500 index.
- Puts and calls on foreign currencies.
- Puts and calls on short- and long-term bonds.
- Puts and calls on metal and agricultural commodities.
- Puts and calls on traded futures contracts.

The following is a short discussion of some of the most common options found in financial management.

Options on Common Stock

The most common options written today are puts and calls on common stock. The common stock option is the most frequently written option. Since the Chicago Board Option Exchange was founded in 1975, hundreds of option contracts have been offered. These include many traded stocks as well as stock indices, bonds, and futures contracts. Other forms of options on common stocks include warrants and bond convertibility features. A **warrant** is a call option on common stock sold in conjunction with a bond sale to enhance its desirability. A **convertibility feature** is a provision embedded in a bond contract that provides the owner with the option to convert the principal value of the bond into shares of common stock in the same company at a specified price on or before a specified date.

INTERNATIONAL ✦ FOCUS

U.S. DOMINATION OF DERIVATIVES THREATENED

The United States has always been the undisputed leader in futures and options innovations and trading. Chicago, the heart of the agricultural Midwest, took the leadership position with its Chicago Board of Trade and Chicago Mercantile Exchange. With the addition of financial derivatives in the 1970s, the markets boomed.

The growth in derivatives for foreign securities, especially the German and Japanese, has resulted in significant growth in derivatives trading outside the United States. Adding to U.S. problems is the growth in computerized trading and over-the-counter trading between dealers. The open outcry trading in the pits limits trading hours, whereas international financial markets know no time limits.

The CBOT is fighting back with an electronic system of its own, called Globex. Most experts, however, feel that the United States will continue to fight a defensive battle for world domination on the derivative markets.

Source: "Has Chicago Lost Its Edge?" *Business Week*, March 9, 1992, pp. 76–78.

Commitments and Lines of Credit

Many financial institutions offer borrowers financial commitments to borrow money. This is the option equivalent of selling the prospective borrower a put on a debt asset written against that borrower. These commitments can usually be written at a fixed or floating interest rate. The fact that a borrower has a commitment, however, does not mean that the borrower must borrow the money. The borrower has the option to deliver the debt asset to the lender. Most commitments are of the American variety.

A good example of a loan commitment is the commitment a mortgage lender gives a borrower on a home mortgage. Typically, the lender will give the borrower a commitment to borrow up to a specified amount of money at a specified interest rate. The option is usually written for 60 to 90 days. This option is a put option owned by the borrower providing the ability to sell a mortgage to the lender within the option period, an American option.

Lines of credit, even if written at a market or floating interest rate, involve a risk to the lender that funds may be very difficult for the lending institution to obtain when the customer decides to exercise the option and borrow the money. Consequently, lenders typically charge a commitment fee for the unused portion of a line of credit.

Business Options

One option that most analysts would likely not recognize is an option on future business opportunities. A business that establishes a market presence in a new market in order to develop name recognition with the hope that business will grow is a business option. McDonald's Corporation's well-publicized entry into Moscow in the late 1980s was certainly a costly proposition with little near-term chance of profit given the state of the USSR. However, the dissolution of the

Soviet Union and increased ability to expand operations in the republic of Russia may make this business option very valuable to McDonald's. PepsiCo invested in a similar option to sell Pepsi in the USSR in the 1970s. The payoff on this option took somewhat longer than McDonald's.

Prepayment Options in Mortgages and Installment Loan and Call Provisions on Bonds

Most mortgages and installment loan contracts, particularly those written to consumers for durable goods and residential properties, have a provision in the contract allowing for prepayment of principal before the contractual maturity of the loan. This prepayment option is a call option, which allows the borrower to purchase the loan outstanding at its par value any time before maturity—an American option.

It is clear that if market interest rates fall appreciably below the contract rate on the existing mortgage, then a prepayment can be expected to occur. This prepayment option is the equivalent of a call option on a bond issued by a corporation.

Many bonds also have call options. These provisions are just like the prepayment case above, but they are not typically as advantageous to the borrower. Most call provisions require that, upon a call, the borrower must pay the investor a premium above the outstanding obligation. Also, the call provision is usually restricted to a single date in the future, as in a European option.

UNDERSTANDING THE OPTION TRANSACTION

Obviously, an option only has value if there is some positive probability that the owner will be able to buy or sell a financial asset by exercising the option and earning a profit. Profit is earned when the market value of the optioned asset is greater (less) than its option exercise price in the case of a call (put). For example, if you own a call option to buy a share of Sears, Roebuck & Co. stock at $55 per share when the current price of Sears is $53 per share, then the option will have a positive value only if there is some positive probability that Sears stock will trade at a price higher than $55 per share during the period the option is outstanding. If such a positive probability is expected, then it is likely someone will be willing to pay a positive price for that option.

The owner of an option can be thought of as an investor, or speculator, in price volatility. Alternatively, the owner of the option may already be exposed to price volatility relating to a specific asset and may want to own an option to offset the price risk, in which case the option is used as a hedge. The greater the volatility in the underlying price of a particular financial asset, the more likely the investor exposed to this price risk will be interested in owning an option. Similarly, the greater the price risk of an asset, the greater will be the incentive for a speculator to be drawn into writing an option on that asset.

The owner of an option is also interested in financial leverage. The owner of an option can receive the benefits from the price volatility of a financial asset by purchasing an option, which will sell at a fraction of the price of the asset itself. This option transaction may be quicker and involve lower transaction costs than purchasing the financial asset directly and borrowing funds against the asset to produce the same financial leverage effect. The investor can buy a call option on 100 shares of Sears stock or buy the stock itself on margin. If the option is purchased, the investor will forgo any dividends paid on the stock and will also be relieved from any interest on the margin loan. Most important, the holder of the option limits the potential loss, which could occur as a result of a sharp decline in the market price of the call-optioned asset. The ability to leverage and limit loss using options, however, has a price—the option premium paid to the writer of the option. A typical quote listing from a financial publication for options on the stock of Disney Corporation is shown in Exhibit 16.3.

Options are referred to as *in-the-money, at-the-money,* or *out-of-the-money* options. An **in-the-money option** has an immediate economic incentive to be exercised. This is a put (call) option whose exercise price is above (below) the market price of the asset. The call options on Disney that can be exercised at the strike prices of $100 and $110 would be in-the-money. An **at-the-money option** has a market price of the asset equal to the exercise price. An **out-of-the-money**

EXHIBIT 16.3

Reading the Financial Page
Stock Option Quotation
Disney Corporation
(typical listing)

American Exchange
Disney

Closing Price*	Strike Price	Calls			Puts		
		Jan.	Feb.	Mar.	Jan.	Feb.	Mar.
135 3/8	100	35	nt	nt	no	1/8	1/4
	110	24 1/2	25 1/2	25 3/4	3/8	5/8	3/4
	140	1 1/8	1 7/8	5	8 1/4	10 1/2	11 7/8

nt: No trades
no: No option.
*Closing price: New York Stock Exchange.

The listing above shows the last traded prices of three call and put options for Disney stock. The prices reflect the price of the option per share of stock. This listing shows three different strike prices. However, for a stock that was as volatile as Disney, strike prices are available in $5 increments. Not all strike prices are shown here. A 100-share call option expiring in February at a strike price of 110 would cost $25.50 per share, or $2,550 for a 100-share block. There are contract months other than those shown in the table. Most listings do not provide all the contracts. Typically the near-term contract months are shown.

put (call) option has an exercise price that is below (above) the market price. The Disney call options at the strike price of $140 are out-of-the-money.

OPTION PAYOFFS

One easy way to understand how an option works is to present graphically the payoff schedule of holding an option. Consider the situation of the holder of a call option on one share of Bricks, Inc., stock. The exercise price is $25 per share and the current market value is $23. The price of the call option is $3 per share. Exhibit 16.4 shows the profit or loss position of the option buyer for a wide range of possible prices for Bricks, Inc. stock. It is clear from the exhibit that the price of Brick's stock must rise above the exercise price by the amount of the option price or premium paid before a profit is possible. Clearly, the option holder has limited losses. The holder of the option cannot lose more than the price of the option no matter how low the price of the stock goes.

Exhibit 16.5. shows a payoff schedule for a put option. It shows the profit or loss from holding a put option on a stock with a market value of $30, an exercise price of $28, and a option premium price of $3. The exhibit shows that it takes a drop in the price of the stock from $30 to $25 before the holder of the

EXHIBIT 16.4

Payoff on Stock Call Option

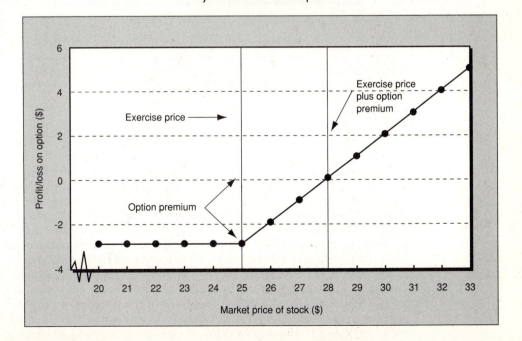

EXHIBIT 16.5

Payoff on Stock Put Option

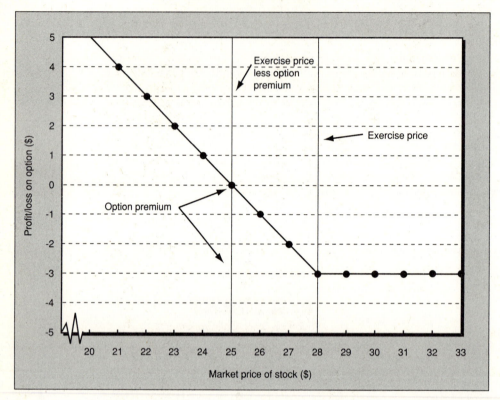

option breaks even. Again, the potential loss to the option holder is limited to the amount of the option premium.

HEDGING WITH OPTIONS

Options are used to hedge price risk. The advantage of using an option is that the cost of obtaining the price risk insurance can be determined precisely. Consider an investor that holds 100 shares of stock in Merck Corp. The stock was purchased years earlier and has appreciated significantly. The investor is planning to sell the stock the next year to fund the purchase of a business. However, the investor would like to avoid the tax liability that would occur if the stock is sold immediately. In addition, the investor would like to avoid the possibility that the stock's value declines significantly in the months ahead. Such an investor can protect against a price decline by purchasing a put option. If the price of Merck is $105.00 per share and the price of a put exercised at $100.00 can be purchased for $2.50 per share, then the investor can be assured of receiving no less than $97.50 per share ($100.00 excercise price less $2.50 option premium). The possible payoffs to the investor depends on the price of Merck stock when the option expires.

Consider the possibilities in Table 16.2, which shows various prices for Merck stock at the expiration date of the option. The amount of funds received by the stockholder after the cost of the option has been considered is shown in the table. It shows that the put hedge limited the loss to the amount of the exercise price less the option premium paid for the put. It is also possible to calculate the percentage cost of price protection from this example. For all market prices of $100.00 or less, the cost of the hedge is ($2.50/$105.00) = 2.3810%.

TABLE 16.2

Net Proceeds from Put Hedge on Merck Stock

Market Value of Stock at Expiration Date (a)	Cost of Option (b)	Exercise Price (c)	Net Proceeds [Greater of (c − b) or (a − b)]
$ 90.00	$2.50	$100.00	$ 97.50
95.00	2.50	100.00	97.50
100.00	2.50		97.50
105.00	2.50		102.50
110.00	2.50		107.50

INTRINSIC VALUE AND TIME VALUE OF OPTIONS

An in-the-money option is said to have *intrinsic value,* which is the positive difference between the call option's exercise price and the spot price of the financial asset. For a call option to have intrinsic value, its exercise price must be below the current spot price of the financial asset on which it is written. Put options will have intrinsic value if the current market price of the optioned assets is below the excercise price. Options with intrinsic value are in-the-money options. If you hold a call option on 100 shares of IBM stock with a exercise price of $99, and the current market or spot price is $102, then the intrinsic value of this option is ($102 – 99) = $3 per share. If the exercise price is $99 or below, it has no intrinsic value. Table 16.3 provides the intrinsic value of a call and put option for one share of GM stock.

Typically, a marketable option will sell for more than its intrinsic value. Virtually all call options that are written at exercise prices below the asset's spot price sell at some positive value. Also, in-the-money marketable options sell for more than their intrinsic value. The difference between an option's market price and its intrinsic value is known as *time value.* The time value of an option falls quickly as the option nears its exercise date. Table 16.4 shows the intrinsic and time values of a call option on one share of GM stock. It is important to note that even though a stock has no intrinsic value, it still has time value. The time value derives from the fact that there is a positive probability that sometime before expiration the stock will rise above its exercise price.

TABLE 16.3

Intrinsic Values of Call and Put Options on GM Stock

Market Price	Exercise Price	Call Option Intrinsic Value	Put Option Intrinsic Value
$32	$35	$0	$3
33	35	0	2
34	35	0	1
35	35	0	0
36	35	1	0
37	35	2	0
38	35	3	0
39	35	4	0
40	35	5	0

TABLE 16.4

Intrinsic and Time Values of Call Options on GM Stock

Market Price	Exercise Price	Market Price of Option (a)	Intrinsic Value (b)	Time Value (a − b)
$32	$35	$ 1/4	$0	$ 1/4
33	35	3/8	0	3/8
34	35	1/2	0	1/2
35	35	1	0	1
36	35	2 1/4	1	1 1/4
37	35	3 3/4	2	1 3/4
38	35	5 1/4	3	2 1/4
39	35	6 3/8	4	2 3/8
40	35	8 1/4	5	3 1/4

FACTORS THAT INFLUENCE THE VALUE OF AN OPTION

A number of factors are likely to affect the option premium, or market value, of an option. These include the following:

1. The price of the underlying financial asset.
2. The predetermined exercise price.
3. The amount of time until the option expires, the expiration period.
4. The interest rate, R_F, on risk-free assets.
5. The underlying volatility of the rate of return on the optioned financial asset.

6.   The interest or dividend received on the optioned financial asset during the period the option is outstanding.

Consider how each of these factors impact the value of a call option, *C,* by viewing each factor in isolation.

Price of the Underlying Asset

The higher the market price, *P,* of the underlying optioned financial asset, the higher will be the value of the option written against that asset. Given a specified exercise price, a higher market price will make it more likely the option will be exercised. This makes the option more valuable.

Relationship: Higher P → Higher C

Exercise Price

The higher the exercise price, *E,* the lower will be the value of the option. A higher exercise price, given a particular market price, the less the chance the option will be in-the-money. This makes the option less valuable.

Relationship: Higher E → Lower C

Period until Expiration

The length of time of the option period, *t,* will affect the value of an option. The longer the option period, the higher will be the option's value. The longer the option period, the greater the chance that the option will come in-the-money. Table 16.5 shows the market value of an option on a call option on one share of U.S. Surgical Co. common stock with a exercise price of $75 per share. The market price of U.S. Surgical stock was $74 per share when these prices were obtained. Note that the value of the option increases as the option period increases.

Relationship: Higher t → Higher C

TABLE 16.5

Price of Call Option for One Share of U.S. Surgical Co.

Exercise Period	Market Price of Option
One month	$1⅞
Two months	3¼
Three months	4¾

Financial Asset's Price Volatility

The higher the price volatility of the price of the underlying optioned asset, the higher will be the value of an option written against that asset. If the range of prices that the underlying asset may take during the option period is considered a probability distribution, then the asset with the highest standard deviation of expected returns, σ, will have a greater value. This assures that both assets have the same mean expected return, because the greater the volatility of the stock's price, the greater the probability that the option will be exercised at a large profit.

Relationship: Higher $\sigma \rightarrow$ Higher C

The Risk-Free Interest Rate

The higher the interest rate, R_F, related to the cost of financing the underlying asset, the higher the option price. Using an option allows the investor to control an asset without tying up funds owning it. Therefore, the higher the interest rates, such as the cost of a margin loan to finance the asset, the more valuable the option.

Relationship: Higher $R_F \rightarrow$ Higher C

Income on the Optioned Asset

If the optioned asset produces income, I—such as stocks paying dividends or bonds interest—then the higher the income, the lower will be the option value. The fact that a financial asset pays income reduces the cost of holding the asset compared to holding the option.

Relationship: Higher $I \rightarrow$ Lower C

VALUING OPTIONS: THE BLACK-SCHOLES OPTION PRICING MODEL

In 1973, Fisher Black and Myron Scholes developed a model to value particular types of options. This model, commonly called the **Black-Scholes option pricing model,** and its many derivations have been used extensively in establishing the value of an option. Sophisticated models are used to determine the appropriate relationship between the price of an option trading on an organized exchange and the cash market price of the underlying financial claim.

The Black-Scholes model includes the first five factors in its specification:

1. The spot price.
2. The exercise price.
3. A measure of price volatility.
4. The risk-free rate.
5. The length of the option period.

This model cannot be used to incorporate income, I, received on the financial claim, however.

The model originally developed by Black-Scholes was designed for European call options. This discussion is concerned with one used to value a call option of the American variety. The model assumes no return on the underlying financial claim and that the options are marketable—that is, they can be bought and sold. This is a very important assumption since many of the options discussed earlier in this section cannot be transferred. This means that the value of these options, absent transferability, will be less than would be calculated using the Black-Scholes methodology. The model also assumes that transaction costs are minimal and that all parties to the transaction have the same marginal tax rate.

Given these limitations, the model has been successfully used to value many types of options. The objective of the model is to estimate the market value of a call option, C. Consider a six-month call option to purchase 100 shares of IBM stock at $100 per share. This is the type of option that can be valued using a Black-Scholes type of model.

The model specification is given in Equation 16.2.

$$C = P\ N(d_1) - E\ e^{-(R_F t)}\ N(d_2) \tag{16.2}$$

where:

C = *Price of the call option, or the value of the option*

P = *Spot price of the underlying financial claim*

E = *Exercise price at the option's maturity*

$ln(P/E)$ = *Natural logarithm of P/E*

e = *Natural log e ≅ 2.7183 . . .*

R_F = *Continuous compound risk-free interest rate*

t = *Remaining life of the option, expressed in years and percentages thereof*

$N(d_1)$ = *Cumulative probability distribution from a normal distribution for the value d_1*

$N(d_2)$ = *Cumulative probability distribution from a normal distribution for the value d_2.*

The values for d_1 and d_2 in the specification are:

$d_1 = \{[ln(P/E) + R_F t]/(\sigma\sqrt{t})\} + .5\ (\sigma)\ \sqrt{t}$

$d_2 = d_1 - \sigma\sqrt{t}$

σ = *Standard deviation of the continuously compounded rate of return on the underlying financial claim.*

It is possible to work out an example of an option value using the Black-Scholes model. The model uses inputs that are generally available. However, it is structured for financial claims that do not pay interest or dividends. Thus, financial options on bonds generally do not fit. The values must be estimated since the distributions of returns in the future are not known. This requires using past data to estimate these parameters.

| DEMONSTRATION PROBLEM | USING BLACK-SCHOLES TO VALUE A CALL OPTION |

Situation

Consider an option to purchase a share of stock in Digital Equipment Corporation at $65.00 when the price of the stock is $62.50. The option will expire in four months, or 120 days. The risk-free interest rate is 5%. The volatility of Digital Equipment stock as measured by the standard deviation of the return on the stock for the 120-day future period is estimated to be .40. Martin has been asked to use the Black-Scholes option pricing model to estimate the value of this option.

Results

The first thing Martin did was to summarize these data as follows:

C = *Unknown option value, what we are solving for*

$P = \$62.50$

$E = \$65$

$R_F = .05$

$t = .33$ *years*

$\sigma = .40$

$d_1 = \{[[ln(62.5/65)] + .05(.33)]/(.40)\sqrt{(.33)}\} + .5(.4)\sqrt{(.33)}$

$d_1 = [((-.03922) + .0165/.229783] + .114891$

C = *Unknown option value, what we are solving for*

$d_1 = .016012$

$d_2 = .016012 - .229783 = -.213771.$

Using our estimates of d_1 and d_2, we are in a position to determine the values for the cumulative density of the normal probability distribution with a mean of zero. To do this, we must use Table 16.6, which gives the cumulative probability under the unit normal probability distribution for d_1 and d_2 values of minus 3.00 to plus 2.95. Using this table, it is necessary to interpolate the values of N(d) for values of d between those given in the table. For example, d_1 is .016012 in Table 16.8. It falls between N(d) values of .5000 and .5199. Since .016012 is between the table d_1 values .00 and .05, we interpolate:

$$.016012/(.00 - .05) = 32.0240\%.$$

TABLE 16.6
Cumulative Normal Unit Probability Distribution: N(d)

d	N(d)	d	N(d)	d	N(d)	d	N(d)	d	N(d)	d	N(d)
−3.00	.0013	−2.00	.0228	−1.00	.1587	.00	.5000	1.00	.8413	2.00	.9773
−2.95	.0016	−1.95	.0256	− .95	.1711	.05	.5199	1.05	.8531	2.05	.9798
−2.90	.0019	−1.90	.0287	− .90	.1841	.10	.5398	1.10	.8643	2.10	.9821
−2.85	.0022	−1.85	.0322	− .85	.1977	.15	.5596	1.15	.8749	2.15	.9842
−2.80	.0026	−1.80	.0359	− .80	.2119	.20	.5793	1.20	.8849	2.20	.9861
−2.75	.0030	−1.75	.0401	− .75	.2266	.25	.5987	1.25	.8944	2.25	.9878
−2.70	.0035	−1.70	.0446	− .70	.2420	.30	.6179	1.30	.9032	2.30	.9893
−2.65	.0040	−1.65	.0495	− .65	.2578	.35	.6368	1.35	.9115	2.35	.9906
−2.60	.0047	−1.60	.0548	− .60	.2743	.40	.6554	1.40	.9192	2.40	.9918
−2.55	.0054	−1.55	.0606	− .55	.2912	.45	.6736	1.45	.9265	2.45	.9929
−2.50	.0062	−1.50	.0668	− .50	.3085	.50	.6915	1.50	.9332	2.50	.9938
−2.45	.0071	−1.45	.0735	− .45	.3264	.55	.7088	1.55	.9394	2.55	.9946
−2.40	.0082	−1.40	.0808	− .40	.3446	.60	.7257	1.60	.9452	2.60	.9953
−2.35	.0094	−1.35	.0885	− .35	.3632	.65	.7422	1.65	.9505	2.65	.9980
−2.30	.0107	−1.30	.0968	− .30	.3821	.70	.7580	1.70	.9554	2.70	.9965
−2.25	.0122	−1.25	.1057	− .25	.4013	.75	.7734	1.75	.9599	2.75	.9970
−2.20	.0139	−1.20	.1151	− .20	.4207	.80	.7881	1.80	.9641	2.80	.9974
−2.15	.0158	−1.15	.1251	− .15	.4404	.85	.8023	1.85	.9678	2.85	.9978
−2.10	.0179	−1.10	.1357	− .10	.4602	.90	.8159	1.90	.9713	2.90	.9981
−2.05	.0202	−1.05	.1469	− .05	.4801	.95	.8289	1.95	.9744	2.95	.9984

This percent of the range between .5000 and .5199 equates to [(.5199 − .5000) × 32.024% =] .006373, which is the value added to .5000 we use for $N(d_1)$. These values and our estimate of the value of C are shown in Equation 16.3.

$$N(d_1) = .506373$$

$$N(d_2) = .415357$$

$$C = P\ N(d_1) - E\ e^{-(R_F t)}\ N(d_2)$$

$$C = 62.5\ (.506373) - 65\ (e^{-.05(.33)})\ (.415357)$$

$$C = \$5.0919 \qquad\qquad [16.3]$$

Martin's estimate of the value of the call option is $5.09 per share.

SENSITIVITY ANALYSIS AND OPTION VALUES

Table 16.7 shows the Black-Scholes determined option values for exercise price, X, risk-free rate, R_F, time to expiration, t, and σ. The table provides a sensitivity analysis of option values to changes in their parameters. In the analysis, σ takes the values of .4 and .6; X the values of $65, $67.5, and $70; R_F the values of 5% and 7%; and t the values of .33 and 1 in years.

TABLE 16.7

Sensitivity of Option Values to Changes in Parameters Using the Black-Scholes Option Pricing Model
(option values in dollars)

$t = .33$ years

X	$65		$67.5		$70	
R_F	5%	7%	5%	7%	5%	7%
$\sigma = .4$	5.09	5.27	4.15	4.31	3.35	3.49
$\sigma = .6$	7.95	8.12	7.00	7.16	6.16	6.30

$t = 1$ year

X	$65		$67.5		$70	
R_F	5%	7%	5%	7%	5%	7%
$\sigma = .4$	10.19	10.73	9.21	9.73	8.31	8.78
$\sigma = .6$	14.99	15.48	14.10	14.57	13.26	13.71

As the table shows, the values of the options given by the Black-Scholes model vary considerably. The impact of changes in time to expiration have particularly large impacts on value. The risk-free rate and the exercise price have less impact for the ranges used in this analysis. A number of computer programs have been developed to permit analysts to calculate quickly the option values using this model and variations of it, greatly simplifying the calculations for this relatively complicated formula.

PUT-CALL PARITY AND PUT VALUATION

The value of a put option is related to the value of a call option. This relationship holds if the put and call options are written on the same financial claim, have the same strike price, E, and time to expiration, t. This relationship for European puts and calls on financial assets that pay no interest or dividend is called *put-call parity*,[4] expressed as Equation 16.4 below:

$$P_v = C - P + E(1 + R_F)^{-t} \qquad [16.4]$$

---

[4]There are a number of rigorous assumptions that must hold for put-call parity to be valid. Some of the most important include: (1) no transaction costs; (2) no bid-ask spread; (3) no taxes; and (4) no margin requirements.

Put-call parity shows that the value of a European put, P_v, is related to the market value of the call, C. To conceptually understand this relationship, consider the following attributes of a call. A call option is comparable to the 100% leveraged ownership of the optioned asset. The rate paid on this loan is assumed to be the risk-free rate, R_F and repaid at the expiration of the option. The amount received on the loan is the present value of E, $E(1 + R_F)^{-t}$. Any increase in the market price of the optioned asset above the exercise price creates a profit to the ower. Unlike the owner of the stock, however, a call owner cannot lose more than the option premium if the price of the asset falls. Consquently, the call owner can be thought of as also owning a put on the asset with the same exercise price as the call. This put allows the 100% leveraged investor to avoid any loss in the value of the stock. If the stock falls to a price below the exercise price, the investor will exercise the put.

The important point of this discussion is that it shows that there is a functional relationship between the market value of a call option and the market value of a put on the same asset with the same exercise price and expiration date.[5]

CALCULATING A PUT VALUE WITH A KNOW CALL VALUE	DEMONSTRATION PROBLEM

Situation

On May 10, 1994, an October call option on Chrysler Corp. last traded at a price of $5.125 per share. The excercise price was $45.00 per share and Chrysler common stock closed at a price of $46.125 per share. You noted that a put with the same expiration date and price last sold at $3.75 per share. You have been asked to determine the put-call parity value of the put. The risk-free rate, R_F, is 4%. The option expires on the third Friday of October, or in 163 days.

Results

Using the put-call parity equation, it is possible to calculate the theoretical value of the put by using equation 16.4:

$$P_v = C - P + E(1 + R_F)^{-t}$$

$$P_v = \$5.125 - \$46.125 + \$45(1 + .04)^{-0.4466}$$

$$P_v = \$5.125 - \$46.125 + \$45(.9826) = \$3.217$$

Theoretical value $3.217 \neq$ Market value of $3.75

---

[5]The relationship between put and call prices provides the opportunity for arbitrage transactions involving the simultaneous purchase and sale of call and put contracts on the same stock with similar exercise prices and expiration dates. Equation 16.4 indicates that the market value of the call and put should be known with a fairly high degree of precision . Yet, there are frequent violations of the put-call parity relationship. These differences do not always relate to transaction costs and provide for interesting arbitrage profit transactions.

The difference, although relatively small, could be due to nonsynchronous trades related to the fact that the last prices recorded for the trades of the call, put, and stock all occurred at different times in the day when the price of Chrysler stock was at different levels. It may also be due to bid-ask differences.

MARKETABILITY AND THE VALUE OF OPTIONS

Many options are marketable. Marketability insures that in-the-money options are exercised. This marketability assumption is very important to the valuation of options. Options are more valuable if they can be sold, because the holder of an in-the-money option can be assured of receiving its value even if the holder is unable to exercise it.

Many options are not marketable. The discussion of financial options disclosed a number that can only be exercised by one party, such as a loan commitment and prepayment option. Frequently, in-the-money options that would be expected to be exercised are not. This is because the holder of the option may be unable to meet all the conditions necessary to exercise. Or, it may not be rewarding enough to incur all the transaction costs related to exercising the option. For example, many homeowners do not refinance a high-rate mortgage because they must pay large closing costs to exercise the prepayment option.

When making analyses of options that are executable by one entity, it is necessary to develop a probability distribution that provides an estimate of the probability that an in-the-money option will be exercised by those holding it. If only 50% of a particular type of in-the-money options are traditionally exercised, then the cost of writing that option would be 50% less than if the option were marketable.

✓ Checkpoints

16-7 What is an option? What is the difference between a put and a call?

16-8 What kinds of options are commonly found embedded in financial assets or common in business transactions?

16-9 What is the difference between an American and European type option?

16-10 Which option of those below would have the greatest value if all other factors were held constant?

   a. An option written on an asset with a highly volatile price or stable price?

   b. A short- or long-term option?

   c. A call option written on an asset whose exercise price is close to the current price or well below it?

16-11 You hold an option to buy 100 shares of ABC corporation at $25 per share. ABC last traded at $21 per share. Is it an in-the-money or out-of-the-money option?

16-12 Explain the Black-Scholes option pricing model. What is it used for? What are its limitations?

Interest Rate and Currency Swaps

One of the fastest-growing risk management tools used in business is the **financial swap.** These financial contracts can be classified into two large segments: **interest rate swaps** and **currency swaps.** These contracts are contractual agreements between two parties who agree to make periodic payments to one another. An interest rate swap typically has one party receiving payments on a fixed nominal amount of principal based on a specified long- or intermediate-term interest rate while the other party receives payments based on a short-term interest rate which floats over the term of the agreement. In the case of a currency swap, the two parties agree to exchange two different currencies at the current prevailing exchange rate and then reverse the exchange at the same exchange rate at some agreed-upon future date. The currency swap will be discussed in Chapter 19.

THE INTEREST RATE SWAP

The concept of the interest rate swap is to assist both parties. Some consider the transaction to be motivated by a condition in which both parties have a comparative advantage in raising funds—one party with a comparative advantage in the short-term market and the other in the longer-term market. This comparative advantage condition provides the motivation for each party to enter into an interest rate swap.

The primary purpose of the swap is to assist each firm to alter its financial obligations. A firm with long-term capital investment requirements might choose to convert its short-term borrowings that float with short-term rates into a longer-term commitment using a swap tied to a longer-term rate. A firm might also find that after issuing a long-term bond, its circumstances change. It may have sold assets financed with long-term bonds and then determined that it would rather have a certain amount of those liabilites tied to a floating rate.

THE TYPICAL SWAP

The typical interest rate swap has two primary players and frequently a third-party player. The two primary players are the institutions that want to alter the cash flow on a specified amount of **notional principal,** the amount specified in the contract on which interest will be paid to each party. In an interest rate swap, actual principal does not change hands. Exhibit 16.6 shows an interest rate swap in which party A agrees to pay a floating rate of 2.5% over the 26-week T-bill rate on $15 million of notional principal for five years. Party B, on the other hand, agrees to pay a fixed rate of 9.5% on $15 million of notional principal for five years. The payments are made semiannually in this case. The two parties may be brought together by a broker, but more typically, the swaps are arranged by a third-party acting as an intermediary. This third-party is frequently a commercial bank or investment banker.

FUTURES OPTIONS AND SWAPTIONS

How

it

Really

Works

Just when you think you understand it all, a new innovation occurs. Today, the derivative market is so complex that literally hundreds of different types of financial contracts have been created. Creating these contracts is known as *financial engineering*. The tools of the trade are sophisticated financial models run on fast computers that allow financial architects to simulate how different contract creations change in price under a variety of economic scenarios.

Two relatively new derivatives are **futures options** and **swaptions**. A futures option is an option to buy or sell a futures contract. The swaption is an option on a specified swap contract. Creating these new financial assets has been a boon for Wall Street and the mathematically skilled financial types who create and trade these contracts. Valuation is particularly difficult. Since many of these contracts are not traded frequently, a dealer must be very certain about the valuation model it uses to price them.

Exhibit 16.7 shows the swap arrangement with the commercial bank as the intermediary. The commercial bank is typically compensated by increasing the rate to parties A and B and keeping this interest rate spread as a profit. As a result, in Exhibit 16.7, party A pays 2.625% over the 26-week T-bill rate and party B, a 9.625% fixed rate. The bank pays party B a floating 2.50% over the 26-week T-bill rate and party A a 9.5% fixed rate. This allows the bank to obtain a profit

---

EXHIBIT 16.6

Interest Rate Swap
Payment Made between Two Parties

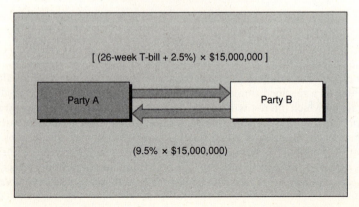

[(26-week T-bill + 2.5%) × $15,000,000]

Party A

Party B

(9.5% × $15,000,000)

EXHIBIT 16.7

Interest Rate Swap with Bank Intermediary

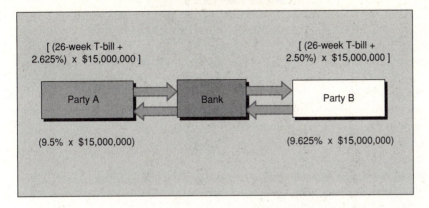

[(26-week T-bill + 2.625%) x $15,000,000]

[(26-week T-bill + 2.50%) x $15,000,000]

Party A

Bank

Party B

(9.5% x $15,000,000)

(9.625% x $15,000,000)

of .25% for the five-year life of the contract. The bank is compensated this .25% spread for providing three services: (1) for acting as a broker bringing both parties together; (2) for acting as an originator of the transaction, which involves legal documentation and underwriting costs; (3) for acting as an intermediary, which involves accepting the credit risk that one or the other party will default on the swap.

In Exhibit 16.7 the commercial bank is an intermediary between the two parties. This does not have to be the case. The bank could write a swap agreement with just one of the two parties. In that case, the bank could assume interest rate risk. If it wrote only the swap to party B, for example, and a rise in short-term interest rates caused its cost of funds to rise, it could face an interest rate squeeze since it would be receiving a fixed return from party B. Many commercial banks act as primary dealers in swaps where they take credit and interest rate risks.

Interest rate swaps are used to reduce the differences between income received by a firm and the obligations it must pay. Many times, the opportunity to participate in an interest rate swap depends on the comparative advantage a firm might have in borrowing in the short- or long-term financial markets. Financial depository firms typically have no trouble raising short-term funds at favorable rates in the deposit markets. Large commercial and industrial firms that regularly borrow in the long-term bond markets have comparatively good access to long-term funds. These comparative advantages provide the economic motivation behind many interest rate swaps.

✓ Checkpoints

16-13 How would you describe a typical interest rate swap?

16-14 Why would two firms be interested in an interest rate swap?

16-15 What role do commercial banks and investment bankers play in the swap market?

PROCTER & GAMBLE CO. SPECULATES WITH DERIVATIVES

How

it

Really

Works

Financial professionals around the world reevaluated their derivative financial strategies in light of Procter & Gamble's (P&G) press release reporting that it had suffered a $157 million pre-tax loss on several derivative transactions. It was clear from the release that P&G was not using derivatives to hedge risk but rather to speculate on future interest rate changes.

One of the transactions involved P&G taking on the obligation to pay a floating rate on a specified amount of notional principal. They also received a handsome payment in the form of an option premium. In return, they gave the counterparty, Bankers Trust Co., a large New York Bank, put options on U.S. Treasury bonds. The transaction was a huge bet that interest rates would stay low or fall. When the opposite occurred, and both short- and long-term rates rose (and long-term bond prices plummeted) in early 1994, P&G suffered huge losses on the puts.

P&G's experience made it clear that derivatives provide the ability to create a highly leveraged speculative position on changes in security or currency prices. It also makes clear that taking this price risk is not limited to financial firms.

Source: "Just What Firms Do with 'Derivatives' Is Suddenly a Hot Issue," *The Wall Street Journal*, April 14, 1994, pp. A1–A6.

SUMMARY AND REVIEW

1. **Describe a futures contract and the types of futures positions.**

   Financial futures contracts are legal agreements to buy (go long) or sell (go short) a specified quantity and quality of a financial asset on a specified date and place. A very small percentage of futures contracts involve delivery of the financial asset since it is customary to offset a futures position with an offsetting position before the contract expiration date.

2. **Discuss the factors that influence the value of a futures contract.**

   The relationship between the spot price of a financial asset and its futures contract price is shown by the following equation:

   Futures contract price = Spot cash market price + Cost of carry of the cash asset – Return on holding cash asset

3. **Discuss the role of margin in the futures market and how to calculate changes in required margin.**

   Users of the financial futures markets must be aware of the requirement to put up **margin** with a clearing house of the exchange. Margin is used to reduce the potential for a party failing to settle on the terms required in a future's contract.

4. **Describe options and the types of options.**

   Options are found in a wide variety of financial transactions and embedded in financial assets. Sometimes they are hard to recognize. Options are classified as **puts** or **calls.** Puts (calls) give the option owner the right to deliver (receive) a financial asset at an agreed-upon price. The option may be an **American option** which is exercisable at any time before its exercise date or a **European option,** exercisable only on its expiration date.

5. **Discuss the factors that impact the value of options and the direction of those impacts and explain the Black-Scholes model and how it is used to value options.**

   The **value of a call option,** C, is a function of six primary variables. These include:

   1. The spot price of the asset, P: Higher $P \rightarrow$ Higher C.
   2. The optioned asset's exercise price, E: Higher $E \rightarrow$ Lower C.
   3. The length of the period until expiration, t: Higher $t \rightarrow$ Higher C.
   4. The underlying volatility of the asset's expected investment return, σ: Higher $\sigma \rightarrow$ Higher C.
   5. The level of interest rates, R_F: Higher $R_F \rightarrow$ Higher C.
   6. The income earned on the optioned asset, I: Higher $I \rightarrow$ Lower C.

   The **Black-Scholes** model is used to value marketable call options on financial assets that don't pay a current return.

6. **Describe interest rate and currency swaps and explain how they are used.**

   Interest rate swaps are the fastest-growing financial technique for altering the interest rate obligations of a firm. Interest rate swaps involve two parties that wish to alter the interest rate they pay on a fixed amount of notional principal. **Currency swaps** permit firms to borrow foreign currencies to be paid back at an agreed-upon foreign exchange rate.

FUTURES AND SPOT PRICES	SELF-TEST PROBLEMS

ST-16-1

You have purchased a one-year futures contract for a $100,000 ten-year Treasury bond at a price of 100% of par, 100 0/32 nds. The Treasury bond has a yield of 6.00%. You can borrow funds for one year at a rate of 3.5%. Will the spot price of a similar ten-year bond be higher or lower than the future's price? By how much?

Answer on page 484.

OPTION PAYOFF AND VALUE

ST-16-2

You purchased a put option for 100 shares of Cycle, Inc. The option exercise price is $45.00. The purchase price of the option was $4.50 per share. The price of Cycle stock has fallen to $42.00 per share. The option has 60 days left until expiration and sells for $6.00 per share.

1. What is the payoff on this option, assuming it is maturing today (and cannot be sold) instead of 60 days from now?
2. What is the intrinsic and time value for this option?
3. What is the gain or loss on this option transaction, assuming you sell it today for $6.00?

Answer on page 484.

Answer on page 484.

PROBLEMS | **MARGIN AND VALUE OF A FUTURES CONTRACT**

16-1

On January 14, Franklin Bank bought the March Treasury bond futures contract with a $100,000 par value at a closing price of 82 17/32 nds., which also turned out to be the settlement price that day. The next day, the opening price rose to 83, and later in the day the price fluctuated, reaching a high of 83 16/32 nds. and eventually closing at a settlement price of 83 10/32 nds. The account is marked-to-market.

a. Show the contract value changes during the trading day (open, high, and close).
b. How much is credited to the bank's margin account?

FUTURES BASIS

16-2

A futures contract on Treasury bonds is available. The current yield on T-bonds is 9.8%. The repo rate that can be used to finance bonds is 5.9%. Based on this information, will the basis between the futures contract price and the spot or cash price for T-bonds be positive or negative? Give a reason for your answer.

FUTURES BASIS

16-3

The cash price of gold is $300 per ounce. The cost of safe storage and insurance is $5 per ounce, and the cost of financing the gold is $10 per ounce. The futures price should be close to what price?

FUTURES MARKET HEDGE

16-4

You work for a commercial bank. The bank has committed to underwrite a two-year term loan of $5 million for a business. In 60 days, $3 million of the loan will be sold to a participating commercial bank investor at the then-prevailing rate which is based on the two-year T-note rate. A hedge can be accomplished by selling two-year T-note futures contracts at a price of 100 8/32 nds.

After 60 days, interest rates have risen and the futures contract has fallen to a price of 98 0/32 nds. The term loan is sold for a price of 97.5% of par value. What was the gain or loss on the hedge compared to the cash sale of the loan? (Disregard commissions and other transaction costs.)

INTRINSIC AND TIME VALUE OF AN OPTION

16-5

You pay $4 for a call option on common stock with a $40 exercise price. What is the intrinsic and time value of this option if the stock sells for $41?

PUT OPTION PAYOFF

16-6

You pay $5.50 for a put option on common stock with an exercise price of $56. The stock's price on expiration date is $51. Disregarding commissions, what is your net profit or loss?

CALL OPTION PAYOFF

16-7

You pay $6.25 for a call option on a common stock with an exercise price of $105.00. The stock sells for $108.00 on expiration date. Disregarding commissions, what is your net profit or loss?

BLACK-SCHOLES OPTION VALUATION

16-8

A call option on Morgan Corporation common stock is available. The stock sells for $40 per share. It pays no dividend. The option has a nine-month exercise period. The call exercise price is $43 per share. Treasury yields are 4%. The option is available at a price of $4.90.

A security firm estimates the standard deviation of the return on Morgan's stock to be .35. You have completed an analysis of the economic environment and the business activities of Morgan. Both suggest greater uncertainty in the earnings prospects of the company in the period ahead as compared to the past. As a result, you estimate the standard deviation of the return to be .55.

Use the Black-Scholes model to estimate the value of the option at a standard deviation of .35 and .55. Do you think the current price of the option is too high or low? Use Table 16.7 as a guide.

SWAP CASH FLOW POSITION

16-9

Assume that you are a swap dealer. You have just acted as a counterparty in an interest rate swap between two firms. The notional principal for the swap is $10 million. You are obligated to make three annual interest payments to your counterparty at a rate of 6.5%. The floating rate paid by the other party is currently set at 8%. If interest rates don't change in the next year, what will be your net cash flow for the year?

SELF-TEST PROBLEM | **SOLUTIONS**

ST-16-1

Solution:
Since it is possible to borrow at 3.5% and reinvest in a $100,000 ten-year Treasury and sell it in the futures market a year from now, the futures price will have to be below the spot price in order to eliminate any chance of an arbitrage profit. Therefore, the spot price will be above the future's price. The profit will be (6.00% − 3.50%) = 2.5% if the spot and futures prices are equal. However, to eliminate this profit the futures price should be 2.5% below the spot price.

Futures price = Spot cash market price + Cost of carry of the cash asset − Return on holding the cash asset

Futures price = 100 0/32 nd = Spot cash market price + .035 × $100,000 − .06 × $100,000

Futures price = 100 0/32 nd + $3,500 − $6,000 = <u>97 16/32 nds</u>.

ST-16-2

Solution:
1. The payoff, assuming it matures today, would be: Option exercise price − Stock price ($0 if this is negative) − Option premium = $45 − $42 − $4.50 = <u>−$1.50</u>
2. Intrinsic value: Option exercise price − Stock price ($0 if this difference is negative) = $45 − $42 = $3.00. Time value = Market price − Intrinsic value = $6.00 − $3.00 = <u>$3.00</u>.
3. Gain or loss is: Selling price − Purchase premium = $6.00 − $4.50 = <u>$1.50 gain</u>.

PROJECT 16.1

DRAFTING AN OPTION

Draft a hypothetical call option on ten acres of land. What are the most important provisions you have included? Will you permit your option to be bought and sold? What impact does this have on its value?

C A S E   1 6 . 1

THE HOT NEW ACCOUNT

Southland Federal Savings Bank is an aggressive newly chartered federal savings bank located in the competitive Southern California market. Chartered in 1982, the bank had grown to $154 million in a single location. Its growth was fueled by fairly high rates paid in their single location, as well as the use of brokered deposits.

In 1995, Southland opened a new office in a very competitive and high-income section of their primary standard metropolitan statistical area. In order to promote the new office, the president, Mr. Green, asked the marketing group to come up with some new ideas.

In March, several months before the office opened for business, Bob Stanley requested a meeting with Mr. Green. Bob was the head of marketing and branch operations. He indicated that he had a great idea for a new account.

The next week at the meeting, Bob briefed Mr. Green on the new account concept. He even provided a sample of the ad copy that would be used to promote the account (See Exhibit C16.1). Bob was very excited with the concept. He indicated that none of the competition were offering anything like it. Moreover, focus group interviews indicated that savers considered the idea a great one. They received overwhelming support from the groups that looked at the new product.

Here is how the account was explained to Mr. Green. The account could be opened for as little as $2,500. The initial term would be nine months. The saver could add to the account any time in the first nine months up to a $50,000 total balance. The saver would still earn the rate that prevailed at the time the account was opened.

The account had another special feature. At the end of nine months, the account could be renewed at the same rate that prevailed at the time it was opened. If, however, interest rates were to rise, the account would earn the higher rate at renewal time. Or the saver could close the account.

The first question Mr. Green asked was what the current Treasury bill rates were for comparable 9- and 18-month securities. He was given the information shown in Table C16.1. He was also told that Treasury securities with a 7.75% coupon maturing in 9 months were selling at 100 28/32 and maturing in 18 months at 101 4/32.

Sample Ad Copy for Southland's New Account

> Southland Federal Savings Bank
> 7.75% Actual
> 8.13% Effective
>
> Open a minimum $2,500 account with a
> nine-month initial maturity. Add at any
> time to a maximum of $50,000.
> At maturity, the account can be renewed
> for another nine months at 7.75%, or higher
> if rates rise. If rates fall, continue to earn
> 7.75%. You can't lose with Southland's
> "Competition Beater."

At this point in the meeting, Mr. Green called you in to answer several questions:

1. Does this account have any options embedded in it? Describe the option(s) as put or call. Describe the option(s) as clearly and carefully as possible.

2. If there are any options, are they American or European type? Describe the option(s) as in-the-money or out-of-the-money.

3. Given the pricing recommendation for this account, does the institution seem to be pricing the account profitably? Why or why not?

4. Based solely on the information provided here, would you offer this program? Why or why not?

TABLE 16.1

Prevailing Treasury Bill Rates

9-month bill	6.54%
18-month bill	7.05%

CASE 16.2

THE "FUND KILLER": COMPETING AGAINST MUTUAL FUNDS

The bull market in common stock equities was raging in late 1995. Many holders of bank and thrift low-yielding certificates of deposit were being enticed into equity-based mutual funds. Indeed, many of the larger-sized commercial bank holding companies and stock-owned thrift holding companies had established retail broker-dealers to offer mutual funds to their customers.

Martin, a financial analyst at Bloomington State Bank was asked to attend a meeting of the bank's retail banking group. The subject was a new account proposal, code named *Fund Killer*. The account was aimed directly at common stock mutual funds.

Juanita, the bank's vice-president for retail savings, opened the meeting by distributing Exhibit C16.2, a preliminary fact sheet of the major attributes of the new account.

Martin listened carefully to the presentation. It took a few minutes for him to understand exactly what the financial attributes of this account really were. On the surface, it seemed to him that such an account could be popular—earning a stock-market return when stock prices rise in an account that guarantees no loss of principal.

EXHIBIT C16.2

Fund Killer Fact Sheet

1. *Minimum account:* The minimum balance for a new account is $5,000.
2. *Term:* The term of the account is one year.
3. *Guaranteed interest return:* The account would pay a guaranteed zero interest rate.
4. *Stock-indexed return:* Any return on the account would be based on the change in the Standard & Poor's 500 Composite Stock Index (S&P 500). A return would be paid on the account only if the S&P 500 went up over the account holding period. The computation of the return would be determined as follows:
   - The initial value for the S&P 500 would be set at the closing daily value of the S&P 500 on the last business day of the month in which the account was opened.
   - The final value for the S&P 500 would be set at the closing daily value of the S&P 500 for the last day of the month in which the account experiences its one-year anniversary.
   - The return on the account would be computed as: [(Final value – Initial value)/Initial value].
   - A return would be paid only if the S&P 500 went up in value. If the return computed above were negative, the account would earn a zero return.
5. *Principal preservation:* If the S&P 500 were to fall in value, the return on the account would be zero. No loss of principal would be possible.
6. *Example:* A $10,000 account is opened on March 24, 1995. The S&P 500 value is 423 on the last day of March 1995. The S&P 500 index rises to 465 on the last business day of March 1996. The return paid on this account would be: [465 – 423)/423] = 9.929%.

Martin began writing down a list of questions that would have to be answered before he could provide useful input on this proposal:

1. Does this account have a option characteristic? If so what is it?

2. The example shown in the fact sheet (Exhibit C16.2) shows a return of almost 10%. Bloomingfield is currently paying only 5% on one-year accounts. The way the return is calculated in this account appears too generous. What market prices can be reviewed to determine the value of this type of computed return to the depositor?

3. If senior management were to want to hedge an account tied to the S&P 500, how would the firm go about doing so? Are their any financial derivative contracts that would allow the firm to hedge the cost of this certificate? How much would the hedge cost?

CHAPTER 17

*M*easuring Interest Rate Risk

Learning Goals

After studying this chapter, you should be able to:

1. Define interest rate risk in terms of the market value of assets and liabilities, the income statement, and off-balance sheet assets and liabilities and explain how it is measured.
2. Describe the periodic *GAP* and show how it is used and calculated.
3. Describe duration, duration *GAP,* the interest rate elasticity, *E,* and the elasticity of the market value of equity, *MVE.*
4. Describe mark-to-market and explain how it is used to assess the interest rate risk of a financial firm.
5. Explain the use of income simulations in assessing the impact of interest rate risk on financial firms.

Interest rate risk relates to the impact that changes in interest rates have on the market value of an institution's assets, liabilities, and income stream. Although financial institutions have alway carried interest rate risk, the potential severity of this risk became quite clear during the period of record high interest rates in the late 1970s and early 1980s. Virtually all savings and loans became insolvent if they had sold their assets at market value and paid off their liabilities; and most experienced substantial operating losses regardless. Without regulatory forbearance, now considered most unfortunate, the government would have taken over most savings and loans by 1983 or else forced these institutions to increase their capital base.[1]

This experience resulted in major efforts to improve interest rate risk management measurement tools and develop new risk management strategies. In addition, financial regulators began requiring savings and loans to provide interest rate risk reports.

---

[1] Some S&Ls were taken over by commercial bank holding companies in the early 1980s. The number of S&Ls purchased by commercial banks or bank holding companies would have been much higher if regulations had permitted such acquisitions. Another limitation that reduced the number of acquisitions by commercial banks was the restrictions on interstate branching.

This chapter explains how to use the three primary interest rate risk management tools: periodic *GAP*, duration, and mark-to-market. Each provides a somewhat different view of a firm's interest rate risk position. This chapter also provides some income simulation tools, for measuring the impact of changes in interest rates on a firm's accounting income statements and balance sheets.

Defining Interest Rate Risk

Interest rate risk relates to the changes in market value and interest revenue and costs of the assets of the firm in relation to its liabilities caused by changes in market interest rates. It is important to keep in mind these two dimensions of interest rate risk. The first, and financially most important dimension, relates to changes in market values of the firm's assets and liabilities. Depending on the asset and liability structures management selects, changes in market interest rates will affect the market values of these financial assets. If changes in market interest rates cause the firm's asset values to rise (fall) and this rise (fall) is perfectly offset by a rise (fall) in the market value of the firm's liabilities, then the firm is said to have no interest rate risk exposure. For this reason, a mutual fund bears no interest rate risk. Changes in a mutual fund's asset values are perfectly offset by changes in the fund's outstanding shares. This is not true for a depository institution. In this case, the firm's assets are likely to experience changes in market value that are not perfectly offset by changes in the firm's liability values. Consequently, these firms are typically concerned about interest rate risk.

The second dimension of interest rate risk relates to the firm's income stream. One aspect of interest rate risk is that a firm with high interest rate risk will rarely have a stable relationship between its interest revenues and costs. If a firm has long-term fixed rate assets financed with short-term liabilities, a rise in open market interest rates will cause the firm's interest costs to rise relative to its interest revenue. This situation is simply another consequence of the presence of interest rate risk. However, unless changes in market values of both assets and liabilities are immediately reflected on the income statement, the impact of interest rate risk will typically lag behind changes in market rates. This situation is being reduced as firms are forced to adopt mark-to-market accounting methodologies, which will be discussed later in this chapter.

AN EXAMPLE OF INTEREST RATE RISK

The concept of interest rate risk is presented in Table 17.1, which shows the balance sheet for a hypothetical financial intermediary, High-Risk Federal. This intermediary invests in long-term U.S. Treasury bonds and finances these bonds with short-term one-year liabilities and equity. It maintains a ratio of 5% equity to total assets.

At the time this balance sheet was developed, the yield on the bonds when they were purchased and the current market yield on the bonds were both at 10%.

Thus, the market value of the bonds was equal to the book value of the bonds. Consequently, the firm could liquidate its bond holdings at its book value and experience no gain or loss on the transaction, except transaction costs.

The liabilities also carry a current market yield that is equal to the market yield when the liabilities were issued, enabling the firm, in theory, to repurchase its liabilities in the secondary market at its book value, effectively paying off these liabilities. Again, there would be no gain or loss from this transaction, save that associated with transaction costs.

TABLE 17.1

Balance Sheet for High-Risk Federal
(dollars in millions)

Asset	Assets				Liability	Liabilities			
	Market Yield When Purchased	Current Market Value	Book Value	Market Value		Market Yield When Issued	Current Market Value	Book Value	Market Value
Ten-year T-bonds	10.0%	10.0%	$100	$100	One-year marketable paper	7.0%	7.0%	$ 95	$ 95
					Equity			5	5
Total			$100	$100	Total			$100	$100

To see how interest rate risk manifests itself, let's consider the following. The day after this balance sheet was developed, the management of High-Risk Federal woke up to find that interest rates had risen 4% over the entire term structure of interest rates. The term structure rose 4% in a parallel move. The yield for one-year liabilities rose to 11% from 7%, while the yield on Treasury bonds rose to 14% from 10%.

Table 17.2 shows the balance sheet of High-Risk Federal with the market rates and market values of its assets and liabilities updated to reflect the higher market interest rates.

Here, the current market values for the firm's ten-year Treasury bond assets and its one-year liabilities are compared to their old market values. The result is shocking. The value of the assets deteriorated by over 21% to the new market value of $78.81 million. This sharp decline in market value was due to the fact that these assets were long term and fixed rate. The liabilities, on the other hand, were short term in maturity. They declined in value by only a little over 3.5%. The 7% coupon one-year liabilities actually had a market value of 97.64% (92.76/95.00) of their original par value. Because High-Risk Federal took a considerable risk by purchasing long-term fixed-rate assets with short-term liabilities, the intermediary would be bankrupt if it were liquidated. Its assets would be sold for $78.81 and its liabilities would be paid off at $92.76. High-Risk Federal's shareholder's equity would be −$13.95.

TABLE 17.2

Balance Sheet for High-Risk Federal Adjusted for Rise in Open Market Interest Rates
(dollars in millions)

	Assets					Liabilities			
Asset	Market Yield When Purchased	Current Market Value	Book Value	Market Value	Liability	Market Yield When Issued	Current Market Value	Book Value	Market Value
Ten-year T-bonds	10.0%	14.0%	$100	$78.81	One-year marketable paper	7.0%	11.0%	$ 95	$92.76
					Equity			5	-13.95
Total			$100	$78.81	Total			$100	$78.81

High-Risk Federal does not have to liquidate its assets and liabilities or show an operating loss, even though it is effectively insolvent. Why? Because under GAAP, as long as High-Risk Federal intends to hold these assets until maturity, it is not obligated to value them at their new lower market value. Moreover, there will be no impact of this rise in open market interest rates on High-Risk Federal's income statement until its one-year liabilities come due. This is because, for accounting purposes, High-Risk Federal will still be earning interest on its assets at 10% and paying 7% for its liabilities. However, after a year, if interest rate levels remain at the new higher level, High-Risk Federal will have to replace the 7% liabilities with 11% liabilities and experience a large negative spread between its asset and liability yields.

This example dramatically shows the impact of interest rate risk on the viability of a financial intermediary. In the late 1970s and early 1980s, savings and loans had long-term assets and short-term liabilities that created losses as significant as those for High-Risk Federal.

INTEREST RATE RISK IS A PORTFOLIO CONCEPT

In controlling interest rate risk, managers must recognize that interest rate risk involves analysis of the firm's entire portfolio of assets and liabilities. Except in a few circumstances, it is virtually impossible for a financial firm to manage interest rate risk by acquiring assets that have the same cash flow characteristics as their liabilities. The exceptions are mutual funds, real estate investment trusts, and limited partnerships. Most intermediaries also have many assets—mortgages are one example—that have embedded options that cannot be offset with liabilities with comparable characteristics. This is why all the tools used for interest rate risk management involve analysis of the entire portfolio. The interest rate risk position of the firm requires measurements based on the entire profile of assets and liabilities in order to understand their interaction.

Considering how off-balance sheet assets and liabilities affect the interest rate risk of the firm is also important. A commercial bank with a large mortgage-servicing portfolio reflected off the balance sheet must include those servicing contracts in its interest rate risk measurement analysis. This is also important for firms that have large outstanding financial commitments to buy or sell loans or securities.

✓ Checkpoints

17-1   What is interest rate risk?

17-2   How is interest rate risk a portfolio concept?

Periodic GAP

The **periodic** *GAP* is the simplest and most easily understood of all the interest rate risk management measurement tools available to financial institutions. The periodic *GAP* is defined as the dollar volume of assets that mature or reprice during period *t*, less the dollar volume of liabilities maturing or repricing during period *t*. This tool is widely used because of its simplicity.

The concept of periodic *GAP* is straightforward. It measures the potential that a change in interest rates will have a proportionately larger or smaller impact on the market value of the assets and interest revenue of the firm than it will on the firm's market value of liabilities and interest costs. A firm has a positive (negative) periodic *GAP* if it has a greater (smaller) dollar amount of assets maturing or repricing than it has liabilities maturing or repricing within period *t*. If interest rates rise, a firm with a positive (negative) periodic *GAP* can be expected to experience a rising (declining) net interest margin. The opposite will occur if interest rates decline.

The periodic *GAP*, GAP_t, of period *t* is shown in Equation 17.1. Here, RPA_t is the quantity of the firm's assets that will mature or reprice during the period from the present until period *t*, and RPL_t is the quantity of liabilities that will reprice or mature during the same period.

$$\text{Periodic } GAP_t = RPA_t - RPL_t \qquad [17.1]$$

The periodic *GAP* can be calculated for any period *t*. This is why it is referred to as the periodic *GAP*. *GAP*s can be calculated as a one-year *GAP*, a three-year *GAP*, or any other period one chooses. They are also calculated for interim periods, such as between 90 and 180 days. Periodic *GAP*s help determine both short-term and long-term exposures to interest rate risks. The length of the chosen period is determined by selecting those periods over which a high percentage of the firm's assets and liabilities will mature or reprice. A ten-year *GAP* report, for example, is of little value for a firm that has 95% of its assets and liabilities maturing in two years. Management uses its knowledge about bunching maturities or repricing assets and liabilities to select the most useful periods for constructing *GAP* reports.

AN EXAMPLE OF A PERIODIC *GAP* REPORT

Table 17.3 shows the balance sheet for a small commercial bank. Assets and liabilities are shown with information about when they mature or reprice.

Given this balance sheet, those assets and liabilities that will mature or reprice within the period chosen for the *GAP* report must be identified. Consider a one-year *GAP*, GAP_1. To create this report, those assets that will mature or reprice within one year must be identified. For assets such as mortgages, it is necessary to estimate the percentage that will prepay during the year. For liabilities, such as NOW accounts and passbook accounts, it is necessary to determine whether the bank will treat them like a fixed-rate account or a repriced account. This will depend on the experience of the bank. Many banks do not frequently change interest rates paid on most transaction accounts, despite changes in open market rates. They may, therefore, use an estimated maturity of two or three years for some of these accounts. If these accounts are treated as fixed rate, then it is necessary to determine the percentage that would be lost if open market rates increased significantly.

TABLE 17.3

Balance Sheet First National Bank of St. George
(dollars in millions)

Assets		Liabilities	
Cash and due from banks + short-term liquid asset (less than 6 months)	$ 1	Demand deposits	$ 3
Government and agencies (more than 1 year)	12	Money market demand deposits	12
Reverse repo agreements (less than 1 month)	1	Passbook accounts	12
Auto loans (initial maturity 48 months)	54	CDs	
		less than 3 months	34
		3–6 months	38
		6–12 months	40
		over 12 months	20
Fixed-rate mortgages (initial maturity 30 years)	50	Federal Home Loan Bank borrowing (maturity 5 years)	70
Adjustable-rate mortgages (index 1-year Treasury)	87	Capital note (maturity 7 years)	10
Loans tied to prime	51	Capital accounts	32
Credit card receivables	15		
Total	$271	Total	$271

Table 17.4 shows the schedule for repriced assets RPA_1. The assets have been divided into two groups. One group consists of those assets in which the analyst can make an accurate forecast of the percentage that will reprice or mature during the one-year period. The second group are those assets that require a forecast or estimate concerning their expected maturities. Table 17.5 shows a comparable schedule for repriced and maturing liabilities, RPL_1.

TABLE 17.4

Maturing or Repriced Assets
Within One Year, RPA_1 First National Bank of St. George
(dollars in millions)

No Estimation of Repricing or Maturity is Necessary:	
Cash and due plus short-term liquidity	$ 1.0
Loans tied to prime	51.0
Reverse repurchase agreements	1.0
Credit card receivables	15.0
Adjustable-rate mortgages	87.0
Assets in Which Estimation of Repricing or Maturity is Necessary:	
Auto loans (assume 20% maturity in first year)	10.8
Fixed-rate mortgages (assume 12% prepay in first year)	6.0
Total RPA_1	$171.8

TABLE 17.5

Maturing or Repricing Liabilities
Within One Year, RPL_1 First National Bank of St. George
(dollars in millions)

Liabilities in Which No Estimation Is Necessary:	
CDs less than one year	$112.00
Money market demand deposits	12.00
Liabilities in Which Estimation Is Necessary:	
Passbook accounts plus demand deposits (assume 15% loss)	2.25
Total RPL_1	$126.25

In the case of Table 17.4, it was necessary to estimate the percentage of auto loans and fixed-rate mortgages that would prepay in one year. The analyst used an estimate of 20% of the principal balances for the auto loans and 12% for the mortgages based on past experience of the bank. Table 17.5 makes estimates for the potential loss of passbook and demand deposits during the one-year period. The estimates assume that these accounts would not be repriced and that a certain percentage would be lost to competitors over the period. The estimate of deposit loss is 15% for the one year.

The resulting one-year *GAP* is shown in Table 17.6; the firm has a positive GAP_1 of $45.55 million. This simply means that during the next 12 months the firm can expect that $45.55 million more in assets will reprice or mature than liabilities. If everything except market interest rates is held constant, this firm can be expected to improve its net interest margin if open market rates rise and to reduce its net interest margin if open market rates fall over the next 12-month period if its size is unchanged. A positive *GAP* will improve the firm's net interest margin during a period of rising interest rates because more lower-rate assets will be replaced by current higher-rate assets than will lower-rate liabilities be replaced by current higher-rate liabilities.

TABLE 17.6

One-Year Periodic GAP_1 First National Bank of St. George
(dollars in millions)

Total repriced assets (RPA_1)	$171.80
Total repriced liabilities (RPL_1)	126.25
One-year periodic $GAP = (RPA_1 - RPL_1) =$	$ 45.55

Another way to express the GAP_t is as a percentage of the firm's total assets at $t = 0$. This quantity, called the GAP_t *percentage*, scales the measure to standardize for asset size and permits the GAP_t of one firm to be compared over time with itself and with other peer group competitors. This expression is shown in Equation 17.2.

$$GAP_t \ percentage = GAP_t/Total \ financial \ assets_t$$

$$= \$45.55/\$271.00 = 16.81\% \hspace{2cm} [17.2]$$

Another similar measure is to take the ratio of RPA_t to RPL_t, as shown in Equation 17.3. This is called the *GAP ratio*.

$$GAP \ ratio = RPA_t/RPL_t$$

$$= \$171.8/\$126.25 = 1.36 \hspace{2cm} [17.3]$$

The *GAP* ratio is another measure that permits the firm to make comparisons with itself over time and with other firms.

GAP BUCKETS

Periodic *GAP* statistics are also computed for interim periods. Consider the *GAP* report shown in Table 17.7. This report was developed for assets and liabilities that mature between several periods up to 365 days. These interim periods, t and $t + 1$, are sometimes referred to as *GAP buckets*.

The analyst can use a *GAP* report divided into buckets to identify specific periods in which changes in the firm's asset and liability structure may be needed in order to reduce interest rate risk.

LIMITATIONS OF GAP REPORTS

Periodic *GAP* reports have some important limitations, which stem from the fact that *GAP* reports are computed at a point in time and cannot properly account for uncertain cash flows and for the repricing limitations of certain assets and liabilities. The following are some of the limitations of *GAP* reports.

	TABLE 17.7			
	GAP Bucket Report			
	Period of Maturity or Repricing			
	0–90 Days	91–180 Days	181–365 Days	365+ Days
Assets maturing or repricing ($RPA_{t+1,t+2}$)	121	72	62	255
Liabilties maturing or repricing ($RPL_{t+1,t+2}$)	132	93	52	232
$GAP_{t+1,t+2}$	−11	−21	+10	+23

Repricing or Maturity Bunching

The GAP_t report only shows the relationship of repricing assets and liabilities during the period *t*. It does not show the interest rate position of the firm after period *t* or between two periods. This creates a problem when a firm has a large volume of assets or liabilities repricing or maturing during a period between two *GAP* periods, $GAP_{t+1,t+2}$. The periodic *GAP* report will not disclose the bunching of asset or liability maturities or repricings. Although the analyst producing the *GAP* report is probably aware of these bunching problems, this is still a limitation of the methodology.

Estimates of Cash Flows

The *GAP* report is only as good as the analyst's estimates of asset and liability cash flows. It is very likely that some of the assets and liabilities that reprice have prepayment options embedded in them. This is true with mortgages, for example. This means that the *GAP* report must rely on estimates of the percentage of mortgage principal that will repay during period *t*.

Another problem concerns assets whose repricing is discretionary. Some assets that may be repriced under the terms of the claim contract are rarely repriced, even during periods of interest rate volatility. Credit card receivables, for example, can be repriced within a short period of time, but they are rarely repriced in practice—even if market rates change by moderate amounts. Other examples are passbook accounts at commercial banks and thrifts and interest-paying negotiable order of withdrawal (NOW) accounts. The rates on these accounts are rarely changed. This means the analyst is left with the task of making assumptions about whether these assets are in practice more like adjustable-rate or fixed-rate assets. The analyst must then calculate the *GAP* statement by incorporating these assumptions.

Rate-Indexed Assets and Liabilities

Another limitation of the *GAP* report relates to the fact that when rate-indexed assets and liabilities reprice, there may be caps or other limitations on the magnitude of the adjustment. This usually occurs when the asset includes an **interest rate cap,** a contractual limit on the maximum level of the interest rate on an adjustable interest rate financial claim. These caps are found in many adjustable-rate mortgages, for example. Consequently, a firm with many capped adjustable-rate mortgages will appear from the *GAP* report to have a low interest rate risk exposure even though the assets facing upward adjustments are constrained by the cap.

Income Statement

Another limitation of the *GAP* report is that there is no stable mathematical relationship between the firm's *GAP* and its profitability. While it is possible to say that a firm with a positive *GAP* should perform better in a rising interest rate environment than in a declining rate environment, it is difficult to determine the extent of the income variation.

Off-Balance Sheet Risks

GAP reports usually do not disclose the interest rate risks related to off-balance sheet claims and commitments. Firms with large off-balance sheet investments in loan servicing contracts, for example, do not reflect the risks of prepayment of these assets. The interest rate risks related to options granted by an institution in the form of loan commitments and forward loan sales are also not reflected. These risks must, therefore, be incorporated in other ways into the overall risk assessment of the institution.

WHAT IS THE RIGHT PERIODIC *GAP*?

The computation of the periodic *GAP* is relatively easy. Determining the right *GAP* for a financial institution is far more difficult. If assets and liabilities did not have complications, such as embedded options, then the simple answer would be to have a zero *GAP*. This would be the right strategy for the interest rate risk averse institution. Such a firm might subscribe to the theory that predicting interest rates is impossible. After all, there is little evidence that forecasters are able to systematically forecast interest rates. For these firms, minimizing interest rate risk might be a sound strategy.

Unfortunately, for a firm desiring to minimize interest rate risk, a zero *GAP* is too simplistic an approach. Special risks such as assets with prepayment options, interest caps, and off-balance sheet assets and liabilities that create interest rate risk must be considered. Additional analyses may dictate a move to a positive or negative *GAP*.

Other firms rely on interest rate forecasts to adjust their interest rate risk position. These firms seek a positive *GAP* when interest rates are expected to rise and a negative *GAP* when rates appear headed lower. Still others believe that the term structure is more likely to be upward sloping or normal most of the time due to the liquidity preferences embedded in the term structure. These firms will desire to have a slight negative *GAP* most of the time.

GAP AND FORECASTING BUSINESS CYCLES

The financial institutions that are willing to expose themselves to additional levels of interest rate risk generally use interest rate forecasts based on the business cycle. These firms feel they can predict interest rates according to major turns in the business cycle. They believe that short-term interest rates are likely to rise in the middle to late stages of a cyclical recovery and fall during the middle to late stages of a recession. If they feel strongly about their forecast, then they would position the firm to have a positive *GAP* in the middle stages of a recovery and a negative *GAP* at the middle stage of recession. Table 17.8 shows how the firm that is willing to take interest rate risk over the business cycle might choose to position itself.

TABLE 17.8

Periodic *GAP* Position during Business Cycle

Stage of Business Cycle	Expected Change in Rates	GAP Position
Middle stage of recession	Fall	Negative
Late stage of recession	?	Close to zero
Middle stage of recovery	Rise	Positive
Late stage of recovery with accelerating inflation	?	Close to zero

✓ Checkpoints

17-3 What is periodic *GAP*, and what is(are) the appropriate *GAP* period(s) *t*?

17-4 Why are cash flow estimations so important in *GAP* reports, and what types of assets and liabilities have difficult-to-estimate cash flows?

17-5 Which is riskier from an interest rate risk perspective, a positive one-year *GAP* percentage of 23% or a negative one-year *GAP* percentage of −23%?

17-6 What are some of the major limitations of *GAP* reports?

17-7 Should a financial firm manage its *GAP* based on an interest rate forecast? Why or why not?

Duration

Unlike *GAP*, **duration** is a financial concept that has been around for a long time. The concept was developed by Frederick Macaulay in a volume published by the National Bureau of Economic Research in 1938. Still, it did not find a wide audience in the financial literature and among practitioners until quite recently. One reason is that powerful computers are required to compute duration statistics. The emergence of powerful personal computers in the last decade has resolved this problem.

Duration is defined as the weighted average period of time over which the cash flows of an investment are expected to be realized. The weights used in duration are equal to the ratio of the present value of the cash flows received to the present value of all the cash flows. The discount rate used for all the cash flows is the market interest rate.[2] The weights for the early cash flows for an annuity will be higher for the early payments than the later payments since their discounted value is higher. Duration is used as an alternative measure of the maturity of an investment. It has some superior attributes, since it takes into consideration the timing and amount of cash flows received before the last payment of principal, as in the case of a typical bond. In the case of high-coupon bonds, mortgages, installment loans, and annuities where the cash flows in early periods are usually substantial, the financial claim's duration is shorter than the claim's stated maturity.

Duration can be used to compare the cash flow profiles of a financial firm's assets and liabilities. The closer the weighted-average duration of the firm's assets is compared to its liabilities, the lower the interest rate risk of the firm.

CALCULATING DURATION

The formula for duration, *DUR,* is shown in Equation 17.4. It is the product of two summations. In the numerator, the sum of the discounted cash flows is calculated from any particular investment weighted by the period in which they are received. The discount rate in duration is the market interest rate, r. The first periodic cash flow, C_1, is weighted by the period it arrives, namely, $t = 1$. The last cash flow, C_n, is weighted by the period it arrives, $t = n$. From this, it is easy to see that for two equal cash flows stemming from an investment, the one that arrives latest will have the more significant impact on the numerator of the duration equation. Late cash flows tend to increase the duration statistic. For this reason, a 10%, ten-year interest-paying bond will have a much longer duration than a 10% fully amortizing loan. This is because the principal cash flows on the bond arrive later.

The denominator of the duration formula is simply the present value of the investment's cash flows discounted at the market interest rate, r. The numerator is the time-weighted present value of the cash flows discounted at the same market rate.

$$DUR = [\Sigma_{t=1}^{n} \, C_t \times t \div (1 + r)^t] \, / \qquad\qquad [17.4]$$

$$[\Sigma_{t=1}^{n} \, C_t \div (1 + r)^t]$$

---

[2]The same discount rate is used for near-term cash flows and those received far in the future. In practice, short-term and long-term interest rates do not move in parallel, and short rates are more volatile than long rates. Still, the duration measure is hard to improve on.

where:

C_t = *Asset cash flow in period t*

r = *Periodic open-market interest rate (discount rate)*

n = *Number of periods the claim is outstanding.*

CALCULATING THE DURATION ON A COUPON BOND	**DEMONSTRATION PROBLEM**

Situation

Diane has been asked to calculate the duration of a three-year $1,000 principal bond with a coupon rate of 8%, calculated at an open market interest rate of 8%, paying semiannual interest.

Result

Diane notices that because the bond pays interest semiannually, six periods, $n = 6$, are used. Using Equation 17.4, she develops Equation 17.5:

$$DUR = \{[\$40 \times (1)/(1 + .04)^1 + \$40 \times (2)/(1 + .04)^2 + \$40 \times (3)/$$
$$(1 + .04)^3 + \$40 \times (4)/(1 + .04)^4 + \$40 \times (5)/(1 + .04)^5 + \$40 \times (6)/$$
$$(1 + 0.4)^6 + \$1000 \times (6)/(1 + 0.4)^6$$

divided by

$$[\$40/(1 + .04)^1 + \$40/(1 + .04)^2 + \$40/(1 + .04)^3 + \$40/(1 + .04)^4 +$$
$$\$40/(1 + .04)^5 + \$40/(1 + .04)^6 + \$1,000/(1 + .04)^6]\}$$

$$= 5.452 \text{ semiannual periods}$$

$$= 5.452/2 = 2.723 \text{ years.} \qquad [17.5]$$

Table 17.9 calculates each of the terms of Equation 17.4 for a bond with a ten-year maturity, a coupon rate of 5%, and a $1,000 principal balance. The market rate used is 8%. The table shows a duration of 7.697 years versus a stated maturity of ten years. Table 17.9 was developed using one of several commercially available software spreadsheets.

PROPERTIES OF THE DURATION MEASURE

The duration measure has certain interesting properties that make it a very useful tool for the financial manager. These properties of duration relate to maturity, coupon rate, and market rate.

TABLE 17.9

Duration Calculation
Ten-Year, 5.00% Semiannual Coupon, $1,000 Principal Bond
Market Rate = 8.00%

Period t	Cash Flow C_t	Present Value of Cash Flow Discounted at $r = 8\%$ $PVIFA_{4.00,\ t}$	Present Value of Cash Flow Times Period $t \times PVIFA_{4.00,\ t}$
1	$ 25	$ 24.038	$ 24.038
2	25	23.113	46.227
3	25	22.225	66.675
4	25	21.370	85.480
5	25	20.548	102.740
6	25	19.758	118.547
7	25	18.998	132.986
8	25	18.267	146.138
9	25	17.565	158.082
10	25	16.889	168.891
11	25	16.239	178.634
12	25	15.615	187.379
13	25	15.014	195.187
14	25	14.437	202.116
15	25	13.882	208.224
16	25	13.348	213.563
17	25	12.834	218.184
18	25	12.341	222.132
19	25	11.866	225.455
20	1,025	467.797	9,355.932
		Total $796.145	Total $12,256.614

Duration in half-year periods (t) = 12,256.614/796.145 = 15.39495 periods.

Duration in years (duration in half-years ÷ 2) = 15.39495/2 = 7.6974751 years.

Duration and Maturity

As a general rule, the relationship between a bond's duration and its stated maturity, assuming the bond has no sinking fund and is not a zero interest bond, is positive. An increase in maturity, if everything else is held constant, will increase the duration of a bond. Nevertheless, the duration will still be less than its stated maturity. The only exception is the case of a zero-coupon security, which has a duration equal to its maturity.

Duration and Market Interest Rates

The duration of a bond will decrease as market interest rates rise.

Duration and Coupon Rate

The duration of a bond will decrease as the coupon rate on the bond increases. This is because the higher coupon bond will generate larger cash flows in the early periods. As the coupon rate approaches zero, as in the case of a zero coupon bond, the duration approaches its stated maturity.

DURATION AND INTEREST RATE ELASTICITY

One measure of a financial asset's price behavior is the extent to which the price will be affected by a rise or fall in open market interest rates. This change in price, ΔP, of a financial debt claim in relation to a specified 1% change in the open market interest rate, r, is referred to as *interest rate elasticity*. The duration measure provides a reasonable approximation for establishing the interest rate elasticity of a bond.

Equation 17.6 provides the relationship between the change in the price of a debt claim and a given change in the interest rate.

$$\%\Delta P = -DUR \times [1\%\Delta r] \times [r/(1 + r)] \qquad [17.6]$$

where:

$$r = Market\ interest\ rate$$

$$P = Price\ of\ the\ claim$$

In this expression, Δr refers to the number of basis points change in the open market interest rate that equates to a 1% change in the base rate, r. A 1% change in the open market rate from a base rate of 8% would be 8 *bp* (.01 × 8%). Note that the relationship of $\%\Delta P$ to a positive change in market interest rates for a financial debt claim is negative, since $-DUR$ (a negative term) is multiplied by the term $1\%\Delta r$, which is positive. This is a normal relationship between a bond's value and a rise in market rates.[3] This equation can be converted into a measure of interest rate elasticity by dividing both sides by $1\%\Delta r$. This gives us Equation 17.7, which is our measure of elasticity, E.[4]

$$E = (\%\Delta P)/(1\%\Delta r)$$

$$= -DUR \times [r/(1 + r)] \qquad [17.7]$$

---

[3]A portfolio of assets with a weighted duration of four years should experience the same price change as a zero-coupon bond with a duration of four years.

[4]The relationship between interest rate and price change is calculated at a point on a curve. Thus, the elasticity measure is only accurate as a point estimate. For larger Δr, the approximation becomes less accurate. The difference between the linear approximation and true curvilinear relationship is referred to as *convexity*.

CALCULATING THE PRICE ELASTICITY OF A BOND USING DURATION

Situation

Diane would like to calculate the elasticity of the bond shown in Table 17.9. She will use Equation 17.7 to make this calculation.

Result

Using the equation results in Equation 17.8; notice that the duration Diane calculated is measured in the same time units as the interest rate. In the example, both are annual. The open market rate is 8%. A 1% change would be 8 basis points or .08%.

$$E = -7.697 \times [.08/1.08]$$

$$= -0.57\% \qquad\qquad\qquad [17.8]$$

Elasticity is interpreted as the percent change in the price of the bond for a given 1% change in open market interest rates. In this case, the initial open market discount rate equals 8.00%. A 1% change in this rate would be 8 basis points. Given an elasticity of −.57%, this 8 *bp* increase in open market rates would result in a .57% decrease in the value of the bond. If an investor held $1 million of market value of these bonds, the 8 *bp*, or 1% change, in open market rates would decrease the value of the bonds by (−.0057 × $1,000,000 =) −$5,700.

The relationship between the price change on a financial claim and changes in open market interest rates is not linear, as suggested by this equation. Thus, Equation 17.7 only gives an accurate estimate of the elasticity for very small changes in *r*. For these small changes in interest rates, it works quite well; but for large changes in *r*, the estimate is less satisfactory.

PORTFOLIO DURATIONS

Managers of financial firms interested in measuring interest rate risks are not particularly interested in the duration of a particular asset or liability, but rather in the duration of a portfolio of assets (DUR_A) and liabilities (DUR_L). Fortunately, the duration measure has a very convenient additive property. It is possible to calculate the duration of each asset or liability separately and then calculate the duration of a portfolio of assets or liabilities by computing the weighted average of the durations of each asset or liability. The weights are the percentage of the firm's total financial assets or liabilities represented by each asset or liability.

The firm's net worth is excluded from a duration analysis. Although net worth, either as retained earnings or newly issued equity, is a financing alternative for all financial firms, its duration is essentially infinite. For purposes of a duration analysis, however, it doesn't make sense to use infinity as the duration of net worth. In portfolio duration analysis, net worth is ignored and treated as a residual. It is the change in net worth that needs to be analyzed after changes in open market interest rates affect the value of the firm's assets and liabilities.

For example, Table 17.10 shows the weighted-average portfolio durations for a small life insurance company. The table shows the duration for each of its financial assets and liabilities. Then, a weighted-average duration is calculated using a weight representing the percentage that each financial asset and liability represents of the total financial assets and liabilities. The result of computing these weighted average portfolio durations is 5.67 years for assets, DUR_A, and 8.14 years for liabilities, DUR_L.

TABLE 17.10

Weighted-Average Portfolio Duration
Benefit Life Company of Cleveland

	Percent of Total Assets (1)	Duration Years (2)	Weighted Duration (1) × (2)
Financial Assets—$266.67 Million			
Cash and government < 1-year bonds	5%	.30	.015
1–2 years	4	1.20	.048
2–3	10	1.90	.190
3–5	12	3.00	.360
5–7	16	5.25	.840
7–10	15	6.30	.945
10–15	8	8.10	.648
15+	5	8.90	.445
Mortgages fixed rate (remaining maturity 20 years)	25	8.70	2.18
Weighted duration (DUR_A)	**100%**		**5.67**

	Percent of Total Liabilities (1)	Duration Years (2)	Weighted Duration (1) × (2)
Financial Liabilities—$200 Million			
Insurance reserves: Term life	22%	.40	.09
Insurance reserves: Whole life and annuity	63	10.70	6.74
Guaranteed investment contracts	15	8 .70	1.31
Weighted duration (DUR_L)	**100%**		**8.14**

Net worth: $66.67 million

USING DURATION *GAP* FOR INTEREST RATE RISK MANAGEMENT

Having reviewed the properties of duration, it is now appropriate to calculate it for specific financial claims as well as portfolios of assets and liabilities. This portfolio duration is used for analyzing a financial firm's interest rate risk position. With the estimates of portfolio durations for financial assets and liabilities, it is possible to calculate the duration *GAP*. This is a measure of the difference between the duration of the firm's financial assets less liabilities weighted by the percentage of financial assets financed by financial liabilities. The duration *GAP*, DUR_{GAP}, is defined as shown in Equation 17.9:

$$DUR_{GAP} = DUR_A - [(w_L) \times DUR_L] \qquad [17.9]$$

In the equation, w_L is defined as the decimal ratio of the dollar market value of financial assets divided by the dollar market value of financial liabilities financing those assets.[5] This is shown in Table 17.10 to be $200 million of financial liabilities divided by $266.67 million of financial assets of ($200/$266.67) = .75. The w_L weight is used to adjust for the fact that the volume of assets and liabilities affected by a change in market rates is rarely equal.

The estimate of the duration *GAP* for Benefit Life is shown in Equation 17.10.

$$DUR_{GAP} = 5.67 - [.75 \times 8.14] = -.44 \qquad [17.10]$$

A DUR_{GAP} of –.44 years is quite low (it is close to zero).[6] The firm, therefore, would experience little change in its market valuation as a result of a change in interest rates in the open market.[7] The negative duration *GAP* means that a rise in market rates would lead to a larger decline in the market value of the firm's liabilities than in the value of its assets. This condition would increase the value of equity of the firm.

Duration *GAP* can be used just like periodic *GAP* to measure the relative exposure of the firm to interest rate risk. In the case of DUR_{GAP}, however, a positive and negative DUR_{GAP} have the exact opposite interpretation compared to periodic *GAP*. Unlike periodic *GAP*, a positive DUR_{GAP} implies that the firm will be hurt by rising interest rates.

DURATION AND THE MARKET VALUE OF EQUITY

Earlier in the chapter, an elasticity measure using the duration statistic was developed. Since the portfolio duration *GAP* is a cumulative weighted-average measure of the asset and liability portfolio durations, then it follows that the elastic-

---

[5]This calculation should use the market values of financial assets and liabilities. For simplicity book values are used here. Usually the differences are not material.

[6]A portfolio of financial assets and liabilities whose duration *GAP* is zero when calculated at market values is said to be *immunized* or *duration matched*.

[7]The measurement and management of interest rate risk using duration *GAP* is a dynamic process. As time passes, the timing of the cash flows in the portfolio of any firm changes. The cash flows of existing assets shorten. This causes the duration of assets and liabilities to change even for a firm holding the same assets financed with the same liabilities. The changes in duration over time is known as *duration drift*. The analyst must be prepared to make duration calculations with some frequency to assess the degree of drift taking place.

ity of the duration *GAP* provides a measure of the sensitivity of the firm's equity to changes in interest rates. Changes in the equity account are the result of changes in the market value of assets less the market value of liabilities. This change is what the duration *GAP* measures when it is converted into an elasticity. This statistic provides another powerful tool for measuring a firm's interest rate risk exposure.

The equity or net worth account is the residual account on the balance sheet that is impacted by changes in the value of assets less liabilities. The statistic that estimates the change in market value of equity for a specified change in open market interest rates is called the *interest rate elasticity of the market value of equity, MVE*.

This approach to interest rate risk management assumes the following:

1. All the assets and liabilities are readily marketable.
2. Any changes in their respective values are accounted for immediately.
3. There is no corporate taxation.

Since none of these assumptions hold in the real world, the elasticity calculated from the duration *GAP* is used simply as an estimation procedure to provide a rough estimate of the impact of changes in interest rates on the residual market value of the firm. This analysis cannot, however, be used to simulate what occurs in the income statement or balance sheet under GAAP.

Another assumption related to the use of the duration *GAP* elasticity statistic is that when it is used, it is assumed that any change in interest rates is the same amount for interest rates of all maturities. This is known as a *parallel shift in the term structure*. From our study of the term structure, we know that a parallel shift in the term structure of interest rates is quite unlikely. However, the calculation of a portfolio duration normally incorporates the implicit assumption that interest rates over the entire term structure will rise uniformly by 1% from their base level.

Despite these limitations, the elasticity measure used to determine the percent change in the market value of equity is still a very useful interest rate risk measurement tool. Equation 17.11 shows the elasticity using the duration *GAP*, $E_{DUR\ GAP}$, calculated at an interest rate of 9%.

$$E_{DUR\ GAP} = -DUR_{GAP} \times [r/(1 + r)] = -(-.44) \times [r/(1 + r)]$$

$$= .44 \times [.09/(1 + .09)] = .44 \times [.08257] = .0363 \qquad [17.11]$$

Using this statistic, it is possible to calculate the percentage change in the market value of equity. A base interest rate of 9% is assumed. Then a rise in open market rates to 9.40% is simulated. The equation for the market value of equity is shown as *MVE* in Equation 17.12.

$$MVE = E_{DUR\ GAP} \times [\Delta(r) / (r)]$$

$$= .0363 \times [(9.40 - 9.00) / 9.00] = .0363 \times .0444$$

$$= .001612 \qquad [17.12]$$

If Benefit Life Company had financial assets of $266,670,000, a 40-basis-point instantaneous parallel increase in open market interest rates would increase the market value of equity by (.001612 × $266,670,000 =) $429,872. In the Benefit Life Company example, equity was $66,670,000. Consequently, this change in rates of plus 40 basis points would increase equity by only ($429,872/ $66,670,000 =) .645%. Recall that Benefit Life had a negative duration *GAP*. Thus, it should be anticipated that a rise in open market rates will increase equity.[8]

PROBLEMS AND LIMITATIONS IN CALCULATING DURATION

The duration calculation is not easy to handle without fairly powerful computers. Even with computers, however, the analyst must first precisely specify the cash flows of each asset or liability, which can be very difficult. Mortgages and installment loans have prepayment options, and many liabilities such as certificates of deposit and annuity life insurance reserves have early withdrawal options embedded in them. These make the cash flow estimation process very difficult.

Consequently, duration, like periodic *GAP*, must necessarily rely on approximations of cash flows that may turn out to be inaccurate. Duration also suffers from the limitation of not being able to capture the impact of many off-balance sheet transactions that impact interest rate risk. In this regard, it mirrors the limitations of periodic *GAP*.

✓ Checkpoints

17-8   What are the properties of the duration calculation? How does the duration of a bond relate to the bond's maturity? How does duration relate to market interest rates? How does duration relate to a bond's coupon rate?

17-9   How would you use duration's measure of a bond's interest rate elasticity?

17-10   What does this statement mean to the manager of the financial firm: "Durations of a firm's assets and liabilities are additive when weighted"?

17-11   If a firm has assets 90% financed by liabilities with a portfolio duration of 2.3 years and liabilities with a portfolio duration of 4.3 years, what would you expect to happen to the firm's profit margin if interest rates drop? What if rates rise?

---

[8]There will be times when the calculation for the theoretical market value of equity is negative for a firm with a positive market value of common stock. This was the case for many S&Ls in the 1980s. The positive common stock value for many of these firms was related to the fact that regulators allowed the firms to add profitable new assets to their portfolio. This gave the shareholders what was in effect a call option on the equity of the firm should it eventually possess positive economic value at some point in the future. The regulators eventually ended this forbearance program in the late 1980s.

17-12 How would you explain the concept of the duration market value of equity?

Mark-to-Market

Many firms have interest rate risk management needs that require very precise techniques for measuring this risk. The most precise technique available is **mark-to-market.** Mark-to-market, sometimes referred to as *market value accounting,* is used to establish the value of assets used in trading portfolios. Unfortunately, as a tool for measuring interest rate risk, such precision is difficult to attain. Mark-to-market is a process whereby the financial assets and liabilities of the firm, or a subgroup thereof, are valued at their current market value calculated at a point in time.

The need for some firms to use mark-to-market relates to: (1) the need to establish the value of the assets of the firm for operating purposes, as in the case of a mutual fund that must mark-to-market in order to be prepared to redeem old and sell new shares; (2) the requirement to mark-to-market in order to meet security or loan sale and trading accounting requirements under GAAP; and (3) the need for additional interest rate risk management measurement information.

In the first two situations, mutual fund operators and security traders and dealers act as market makers for various securities. They must mark-to-market under GAAP accounting rules. The mutual fund operator must be prepared to sell and redeem shares at market value. The management of security trading firms must know the value of their portfolios throughout the trading day to ensure against loss due to volatile interest rate conditions. Likewise, a mortgage banker or other originator of mortgages having outstanding mortgage commitments to sell in the secondary market must monitor the value of these mortgages against the price at which they have been committed to be sold. Under GAAP, these firms must account for their transactions and asset holdings using the mark-to-market methodology. The need to mark-to-market certain security portfolios in which sales occur was extended to depositories and insurance companies by the Financial Accounting Standard Board (FASB) in 1993, effective in 1994.

In the third situation, still other firms use mark-to-market not because they have to, but because it provides yet another interpretation of the interest rate risk position of the firm. These firms are interested in using mark-to-market as a tool to analyze the impact of changes in interest rates on the value of all their firm's assets and liabilities.

Mark-to-market is not used more frequently primarily due to the difficulty in developing mathematical functional relationships between open market interest rates and the value of specific loans and investments.

MARK-TO-MARKET EQUITY VALUATIONS

The last section developed the concept of the duration market value of equity. This statistic was used to monitor the impact of changing interest rates on the residual value of the firm, its equity value. This is computed by subtracting the

MARK-TO-MARKET RULING UPSETS BANKERS

How

it

Really

Works

Concern by depository regulators and the Securities and Exchange Commission over the adequacy of financial institution financial statements prompted the Federal Accounting Standards Board (FASB) to consider new accounting rules for depositories and insurance companies. These rules alter the old convention where securities to be held to maturity were valued on the balance sheet at their the initial cost, even if their market value fell after purchase. The exceptions were securities held for the purpose of sale before maturity, such as trading portfolios. Accountants typically allowed these institutions to sell a portion of each type of bond before maturity without requiring them to mark-to-market the rest of their holdings of similar bonds. In 1993, FASB issued Statement of Financial Accounting Standards No. 115 which altered the rule. FASB developed a new bond-valuation rule which requires that any sale of bonds of a particular type will necessitate a mark-to-market for all the rest of similar bonds held. Financial institutions are now forced to classify their debt securities in one of three classes with the following accounting implications:

1. *Held-to-maturity:* Accounted for at amortized cost.
2. *Trading:* Accounted for at fair market value with changes reported as changes to net income.
3. *Available-for-sale:* Accounted for at fair market value with changes reported as adjustments to shareholders' equity.

Financial institution operators argued that the new rule will result in excessive record keeping and excessively volatile changes in capital accounts. They argue that financial institutions won't hold long-term fixed-rate securities because of their excessive interest rate risk.

market value of assets from the market value of liabilities. Mark-to-market valuation is also used to estimate the residual mark-to-market valuation of equity for financial firms.

Mark-to-market has an advantage over duration market value of equity because the marketplace impacts the market value of financial assets in ways that cannot be measured by duration alone. Duration only considers the impact of changes in interest rates on value. In the money and capital markets, however, the market value of financial claims is affected by factors in addition to interest rate changes—factors which are sometimes equally important in the valuation process. These include:

1. Changes in the relative default risk premium.
2. Changes in the marketability premium.
3. Changes in the value of embedded options in the claim.
4. Changes in the supply-and-demand conditions for a particular asset.

In other words, mark-to-market aims to capture the impact of as many of the factors that impact on the value of a particular financial claim as possible. Looking at the duration percentage change in the market value of equity, for example, means looking solely at the impact of interest rates on the price of the financial claim.

Most mark-to-market accounting systems base their valuations on actual estimates of the market values of assets and liabilities. These values are typically based on secondary market price quotations. Where price quotations are unavailable, it is necessary to establish valuation models that relate in some functional way the value of specific assets and liabilities on the books of the institution to financial claims that trade in an established secondary market. Sometimes this is a very imprecise process.

MARK-TO-MARKET VALUATION OF EQUITY SENSITIVITY ANALYSIS

Mark-to-market equity valuations are also used for managing interest rate risk. This process involves the use of **sensitivity analysis,** that is, estimating the value of assets and liabilities under different interest rate scenarios. The analysis to be carried out here will involve a mark-to-market valuation of equity sensitivity on the assets and liabilities of a medium-sized credit union named the Woodlawn Community Credit Union. The management and directors of this small firm want to learn how the firm's assets and liabilities will change in market value as a result of a change in open market interest rates. They will accomplish this by creating a mark-to-market equity sensitivity analysis of the firm.

The objective of this sensitivity analysis is to determine how the existing portfolio of assets and liabilities will change in value assuming interest rates rise or fall by a specified amount—say, by 100 and 200 basis points from their current levels. To make these estimates, the cash flows of each asset and liability must be modeled. In the case of mortgages and installment loans with embedded prepayment options, it is important to properly estimate how these assets will prepay in different interest rate environments since the market value of these assets will be influenced by these cash flow changes. Notice that the liabilities of the firm are also marked-to-market. The concept here is to treat the liabilities as if they were all traded in a secondary market and could be purchased by the firm at their secondary market prices.

In this analysis, an instantaneous change in interest rates is assumed. It is as if one day the entire term structure of interest rates had risen or fallen by 100 or 200 basis points. This is not a realistic assumption, of course, but it provides a basis for measuring the sensitivity of the firm's assets and liabilities to interest rate shocks. It also greatly simplifies the computational procedures. Of course, any schedule of interest rates can be used to mark-to-market.

Tables 17.11, 17.12, and 17.13 show the balance sheet, expected percentage of the firm's assets that will amortize or pay off under several assumptions about changes in open market rates, and the initial market discount rates used to discount assets and liabilities under the assumed prevailing term structure. The tables also include off-balance sheet assets and liabilities, which, in this case, include a portfolio of mortgage servicing contracts that had a market value of $650,000 on December 31, 1995. Exhibit 17.1 shows the five term structures used in the analysis.

TABLE 17.11

Woodlawn Community Credit Union Balance Sheet December 31, 1995
(dollars in millions)

Assets		Liabilities	
Cash and short-term and agency securities	$ 8.0	Savings accounts	$35.0
Auto loans	23.0	NUCIF advance (three-year)	1.0
Mortgage loans	9.0	Term certificates (two-year)	8.0
Mortgage securities	6.0	Net worth (reserves)	3.0
Reverse repurchase agreements	1.0		
Total	$47.0		$47.0

Off-Balance Sheet

Mortgage servicing portfolio of $45 million at 37.5 basis points per annum	Valued at a 11% discount rate = $650,000

TABLE 17.12

Payoff and Prepayment Assumptions Annualized Payoff and Amortization Rate*
(five interest rate levels assumed)

Asset	−200 bp	−100 bp	Current Rates	+100 bp	+200 bp
Impacted auto loans	25%	15%	12%	11%	10%
Mortgages	18	13	8	7	5
Mortgage securities	15	12	7	6	5
Mortgage servicing	14	10	8	7	5

*Based on initial principal balances.

From these data, a statement showing the impact of a change in the market value of the firm's assets and liabilities resulting from a parallel change in open market rates of (+/−) 200 bp and (+/−) 100 bp is developed. The cash flow payoff and prepayment assumptions represented by Table 17.12 and the cash flows for each of the other assets and liabilities are discounted at interest rates that are 100 bp and 200 bp higher and lower than those shown in Table 17.13. The result of this discounting process is shown in Table 17.14. The mark-to-market equity sensitivity analysis reveals that the Woodlawn Community Credit Union has considerable interest rate risk. If interest rates rise unexpectedly by a large amount, the credit union will experience a dramatic decline in the firm's equity, the market value of its assets less liabilities. The results of this type of analysis can be depicted in a graph. In Exhibit 17.2, the actual mark-to-market value of

---

TABLE 17.13

Initial Market Discount Rates for Assets and Liabilities December 31, 1995

Asset and Liability Class	Current Market Discount Rate
Cash and agency securities	6.50%
Auto loans	11.25
Mortgages	9.65
Mortgage securities	9.30
Reverse repurchase agreements	6.25
Savings accounts	5.25
NUCIF advance	7.50
Term certificate	7.10%
Off-Balance Sheet	
Mortgage servicing portfolio	11.00%

EXHIBIT 17.1

Term Structures Used for Sensitivity Analysis
(base and change base +/− 100 and 200 basis points)

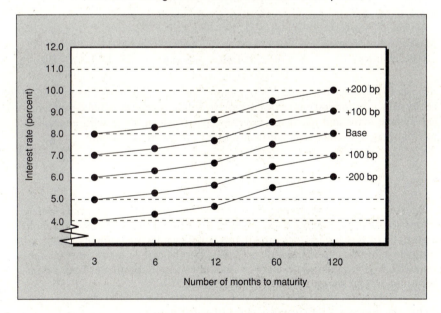

equity is shown with a hypothetical line called the *hypothetical low-risk mark-to-market*. This line represents the profile that a risk-adverse firm would prefer, if attainable.

The decline in the mark-to-market value of equity is primarily because Woodlawn holds long-term fixed-rate mortgages in whole loans and mortgage

---

TABLE 17.14

Mark-to-Market Equity Valuation Sensitivity Analysis for Parallel (+/−) 100 and 200 bp Changes in Open Market Interest Rates
(dollars in millions)

	−200 bp	−100 bp	Current Rates	+100 bp	+200 bp
Assets					
Cash and agencies	$ 8.00	$ 8.00	$ 8.00	$ 8.00	$ 8.00
Auto loans	25.00	24.00	23.00	22.00	20.00
Mortgages	9.50	9.30	9.00	8.50	8.10
Reverse repurchase agreements	1.00	1.00	1.00	1.00	1.00
Mortgager securities	6.30	6.20	6.00	5.80	5.60
Mortgage servicing	.45	.52	.65	.71	.76
Total	$50.25	$49.02	$47.65	$46.01	$43.46
Liabilities					
Savings accounts	$35.00	$35.00	$35.00	$35.00	$35.00
NCUIF advance	1.05	1.02	1.00	.98	.96
Term certificates	8.90	8.60	8.00	7.60	7.20
Total	$44.95	$44.62	$44.00	$43.58	$43.16
Mark-to-Market Value of Equity					
Market value of assets less liabilities	$ 5.30	$ 4.40	$ 3.65	$ 2.43	$ .30

securities. These are not offset by long-term fixed-rate liabilities. The institution could reduce its interest rate risk position by selling some of its fixed-rate mortgage whole loans and mortgage securities and replacing them with adjustable-rate mortgages or additional auto loans that have shorter duration.

LIMITATIONS OF MARK-TO-MARKET

Mark-to-market is a simple process for some financial firms that hold widely traded securities on organized exchanges. Most mutual funds, for example, hold a portfolio of very liquid stocks and bonds, whose values are normally readily ascertainable in the organized markets. This is not the case in many other circumstances, however. As a result, mark-to-market valuation techniques have a number of limitations that make them difficult to use.

Establishing the Value of Infrequently Traded Assets

Mark-to-market is a very difficult process for firms that hold loans and other investments that are infrequently traded. These might include assets such as high-yield corporate bonds, commercial loans, and consumer loans. Some of these assets have no organized exchange or group of dealers that are able to quote market prices precisely. As a result, to use mark-to-market means relying on estimation techniques that are imprecise and complicated to administer. Despite this limitation, the analyst usually can make an informed judgment about the value of less-marketable assets, which makes the mark-to-market approach a useful measure of interest rate risk.

The firm using mark-to-market valuation techniques may attempt to establish valuation benchmarks based on information from dealer groups and others who have a working knowledge of the value of a particular loan or investment. Other firms rely on analytical models that provide statistical relationships between the value of a marketable security and the less-marketable security held by the firm. In this case, the value of a less-marketable security is based on a historical mathematical relationship to another highly marketable security.

MARK-TO-MARKET DIFFICULTIES FOR THE FINANCIAL FIRM'S LIABILITIES

It is also difficult to mark the liabilities to market. Many liabilities do not trade at all, such as insurance reserves held for policyholders. Establishing the market value of a certificate of deposit in a changing interest rate environment is much easier but still requires the analyst to make a number of simplifying assumptions.

THE ASSUMPTION OF PARALLEL TERM STRUCTURE SHIFTS

In most cases, the analyst using mark-to-market to perform a sensitivity analysis for changes in the firm's asset and liability values will do so by estimating equal nominal percent changes in interest rates along the entire term structure, referred to as *parallel changes in the term structure*. In reality, changes in the economy normally result in other-than-parallel shifts. This causes the mark-to-market estimates to be less than realistic. Analysts can, of course, make any assumptions they want about how interest rates will change in the next period.

PICKING BID OR ASK PRICES

Another knotty problem is that there are sometimes large spreads between the bid and ask prices on various assets to be marked-to-market. This gives the analyst using mark-to-market a range of prices upon which to establish value. The firm using mark-to-market has to decide how to handle this seemingly innocuous dilemma.

Take the case of a firm that just purchased a portfolio of commercial mortgage loans in the secondary market at the ask price. Such a transaction might have a difference of one-half to three-quarters of a point between the bid and ask price for the asset. If interest rates did not change and the firm marked-to-market this portfolio the next day using the bid price, the firm would have lost the one-half to three-quarters of a point according to its mark-to-market report. For a financial firm with only 5% to 6% equity, this is a major reduction in value. This sit-

EXHIBIT 17.2

Market Value of Equity Sensitivity Analysis

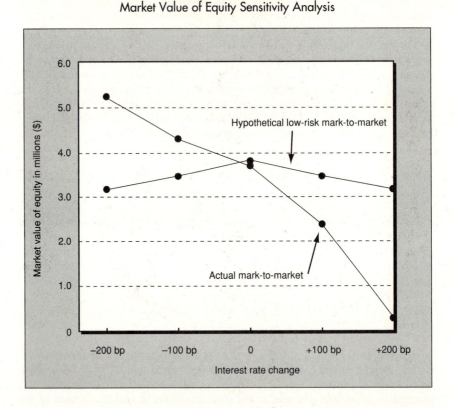

For purposes of simulating changes in equity value, it is probably wise to use the average between the bid and ask price when it is available. In any case, it is important to recognize the computational problem created by the bid-ask spread and to apply the methodology consistently over time.

uation dramatizes one of the limitations of mark-to-market. In the valuation of less-marketable assets, the bid-ask spread can be very wide. This distorts the valuation process. It may lead to too high a valuation of assets if the ask price is used and the opposite if the bid price is used.

For purposes of simulating changes in equity value, it is probably wise to use the average between the bid and ask price when it is available. In any case, it is important to recognize the computational problem created by the bid-ask spread and to apply the methodology consistently over time.

MARK-TO-MARKET CAPITAL REQUIREMENTS

Now that you have a working knowledge of mark-to-market techniques for measuring interest rate risk, it is time to see how some financial institution regulators are using the concept. The Federal Deposit Insurance Corporation Improvement Act of 1991 (discussed in the Appendix 4B) required that banking agencies review their risk-based capital guidelines to take adequate account of interest rate risk. In late 1993, the Office of the Comptroller of the Currency, the Federal Reserve System, and Federal Deposit Insurance Corporation jointly issued a proposed rule concerning how financial institutions should measure their interest rate risk and the capital requirements related to this risk. Although the details of this complicated regulation will change over time, the basic framework is based on a mark-to-market structure.

The basic approach involves classifying assets and liabilities into categories that reflect the degree of price exposure they have relative to changes in interest rates. Then a given increase and decrease in interest rates is assumed and the impact on the value of the firm's assets and liabilities is simulated. The difference between the gain or loss on the value of the assets is compared to a like measure for the liabilities. Firms that show too large a net loss as a result of a change in interest rates must augment their capital to reflect this risk. Specifically the regulation involves the following steps.

1. Segment assets and liabilities by maturity or period of repricing—the regulation proposed classification into seven time bands:

   Up to 3 months.

   3–12 months.

   1–3 years.

   3–5 years.

   5–10 years.

   10–20 years.

   More than 20 years.

   2.Classify assets by the instrument's cash-flow characteristics—the regulation proposes five classifications, including:

   Adjustable-rate mortgages and adjustable-rate mortgage securities.

   Fixed-rate mortgages, mortgage securities, and asset-backed securities.

   Zero- or low-coupon securities (securities with coupon rates of 2% or less).

   All other instruments assumed to involve scheduled periodic payment of principal and interest.

   Mortgage derivative securities, such as interest and principal-only, CMOs, and REMICs, would be classified by whether they are high risk or nonhigh risk based on another regulation.

3. Classify the firm's liabilities according to type of funding source, including:

   Nonmaturity liabilities such as demand deposits, NOW accounts, money market demand accounts, and savings (or passbook) accounts.

   Off-balance sheet positions that impact on interest rate risk.

   Time deposits and purchased funds.

4. Determine the appropriate risk weights (generally given by the regulator) which relate to the type of asset and liability, the maturity of the instrument, and the economic interest rate scenario. The risk weight is a measure of the percentage increase or decrease in the value of the asset and liability related to a specified nominal percent change in open market interest rates. For example, a risk weight of −8.80% for fixed-rate mortgages with maturites of 15 years given a +2.00% increase in open mar-

ket interest rates would mean that the value of the firm's mortgages of this type would decline by 8.80% from their book value level. The risk-weight classifications would include:

Seven amortizing risk weights for mortgages and other amortizing instruments.

Seven zero- and low-coupon risk weights.

Seven all-other risk weights.

Seven liability risk weights.

5. Development of an interest rate risk worksheet to determine the net impact of an assumed instantaneous change in interest rates on the firm. An abbreviated sample of a worksheet would look like Table 17.15.

6. Determine the acceptable threshold level for the net risk weighted position established by the regulators and use it to calculate the firm's excess risk exposure, if any. The regulators will establish an acceptable net risk weight position for a given economic scenario. If the regulator determines that the largest negative net risk-weighted position acceptable is 1% of assets, then the firm would calculate its excess measured exposure using the equation:

$$\textit{Measured exposure} - (.01 \times \textit{Total assets}) = \textit{Excess measured exposure}$$
$$\$766 - (.01 \times \$19,600) = \$570$$

7. The firm would face an additional increase in its minimum risk-based capital requirement (see Chapter 22) equal to its excess measured exposure of $570 or some multiple of that amount.

It is clear that the concept of mark-to-market has become extremely important in recent years. Although the approach outlined here will change over time, it is likely that the mark-to-market structure will remain unchanged.

✓ Checkpoints

17-13 What types of intermediaries use mark-to-market techniques to value their assets and liabilities?

17-14 What are some limitations of marking-to-market?

17-15 What are the advantages of mark-to-market as an interest rate risk management measurement tool?

17-16 How would you use mark-to-market situations to determine the sensitivity of the firm's equity to changes in interest rates?

17-17 What is a parallel shift in the term structure of interest rates relative to duration market value of equity analysis and mark-to-market valuation of equity sensitivity analysis?

17-18 How do financial institution regulators use the mark-to-market concept in evaluating a bank's capital position?

TABLE 17.15

Hypothetical Interest Rate Risk Worksheet
200 Basis Point Rising Rate Scenario

Asset and liability (thousands)	Total A	Risk Weights B	Risk-Weighted Position A × B	Total Risk Weighted Position
Interest Sensitive Assets				
ARMs, FRMs, and other amortizing:				
Up to 3 months	$ 4,500	−.10%	($4.5)	
3–12 months	3,600	−.50	($18)	
1–3 years	0	−1.60		
3–5 years	0	−3.00		
5–10 years	1,500	−5.50	($82.5)	
10–20 years	2,000	−8.80	($176)	
More than 20 years	5,000	−9.20	($460)	
Zero- or low-coupon:				
Up to 3 months				
All other:				
Up to 3 months				
High-risk mortgage securities	1,000	−38.00	($380)	
Total interest-sensitive assets	17,600		($1,121)	($1,121)
All other assets	2,000			
Total assets	$19,600			
Interest Sensitive Liabilities				
Non-maturity, time, savings, and all other:				
Up to 3 months	$ 5,100	.25	$13	
3–12 months	8,000	1.20	$96	
1–3 years	3,000	3.70	$111	
3–5 years	2,000	6.90	$138	
5–10 years		11.60		
10–20 years		18.70		
More than 20 years		24.00		
Total liabilities	$18,100		$358	$358
Total equity	$1,500			
Off-Balance Sheet Positions:				
Up to 3 months	$1,000	−.25%	($3)	($3)
Net risk weighted position				($766)
Net position/assets (−$766 ÷ $19,600 =)				−3.91%

Income Simulation

Each of the interest rate risk measurement techniques assists in measuring how changes in interest rates affect the repricing of assets and liabilities in relation to one another and the market valuation of the firm. However, as useful as these measurement tools are, none of these approaches is useful in determining the impact of open market rate changes on the accounting income of financial institutions. This is because, except for trading portfolios, accounting under GAAP does not require marking-to-market the assets and liabilities of the firm. Consequently, market gains or losses due to interest rate changes generally are not recognized in the income statements of depositories, finance companies, and insurance companies, except over time.

In order to determine the impact of interest rate changes on the reported accounting income of a financial intermediary, it is generally necessary to use an income simulation model. This permits the firm's management to simulate accounting statement income resulting from changes in interest rates and from changes in interest rate risk strategies.

Simulation models have been used for decades to help guide management in selecting various asset and liability strategies. Today, it is possible to develop relatively robust simulation models using personal computers with spreadsheet software. The problems in developing these models are the same faced in the periodic *GAP,* duration *GAP,* and mark-to-market techniques discussed previously—namely, determining reasonable assumptions for cash flows of assets and liabilities that have embedded options.

It is also difficult to model changes in the relationship between the prices and yields of various assets and liabilities. That is, the market price or yield on a particular asset or liability may experience a change in its relationship to the price or yield of the firm's other assets and liabilities. These changes may be totally unrelated to changes in the term structure of interest rates. A particular deposit, for example, may become relatively more costly to the firm as a result of local competitive conditions that require paying more to retain that deposit. Consequently, the price and yield of this liability will change relative to the firm's other assets and liabilities. Such changes are generally unpredictable. However, simulation models can be used to perform sensitivity analyses of these changes.

Management generally will use a simulation model in conjunction with the interest rate risk management measurement tools presented in this chapter to obtain a more comprehensive understanding of how the firm is impacted by interest rate risk changes.

EXAMPLE OF AN INCOME SIMULATION

Security Federal Savings Bank is a traditional savings institution with a large portfolio of fixed-rate mortgages. Despite a major effort by the firm in recent years, it has been unable to originate adjustable-rate mortgages. During the early 1990s, this situation produced profitable results, since interest rates in the open market fell from 1989 through most of 1993. The directors of Security have become very concerned about its large holding of fixed-rate mortgages that are financed with short-term liabilities. At year-end 1993, the financial officer prepared a periodic *GAP* report. This report is shown in Table 17.16.

The periodic *GAP* report indicates that the institution has a very severe interest rate mismatch. This means that an increase in open market interest rates could have a severe impact on the solvency of the company. With this information at hand, the directors have requested a simulation using a rising open market interest rate scenario. The forecast interest rates to be used in the simulation are shown in Table 17.17.

Security's directors have decided to reinvest all of the firm's cash flow into new adjustable-rate mortgages. They are interested in what will happen to reported income. The simulation result of this strategy is shown in Table 17.18.

As the directors anticipated, the simulated rise in open market rates would be extremely harmful to Security Federal. The income simulation allowed the management and directors to see just what type of impact a rise in rates would actually have on the pro forma income statement. The simulation confirmed the information supplied in the periodic *GAP* report indicating a substantial interest rate risk problem. While this simulation is an extremely simple model, it serves to show how a simulation can be used to create pro forma income statements under a variety of economic scenarios and investment strategies.

TABLE 17.16

Security Federal Savings Bank One-Year Periodic GAP_1 Analysis Report
December 31, 1993

Assets:

Cash and short-term liquid assets (less than one year)	$10,000,000
Fixed-rate mortgages and mortgage securities	
(Prepay 12% of $95,000,000)	11,400,000
Total assets maturing or repricing in one year (RPA_1)	21,400,000

Liabilities:

Money market accounts	10,000,000
Three-month CDs	85,000,000
Total liabilities maturing or repricing in one year (RPL_1)	95,000,000

$$RPA_1 - RPL_1 - \$73,600,000$$

Periodic GAP percentage (GAP/financial assets) $= -\$73,600,000/\$105,000,000$
$$= -70.1\%$$

Periodic GAP ratio (RPA_1/RPL_1) $= \$21,400,000/\$95,000,000 = 22.5\%$

TABLE 17.17

Interest Rate Forecast for Simulation

Claim	Quarter 1	Quarter 2	Quarter 3	Quarter 4
Money market accounts and CD rates	6.00%	6.5%	7.00%	8.5%
Mortgage rates	7.00	7.5	7.75	8.0
Liquid asset earning rates	6.00	6.5	7.00	8.5

TABLE 17.18

Income Simulation: Security Federal Savings Bank

	Quarter 1	Quarter 2	Quarter 3	Quarter 4
Interest income:				
Old mortgages	$1,662,500	$1,612,625	$1,562,750	$1,512,875
New mortgages		53,438	110,438	171,000
Liquidity	$ 75,000	$ 81,250	$ 87,500	$ 106,250
Interest expense:				
Savings	1,425,000	$1,543,750	$1,662,500	$2,018,750
Net interest income	312,500	203,563	98,188	–228,625
Other income	125,000	125,000	125,000	125,000
Operating expenses	375,000	375,000	375,000	375,000
Net profit before tax	$ 62,500	$ –46,437	$ –151,812	$ –478,625

✓ Checkpoint

17-19 It is said that measures of interest rate risk exposure obtained from periodic *GAP*, duration *GAP*, and mark-to-market analysis do not translate into useful forecasts of earnings. Why? What methodology might you use to obtain useful earnings forecasts?

SUMMARY AND REVIEW

1. **Define interest rate risk in terms of the market value of assets and liabilities, the income statement, and off-balance sheet assets and liabilities and explain how it is measured.**

   Interest rate risk is defined as the impact that changes in open market interest rates have on the value of a financial firm's assets and liabilities and its income stream.

   Interest rate risk is measured by considering all the firm's assets and liabilities as well as off-balance sheet commitments. Because interest rates affect values of specific assets and liabilities differently, interest rate risk measurement should be implemented as a **portfolio concept.**

2. **Describe the periodic *GAP* and show how it is used and calculated.**

   Periodic *GAP*, (GAP_t), is defined as the difference between the dollar amount of assets, (RPA_t), and liabilities, (RPL_t), that mature or reprice within a specified period of time. Periodic *GAP* is defined as $GAP_t = RPA_t - RPL_t$

3. **Describe duration, duration *GAP*, the interest rate elasticity, *E*, and the elasticity of the market value of equity, *MVE*.**

Duration is an alternative measure of a financial claim's maturity that more accurately weighs the cash flows of a financial claim as they occur over time. Duration is defined as: $DUR = [\Sigma_{t=1}^{n} C_t \times (t)/ (1 + r)^t]/[\Sigma_{t=1}^{n} C_t/(1 + r)^t]$ where: C_t = Asset cash flow in period t; r = Periodic open market interest rate (discount rate); and t = Number of periods the claim in outstanding. **Portfolio durations** can be simply computed by calculating the weighted-average durations for the firm's assets and liabilities. From these asset and liability portfolio durations, DUR_A and DUR_L, a **duration GAP**, DUR_{GAP}, measure can be calculated by using the following formula: $DUR_{GAP} = DUR_A - [(w_L) \times DUR_L]$. w_L is defined as the percentage of financial assets financed with financial liabilities. Duration measures have the valuable property that they can be used to calculate the change in value of a financial claim resulting from small changes in the level of interest rates. This is known as *interest rate elasticity, E.* It is defined as $E = -DUR \times [r/1 + r]$. Using portfolio duration GAP statistics, it is possible to calculate the change in value of a financial firm's portfolio of assets and liabilities due to a small change in interest rates. This is known as the *interest rate elasticity of the market value of equity, MVE.* This is defined as $MVE = -DUR_{GAP} \times [(r)/(1 + r)]$. This is a very important measure of the impact of changes in open market interest rates on the shareholders' equity in the firm.

4. **Describe mark-to-market and explain how it is used to assess the interest rate risk of a financial firm.**

   Mark-to-market is a interest rate risk tool and accounting methodology that serves as a required approach to the valuation of a firm's assets and liabilities for certain firms, such as mutual funds and firms that trade financial claims, and also as a powerful **sensitivity analysis tool** for measuring the impact of changes in open market interest rates on the equity of the firm. Conceptually, mark-to-market is a straightforward methodology for performing sensitivity analysis whereby the firm values its assets and liabilities at different levels of open market interest rates. With several of these valuations calculated at different interest rate levels, a **mark-to-market valuation of equity sensitivity analysis** is developed that provides estimates for how the firm's equity value, viewed as the residual of the market value of assets less the market value of liabilities, changes as the level of interest rates changes.

5. **Explain the use of income simulations in assessing the impact of interest rate risk on financial firms.**

   Because each of the previously mentioned interest rate risk measurement methodologies does not provide good estimates of how changes in interest rates will impact the reported financial income of the firm, **income simulation** techniques are used. Income simulations forecast how changes in interest rates, given specified financial asset and liability strategies, will impact the reported accounting income of the firm.

PERIODIC GAP

ST-17-1

A credit union has total financial assets of $35.0 million and total financial liabilities of $ 33million. Within the next year, $12.0 million in assets and $15 million in liabilities are subject to maturity or repricing.

1. What is the firm's one-year periodic *GAP?*
2. What is the *GAP* percentage and *GAP* ratio?
3. Would the firm expect to see its net interest margin rise or fall if market interest rates fall during the next year? Why?

  Answers on page 528.

DURATION

ST-17-2

Calculate the duration for a two-year bond paying a 3.0% coupon return. The market interest rate is also 3.00%.

DURATION GAP

ST-17-3

Williams Bay Savings has computed its liability duration to be 3.5 years. The firm's total financial liabilities are $98 million. The firm's assets have the following characteristics:

	% of Total Assets (1)	Duration Years (2)
Financial assets—$ 105 Million		
Cash and government < 1-year bonds	5%	.30
U.S. Government bonds	24	3.20
Auto loans	25	2.60
Adjustable-rate mortgages (tied to 1-year Treasuries)	26	.90
Fixed-rate mortgages (remaining maturity 20 years)	20	8.70
Total financial assets	100%	

Using these data, determine the duration *GAP* of this firm. What is the elasticity of the firm's duration *GAP* assuming market rates are 4.0% and interest rates rise 4 basis points? If Williams Bay Savings experiences a substantial rise in open market interest rates, is this likely to increase or decrease the firm's net interest margin?

PERIODIC GAP

17-1

A thrift institution has total assets of $520 million and total liabilities of $476 million. Within the next year, $212 million in assets and $330 million in liabilities are subject to maturity or repricing if interest rates change.

1. What is the firm's one-year periodic *GAP?*
2. What is the *GAP* percentage and *GAP* ratio?
3. Would the firm expect to see its net interest margin rise or fall if market interest rates rise during the next year? Why?

PERIODIC GAP

17-2

A commercial bank has total assets of $1.35 billion and total liabilities of $1.08 billion. Within the next year, $464 million in assets and $420 million in liabilities are subject to maturity or repricing.

1. What is the firm's one-year periodic *GAP?*
2. What is the *GAP* percentage and *GAP* ratio?
3. Would the firm expect to see its net interest margin rise or fall if market interest rates rose during the next year? Why?

DURATION AND ELASTICITY

17-3

You own a $1,000 bond with a term of maturity of four years. The coupon rate is 9%, paid semiannually. The current market yield on similar bonds is 8.25%.

1. What is the duration of the bond?
2. What is the market value of the bond?
3. What is the interest rate elasticity of the bond at the current market interest rate?
4. What would you expect the market value of the bond to be if market interest rates should fall to 8%?

DURATION ELASTICITY/PORTFOLIO DURATION

17-4

As portfolio manager for a large bank you have a choice of three equally risky assets to invest in with the following durations:

Asset A DUR = 3.5 years

Asset B DUR = 6.0 years

Asset C DUR = 15.5 years

1. Assume the current term structure is relatively flat and that market yields for each of these instruments is currently at 9%. Compute the interest rate elasticity for each asset.

2. Compute the duration and interest rate elasticity of a portfolio consisting of 20% of Asset A, 35% of Asset B, and 45% of Asset C. Assume market rates are 9%.

3. If you commit half your portfolio to Asset A, what portions of Assets B and C would you need to purchase to have a portfolio duration of 7.5 years? What would be the interest rate elasticity of that portfolio if market rates are 9%?

PORTFOLIO DURATION/DURATION GAP

17-5

Midwest National Bank has the Following Balance Sheet:

Midwest National Bank
Balance Sheet
December 31, 1995

	$ Millions	Avg. DUR (years)
Assets		
Cash	$ 3	0.0
Short-term Treasuries	20	0.4
Long-term Treasuries	18	7.5
Commercial loans	30	3.2
Real estate loans	25	9.1
Property, plant, equipment	4	—
Total assets	$100	
Total financial assets	$ 96	
Liabilities		
Demand deposits	12	—
1-year certificates	35	0.7
5-year certificates	35	4.3
Other liabilities	7	3.8
Total liabilities	$ 94	
Net worth	6	
Total Financial Liabilities	$ 94	

1. Compute the weighted-average duration of the bank's assets. Compute the weighted-average duration of the bank's liabilities.

2. Compute the duration *GAP* and the interest rate elasticity of the market value of equity for the bank. Market rates are averaging 7%.

3. From your answers in Number 2, by how much would you expect the market value of the bank's equity to change if market interest rates moved to 8%?

PORTFOLIO DURATION/DURATION GAP

17-6

Providence Savings and Loan has the following balance sheet:

Providence Savings and Loan
Balance Sheet
December 31, 1995

	$ Millions	Avg. DUR (years)
Assets		
Cash	$ 22	0.0
First mortgage loans	180	14.5
Second mortgage loans	53	6.6
Auto loans	75	3.0
Other assets	12	7.2
Property, plant, equipment	8	—
Total assets	$350	
Total financial assets	$342	
Liabilities		
NOW accounts	40	0.0
Passbook accounts	36	0.0
One-year time deposits	84	0.8
Two-year time deposits	78	1.5
Three-year time deposits	42	2.7
Other liabilities	50	5.4
Total liabilities	$330	
Net worth	20	
Total financial liabilities	$330	

1. Compute the weighted-average duration of the firm's assets. Compute the weighted-average duration of the firm's liabilities.

2. Compute the duration *GAP* and the interest rate elasticity of the market value of equity for the firm. Market rates are averaging 6.5%.

3. From your answer in Number 2, by how much would you expect the market value of the firm's equity to change if market interest rates moved to 6.25%?

SELF-TEST PROBLEM   SOLUTIONS

ST-17-1

Solution:
1. The firm's one-year *GAP* is $RPA_1 - RPL_1$ = $12 million – $15 million = –$3 million.
2. The *GAP* percentage is $GAP_t = GAP_t/$Total financial assets$_t$ = –$3 million/$12 million = –25%
   The *GAP* ration = RPA_t/RPL_t = $12 million/$15 million = .80
3. The firm would experience a rise in its net interest margin in the event of a decline in rates since a greater amount of liabilities than assets would mature or reprice.

ST-17-2

Solution:
Using a $1,000 principal value bond:

$$DUR = \{[\$15 \times (1)/(1 + .015)^1 + \$15 \times (2)/(1 + .015)^2 + \$15 \times (3)/(1 + .015)^3 + \$15 \times (4)/(1 + .015)^4 + \$1,000 \times (4)/(1 + 0.15)^4$$

divided by

$$[\$15/(1 + .015)^1 + \$15/(1 + .015)^2 + \$15/(1 + .015)^3 + \$15/(1 + .015)^4 + \$1,000/(1 + .015)^4]\}$$

$$DUR = [\$15/1.015 + \$30/1.03023 + \$45/1.04568 + \$4,060/1.06136]/ [\$15/1.015 + \$15/1.03023 + \$15/1.04568 + \$1,015/1.06136]$$

$$DUR = [\$14.77833 + \$29.11971 + \$43.03420 + \$3825.28077]/ [\$14.77833 + \$14.55986 + \$14.34473 + \$956.32019] = \$3,912.21/\$1,000$$

$$= 3.91221 \text{ semiannual periods}$$

$$= 3.91221/2 = 1.956105 \text{ years}$$

ST-17-3

Solution:
The firm's duration *GAP* is found by computing the firm's asset and liability durations, DUR_A and DUR_L. Then it is necessary to determine the weight percentage, w_L, for the percentage of assets financed by liabilities.

	% of Total Assets (1)	Duration Years (2)	Weighted Duration (1) – (2)
Financial assets—$ 105 Million			
Cash and government < 1-year bonds	5%	.30	.015
U.S. government bonds	24	3.20	.768
Auto loans	25	2.60	.650
Adjustable-rate mortgages (tied to 1-year Treasuries)	26	.90	.234
Mortgages fixed rate (remaining maturity 20 years)	20	8.70	2.18
Total financial assets	100%		3.847

$$w_L = \$98 \ million/\$105 \ million = 93.33\%$$

Duration GAP:

$$DUR_{GAP} = DUR_A - [(w_L) \times DUR_L]$$

$$= 3.847 \ years - [.9333 \times 3.5 \ years] = .58045 \ years$$

Elasticity of duration GAP:

$$E_{DURGAP} = -DUR_{GAP} \times [r/(1 + r)]$$

$$E_{DURGAP} = -.58045 \ years \times [.04/(1 + .04)] = -.02233$$

If interest rates rise, Williams Bay Savings will experience a decline in the value of its financial assets that is greater than the decline in the value of its liabilities. This is borne out by the negative elasticity of the duration *GAP*. This will tend to reduce the firm's net interest margin.

CASE 17.1

GAP MEASUREMENT OF INTEREST RATE RISK FOR BAY CITY SAVINGS BANK

Introduction

Bay City Savings Bank is a shareholder-owned institution located in the upper Midwest. The company was chartered in 1952 as a mutual institution and was managed by Robert Rine from its formation until Mr. Rine retired in 1993. The company experienced significant difficulties in the late 1970s and early 1980s due to the high market interest rates, its large holdings of fixed-rate mortgages, and the deregulation of savings deposit rates in 1980.

Bay City SB is now managed by Martin Went. The board hired Mr. Went from outside the organization to accomplish several objectives. He was first asked to accomplish a mutual conversion of the institution into a stock-held company, which he completed in the spring of 1994. He was also asked to implement a portfolio diversification program that would substantially reduce the company's holdings of fixed-rate mortgages by increasing the company's investment in adjustable-rate mortgages, consumer loans, and business loans tied to the prime rate. The board has made it very clear that they want to reduce the firm's interest rate risk.

Bay City SB is a very dominant institution in a three-county area. Unfortunately, the demand for loans is relatively weak. This means that finding a suitable supply of loans that reprice or mature in a short period has proved difficult. Reducing the firm's interest rate risk has been a very slow process and not altogether successful.

The Problem

Mr. Went has asked you to review his firm's overall operating position. In particular, he is interested in the firm's interest rate risk position. He would like you to identify where the firm stands with respect to interest rate risk. He would also like your ideas concerning what can be done to reduce it.

Some of the firm's primary operating statements for the year 1994 are shown in Tables C17.1 and C17.2.

TABLE C17.1

Bay City Savings Bank 1994 Income Statement

Interest on mortgages	$145,119,000
Interest on investments	7,315,000
Interest on other loans	26,070,000
Total interest income	$178,504,000
Less:	
Cost of deposits	$107,340,000
Cost of borrowings	17,675,000
Cost of other liabilities	9,200,000
Total interest cost	$134,215,000
Net interest margin	$ 44,289,000
Plus:	
Fee and other income	6,500,000
Less:	
Loan loss provision	7,990,000
Less:	
Operating expenses	34,000,000
Net before tax income	$ 8,799,000
Less:	
Federal and state taxes	3,518,000
After tax income	$ 5,281,000

TABLE C17.2

Bay City Savings Bank Balance Sheet December 31, 1994
(dollars in millions)

	$ Amount	Rate in %
Assets		
Cash and short term investments	$ 110	6.65
Auto loans (60 months)	75	10.75
Credit card receivables	35	19.75
Second mortgages		
Fixed (15-year)	32	11.50
Variable (15-year)	12	10.50
First mortgages		
Fixed (30-year)	658	8.25
Variable (30-year) tied to cost of funds	234	7.50
Variable (30 year) tied to 1-year Treasury	276	7.75
Variable (30-year) tied to 5-year Treasury	321	7.40
Business loans tied to prime rate	98	11.50
Building and fixtures	87	0.00
Foreclosed and repossessed assets	34	0.00
Total	$1,972	
Liabilities		
Demand deposits	$ 78	0.00
Money market demand accounts	233	6.75
Savings passbook deposits	254	5.00
Retail certificates of deposit	930	7.80
Certificates over $100,000 (less than 6 months)	85	7.50
Federal Home Loan Bank borrowing	202	8.75
Collateralized mortgage bond	100	9.20
Retained earnings and paid in surplus	90	
Total	$1,972	

Gathering Data

In discussing the consulting assignment with Mr. Went, it was determined that a periodic *GAP* report should be prepared for Bay City SB. This report would include the one- and three-year *GAP* for the bank. Mr. Went would like you to explain the overall *GAP* position of the firm.

To prepare the *GAP* report, you met with Mr. Bender, the chief financial officer, to determine various assumptions for the maturity, cash flows, and repricing of the various liabilities.

In discussing the mortgage portfolio, Mr. Bender indicated that the large portfolio of fixed-rate mortgages was expected to prepay at a rate of approximately 12% per annum over the next five years. The adjustable-rate portfolio was expected to prepay at the rate of 8% per annum. The second mortgage portfolio, both fixed and adjustable, was expected to prepay at the rate of 15% per annum. The adjustable second mortgages are tied to the one-year Treasury.

The five-year adjustable-rate mortgages are tied to the five-year Treasury. Mr. Bender feels that it is safe to assume that they will reprice by equal amounts each yearly period. The cost of funds adjustable mortgages reprice monthly.

The other loans are all essentially adjustable at any time, except for the auto loans which Mr. Bender indicated are likely to mature equally over the next five years. On the liability side, Mr. Bender has prepared Table C17.3 showing the remaining terms of the certificates of deposit and the borrowing.

TABLE C17.3

Maturity Structure of Certificates of Deposit and Borrowings
(dollars in millions)

Retail certificates:	
Less than 90 days	$130
90 days to 6 months	250
6 months to 1 year	350
1–3 years	200
FHLB borrowings:	
Less than 1 year	120
1–3 years	50
Over 3 years	32
Mortgage collateralized bond:	
Over 5 years	100

Reviewing Other Operating Statistics

Once the GAP report is complete, Mr. Went would like you to review some of the other conditions of the firm. In particular, he is concerned that the net interest margin is quite weak. The industry average for 1994 was 2.75%. He would like you to measure Bay City SB's net interest spread and see how it stacks up to the industry. (Note: You can calculate this by determining the weighted-average yield on assets and liabilities.) He would also like you to provide ideas for improving the interest rate position of the firm if you feel it needs improvement.

Questions

1. Prepare a one- and three-year GAP report for the bank. Compute the GAP_1 percentage and ratio.

2. Analyze the report concerning the interest rate risk position of the bank. Discuss what would likely happen to the net income of the institution if interest rates rose or fell by a significant amount.

3. Compute the weighted yield on earning financial assets and liabilities. (This is similar to the net interest spread discussed in Chapter 10, except you can use the actual current yields and balances rather than average balances. Note that demand deposits is included in interest-paying liabilities.) How does the net interest spread compare to the industry? What can management do to improve it?

CHAPTER 18

Managing Interest Rate Risk

Learning Goals

After studying this chapter, you should be able to:

1. Discuss the trade-off between interest rate risk and income for most financial firms and list the primary risk management tools.
2. Describe financial futures contracts and how to use them to reduce interest rate risk.
3. Describe options and futures options and how to use them to reduce interest rate risk.
4. Describe interest rate swaps and how to use them to reduce interest rate risk.
5. Describe adjustable-rate financial contracts and the most common provisions found in them.
6. Describe caps, floors, and collars and explain how they are used to manage interest rate risk.

How does a firm alter its interest rate risk profile? If you mastered the techniques for measuring the interest rate risk position of the firm, then you should be ready to tackle this new managerial challenge. During the last decade, there has been a significant increase in the number and sophistication of interest rate risk management techniques, coincidental with the increase in interest rate volatility in the late 1970s.

This chapter provides you with a number of major risk management tools, such as:

1. The financial futures and forward cash markets.

2. The options market.

3. The futures options market.

4. The interest rate swap market.

5. The use of adjustable-rate lending.[1]

---

[1] It is possible to use futures contracts and certain financial options to hedge against credit risk. For example, a lender highly exposed to risky commercial and industrial loans to companies highly dependent on the business cycle might purchase put options on a stock market index or sell short a stock market index contract. If the economy entered recession, the stock indices would likely fall, creating a profit to offset looses in the loan portfolio.

The selection of one of these approaches over the others relates to the objective to be accomplished, the length of time over which the transaction will extend, and the profit impact of producing a given change in the company's interest rate risk profile.

The Income and Interest Rate Risk Trade-off

Students of finance should by now believe in the often-cited adage, "There's no such thing as a free lunch." This applies equally well to the reduction of interest rate risk. Interest rate risk management techniques involve difficult trade-offs. The primary trade-off is usually lower current income for the probability of less-volatile future income under certain undesirable future economic scenarios. Reducing interest rate risk, however, almost always has a negative expected value with respect to future income in an environment of unchanged interest rates. This is why it is so important to consider the costs as well as the benefits of reducing interest rate risk.

Consider the case of a firm with a high negative periodic *GAP*. This firm's objective is to reduce its interest rate risk by reducing its negative one-year periodic *GAP* on $50 million of assets and liabilities. To do so, management has identified the following three strategic policy options covering $50 million of assets and/or liabilities:

1. Stop originating the next $50 million of 8.5% fixed-rate mortgages and begin origination of 7.25% adjustable-rate mortgages to hold in portfolio.

2. Replace $50 million of maturing three- and six-month liabilities costing 5.25% with longer-term maturity liabilities over one year costing 6.75%.

3. Complete an interest rate swap of $50 million of short-term liabilities to receive a floating rate tied to the 30-day Treasury bill rate currently at 5.4% for a fixed-cost five-year liability obligation costing 6.70%.

Each of these strategies will reduce the firm's interest rate mismatch and will also reduce the firm's income in the short run under scenarios of unchanged interest rates or lower interest rates. These transactions will only help the firm in the case of rising interest rates—the most undesirable economic scenario.

In order to analyze this trade-off, it is necessary to complete an analysis to determine the impact these strategy options have under alternative economic scenarios. The customary approach is to use an income simulation model. Consider Table 18.1. It shows the impact on the pro forma pretax income of Second National Bank for the next 12 months under several interest rate scenarios after simulating the implementation of the three strategies. The process of developing this schedule involves simulating income under five different interest rate strategies (0, +/− 100, and +/− 200 basis point changes in interest rates) for each of the three new strategies and a sixth alternative, a 0 change in rates for the present strategy. The simulation of the current strategy with interest rates unchanged will be used as the baseline income level to which each of the other strategies will be compared.

It is obvious from the table that implementing interest rate risk-reducing strategies can be costly. This is why so much analysis is required to evaluate different strategies for improving the interest rate risk position of the firm. In order to select the least costly strategy, a probability can be applied to each of the five scenarios and the expected value of each strategy can be calculated. For the firm that applies a simple probability of 20% to each interest rate scenario, the expected values of the three scenarios are –$145,000, –$280,000, and –$131,200, respectively. This can be interpreted as the cost of reducing the firm's interest rate risk on $50 million of assets and liabilities. In this case, management would choose Option 3 to reduce their interest rate risk.

TABLE 18.1

One-Year Income Impact Compared to Baseline Income of Implementing Three *GAP*-reducing Strategies for Five Interest Rate Scenarios and Expected Values for Each
(change in interest rate forecast)

+200 bp	+100 bp	0 bp	–100 bp	–200 bp
		Option 1		
+$375,000	+$187,500	–$62,500	–$450,000	–$775,000
		Option 2		
+$525,000	+$270,000	–$467,000	–$678,000	–$1,050,000
		Option 3		
+$467,000	+$205,000	–$178,000	–$425,000	–$725,000

Expected Values

Option 1.

$$\$375,000 \times .20 + \$187,500 \times .20 + (-\$62,500 \times .20) + (-\$450,000 \times .20)$$
$$+ (-\$775,000 \times .20) = -\$145,000$$

Option 2.

$$\$525,000 \times .20 + \$270,000 \times .20 + (-\$467,000 \times .20) + (-\$678,000 \times .20)$$
$$+ (-\$1,050,000 \times .20) = -\$280,000$$

Option 3.

$$\$467,000 \times .20 + \$205,000 \times .20 + (-\$178,000 \times .20) + (-\$425,000 \times .20)$$
$$+ (-\$725,000 \times .20) = -\$131,200$$

✓ Checkpoints

18-1 Why does reducing interest rate risk at intermediaries normally involve reducing the short-term reported income for these firms?

18-2 What are several important approaches to managing interest rate risk?

Financial Futures and Forward Cash Markets

Chapter 16 discussed financial futures and forward cash markets in some depth. Because of the greater operational difficulties in using the futures market, it will be emphasized in this chapter. However, keep in mind that many hedging transactions that can be accomplished in the financial futures market can also be accomplished in the forward cash markets operated by security dealers, GSEs, and foreign exchange dealers.

FUTURES AND FORWARD CASH MARKET HEDGES

The function of futures and forward cash market hedges is to offset price fluctuations of a cash market claim held by an institution or a claim committed to be bought or sold with another contract whose price changes are perfectly negatively correlated with the cash market position. These offsetting positions can be in either the forward cash markets or the futures market.

Active forward cash markets are maintained by dealers in Treasury securities, mortgage-backed securities, and foreign exchange.[2] The major GSEs in mortgages, the FNMA and FHLMC, maintain active forward markets in residential mortgages. These forward markets make it possible to sell, and sometimes buy, mortgages and mortgage-backed securities for forward delivery. This can eliminate price risk for an institution that holds or contemplates investing in these claims and does not want to accept the risk of price fluctuations between the current period and the future period when purchase or sale is contemplated.

One of the first duties of the analyst is to determine whether the forward cash market or futures market is best for reducing interest rate risk. This decision is not always easy and it usually depends on the unique circumstances of the institution and its relationship to dealers. Some of the important differences between the forward cash and futures markets include the following:

1. Futures contracts have established margin requirements that reduce credit risk between the parties to the transaction.

2. The forward market may provide a lower cost due to lower margin requirements.

3. Forward contracts are more flexible in terms of timing and type of claim.

4. Futures contracts are generally easier to offset than forward cash contracts.

5. Futures contracts may be more marketable.

---

[2]The largest forward market is the when-issued Treasury security market, which is run by large commercial banks and security dealers. These firms make forward delivery commitments to sell Treasury securities to their customers before they are issued.

A main point to remember is that futures prices and forward prices move closely together in active markets. As a result, the efficiency of the hedge is not seriously compromised by the selection of one of these markets over the other.

The greater complexity of the financial futures market, however, necessitates a closer look at the mechanics of determining the **hedge ratio** for a financial futures hedge. This is an important problem because frequently the claim to be hedged does not have a futures contract equivalent. When a hedge takes place using a futures or forward contract in a financial asset different from one exposed to price risk in the cash market, it is called a *cross-hedge*.

HEDGE RATIO

A major problem in using the futures market is determining the number of futures contracts needed to hedge the cash market position. The objective is to find the best type and number of futures contracts that provide the highest correlation between the price changes of the cash market position and the futures market position. The hedger wants to create a situation in which, as nearly as possible, the change in price of the contract used to hedge, such as a futures contract, will offset the change in price of the cash market position. The target hedge ratio is the quantity of futures contracts needed to provide the most effective hedge for a given cash market position.[3] It is given by Equation 18.1.

$$\textit{Hedge ratio} = [PV_{cc}/PV_{fc}] \times b_{cc/fc} \qquad [18.1]$$

The hedge ratio is made up of two parts. The first, PV_{cc}/PV_{fc}, is the relationship of a price sensitivity for the cash market claim divided by the price sensitivity of the futures contract. The second part is the correlation between the actual yield change of the cash market claim and the futures market claim.

The first part of the hedge ratio requires establishing the relationship between changes in the price of the cash market claim and the futures market contract in relation to a specified change in open market yields. This is defined by the ratio in Equation 18.2.

$$\textit{Price value of one basis point change in cash claim}$$
$$\div \textit{Price value of one basis point change in futures contract}$$
$$= PV_{cc}/PV_{fc} \qquad [18.2]$$

The quantity in Equation 18.2 is simply the elasticity of the price of the cash market claim, PV_{cc}, in the numerator divided by the elasticity of the price of the futures contract claim, PV_{fc}, in the denominator. These elasticities will depend on the market interest rate, maturity of the cash and futures market claims, and the coupon rate on each. These elasticities therefore must be calculated carefully

---

[3]A similar but less popular method for calculating a hedge ratio is to take the most recent ratio of the change in the cash and futures prices and use it to establish the number of contracts. This method suffers from being based on only one observation. Since basis risk does exist, a single observation model is not recommended. However, regulated financial institutions such as commercial banks and thrifts should establish how their regulators are going to evaluate their hedging techniques and accounting methodologies.

for the cash and futures claim. Moreover, as market conditions change during the life of the hedge, market yields and maturities change; consequently, the hedge ratio that is needed to provide the most efficient hedge will change, making it necessary to change the number of futures contracts in the hedge during the hedge period.

Consider the change in the price of a high-grade ten-year corporate bond with a coupon rate of 10% and a yield to maturity of 9%. A one basis point change in rates to 9.01% will result in a decline in price of −.0639% of par. If a ten-year Treasury futures contract is used with an 8% coupon and 8% yield to maturity, then a one basis point change in yield to maturity to 8.01% will decrease price by −.0680 percent of par. The factor in Equation 18.2 would be −.0639/−.0680 = .9397. In this example, the price of the futures contract will change more than the price of the cash market claim for a given change in interest rates. Therefore, fewer futures market contracts are needed as compared to the dollar amount of cash market claims being hedged. In the previous chapter, duration was used to determine the price elasticity of a financial debt claim. The duration price elasticity measure, discussed in Chapter 17, can also be used to determine the hedge ratio.

The second part of the hedge ratio concerns the relationship between the yield movement of the cash market claim and the futures market contract. This is shown as Equation 18.3.

$$\textit{Change in the yield of the cash market claim} \div$$
$$\textit{Change in the yield of the futures market contract}$$
$$= b_{cc/fc} \qquad\qquad [18.3]$$

The relationship in Equation 18.3 is nothing more than the beta, b, in a simple correlation [(Y: Change in yield of cash market claim) = $a + b$ (X: Change in yield of the futures contract) + Error]. In these correlations, the length of time over which changes in yields are collected should correspond to the length of the hedge period. For short hedges of several days, then, the beta should be calculated using daily changes in yield to maturity for the futures and cash market claims. For hedges of several months, changes in yield to maturity measured over weekly or monthly periods will be appropriate. An example of a daily yield correlation is shown in Exhibit 18.1.

A high correlation between the yield on the cash and futures claims would be reflected by a high coefficient of determination, or R^2. R^2 values range from a low of 0 to a perfect correlation of 1.00. A high correlation between the yield change of the cash and futures market claim does not ensure a riskless hedge, however.

In our example, the beta for the correlation between the change in yields between a ten-year high-grade corporate and ten-year Treasury is .92. This means changes in the yield of ten-year corporate securities change only 92% as much as the ten-year Treasury. Thus, fewer futures contracts are needed to hedge the change in the corporate securities than if the beta were 1.0 or higher. The hedge ratio is computed by taking the product of Equation 18.2 and Equation 18.3.

Hedge ratio = .9397 × .92 = .8645

The hedge ratio of .8645 indicates that less than one dollar of the Treasury futures contract is needed for each dollar of cash claim to be hedged. In this example $.8645 of Treasury bond contracts is required for each dollar of corporate bonds to be hedged.

The hedge ratio shows the price relationship between one dollar of the cash market claim to be hedged and one dollar of the futures contract. Unfortunately, futures contracts do not come in one-dollar denominations. Therefore, it is necessary to compute the number of futures contracts for each hedge transaction. This is easily done by multiplying the hedge ratio by the ratio of the dollar amount of the cash market claims being hedged divided by the dollar amount of the futures contracts.

In the previous example, the hedger is interested in hedging $3,000,000 in corporate bonds. The Treasury bond contract is offered in $100,000 units. Therefore, to hedge $3,000,000 in corporate bonds requires multiplying the hedge ratio by the ratio of the dollar of cash claims to the dollar amount on the futures contract chosen.

Number of futures contracts = Hedge ratio × $3,000,000/$100,000
= .8645 × 30 = 25.94, or 26 contracts.

EXHIBIT 18.1

Correlation Between Yield Changes for Cash and Futures Claim

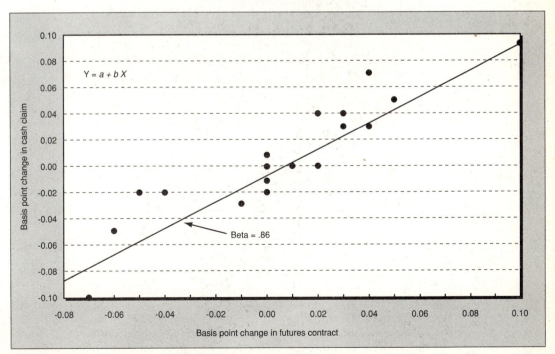

FUTURES HEDGE

Situation:

A pension fund manager expects a $20 million corporate contribution into the plan in 60 days. The funds will be invested in agency mortgage-backed securities at that time. The pension fund manager is concerned that interest rates will fall. Consequently, she considers hedging the price risk by going long on Treasury bond futures.

On the day of the transaction the pension manager has assembled the following information needed to design the correct hedge:

Data Input:

(December 5, 1995)
   Spot price of 8% coupon Treasury bonds 100–03.
   Spot price of 8% mortgage security,
      8% FNMA 99–22.
   March price of 8% coupon futures
      contract for Treasury bonds, March 1996 delivery 99–07.
   Beta (Treasury bond versus mortgage security) .84.
   PV_{fc} per 8% Treasury bonds –.08415.
   PV_{cc} per 8% mortgage security,
      8% FNMA –.08723.

Establishing Hedge Transaction:

Step 1: Determine hedge ratio:

$$Hedge\ ratio = PV_{cc}/PV_{fc} \times b_{cc/fc}$$

$$= -.08723/-.08415 \times .84$$

$$= .8707.$$

Step 2: Determine number of futures contracts:

$$Number\ of\ contracts = \$20,000,000/\$100,000 \times .8707 = 174.1$$

$$= 174\ contracts.$$

Step 3: Buy 174 long contracts on Treasury bonds.

Data Input:

(Feb. 15, 1996)
   Treasury bond futures price, March 1996 contract 101–08.
   Mortgage security, 8% FNMA 101–12.

Results:

Cost without futures hedge:
  Purchase 8% FNMA, $20 million par value
  March 15, 1996 cost = $20,000,000 × 101–12   = $20,275,000

Cost with futures hedge:
  Purchase 8% FNMA, $20 million par value
  March 15, 1996 = $20,000,000 × 101–12   = $20,275,000
  Futures gain [(101–08) – (99–07)]% × 174
    × $100,000   –358,875

  Cost with futures hedge: $19,916,125

Futures hedge reduced cost of mortgage securities resulting from the fall in interest rates.

TYPES OF RISK-REDUCING HEDGING TRANSACTIONS

As discussed in Chapter 16, there are two types of futures positions. The first is a **long futures position,** which is analogous to buying the financial claim with an obligation to sell it on or before a specified date at the market price prevailing at the time of sale. This position is used for hedging when the firm has sold or is committed to sell a financial claim in the forward cash market that it does not own. In this case, the hedger is concerned about a rise in price. The firm has an outstanding contract to deliver a claim at a predetermined price but does not yet own the claim. A **short cash position** involves selling the claim in the forward cash market and is used to hedge the price risk on a financial claim that is owned or if there exists a firm commitment to buy. The firm, however, has no contract to sell at a predetermined price. In this case, the hedger is concerned about a possible drop in price on the claim in the future when the sale takes place.

The trading activities of commercial banks and investment banking firms routinely involve selling financial claims to customers with the expectation that they will cover their short position at some future time. This situation frequently involves the need to hedge. Another example is an insurance company that sells a guaranteed investment contract to a pension fund at a fixed yield when the sale will not fund for a specified period. The insurance company has committed to a fixed-cost liability without locking in the yield on the assets to ensure a positive interest margin. Such a firm could be thought of as being short fixed-rate assets. In the futures market, the firm could go long on a futures contract in a long-term bond in order to lock in the value of assets to be acquired in the cash market at some future point.

The other basic futures transaction is a **short futures position.** This position is analogous to selling a financial claim in the forward cash market with an obligation to buy it back on or before a specified date at the prevailing price. There are many circumstances in which a financial firm will find itself needing to hedge a long cash position. Financial firms routinely commit to make loans at an agreed-upon rate to be funded at some future date, creating a long cash position.

A firm that has not yet funded this commitment or sold the loan in the secondary market, as in the case of a mortgage commitment, would be exposed to interest rate risk.

A common example of such a situation would be a mortgage banking firm that has made commitments to homebuyers to fund mortgages at a specified rate. Such commitments usually take 60 days or more to fund. With this long cash position, the firm might consider using the futures market to create a short sale of a futures contract to cover their long position. Another example would include a firm that has very short-term liabilities and longer-term assets, a large negative periodic *GAP*. Such a firm could be thought of as being long on long-term assets. To hedge such a position, the firm could go short in the futures market for long-term bonds.

Exhibit 18.2 shows a number of common unhedged positions in which financial institutions might find themselves. There are two types of hedges shown. A **macro hedge** refers to a hedge involving the interest rate price risk of a firm's entire portfolio of financial assets and liabilities such as that related to correcting a large positive or negative *GAP*. **Selective hedging** involves reducing the price risk on a specific asset or liabilility or transaction such as a loan commitment. These positions could create the need for an offsetting futures market hedged position. The exhibit also shows a hypothetical futures position that might be used to hedge the risk of the cash position.

HAZARDS OF FUTURES MARKET TRANSACTIONS

Although the concepts involved in futures market transactions appear straightforward, the actual mechanics of using the futures market are complex and represent potential risks. Several of the more common problems in using the futures market for hedging the types of transactions shown in Exhibit 18.1 include:

1. Managing basis risk.
2. Hedging options risk with futures contracts.
3. Accounting for futures transactions.

Basis Risk

A primary underlying assumption in using the futures market for hedging price risk is that the price of the futures contract will closely track the movements of the price of the claim in the cash market. *Basis risk* is defined as the probability that the price of two financial claims do not closely correlate to one another over time. That is, the functional price relationship between two financial claims shows low correlation, as in the calculation of the hedge ratio. This statistic was defined for the hedge ratio as R^2. This coefficient is the correlation between the change in yield of the cash market claim and the change in yield for the futures contract.

EXHIBIT 18.2

Common Unhedged Financial Positions of Financial Institutions and the Futures Position to Hedge Them

Cash Market Position	Futures Market Position	Futures Market Transaction
Hedging Commitment Lender makes a fixed-rate loan commitment to borrower to be funded in 60 days: long cash position in fixed-rate assets	Lender requires a short futures bond contract *Concern:* Rates will rise	Sell (go short) a Treasury note or bond contract due 60+ days
Reducing Negative Periodic *GAP* Intermediary has a large negative periodic *GAP* between assets and liabilities: long cash position in fixed-rate assets	Intermediary requires a short futures bond contract *Concern:* Rates will rise	Sell (go short) a Treasury note or bond contract due long term
Reducing a Positive Periodic *GAP* Intermediary has a large positive periodic *GAP:* short cash position in fixed-rate assets	Intermediary requires a long futures contract *Concern:* Rates will fall	Buy (go long) a Treasury note or bond contract due long term
Locking in Borrowing Rate Intermediary has a collateralized borrowing coming due in three months and would like to lock in today's interest rate on the refunding: long cash position in a fixed-rate asset	Intermediary requires a short futures position *Concern:* Rates will rise	Sell (go short) a Treasury note or bond contract due after refunding date
Locking in Asset Yield Intermediary has sold a fixed-rate liability due to be funded in 90 days and wants to lock in an asset yield: short cash position in fixed-rate assets	Intermediary requires a long futures position *Concern:* Rates will fall	Buy (go long) a Treasury note or bond contract due after funding date

Clearly, basis risk is very important in futures market hedging transactions, because the primary purpose of a hedge is to go long or short on a futures contract whose price will be perfectly negatively correlated with the cash market claim's price. Such perfect negative correlation will provide an effective portfolio hedge.

The following example will show vividly how basis risk can adversely impact the success of a futures market hedge. Consider an institutional investor that is interested in using a portfolio of high-yield securities (junk bonds) as collateral in a collateralized bond obligation. Such an issue is to be priced at a yield premium over the five-year Treasury note. The securities chosen as collateral are five-to ten-year high-yield bonds with a weighted-average yield-to-the-call of 14%. The bond issuer is concerned that interest rates will rise, reducing the spread between the weighted return on the high-yield bonds and the collateralized financing.

In order to hedge this position, the finance department concludes that the firm should sell a five-year Treasury note futures contract. If interest rates rise, then the firm will be able to cover (buy back) the futures contract at a lower price, creating a gain to offset the expected loss in the price of the high-yield bonds. The department believes that if the general level of interest rates falls, it will impact the high-yield market as much as the Treasury market. In other words, it computes the $b_{cc/fc}$ to be 1.0. However, the R^2 is only .3, a very poor correlation. To the extent the correlation is poor, it represents basis risk to the firm.

The firm's hedge works as follows. The firm sells $5 million of five-year Treasury securities in the futures contract. At the end of 60 days, the firm completes preparations to issue the collateralized bond obligation. A major event takes place, however, to complicate the situation for the firm: ten days before the bond issue, the nation's largest high-yield bond dealer files for bankruptcy, sending the high-yield bond market into a tailspin. The price of the portfolio of high-yield bonds falls by 4%. In the meantime, the Treasury market rallies and the five-year Treasury note increases in price by 2 3/32. The result of the hedge program is shown in Table 18.2.

TABLE 18.2

Result of Hedge Program

	Position	Amount	Change in Price	Change in Value of Position
High-yield bonds	Long	$5 million	−4%	−$200,000
Treasury futures	Short	$5 million	+2 3/32	−$104,678
Gain or loss on hedge				−$304,678

Clearly, in the example, the finance department did not fully understand the potential impact of basis risk represented by the low R^2. The relationship between the value of the high-yield bonds and the Treasury securities was very unstable. In this particular case, the relationship was actually negative for a short period of time, during which the price of the futures contract and Treasury securities rose while the price of the high-yield bonds fell. The hedge actually exacerbated the loss to the firm. This is an extreme example, but it does serve to show the potential impact of basis risk on the effectiveness of a hedge.

Mixing Futures and Options

Exhibit 18.2 showed a number of situations in which a firm might want to hedge a financial position. A careful look at the exhibit will indicate that a financial firm has actually issued an option in one of the hedge positions. It is very risky to hedge option price risk with a futures contract.

In this case, the firm has an outstanding fixed-rate loan commitment. This type of commitment is an option owned by the prospective borrower. Such a situation could result in a dangerous use of a futures market hedge. Consider a mortgage banking company that makes fixed-rate mortgages whose customary practice is to make a mortgage commitment to a potential homebuyer at the prevailing fixed-rate mortgage rate. The commitment will be honored if the loan is funded within 60 days. This is tantamount to the lender writing an option to a homebuyer to deliver (put) a mortgage at a specified price and interest rate on or before a specified date.

What might happen if the mortgage banker uses the futures market to provide price protection between the time the commitment is made and the loan is sold in the secondary market? The mortgage lender decides to use the ten-year Treasury to hedge the risk of price volatility in the value of the mortgage to be delivered to the secondary market agency within 90 days. As conditions unfold over the course of the 60-day commitment period, the trend of interest rates is down. The commitment made to the homebuyer at a rate of 10.25% for a 30-year mortgage can now be obtained from a competing lender at a rate of 9.5%. The homebuyer discovers this and decides to obtain a loan commitment from another lender. Table 18.3 illustrates this transaction.

In this example, the firm used a futures contract to hedge an option. The futures contract requires that the firm fulfill the obligation to deliver. The option does not. Consequently, the firm lost money on the futures position with no offsetting gain in the mortgage cash market. The firm attempted to hedge option risk with a futures contract.

TABLE 18.3

Result of Hedge Program

	Position	Amount	Change in Price	Change in Value of Position
$200,000 ten-year Treasury futures	Short	$200,000	+3.25%	–$6,500
$200,000 mortgage	Long	0	N/A	N/A
Gain or loss on hedge				–$6,500

Despite the obvious risk in using futures contracts to hedge the risks of options, it is frequently done in practice. In the case of the mortgage banker, it is typical to determine an average percentage of loans that close as a percentage of the total dollar amount of commitments written. The **closed loan ratio** is used to determine the number of futures contracts to use. This ratio is adjusted higher during periods of rising open market interest rates, when a high percentage of the outstanding commitments move to an in-the-money condition and, therefore, are expected to be exercised. The ratio is decreased in a falling interest rate environment, when a high percentage of outstanding commitments are out-of-the-money and therefore, are expected not to be exercised. The closed loan ratio is raised when open market rates are rising and lowered when rates fall. However, the possibility still remains that if interest rates fall, the firm will have a large loss on the futures position and no offsetting gain in the cash market.

Accounting Issues

Making matters somewhat more complicated in the world of futures are the GAAP requirements affecting futures transaction accounting. Although accounting for a futures position does not affect the economic consequences of the transaction, it could affect the timing of when gains or losses are reported. Accounting for a futures position requires that the futures position be marked-to-market if the firm is unable to specify the cash market financial claim being hedged that has potential price volatility.

If the firm can identify a specific financial claim cash market position or outstanding commitment that represents a financial risk due to price fluctuation, then the firm would account for it by offsetting the gain or loss of the futures contract against the gain or loss in the cash market at the time the positions are closed out. If there is no current cash gain or loss, then the gain or loss on the futures contract is used to adjust the cost basis of the hedged cash market instrument. This results in the amortization of the gain or loss over the life of the hedged asset or liability.

The problem with using the accounting rules relates to circumstances in which a specific cash market claim cannot be identified easily, as in the case of an entire asset portfolio being hedged to reduce a large positive or negative periodic *GAP*. This is also the case when the relationship between the change in the futures market price and the hedged cash market claim price is not highly correlated, with a low R^2, due to high basis risk. In these circumstances, accounting for the transaction would require that the futures contract be marked-to-market and the cash position accounted for at the lower of cost or market. The firm could be experiencing a successful hedge but would be required to report the futures gain or loss without reporting the offsetting cash market gain or loss. This accounting problem should become less important as more financial firms adopt mark-to-market accounting for financial assets held.[4]

---

[4]Accounting for futures transactions is guided by the Financial Accounting Standards Board *Statement Number 80* "Accounting for Futures Contracts," 1984. Despite the rules established for accounting, there continue to be disagreements between management, accountants, and regulators over whether a transaction is a hedge or speculation and, whether it is efficient enough to have gains and loses taken over the life of the cash position (if classified a hedge) or immediately marked-to-market (if deemed a speculation).

This accounting practice effectively reduces the desire to implement the macro hedge listed in Exhibit 18.2, even though such a hedge could be used effectively to improve the firm's overall periodic or duration *GAP* position. To avoid having to mark-to-market a futures position, a firm would have to pick a specific group of assets or liabilities to hedge. It would also have to demonstrate that the hedge contract's price was highly correlated with the cash claim's price.

✓ Checkpoints

18-3 What is a futures contract?

18-4 Financial futures contracts are used to hedge the price fluctuations related to changes in interest rates. What kinds of situations might suggest the use of a futures market hedge?

18-5 What is meant by a long and short futures position? What is meant by the expressions *macro hedge* and *selective hedge*?

18-6 What is basis risk, and why is it important in hedging using the futures market?

18-7 Why is it risky to hedge the risk of writing an option with a futures market hedge?

18-8 What are some of the accounting issues that relate to using the futures market?

18-9 In the futures market, what is meant by *margin*? Who must put up margin?

18-10 What is the hedge ratio as it relates to using the futures market? How is it calculated? Why is a correct hedge ratio so important?

Options and Futures Options

Fortunately, there is an alternative market for hedging the price risk associated with being the writer of options such as loan commitments. These are the options and options on futures markets. Since options were discussed in Chapter 16, futures options will be the focus here. **Futures options** contracts are options to buy or sell a specified futures contract prior to its expiration at an agreed-upon price.

In October 1982, the Chicago Board Options Exchange (CBOE) of the CBOT began trading options contracts on Treasury bond futures contracts. These contracts, known as *futures options,* are offered on Treasury bonds, notes, and bills; a municipal bond index; interest rate swaps; Eurodollar bonds; LIBOR bonds; British gilts; and mortgage-backed securities. Despite all these contracts, the largest volume of outstanding contracts is concentrated in Treasury bonds and Eurodollar bonds.

The logic of having options written against futures contracts may not seem readily apparent. However, the standardization of futures contracts, the organized trading of futures contracts that creates marketability, and the future's market exchange margin system all make the futures contract a good alternative for writing option contracts. This is especially true since it has been shown that futures prices closely track forward cash market prices. Therefore the futures contract provides an excellent vehicle to establish an option for hedging price risk. These advantages do not mean that investment dealers do not write and broker negotiated price options directly. They do. However, the futures options market has several advantages over the dealer market—the two most important being marketability and standardization.

FUTURES OPTIONS: A DESCRIPTION

Recall from Chapter 16 that options are written as either *call* (a right to buy) or *put* (a right to sell) options. A call (put) option written on a futures contract provides the owner with the right to buy a long (short) futures contract. That is, the call (put) option on a futures contract is a right to go long (short) on a futures contract. The advantage of the option is that the price of the futures contract is set at the time the option is written. And, like all options, a futures option is exercised at the discretion of the holder.

Futures options are written to coincide exactly with traded futures contracts. Indeed, they are written against existing traded futures contracts. Thus, the exercise dates of the options are the expiration dates for the futures contracts. Exhibit 18.3 shows typical quotes as they might appear in the financial press for several

EXHIBIT 18.3

Reading the Financial Page
Futures Options
(typical listing)

Treasury bonds $100,000 bonds; 64ths of 100%
Chicago Board of Trade

Strike	Calls			Puts		
Price	Jan.	Mar.	June	Jan.	Mar.	June
98	2–14	3–41	3–56	0–08	0–25	1–14
100	0–12	1–31	1–42	0–10	1–01	2–01
102	0–02	0–42	1–45	1–05	2–06	3–20
104	0–01	0–25	0–52	3–20	4–11	5–21
106	—	0–02	0–06	—	6–02	7–01
108	—	—	—	—	8–00	8–42

Estimated volume: 75,000
Previous volume: 52,000
    23,000 calls; 29,000 puts
Open interest: 340,000 calls; 185,000 puts

This table shows a typical listing for futures options contracts on Treasury bonds. The options are written against futures contracts listed on the CBOT. The prices are expressed as points and 64ths of 100%. Thus, a price of 1–31 for the $100,000 March contract at a strike of 100 would cost (1 31/64% x $100,000) = $1,484.375.

futures options on Treasury bonds. Notice that there are three call and put contracts at six different strike prices.

Consider the March call at 100. The contract amount is for $100,0000 par value of bonds. This option provides the owner with the right to purchase a long futures contract at a price of 100 $^{31}/_{64}$ percent of par on or before March. The call premium, or price, of this option is 1 $^{31}/_{64}$. Each $^1/_{64}$ is worth ($^1/_{64}$% × $100,000 =) $15.625. Thus, the price of one call at a strike price of 100 would be ($^{95}/_{64}$ × $15.625 per $^1/_{64}$ =) $1,484.38.

At the time this option could be purchased, the March T-bond futures contract was selling at 99 $^7/_{32}$. Consequently, the option in question would be considered to be out-of-the-money. This means that there would be no profit from exercising the option at the current price of the futures contract. If the futures contract were selling for 100 $^5/_{32}$, however, the option would be considered to be in-the-money since the option could be exercised immediately at 100 and the futures contract sold at 100 $^5/_{32}$.

USING TRADED FUTURES OPTIONS

In practice, futures options are used for two primary purposes. First, they are used to hedge the price risk of writing options. On many occasions, financial institutions write options to customers. A loan commitment with a rate set in advance is a good example of a put option sold to a potential borrower. In this situation, the lender has written a put option to accept a borrower's debt claim at a specified interest rate on or before a specified date. If interest rates rise, the borrower can be expected to exercise the option and deliver the debt claim. If rates fall, however, the borrower will likely borrow at a lower rate elsewhere.

One way to hedge the risk inherent in writing this put is for the lender to buy an offsetting put futures option that expires around the time of the loan commitment. If interest rates rise, the lender will lose on the loan commitment and gain on the put futures option. Thus, a futures put (call) option can be used to hedge a cash market put (call) option written in the cash market.

The second primary purpose of futures options is to purchase price insurance. The owner of an option stands to lose only the option premium paid but stands to gain an unlimited amount if the price of a futures contract rises in the case of a call option or falls in the case of a put. Consequently, a futures option may be purchased to provide protection from an adverse price change in a cash market position without giving up a potential gain from a favorable price change.

Exhibit 18.4 provides several examples of how futures options can be used to manage interest rate risk.

The primary advantages of futures options relate to the fact that, unlike futures contracts, an option provides a safer hedge for options written by the institution than do futures contracts. In theory, options price risk should be hedged with offsetting options. Another advantage of options is that there is no margin required.

One disadvantage of futures options is that options do not provide offsetting price protection until the futures price exceeds the strike price by the amount of the option premium. Options are not cost-effective for small adverse price moves.

EXHIBIT 18.4

Selected Futures Options Transactions for Managing Interest Rate Risk

Cash Market Transaction	Cash Market Risk Position	Option Used to Hedge Interest Rate Risk
Fixed-rate commitment outstanding	Sold put option on loan	Buy futures option put on debt similar to loan
Hold large bond portfolio. Concerned over possible change in Fed policy raising rates	Long cash position on Treasury bonds	Buy futures option put on Treasury bonds
Sold certificates of deposit with clause permitting additional deposits at existing interest rate	Sold call option on additional CDs	Buy futures option call on debt claim similar to CD

DEMONSTRATION PROBLEM | **FUTURES OPTION HEDGE**

Situation:

A mortgage lender has made a $1 million commitment to a borrower on March 2, 1996. The loan has a rate of 9.25% and a 20-year maturity. It must be closed within 60 days.

The lender is concerned that if interest rates fall, the loan will not close. This is a problem since the loan has been presold to a life insurance company to yield the life company 9%. Consequently, if the loan does not close, the lender will have to purchase another loan in the secondary market to yield the rate promised to the life company. If rates fall, buying a loan to cover the committed sale to the life company will result in a loss.

The solution is purchasing a call option on a long-term futures contract to offset the put option offered the borrower.

Data Input:

(March 2, 1996)

Spot price of 8% coupon Treasury bonds	96–03
Spot price of 9% mortgage	100–22
March price of 8% coupon futures contract for Treasury bonds, June 1996 delivery	95–07

Data Input: *(cont.)*

Beta (Treasury bond versus mortgage)	.82
PV_{fc} per 8% Treasury bonds	−.8415
PV_{cc} per 9% mortgage	−.8945
June Treasury bond call option price, strike price 97	1–50

Establishing Hedge Transaction:

Step 1: Determine hedge ratio:

$$Hedge\ ratio = PV_{cc}/PV_{fc} \times b_{cc/fc} = -.8945/-.8415 \times .82 = .8716$$

Step 2: Determine number of futures options contracts:

$$Number\ of\ contracts = \$1,000,000/\$100,000 \times .8716$$

$$= 8.716 = 9\ contracts$$

Step 3: Buy nine call options at 1–50 per option = 9 × $1,781.25
$$= \$16,031.25$$

Data Input:

Rates fall, loan does not close, lender must purchase mortgage in secondary market to deliver to life company.
(May 4, 1996)

Treasury bond futures price, June 1996 contract	100–08
Mortgage, 9%	102–30
June Treasury bond call option price, June 1996	6–50

Results:

Cost without futures options hedge:

Purchase 9% mortgage = $1,000,000 × 102–30	= −$1,029,375
Deliver 9% mortgage = $1,000,000	+1,000,000
Loss	−$29,375

Cost with futures options hedge:

Purchase 9% mortgage = $1,000,000 × 102–30	= −$1,029,375
Cost of options	−16,031
Deliver 9% mortgage = $1,000,000	+1,000,000
Futures options gain [6–50−(1–50)]% × $100,000 × 9 = $5,000 × 9 =	45,000
Loss	$ −406

Futures options hedge reduced the loss. The loan commitment was not exercised, and the lender had to buy a mortgage in the secondary market to meet its obligation to the life company.

Note: Futures and cash quoted in 32nds and options in 64ths of 100%.

✓ Checkpoints

18-11 What is a futures option? What advantage is there to writing an option on a preexisting futures contract?

18-12 How can a futures option be used to reduce interest rate risk for a firm with a commitment to lend money at an agreed-upon rate three months in the future?

Interest Rate Swaps

The interest rate swap is one of the fastest growing interest rate risk management tools. The first interest rate swap was accomplished in England in 1981. The United States got into the act in 1982 when the Student Loan Marketing Association completed one of the transactions. The growth in swaps has been rapid, with approximately $1 billion in swaps being accomplished each year.

As discussed in Chapter 16, the basic use of the interest rate swap is to convert a liability priced at one term to maturity into another. A liability priced at a fixed rate can be converted into a short-term indexed liability, or vice-versa. This gives management considerable flexibility. It provides a very efficient way to alter the interest rate profile of the firm substantially without changing the firm's asset-liability mix. This is important because firms each have special comparative advantages in the types of assets and liabilities they originate. This mix may not produce the most desirable interest rate risk position, however. That's where the interest rate swap comes into play. Leaving the firm's asset-liability structure in place, the firm can execute a swap and alter its interest rate risk position to a more desirable one.

DEMONSTRATION PROBLEM   **INTEREST RATE SWAP**

Situation:

Southern Savings Bank has a large negative one-year periodic GAP_1. This situation can be improved by completing an interest rate swap. The bank will accept a fixed-rate obligation for five years at a fixed rate of 7%. In return, it will receive income at the three-month Treasury bill rate plus. 50%. The term of the swap will be five years.

Data Input:

The bank's quarterly income statement, ignoring operating expenses and loan losses, is shown below. The bank's GAP_1 is negative $3 million. The bank is contemplating a $3 million notional principal swap.

Quarterly Net Interest Margin

Interest income	$8,500,000
Interest expense	6,250,000
Net interest margin	$2,250,000

Interest swap $3 million notional principal five years fixed @ 7.00%
Interest swap $3 million notional principal, floating quarterly, @ three-month
bill + .50%, current bill rate 4.5%

Result:

The result of this swap will depend on future changes in interest rate levels.
Table 18.4 shows the change in the net interest margin for changes of (+/–)
0%, 1%, and 2% changes in the level of interest rates. (For simplicity, assume
all assets and liabilities, except the swap, reprice or mature after the period
shown in the sensitivity analysis.)

TABLE 18.4

Sensitivity Analysis of Net Interest Margin
Changes in Interest Rates of (+/–) 0%, 1%, and 2%
(dollars in thousands)

Change in Interest Rates

	–2.00%	–1.00%	0	+1.00%	+2.00%
Without swap					
Interest income	$8.50	$8.50	$8.50	$8.50	$8.50
Interest expense	5.95	6.10	6.25	6.40	6.55
Net interest margin	$2.55	$2.40	$2.25	$2.10	$1.95
With swap					
Interest income	$8.50	$8.50	$8.50	$8.50	$8.50
Interest expense	6.70	6.55	6.40	6.40	6.40
Net interest margin	$1.80	$1.95	$2.10	$2.10	$2.10

Southern Savings Bank's swap has the impact of insulating its net interest margin from increases in open market interest rates. There is a cost to doing this,
however. The firm will experience a decline in its net interest margin initially
(under the 0 change in rate scenario), since the cost of the five-year swap payments is 2% higher than the current receipts under the short-term swap. This
is because the term structure is upward sloping at the time of the swap.
Another cost of the swap is the spread that the counterparty takes out of the
transaction. This is a net loss shared by the two swapping organizations.

COMMERCIAL BANK PROFIT FROM THE SWAP

In the case of Exhibit 18.5, the commercial bank has written two swap agreements that provide a .125% margin each between the interest payments it receives and the interest payments it makes. This amounts to .25% on $15 million
of total principal. The profit from this transaction can be considered the present
value of these interest rate margin cash flows. The swap is outstanding five years
or ten periods ($n = 10$). When discounted at a weighted cost of capital of, say,

12%, the present value of an n period swap to the bank, ignoring administrative costs and credit risk, would be shown by the equation below:

$$Present\ value\ of\ swap = \Sigma_{n-1}^{10}\ [(.0025\ /\ 2) \times \$15,000,000]\ /\ [(1 + .12\ /\ 2)^n]$$

$$= \$146,282$$

EXHIBIT 18.5

Payments Made Semiannually Among Three-party Swap
with Bank as Intermediary

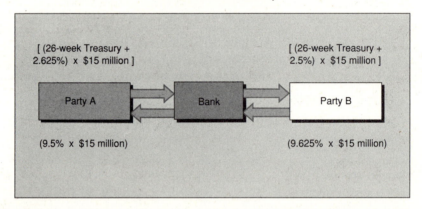

In January 1989 the Federal Reserve Board issued regulations establishing the capital requirements required of commercial banks holding a swap portfolio. Until that time, the swap portfolios of commercial banks required no capital. This was due in part to the fact that swap transactions are off-balance sheet transactions since the notional principal of swap transactions is not shown on the balance sheet.

In order to recognize the credit and interest rate risks inherent in swaps written by commercial banks, the Federal Reserve developed a methodology that determines the minimum capital requirement to be held against swaps. The amount of this reserve is based primarily on a mark-to-market calculation using the notional principal, swap coupon rate, and prevailing market interest rate.

Consider a commercial bank that has written a swap with four remaining years to maturity, calling for a 10.5% fixed-coupon payment. If after a one-year period, the current prevailing swap rate for the remaining three-year term on this swap is 7.5%, then it is clear that the bank could lose 3% per annum to replace the swap if the counterparty that was making the 10.5% payment to the bank defaulted. The risk-based capital requirement is based on the recognition of this potential loss to the bank.

RISKS IN MANAGING SWAP PORTFOLIOS

An institution managing a large swap portfolio must understand the risks involved. These risks include credit, interest rate, and basis risks.

Credit Risk

Swap credit risk is the risk that a counterparty will default on a swap agreement at a time when the replacement of the swap would represent a loss to the intermediary.

Interest Rate Risk

Swap interest rate risk is the risk that a swap that is written by the intermediary is unhedged by offsetting swaps or other assets and liabilities. This unhedged swap position would occur if an intermediary were making floating payments to a counterparty under a swap agreement when the firm had a large negative periodic *GAP*. Such a swap would exacerbate the interest rate mismatch of the organization.

Basis Risk

The intermediary accepts basis risk to the extent that one floating rate swap payment is tied to one index and an offsetting swap tied to another. If these two indices are not perfectly correlated, then the firm will face basis risk. If an intermediary contracted to pay six-month LIBOR + 2.25% to a counterparty and accepted a payment of 26-week Treasury +2.50% and the relationship between the two rates changed, then the intermediary would be exposed to basis risk.

INTEREST RATE SWAPS AND INTEREST RATE RISK MANAGEMENT

The usefulness of interest rate swaps in interest rate risk management should be obvious at this point. The interest rate swap can be used to convert liabilities whose cost is predominantly short term into fixed-rate liabilities, and vice versa. The swap can be used very much like the interest rate futures contract to hedge against the price risk of debt securities. The advantage of the swap is that the term of a swap can frequently far exceed that of a futures contract. Some swaps are written for up to 20 years. In addition, swaps provide more flexibility due to the negotiated nature of the transaction.

A financial institution with high interest rate risk due to a large positive or negative periodic *GAP* would use the swap as shown in Exhibit 18.6.

EXHIBIT 18.6

Use of Swap for Interest Rate Risk Management

Interest Rate Risk Position	Indicated Swap
Large negative periodic *GAP*	Assume fixed-rate interest payment for short-term interest receipt
Large positive periodic *GAP*	Assume short-term interest payment for fixed-rate interest receipt

✓ Checkpoints

18-13 Why are commercial banks involved in the swap market?

18-14 How does a commercial bank or other intermediary writer of swaps make a profit on swap transactions?

18-15 What types of risk are inherent in swap transactions?

18-16 How would you use an interest rate swap to help manage interest rate risk?

Adjustable-rate Lending

Many financial contracts have adjustable-rate interest provisions. Loans tied to the prime rate, Treasury bill yields, and LIBOR are common examples. The reason so many financial intermediaries lend using adjustable-rate contracts is to reduce interest rate risk. Most depositories, for example, have limited access to long-term liabilities. However, they have ample short-term liabilities, since this is the depositors' preference. As a result, these lenders prefer loans whose interest rate closely tracks the changes in short-term liability costs.

The problems in the thrift industry in the late 1970s and early 1980s were the impetus for the development and widespread adoption of adjustable-rate mortgage (ARM) programs for residential housing. It also led to the adoption of adjustable-rate indexed claims in other contracts as well. Until the early 1980s, only a handful of state-chartered institutions had the clear legal ability to write these mortgages. Even in those states that permitted ARM lending, however, the majority of state-chartered institutions made fixed-rate mortgages (FRMs). In the early 1980s, however, that changed as the thrift and commercial bank regulators adopted regulations permitting ARMs. Until that time, ARMs were criticized by groups of homebuilders and real estate sales groups who felt that the "inferior" ARM would drive "superior" FRMs out of the market. These groups contended this would hurt the sales of new and existing houses. With the deregulation of deposit rates, however, the pressure for regulators to authorize ARMs was overwhelming.

Regulators in the early 1980s demanded that the nation's savings and loans reduce their interest rate risk positions. They strongly encouraged institutions to originate these loans for portfolio investment. By the mid-1980s, close to 50% of all newly originated mortgages were ARMs. By 1992, still only about 30% of the nation's single-family mortgage stock were ARMs. These percentages compare to virtually no ARMs in the mid-1970s. The percentage of home mortgages that are ARMs is not likely to grow signficantly as long as the GSEs continue to dominate the mortgage market and can create hybrid mortgage securities such as CMOs and REMICs from pools of fixed-rate mortgages.

THE BASIC ARM FEATURES

The ARM has been the source of significant innovation over the last decade. Several features of ARMs, however, have to be established at the time they are originated. Because there are so many features, it is easy to see why ARMs have been the source of so much innovation and consumer confusion. The main features include:

1. The interest rate index.
2. The margin over the index.
3. The adjustment period.
4. The option of using interest rate caps and floors.
5. The option of a lower-than-coupon initial rate (sometimes known as *teasers*).
6. The option of payment limits.
7. The option of negative amortization.

The first three of these provisions are necessary in any adjustable rate contract, and the others are optional.

EXHIBIT 18.7

Common ARM Indices

One-year Treasury
Three-year Treasury
Various LIBOR rates
Cost of funds index, various Federal Home Loan Banks
Cost of funds index, national

Interest Rate Index

The **interest rate index** specifies the base upon which the mortgage's interest rate is established. Exhibit 18.7 shows a number of the more commonly used indices.

Interest Rate Margin

The **interest rate margin** determines the percentage amount of spread the borrower's rate is established over the index. The index is determined at a specified time and the margin is added to it. For example, the 11th District cost of funds index for the Federal Home Loan Bank of San Francisco is determined to be 8.02% in March 1994. The margin on a particular mortgage is 2.25%. The rate on the mortgage would be 10.27% (8.02% + 2.25% = 10.27%).

Adjustment Period

The **adjustment period** determines the amount of time between adjustments to the mortgage rate. Within the adjustment period, the changes in the index do not influence the rate on the mortgage. However, at the adjustment period, the index value will affect the mortgage rate. Adjustment periods are typically monthly (on cost of funds ARMs), semiannually, annually, or every three years (on certain Treasury and LIBOR ARMs).

Interest Rate Life-of-loan Caps and Floors

An ARM can be written to incorporate a maximum rate **life-of-loan cap**, which establishes the highest rate the index plus margin can rise to, regardless of the rise in the index. The mortgage may also incorporate a **life-of-loan floor**, which is the minimum rate to which the index and margin can fall.

Initial Rate Discount or Teaser

It is common to have ARMs quoted in the market with an initial rate that is below the index plus margin. This lower rate has come to be known as a **teaser**. The teaser has been used to encourage the use of the ARM at the expense of the FRM. Occasionally, the lender allows the borrower to qualify for the mortgage at the lower monthly payment computed at the teaser. This allows some borrowers to qualify for a larger mortgage.

Payment Change Limits—The Annual Life-of-loan Cap

Some ARMs have a maximum payment increase feature built into them. This is known as an **annual life-of-loan cap.** These ARMs will constrain the rise in the index to say, 1% or 2% within any 12-month period. In the case of a cost of funds ARM, the limit frequently has been set so that the maximum adjustment in rate will be limited to no more than what will produce a maximum, say, 7.5% payment increase in any annual period. This feature is designed to limit the payment "shock" to the borrower and lessen the probability of default.

Negative Amortization

Most mortgages provide for a portion of each monthly payment to reduce the principal balance on the mortgage. This is called *amortization*. Some ARMs have a negative amortization feature. The principal goes up instead of down. This occurs when the index plus margin increases but the payment is held constant or is not permitted to rise enough to pay all the interest, thus creating a negative amortization situation. A mortgage with a 7.5% payment increase limit, as in the previous example, might include a negative amortization feature.

These ARM features can be put together in an infinite variety of combinations and have clearly been a major tool in reducing interest rate risk at the nation's depository institutions.

Many depositories will originate ARMs for portfolio investment and FRMs for sale in the secondary market. This permits the institution to create two valuable income streams that act as an interest rate hedge against rising interest rates. In the firm's portfolio, it will have an adjustable-rate asset whose rate increases as open market interest rates rise. In addition, the firm will also produce a servicing contract that also acts as a hedge against rising interest rates. A servicing contract will tend to rise in value as open market interest rates rise, due to the slower prepayment experience anticipated during a period of rising interest rates.

OTHER ADJUSTABLE LOANS

The success of the ARM has led intermediaries to develop a wide array of adjustable-rate consumer loan contracts. Today, the adjustable-rate feature is used on second mortgages, credit card receivables, lines of credit, and security loans. On other than first mortgages, the more popular indices include the prime rate, Treasury bill rate, and cost of funds.

✓ **Checkpoints:**

18-17 Why has there been an increase in the use of adjustable-rate financial contracts?

18-18 What are the basic features of most adjustable-rate financial claims?

18-19 What are some of the problems in the valuation of financial claims with caps, floors, payment change limits, teasers, and other features found in many adjustable-rate financial claim contracts?

18-20 What are the most common indices used in adjustable-rate financial claim contracts?

18-21 Increasing the use of adjustable-rate loans in the portfolio will decrease interest rate risk for most depositories, but this action could also decrease the firm's interest rate margin. Why is this so?

Caps, Floors, and Collars

Over the last decade, a new class of option contracts have been developed called **caps, floors,** and **collars.** These options provide that the writer pay the option holder interest payments on a fixed amount of notional principal should the interest rate index stipulated by the contract rise above a predetermined level, a cap, or below a predetermined level, a floor. A collar is a combination of a cap and floor contract.

Caps and floors are used for hedging interest rate risk. A financial institution which is using short-term rate-indexed liabilities to invest in intermediate-term assets would be exposed to the risk that short-term rates rise. Such a firm would be a candidate for a cap option. The opposite case would be a firm with short-term rate-indexed assets financed with intermediate-term liabilities. This firm is exposed to declining profits if interest rates fall. Table 18.5 provides the payoff schedule for a cap and floor written for one six-month period at an initial rate of 6.00%. These cap and floor options provide that at the end of six months the writer of the option will pay the difference between the initial rate and market rate times the amount of notional principal for six months. The table shows that at a market rate of 4% on July 1, 1996, the floor writer would be obligated to pay $\{[(6.00\% - 4.00\%) \times \$10,000,000] \div 2 = \}$ $50,000. The cap option only pays off if the market rate on the exercise date(s) is above 6%. The collar option provides protection against both increases and decreases in interest rates since it combines a cap and floor.

TABLE 18.5

Payoff Schedule for a Cap, Floor, and Collar

Initial rate: 6.00%
Notional principal: $10,000,000
Date of purchase: Jan. 1, 1996
Exercise date: July 1, 1996

Possible Market Interest Rate Level	Cap	Floor	Collar
4.00%	$ 0	$100,000	$100,000
5.00	0	50,000	50,000
6.00	0	0	0
7.00	50,000	0	50,000
8.00	$100,000	$ 0	$100,000

Needless to say, an option that has such a large potential payoff does not come cheap. The buyer of these options must pay an option premium that can be quite expensive, especially in periods of volatile interest rates. To assist in determining the value of such an option, it is necessary to determine the probability of various interest rate scenarios. Consider the example in Table 18.6. The financial manager has assigned the following probabilities to the interest rate scenarios. The expected value is calculated by multiplying the probability times the payoff; this is then discounted by the discount rate relevant over the period between the contract date and when the payoff is received. In this case it would be the periodic rate for six months (6.00/2 =) 3%.

TABLE 18.6

Expected Value of Cap, Floor, and Collar under Various Interest Rate Scenario Probabilities
July 1, 1996

Possible Interest Rate Scenarios	Cap Payoff	Floor Payoff	Probability of Interest Rate Scenario	Present Value of Expected Payoff at Initial Six-Month Rate
4.00%	$ 0	$100,000	10%	Floor: $100,000/(1 + .06/2)^1$ = $ 9,708.74
5.00	0	50,000	25	*Floor:* $12,500/(1 + .06/2)^1$ = $12,136.92
6.00	0	0	30	$ 0
7.00	50,000	0	25	*Cap:* $12,500/(1 + .06/2)^1$ = $12,136.92
8.00	$100,000	0	10	*Cap:* $10,000/(1 + .06/2)^1$ = $ 9,708.74

The table indicates that the expected value of the cap and floor under the interest rate scenario probabilities provided is ($9,708.74 + $12,136.92 =) $21,844.66. The price of a cap typically is expressed as a premium percent of the amount of notional principal. Thus, the cap and floor discussed above would be expected to have a premium of ($21,844.66/$10,000,000 =) .002184 or 0.2184%. The collar would have an expected value equal to the sum of the value of the cap plus the floor or (2 × $21,844.66 =) $43,689.32. Its premium would be (2 × .002184 =) .004369 or 0.4369%.

HEDGING WITH CAPS AND FLOORS

Consider a financial institution with a positive duration *GAP*. This firm is concerned about a rise in interest rates. One way to reduce this exposure is to buy a cap and simultaneously write a floor. If rates rise, the cap will act to offset the fall in the firm's equity value. If rates fall, the floor will act to reduce the windfall increase in the firm's equity value. The premium obtained from writing the floor would help pay for the cap. The net cost (*NC*) of this transaction is shown in Equation 18.4.

$$NC = \$c \times Pc - \$f \times Pf \qquad [18.4]$$

where:

$$NC = Net\ cost$$

$$\$c = Notional\ dollar\ amount\ of\ cap$$

$$Pc = Premium\ percent\ of\ cap$$

$$\$f = Notional\ dollar\ amount\ of\ floor$$

$$Pf = Notional\ premium\ of\ floor.$$

DEMONSTRATION PROBLEM | **NET COST OF CAP AND FLOOR HEDGE**

Situation:

Consider a firm with a positive duration *GAP* that would like to buy a cap priced at a premium of .5% on notional principal of $50 million. The same firm can write a floor and receive a premium of .4%. If the firm wrote a $50 million floor, they would like to determine the net cost. They would also like to know what amount of floor notional principal option they could write such that the net cost would be $0.

Result:

Using Equation 18.4 the net cost can be computed.

$$NC = \$50,000,000 \times 0.5\% - \$50,000,000 \times 0.4\% = \$50,000$$

In order to determine the amount of notional principal for the floor which could be sold to produce a net cost of $0, it is necessary to solve for *$f* in the same equation which has substituted *$f* for $50 million and set *NC* equal to $0:

$$NC = \$50,000,000 \times 0.5\% - \$f \times 0.4\% = \$0$$

$$\$f = (\$50,000,000 \times 0.5\%) \div 0.4\% = \$62,500,000$$

✓ Checkpoints

18-22 What are interest rate caps, floors, and collars?

18-23 How can caps and floors be used to reduce interest rate risk?

SUMMARY AND REVIEW

1. **Discuss the trade-off between interest rate risk and income for most financial firms and list the primary risk management tools.**

   Reducing interest rate risk normally involves actions that reduce the short-term income of financial firms. A firm with a large negative periodic *GAP* will generally face lower revenue by lengthening liabilities, for example. The primary tools used to reduce interest rate risk are financial **forward and futures contracts**, **options** and **options on futures**, **interest rate swaps**, **adjustable-rate loans**, and **caps, floors, and collars**.

2. **Describe financial futures contracts and how to use them to reduce interest rate risk.**

   Financial futures contracts are legal contracts that commit the buyer (**long position**) to take delivery of the financial claim for which the contract is written or to repurchase the contract (cover the position) before its expiration date at the prevailing market price. A seller (**short position**) of a futures contract is committed to deliver the financial claim at the contract expiration date or repurchase the contract at its prevailing market price anytime before expiration. **Hedging** in financial futures involves identifying the cash market financial claim that presents price risk to the firm and offsetting that cash market position with an opposite position in the futures market. The mechanics of using the futures market can be very complicated. Futures transactions require holding **margin** in the form of cash or certain marketable securities to cover any potential loss that may occur should the firm immediately reverse its futures market position. Futures market hedging also involves determining the correct relationship between the price changes in the cash market claim and the contract used in the futures market. This involves calculating a **hedge ratio**, which is defined as follows:

   [Price value of one basis point change in cash claim] ÷

   [Price value of one basis point change in futures contract]

   $$= PV_{cc}/PV_{fc}$$

   [Change in the yield of the cash market claim] ÷

   [Change in the yield of the futures market contract]

   $$= b_{cc/fc}$$

$$\textit{Hedge ratio} = [PV_{cc}/PV_{fc}] \times b_{cc/fc}$$

The relationship between the yield of the cash market claim and the futures market claim is rarely a perfect correlation. This presents the hedger with basis risk, the risk that the interest rate change of the cash market claim is not perfectly correlated to the futures market claim. Basis risk can produce unexpected losses and gains to the hedger.

3. **Describe options and futures options and how to use them to reduce interest rate risk.**

   Options and **futures options** provide the most theoretically sound approach for hedging the price risk associated with writing options. Futures options are options written on outstanding traded futures contracts. They allow the owner to purchase (call) or sell (put) a long or short futures contract at an agreed-upon price prior to the expiration date of the futures contract.

4. **Describe interest rate swaps and how to use them to reduce interest rate risk.**

   Interest rate swaps are the fastest growing financial technique for altering the interest rate risk position of a firm. Swaps involve two parties that wish to alter the interest rate they pay on a fixed amount of nominal dollar principal. One party that is currently obligated to make a fixed-rate payment wants to convert to a floating rate, and the other party the opposite. Typically a third-party, such as a commercial bank or investment banker, will act as a principal in a swap transaction between the other two parties. This is performed to earn a profit for providing origination, portfolio management, and brokerage services. The compensation is earned through acquiring an interest margin.

5. **Describe adjustable-rate financial contracts and the most common provisions found in them.**

   Adjustable-rate financial contracts are widely used by financial firms to modify their interest rate risk position. A major increase in adjustable-rate lending has occurred in the residential mortgage market. Adjustable-rate financial contracts require that certain provisions be specified. The necessary provisions include **interest rate index, adjustment period,** and **interest rate margin.** Other provisions found in adjustable-rate claims are optional.

6. **Describe caps, floors, and collars and explain how they are used to manage interest rate risk.**

   Caps, floors, and **collars** are options that provide the owner with interest payments on a stated amount of notional principal in the event that the interest rate indexes on which they are written rise above a stated level in the case of a cap, fall below a stated level in the case of a floor, or both in the case of a collar. These contracts are used to offset gains or losses of equity due to changes in market interest rates.

HEDGE RATIO   **SELF-TEST PROBLEMS**

ST-18-1

Martin Inc. is contempting a ten-year $100 million bond issue. It will take 60 days to complete the offering material and distribute the issue. The financial officer of Martin is contemplating a hedge.

There is a ten-year Treasury bond futures contract with a delivery date coming near the time of the security issuance. The contract represents $100,000 principal value of bonds. The financial officer has determined the price elasticity of the Martin bond to be .0021% for a 1% change in its interest rate. The Treasury bond price elasticity is .0018%. The beta between the futures contract and the Martin bond shows that for every basis point the Treasury bond yield changes, the Martin bond changes by 1.1 basis point.

Should Martin Inc. go long or short in the futures market?

How many contracts should be bought or sold at the onset of this transaction?

Answers on page 567.

FUTURES OPTIONS

ST-18-2

Your financial institution has purchased a portfolio of five-year, high-yielding corporate bonds with a near-term call provisions. It is concerned that interest rates will fall and the bonds will be called away. It is considering various ways to lessen the financial consequences of this possiblity. There is a futures contract on five-year Treasury bonds. There is also a five-year Treasury bond option available on the five-year Treasury futures contract.

What type of contract would act as a good hedge in this circumstance?

CAP AND FLOOR HEDGE

ST-18-3

Brisbane Savings Bank is concerned about its negative duration *GAP*. It has decided to reduce the firm's interest rate risk by purchasing a floor on $20 million of notional principal. The premium they were quoted was 0.7%. They would like to offset the cost by selling a cap. What size cap would they have to sell to offset the cost of the floor if they receive a premium of 0.6%?

PROBLEMS | **HEDGING**

18-1

You are a mortgage banker and have just agreed to make a $3 million apartment loan. It will take 60 days to process the loan, at which time you will sell it in the secondary mortgage market at the then-prevailing interest rate.

1. You decide to hedge your position with the five-year Treasury note futures contract. You sell $3 million worth of contracts at a price of 100 8/32. After 60 days, interest rates have risen and the futures contract price has fallen to 98 12/32. The mortgage can only be sold for 97.5% of par. What is the net gain or loss from the hedge?

2. Was this a perfect hedge? Why or why not?

HEDGING

18-2

As portfolio manager for a commercial bank, you are examining the refunding of $55 million in brokered CDs, which are maturing in six months. You would like to construct a hedge that will protect you from rising interest rates that would increase your refunding costs.

1. You choose the five-year Treasury note futures contract as your hedge instrument. What will rising interest rates do to the price of the contract? Should you sell the contract (short futures position) or buy the contract (long futures position)? Why?

2. What will be the effect of the hedge if interest rates fall? What will be the effect of falling interest rates if you don't use a hedge?

OPTIONS, FUTURES, AND FUTURES OPTIONS

18-3

Determine from the list of available option and futures option contracts the best contract for hedging in the following situations:

1. Your firm has sold a certificate of deposit that upon maturity may be cashed out or converted to a new certificate at the initial interest rate.

2. Your firm has issued a commitment to a takeover firm giving it the opportunity to borrow at 5.00% for five years anytime in the next three months.

3.   Your firm has a portfolio of five-year corporate bonds that must be sold in the next 90 days. The concern is that the bond prices will fall before they are sold.

4.   Your firm has sold some fixed-rate liabilities and holds the funds in liquid investments. It has not had the opportunity to invest these funds in the long-term assets they eventually want to hold.

Contracts available:

Long futures contract.

Short futures contract.

Put option or put futures option.

Call option or call futures option.

CAPS, FLOORS, AND COLLARS

18-4

Las Vegas Second National Bank suffers from a large positive periodic two-year *GAP*. The management would like to know if buying and selling a cap and floor can reduce the impact of the positive periodic *GAP*. They can buy or sell a cap for 0.4% of the notional principal and a floor for 0.3%. They need to offset $50 million of notional principal. What combination of cap and floor would produce no out-of-pocket cost?

SOLUTIONS   SELF-TEST PROBLEM

ST-18-1

Solution:

   Since Martin is obligated to deliver bonds in 60 days, it is short bonds. Therefore, it will want to go long in the futures market. Martin is concerned that if interest rates rise it will sell its bonds at a lower price. If it goes long in the futures market, it can buy back its contracts at an offsetting lower price in the event of a rise in interest rates.

   The hedge ratio is determined by using the equation:

$$Hedge\ ratio = [PV_{cc}/PV_{fc}] \times b_{cc/fc}$$

$$Hedge\ ratio = .0021/.0018 \times 1.1 = 1.28333$$

$$Number\ of\ contracts = (\$100,000,000 \div \$100,000) \times 1.28333$$

$$= 1,283.33 \cong 1,283\ contracts$$

ST-18-2

Solution:

The firm has taken the risk that if interest rates fall, the bonds it owns will be called away. One way to reduce this risk is to buy a contract that will give it the option to buy bonds at today's prices if rates fall. To replace the called bonds, the firm would need a futures contract that would permit it to buy Treasury bonds at a price determined today even though prices may rise (and rates fall) later. To eliminate the possibility of loss if market rates rise, which is unavoidable in a straight long futures contract, a futures option would be selected. Again, the firm wants the option to purchase the Treasuries if rates fall and prices rise, so it would buy a call futures option.

ST-18-3

Solution:

$$NC = \$0 = \$20,000,000 \times 0.7\% - \$c \times 0.6\%$$

$$(\$20,000,000 \times 0.7\%) \div 0.6\% = \underline{\$23,333,333}$$

CHAPTER 19

Foreign Exchange Risk Management

Learning Goals

After studying this chapter, you should be able to:

1. Explain the basis and the significance of foreign exchange rates.
2. Define and calculate interest rate parity and describe how arbitrage affects the relationship between current and forward exchange rates.
3. Discuss the concept of purchasing power parity and the law of one price.
4. Describe how differential inflation rates among countries affect exchange rates.
5. Explain how to use the forward cash and futures markets in hedging currency risk.
6. Explain how to use options on foreign exchange and how to compute the cost of such an option in hedging currency risk.
7. Explain how to use currency swaps in hedging currency risk.

If you've ever traveled or studied abroad, then you're probably familiar with some of the challenges to completing international business transactions: language barriers, contrasting social customs and practices, diverse legal and regulatory systems, and perhaps even conflicting institutional structures. By now, you should understand how the rapid growth of trade and technological improvements in the communications media and data processing have integrated financial markets and markets for goods and services worldwide. You should also recognize that virtually all companies today must consider international market opportunities for both the sale and the production of products and the effects of increased foreign competition. But what's the most serious risk that distinguishes international transactions from domestic ones? The chapter title gives the answer away: changes in foreign exchange rates.

In two sections, this chapter establishes a framework for understanding the foreign exchange mechanism, how foreign exchange is a source of risk, and how foreign exchange markets operate compared to other markets studied thus far. The first section introduces you to exchange rates, what they are, and how they are determined. The second section covers the risks associated with changes in exchange rates and the methods for managing such risk.

International Financial Issues

Since this book has repeatedly raised international financial issues, the following section summarizes those addressed thus far and expands upon a few. Acceleration of international trade, globalization of financial markets, and growth in international transactions have required that the finance professional be able to:

1. *Evaluate the cost of foreign borrowing:* Chapter 14 related changing foreign exchange rates to the cost of borrowing in international markets; a financial manager must consider these changes when comparing the cost of borrowing in foreign and domestic markets.

2. *Account for changes in asset and liability values:* Multinational corporations (MNCs) and financial institutions engaged in international transactions must account for changes in value of the assets and liabilities held in foreign countries. Changes in exchange rates can influence the flow of income from foreign operations and the value of these firms' foreign assets and liabilities.

3. *Anticipate foreign laws and regulations:* Foreign operations and operations in particular countries are subject to risk resulting from changes in tax, trade, labor, and environmental laws and regulations, and through war, local economics, and politics.

4. *Use global capital markets:* International financial institutions can diversify through securities of foreign institutions but must obtain considerable information about these foreign security issuers.

5. *Hedge foreign exchange risk:* Changes in exchange rates represent potentially large risk to international financial institutions and MNCs dealing with foreign securities, because exchange rate changes affect the firm's sales competitiveness, asset and liability values, and cost of borrowing.

6. *Diversify international investments:* The globalization of financial markets has placed international investment within the reach of virtually all investors. International investments enable investors not just to diversify risk across international boundaries but also to obtain higher returns for any given level of risk.

✓ Checkpoints

19-1   Why should business people worry about changes in foreign exchange rates?

19-2   How might a change in the foreign exchange rate affect the business of someone who sells product in a foreign market?

EUROPE'S EXCHANGE RATE SYSTEM COMES UNGLUED

In 1979, the members of European Common Market set up the European Monetary System (EMS). Although a member of the European Common Market, the United Kingdom didn't join the EMS until 1990. The purpose of the system was to facilitate trade by forcing each member to maintain exchange rates with one other that could change only within very small bands. This would serve to reduce exchange rate risk and thereby improve trade. The other desired effect was to force each country to pursue macroeconomic policies that were consistent with one another.

The merger of East and West Germany in 1990 served to upset the EMS. The new Germany experienced a rise in inflation in 1991–92 as the costs of unification increased budget deficits. This led the notorious inflation fighter, the German central bank, the Bundesbank, to raise interest rates, resulting in capital from all over Europe flowing into the higher-yielding German investments and putting downward pressure on the value of the other European currencies. As a result, in September 1992, several of the European countries pulled out of the EMS and let their currencies float to new lower equilibrium values. The most important departure from the system was the United Kingdom.

How significant was the change in the U.K. pound value relative to the U.S. dollar? Consider this: in early September 1992, the cost of one British pound was over $2.00 U.S. By February 1993, after only five months, the cost of the British pound was down to less than $1.45 U.S. That is a decline of over 27.5%. At an annual rate, the decline was well over 55%. The U.S. investor in a six-month British security in August 1992 would have lost a large percentage of the principal value by February 1993.

How

it

Really

Works

Foreign Exchange Markets, Trading, and Exchange Rates

This section covers the basics of foreign exchange and answers the questions: Who needs foreign exchange? How do economic units trade in the foreign exchange markets? What is a foreign exchange rate? The section also looks at both cash and forward foreign exchange markets, compared to forward and cash markets in domestic financial assets.

WHO USES FOREIGN EXCHANGE?

Foreign exchange involves the supply and demand for another country's currency and deals with the expression of one currency in terms of another. The exchange depends on several of the economic activities described below.

Exporters and Importers

These firms supply goods to foreign buyers. In return, they either receive foreign currency directly or are paid in their domestic currency which has been purchased by the overseas importer with a foreign currency. For example, U.S. exporters are associated with the supply of foreign currency into the United States, while U.S. importers are associated with the demand for foreign currency by the United States.

Foreign Investors

Foreign investors who invest in a foreign country's assets supply foreign currency to the country in which they are investing. A foreign investor in a U.S.-owned hotel supplies foreign currency that is subsequently converted into U.S. dollars. The Japanese, for example, have used a large portion of their balance of trade surpluses of foreign currencies to make major investments in the U.S. financial and real asset markets.

Speculators

A speculator or trader is regarded as an economic unit who operates in the foreign exchange markets so as to make a profit from the activity of buying and selling foreign exchange.

Tourists

Tourists are a type of importer of another country's goods and services. They are a major source of foreign exchange to a number of countries. Some countries earn most of their foreign exchange from tourism.[1]

FOREIGN EXCHANGE TRADING

Foreign exchange trading has become a significant activity in the last ten years, running as high as $1 trillion a day in the 1990s. There is no organized exchange in foreign exchange. Rather, like the market for Treasury securities, the foreign exchange market is a dealer-to-dealer market. It is primarily made up of large international commercial banks and international investment banking firms. The primary currencies involved in foreign exchange trading are the German mark, Japanese yen, British pound, Swiss franc, and Canadian and U.S. dollars. Trading in the spot market is carried out between institutions with a two-day settlement period.

Commercial banks active in foreign exchange trading also speculate on changes in exchange rates by taking positions on foreign bonds or by borrowing

---

[1]Tourists can be considered importers of services from the countries they visit. However, they are separated out here due to their significance in certain countries.

foreign currencies. A speculator will hold foreign-denominated securities if it believes the value of the foreign currency will rise above its interest rate parity forward value. Alternatively, the bank could borrow foreign currencies from another bank to invest in U.S. securities in hopes that dollars will rise in value above their interest rate parity forward value. Remember, the interest rate parity forward value is the forward price of a currency that eliminates an arbitrage profit opportunity.

FOREIGN EXCHANGE RATES

The most important relationship in foreign exchange trading is the **exchange rate,** a price of foreign currencies measured in domestic prices. For an American, the exchange rate for the British pound would be expressed as $1.75 per pound. This is also known as the *American term.* The exchange rate could be expressed as the *European term* and would become the amount of a foreign country's currency needed to purchase $1.00, say, .5714 pounds. The European term exchange rate is simply the reciprocal of the American term. For example, the Belgian franc was worth $.02773 on Friday June 7, 1991, as quoted on the American term. The European term was quoted at 36.06 Belgian francs per $1.00. Equation 19.1 shows the reciprocal relationship between the two terms.

$$\$.02773/Belgian\ franc = 1 \ / \ [36.06\ Belgian\ francs/ \ \$1.00]$$

$$American\ term = 1 \ / \ European\ term \qquad [19.1]$$

Table 19.1 shows the European term exchange rates for the U.S. dollar versus several major currencies over the last few years. A foreign currency is said to be *appreciating in value* if its price rises in relation to the domestic currency. In the table, the currencies of all the countries shown, except for Canada and Japan, depreciated in value relative to the U.S. dollar between 1987 and 1993. That is, the price of one U.S. dollar rose as measured in terms of the foreign currency. Table 19.1 shows that the cost of one dollar measured in terms of the Japanese yen dropped from 138.07 yen/$ in 1989 to 126.78 yen/$ in 1992. The yen appreciated in value. Several currencies that have experienced very pronounced changes in value between 1989 and 1992 are shown below.

$$Change\ in\ foreign\ exchange\ rates,\ ERt:\ [(ER1989 - ER1992)/(ER1989)]$$

$$France\ [(6.3802 - 5.2935)/(6.3802)] = +17.0324\%$$

$$Japan\ [(138.07 - 126.78)/(138.07)] = +8.1770\%$$

$$Switzerland\ [(1.6369 - 1.4064)/(1.6369)] = +14.0815\%$$

| TABLE 19.1 |

European Term Exchange Rates Annual Average 1987–1993
(foreign exchange units per U.S. dollar)

Country	1987	1988	1989	1992	1993
Canada	1.3259	1.2306	1.1842	1.2085	1.2902
France	6.0122	5.9595	6.3802	5.2935	5.6669
Germany	1.7981	1.7570	1.8808	1.5618	1.6545
Japan	144.6	128.17	138.07	126.78	111.08
Switzerland	1.4918	1.4643	1.6369	1.4064	1.4781
United Kingdom	0.6098	0.5614	0.6109	0.5662	0.6660

Source: *Federal Reserve Bulletin*, May 1994.

CROSS RATES

Cross rates represent the relationship of any two foreign currencies to a third. Foreign exchange traders attempt to profit by exploiting any inconsistencies in the relationships between foreign exchange rate relationships. Consider the following foreign exchange relationships for the U.S. dollar, German mark (DM), and French franc (FF):

$$\$1 \ U.S. = 3 \ DM \ or \ \$.33/DM$$

$$1 \ DM = 1.5 \ Ff \ or \ .67DM/Ff$$

Given these relationships, it is simple to calculate the American term cross rate between the U.S. dollar and French franc. To do this, we simply multiply the American term exchange rate for the DM by the DM exhange rate for French francs. We obtain:

$$\$.33/DM \times .67DM/Ff = (\$.33 \times .67)/Ff = \$.221/Ff$$

If this relationship does not hold, then it is possible for foreign exchange traders to exploit the mispricing to earn a profit.[2]

---

[2]This is known as a *triangular arbitrage*. For example, if the exchange rate between the U.S. dollar and French franc were $.20 U.S./Ff, then it would be profitable to take one (or more) U.S. dollars and buy five French Francs, use the the francs to buy (5 × .67 DM/Ff) = 3.35 German marks, and then convert the DM into (3.35 DM × $.33 U.S./DM) = $1.106, producing a $.106 profit per dollar. This profit should not exist if foreign exhange markets are operating efficiently.

✓ Checkpoints

19-3 Who uses foreign exchange?

19-4 How do the American and the European term exchange rates differ?

Forward Foreign Exchange Market and Interest Rate Parity

There is a very active forward market in foreign exchange. This market allows users of foreign exchange to purchase or sell it for delivery in the future. The price of a currency in the forward market can be above or below the current or spot price. A foreign currency is said to be *selling at a discount* in the forward market if a dollar purchases more units of the foreign currency for forward delivery than its does for spot delivery. For example, if the dollar purchases 1.50 DM in the spot market and 1.51 DM in the 90-day forward market, the German mark is said to be selling at a discount in the forward market. If the German mark sold for 1.49 DM = \$1.00 for forward delivery compared to 1.50 DM = \$1.00 in the spot market, then it is said to be *selling at a premium* in the forward market. Exhibit 19.1 shows the spot and forward exchange rates for several major currencies as they appear in the press.

The reason that currencies sell at different exchange rates in the spot and forward markets relates to the level of interest rates domestically and in the country of the foreign currency in question. **Interest rate parity** relates to arbitrage pricing theory which explains the relationship between spot and forward prices of foreign exchange.

To understand interest rate parity, financial managers must know the spot price of foreign exchange, ER_s, the interest rates for specific maturity deposits in the foreign currency, r_f, and the domestic currency, r_d, and the period over which the forward contract is drawn, t. Assume that r_f and r_d are periodic interest rates for the period of time t. Also assume, for simplicity, that foreign currency can be bought and sold at a bid and ask price that is the same. Arbitrage interest rate parity works in the following way:

A trader borrows dollars in the United States at an interest rate of r_d. The trader then turns around and purchases a foreign currency at a spot exchange rate (ERs) of say, a price of \$.5 = 1 DM. The trader then sells the DM and any interest to be earned in the forward cash market for delivery at the end of period t. During period t, the currency is invested in German deposits at an interest rate of r_f. The amount of German marks sold forward is 2 DM $\times (1 + r_f)$ per dollar exchanged for marks. Two things about this transaction are known. First, the amount of borrowed dollars to be repaid is known. This will be \$1.00 $\times (1 + r_d)$ per dollar borrowed. Next, the amount of DM that will be sold at the end of period t to meet the forward sale of DM can also be calculated. It is 2 DM $\times (1 + r_f)$ per dollar converted into DM.

EXHIBIT 19.1

Reading the Financial Page
Spot and Forward Foreign Exchange Rates
(typical listing)

Country	American $ per Foreign Currency Unit		European Foreign Currency Unit per $	
	Tuesday	Monday	Tuesday	Monday
Britain (pound)	1.7910	1.8160	.5583	.5507
30-day forward	1.7810	1.8059	.5615	.5537
90-day forward	1.7623	1.7868	.5674	.5597
180-day forward	1.7357	1.7602	.5761	.5681
Canada (dollar)	.8666	.8711	1.1540	1.1480
30-day forward	.8642	.8687	1.1572	1.1512
90-day forward	.8601	.8645	1.1627	1.1567
180-day forward	.8546	.8590	1.1701	1.1642
France (franc)	.18519	.18771	5.4000	5.3275
30-day forward	.18425	.18677	5.4275	5.3543
90-day forward	.18254	.18501	5.4783	5.4050
180-day forward	.18017	.18250	5.5503	5.4795
Germany (mark)	.6321	.6410	1.5820	1.5600
30-day forward	.6292	.6381	1.5892	1.5671
90-day forward	.6238	.6327	1.6032	1.5806
180-day forward	.6161	.6248	1.6232	1.6005
SDR	1.41232	1.42828	.70805	.70014
ECU	1.30578	1.33538	.76583	.74885

This exhibit shows the American and European term exchange rates based on trading among the largest U.S. foreign exchange dealers. The American term represents the cost of one unit of the foreign exchange priced in dollars. The European term is the price in foreign currency of one U.S. dollar. The table represents the exchange rates for transactions typically over $1 million. The cost to an international traveler would be considerably different, due to the higher transaction costs and lower volume represented by an individual transaction.

The exhibit also shows the forward rates of exchange. These are the rates for forward delivery of the foreign exchange in question. In the table, the 180-day forward American term exchange rate for German marks on Tuesday was U.S. $.6161/DM. The table also shows the exchange rates for the Special Drawing Rights (SDR) and European Currency Unit (ECU). The SDR is an international reserve currency used for exchange settlements between countries and is a weighted average of the values of a number of major currencies. The ECU is similar to the SDR, except that it comprises of a basket of currencies representing the European Economic Community. It is the forerunner of the unified Common Market currency that could be implemented in 1999.

The effect of interest rate parity in action is to ensure that a risk-free or pure arbitrage profit cannot take place. Interest rate parity will ensure that the forward market exchange rate, ER_f, will be set at a value that would preclude an arbitrage profit. Under interest rate parity, the forward exchange rate will be Equation 19.2. This condition will hold to eliminate any possibility for an arbitrage profit.

Forward six-month exchange rate: $ER_6 = ER_s\ [(1 + r_d)/(1 + r_f)]$ [19.2]

Financial managers can use the interest rate parity condition to determine the expected foreign exchange price of German marks in six months as in the following demonstration problem.

USING INTEREST RATE PARITY TO PREDICT FORWARD EXCHANGE PRICES	DEMONSTRATION PROBLEM

Situation

Consider the following data and assume the initial conditions:

Spot exchange rate ER_s is $.5 = 1 DM (domestic price of foreign currency).

Domestic periodic interest rate is r_d = .04 for six months.

German periodic interest rate is r_f = .02 for six months.

Time period t = six months.

Given these conditions, what would the forward exchange rate for DM have to be to eliminate a profitable arbitrage?

Result

Using Equation 19.2, the breakeven forward exchange rate for DM would be:

ER_6 = $.5/DM × [(1.04)/(1.02)] = $.5098/DM.

   As shown, the forward price of DM, $.5098 = 1.00 DM, must be higher than the spot price of $.5 = 1 DM, as measured by the American term in order to eliminate the potential for arbitrage. But, at $.5098 = 1 DM, no profit can be made. If the forward price of the DM were higher than $.5098 / DM, however, the trader would continue to sell dollars for DM and buy DM bonds and sell the principal and interest to be received on these bond investments in the forward $/DM market. If the forward exchange rate for DM were below the interest parity level of $.5098 / DM, then it would pay to convert DM into dollars, invest in dollar securities, and sell dollars in the forward dollar market for DM. This problem explains arbitrage at work in the foreign exchange market.

DEMONSTRATION PROBLEM	YIELD ON A FOREIGN INVESTMENT

Situation

Marion Corporation has a relationship with a firm in France. The French firm would like to borrow funds from Marion for six months at a six-month periodic rate of 3.5%. The loan will be made in French francs, Ff. Marion has sufficient liquid assets to make the loan. Marion was expecting to invest the excess funds in Treasury bills at a six-month periodic rate of 2.5%. The current exchange rate is $.37/Ff. The six-month forward rate is $.36/Ff. Marion believes the loan to be virtually risk free.

Results

Calculate the breakeven interest rate for the French investment that would eliminate any arbitrage possibility. This is the breakeven interest rate where interest rate parity is in effect as shown in Equation 19.2. Using the data above we have:

$$\$.36/Ff = \$.37/Ff \left[(1 + .025)/(1 + r_f)\right]$$

$$(1 + r_f) = \left[(\$.37/Ff)(1 + .025)\right]/(\$.36/Ff)$$

$$(1 + r_f) = 1.053472$$

$$r_f = 5.3472\%$$

The breakeven six-month rate for a French investment that results in interest rate parity is 5.3472%. This is much higher than the 3.5% the French firm has offered, so it is not worthwhile to make the loan.

Traders cannot borrow and invest at the interest rates implied in the interest rate parity theory; they must use actual, not hypothetical, interest rates to set foreign exchange rates. The interest rates generally used are the rates on eurocurrency deposits. With these rates, the interest parity condition closely approximates the relationship between spot and forward foreign exchange rates. Foreign exchange dealers use rates that differ from the interest rates that a private company or individual might pay to a borrower or earn on investments. As a result, the interest parity condition will differ for a private entity having a different set of borrowing and investing alternatives. Moreover, the example assumes no difference between the bid and ask prices for currencies or other transaction costs. Consequently, the equation would need to be adjusted to conform to these realities.

✓ Checkpoints

19-5 What is a forward market in foreign exchange?

19-6 What is interest rate parity, and how does it affect the relative exchange rates between spot and forward exchange prices?

Why Exchange Rates Change

Many theories have been offered to explain changes in exchange rates, most of which have been subjected to empirical analysis as well. Unfortunately, no theory, as yet, seems to explain the volatility that has been evident in the market.

The simplest place to begin an investigation of exchange rate movements is to review the concept of **purchasing power parity (PPP)**. If currencies represent purchasing power over a certain amount of a particular country's goods and services, then the exchange rate should represent the relationship of the cost of goods and services in one country versus that of another. This idea aligns with the PPP concept of the **law of one price,** which simply states that a commodity should cost the same in two countries, adjusted by the exchange rate between the currencies of the countries and costs of transportation and importing.

For example, if an ounce of gold costs $300 in New York and 171.43 pounds in the United Kingdom, then the spot exchange rate, ER_s, using the American term must be as shown in Equation 19.3 if the law of one price holds:

$$\$300 = 171.43 \; pounds \times ER_s$$

$$ER_s = \$300/171.43 \; pounds = \$1.75/pound \qquad [19.3]$$

There are several simplifying assumptions built into the law of one price that must be met for it to hold strictly. These include the following:

1. *There are no transaction costs.* That is, gold bought in London can be transported to New York at no cost. The law also dictates that there be no difference between the bid and ask prices for the good or service.

2. *There are no trade barriers.* For the law of one price to hold, goods and services must be freely traded. Trade barriers such as import quotas, tariffs, import taxes, and other constraints will act to negate and frustrate the law of one price.

3. *The good or service is of equal quality.* The law of one price must be used to compare truly equal goods and services. Quality differences will certainly frustrate the law of one price.

In practice, the concept of purchasing power parity is difficult to measure since there are many different prices of goods and services. Quality differences exist, and the relative consumption of particular goods in any two economies differs significantly.[3]

PPP considers changes in exchange rates to be primarily a monetary phenomenon. That is, changes in exchange rates under PPP largely reflect the changes in price levels in different countries induced by monetary policy's impact on infla-

---

[3]The concept of purchasing power parity is very appealing. Unfortunately, there is little predictive power in the relationship. For most developed economies, imports and exports are only a small percentage of total goods and services sold or consumed. Many goods and services simply cannot be exported, such as rail service or a near-by movie or restaurant meal. For this reason and others, disparities in prices from purchasing power parity predicted levels exist.

tion. Countries that experience rapid changes in prices relative to another country will also experience depreciating exchange rates in relation to countries with more modest changes in price levels.

Considerable empirical analysis has been carried out in an effort to confirm PPP. Unfortunately, little of this work has confirmed the expected relationships between changes in prices and exchange rates, excepting countries with rapid inflation. These countries experience offsetting depreciation of their currency values. Monetary policymakers use PPP calculations to estimate the potential that a certain currency may be undervalued or overvalued, according to some equilibrium valuation calculation of PPP.

Although differential inflation rates are the primary cause of changes in exchange rates, there are other factors as well: differential changes in interest rates, differential income levels, and differential expected returns on real investments between two countries.

DIFFERENTIAL INTEREST RATES

An investor is able to convert dollars into francs in the spot or cash market and sell francs for dollars in the forward cash market. The proceeds of this transaction is then put into French bonds. This is the interest rate parity transaction we discussed earlier. Now consider what would happen if French monetary authorities pushed French interest rates up. This would increase the demand for French francs to buy French bonds. The result would be a higher price of French francs in terms of dollars. That is why the value of a country's currency will rise (fall) whenever its interest rates rise (fall) relative to other country's rates.

DIFFERENTIAL INCOME LEVELS

If the United States enters into a recession and the economy in Germany accelerates its growth, then U.S. importers will reduce purchases in Germany while German importers will purchase more U.S. goods and services. This action will decrease U.S. demand for German marks and increase German demand for dollars. The result will be a declining mark price measured in terms of dollars.

DIFFERENTIAL EXPECTED RETURNS ON INVESTMENTS

Chapter 14 hypothesized about a situation in which a small country discovers oil. Investors will seek investment opportunities in this country. As a result, the value of the currency with the higher expected returns on capital will experience an increase in the value of its currency relative to the other country's with lower expected returns on investment. Unfortunately, determining the expected returns on invested capital in various countries is no easy task. One approach is to try to estimate real interest rates, but major measurement problems remain.[4]

As plausible as these theories of exchange rate movement are, empirical work corroborating these hypotheses is not available. Completed studies do not expand much upon changes in exchange rates. Exchange rate speculation can be extremely risky, which makes managing currency risk that much more important.

✓ Checkpoints

19-7 Why do foreign exchange rates change?

19-8 Why is purchasing power parity significant?

19-9 What is the law of one price?

19-10 How does the inflation rate in one country affect the value of its currency relative to another country's currency, according to the theory of purchasing power parity?

19-11 What are some of the major factors that account for change in exchange rates?

Managing Currency Risk

Managing currency risk is very similar to managing other price risks. The forward market, options, futures market, and swaps are used to reduce the firm's sensitivity to price changes of financial claims. The same tools are available in the foreign exchange markets to manage the risks of changes in foreign exchange prices.

THE VOLATILITY OF FOREIGN EXCHANGE MARKETS

Exchange rates have become so volatile that managing foreign exchange risk is a very important activity for financial and nonfinancial firms operating in foreign markets. Table 19.2 shows the number of six-month periods from 1973 to 1989 when the U.S. dollar exchange rate with the British pound, German mark, and Japanese yen changed by more than ± 15%. These represent very large changes for such a short period of time. These large changes dramatically indicate the risks associated with foreign exchange transactions.

---

[4]Empirical data on the correlation between yields on long-term bonds among developed countries by Ibbotson and Siegel suggest that international capital markets do shift capital from countries with lower nominal returns on bonds to countries with higher nominal returns. These capital flows tend to equate the real returns on invested capital between countries. However, the results of the analysis suggest that while the relationships are positive, they are anything but perfect. See R. G. Ibbotson and L. B. Siegel, "The World Bond Market: Market Values, Yields, and Returns," *Journal of Fixed Income*, June 1991, pp. 90–99.

TABLE 19.2

Six-month Percentage Changes in the Exchange Rate between the Dollar, Pound, Mark, and Yen June 1973 to December 1989

Dollar to Pound*		Dollar to Mark*		Dollar to Yen*	
Ending Date	Change	Ending Date	Change	Ending Date	Change
July 1981	25.1%	Feb. 1986	−22.6%	Feb. 1986	−27.8%
Aug. 1985	−25.0	June 1981	19.9	Oct. 1978	−23.6
Feb. 1985	18.4	Aug. 1985	−17.8	Apr. 1979	21.6
Sept. 1975	16.6	Oct. 1978	−17.4	Mar. 1978	−17.7
May 1989	16.0	Jan. 1974	16.8	Dec. 1987	−17.4
Dec. 1987	−15.1	Nov. 1986	−15.7	Oct. 1982	16.5
		Sept. 1984	15.5	Sept. 1980	−16.3
		Feb. 1975	−15.4	May 1989	15.9
				Apr. 1983	−15.7
				July 1981	15.7
				Sept. 1986	−15.6

*Positive values indicate appreciation in the value of the dollar while negative values indicate depreciation in the value of the dollar relative to the other currencies shown.

Source: Joseph A. Whitt, Jr., "Flexible Exchange Rates: An Idea Whose Time Has Passed?" *Economic Review,* Federal Reserve Bank of Atlanta, Sept./Oct. 1990, adapted from Tables 1, 2, and 3, pp. 9–11.

FORWARD CASH MARKETS

The market most frequently used to hedge the price volatility of exchange rates is the forward cash market in foreign exchange. This over-the-counter market is operated by commercial banks and investment bankers who manage large foreign exchange trading activities. The primary way in which international firms can hedge a foreign exchange position of relatively short maturity, say a week to 12 months, is by using the forward exchange market. A firm that owes an entity a foreign currency for future delivery or has an account receivable representing a claim on a certain amount of foreign currency for future delivery has exchange risk exposure.

The firm that owes foreign exchange faces the risk that the value of the currency owed will increase relative to the currency customarily used in daily dealings. If it is owed a foreign currency, then it faces the possibility that the value of the currency received will fall relative to the value that the firm anticipated when it consummated the transaction.

The forward cash market can be used to reduce the risk of currency fluctuation. If a firm owes a foreign currency, then it can purchase the currency today in the forward market for delivery at a set date. This effectively eliminates the price volatility risk. Alternatively, if the firm is to receive a foreign currency at some near-term future date, it can eliminate price volatility by selling the currency in the forward exchange market on a date to coincide with the date it receives the foreign currency. These represent foreign currency hedges.

These transactions may require that the user provide collateral to cover the difference between the forward agreed-upon price and the current cash price, which protects the dealer should the market go against the hedger. This is a type of margin that the dealer will require to ensure that the transaction is settled as agreed.

The forward market has the disadvantage for some users that the transactions are typically quite large, generally in minimum $1 million amounts or their foreign currency equivalent. Forward contracts can be traded, however, as dealers will broker outstanding contracts. The major advantage of the forward contract is that some users of this market can avoid putting up margin, always required in the futures markets. This move may make the forward cash market a more cost-effective hedging alternative for some users.

FUTURES MARKETS IN FOREIGN CURRENCIES

A futures market in foreign currencies that permits hedging of foreign exchange price risk has developed during the last 20 years. The International Monetary Market (IMM), run by the Chicago Mercantile Exchange, and the London International Financial Futures Exchange (LIFFE) are the largest markets for foreign exchange futures. The primary currencies offered by the IMM in 1993 are shown in Table 19.3.

TABLE 19.3

Major Foreign Exchange Contracts on the IMM

Contract	Face Amount
Australian dollar	100,000 dollars
British pound	62,500 pounds
Canadian dollar	100,000 dollars
German mark	125,000 marks
Japanese yen	12,500,000 yen
Swiss franc	125,000 francs

The IMM contracts are settled in March, June, September, and December. Most of the activity is in contracts of nine months or less. Exhibit 19.2 shows hypothetical listings for British pound futures contracts as they would appear in the financial press.

Conceptually, practitioners use the futures market and the forward cash market similarly. If a firm is owed a foreign currency to be received in the future (a long position), it would go short on a futures contract in that currency or a currency traded on the exchange whose value is closely correlated to one being hedged. If a firm owes a foreign currency for future delivery (a short position), it would want to go long in the futures contract of that currency.

The relationship between forward cash prices and futures prices is very close. Indeed, the markets tend to move in tandem, which makes either market an equally efficient hedge for foreign exchange risk.

EXHIBIT 19.2

Reading the Financial Page
Exchange Futures Contracts
(typical listing)

British pound (IMM)—62,500 pounds—$ per pound

Date	Open	Contract High	Low	Settle	Change pt = $.0001	Open Interest	Contract High	Low
Mar.	1.7412	1.7414	1.7409	1.7410	−02	31,000	1.7612	1.7323
June	1.7134	1.7156	1.7133	1.7137	−03	23,000	1.7345	1.7087
Dec.	1.6900	1.6913	1.6956	1.6943	−04	123	1.7123	1.6845

Estimated volume: 12,765
Yesterday's volume: 23,000

This exhibit shows the futures quotations for future contracts in British pounds. The contract is for 62,500 pounds. It shows the open price, high, low, and settlement (close) price expressed in the American term exchange rate. The change in price is expressed at 1/100 of a cent or $.0001. The open interest shows the number of contracts outstanding. The high and low prices are for the contract's life. The volume of contracts purchased or sold are shown as estimated volume for the day shown and actual volume for the previous day.

OPTIONS ON FOREIGN EXCHANGE

Options, the subject of Chapter 16, are also available for hedging foreign exchange risk. Over-the-counter options in foreign currencies are available through dealers and also provided by organized exchanges such as the Chicago Board Options Exchange (CBOE), the Philadelphia Stock Exchange (PHLX), and several foreign exchanges. The currencies used by the CBOE and PHLX are the same. There is a major difference in the nature of the contracts, however. The contracts traded on the CBOE are European options, which can only be exercised on a specific date, while the PHLX options are European and American options, the latter of which can be exercised anytime during the contract life. A hypothetical listing of several contracts listed on the PHLX is shown in Exhibit 19.3 as they would be shown in the financial press.

In options contracts, there are two parties. The buyer of the option can purchase a put, which is the right to sell at an agreed-upon price on (European option) or before (American option) a specified date. A call option is the right to purchase. The other party to an option contract is the writer of the option. The writer can be a pure speculator, who does not care about ever owning the currency being optioned (described as an uncovered position or naked option), or an owner of the foreign exchange (covered option).

Options can be considered a form of price insurance. If a person owns a call on a foreign currency at a specified price in U.S. dollars, then the person has in-

EXHIBIT 19.3

Reading the Financial Page
Exchange Options

Option and Current Price	Strike Price	Calls Dec.	Jan.	Mar.	Puts Dec.	Jan.	Mar.
German mark—62,500 marks —American style—cents per unit							
61.23	60	.80	1.23	*r*	.10	.60	*r*
61.23	60 1/2	.45	.83	1.30	.20	.83	1.67
61.23	61	.40	.67	*r*	.45	1.23	*s*
German mark—62,500 marks—European style—cents per unit							
61.23	61	.33	.56	*s*	.41	.98	*s*

This table shows the prices of three contract exercise dates—December, January, and March—for call and put options on German marks. The table indicates the type of currency and the underlying spot price for the mark, 61.23 cents per mark. The prices of the options are based on cents per number of units in a contract. Thus, a call option at a strike price of 60 1/2 for January delivery would be .83 cents times 62,500 units in the contract or (.0083 x 62,500 =) $518.75. The trading in options is not that active, so that an *r* represents no trading that day and an *s* indicates that no option is outstanding. The PHLX exchange has both American and European options in the German mark.

surance that if the value of the foreign currency rises significantly, relative to the dollar, the price is fixed. The maximum hedged price, FX_{xx}, for an *xx* day option, will be equal to the option strike price, $Option_{xx}$, plus the cost of the option call premium paid, *CP*, shown as Equation 19.4.

$$FX_{xx} = Option_{xx} + CP \qquad [19.4]$$

where:

FX_{xx} = *Maximum price of foreign exchange in XX days*

$Option_{xx}$ = *Call contract option strike price for settlement in XX days*

CP = Call premium paid for option

XX = Option period in days

For example a firm might need 3 million British pounds to settle a contract with a British firm. The settlement will be in 180 days, which expires on December 31, 1996. It is now June 30, 1996. The current price of pounds is $1.6909 per pound. A European-type call option is offered on the CBOE for December settlement at a strike price of 172.5 cents per pound. The maximum price is shown as:

	Strike Price$_{180}$	Call Premium
British pound$_{180}$ =	172.5 cents/pd	+ 3.40 cents/pd

When viewed as insurance against adverse foreign exchange price changes, the hedged ceiling price, FX_{180}, of the pound for December 1996 settlement will be as follows:

Ceiling Price FX$_{180}$ = 172.5 cents + 3.40 cents/pd = 175.90 cents/pd

In this case, the price of insurance is (175.9 cents – 169.90 =) 6.00 cents per pound. This represents a 3.531 percent premium over the current price of pounds.

DEMONSTRATION PROBLEM   **COST OF OPTION PRICE INSURANCE**

Situation

John received 200 shares of stock in a foreign firm when he was born. The stock was valued at 180 German marks per share. The stock appreciated and split several times. He now has 800 shares, which are currently valued at 350 marks per share.

John is concerned that too much of his net worth is tied up in one stock. He wants to sell 500 shares to diversify risk. However, he does not want to incur the tax liability for the sale until next year. He is concerned that the value of the German mark will decline between now and when he plans to sell the stock.

He learns that he can purchase a put option on German marks which has a strike price of 1.46 marks per U.S. dollar and expires in February of the following year, 90 days from now. The spot exchange rate is 1.44DM/$. The put option cost is .02DM/$.

He would like to know the cost of this price insurance.

Results

The minimum exchange rate, FX_{90}, to break even is that exchange rate that covers the cost of the option premium and the difference between the spot exchange rate of 1.44DM/$ and the option price, Option$_{90}$ of 1.46DM/$.

FX$_{90}$ = 1.46DM/$ + .02DM/$ = 1.48DM/$

This price represents the lowest DM/$ price John can receive if he purchases the options. The total cost of the price insurance figured at 1.44DM/$ is .04DM/$ or 2.7% (.04DM/$/1.44DM/$) above the current market price of dollars. This represents the cost of the price insurance.

The buyer of an option must be concerned about the credit risk related to the writer of an option. If the optioned currency turns out to be worth more than the strike price in the case of a call or less in the case of a put, then the writer of the option must deliver the currency, if a call, or purchase currency, if a put. This obligation could be very costly for the writer of the option and it might encourage the writer to default, which would not trouble the organized exchanges that require the writer to have sufficient margin in the form of optioned currency on deposit, an irrevocable letter of credit, or cash margin. On the other hand, in over-the-counter option transactions, the buyer of the option must worry about the credit quality of the option seller. Usually the dealer will put its credit behind these transactions.

CURRENCY SWAPS

A typical **currency swap** is an agreement between two parties to exchange two currencies at the spot or current exchange rate, with the agreement that they will reverse the exchange at some agreed-upon future date, at the same exchange rate that prevailed at the time of the initial exchange. The agreement also calls for the party that obtains the currency from the country with the higher interest rate to pay the difference between the interest rate in its country and the rate in the lower interest rate country. Currency swaps are major activities at large international commercial banks and investment banking firms. These firms act as brokers and intermediaries in swap transactions.

EXHIBIT 19.4

Typical Currency Swap

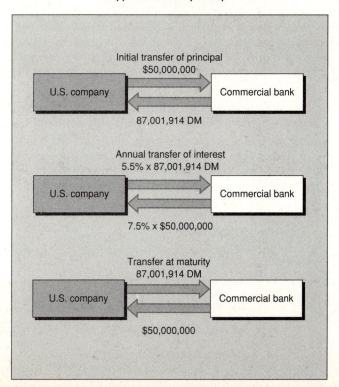

For instance, a five-year currency swap with a commercial bank provides German marks for U.S. dollars. The U.S. company has $50 million that it would like to swap for marks at an exchange rate of $.5747/DM. This would involve a swap of ($50,000,000/.5747 =) 87,001,914 DMs. If the U.S. interest rate on five-year money is 7.5%, and the German rate 5.5%, then the bank would pay the U.S. company swapping the $50 million a rate of 7.5% per annum in U.S. dollars. The U.S. company would pay the bank 5.5% in German DMs. At the end of five years, the bank would pay the company back $50 million and the U.S. company would pay the bank 87,001,914 DMs. Exhibit 19.4 shows the transactions associated with this swap.

✓ Checkpoints

19-12 What is the advantage of using the futures market in foreign currencies instead of the forward cash market?

19-13 How would you use an option contract in foreign currencies?

19-14 Who participates in the currency swap market?

SUMMARY AND REVIEW

1. **Explain the basis and the significance of foreign exchange rates.**

   Foreign exchange is demanded to settle international transactions for importing and exporting, investments, speculation, and tourism. Foreign exchange rates are quoted under the **American term**, which represents the number of dollars needed to purchase one unit of foreign exchange ($1.80 per British pound) or the **European term**, which expresses the number of foreign currency units needed to purchase one dollar (1.5 German marks per one U.S. dollar).

2. **Define and calculate interest rate parity and describe how arbitrage affects the relationship between current and forward exchange rates.**

   Interest rate parity represents an arbitrage condition that establishes the relationship between spot and forward exchange rates. The forward exchange rate is affected by arbitrage and establishes the relationship between the forward and spot exchange rate according to the following interest parity equation:

   $$\text{Forward exchange rate: } ER_f = ER_s[(1 + r_d)/(1 + r_f)]$$

   where:

   $$ER_s = \text{Spot exchange rate (domestic price of foreign currency)}$$
   $$ER_f = \text{Forward exchange rate}$$
   $$r_d = \text{Domestic periodic interest rate}$$
   $$r_f = \text{Foreign periodic interest rate.}$$

3. **Discuss the concept of purchasing power parity and the law of one price.**

    Purchasing power parity (PPP) is a theory that states the exchange rate between two countries will change in relation to changes in their relative inflation rates. The **law of one price** is a condition that must hold for PPP to operate. It states that a commodity should cost the same in two countries, adjusted by the exchange rate between the two countries and the cost of transportation and importing.

4. **Describe how differential inflation rates among countries affect exchange rates.**

    Purchasing power parity holds if increases in the general price levels of two countries are reflected in offsetting changes in the exchange rates between those two countries. Forward cash markets in foreign currencies are the most widely used technique for hedging currency risk. The forward cash markets, operated by foreign currency dealers, provide the ability to buy and sell foreign currency for future delivery.

5. **Explain how to use the forward cash and futures market in hedging currency risk.**

    The **foreign currency futures and forward cash markets** provide the ability to purchase futures contracts in foreign currencies. The futures market is an organized market with specific contracts, settlement dates, and margin requirements.

6. **Explain how to use options on foreign exchange and how to compute the cost of such an option in hedging currency risk.**

    Options on foreign exchange are available on several organized exchanges. They provide the ability to purchase put and call options in foreign currencies. The XX day forward price of foreign exchange, FX_{xx}, which will cover the cost of the options premium, CP, is shown in the following equation:

    $$FX_{xx} = \text{Option}_{xx} + CP$$

    where:

    $$FX_{xx} = \textit{Maximum price of foreign exchange in XX days}$$

    $$\text{Option}_{xx} = \textit{Call contract option strike price for settlement in XX days}$$

    $$CP = \textit{Call premium paid for option}$$

7. **Explain how to use currency swaps to hedge currency risk.**

    Currency swaps allow two parties to exchange currency at the spot exchange rate with the agreement that they will reverse the exchange at some future point. A currency swap also requires the party receiving the currency with a higher interest rate in that country's currency to pay interest to the counterparty at a rate that represents the interest rate differential between the two countries.

SELF-TEST PROBLEMS	INTEREST RATE PARITY

ST-19-1

MKY Corporation has issued debentures in Australia denominated in Australian dollars and in the United States denominated in U.S. dollars. Both debentures mature in one year. Both bonds have similar covenants and are therefore equally risky. You are considering investing in these bonds for a one-year period until they mature. The bonds have a yield of 7.5% in Australia and 4.2% in the United States. The current exchange rate between Australian and United States dollars is .675 U.S dollars per Australian dollar (A$). You notice that the one-year forward exchange rate is $.673 U.S./A$. If interest rate parity conditions held, what would you calculate the forward exchange rate to be? Which bond should you invest in to receive the highest return?
Answer on page 592.

PURCHASING POWER PARITY

ST-19-2

Suppose a new CD recording cost 12DM in Germany. The cost of shipping to the United States is 1DM. The current exchange rate between U.S. dollars and DM is $.40U.S./DM. If purchasing power parity holds, what is the price of the CD in the United States assuming no other costs are involved?

PROBLEMS	QUOTING EXCHANGE RATES

19-1

Convert the following exchange rates from the American term to the European term, or vice-versa.

American Term	European Term
128 yen/$	
	$.25/ French franc
3 Swiss Francs/$	

CHANGE IN EXCHANGE RATES

19-2

Compute the percentage change in the following exchange rates between the two periods shown:

Period t	Period $t + 1$	Percent Change
125 yen /$	145 yen/$	
4.5 French francs/$	3.75 French francs/$	
.45 DM/$	.425 DM/$	

QUOTING EXCHANGE RATES—AMERICAN AND EUROPEAN TERM

19-3

The spot rate of Canadian dollars is quoted on the European term as follows:

Bid: C$1.3060/US$

Ask: C$1.3078/US$

What are the bid and ask prices quoted on the American term?

PURCHASING POWER PARITY

19-4

The average price of a specific good in the United States is $5,000. The average price of the same good in Switzerland is 8,000 SF. If purchasing power parity holds, what is the exchange rate between the United States and Switzerland measured on the American term?

FORWARD EXCHANGE INTEREST PARITY

19-5

The spot exchange rate of U.S. dollars to Swiss francs is SF1.5085/US$. The Eurodollar interest rate is 8% for one year and the comparable Swiss rate is 4%. What would you expect the forward exchange rate to be for delivery in one year?

FOREIGN EXCHANGE INTEREST PARITY

19-6

The spot foreign exchange rate (American term) between the United States and Japan is $.032 = 1 yen. The six-month T-bill rate in the United States is 7%. The comparable six-month rate on Japanese bonds is 3%. If interest parity holds, what is the six-month forward exchange rate FX180 between the United States and Japan?

EXCHANGE RATE RISK

19-7

You are evaluating a one-year equity investment in the U.S. or German stock markets. Your analysts expect an 11% return on U.S. equities and 9% on German equities. Your foreign exchange analysts expect the exchange rate between U.S. dollars and German marks to fall from 1.60 DM/$1 to 1.35 DM/$1 in the next year. Given these expectations, which country's equities would you buy and why?

FOREIGN EXCHANGE ARBITRAGE

19-8

The spot foreign exchange rate (American term) between the United States and United Kingdom is $1.80 = 1 pound. The six-month rate on Europound securities is 12%. The six-month Eurodollar rate is 6%. The six-month forward exchange rate is $1.75 = 1 pd. An arbitrage consisting of borrowing U.S. dollars to purchase pounds, investing in British debt, and buying dollars forward would cost $5,000 in transaction costs per $1 million of trading. Would such an arbitrage be profitable? What would be your gain or loss?

SELF-TEST PROBLEM	SOLUTIONS

ST-19-1

Solution:

The spot exchange rate is .675 U.S$/A$ using the American term.

To solve for the forward exchange rate, ER_{365}, assuming the interest rate parity condition results in:

$$ER_{365} = ER_S [(1 + r_d)/(1 + r_f)]$$

$$ER_{365} = .675U.S.\$/A\$ \times [(1 + .042)(1 + .075)]$$

$$= .675U.S.\$/A\$ \times .96930 = .65428U.S.\$/A\$$$

Since the forward price of the U.S. dollar is $.673U.S./A$, which is above the interest parity condition value of $.65428U.S./A$, then the return on the Australian investment will offer the higher return of the two possibilities.

ST-19-2

Solution:

Solving for the U.S. price using Equation 19.3 gives us:

$$\$X = (12DM + 1DM) \times \$.40U.S./DM = \$5.20$$

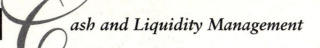

ash and Liquidity Management

Learning Goals

After studying this chapter, you should be able to:

1. Describe the process of cash management as it relates to determining optimal cash holdings and making and receiving payments.
2. Discuss liquidity management in terms of its impact on profitability, the processes to accomplish it, the sources of liquidity, the impact of regulatory liquidity requirements, and the selection of liquid assets.
3. Define and describe several measures of liquidity for financial institutions.
4. Describe the process of meeting Federal Reserve mandated reserve requirements and discuss the contemporaneous accounting technique.

Which amount is greater: the cash flowing through a typical financial institution, or the cash flow through a comparably sized commercial or industrial firm? Considering that financial institutions are in the business of managing cash and other financial assets, the answer should be obvious: Liquidity management, including cash management, begins the portfolio management activities of financial institutions. Consequently, these firms must adopt sound cash management procedures.

Financial institutions are also the primary suppliers of liquid assets to government, business, and household sectors. On December 31, 1993, commercial banks and thrift institutions had transaction liabilities of $403 billion in demand deposits and another $419 billion in checkable deposits, including NOW accounts, automated transfer service balances, and credit union share drafts. The creation of these liquid liabilities is one of the basic transformation products that these institutions can offer. Providing this quantity of liquid liabilities necessitates managing the liquidity of the institution optimally. This chapter discusses how managers of financial firms can develop and implement cash management procedures and liquidity management strategies.

Cash Management

Financial firms hold cash to:

- Meet obligations of customers and others who have checks drawn against the firm.
- Provide cash for customers seeking to consume or make other payments.
- Assist in meeting reserve requirements, when required.
- Insure settlement of outstanding loan and investment commitments.

Holding cash provides no revenue for the financial firm. Since the cash must be financed, financial firms try to minimize their holdings of cash and other non-earning near-cash items. This section considers both the holding of cash by financial institutions and the processing of incoming payments.

The challenge of liquidity management differs greatly from one type of financial institution to another. Some institutions, such as large depositories, have many sources of liquidity, such as emergency borrowings from Federal Reserve Banks and longer-term resources from Federal Home Loan Banks, and government insured deposits. For these firms, managing liquidity is a bit easier.

Other financial institutions do not have the advantage of so many sources of generating cash, so that liquidity management becomes quite challenging. In recent years, life insurance companies that issue large volumes of annuities, have experienced liquidity problems when customers concerned about the firms' safety have redeemed large numbers of policies. Property and casualty companies are also vulnerable to large claims, such as those from natural disasters, which can tax their liquid resources. Finance companies, relying primarily on the money and capital markets to obtain cash, often hedge their liquidity risk by establishing lines of credit at commercial banks to insure that cash will be available when conditions in the money and capital markets make security issuance difficult.

HOLDING CASH

The Federal Reserve defines cash as the following: (1) currency; (2) travelers' checks; (3) demand deposits; and (4) other checkable deposits. As of December 1993, these represented a balance of over $1.129 trillion, over 70% of which was in demand deposits and other checkable deposits and the remainder in currency and travelers' checks. Depository institutions must be particularly adept at cash management procedures because they supply individuals and businesses the currency and transaction account services to facilitate commerce.

Depositories obtain cash from local Federal Reserve banks or a correspondent bank. Excess cash is delivered and surplus cash taken from branch offices when needed. Usually these cash needs are predictable, so that a delivery schedule can be established. The delivery of cash to depository offices, its safekeeping, and the holding currency for customer needs are major costs to depositories. Depositories

FEDERAL RESERVE SUPPLIES GREENBACKS FOR MUCH OF THE DEVELOPING WORLD

As more countries move from centrally planned to private-based economies, the need for a currency representing a stable store of value and an acceptable medium of exchange has become more important. The converting countries of the former Soviet Union and several developing countries in Central and South America have found that the U.S. currency provides an excellent store of value as well as worldwide acceptance as a medium of exchange. Consumers and business people who do not want to risk holding inflating domestic currencies feel comfortable using dollars for store of value and exchange.

Federal Reserve officials have estimated that in 1992 approximately two-thirds of all U.S. currency is used outside the United States. One great advantage to the United States is that the cash used in foreign countries represents a zero-interest loan to the U.S. Treasury. Some analysts claim that these large holdings serve to keep U.S. monetary authorities from inflating the dollar, because if inflation became severe, it might lead to a worldwide flight from the dollar, thus ending U.S.'s zero-interest loan.

How

it

Really

Works

develop policies and procedures designed to minimize the holdings of currency and to insure safekeeping of currency held by the firm.

PROCESSING INCOMING CASH

Financial institutions also receive huge amounts of payments coming into the institution for covering obligations held against others, primarily loans and investments. Many of these loans involve periodic payments, some of which involve massive payment processing activities. Checks sent to financial firms for payments on loans, credit cards, and security purchases must be processed as quickly as possible to minimize float and maximize the return on investable funds. **Float** represents checks in process of collection for which the payer and payee are both credited with the balance of the check. Financial institutions work with postal authorities to obtain access to incoming mail as quickly as possible, and larger institutions operate around-the-clock payment processing centers to account for payments and process incoming checks.

Some actions financial institutions take to optimize the crediting of deposits on incoming payments and maximize float advantages on outgoing check payments include:

- Encouraging loan customers to pay periodic payments using **pre-authorized payment programs,** which permit the receiving bank to debit the transaction account of the loan customer on a specified date.

- Making periodic payments to customers using slow postal services and delaying mailing until the latest contractual date permitted.

- Reducing the **grace period** which specifies a number of days after the payment due date in which the payment will be accepted as on time.

- Encouraging loan customers to use a transaction account at the same institution to make payments, thus eliminating the delay in clearing the check against another institution.
- Developing machine-readable payment invoices to expedite the processing of incoming payments.

These are but a few of the techniques used by financial institutions to improve cash management procedures. Each firm should review carefully each step in the process of incoming and outgoing payment processing, contractual loan terms, and use of technology to improve its cash management.

✓ Checkpoints

20-1 Why must management of financial institutions focus on fine-tuning their cash management skills?

20-2 How do financial institutions reduce cash holdings, expedite cash receipts, and delay expenditures.

How it Really Works

CENTRAL BANK'S ROLE IN CASH MANAGEMENT

The largest source of float is caused by delays in check processing. Checks in transit accounts for most of it. In order to reduce float, the Federal Reserve has worked on a number of programs since the 1970s. The 1970s recorded a record increase in the amount of float as well as the in the economic distortions caused by it. As check use rose in the 1970s, interest rates were also rising. As a result, there was a large and growing value to the beneficiaries of float balances. Since the Federal Reserve frequently credited two banks with balances on the same check, the Federal Reserve was the largest creator of float.

In order to deal with this problem, the government took three major steps. First, it improved its own check clearing processes. This involved setting up 48 regional check processing centers outside the Federal Reserve Bank cities. Air charter services were improved. All this served to slow the growth in float.

The second action took an act of Congress. In 1980, Congress passed legislation that instructed the Fed to charge banks directly for the use of float they obtained through the check processing delays. This action really was effective: in only three years, average Fed float dropped from $6.7 billion to $1.8 billion. The decline indicated how much individual banks were contributing to the creation of float.

In 1983, the Fed instituted new procedures to reduce float, including the establishment of new policies designed to increase the number of checks that could be collected overnight, thus reducing presentation delays and further reducing float. By 1990, float was down to below $500 million.

Source: "Float," *Fedpoints*, Federal Reserve Bank of New York, no. 8 (March 1992).

Liquidity Management

Liquidity management involves the cash management issues discussed above as well as the larger issues of holding liquid assets in addition to cash. This section considers the impact of liquidity on profitability, the process of liquidity management, the need for liquidity, and the impact of government requirements that involve liquidity.

LIQUIDITY, PROFITABILITY, AND REGULATORY REQUIREMENTS

The management of liquidity is important to the profitability of the institution for two reasons. First, the need to hold highly liquid, low-credit-risk, short-term assets makes it difficult to show a suitable positive interest rate spread on this portion of the firm's assets. In this respect, regulatory liquidity requirements act as a form of tax on the institution by adversely affecting profitability. Certainly, the reserves required by the Federal Reserve, which are held in a noninterest-bearing Federal Reserve account or vault cash, act as a major drag on profitability. Holding excess interest-earning liquid assets at a time when other investment opportunities provide higher returns also acts to reduce earnings.

Second, liquidity requirements are important because assets that are held to meet regulator requirements alter the overall investment strategy of the firm in such a way as to adversely impact profitability. A minimum liquidity requirement ties up assets in liquid form that would otherwise be lent or invested in assets in higher-yielding markets. Moreover, assets held to meet regulator requirements are not available to meet normal liquidity needs without penalty, because these assets are held primarily to avoid regulator sanctions and financial penalties rather than to meet forecast cash flow or emergency cash needs. As a result, firms must hold liquid assets generally in excess of the regulatory minimums established.

THE LIQUIDITY MANAGEMENT PROCESS

The process of liquidity management involves a number of financial activities. First, it involves completing a highly detailed pro forma cash flow statement for the firm. Because most financial institutions have large and frequently volatile cash flow needs, the financial manager responsible for liquidity management usually must provide these statements daily. The pro forma cash flow statement serves to determine whether the firm anticipates an excess or deficient cash flow position for the period under review.

Second, the firm's liquidity manager must determine how to raise cash if the cash flow statement shows a deficiency or utilize cash if a surplus results. This involves an analysis of sources of liquidity. These alternatives can be looked at as alternative ways of raising cash or utilizing excess cash.

Third, liquidity management requires determining the types of investments in which the liquidity portfolio will be invested. Such factors as the marketability of the investments held, credit risk, maturity, basis risk, and taxation are important in selecting a liquidity portfolio strategy.

Fourth, the financial manager must develop a separate liquidity strategy for each approach to raising cash. This strategy involves raising cash by identifying: (1) assets that may be liquidated, (2) liabilities that may be issued quickly, and (3) assets that can be used as collateral. Each of these alternatives must be analyzed in some detail to determine the optimal liquidity raising strategy.

DEVELOPING PRO FORMA CASH FLOW STATEMENTS

Developing pro forma cash flow statements for the financial intermediary is the first step in the liquidity management process. The financial manager must identify all the items on the balance sheet, income statement, and off-balance sheet statements that impact cash flow. Table 20.1 represents a sample pro forma cash flow statement.

TABLE 20.1

Commercial World Bank
Pro Forma Cash Flow Statement
for March and April 1995

Sources of Pro Forma Cash	March	April
Loan repayments	$ 34,000,000	$ 23,000,000
Loan prepayments	5,000,000	4,000,000
Interest receipts	122,000,000	123,000,000
Net (+ −) demand deposits	23,000,000	−5,000,000
Net (+ −) savings and time deposits	45,000,000	−12,000,000
Sale of loans and investments	12,000,000	4,000,000
Maturing securities	22,000,000	21,000,000
Total sources	$263,000,000	$158,000,000
Uses of Pro Forma Cash		
Loans funded	$110,000,000	$ 98,000,000
Investments purchased (settlements)	35,000,000	25,000,000
Operating expenses (cash)	14,000,000	14,000,000
Cash interest paid on liabilities	22,000,000	23,000,000
Lines of credit taken down	8,000,000	0
Nondeposit liabilities maturing	34,000,000	32,000,000
Total uses	$223,000,000	$192,000,000
Cash excess or (deficiency)	($ 40,000,000)	$ 34,000,000

For an institution large enough to use it, a full-time cash management function is usually justified. This function is responsible for integrating with all the operating units to ensure that all asset and liability decisions that impact cash flow are identified. This function is also responsible for identifying ways to improve cash flow within the firm by making recommendations to alter operations in ways that will reduce float, increase the timing of cash flows, and reduce outflows. Out of these analyses frequently come ideas for changing bill-paying methods, changing the timing of sending out interest payments, improving payment processing, altering product design, and modifying funding methods.

SOURCES OF LIQUIDITY: ASSETS, LIABILITIES, AND COLLATERAL

One myth of liquidity management is that the primary source of liquidity or cash is the maturity or sale of the institution's liquid assets. This does not hold true for many institutions, because they have many other sources of cash that may be easier to access. Another reason is that a regulator may require an institution to hold a certain percentage of its liquid assets. As a result, these assets are not truly liquid.

Thus, the financial manager will want to look at the following alternatives to raise cash:

1. Saleable assets.
2. Assets that can be pledged for borrowing purposes.
3. Lines of credit.
4. Wholesale deposit sources.
5. Government sources, such as the Federal Reserve's discount window, the FHLBs, and the Credit Union Liquidity Fund.

Saleable Assets

Most financial institutions hold assets other than those that can be sold in highly liquid markets. Many banks hold Treasury securities while many thrifts hold government agency mortgage-backed securities. Selling these assets may be an effective way to generate cash.

Pledgable Assets

Many institutions can easily raise cash by using assets on their books as collateral for a short-term loan. The repurchase agreement was designed as a way to use assets to raise cash quickly and inexpensively. There are very large repo markets in virtually all Treasury, agency, and agency guaranteed mortgage-backed securities. In addition, security dealers will provide repo programs for most other securities held by financial firms. Because collateral is so important to the ability of firms to generate cash, many financial institutions have someone responsible for keeping track of eligible assets that can qualify as collateral for borrowing.

Lines of Credit

Stronger financial institutions—primarily large, well-capitalized commercial banks—establish lines of credit with other financial institutions. The most frequently used is the federal funds market. Many smaller banks and thrifts have excess liquidity they want to invest overnight or for a few days. The federal funds market is also a good investment for these institutions.

Wholesale Deposit Sources

The wholesale funds market has significantly increased in scope and activity over the last decade. While wholesale deposits have been available to large commercial banks for years through the negotiable CD market, it has only been in the last decade that smaller institutions have been able to participate through the brokered insured deposit market. The brokered insured deposit market will be less important in the future because the FDICIA of 1991 put restrictions on the types of institutions that can use this market and constraints on the rates that can be offered. The availability of negotiable CDs and brokered insured deposits provides another efficient way for financial institutions to raise cash quickly.

Government Liquidity Sources

There are several government agencies available to financial institutions that need to raise cash quickly. The major programs include the Federal Reserve's discount window, the FHLB's advance window, and the Credit Union Liquidity Fund. Although each of these handles its lending differently, all are in the business of lending to their member firms with acceptable collateral.

LIQUIDITY AND REGULATORY REQUIREMENTS

For a portion of the liquid assets held, the asset strategy is sometimes controlled by the regulator. The Federal Reserve requires that the reserves held against transaction deposits be held in noninterest-bearing deposits in the Federal Reserve or with another qualifying institution and vault cash. For thrift institutions regulated by the OTS, the liquidity requirements dictate the percentage of specified liabilities that must be held in a specified group of eligible investments. These investments include U.S. government securities, agency securities, high-grade corporate investments, and deposits. The requirements also specify that a certain percentage of these liquid assets be in short-term investments having maturities of less than two years, while the remainder must be less than five years. The National Credit Union Administration (NCUA) also has the authority to require credit unions to hold a specified percentage of their assets in liquid form. Since credit unions now must hold reserves at the Federal Reserve, the NCUA does not now impose liquidity requirements.

This leaves many financial institutions in the perplexing situation that a certain portion of liquid assets are really not liquid at all, making liquidity management more difficult, since it is necessary to optimize liquidity management subject to a number of regulatory constraints that act to reduce profitability for the institution. This objective of liquidity management is to reduce the negative drag on earnings caused by the regulator's imposed liquidity requirements.

SELECTING THE LIQUIDITY ASSET PORTFOLIO

Once an institution determines the amount of liquid assets to be held, it must decide which liquid assets to hold. Developing a liquidity portfolio strategy requires identifying the following characteristics of the liquid assets to be held:

- Types of liquid assets.
- Maturities.
- Credit risks.
- Marketability.
- Taxability.

This section considers the criteria that should be considered in the selection of liquid assets. Although liquid assets are treated in this section as if they are managed in isolation from the rest of the firm's portfolio, they are not. Indeed, they are a component part of each firm's portfolio and must be considered a part of the same risk-return framework as all other assets.

Types of Liquid Assets to Hold

Liquid assets fall into four classifications: (1) U.S. government and agency securities, (2) short-term corporate securities, (3) deposits in regulated institutions such as negotiable CDs, and (4) short-term state and municipal securities of investment grade. Each of these can be represented in liquidity portfolios, depending on acceptance by the regulator and on the liquidity investment strategy management chooses.

The development of this strategy relies on the four additional aspects of the portfolio. Investment strategies have also been designed around each of the following elements of the portfolio.

Maturity

The maturity structure of the liquidity portfolio impacts the interest rate risk position of the firm's entire asset portfolio. Consequently, the maturity structure of liquid assets should be an element of the firm's interest rate risk strategy. A portfolio manager who attempts to minimize interest rate risk will concentrate on short-term investments, while one willing to accept greater interest rate risk exposure will do the opposite.

Financial managers can implement three strategies provided that the plans support the firm's overall interest rate position: the ladder of maturities liquidity strategy, the barbell liquidity strategy, and the riding the yield curve liquidity strategy.

The **ladder of maturities liquidity strategy** is the simplest. This strategy would have the institution make an interest rate neutral forecast of future interest rates.

Given this forecast, the firm spaces the maturities of its liquid assets evenly over the liquidity portfolio's holding period, say two or three years. The ladder of maturities strategy is described graphically in Exhibit 20.1.

EXHIBIT 20.1

Ladder of Maturities Liquidity Strategy

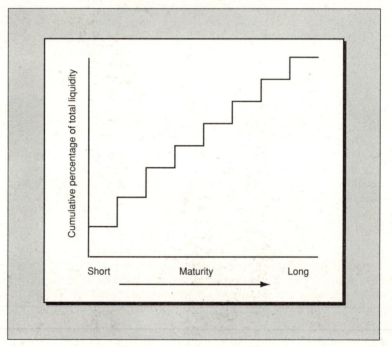

A **barbell liquidity strategy,** on the other hand, would have the liquidity manager invest a high percentage of all discretionary liquid funds in a particular maturity or risk class of liquid investments. Usually, the barbell would be between very short- and very long-term liquid assets. If the liquid asset holding period is two years, for example, the firm would alter the average maturity of its liquid asset portfolio between 6 and 18 months. The average maturity would depend on the firm's forecast of future interest rates. An example of a barbell strategy is shown graphically in Exhibit 20.2. Another barbell strategy relating to credit risk would be between holding very low credit risk assets such as U.S. Treasuries and riskier liquid instruments such as corporate money market instruments. The liquidity investment manager would move between the two classes depending on the relative yield relationships, or basis, between the two groups of money market instruments. When the basis is wide, as measured by the yield differential between the two, the decision rule would be to sell the relatively high-priced asset and buy the relatively low-priced asset.

EXHIBIT 20.2

Maturity Barbell Liquidity Strategy

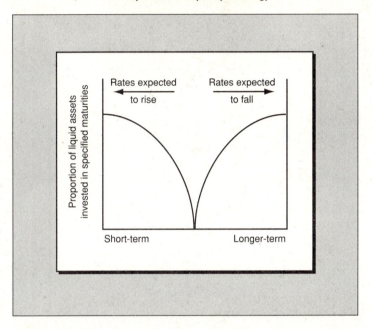

The **riding the yield curve liquidity strategy** takes the position that an upward-sloping yield curve is the norm. For an investor expecting an upward-sloping yield curve to persist for long periods of time, it would make sense to bunch the bulk of the firm's liquid assets in maturities on the long-term end of its liquidity maturity spectrum. Moreover, it would make sense to sell shorter-term liquid assets purchased some months or years earlier and use the funds raised to buy longer-maturity liquid assets. A simple riding the yield curve strategy might have the firm purchasing liquid assets with maturities of 18 to 24 months and selling liquid assets when their maturities fall to 3 to 6 months. The riding the yield curve strategy is described graphically in Exhibit 20.3.

Credit Risk

Credit risk impacts on liquidity management. Liquidity managers must make judgments about the risk versus return expectations for the allowable types of liquid investments. This assessment can be used in the barbell liquidity strategy.

Marketability

During periods of financial stress, an institution is most concerned about the marketability of its liquid assets. Not all liquid assets are equally marketable. Marketability is a matter of degree. Chapter 14 defined *marketability* as the difference between bid and ask prices. During stress periods, a high concentration

EXHIBIT 20.3

Riding the Yield Curve Liquidity Strategy

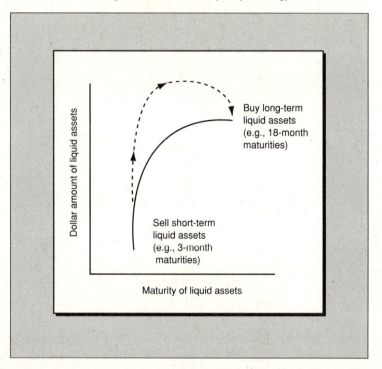

of the most marketable U.S. government and agency securities is a common strategy. This may also be a good strategy for the institution that relies primarily on the sale of liquid assets as the optimal way to raise cash.

Taxability

Some institutions are able to invest their liquid assets in tax-exempt securities. They find that the after-tax yields on tax-exempt securities are higher than the taxable yields on other liquid investments, meaning that tax-exempt securities might have a place in the institution's liquidity portfolio. One concern is that the Tax Reform Act of 1986 has made tax-exempt state and local bonds less attractive to intermediaries, as we discussed in Chapter 14.

✓ Checkpoints

20-3 How does holding liquid assets, especially to meet regulatory reserve requirements, affect the profitability of financial firms?

20-4 How can a financial manager design and carry out sound liquidity management policies?

20-5 What are the differences between the primary asset and liability sources of liquidity at financial institutions?

20-6 How do regulatory reserve requirements affect liquidity management?

20-7 What factors should managers consider when developing a liquidity portfolio?

20-8 What are the differences and similarities among the ladder of maturities liquidity strategy, the barbell liquidity strategy, and the riding the yield curve liquidity strategy?

Measuring Liquidity of Financial Institutions

As shown above, liquid assets can be measured as a balance sheet item or as alternative methods not reflected on the balance sheet for raising liquid assets through sale of assets and borrowing. This presents a problem in developing measures that can monitor the liquidity position of financial firms over time. Because no single liquidity measure or ratio is really sufficient to accomplish the task, it is necessary to develop a conceptual framework that will serve to identify the various aspects of liquidity management and provide specific measures for each, rather than attempt to develop a global measurement of liquidity adequacy. The aspects of liquidity adequacy that we will focus on here include:

- Assets convertible into cash.
- Liabilities available to raise cash.
- Riskiness of raising the liabilities.

We will discuss each of these aspects of liquidity and its measurement.

ASSETS CONVERTIBLE INTO CASH

For depository institutions, finance companies, and investment bankers, the holding of assets, that can be quickly sold with little possibility of loss, is a primary source of liquidity. The most liquid assets are generally thought to be:

- U.S. government, agency, and high-grade municipal and corporate securities with maturities less than one year, and which are not pledged to others *(LSA)*.
- Federal funds sold and reverse repurchase agreement (securities purchased under an agreement to resell) *(FFRR)*.
- Deposits held in depository institutions with maturities less than one year *(D)*.

These assets are the easiest to convert to cash. The ratio of liquid assets to total assets *(LATA)* can be used to track this aspect of liquidity, shown Equation 20.1:

$$LATA = (LSA + FFRR + D)/TA \qquad [20.1]$$

where:

$$LATA = Liquid\ assets\ to\ total\ assets$$

$$LSA = Liquid\ security\ assets$$

$$FFRR = Federal\ funds\ sold\ and\ reverse\ repos\ held$$

$$D = Short\text{-}term\ deposits$$

$$TA = Total\ assets$$

LIABILITIES AVAILABLE TO RAISE CASH

The other primary method to raise cash is simply to borrow it. Many financial firms establish **lines of credit** with other financial institutions which can be drawn down quickly. These lines of credit can be set up with private institutions such as by establishing federal funds lines. Most financial institutions also carefully track their holdings of assets that can serve as collateral secured credit lines or, alternatively, be used to raise cash under repurchase agreements. There are many financial assets that can be used as collateral for credit lines or as assets that can be sold under repurchase agreements. Some of the most common include:

- U.S. government and agency securities.
- Corporate securities.
- Home mortgages that can be sold to GSEs.

Although these are the most commonly used collateral, the fact is that large commercial banks and investment bankers will negotiate credit lines and repurchase agreements for most types of financial assets. The less liquid the asset, the less the amount of a loan that can be obtained using the asset as collateral. The percentage difference between the asset's market value and the amount that can be lent against it is known as a *haircut.* If the asset's market value is $100,000 and the amount that a lender will lend you against that collateral is $95,000, then the haircut would be [($100,000 – $95,000)/$100,000] = 5%. Even a junk bond might serve as collateral, but a haircut of 50% might be expected. It is important that credit lines and repurchase programs be established long before they are needed. Agreements dealing with the physical handing and inspection of collateral, pricing, and other terms and conditions must be established before any such program can be used.

Another major source of credit lines and repurchase programs are the GSEs. Federal Home Loan Banks, the Federal National Mortgage Association, and the

Federal Home Loan Mortgage Corporation are sources of funds where mortgage securities and mortgage loans that qualify for sale to FHMA and FHLMC are used as collateral. They also operate repo programs.

One way to track these sources of cash is to compute the ratio of total pledgable assets *(TPA)* to total assets *(TA)*, shown in Equation 20.2.

$$PATA = TPA/TA \qquad\qquad [20.2]$$

where:

> *PATA = Pledgable assets to total assets*
>
> *TPA = Total pledgable assets*
>
> *TA = Total assets*

RISKINESS OF RAISING THE LIABILITIES

Financial institutions with volatile liabilities must be more concerned about access to liquidity than those with stable sources of liabilities. The volatility of liabilities is generally thought to be a function of the source of the liabilities, their average size, and their credit risk. Financial institutions whose liabilities are generated from institutional sources offering large average-sized liabilities that are of lower credit rating will face higher risk in raising liabilities than financial institutions whose liabilities are the opposite.

For depository institutions, there is a distinction between core and wholesale deposits which impacts the riskiness of these liabilities. **Core deposits** are those that have been shown to be more stable and less interest-rate sensitive than wholesale funding sources. Core deposits are usually defined as transactions accounts, passbook savings, money market accounts, and certificates of deposit that are held by individuals in accounts below $100,000.

Determining which accounts are stable and which are risky requires analysis of past experience with the funding sources. Where there is no experience with the liability, it requires judgment to differentiate. Once this analysis is performed, the ratio of stable (or core) liabilities to total liabilities *(SLTL)* can be calculated as shown in Equation 20.3.

$$SLTL = SL/TL \qquad\qquad [20.3]$$

where:

> *SLTL = Stable liabilities to total liabilities*
>
> *SL = Stable liabilities*
>
> *TL = Total liabilities*

CALCULATING LIQUIDITY MEASURES

Situation

Williams Shore Bank has the balance sheet shown in Table 20.2. Marcy has been asked to assess the firm's liquidity position by comparing several appropriate financial ratios with those computed three months earlier.

TABLE 20.2

Williams Shore Bank Balance Sheet
March 31, 1997
(dollars in millions)

Assets		Liabilities and Net Worth	
U.S. government	$ 12	Transaction accounts	$ 50
Agency securities	8	Passbook accounts	70
Fed funds and reserve repos	10	CDs less than $100,000	550
Deposits held in commercial banks	15	CDs over $100,000	75
		Other liabilities	75
Home mortgages (qualified for sale to GSEs)*	125		
Home mortgages (not qualified for sale to GSEs)	200		
Mortgage-backed securities*	50		
Commercial and business loans	350		
Commercial mortgages	50	Capital accounts	70
Other assets	70	Total liabilities and	
Total assets	$890	net worth	$890

*GSE qualified mortgages are pledgable assets for repurchase agreements.

Several liquidity ratios at the bank for year-end 1996 include the following:
Liquid assets to total assets (LATA) = 6.76%
Total pledgable assets to total assets (PATA) = 25.87%
Stable liabilities to total liabilities (SLTL) = 82.56%

Results

Marcy computed the March 31, 1997, ratios for *LATA*, *PATA*, and *SLTL* to compare to the year-end 1996 levels. These March levels are:

$$LATA = (\$12 + \$8 + \$10 + \$15)/(\$890) = 5.056\%$$

$$PATA = (\$125 + \$50)/(\$890) = 19.663\%$$

$$SLTL = (\$50 + \$70 + \$550)/(\$890) = 75.281\%$$

Marcy has determined that Williams' liquidity position has deteriorated significantly in the last three months. All the ratios she calculated were less favorable on March 31, 1997, than at year-end 1996.

✓ Checkpoints

20-9 What three aspects of a financial firm's liquidity position should be monitored and measured over time?

20-10 Which liquidity measures relate to the liquidity of the firm's assets and liabilities? How does the riskiness of a firm's liabilities affect liquidity?

Depository Legal Deposit Reserve Requirements

Depository institutions that offer transaction accounts above a certain amount ($3.8 million as of December 1992) must be concerned about maintaining adequate reserves called for by the Federal Reserve Board's Regulation D. These regulations specify the percentage of deposits held in Federal Reserve Banks, vault cash and acceptable pass-through deposits held in a Federal Home Loan Bank, or the Central Liquidity Fund for institutions that are not members of the Fed.[1]

The amount of reserves to be held is a function of the reserve requirement percentage called for under the regulation, *rr*, and the amount of deposits, *D*, of certain types which are subject to reserve requirements.[2] Table 20.3 shows the reserve requirement percentages and the deposits for which they apply.

TABLE 20.3

Reserve Requirement Percentages
(July 1994)

Type of Deposit	Total Amount of Deposits Applicable	Reserve Requirement Percentage, *rr* and (range)
Transaction accounts	$0 to $51.9 million	3% (none)
	over $51.9 million*	10% (8–14%)
Nonpersonal time deposits		0%† (0–9%)
Eurocurrency liabilities		0%† (0–9%)

*The amount of transaction accounts subject to the higher reserve percentage changes each year by 80% of the percentage change in total transaction accounts held by all depositories.

†Reduced from 3% to 0% on December 17, 1991.

---

[1]The total reserve balance as of December 31, 1993, was $62.9 billion. Of that amount, $29.4 billion was held as balances in Federal Reserve banks and $36.8 billion in vault cash.

[2]Deposits on which transaction account reserve requirements are imposed include all deposits against which the negotiable withdrawals and preauthorized transfers in excess of three per month are permitted.

Maintaining adequate reserves is not as easy as it looks, even though the concept is simple enough. The amount of reserves is determined by calculating the relevant deposit balances, *D,* each day for a given period. Then the institution must hold actual reserves equal to those required during another specified period. How this works is less straightforward.

In 1984, the Federal Reserve went to a reserve accounting system called *contemporaneous reserve accounting.* This system requires that financial depositories maintain a specified amount of reserves measured by an arithmetic average calculated over a 14-day period beginning on a Thursday and ending on the second following Wednesday. This period is called the *maintenance period.* To determine the transaction deposit balances, *T,* upon which the reserve percentage, *rr,* is to be calculated, it is necessary to define the computation periods. There are two computation periods relevant to determining the required reserves to be held during the maintenance period. The first is called the *two-week lagged computation period* which covers vault cash (and nontransaction accounts and Eurocurrency when reserves are required against them). This computation period is two weeks long, but is not the same as the maintenance period. The lagged computation period begins on a Tuesday four weeks before the Thursday of the maintenance period. The second computation period is called the *two-week contemporaneous computation period* and it measures net transaction account balances, *T.* This period begins on the Tuesday preceding the relevant Thursday maintenance period. It begins four weeks after the two-week maintenance period. This sequence of computation periods and maintenance period immediately follow one another, creating overlap. The following demonstration problem should clarify this somewhat complicated procedure.

DEMONSTRATION PROBLEM	CALCULATING RESERVE REQUIREMENTS

Situation

Reserve requirements as shown in Table 20.3 are in effect. The exempt amount for transaction deposits is $3.8 million. The following calendar shows the day of the week and amount of vault cash *(V),* nontransaction liabilities *(NTL),* and net transaction accounts *(T). V* and *T* are measured in millions of dollars.

Lagged computation period is Tuesday 3rd to Monday 16th.

Contemporaneous computation period is Tuesday 31st to Monday 13th.

Maintenance period is Thursday 2nd to Wednesday 15th.

Vault cash average = $5.043 million.

Transaction account average balance = $639.57 million.

Results

Using the data in the calendar, the calculation for average vault cash for the lagged computation period, and transaction accounts for the contemporaneous computation period, the required reserves can be calculated. Table 20.4. shows these calculations.

Sunday	Monday	Tuesday	Wednesday	Thursday	Friday	Saturday
1	2	3 V = $5.1 NTL = 0	4 V = $4.9 NTL = 0	5 V = $5.0 NTL = 0	6 V = $5.2 NTL = 0	7 V = $5.4 NTL = 0
8 V = $4.5 NTL = 0	9 V = $5.1 NTL = 0	10 V = $5.4 NTL = 0	11 V = $5.3 NTL = 0	12 V = $4.8 NTL = 0	13 V = $5.4 NTL = 0	14 V = $4.4 NTL = 0
15 V = $4.7 NTL = 0	16 V = $5.4 NTL = 0	17	18	19	20	21
22	23	24	25	26	27	28
29	30	31 T = $650	1 T = $655	2 T = $642	3 T = $623	4 T = $640
5 T = $640	6 T = $640	7 T = $654	8 T = $634	9 T = $640	10 T = $634	11 T = $634
12 T = $634	13 T = $634	14	15	16	17	18

TABLE 20.4

Required Reserve Calculation
(dollars in millions)

Deposit Type	Amount	Reserve Percentage	Requirement
	Tuesday 31st to Monday 13th		
Nontransaction liabilities	$ 0	0%	$0
Transaction average	639.57		
Up to $51.9 million	51.90	3	1.557
Over $51.9 million	$587.67		
Less: exempt amount	3.80		
	583.87	10	5.8387
Total requirement			$7.3957
	Tuesday 3rd to Monday 16th		
Vault cash average			5.0430
Net reserve requirement			$2.3527

✓ Checkpoints

20-11 What is the Federal Reserve Regulation D reserve requirement?

20-12 How do financial managers use the contemporaneous accounting system to determine required reserves? What are the differences among the two-week lagged computation period, two-week contemporaneous computation period, and two-week maintenance period?

SUMMARY AND REVIEW

1. **Describe the process of cash management as it relates to determining optimal cash holdings and making and receiving payments.**

   Financial institutions must practice strong **cash management** techniques in order to meet the cash needs of customers while at the same time minimizing the holdings of this nonearning cash asset. Financial institutions as major processors of payments must develop processes to quickly process incoming payments and delay disbursements, thereby maximizing **float** on ongoing payments.

2. **Discuss liquidity management in terms of its impact on profitability, the processes to accomplish it, the sources of liquidity, the impact of regulatory liquidity requirements, and the selection of liquid assets.**

   Given the dominance of an upward-sloping term structure, holding of cash and short-term liquid assets typically act to retard earnings. **Liquidity management** involves developing **pro forma cash flow statements, identifying sources of liquidity, developing a liquidity investment strategy,** and **selecting appropriate liquid assets.** Regulations on some financial institutions have an impact on the liquidity strategy selected. The liquid assets selected should reflect analysis of **types of assets, marketability, maturity, credit risk,** and **taxability.** There are three common liquidity management strategies, the **ladder of maturities, barbell,** and **riding the yield curve** strategies.

3. **Define and describe several measures of liquidity for financial institutions.**

   Measures of liquidity for financial institutions are used to analyze the **liquidity of assets, potential liquidity of liability options,** and the **riskiness of liabilities** used to finance the firm. Three common ratios used to measure liquidity include the ratios of (1) **liquid assets to total assets (LATA);** (2) **total pledgable assets to total assets (PATA);** and (3) **stable liabilities to total liabilities (SLTL).**

4. **Describe the process for meeting Federal Reserve mandated reserve requirements and discuss the contemporaneous accounting technique.**

   Depositories issuing transaction accounts must hold **Federal Reserve required reserves** in the form of **vault cash** or **acceptable deposits** equal to a specified percentage of those deposits. The method for calculating this requirement is called the **two-week contemporaneous accounting method.** It involves determining vault cash over a period called the **two-week lagged computation period,** transaction deposits over a period called the **two-week contemporaneous computation period,** and average actual reserve holdings over a period called the **two-week maintenance period.**

CASE 20.1

MANAGING COLLATERAL AND LIQUIDITY

Advance Credit Corporation (ACC) was founded in 1923 as a subsidiary of the Gilson Manufacturing Co. Gilson, a manufacturer of heavy equipment, formed ACC to finance customer purchases of Gilson equipment.

Over the years, Gilson fell on hard times, unable to advance technologically and meet foreign competition, and experienced dramatic declines in market share and profitability. ACC's management, recognizing Gilson's problems, expanded into consumer credit through the opening of small loan offices. In the 1960s, they began offering a credit card. Over the years, their consumer loan business eventually replaced the dying business finance activity. In fact, by 1992, what was left of Gilson was sold to a large competitor and ACC no longer had a viable business equipment financing activity.

As a condition of the Gilson acquisition, ACC was to be made a private company through an initial public offering (IPO) of common stock. Its stock was sold to management and the public in early 1993. For two years following the IPO, the purchaser of Gilson agreed to guarantee ACC's commercial paper. After that period, ACC would be on its own.

With its independence, ACC had to deal with critical liquidity management issues. The commercial paper guarantee had expired six months ago. Without the guarantee of its commercial paper, it could no longer rely on a quick sale of additional commercial paper if it experienced a liquidity crunch. The consumer loan business's high cyclicality added to the liquidity management complexity. ACC had only limited sources of liquidity to draw on, creating a need for effective and accurate cash-flow pro formas and liquidity management skills. Table C20.1 provides the balance sheet for ACC at year-end 1994 and 1995.

TABLE C20.1

Advance Credit Corporation
Balance Sheets for Year-End 1994 and 1995
(dollars in millions)

	December 31, 1995	December 31, 1994
Assets		
Cash and bank CDs	$ 3	$ 2
U.S. Goverment and agencies	3	3
Consumer installment	234	210
Credit card receivables	345	321
Less: Reserves for unearned income	(58)	(54)
Reserves for losses	(6)	(5)
Other assets	45	43
Total assets	$566	$520
Liabilities and Capital		
Bank loans	$ 12	$ 10
Commercial paper	412	375
Long-term bonds	50	50
Other liabilities	14	12
Net worth	78	73
Total liabilities and net worth	$566	$520

TABLE C20.2

Pro Forma Consumer Loan Extensions and Repayments
Monthly for 1996
(dollars in millions)

Month	Installment Loans Made	Installment Loans Repaid	Credit Card Receivables Extended	Credit Card Receivables Repaid	Net Increase (Decrease) in Credit Outstanding
Jan.	$18	$16	$21	$13	$10
Feb.	16	16	12	14	(2)
Mar.	14	17	13	14	(4)
Apr.	14	17	14	14	(3)
May	12	16	15	14	(3)
June	17	18	17	15	1
July	19	18	18	15	4
Aug.	20	19	18	15	4
Sept.	20	18	16	16	2
Oct.	21	18	17	16	4
Nov.	30	17	26	15	24
Dec.	34	17	27	14	30

The firm had just completed its pro forma planning concerning its lending activities for 1996. These data are included in Table C20.2. The table shows the pro forma installment loan extensions and repayment for installment loans and credit card receivables for each month of 1996. The table indicates a strong seasonal variation with high extensions of credit in November, December, and January and repayment from February through May.

The firm has developed a table showing the maturity of its commercial paper outstanding and the amount of its corporate bond that must be repaid under the bond's sinking fund requirement which calls for 10% of the bond's principal to be redeemed in July. This bond is collateralized by $75 million of installment loans and credit card receivables. The financing repayment schedule for 1996 is shown in Table C20.3. ACC's commercial paper is issued in maturities from 90 days to 1.5 years. The vast majority is issued for 90 days.

TABLE C20.3

Debt Repayment Schedule for 1996
(dollars in millions)

Month	Amount of Debt Principal Due
Jan.	$35
Feb.	30
Mar.	35
Apr.	20
May	35
June	40
July	5 + 30
Aug.	20
Sept.	35
Oct.	40
Nov.	25
Dec.	37

ACC has arranged with a national investment banker to issue one-year commercial paper monthly in amounts up to a maximum of $50 million. This paper is issued with collateral made up of the firm's installment loans and credit card receivables. The firm is able to issue paper equal to 90% of the nonpledged installment loans and credit card receivables outstanding.

ACC has arranged an unsecured credit line at a large regional bank for up to $40 million. The cost of this line is prohibitive, however, at roughly 2% more than the firm's commercial paper for comparable maturity credit.

ACC has also considered issuing another corporate bond. These bonds are not economical to issue in amounts less than $50 million. The maximum term for which ACC could obtain a reasonable rate would be five years. The maximum amount of a bond would be $75 million. Such a bond would require collateral equal to 1.5 times the principal amount of the bond. Given the plans for ACC's growth in the years ahead, management of ACC believes that issuing the bond would be a good idea. Management has also determined to keep a minimum amount of assets in cash and U.S. Government and agency securities equal to $8 million.

ACC expects to be profitable again in 1996. It also will be adding to its loss reserves. However, for purposes of liquidity planning, both of these factors are to be ignored.

PROBLEMS

1. Determine ACC's liquidity needs on a monthly basis for 1996. Using the firm's statement of credit extensions and repayments and debt maturity schedule, determine the credit needs of the firm each month, assuming it will maintain the necessary amount of liquid assets.

2. Describe the funding alternatives available to ACC. Does ACC have enough collateral to meet its entire funding requirements with commercial paper? To simplify the calculations, assume all the commercial paper issued matures in 12 months or later. (Ignore any changes in loan loss reserves and in net worth for purposes of this analysis.)

3. Do you expect that ACC will be required to utilize its bank credit line at any time during the year?

4. Do you advise ACC to issue a corporate bond? If so, when, and for how much?

CHAPTER 21

Asset Management and Pricing

Learning Goals

After studying this chapter, you should be able to:

1. Describe the factors that management must consider in determining the firm's asset structure.
2. Explain the importance of capital structure and how to calculate and use the weighted cost of capital and the breakeven risk adjusted asset yield in analyzing potential asset acquisitions.
3. Explain why financial institutions have become major sellers of loans through participations and syndications.

What does asset management involve? It involves three activities: developing an overall asset strategy for the firm; managing liquid assets; and pricing loans, including the minimum required yield on asset acquisitions. The portfolio management unit typically handles these activities.

Asset management is one of the most dynamic activities within any financial firm because the expected returns and risk on assets change constantly. A manager's objective is to make only those loans and investments that will be profitable enough to provide shareholders with their target return on equity. However, the optimal asset structure can change from one week to the next. Asset management requires constant monitoring of the competition's actions, the economic environment, the conditions within financial markets, and the changes in the regulatory and legal environments.

Determining the Asset Structure

The development of the optimal asset structure is of critical importance to a financial institution. Since portfolio management income is the largest source of income for depositories, life insurance companies, and pension funds, the portfolio structure decision will impact profitability the most. The portfolio decision is constrained by a multitude of factors, including:

1. Laws and regulations that constrain management's asset portfolio options.
2. Diversification options available.
3. Local market supply and demand conditions and market pricing.
4. Fixed costs that may affect the economic size needed to effectively operate in certain markets for particular types of claims.

LAWS AND REGULATIONS

Most financial intermediaries must accept certain constraints on the allowable assets they may hold. These are usually incorporated in their charter and typically differ by type of institution, by whether a state or national authority grants the charter, and by state-issuing authority. Most other financial institutions have greater leeway in their asset portfolio management decisions.

On the surface, it may appear somewhat counterproductive that financial institutions have constraints on the types of assets they hold. Chapter 11 discussed the importance of diversification in reducing credit risk. Asset constraints such as those that apply to S&Ls and credit unions, for example, would appear to be inconsistent with the need to provide for prudent diversification of credit risk. This inconsistency is explained by the public policymakers that create the charters for these institutions having other objectives in addition to promoting risk-reducing diversification. One objective of the regulation of financial institutions is allocating credit. S&Ls were chartered to increase access to home mortgages, and credit unions were chartered to add to the supply of consumer loans.

By constraining asset powers, the regulators of these institutions are able to simplify the supervision of these institutions. The rapid diversification of S&Ls in the 1980s convinced many in Congress that the risk of inadequate asset diversification was less than the risk of diversification combined with inadequate supervision and capital.

DIVERSIFICATION OPTIONS

Diversification of credit risk is a major concern of the portfolio manager. Unfortunately, achieving diversification is no simple matter. The average size or type of loan may make it impossible to achieve law of large numbers diversifica-

CONGRESS OUTLAWS JUNK BONDS AND SINKS SOME THRIFTS

How

it

Really

Works

The passage of the Financial Institution Reform, Recovery, and Enforcement Act of 1989 was designed, among other things, to stop thrifts from investing in risky assets. Among the risky assets identified by Congress were junk bonds. The law stated that thrifts could no longer acquire additional junk bonds and were required to liquidate their existing holdings within five years. The result was that accountants required that the bonds be marked-to-market, since they were no longer going to be held as investments until maturity.

Eliminating thrift buyers and forcing the sale of bonds led to significant declines in junk bond values in 1989 and 1990. Over the course of late 1989 through 1990, indices of average junk bond values dropped over 20%, causing a number of thrifts to fail since the decline in values had to be immediately reflected in current earnings and capital levels. After the Resolution Trust Corporation took over the institutions and liquidated a large percentage of the bonds, their values rebounded. Between late 1990 and mid-1993, junk bond prices were up over 30%. The experience provided clear evidence about the significant impact that government has on financial institution asset structures.

tion. Diversification is also limited by the market demand in the area served by the financial institution. Commercial banks and thrifts in Texas, Oklahoma, and Colorado suffered as a result of their heavy concentration of real estate assets lent in those states in the 1980s. Most of those institutions were too small to diversify by opening lending offices outside of those markets.

Many smaller firms must invest a much higher percentage of the firm's assets in low-risk securities because of their inability to diversify. Consequently, small commercial banks, thrifts, and insurance companies usually have a much higher percentage of assets in low-risk, highly marketable securities.

MARKET DEMAND LIMITATIONS AND PRICING

Local credit demand is also a major determinant of a depository's asset structure. Local markets can be categorized as *capital surplus* or *capital deficit* markets. Capital surplus markets are stable or declining areas that generate more savings than they borrow. Capital deficit markets are growing markets that must import capital. The intermediaries in capital surplus markets are forced to consider investments that were originated outside their market or were purchased in the secondary markets. Firms in capital deficit areas are likely to be sellers of loans to investors through secondary markets. The types of loans that are available will be influenced by the local economy. Fast-growing areas will experience strong demand for real estate loans; rural areas will emphasize agricultural loans; major cities will have a relatively larger demand for business lending.

Each financial firm must complete a thorough analysis of its local market. Managers cannot assume that, because an area is growing rapidly in population and employment, real estate lending will be profitable. Today, lenders have loan origination offices in markets outside their local areas. These offices can be opened and closed quickly and relatively inexpensively. As a result, a market that has strong demand can still face excess supply. Many financial institutions from the slow-growing agricultural states such as Kansas, Iowa, and Nebraska were major lenders in the Texas and Colorado markets during the mid-1980s. Continental Illinois National Bank was a major lender financing oil and gas exploration in Texas and Oklahoma in the early 1980s. The interaction of supply and demand determines pricing. Profitable pricing levels are not always found in markets experiencing strong demand.

How

it

Really

Works

DO MORTGAGE LENDERS REDLINE?

Despite the difficulty in finding sound assets in which to invest, accusations of redlining persist. *Redlining* is defined as the refusal of lenders to originate mortgages in given geographic areas despite the creditworthiness of prospective borrowers. Since the 1970s Congress has passed numerous laws to eliminate the practice, but the controversy continues.

In the last few years, a number of academic studies have attempted to determine whether redlining occurs. In one such study, Benston and Horsky conducted interviews with hundreds of actual and potential homebuyers in allegedly redlined neighborhoods. They found no evidence of redlining. An even more recent empirical study by Holmes and Horvitz tested for redlining in minority neighborhoods. These researchers attempted to improve on previous studies by controlling for differences in mortgage demand and credit risk, but they could not find any evidence of redlining, either.

These studies may well be telling us that efforts to eliminate the practice have been successful.

Sources: George J. Benston and Dan Horsky, "The Relationship between the Demand and Supply of Home Financing and Neighborhood Characteristics: An Empirical Study of Mortgage Redlining," *Journal of Financial Services Research*, 1992, no. 5, pp. 235–60; Andrew Holmes and Paul Horvitz, "Mortgage Redlining: Race, Risk, and Demand," *Journal of Finance*, March 1994, pp. 81–99.

Loan pricing and the relationship of pricing to alternative investments are major factors involved in achieving an optimal asset structure. The local markets in which financial institutions operate are dynamic, and most loans exhibit substantial pricing variations between local markets. Changes in macroeconomic policies, local economic conditions, competitive conditions, and financial conditions around the world have a way of impacting the asset structure decision.

The firm's asset structure is heavily influenced by changes in relative asset prices. Changes in the relative prices between two assets is called *basis*. The basis between two financial claims may change because of marketability, changes in the value of embedded options, credit risk expectations, taxation, tempory supply and demand factors, laws and regulations, and other institutional factors. These same factors influence the expected returns on loans and investments. A primary responsibility of the portfolio management function is constantly monitoring the financial markets to track basis changes over time. By doing so, the firm can be positioned to make investments with the highest return for any given level of risk.

Exhibit 21.1 provides annual average interest rates on ten-year Treasury, and Baa corporate bonds from 1986 to 1992. Also shown is the basis between the two computed by substracting the Treasury yield from the Baa yields. Notice that the basis narrowed in the 1989 to 1990 period and then widened. An investor might develop a strategy of buying the higher-risk Baa securities when the basis is wide, as it was in 1986, and holding Treasuries when the basis is narrow, as it was in 1989.

EXHIBIT 21.1

Various Interest Rates and the Basis between Them
1986 to 1993

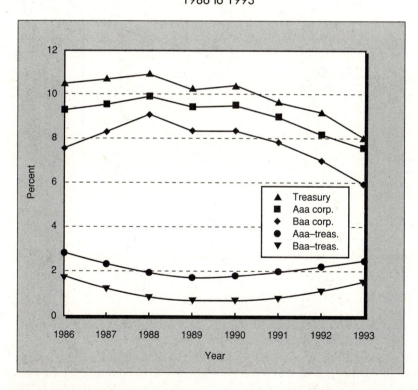

ECONOMIES OF SCALE AND SCOPE

How big should financial institutions be? That depends on whether large institutions are indeed more efficient and able to deliver more services at lower cost. These attributes are referred to as *economies of scale and scope. **Economies of scale*** concerns the relationship between the quantity of a bank service produced and the cost per unit of that service. In other words, it asks, "Can larger banks provide any given service more cheaply than smaller banks?" Exhibit 21.2 shows that three hypothetical relationships of cost per unit are independent of the number of units produced. The linear cost unit line "B" represents a situation in which cost per unit is independent of the number of units produced. The line labeled "C" indicates a product in which costs per unit decline as units produced increase, while the "A" line shows diseconomies of scale with its rising cost per unit.[1]

EXHIBIT 21.2

Economies of Scale

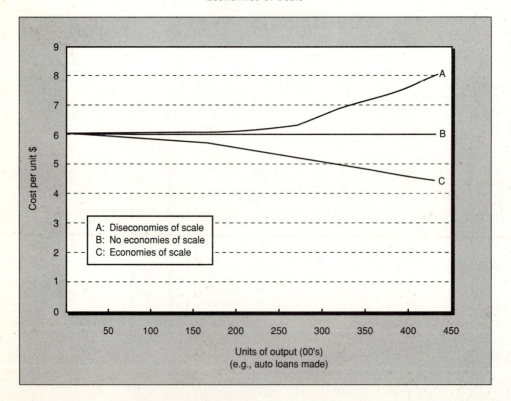

Economies of scope relates to the cost per unit of bank services that are produced jointly by sharing a common production system. For example, if a bank offers both first and second mortgages that are originated and serviced by the same unit within the bank, the cost per unit of the first and second mortgages

---

[1]The economies of scale functions shown in the graph are rather smooth functions. In reality, these functions may include significant jumps and drops as capital limits of a given technology are approached or new more-efficient technologies put in place.

originated and serviced would be less than if two groups provided the product. The issue in economies of scope is, "Can larger banks provide a wider range of services at lower per-unit cost because of shared joint production?"

Bank management and shareholders are interested in producing banking services at the least cost because, in a competitive market, the bank will survive and earn a reasonable profit. If technology, management structure, or a common production system results in lower costs as an activity grows in size, then there is a strong incentive for growing to maximize profits. From the government's perspective, low-cost banking services are critically important to overall economic efficiency. Thus the question of whether the government should encourage or discourage the creation of large banks becomes a very important public policy issue.

Over the years, the great body of operating statistics on commercial banks has permitted extensive research on the subject of economies of scale and scope. Much of this work was done using the Federal Reserve functional cost analysis data, which provides cost and volume data for a large number of banks of various sizes by type of services provided, such as demand deposits, mortgage loans, and others.[2]

Economies of Scale and Financial Functions

Many lenders would like to diversify to a greater extent but find the costs of establishing new lending capacity to be prohibitively high. Each new financial function for each financial claim, such as a new lending program, requires putting in place all the origination and servicing capabilities discussed in Chapter 2. There are high costs associated with each new type of loan that is added to the firm's menu. These costs add up quickly as the firm grows and diversifies, and many are subject to economies of scale which must be considered in order to be operationally competitive.

The risk and return characteristics of a particular type of loan also change rapidly. If the firm sets up a business loan origination group, for example, it may find that its competitors make the same choice. The result would be that this additional competition drives down loan rates and lowers volume per institution. The firm still has to pay the staff and service the business on the books, but it cannot achieve adequate scale economies.

✓ Checkpoints

21-1 What are some recent instances where laws and regulations have influenced asset management by prescribing the loans and investments that financial firms can make?

21-2 Why do small financial intermediaries have trouble diversifying?

---

[2]There are many limitations of the many empirical studies concerning economies of scale. They include: (1) determining the correct output of a financial institution; (2) recognizing the dynamic nature of technology on information and communication companies such as financial institutions; (3) lack of data properly itemizing costs; (4) determining how to deal with off-balance sheet contingent liabilities that require costs to create but don't show on the balance sheet; and (5) correctly estimating cost functions that do not lend themselves to the smooth functions used in most studies.

21-3 How can a specific local financial market for a certain type of claim experience strong demand but still be unprofitable for the originating firm?

21-4 How do economies of scale and scope influence the assets originated and held by a financial intermediary?

Financial Depository Pricing of Loans

This section develops a methodology for pricing loans at depository institutions by incorporating information about financial alternatives and all costs and financial risks that must be covered in order to ensure a loan's profitablility.[3] To accomplish this, the financial intermediary must understand its optimal capital structure and related regulatory equity requirements, marginal cost of funds, credit risks, and servicing costs for each of its loan classes. Each of these elements is needed to complete the development of the pricing methodology.

REGULATORY CAPITAL REQUIREMENTS

Establishing a marginal capital requirement for each new asset is the first step in developing our pricing algorithm. *Marginal* means the dollar change in equity for a given dollar change in the asset or off-balance sheet factor. These marginal equity or capital percentages are determined by management for depository institutions and are based on management's determination of the firm's optimal capital structure. The regulator's risk-based minimum capital requirement may be considered an important factor in setting the level for each firm. Indeed, many depository firms use the minimum capital requirements for each type of asset as specified by the risk-based capital requirements discussed in Chapter 10. Of course, depository institutions can use a higher or lower capital standard than the minimum imposed by the regulator. The objective in either case should be to minimize the firm's weighted cost of capital and still attain the selected capital minimum.

CALCULATING THE WEIGHTED AVERAGE COST OF CAPITAL

As discussed earlier, financial depositories will likely establish a capital structure calling for higher equity levels than required by the minimum risk-based

---

[3]The analysis used here is useful whether the institution has the market power to set loan rates with some discretion or is simply a price taker. If the firm is analyzing marketable securities, it will act as a price taker. On the other hand, for some types of loans, the firm may have a strong market position which permits it to establish interest rates with some discretion even though competition exists. The objective in either case is to determine whether the asset once put on the books of the institution will cover the cost of capital and the risks associated with the asset.

standards. Once these are established, the firm is in a position to determine the relative ratio of debt and equity for the acquisition of each asset to be acquired on the margin. The cost of capital for the next asset acquired is defined as the weighted average cost of capital, *WACC*, shown in Equation 21.1. The before-tax cost of debt is used, as long as the before-tax cost of equity is used. Since financial asset yields are typically quoted on a before-tax or taxable equivalent basis, this approach greatly simplifies the computational process. It saves us from computing asset yields on an after-tax basis.

$$WACC = C_e\,(W_e) + \Sigma_{i=1}^{N}\,C_{di}\,(W_{di}) \qquad [21.1]$$

where:

$N = $ *Number of liabilities*

$C_e = $ *Cost of equity before tax*

$W_e = $ *Equity percent of funding*

$C_{di} = $ *Cost of debt of type i before tax*

$W_{di} = $ *Weight of debt of type i*

The relevant cost of equity, C_e, in the case of a new issue of common stock would be estimated from one of the three capital market equilibrium models: the capital asset pricing model, arbitrage pricing theory, or discounted cash flow models (such as the Gordon dividend growth model). Alternatively, the cost of equity, C_e, could be the firm's cost of retained earnings or newly issued preferred stock.

The relevant cost of debt for type i, C_{di}, should it be a deposit, must include the origination costs, the servicing costs, the Federal Reserve required reserves, required insurance of account premiums, and brokers' commissions, if any. The cost of debt should be for the lowest-cost source of comparable duration to the asset intended to be purchased or originated.

CALCULATING THE WACC	**DEMONSTRATION PROBLEM**

Situation

Barbara has been asked to determine the weighted average cost of capital using three funding alternatives, A, B, and C. The asset to be acquired is a fixed-rate home mortgage. Financing alternative A will use 6% equity and 94% deposits. Financing alternative B will use 8% equity and 92% deposits. Financing alternative C will use 6% equity; 50% collateralized debt, such as FHLB borrowings, and 44% deposits. Table 21.1 provides a schedule of the cost of each of these funding sources.

TABLE 21.1

Cost of Funding Source Alternatives*

Equity (before-tax return)	16.00%
Collateralized debt	9.75%
Deposits	9.60%

*Includes origination, servicing, deposit insurance, reserve requirements, and brokerage costs where applicable.

Result

Barbara used the funding source costs in Table 21.1 and the weights discussed above to determine the weighted costs of capital using financial alternatives A, B, and C. Table 21.2 provides the *WACC* for each asset to be financed.

TABLE 21.2

Weighted Average Cost of Capital*

Alternative A = (.16)(.06) + (.096)(.94)	= 9.984%
Alternative B = (.16)(.08) + (.096)(.92)	= 10.112%
Alternative C = (.16)(.06) + (.096)(.44) + (.0975)(.50)	= 10.059%

*The rates shown in this example assume that the assets are financed with liabilities of comparable duration to the assets they finance.

BREAKEVEN RISK ADJUSTED ASSET YIELD (BERAY)

The calculation of the *WACC* provides only one-half of the pricing methodology; the other half is far more difficult to develop. It involves analyzing each type of asset to identify all the possible risks and costs that may serve to reduce the gross yield on the asset. The result of this analysis is the development of the **breakeven risk adjusted yield, *BERAY*.**

These risks and costs include credit risk premium, *crp;* marketability risk premium, *mrp;* call option premium, *cop;* delivery option premium, *dop;* and servicing cost, *sc.* The breakeven risk adjusted yield is equal to the *WACC* plus a yield estimate for each of these factors. Equation 21.2 shows how to calculate the breakeven risk adjusted yield.

$$BERAY = WACC + crp + mrp + cop + dop + sc \qquad [21.2]$$

Each of the factors affecting the breakeven risk adjusted yield will be discussed in the list that follows. With the exception of the delivery option premium, each of these factors was discussed in Chapter 14.

- *Credit risk premium, crp:* The credit risk premium relates to the average credit losses expected on any given portfolio of assets. Credit card portfolios might be expected to experience a 2.5% to 4% per annum loss of principal due to credit losses while a portfolio of single-family home loans, with low loan-to-value ratios, might have an anticipated annual loss of principal of 0.25% per annum or less.

- *Marketability risk premium, mrp:* Some assets are inherently more marketable than others. The marketability risk premium could be measured as the yield difference based on the asset's bid and ask prices. Home mortgages conforming to purchase standards of the FHLMC or FNMA are considered very marketable while highly leveraged business loans have low marketability. The lender must be compensated for the lack of marketability.

- *Call option premium, cop:* Many loans, such as auto loans and first and second mortgages, have embedded call options providing for prepayment. This presents a major funding risk for the financial firm. The value of this call option must be subtracted from the gross yield on the loan since it represents nothing more than a premium paid by the borrower for the option, not a profit to the lender. In other words, if the gross yield on a loan is 10.25% and the option is valued at 0.75%, then the true yield to the lender is only 9.50% (10.25% − 0.75%). The 0.75% represents the option price as a percentage of the loan balance converted to a yield equivalent. These option values are estimated using sophisticated option pricing models.

- *Delivery option premium, dop:* Some loans are originated in terms that allow the borrower to have the advantage of fixing the rate on the loan before closing the transaction. On a mortgage, the rate might be set up to 60 days before the transaction is closed. For an auto loan, on the other hand, the rate might be set a week before the loan closes. In both cases, the borrower can go to another lender or walk away from the transaction. This amounts to an option offered to the borrower by the lender which must be hedged. The cost of hedging this option risk could be charged directly to the borrower in the form of a commitment fee, but frequently it is not. When no fee is charged, the cost of hedging this risk should be netted out of the gross yield on the loan.

- *Servicing costs, sc:* The cost of servicing the asset must be considered also. The appropriate cost of servicing will be the marginal cost of servicing the additional asset being analyzed. This involves all the activities of collection, document control, and other servicing activities, but not credit losses. This cost must be included in the gross yield.

Table 21.3 shows how, after considerable analysis, the various components of the cost and risk matrix might look for four types of loans: a single-family 15-year fixed-rate home mortgage, a single-family ARM one-year home mortgage, a 48-month auto loan, and a commercial business loan.

TABLE 21.3

Servicing Costs and Risk Matrix

Risk and Cost Factors	First Home Mortgage (fixed-rate)	High-grade Auto Loan	Business Loan
Credit risk (*crp*)	.12%	.50%	.75%
Marketability risk (*mrp*)	.05	0	.10
Call option (*cop*)	.90	0	0
Delivery option (*dop*)	.15	.05	0
Servicing cost (*sc*)	.12	1.20	.50
Total	**1.34%**	**1.75%**	**1.35%**

The *BERAY* is a rate that allows the financial firm to earn its weighted cost of capital while covering the costs of servicing, credit, marketability, and option risks. The appropriate weighted cost of capital for each asset must provide funds with a duration that matches the asset. The duration match is important for pricing, but it does not obligate the firm to use a particular liability to fund an asset.

Table 21.2 compared the *WACC* using the appropriate financing options for a single-family fixed-rate first mortgage under three financing alternatives. To these weighted cost of capital estimates, add the total of the column in Table 21.3, or 134 basis points. This produces a breakeven risk adjusted loan rate, *BERAY*, using financing alternative A of 11.324% (9.984% + 1.34%) assuming a financing mix of 96% deposits and 4% equity. Financing alternative B produces 11.452% (10.112% + 1.34%) assuming a financing mix of 92% deposits and 8% equity, and financing alternative C produces 11.399% (10.059% + 1.34%), assuming a financing mix of 50% deposits, 44% collateralized debt, and 6% equity.

DEMONSTRATION PROBLEM

DEVELOPING A *BERAY* MATRIX

Situation

Burnham Bank is considering investing in four assets. These include single-family 15-year fixed-rate home mortgages (A), single-family one-year ARM home mortgages (B), 48-month auto loans (C), and business loans priced at the prime rate (D). Management has asked that Franklin prepare a schedule determining the breakeven risk adjusted asset yields (*BERAY*) for each.

Assets A and B will be financed with 94% debt costing 9.65% and 6% equity with a pre-tax cost of 15%. Asset C will be financed with 92% debt costing 7.75% and 8% equity costing a pre-tax 15%. Asset D will be financed with 92% debt costing 6.80% and 8% equity costing a pre-tax 15%. The servicing cost and risk matrix associated with each of these assets is shown below.

Risk and Cost Factors	A	B	C	D
Credit risk *(crp)*	.12%	.17%	.70%	1.25%
Marketability risk *(mrp)*	.05	.05	.15	.20
Call option *(cop)*	.85	.05	.07	.00
Delivery option *(dop)*	.20	.05	.02	.00
Servicing costs *(sc)*	.12	.20	1.30	.50
Total	**1.34%**	**.52%**	**2.24%**	**1.95%**

Result

Using the data on the funding sources and cost and risks for each of these assets, Franklin prepared Table 21.4 providing the loan pricing matrix for several common loans made by depository institutions. In the table, the cost of debt and equity are calculated. Then the appropriate capital structure is determined for the loan, from which the *WACC* is calculated. Added to this are the various additional risk and cost factors mentioned previously. The result is the *BERAY* that the firm must earn in order to cover all costs, to be compensated for all risks, and to achieve the firm's targeted return on equity.

TABLE 21.4

BERAY for Four Types of Loans

Cost Factors	A Single-family 15-year Fixed	B Single-family ARM One-year	C Auto Loan 48-month	D Business Loan at Prime
Cost of debt and equity				
Debt C_d	9.65%	8.25%	7.75%	6.80%
Equity C_e	15.00	15.00	15.00	15.00
Finance weights				
Weight debt W_d	.94	.94	.92	.92
Weight equity W_e	.06	.06	.08	.08
Weighted cost of capital *WACC*				
$[(C_d \times W_d) + (C_e \times W_e)]$	9.971%	8.655%	8.33%	7.456%
Risk factors	1.34	.52	2.24	1.95
BERAY	**11.311%**	**9.175%**	**10.57%**	**9.406%**

Although the demonstration problem features a depository, the analysis would be the same for an insurance company that sells guaranteed investment contracts and invests in bonds, mortgages, or other investments or a finance company that invests in installment paper or warehouse financing. Even though these firms would have different capital structures and costs of equity and debt, the basic pricing algorithm would remain the same.

USING THE *BERAY*

The *BERAY* is used to determine which assets the firm should acquire that are expected to earn a profit. Loans whose yield exceeds the *BERAY* will have a positive net present value based on the firm's *WACC*. It is also necessary to compare the *BERAY* for each loan to the yield charged by the competition in the marketplace. Financial institutions typically take a survey to establish the market yields. For highly liquid assets, the yield would come from a security dealer.

DEMONSTRATION PROBLEM | **USING *BERAY* TO ANALYZE LOAN OPTIONS**

Situation

Franklin has obtained market survey data indicating the rates available on the four loans discussed in the previous demonstration problem. Franklin's manager asked Franklin to prepare a schedule to determine the profitability of each of these loans.

Result

Franklin prepared an analysis comparing the *BERAY* and market survey yields. The result of this comparison is shown in Table 21.5. Franklin's analysis indicates that the two mortgages, A and B, are both unprofitable to the bank. The auto loan and business loan are profitable. Franklin has recommended that the bank stress the auto loans and business loans for portfolio investment.

TABLE 21.5

BERAY of Four Loans Compared to Market Yields

	A Single-family 15-year Fixed	B Single-family ARM One-year	C Auto Loan 48-month	D Business Loan at Prime
BERAY and Market Yields				
BERAY	11.311%	9.175%	10.57%	9.406%
Yields derived from market survey	11.00	7.75	10.75	10.00
Expected profit (or loss) spread	−.311%	−1.425%	.18%	.594%

As indicated earlier in the chapter, supply and demand conditions within local and regional loan markets may have a significant influence on the pricing of particular types of loans. A financial firm attempting to build a large market share for a particular type of loan may price the loan below its *BERAY*. Other institutions in the market must know their *BERAY* to determine whether or not they want to meet the competition.

Another reason that the *BERAY* for one institution may indicate that the loan is profitable while for another it is unprofitable is that different institutions have different cost structures and make different estimates of a loan's credit risk, marketability premium, and value of the options offered. Firms also have different *WACCs*. These differences are what makes a market.

In the late 1980s, for example, many institutions continued to make commercial real estate loans while others dropped out, thinking the market for new commercial properties was overbuilt. The latter institutions put a higher value on the credit risk premium than the former. They turned out to be right.

THE PRIME RATE

The **prime rate,** an administered interest rate used to price adjustable-rate loans at commercial banks, is widely quoted in the financial press because many depository institution borrowers have loans whose interest rate is tied to the prime. Although the prime rate has the exalted reputation of being the interest rate that commercial banks charge their most creditworthy customers, this characterization is not true. The opening of the capital markets to many more firms has put tremendous pressure on banks to be more competitive in their pricing. Today, a majority of commercial bank loans are tied to open market interest rates that float with the marginal cost of funds to commercial banks. Two indices that are used often are the cost of new funds to the bank represented by the federal funds rate and the negotiable CD rate. Another frequently used index rate is *LIBOR (the London interbank offered rate),* which is the interest rate on Eurodollar deposits made between banks outside the United States.

The prime rate has truly fallen from grace. A study of 48 large commercial banks completed by Brady (1985) using 1984 data indicated that approximately 90% of loans with maturities of less than one year were made at a rate below prime while over 50% of loans with maturities over one year were priced below prime. With the domination of open market indexed commercial bank pricing of business loans, the prime rate has become largely an "administered rate," a rate not very responsive to changes in open market conditions. It is primarily used for loans to smaller and less creditworthy borrowers because it is generally above the commercial bank rates tied to LIBOR, negotiable CDs, and federal funds.

✓ Checkpoints

21-5 What factors influence management's choice of capital structure?

21-6 What types of liabilities that financial firms originate incur high distress and agency costs?

21-7 How do regulatory risk-based asset net worth reserve requirements influence the capital structure decision?

21-8 What is the weighted cost of capital for a financial institution, compared to a nonfinancial corporation?

21-9 Would an asset financed with a high percentage of equity have a higher or lower weighted cost of capital than another type of asset? Why or why not?

21-10 What factors must financial managers add to the weighted cost of capital before establishing the minimum price for a loan or investment acquisition?

21-11 What is the delivery option premium?

Loan Participations and Syndications

The separation of the origination, servicing, and portfolio management functions at intermediaries has facilitated the growth of loan participations and syndications. **Loan participations and syndications** are the sale of a fixed percentage of the principal value of a loan to one or more investors or correspondents. Typically, the originating institution will maintain a portion of the loan in portfolio.

Participations and syndications are sold for several reasons. First, these loan sales facilitate diversification of credit risk. Many loans are very large and present excessive credit risk exposure to one borrower. To reduce this large credit exposure, the originator sells a percentage interest in the loan to one or more other investors. Loan participation and syndication sales are also used to increase a firm's origination and servicing revenues. If the firm is particularly profitable in these functions, then the participation permits the firm to originate and service a volume of loans that far exceeds its portfolio capacity.

Loan participation and syndications also permit the firm to leverage the revenue from its investment in a loan by earning a spread between the yield it offers to the participation buyer and the yield it receives from the borrower. This process provides additional compensation for the origination and servicing units within the firm.

In addition, loan participation and syndications are sometimes easier to sell to other investors than whole loans because, since the originator is also an investor, the buyer has additional confidence in the credit underwriting of the loan. This situation translates into the ability of the seller to offer a lower yield to the buyer of the participation or syndication than if the seller had no investment.

Loan participation and syndication sales are used primarily in large real estate and commercial and industrial loan transactions. Many are large-balance loans that would be quite risky if they were held by one institution. The financing of development and construction of large commercial real estate projects and

SYNDICATIONS CREATE EXAMINATION PROBLEMS

The Federal Reserve Board (FRB), Federal Deposit Insurance Corporation (FDIC), and Office of the Comptroller of the Currency (OCC) jointly administer the Shared National Credit Program. The purpose of the program is to ensure that loan syndications are evaluated and supervised in a consistent fashion. A loan sold by a bank supervised by the FRB might sell a portion to a bank supervised by the OCC. The result could be that both the FRB and OCC would be forced to evaluate the credit quality of the same loan. Sometimes differences resulted and duplication occurred. Today, only the lead bank's loan is evaluated with the regulator's credit quality rating shared by the regulator of the other syndicate members.

In 1991, the program developed statistics on outstanding syndications. These statistics showed that the average syndication was a large $131,434,000 for the 4,332 loans surveyed. The average share kept by the lead bank was 34.6%. In some cases, the lead bank kept none of the loan, selling off all of it to other institutions. The highest retention by a lead bank was 98.8%.

Source: Katerina Simons, "Why Do Banks Syndicate Loans," *New England Economic Review*, Federal Reserve Bank of Boston, Jan./Feb. 1993, p. 47.

How

it

Really

Works

large corporate loans used for restructuring, leveraged buyouts, and hostile takeovers are frequent participation and syndication sale candidates.

PROFITING FROM LOAN PARTICIPATIONS AND SYNDICATIONS

When a financial intermediary sells a participation or syndication, the main problem is to identify all the marginal costs and revenues that impact the firm. These involve the costs of origination, earned origination fees, the cost of servicing, and the revenue comprising the excess yield earned on the loan that is not distributed to the participation buyer.

For example, a mortgage lender must decide whether to originate a $50 million mortgage on a regional shopping center. The loan will be made at a rate, r, of 10.5%. The originator will earn a fee of 3% of the loan principal from the borrower at the time the loan is closed.

One reason the originator expressed an interest in this loan is that several other portfolio lenders agreed to purchase up to $40 million, leaving the originator with an investment of $10 million. The $10 million is well below the board of directors' established maximum loan amount. The seller of the participation will offer a participation yield, r_p, of 10.25% and a 2% origination fee on the amount of its investment. The selling institution is interested in estimating the yield on the retained portion of the loan.

TABLE 21.6

Participation Seller's Cash Flows from Origination and Sale of Participation in Loan[*]

Loan disbursement to borrower	−$50,000,000
Origination fees paid by borrower: 3% of $50 million principal	$1,500,000
Less cost of origination: $550,000	−$550,000
Proceeds from participation sale	$40,000,000
Origination fees paid to participants: 2% of $40 million	−$800,000
Net amount of investment	−$9,850,000
n (7 years × 12 months)	84
r (loan rate)	10.50%
r_p (participation rate)	10.25%

[*]Incorporates loan fees, origination costs, and investor fees paid.

The seller estimates that the servicing costs for remitting principal and interest payments to the four participation buyers will be $120 per month. The cost of origination is estimated to be $550,000. The loan has a balloon clause that makes it due and payable in seven years. The loan is nonamortizing and interest is charged monthly. Table 21.6 shows the cash flows representing the selling firm's investment in the loan after it sells the participation.

The present value equation for determining the **participation seller's yield** **(PSY)** on the selling firm's $10 million investment in the loan is shown in Equation 21.3.

$$\$9,850,000 = [\textstyle\sum_{t=1}^{84} [\$8,333.33 + \$89,583.33 - \$120.00] / (1 + PSY)^t] + \$10,000,000 / (1 + PSY)^{84}$$

$$PSY = \underline{12.05\%} \qquad\qquad [21.3]$$

where:

The monthly interest earned on the $40,000,000 sold is

$$(.0025/12) \times \$40,000,000 = \$8,333.33$$

The monthly interest earned on the $10,000,000 retained portion of the loan is

$$(.1075/12) \times \$10,000,000 = \$89,583.33$$

The servicing cost per month is $120.00

The balloon payment at the end of seven years or 84 months is $10,000,000

As can be seen by this example, the yield on the originating firm's investment of $9.85 million is 12.05%, when the additional cash flows received on the sold portion is factored into it. A rough approximation of *PSY* on the retained portion of a loan participation retained in the portfolio of the selling institution can be calculated using Equation 21.4. This approximation ignores origination fees, origination costs, and servicing costs.

$$\textit{Yield on retained portion of PSY} =$$

$$r + \{(r - r_p) \times [\textit{Sold amount/Retained amount}]\} \qquad [21.4]$$

where:

$$\textit{PSY} = \textit{Participation seller's yield}$$

$$r = \textit{Yield paid by borrower}$$

$$r_p = \textit{Yield paid to participant investor}$$

$$\textit{Retained amount} = \textit{Dollar amount of loan retained in seller's portfolio}$$

$$\textit{Sold amount} = \textit{Dollar amount of loan sold to participation investors}$$

The following equation uses the data for the previous example while ignoring both the fee income and servicing costs:

$$PSY = 10.50\% + [(10.50\% - 10.25\%) \times (\$40,000,000/\$10,000,000)]$$

$$= 10.50\% + (.25 \times 4)$$

$$PSY = \underline{\underline{11.50\%}}$$

The yield on the retained $10 million investment is estimated to be 11.50%. This estimate ignores the additional yield related to the discount of $150,000 ($10,000,000 − $9,850,000) used in the earlier calculation, which shows how a participation sale of a loan can substantially increase (or decrease if the yield on the sold portion is higher than the loan rate) the yield to the selling organization. Table 21.7 provides several examples of computations using Equation 21.4 for an original 8% loan.

TABLE 21.7

Yield to Seller on the Retained Portion of a Participation
(coupon rate on loan, r: 8.00%)

Coupon Rate on Participation, r_p	Percent of Loan Sold as Participation (in percent of original loan balance)				
	10.000	30.000	50.000	70.000	90.00
7.00	8.114	8.429	9.000	10.330	17.00
7.50	8.056	8.214	8.509	9.160	12.50
8.00	8.000	8.000	8.000	8.000	8.00
8.25	7.972	7.893	7.750	7.417	5.75
8.50	7.944	7.786	7.500	6.833	3.50

DEMONSTRATION PROBLEM	**EXAMPLE OF PARTICIPATION YIELD**

Situation

Wilderness Bank sells a $9 million participation in a $10 million loan. The yield on the loan, r, is 11%. The 90% participation is sold to yield, r_p, 10.75%. You are to determine the yield on the retained portion of the loan, PSY. You should disregard origination fees, origination costs, and servicing costs.

Result

Using Equation 21.4, you have determined the yield on the retained portion of the loan to be the following:

$$PSY = 11.00\% + (11.00 - 10.75) \times (9 \text{ million}/1 \text{ million})$$

$$= 11.00\% + (.25 \times 9) = \underline{13.25\%}$$

The yield on the retained $1 million investment is approximated to be 13.25%.

ACCOUNTING FOR LOAN SALES

Generally, GAAP accounting rules permit an institution to take into income a portion of any excess yield derived from a loan sale. This excess income is determined by calculating the difference between the rate earned on the portion of the loan retained in portfolio and the yield to the participation buyer. The difference is in the form of a cash flow stream that will be earned for the life of the loan. From this cash flow, the cost of servicing must be subtracted. The remainder can be taken into income by calculating the present value of the excess income stream less servicing costs.

For instance, a mortgage lender originates a $500,000 ten-year fixed-rate non-amortizing loan with a coupon rate of 11.75%. The lender is able to sell a 50% participation at a coupon rate of 11.25%. The accountants determine that a minimum of 0.25% is needed to cover the cost of servicing. This leaves a 0.25% excess yield. If the loan is expected to remain on the books for a loan life of seven years, then the firm can take into income the present value of an ordinary annuity as in Equation 21.5. If the loan is an amortizing variety, then the calculations would be far more difficult.

Present value of excess yield for participation sale

$$= (erm/m) \times (SL) \times [1 - (1 / (1 + (k / m))^{nm})] / (k / m) \qquad [21.5]$$

where:

erm = *Annualized excess interest rate margin*

m = *Number of periods per year payments are received*

SL = *Sold loan amount*

k = *Before-tax cost of capital*

n = *Number of annual periods*

The following solves for the earnings on the $250,000 participation sale and uses a 15% pre-tax cost of capital as the discount rate, k. This equation is simply the present value of an ordinary annuity.

Present value of excess yield for participation sale

$$= (.0025/12) \times (\$250,000) \times \{[1 - (1 / (1 + (.15/12))^{(7 \times 12)})] / (.15/12)\}$$

$$= \underline{\$2,698.90}$$

Once the firm has capitalized the income it will receive in the future, it must be concerned that the loan life is at least seven years. If it is shorter, the firm will not earn the profit that it had earlier recorded on its income statement at the time the participation was sold. This move requires the firm to take a charge against income for the amount of the present value of the income stream it did not receive, which happens frequently when interest rates fall and mortgages prepay earlier than expected. The reverse can also take place as well. If the loan extends beyond seven years, then the firm could earn more than the amount estimated.

✓ Checkpoints

21-12 Why do financial firms use loan participations and syndications?

21-13 How do firms profit from loan participation and syndication loan sales?

21-14 Is prime rate important because commercial banks charge it to their most creditworthy customers.

SUMMARY AND REVIEW

1. **Describe the factors that management must consider in determining the firm's asset structure.**

    Selecting the firm's asset structure requires analyses of **laws and regulations** that determine the allowable investments of the firm, **diversification** impact on the firm's portfolio expected risk and return, asset **supply and demand conditions**, and **asset market pricing.**

2. **Explain the importance of capital structure and how to calculate and use the weighted cost of capital and the breakeven risk adjusted asset yield in analyzing potential asset acquisitions.**

    The **optimal capital structure** for many financial firms is impacted by regulatory capital requirements. Commercial banks, SBs, and S&Ls must meet a set of risk-based capital requirements that are calculated as a weighted average of the firm's asset structure. This sets the minimum level of capital needed to finance a new asset. The firm can then establish higher capital levels.

The selection of assets depends critically on knowledge of the firm's **weighted cost of capital, WACC.** This is determined by estimating the cost of all the debt and equity financing mixes that can be used to finance a particular asset that are consistent with the firm's optimal capital structure.

The yield on a particular asset must be high enough to cover all the costs of financing it as well as the credit risk premium, marketability risk premium, servicing costs, and the value of options for call and delivery. This is calculated as the **breakeven risk adjusted yield, BERAY:**

$$BERAY = WACC + crp + mrp + cop + dop + sc$$

where:

$$WACC = Weighted\ cost\ of\ capital$$

$$crp = Credit\ risk\ premium$$

$$mrp = Marketability\ risk\ premium$$

$$cop = Call\ option\ premium$$

$$dop = Delivery\ option\ premium$$

$$sc = Servicing\ costs$$

The *BERAY* is compared to market yields to determine which assets are expected to meet the return on equity target of the firm.

3. **Explain why financial institutions have become major sellers of loans through participations and syndications.**

These are sales of a fixed percentage of a loan's principal to one or more investors. The objectives of these sales are to (1) **improve portfolio diversification,** (2) **increase origination and servicing volumes** and profits, and (3) **create a positive income stream** by selling a portion of a loan at a yield lower than that paid by the borrower. One way to determine the financial benefit from a loan participation sale is to calculate the yield, *PSY,* on the retained portion of a loan sale using the following formula:

$$Yield\ on\ retained\ portion\ of\ participation =$$

$$PSY = r + [(r - r_p) \times (Sold\ amount/Retained\ amount)]$$

where:

$$r = Yield\ on\ loan\ to\ borrower$$

$$r_p = Yield\ paid\ to\ participant\ investor$$

$$Retained\ amount = Dollar\ amount\ of\ loan\ retained\ in\ seller's\ portfolio$$

$$Sold\ amount = Dollar\ amount\ of\ loan\ sold\ to\ participation\ investors$$

BREAKEVEN RISK ADJUSTED YIELD, BERAY	SELF-TEST PROBLEMS

ST-21-1

Border Bank is preparing to originate second mortgages. The new risk-based asset equity requirements call for 8% equity. However, Border will hold at least 9% against these loans. Border estimates that these loans will experience 0.3% credit losses as a percent of outstanding balances annually. The loans cost 21 basis points per year to service based on outstanding balances. The loans are not marketable, and management suggests that a marketability premium of 5 basis points is needed to cover this. The loans are originated with a four-week delivery option, which is estimated to be valued at 7 basis points. They can also be paid off without penalty. This call provision is valued at 40 basis points in yield.

Calculate the *BERAY* assuming its pre-tax cost of equity is 16% and deposits cost 3.25%.

Answer on page 642.

PARTICIPATION SELLER'S YIELD, PSY

ST-21-2

Winfield Savings has originated a loan of $12 million. The firm plans to sell a participation of $7 million. The yield on the original loan is 6%. Williams will pay the participation buyer a yield of 5.5%. What is the *PSY* on the retained portion of the loan?

WEIGHTED AVERAGE COST OF CAPITAL	PROBLEMS

21-1

You are considering funding a large new loan program with 5% equity at a cost of 21.5 percent, 50 percent collateralized borrowings at a cost of 7.25%, and 45% negotiable CDs at a cost of 9.5%.

1. What is the weighted average cost of capital for the loan program?
2. You have just learned that regulatory changes will require you to fund this program with 10% equity. What is the new cost of capital if you reduce collateralized borrowings to 45 percent?
3. Price competition for this type of asset is strong and you don't want to increase the overall cost of capital. What alternative mix of collateralized borrowings and negotiable CDs would bring the cost of capital back down to the result you obtain in number 1 above?

WEIGHTED AVERAGE COST OF CAPITAL, WACC

21-2

As portfolio manager for a small southeastern bank, you are analyzing the firm's cost of capital. Your staff has prepared the following list of available funding sources and their costs:

Funding Source	Current Weight	Cost	Servicing Costs
Equity	6.00%	18.00%	0.00%
Demand Deposits	15.00	0.00	2.75
Retail Time Deposits	65.00	6.50	1.25
Brokered Deposits	9.00	8.00	.50
Other	5.00	0.00	0.00

1. Compute the total cost of each funding source.
2. Compute the weighted cost of capital for a new loan program to be funded with 8 percent retained earnings (equity) and 92% retail time deposits.
3. Compute the weighted cost of capital for an asset that is funded 6 percent by retained earnings, 40% by retail time deposits, and the remaining 54 percent by brokered deposits.

BREAKEVEN RISK ADJUSTED YIELD, BERAY

21-3

Eastern Savings Bank is considering originating auto loans. The new risk-based asset equity requirements call for 8% equity for auto loans. Eastern estimates that these loans will experience .7% credit losses as a percent of outstanding balances annually. The loans cost 70 basis points per year to service based on outstanding balances. The loans are not liquid and management suggests that a marketability premium of 20 basis points is needed to cover this. The loans are originated with a one-week delivery option, which is estimated to be valued at 5 basis points. They can also be paid off without penalty. This call provision is valued at 15 basis points in yield. Eastern is conservative and is considering holding 10% equity rather than the required 8% behind these loans.

1. Calculate the BERAY assuming its pre-tax cost of equity is 18 percent and deposits cost 7.25%.
2. A competitor of Eastern has estimated that all risks and costs of auto loans will be the same as those estimated by Eastern. This firm's cost of equity and debt are also the same as Eastern's. However, this competitor will use 8% equity rather than 10%. What is the competitor's BERAY?

BREAKEVEN RISK ADJUSTED YIELD, BERAY

21-4

Consider the following thrift institution assets:

> Asset X: 25-year ARM
> Asset Y: 60-month construction loan
> Asset Z: 36-month unsecured consumer loan

The thrift's cost of equity is 18%. The cost of duration-matched debt, the appropriate financing weights, and other risk and cost factors for each asset are shown in the following table:

	X	Y	Z
Cost of debt	8.65%	8.00%	7.75%
Weight of debt	0.95	0.80	0.85
Credit risk premium	0.22	2.25	1.50
Marketability risk	0.08	0.60	0.15
Delivery option	0.28	N/A	N/A
Servicing costs	0.20	0.16	0.65

For each asset, compute the weighted cost of capital, *WACC*, and breakeven risk adjusted yield, *BERAY*.

PARTICIPATION SELLER'S YIELD, PSY

21-5

You have been asked to determine a rough estimate of the yield on the portion of a loan that will be retained in portfolio after a participation is sold. The loan is $8,000,000. You can sell $7,000,000. The yield the borrower will pay is 8%. You promise the participation buyer a yield of 7.80%. What is the PSY on the retained portion of the loan?

PARTICIPATION SELLER'S YIELD, PSY

21-6

Security S&L originated a portfolio of $8,000,000 of home mortgages whose dollar balances exceed the purchase limits of the government sponsored mortgage credit enterprise. The mortgages have a coupon of 8.75%. Security has found a buyer for a 90% participation in the portfolio at 8.50%.

1. What yield will Security receive on the portion of the loans it retains?

2. Security estimates it will cost 12 basis points per year to service the outstanding balances of the loans. Given this information, what would you estimate the yield adjusted for servicing to be on the retained portion of the portfolio held by Security?

SELF-TEST PROBLEMS

SOLUTIONS

ST-21-1

Solution:

The calculation process begins by developing the servicing cost and risk matrix. Then the weighted cost of capital is calculated. Estimating these two quantities results in the breakeven risk adjusted yield, *BERAY*.

Servicing Costs and Risk Matrix

Risk and Cost Factors	Second Mortgage
Credit risk (*crp*)	.30%
Marketability risk (*mrp*)	.05
Call option (*cop*)	.40
Delivery option (*dop*)	.07
Servicing cost (*sc*)	.21
Total	1.03%
Cost of debt and equity:	
Debt C_d	3.25%
Equity C_e	16.00
Finance weights:	
Weight debt W_d	91.00
Weight equity W_e	9.00
Weighted cost of capital, WACC:	
$[(C_d \times W_d)$	2.96
$+ (C_e \times W_e)]$	1.44
Risk factors	1.03
BERAY	5.43%

ST-21-2

Solution:

$$PSY = r + [(r - rp) \times (Sold\ amount/Retained\ amount)]$$

$$PSY = 6.00 + [(6.00 - 5.50) \times (\$7\ million/\$12\ million)]$$

$$PSY = 6.00 + .29167 = 6.29167\%$$

*L*iability Management and Pricing

Learning Goals

After studying this chapter, you should be able to:

1. Distinguish among the uses and types of retail and wholesale funding sources for depositories, insurance companies, and finance companies.
2. Describe the factors affecting the cost of different types of funding sources at financial institutions.
3. Define asset-backed securities and explain why financial intermediaries use them.

Liability management, which concerns selecting and pricing funding sources, is a major issue for depositories, finance companies, and insurance companies because these firms have a great deal of freedom in the selection of liabilities and because the liabilities they sell are primary products, not simply funding sources. For pension funds, mutual funds, REITs, and limited partnerships the liability decision is not a major issue.

The liability management and pricing problems for depositories and insurance companies can be broken down into several parts. The first step is to determine which funding sources are available. The second is to ascertain the marginal cost of each source in relation to the quantity that can be raised. Third, the appropriate mix of liabilities is selected by considering such issues as the firm's optimal capital structure and funding risks.

Identifying Funding Sources: Wholesale and Retail

Depository institutions and insurance companies have many funding sources. These are generally broken down into two primary types. **Retail funding sources** refers to the sale of liabilities in small denominations to consumers. Examples include demand and time deposit accounts and individual life policies. **Wholesale funding sources** include large dollar-denominated liabilities sold primarily to institutions and very wealthy individuals. Wholesale funding sources are sometimes sold by third-party brokers.

Most institutions consider wholesale funding sources to be less dependable and more price sensitive or interest rate elastic than retail funding sources. Most wholesale sources are uninsured, causing investors to be very concerned about the institution's capital structure, profitability, and asset quality. Information that causes concern over the credit quality of the institution can quickly cause wholesale funding sources to dry up.

One exception to the general rule that wholesale funding sources carry higher funding risks than retail sources is the collateralized or asset-backed borrowing. Here the investor is secured by assets that normally provide more than adequate interest cash flow and collateral value to pay off interest and principal on the debt. Many firms with very weak credit ratings are able to issue asset-backed securities with investment-grade ratings.

The positive side of wholesale funding sources is that the firm can quickly attract funds in large quantities if it is willing to pay the marginal rate required of the wholesale market. A slightly higher rate paid in the wholesale market can usually attract funds in quantity. Moreover, the higher rate is paid only to new customers, whereas a higher rate paid to retail customers is also paid to existing customers, many of whom would likely roll over their deposits at a lower rate. It is necessary to identify the most important retail and wholesale funding sources for depositories and life companies.

RETAIL FUNDING SOURCES

Retail sources for depositories include virtually all liabilities attracted through branch offices: a variety of transaction-type accounts including demand deposits, money market demand accounts, negotiable order of withdrawal accounts, and debit-activated accounts. Retail savings and time deposits include savings and passbook accounts and small-denomination time accounts, such as certificates of deposit.

Insurance companies also have a variety of retail funding sources, including retail consumer insurance programs that are sold through large sales forces using direct marketing, telemarketing, and direct mail. The most popular are whole life and single premium annuity policies.

WHOLESALE FUNDING SOURCES

Depository institutions have a variety of wholesale funding sources. Negotiable certificates of deposit, commercial paper, repurchase agreements, insured certificates of deposit sold by broker/dealers, collateralized deposits of government units, and federal funds are examples of wholesale sources.

Insurance companies also market liabilities in the wholesale markets. The primary liability they sell is the **guaranteed investment contract (GIC)**, which is an unsecured liability of the life company and is sold in large denominations primarily to pension funds and employee trusts. The GIC has many of the attributes of a certificate of deposit, except it is uninsured. Insurance companies also sell insurance policies to large corporations for group plans. These include lump sum purchases of annuities used to meet pension fund obligations.

Another major source of funds for depositories and finance companies is asset-backed securities. In the 1980s, the word *securitization* was coined, which refers to the process of using loans and investments as collateral for a hybrid liability. During the last decade, mortgages, both residential and commercial; mobile home loans; auto loans; corporate bonds; credit card receivables; leases; and trade receivables have been used as collateral for securities. Asset-backed securities as a source of wholesale funds will be discussed more fully later in the chapter.

Table 22.1 provides a brief summary of the primary wholesale and retail funding sources of depositories, life companies, and finance companies.

TABLE 22.1

Primary Retail and Wholesale Funding Sources of Depositories, Life Companies, and Finance Companies

Type of Institution	Retail	Wholesale
Depositories	Demand deposits, NOW accounts, and money market demand accounts; passbook accounts and certificates of deposit	Negotiable CDs, commercial paper, asset-backed securities, brokered deposits; collateralized borrowings such as repos and FHLB borrowings
Insurance companies	Term, whole life, and annuities sold to individuals	Guaranteed investment contracts; group insurance annuities sold to pension funds
Finance companies		Commercial paper, asset-backed securities, and debentures

✓ Checkpoints

22-1   How does a wholesale funding source differ from a retail funding source?

22-2   Why do practitioners sometimes consider wholesale funding sources riskier than retail funding sources?

22-3 Why do larger financial intermediaries have more liability alternatives than smaller financial firms do?

Costs of Alternative Depository Funding Sources

Determining the cost of each of the funding sources is not nearly as easy as it might appear at first glance. Each deposit source has its own unique set of cost factors. These costs vary from liability to liability and include such factors as deposit insurance premiums, opportunity costs associated with Federal Reserve Regulation D reserve requirements, servicing costs, commissions, compensating balances, and the cost of equity in which collateral is involved.[1] The true marginal cost of each funding source can be computed only after each of the following cost factors are determined.

DEPOSIT INSURANCE COST

Depositories are required to pay insurance premiums to their respective deposit insurance corporations. For example, as a result of the Financial Institution Reform Recovery and Enforcement Act of 1989, the cost of deposit insurance has changed significantly. The cost of deposit insurance for commercial banks insured by the Bank Insurance Fund and thrifts insured by the Savings Association Insurance Fund in early 1994 ranged from 23 to 31 basis points computed off of deposit balances.

FEDERAL RESERVE REGULATION D RESERVES

All insured depositories are now subject to holding reserves in noninterest-earning accounts or vault cash at a Federal Reserve Bank for specified types of deposits. These reserve requirements were modified extensively in 1980 as a result of the passage by Congress of the Depository Institution Deregulation and Monetary Control Act. At that time, reserve requirements were also applied to thrift institutions. Table 20.3 (page 609) showed the reserve requirements currently imposed.

The fact that depositories must hold reserves in noninterest bearing accounts or vault cash increases the true cost of these deposits. For example, assume a $100,000 demand deposit held by a large commercial bank would require a reserve of 10%. This means that the institution has use of 90% of the deposits raised. If the effective cost of processing these deposits is 3.85%, the reserve requirement would serve to increase the true cost to $[(3.85\%/.90)] = 4.27\%$, or roughly $[(4.27\% - 3.85\%)] = 42$ basis points.

---

[1]Revenue generated by certain liabilities, such as fees earned on checking accounts, should be reflected in determining the cost of raising funds using this type of account. These fees serve to reduce the cost of generating funds from these types of accounts. In checking accounts, these fees include: (1) fees for check printing; (2) monthly service charges; (3) nonsufficient-funds fees; and (4) miscellaneous transaction fees.

INSURANCE FEES MAY SINK SOME THRIFTS

One objective of the Financial Institutions Reform Recovery and Enforcement Act of 1989 (FIRREA) was to separate the costs of liquidating failed institutions from that of creating the new Savings Association Insurance Fund (SAIF). The newly created SAIF began its operations with a fund of only $441 million to insure some $550 billion in deposits, creating a reserve of .08%, or 8 basis points. On September 30, 1993, the Federal Deposit Insurance Corporation reported that there were 116 problem institutions with $66 billion in assets. As a result of the precarious position of the SAIF, the Congress passed the RTC Completion Act of 1993. It extended the receivership authority of the RTC from September 30, 1993, to January 1, 1995, and provided it with $18.3 billion in funds.

The act only delayed the day of reckoning for the SAIF. Under existing law, the remaining thrifts are to provide enough in premiums to pay back interest on $11 billion in bonds issued between 1987 and 1989 to bail out the old FSLIC. Under existing law, the reserves of both the BIF and SAIF eventually are to reach 125 basis points of total insured deposits. As of June 30, 1994, the SAIF fund was $1.7 billion or only 0.24% of deposits. With the potentially large exposure from future failures, the SAIF-insured institutions will have tough going.

The BIF, on the other hand, is quickly approaching 125 basis points. As of June 30, 1994, the BIF fund reached $17.5 billion or 0.92% of total deposits. Estimates suggest they will achieve that level by 1998. When they do, the FDIC can lower its insurance premium. The SAIF-insured institutions must play catch-up. If the BIF insurance premium falls while the SAIF-insured institutions pay the current average 26 basis points or much higher, they will be uncompetitive with BIF-insured institutions. Thrifts have argued that the two funds should be merged in order to bring about a competitive parity.

Source: William P. Osterberg and James B. Thomson, "Making the SAIF Safe for Taxpayers," *Economic Commentary*, Federal Reserve Bank of Cleveland, Nov. 1, 1993.

How it Really Works

SERVICING COSTS

Each source of funds must be serviced. Since the servicing requirements are different for each source of funds, the firm must estimate the marginal servicing cost for each funding alternative. A 1985 Federal Reserve functional cost analysis indicated that the cost of servicing a savings account for one month ranged from $1.97 for small banks to $2.61 for medium-sized banks. The same study estimated the monthly cost of servicing a checking account to be $12.42 for small banks and $18.61 for medium-sized banks.[2]

[2]The data from the Fed's functional cost analyses is suspect. Therefore, it is necessary for each institution to make their own estimates of the marginal cost of servicing various types of liabilities.

COMMISSIONS PAID TO A DISTRIBUTOR

Some wholesale funding sources, such as brokered insured deposits, necessitate paying the distributing broker/dealer a commission to sell the accounts. This commission is usually expressed as an additional interest cost.

COMPENSATING BALANCES OR REQUIRED INVESTMENTS

Some types of borrowings require compensating balances or investments related to the size of the loan. A **compensating balance** is a percentage of the loan that remains on deposit at the lending institution as a condition for obtaining the loan. Some institutions that borrow from the Federal Home Loan Bank, for example, are required to hold stock in a Federal Home Loan Bank up to 1% of the amount borrowed. Compensating balances are also a common feature of many business loans made by commercial banks. The compensating balance effectively increases the cost of the borrowing if the income earned on the compensating balance pays a lower interest rate than the borrowing rate.

Consider a loan that requires the borrower to maintain a compensating investment in a Federal Home Loan Bank equal to 1% of the loan balance. The investment pays a return equal to 5%. This is well below the cost of the loan. In this case, the effective rate, *ER,* of a loan made at a base rate, *BR,* of 9% would be equal to the base rate less the interest earned on the compensating balance, *CBR,* if any, times the amount of the compensating balance percentage, *CB%,* all divided by 1.00 minus the compensating balance percentage. Equation 22.1 solves for *ER* as shown:

$$ER = [BR - (CB\% \times CBR)] / (1.00 - CB\%) \qquad [22.1]$$

where:

$$ER = Effective\ rate$$

$$BR = Base\ rate\ on\ loan$$

$$CB\% = Compensating\ balance\ as\ a\ percent\ of\ loan$$

$$CBR = Interest\ rate\ paid\ on\ compensating\ balance$$

DEMONSTRATION PROBLEM	CALCULATING THE EFFECTIVE RATE WITH COMPENSATING BALANCES

Situation

You have been asked to determine the effective cost of using Federal Home Loan Bank (FHLB) advances. As discussed above, the base rate, *BR,* is 9%, the compensating investment, (CB%), in FHLB stock is 1% of the loan amount and pays a return, (CBR), of 5%.

Result

Using Equation 22.1 you have developed the following estimate for the effective rate for this borrowing:

$$ER = [9.00 - [.01 \times 5.00\%]] / (1.00 - .01)$$

$$[9.00\% - (.05\%)] / (1.00 - .01) = 9.04\%$$

In this case, the impact of the compensating balance is small. However, on many loans made by commercial banks to commercial customers there might be a compensating balance as high as 10% to be held in a noninterest-bearing account. If that were the case using a 9 percent loan, the effective cost would be $[((9.00\%) - (0)) / .90] = 10.00\%$. Compensating balances result in firms having to borrow more than they need.

COST OF EQUITY FOR COLLATERALIZED BORROWING

The use of collateral to raise funds also entails a hidden cost. This is the cost of the equity that the institution must hold on the margin to have the collateral available. Say that the institution wants to use a government guaranteed mortgage-backed security as collateral behind a term reverse repurchase agreement. This would require a 3% equity holding under the risk-based reserve requirement.

Assuming the firm held 3% equity to support the investment in a mortgage security at a 25% pre-tax cost of capital, and the rest is financed at 7%, the weighted capital cost would be $[(.03) \times (.25\%) + (.97) \times (.07\%)] = 7.54\%$. Thus, the marginal cost of equity adds 54 basis points to the marginal cost of this borrowing alternative. This example, of course, assumes the firm has no excess capital. Management may decide to ignore the additional equity cost if it uses the collateral infrequently for borrowing purposes and has excess equity.

Determining the interest rate equivalent cost of each of these factors and adding it to the interest rate paid on the source of funds allows the firm to compare the costs of each funding source in a consistent manner. The result of this analysis is shown in Table 22.2, which shows the cost of alternative funding sources for a hypothetical commercial bank. This table also indicates the expected amount of funds that can be attracted at the rate specified.

PICKING THE OPTIMAL FUNDING MIX: THE FUNDING ALTERNATIVES MATRIX

Once the alternative funding sources have been identified and the marginal cost of each determined, it is time to determine the optimal funding mix. This decision is made in conjunction with the determination of the optimal interest rate risk position of the firm and the extent to which the institution wants to use wholesale versus retail funding sources.

The *funding alternatives matrix* portrays the result of this analysis; it shows each alternative funding source, the quantity of funds that can be obtained, and the marginal cost of each. Using the data from Table 22.2, one could determine the lowest cost source of funds and the quantities of each that can be raised at each interest rate. Table 22.3 shows the funding alternatives matrix.

TABLE 22.2

Cost of Alternative Funding Sources
(dollars in millions)

Type of Six-Month Term Funding

Cost Factors	Retail CD < 100,000	Retail CD > 100,000	Collateralized CD	Brokered Insured CD
Base interest rate	7.23%	7.45%	7.45%	7.30%
Insurance premium	.21	.21	.21	.21
Brokerage fee	N/A	N/A	N/A	.60
Equity cost of holding collateral	N/A	N/A	.54	N/A
Servicing cost	.55	.25	.07	.05
Federal Reserve Regulation D reserves	N/A	.15	N/A	N/A
Total cost	**7.99%**	**8.06 %**	**8.27%**	**8.16%**
Amount available at this rate	$2.00	$5.00	$10.00	$10.00

TABLE 22.3

Funding Alternatives Matrix
Costs and Quantities of Alternative Sources of Funds
(dollars in millions)

Source	Rate and Quantity			
	$0–1	$1–3	$3–5	$5+
Retail CD < 100k	*7.99%*	*7.99%*	8.95%	9.05%
Retail CD > 100k	8.06	8.06	8.06	8.95
Collateralized CD	8.42	8.42	8.42	8.42
Brokered CD	8.16	8.16	*8.16*	*8.16*
Interest rate swap	9.05	9.05	9.05	9.05
Reverse repo (Mortgage-backed security)	8.65	8.65	8.65	8.60
Reverse repo (U.S. Treasury)	8.60	8.60	8.60	8.55
Term fed funds	9.10	9.10	9.10	9.20
Least cost	7.99	7.99	8.16	8.16
Treasury benchmark	7.60%	7.60%	7.60%	7.60%
Lowest-cost source:				
Spread over Treasury	.39	.39	.56	.56

The table also shows the relationship of the cost of each funding source to the amount of funds that can be attracted at each specified interest rate.

With the funding alternatives matrix, the asset and liability manager can make sound judgments about which of the alternative funding sources to utilize. This process is dynamic: yield relationships among the various funding sources and their respective quantities change constantly. For a large institution with many sources of funds, maintaining a current funding alternatives matrix is a full-time activity.

THE MARGINAL COST OF NEW RETAIL DEPOSITS

One of the more difficult decisions faced by depositories concerns the pricing of retail deposits. A primary advantage of retail deposits is that they are less interest elastic than wholesale. In order to profit from this alleged advantage, depositories frequently attempt to avoid paying as high an interest rate to existing customers as they do to attract new customers to the institution. In order to determine whether raising interest rates on retail deposit programs is cost-effective, it is necessary to compute the *marginal cost of new funds (MCNF)*.

Consider a depository attempting to raise $10 million in additional funds. It can go to the negotiable CD market and pay the going rate. Alternatively, it can pay a higher rate in the retail market. However, in the retail market, the existing customers who have accounts maturing may be the major recipients of the higher rate paid, since they have accounts that will be automatically renewed at the higher rate.

In our example, the firm may end up paying a higher rate on $50 million of deposits to obtain only $10 million of new funds. This means that calculating the marginal cost of additional funds at the retail level requires making estimates of the amount of marginal new funds. The marginal new funds equal the dollar amount going into the higher-rate account that is new to the institution and the amount that is renewed by current customers that would have been lost to competitors if the higher rate were not paid. In practice, these estimates are difficult to obtain and most firms must rely on their past experience as a guide. Equation 22.2 shows how to calculate the marginal cost of new funds:

$$MCNF = [(Rn \times \$New) + (Rn - Rnor) \times \$Roll)] / \$New \qquad [22.2]$$

where:

MCNF = Marginal cost of new funds

  Rn = Proposed higher rate to attract new funds and increase market share

  Rnor = Normal rate expected to maintain balances and market share

  $New = New dollars attracted plus dollars rolled over by existing customers that were retained due to higher rate

  $Roll = Dollars rolled over by existing customers at the higher rate that would have been retained without paying the higher rate

CALCULATING MARGINAL COST OF NEW FUNDS

Situation

Honest Federal has been paying a rate, *Rnor,* of 7.50% on 18-month deposits. Since market conditions have not changed, it feels it could continue to pay 7.50% and retain its existing market share. The liability manager has proposed a new rate of 7.75%, *Rn,* designed to attract new customers and increase market share. The savings department anticipates that $50 million will go into the higher-rate account. Of that $50 million, $10 million will consist of new funds plus funds rolled over that would have left the institution if the higher rate had not been paid. The $40 million is estimated to be the amount rolled over into the new higher-rate account that would otherwise have stayed with the firm at 7.50%, *Rnor.*

Data Input

$$MCNF = Marginal\ cost\ of\ new\ funds$$

$$Rn = 7.75\%$$

$$Rnor = 7.50\%$$

$$\$New = \$10\ million$$

$$\$Roll = \$40\ million$$

Result

$$\{(7.75\% \times \$10\ million) +$$

$$[(7.75\% - 7.50\%) \times \$40\ million]\} / \$10\ million = 8.75\%.$$

This equation reveals that the cost of attracting the marginal new funds is 8.75%, or 1% higher than the old rate.

You might observe sometime that when depository institutions have a savings certificate promotion, they will frequently promote a certificate with an unusual number of months to maturity—say, four months. They do this knowing that the most popular certificate maturities are three and six months. By offering a higher rate on a four-month account, the higher rate does not apply to accounts of existing customers, many of whom will automatically roll over their three- and six-month accounts.

✓ **Checkpoints**

    22-4   What factors should financial managers consider when determining the cost of alternative funding sources?

    22-5   How could a practitioner use the funding alternatives matrix as a decision-making tool?

Asset-backed Financing

Asset-backed financing has become a major source of funding for financial institutions in the last decade. Its increased use follows in the tracks of the successful issuance of asset mortgage-backed securities by GNMA, FHLMC, and FNMA. The growth in asset-backed financing continues to be rapid, with mortgage securities representing the largest share of this market. The primary types of collateral used in these securities include:

- Residential mortgages.
- Home equity loans.
- Multifamily mortgages.
- Auto loans.
- Credit card receivables.
- Leases.
- Other consumer loans.
- Trade receivables.
- Manufactured homes.
- Corporate bonds.

REASONS FOR SECURITIZATION

There are eight primary reasons why financial institutions use securities and loans as collateral for asset-backed securities:

1. The ability to transfer interest rate risk.
2. The ability to tap large volumes of funds in a single transaction.
3. The ability to generate a larger volume of origination and servicing profits without commensurate growth in the asset portfolio.
4. The ability of financial institutions with low credit ratings to borrow at the lower interest rates found on highly credit-rated securities.
5. The rising cost of deposit liabilities due to increases in deposit insurance premiums.

6. The incentive to move capital from capital deficit to surplus regional areas.

7. The desire to limit the impact of regulatory capital requirements.

8. The increased efficiency for lenders to monitor credit quality of local borrowers.[3]

One of the most attractive uses of asset-backed securities is to transfer interest rate risk. This has become more important as the volatility of our financial markets has increased. Depositories do not have ready access to large sources of longer-term liabilities because most deposits have short-term maturities. The asset-backed security represents an excellent way to finance longer-term assets, such as mortgages and manufactured housing loans.

The use of the asset-backed security permits the borrowing of large volumes of funds in a single transaction. The typical asset-backed security is issued in a volume of $75 million or more. This is because the high fixed costs of underwriting and distribution must be spread over as large a quantity of borrowed funds as possible. The large size of asset-backed securities effectively denies this financing option for most small institutions.

The demand for asset-backed security financing has been matched by an increase in the supply of funds. The last several decades have witnessed a substantial institutionalization of savings through pension funds and mutual funds. These investors are attracted to asset-backed investments because they are standardized, rated, easy to service, and available in large amounts.

Asset-backed securities also allow the lender to maintain a large origination and servicing market presence without having to put all the loans originated in portfolio. As a result, firms with fairly small asset portfolios can operate large origination and servicing units. The best example of this is the mortgage banking business.

These securities allow financial firms that carry very low credit ratings to borrow using their collateral to obtain an investment-grade rating. Many financial institutions that carry a below investment-grade rating on their unsecured debt can borrow at investment-grade interest rates using asset-backed securities.

Depository institutions face rising costs of deposit liabilities due to rising deposit insurance premium costs and other factors. In some cases, asset-backed securities may be less expensive.

The relative cost of asset-backed financing has been reduced by the significant declines in transaction costs brought about by today's computer technologies which have permitted a degree of financial sophistication in security design and information gathering and dissemination not possible several decades ago. Adding to the cost savings of these securities was the 1982 Securities and

---

[3]A number of models hold that lenders use securitization as well as participation and syndication sales of assets to capitalize on cost advantages related to monitoring costs of local borrowers. The large intermarket monitoring costs make it worthwhile for local lenders to originate and securitize or sell assets directly. A good summary can be found in Charles T. Carlstrom and Katherine A. Samolyk, "Examining the Microfoundations of Market Incentives for Asset-Backed Lending," *Economic Review,* Federal Reserve Bank of Cleveland, first quarter 1993, pp. 27–38.

Exchange Commission's **shelf registration Rule 412,** which permits a firm to obtain permission to issue one or more similar securities under a shelf registration within a specified period of time and up to a specified amount. Shelf registration permits lower issuing costs and greater flexibility for issuers.

Asset-backed securitization is also used to shift funds from capital deficit to capital surplus geographic areas. Regions of the country with a large number of high-return investments (given specified levels of risk) versus other geographic areas that also face capital constraints at local lenders will produce lender incentives to originate and pool loans for sale in asset-backed securities.

ASSET-BACKED FINANCING SPREADS

Asset-backed financings have become widely used by nondepository institutions in recent years. Most popular are credit card financings from large credit card issuers such as AT&T, the financing subsidiary of Speigel Catalog Co., and Federated Department Stores. Deere & Co. looked to finance receivables on agricultural equipment, Ford Motor financed leases on auto production equipment, and Fremont General Corp., an insurance holding company, sought to finance loans guaranteed by the Small Business Administration. Experts put total asset-backed financings at close to $50 billion in 1991 and $45 billion in 1992. The three largest types of issues involve credit card receivables, auto loans, and home equity loans, respectively.

Source: Abby Schultz, "Asset-backed issues are set for rebound," *The Wall Street Journal,* Oct. 17, 1992.

How it Really Works

Government regulatory capital requirements provide a strong incentive for intermediaries subject to them to sell asset-backed securities. The assets that provide the strongest incentive to securitize are the low-risk assets. Home mortgages carry a capital requirement at banks and savings and loans of 4%. Yet, not all home mortgages are equally risky. Low-risk home mortgages may be financed at lower costs through asset-backed securities as opposed to being financed on-balance sheet with 4% equity capital. The regulatory capital requirements treat all mortgages, business loans, and consumer loans as if they were equally risky, when they are not. The fixed percentage capital requirements for various types of assets create the incentive for depositories to finance their least-risky assets with asset-backed debt.

TYPES OF ASSET-BACKED SECURITIES

Asset-backed securities come in four primary structures: pass-through securities, asset-backed bonds, pay-through securities, and real estate mortgage investment conduits (REMICs). The main features of these four structures are shown in Exhibit 22.1.

EXHIBIT 22.1

Primary Attributes of Asset-backed Securities

Type of Asset-backed Structure	Attributes of Security
Pass-through	Security represents a pro-rata share of the assets in the pool. Assets are not shown on the originator's balance sheet since they are treated as a sale of assets. Principal and interest payments are passed through to investors on a schedule similar to the assets.
Asset-backed-bond	Security is a debt obligation. Assets remain on originator's balance sheet. Principal and interest payments are passed through to investors on a schedule that may differ from the asset.
Pay-through	Security is an asset-backed debt obligation. Assets remain on originator's balance sheet. Principal and interest are passed through to investors on a schedule that may differ from the asset.
Real Estate Mortgage Investment Conduit (REMIC)	Payment of principal and interest are passed through to one or more regular classes of securities and one residual class. Assets are transferred to the REMIC in a nontaxable transfer. Allows for creation of CMO-type multisecurity structure without having debt on the balance sheet.

ASSET-BACKED COLLATERAL ATTRIBUTES

One of the most important characteristics of the asset-backed bond is the type of collateral that is used, which has a significant impact on the cost and ease of issuing these securities. The primary characteristics of the collateral that influence the cost of the securitization process are:

1. The complexity of its credit characteristics.
2. The predictability of its cash flow.
3. Its maturity.
4. The delinquency and default rate on it.

5. The degree of diversification of credit risk relating to the number of obligators.

6. The servicing experience and reputation of the servicing organization.

7. The collateral's liquidation value.

This list clearly shows that most loans only score well with respect to a few of these characteristics. For example, mortgages—which comprise the collateral in the largest volume of securities—do not score well on the criteria relating to predictability of cash flows and maturity, but they do score well on most of the others. Despite these many criteria, investment bankers, issuers, and credit-rating organizations have worked to find ways to use a wide variety of loans as collateral for these bonds.

Even in cases where collateral does not measure up to the criteria discussed above, securitization is possible. The primary approaches used for creating asset-backed securities when collateral is not optimal include:

- Use of over-collaterization.[4]
- Use of public and private guarantees.
- Use of well-diversified portfolios.

COMMERCIAL REAL ESTATE MORTGAGES LATEST ASSET-BACKED RAGE

Although commercial mortgages possess few of the attributes of collateral best suited for asset-backed securities, commercial mortgage securities have grown rapidly in recent years. The first commercial mortgage securities used primarily multifamily housing and retail shopping centers because these properties were the most marketable. Today, however, office buildings, mobile home parks, health care facilities, and hotel mortgages are used as collateral for commercial-mortgage securities. In 1993, $14.5 billion of these securities were issued.

Who issued the bonds? The largest issuer has been the Resolution Trust Corporation. Others include property owners and developers, insurance companies, and real estate investment trusts. Conduits are another major issuer. Conduits pool smaller loans on multifamily and small commercial properties and issue securities collaterized by pools of loans.

Source: Carl Kane and Daniel Lisser, "Commercial Mortgage Securities Attract Broader Range of Issuers," *Real Estate Newsline*, Kenneth Leventhal & Company, April/May 1994, pp. 1–8.

How it Really Works

---

[4]Over-collateralization is a common method to create asset-backed bonds with certain types of collateral. A credit card receivable-backed bond might involve taking $225 million in credit card receivables transferred to a trust in which the issuer retains an equity interest in the residual value of any collateral that remains after the bonds are repaid. A bond of $200 million might be issued in this example.

✓ Checkpoints

22-6 Why has asset-based financing become so popular?

22-7 How does a pass-through mortgage-backed bond differ from a pay-through mortgage-backed bond?

22-8 What advantage does a REMIC have over a collateralized mortgage obligation?

Liability Management for Life Insurance Companies

Life insurance companies can be thought of as selling two primary products: the first is pure life insurance, and the second is liabilities that provide retail and institutional investors investments with a variety of credit, return, and maturity options. One advantage of these investments is that the income they earn is deferred for federal and state income tax purposes, an advantage that is heavily exploited in the marketing of certain types of life insurance policies.

The separation of the pure insurance cost component from the investment component is not always straightforward. First, many life policies have fixed premiums, which makes it difficult to determine what portion of a premium is being used to purchase insurance coverage and what portion is used to purchase the investment. Second, a number of life insurance companies are mutual companies that return a portion of the premium to the policyholder at the end of the policy year in the form of a dividend. Because this return of premium is not contractual, it is impossible for the policyholder to know what the true cost of the policy is going to be. The policyholder is forced to make assumptions about the size of the dividend, if any.

In recent years, life insurance companies have faced greater competition. Increasingly, term insurance has been sold as a cost-effective investment strategy when combined with sales of mutual fund shares and other investments. These factors have made it more difficult for life companies to attract liabilities. As a result, they have been forced to offer higher-yielding annuities and GICs.

LIABILITY COSTS AT LIFE INSURANCE COMPANIES

Like the depository institution, the life insurance company has many different options to sell liabilities. Each of these options has different cost parameters that management must estimate. The most important parameters include the guaranteed rate of return on the liability, the cost of marketing and originating the liability, and the cost of servicing.

A simple example will serve to demonstrate the methodology. One of the most competitive policies marketed by life insurance companies in recent years is the single-premium annuity. This policy provides for a guaranteed interest return to the policyholder for a specified period of time, say one to three years. After the guarantee period, the rate is determined by whatever rate the insurance company feels it needs to pay to retain the policy.

These policies are generally marketed by a direct sales force. The commission on these policies might be as high as 8% of the principal invested by the policy-holder. The insurance company also must service the policy, and this is also a costly activity.

Table 22.4 provides a hypothetical example of how an insurance company might estimate the cost of raising funds from this type of policy, assuming it stays on the insurance company's books from one to seven years. A policy like this typically has an early redemption (put) feature so that the policyholder can redeem the policy in the early years of the policy's life but at a discount from the stated policy value. The yield, y, for these funds, ignoring mortality costs, is calculated using Equation 22.3:

$$PP = COM + [[PP (1 + r)^n] (1 - d)] / (1 + y)^n \qquad [22.3]$$

where:

PP = Initial investment in policy and policy principal.

COM = Commission paid to sales person and issuance costs

n = Number of periods policy is outstanding

r = Rate of interest paid on policy

y = Interest yield on policy to insurance company including payment of commissions

d = Discount percentage at redemption

CALCULATING THE COST OF SINGLE-PREMIUM ANNUITY LIABILITIES　　　　**DEMONSTRATION PROBLEM**

Situation

The insurance company you work for has asked you to consider the cost of liabilities generated from a $25,000 single-premium insurance policy. Assume that the redemption discount, d, ranges from 5% at the end of Year 1 to 0% at the end of Year 5. Assume also that the insurance company pays a premium of 0.25% over the seven-year Treasury bond rate, r, of 7%. In this example, r does not change from year to year. From these data, the yield for the number of years the policy is assumed to be outstanding is computed. A 30 basis point per annum cost for servicing has also been incorporated. The company pays a commission of 8%, or $2,000, to the sales person. The early redemption rate, *d*, at the end of Year 3 is 3%. You have been asked to determine the cost of these funds, assuming the policies are redeemed at the end of each of the next seven years. Ignore the pure insurance costs.

Result

In order to estimate the cost of these liabilities, you use Equation 22.3. The cost of these funds to the life company is shown by solving the following equation:

$$\$25,000 = \$2,000 + [[\$25,000(1 + .07)^3 \times (1.00 - .03)]/(1 + y)^3]$$

$$\$25,000 = \$2,000 + [\$30,626 \times (.97)]/(1 + y)^3$$

$$y = 8.90\%$$

Adding servicing costs of 0.30% results in:

$$Total\ cost = y + Servicing\ cost$$

$$= 8.90\% + .30\% = 9.20\%$$

Using the same methodology, you have developed Table 22.4, which shows the cost of these liabilities assuming the policies are terminated at the end of each of seven years. The 8.90%, *y*, is the number shown on the three-year row in column 5 of Table 22.4. It represents the cost of the funds to the insurance company for three years without factoring the cost of servicing or the cost of providing pure insurance coverage. The cost of servicing is added in Column 6 of the table.

TABLE 22.4

**Estimated Cost of Single-Premium Annuity
Over Seven-Year Average Term**

Amount of principal invested in the policy	$25,000
Commission paid at 8%	2,000
Available for investment	23,000
Rate paid on annuity	7.00%

End of Policy Year (1)	Redemption Discount % (2)	Policy Value (3)	Cost Redemption Value (4)	Cost with Servicing to Insurance Company (5)	Added at 30 Basis Points (6)
1	5%	$26,750	$25,413	10.49%	10.79%
2	4	28,623	27,478	9.30	9.60
3	3	30,626	29,707	8.90	9.20
4	2	32,770	32,115	8.70	9.00
5	1	35,064	34,713	8.58	8.88
6	0	37,518	37,518	8.50	8.80
7	0	40,145	40,145	8.28	8.58

The table shows the potentially high cost of these funds to the insurance company as a result of the large marketing costs incurred at the time of sale and the high servicing expenses.

Another way life insurance companies raise funds is through the sale of GICs. GICs provide a fixed rate of return, and the cost to the life insurance company depends largely on the credit quality of the life company selling the GIC. The yields offered by life insurance companies on GIC contracts are higher than comparable-maturity Treasury security yields. The yields typically are 15 to 25 basis points higher for short-term Treasuries and 65 to 75 basis points higher for Treasuries of five-year maturities.

Pension funds have used GICs to provide fixed-rate investments to meet funding requirements. The GIC's advantages to the investor include its higher rate of return as compared to Treasury securities and the investor's ability to purchase the GIC in a maturity to meet its specific needs. The GIC has also been used as an investment for defined contribution retirement accounts such as employee 401k programs, in which employees may make contributions to investments in a trust account in before-tax dollars and employers may also make contributions to the employee's account. The GIC is used to provide fixed-return investment options for the employee in the program.

The GIC came under increased scrutiny in the early 1990s when the First Executive Life Company of California, Mutual Benefit Life Company of New Jersey, and the First Capital Life Company of California ran into financial difficulties and were forced to cease operations. The holders of the GIC contracts were unsecured creditors of these firms. Their unsecured position caused them to redeem their GICs and to seek out additional financial information about the safety and soundness of the insurance companies offering GICs.

The insurance companies that have issued GICs have also had to become more sophisticated in their interest rate risk management policies. Because the GIC is a fixed-return and fixed-term liability, the insurance company has to be sure it can find investments that provide a long-term fixed-rate return. In the early 1980s, a number of life companies issued a high volume of GIC contracts when interest rates were very high. When interest rates fell in the mid-1980s, these life companies found that they did not have sufficient high-yielding noncallable assets to cover the high interest costs of these GIC contracts. This resulted in a sharp squeeze on the interest margins for these firms.

✓ Checkpoints

22-9 Why is the cost of funds raised in annuity policies generally quite high if the policy is redeemed in early years?

22-10 What happened in the market for guaranteed investment contracts after several large insurance companies failed in the early 1990s?

SUMMARY AND REVIEW

1. **Distinguish among the uses and types of retail and wholesale funding sources for depositories, insurance companies, and finance companies.**

   Funding sources are categorized as either **retail** or **wholesale**. Retail funding sources are liabilities that are sold to individuals. These include time and savings deposits, transactions accounts, and life insurance policies. Retail funding sources are thought to be **less price sensitive**, less elastic, than wholesale funding sources. Wholesale funding sources involve large sales of liabilities sold primarily to institutional clients. Wholesale sources include negotiable CDs, GICs, commercial paper, and repurchase agreements.

2. **Describe the factors affecting the cost of different types of funding sources at financial institutions.**

   Liability costs include such factors as **deposit insurance cost, opportunity cost of Federal Reserve Regulation D reserves, servicing costs, commissions, compensating balances,** and the **cost of equity for collateralized borrowings.** This is in addition to the cost of interest paid. Compensating balances increase the effective cost of borrowing. The following equation allows the effective interest rate, *ER,* to be calculated when there is a compensating balance required.

$$ER = [BR - (CB\% \times CBR)] / (1.00 - CB\%)$$

   where:

   ER = *Effective rate*

   BR = *Base rate on loan*

   $CB\%$ = *Compensating balance as a percent of loan*

   CBR = *Interest rate paid on compensating balance*

   The **funding alternatives matrix** serves to identify all sources of funds available to the institution, the full cost of issuing these liabilities, and the volume of funds that can be obtained at the costs specified. From this matrix, the firm can make intelligent choices about which liabilities to issue.

3. **Define asset-backed securities and explain why financial intermediaries use them.**

   Asset-backed securities are securities that pool loans of other securities acting as collateral for newly issued securities. They are increasingly used by financial intermediaries to raise funds. The advantages of asset-backed securities include **transferring interest rate risk, borrowing in large volume, originating and servicing a large volume of loans** without balance sheet growth, **borrowing at investment-grade interest rates,** and **avoiding rising cost** of retail funds. The primary types of asset-backed bonds include **pass-through, asset-backed bonds, pay-through bonds,** and **REMICs.** A wide variety of different loans and securities can be used as collateral in asset-backed financings.

COMPENSATING BALANCES	SELF-TEST PROBLEMS

ST-22-1

Milton Corporation is establishing a line of credit at the bank you work for. They will pay prime, currently 5.5%, plus 0.5%. Your bank requires a compensating balance of 5% in a zero-interest account. Milton's officer has asked you to determine the yield on this loan, giving consideration to the compensating balance required.

Answer on page 665.

CALCULATING THE MARGINAL COST OF NEW FUNDS

ST-22-2

South Dakota Savings Bank has a large amount of certificates of deposit maturing within the next 60 days. These certificates were issued as a promotion two years ago at an especially high rate. Many of the deposits obtained two years ago were from competing institutions. Therefore, if South Dakota is not competitive, it stands to lose a high percentage of these deposits. Currently, South Dakota Savings is issuing two-year certificates at a rate of 3.45%.

The marketing and finance departments have been analyzing two options. The first is to pay a slightly higher rate of 3.65% and retain a much higher percentage of these deposits. This higher-rate certificate is also expected to bring in $5,000,000 of new deposits. They also expect that the institution will retain 90% of the deposits. If they don't pay the higher rate, they can raise all the funds they need by borrowing from a Federal Home Loan Bank at a rate of 3.70% for two years. However, they expect to retain only 75% of the $50,000,000 of maturing certificate deposits if they pay the lower rate. Retaining 75%, as compared to 90% of maturing certificates, means that $7,500,000 less would be retained than if they paid the higher rate.

You have been asked to assist in determining which approach provides the lowest cost of funds.

COST OF SINGLE PREMIUM ANNUITY

ST-22-3

The life company you work for will issue a new single-premium annuity policy. It will pay 8.50% for the first two years on a simple interest basis. The insurance policy can be redeemed at 96% of its principal and accrued interest value in two years.

The sales person is paid a 6% commission, and it costs 25 basis points per year to service the policy. Your supervisor would like to know the cost of funds received in this manner, disregarding the cost of insurance coverage provided, if the policy is redeemed in two years. This problem should be worked out for a $10,000 principal value policy.

PROBLEMS   **WHOLESALE VERSUS RETAIL BORROWING**

22-1

A savings and loan association has a need for $35 million in new funds. It can issue brokered insured deposits at 8.95% plus 15 basis points commission, or it can attract additional deposits through its retail branches. The thrift predicts that it can attract the $35 million by raising its CD rate from 7.65% to 7.95%. However, raising the rate will result in $80 million in deposits that will automatically roll over from the lower rate into the higher rate. These deposits would have stayed with the institution despite the higher rate.

1.   What is the marginal cost of each funding alternative?
2.   Which alternative should the thrift choose?

COMPENSATING BALANCE YIELD IMPACT

22-2

You are about to borrow from the Federal Home Loan Bank. It will lend you $10 million at a rate of 6.40%. However, it expects you to purchase stock in the Federal Home Loan Bank that is fully redeemable at par when the loan matures. The stock will pay a dividend of 2%. You must buy stock equal to 4% of the loan balance. How does the stock purchase affect the cost of the loan?

COST OF EQUITY IN COLLATERALIZED BORROWING

22-3

You are preparing a short-term collateralized borrowing for which you will pledge your portfolio of GNMA securities.

1.   You are required to hold 3% equity against the collateral. Your firm's pretax cost of equity is 21.5%. What is the weighted marginal cost of equity for the collateral in basis points?

2. If the cost of the collateralized borrowing is 6.50% plus servicing and maintenance costs of 25 basis points, what is the marginal cost of the collateralized borrowing?

COST OF ANNUITY FUNDS

22-4

Banner Life will offer a single-premium annuity. It pays 6.75% guaranteed for three years. The commission is 7%. The policy can be redeemed at 96% of principal and accrued interest value at any time. The company can sell guaranteed investment contracts at 7.10%. Ignoring the cost of insurance, if the annuity is redeemed in three years, will the cost of these funds be more or less than the GIC?

SOLUTIONS

ST-22-1

Solution:

Using Equation 22.1:

$$ER = [BR - (CB\% \times CBR)]]/(1.00 - CB\%)$$

$$ER = (6.00\% - 0)/(1.00 - .05) = 6.00\%/.95 = 6.31579\%$$

ST-22-2

Solution:

The marginal cost of new funds in this example is 3.70%, which is the rate at which the firm can borrow new funds. The cost of raising $5,000,000 in net new funds plus the additional $7,500,000 in retained funds that would otherwise be lost resulting from increasing the rate on the two-year account can be estimated by using the equation:

$$MCNF = [(Rn \times \$New) + (Rn - Rnor) \times \$Roll)] / \$New$$

$$MCNF = [(3.65\% \times \$12,500,000) + (3.65\% - 3.45\%) \times \$37,500,000] / \$12,500,000$$

$$MCNF = (\$456,250 + \$75,000) / \$12,500,000 = 4.25\%$$

The cost of raising the rate on the two-year account (4.25%) is much higher than borrowing from the Federal Home Loan Bank (3.70%). Therefore, borrwowing is the least costly strategy.

ST-22-3

Solution:

Using Equation 22.3 results in:

$$\$10,000 = (.06 \times \$10,000) + \{[\$10,000(1 + .085)^2](.96)\}/(1 + y)^2$$

$$= \$600 + [(\$11,772.23)(.96)]/(1 + y)^2$$

$$(1 + y)^2 = \$11,301.36/\$9,400.00$$

$$y = [\$11,301.36/\$9,400]^{1/2} - 1.0 = 9.65\%$$

$$Total\ cost = y + Servicing\ cost = 9.65\% + .25\% = 9.90\%$$

CHAPTER 23

Noninterest Income Sources

Learning Goals

After studying this chapter, you should be able to:

1. Explain why noninterest income is becoming more important for many financial institutions.
2. Explain the advantages and disadvantages of developing noninterest income sources.
3. Describe the sources of noninterest income for most financial firms.

A pop-review quiz: Which four functions of intermediaries are sources of revenue and expenses for intermediaries? If you listed origination, servicing, brokerage, and portfolio management, then you earn a high mark! However, much of the income from these activities does not represent interest earned or expensed on financial assets but income from nonintermediation functions. This chapter explains the importance, sources, and advantages and disadvantages of the noninterest income-generating activities.

Why Is Noninterest Income So Important?

A number of forces have compelled financial institutions to seek sources of revenue that are not dependent on intermediation. These sources of revenue are known as *noninterest income.* They do not involve interest income or expenses. The most important sources of noninterest income are fees charged for services rendered by intermediaries, which is sometimes referred to as *fee-based income.* The long-term downward pressure on intermediation profit margins and rising capital requirements are two principle reasons for the growing interest in noninterest income-generating activities.

NET INTEREST MARGINS UNDER PRESSURE

During the last 20 years, the traditional depository intermediaries have experienced significant new competition and have lost valuable regulatory protections. New powers of thrift institutions and significant competition from nonbank intermediaries such an finance companies, mutual funds, and investment bankers have reduced profit margins of lending and deposit intermediation taking place within depositories' portfolio management function. Thrifts have had to compete with federally sponsored enterprises in mortgage lending, which has reduced their portfolio management profitability. The result has been unprecedented profit pressures, which has led to consolidation and failures.

Profit pressure has been felt most on the net interest margin. Until 1980, depositors earned market interest rates on loans and had their deposit rates held below market level by interest rate ceilings controlled by the Federal Reserve under Regulation Q. To some extent, this guaranteed a positive net interest margin.

These regulations had another interesting impact. They caused most depositories to compete for customers using nonrate-competitive product and service features. Rather than charge customers the full cost of providing services such as automated tellers, transaction accounts, and convenient service, depositories charged below-market prices for these services in hopes of attracting deposit accounts from customers at lower than market interest rates. These nonprice factors had the impact of increasing operating costs and artificially holding down noninterest income that would otherwise have been needed to make these services profitable.

From the 1970s through today, competition from investment bankers has opened up the money and capital markets to many traditional depository business customers. Government sponsored enterprises compete for mortgages, student loans, and farm loans. These factors all create downward pressure on profit margins.

CAPITAL REQUIREMENTS INCREASE IMPORTANCE OF NONINTEREST INCOME

The failure of so many savings and loans, savings banks, and commercial banks in the 1980s and 1990s resulted in legislative- and regulator-mandated increases in capital requirements at insured depositories and insurance companies. Higher capital requirements increase the weighted cost of capital for some intermediaries, as discussed in Chapter 22. This increase in capital costs is another important reason why depository institutions and insurance companies have developed operating strategies that do not rely on leveraging capital by acquiring assets.

Most noninterest-earning activities do not involve adding large amounts of assets to the balance sheet of the firm. This means that the financial institution can pursue revenue-raising activities without incurring additional regulatory capital requirements. For the most part, financial depository institution regulators ignore the operating risks associated with large origination, servicing, and brokerage activities when establishing equity reserve requirements.

GROWTH IN NONINTEREST INCOME

Most depositories have stressed the growth of noninterest revenue sources in the last several decades. This pressure to build noninterest income has accelerated in the 1980s and 1990s. Good measures of the growing importance of noninterest income are shown by the data in Table 23.1. The table shows the net interest margin, noninterest income, and percentage of noninterest income to the net interest margin at all FDIC-insured commercial banks from 1985 to 1993. It also shows the steady rise in the growth of noninterest income and as a percentage of the net interest margin. In this nine-year period, the percentage of noninterest income to the net interest margin rose significantly from 34.1% to 53.8%.

TABLE 23.1

Net Interest Income and Noninterest Income
for Insured Commercial Banks 1985 to 1993
(dollars in billions)

Source of income	Year								
	1985	1986	1987	1988	1989	1990	1991	1992	1993
Net interest income	$90.9	$95.0	$99.9	$107.3	$112.2	$115.5	$121.9	$133.5	$139.3
Noninterest income	$31.0	$35.9	$41.5	$44.9	$51.1	$55.1	$59.7	$65.6	$74.9
Noninterest income/ Net interest income	34.1%	37.8%	41.5%	41.8%	45.5%	47.7%	49.0%	49.1%	53.8%

Sources: Federal Deposit Insurance Corporation, *Statistics on Banking, 1990, 1991;* and Federal Deposit Insurance Corporation, *The FDIC Quarterly Banking Profile,* various issues.

Although not shown in the table, significant increases in noninterest income have occurred at savings and loans, savings banks, and credit unions as well.[1]

Noninterest income is not spread evenly across all size classes of institutions. Larger institutions, like commercial banks, appear to have a far greater ability to generate noninterest income than smaller institutions. Table 23.2 shows the dollar amount of noninterest income as a percentage of the bank's earning assets by size class of bank. Earning assets are those loans, leases, and security investments of banks that earn interest income. It also shows the noninterest income percentage for four size groups for the year 1993.

TABLE 23.2

Noninterest Income as a Percent of Earning Assets by Size of Bank: 1993
(Noninterest income ÷ Earning assets)

Size Class of Bank	All Banks	Less than $100 Million	$100 to $1 Billion	$1–10 Billion	Greater than $10 Billion
	2.37%	1.12%	1.45%	2.59%	2.90%

Source: Federal Deposit Insurance Corporation, *The FDIC Quarterly Banking Profile*, fourth quarter 1993, p. 6.

✓ Checkpoints

23-1　What factors have caused so many financial institutions to focus on noninterest income over the last several decades?

23-2　How did interest rate ceilings on deposits affect the willingness of depositories to stress noninterest income?

Costs and Benefits of Generating Noninterest Income

The pursuit of noninterest-generating activities has both advantages and disadvantages, which we will now discuss.

ADVANTAGES OF NONINTEREST-GENERATING ACTIVITIES

The principal advantages relate primarily to the fact that noninterest income can usually be earned without growing the size of the balance sheet and incurring capital requirements. These and other advantages follow.

---

[1]In 1993, noninterest income as a percentage of earning assets for savings banks and savings and loans was 0.87%. This is well below the comparable figures for commercial banks. The fact that thrifts are considerably more specialized than banks and have a lower percentage of liabilities in transaction accounts explains most of the difference.

Avoidance of Regulatory Capital Requirements

For commercial banks, thrifts, and insurance companies, the need to meet regulatory capital requirements provides a very strong inducement to increase noninterest income activities. The development in the early 1990s of risk-based capital requirements put emphasis on the on- and off-balance sheet contingent liabilities of these firms. However, these capital requirements do not relate to large origination, servicing, data processing, and other noninterest-generating activities that may involve large human resource and technology resources but little in the way of on-balance sheet assets. As a result, intermediaries subject to risk-based capital requirements have a strong incentive to grow those noninterest income-generating activities that will not require additional capital.

Less Subject to Business Cycles

Financial institutions also pursue some noninterest income-generating activities in order to reduce the firm's vulnerability to the business cycle. Business activities tied to gross volume of sales transactions do not fluctuate significantly over the course of the business cycle. Even during recessions, the nominal volume of sales usually rises, which means that noninterest income activities related to payment-system services continue to increase. This tendency helps to offset the cyclical behavior of financial institutions' other activities such as lending and security issuance and sales.

Diversifies Income Sources

Financial institutions pursue noninterest income-generating activities in order to diversify. Many financial institutions are dependent on the economic conditions of particular cities, states, or regions. This makes them susceptible to recessions which may lead to increases in loan delinquencies and losses. Some noninterest-generating activities serve to offset these losses.

Allows for Cross-selling of Existing Customers

Many noninterest-generating activities serve to take advantage of customer relationships that the financial institution has already developed. A customer with an account relationship is generally easier to sell new products to than a person or firm that has no relationship to the firm. This fact provides the rationale for expanding financial firms' product offerings. The concept of the "one-stop financial center" is based on this rationale. Today, many of the larger commercial banks, thrifts, and retail broker-dealers offers a wide range of loan, deposit, security, and insurance services to their customers in order to take advantage of the cross-selling opportunities of their existing customer base.

Takes Advantage of Economies of Scale

Certain types of origination and servicing activities seem to demonstrate significant economies of scale, which was discussed fully in Chapter 21. This is especially evident in servicing. Credit card and mortgage loan servicing organizations seem to benefit from size. To the extent that the average cost per unit serviced falls as the number of servicing units increases, the firm has a greater incentive to expand this activity. Indeed, both the credit card and mortgage loan servicing businesses are highly concentrated.

DISADVANTAGES

The principal disadvantage is that most noninterest-generating activities involve increasing the operating risk of the financial institution by adding fixed costs in the form of plant and equipment and human resources. Discussions of this and other disadvantages follow.

Increases the Operating Risk of the Firm

The principal disadvantage of noninterest-generating activities is that they require increasing the operating risk of financial firms. Most of these activities require investing in plant and equipment and human resources that serve to increase the fixed cost of operating the financial firm. This involves increasing the operating risk of running the firm.

Table 23.3 shows the percentage of noninterest income to average assets and nonintererest expense to earning assets for different-sized commercial banks in 1993. The data show that the percentage of noninterest income to average assets is much higher in larger banks. However, it is also true that the noninterest expenses to average assets is higher for large banks. This finding emphasizes the positive relationship between noninterest-generating activities and higher operating risks.

TABLE 23.3

Noninterest Income and Expenses as a Percentage of Earning Assets for Different-sized Commercial Banks in 1992

	Size Class of Bank			
	Less than $100 Million	$100 to $1 Billion	$1–10 Billion	Greater than $10 Billion
Noninterest income ÷ Earning assets	1.12%	1.45%	2.59%	2.90%
Noninterest expense ÷ Earning assets	3.91%	4.05%	4.62%	4.54%

Source: Federal Deposit Insurance Corporation, *The FDIC Quarter Banking Profile*, first quarter 1994. p. 4.

Economies of Scale May Inhibit Entry

Many noninterest-generating activities involve information-processing activities, such as servicing, which may be susceptible to economies of scale. As a result, producers of large quantities can lower their average costs, which is why large firms dominate the credit card service market. The servicing of credit card portfolios benefits from substantial economies of scale.

✓ Checkpoints

23-3 What are the primary advantages and disadvantages of developing non-interest income-generating activities?

23-4 What role do economies of scale play in developing noninterest income-generating activities?

23-5 How does operating risk relate to financial firms in terms of noninterest income-generating activities?

Sources of Noninterest Income

Fee income is generated as a result of the three information-processing functions of intermediaries—origination, servicing, and brokerage. Some noninterest income is also generated by the portfolio management activities, but this revenue is not reported as part of the net interest margin under GAAP. Consequently, these sources are also discussed in this section. The following are primary sources of fee income that relate to each of these functions.

ORIGINATION SOURCES OF FEE INCOME

The origination function is a lucrative source of fee income. Many financial institutions charge fees to customers to help offset the high costs normally attributed to the origination of financial assets. The best known of these are underwriting fees charged by investment bankers. Most other intermediaries charge origination-related fees for such loans as mortgages, business loans, and installment loans. Some of the most important fees associated with the origination function are discussed below.

- *Loan origination fees:* Many types of loans require the borrower to pay an origination fee, which is normally assessed at the time the loan is funded. These fees are very common on real estate loans of all types, including home mortgages, second mortgages, and equity lines of credit.

- *Security underwriting fees:* Another form of loan origination fees are underwriting fees. Investment banks and commercial banks earn underwriting fees for the creation of securities and syndicated loans. The fees represent compensation for origination activities relating to the claim, as well as the brokerage expertise that the institution brings to bear in order to ensure that the claim is distributed to investors.

    Until 1990, the Federal Reserve Board (FRB) prohibited commercial bank holding companies (BHCs) from underwriting and distributing corporate securities even though commercial banks had already been engaged in the underwriting of state and local bonds.[2] In 1990, the FRB provided authority to certain BHCs to underwrite and distribute corporate securities.[3] The new BHC authority, initially granted by the Federal Reserve to a very limited group of firms, has further blurred the distinction between

---

[2]BHCs had been granted the approval to underwrite state and local municipal bonds and asset-backed securities in 1987. The Fed required that these activities be conducted through nonbank subsidiaries.

[3]The first BHC to receive the Fed-granted authority was J.P. Morgan & Co.

commercial and investment banks and has given BHCs another source of generating noninterest income.

Not to be outdone by banks seeking to enter the security underwriting business, CS First Boston Inc. and Merrill Lynch & Co., two of the U.S.'s largest investment bankers, announced in June 1994 that they planned to originate large commercial loans. The plan was to concentrate on large and medium-sized companies with noninvestment-grade credit ratings. The investment banking firms would hold some of the loans in portfolio and syndicate out the balance.

- *Real estate appraisal fees:* Virtually all real estate loans involve the assessment of the cost of a real estate appraisal. This might be done by the lender's staff appraiser or an outside contract appraiser.

SERVICING SOURCES OF FEE INCOME

Servicing is a very substantial source of noninterest income for most financial institutions. Servicing activities are provided to commercial and retail customers. Generally, these services are priced using explicit fees, such as an annual fee on a credit card, or as an increment to the interest rate charged, such as on commercial, mortgage, and installment loans. The most important servicing fee income sources include those related to investing and operations and to running the nation's payment system. These two sources are discussed below.

Investment and Operational Sources of Noninterest Income

Financial institutions usually look for opportunities to increase revenue by selling a service they provide to their customers to other institutions, which in turn distribute the product to their customers. Many of these services involve data processing and other asset and liability servicing functions that can be extended to other institutions who feel they are too small to service the product efficiently. There are a host of these so-called **correspondent services** provided by large commercial banks and other financial institutions. Financial asset management services also have been offered to new and existing customers by leveraging off of the asset management skills of financial institutions.

- *Commercial bank correspondent and data processing services:* Large commercial banks historically have provided a number of services for smaller commercial banks and thrifts over the years. The most important of these is check-processing services. Larger banks also process credit card receivables and other accounts for smaller financial depositories.[4] Some commercial banks also have developed computer service bureaus which provide a full range of information processing (EDP services), general-ledger accounting, human resource, and payroll services for smaller institutions.

---

[4]The most important correspondent services provided by large commerical banks include check clearing, data processing, short-term credit lines, and security brokerage.

Most of these servicing activities are highly automated. The leading firms have developed very expensive proprietary software. These firms will frequently sell or license the use of the software or process the work of other financial firms for a fee. There are hundreds of different types of services financial institutions perform for each other. These can be priced separately for each service, or the services can be bundled and a single fee assessed.

The most common data processing services include checking account, savings account, credit card, mortgage loan, general ledger, payroll, and commercial and industrial loan processing. American Express Company, for example, is the nation's largest supplier of data processing systems for credit cards.

- *Security transfer and registration:* A small number of commercial banks are active in the data processing activities required in the transfer and registration of securities. These banks generate significant revenue from this non-interest-generating activity.

- *Trust services:* Providing trust services is an important revenue source for a number of financial institutions. This activity involves managing a client's financial and real assets. The trust entity normally provides safekeeping, advisory, accounting, recordkeeping, and management services for the client. Trust fees are normally assessed on the amount of assets under management. A number of bankers consider trust services to have significant

WRAPPING FOR GREATER PROFITS

The U.S. brokerage industry devised a new product in the 1980s that has experienced rapid growth in the 1990s—the portfolio management wrap business. Brokerage firms and others will provide brokerage services and portfolio management services for a fee based on total assets managed. The objective is to compete with the lower-cost discount brokers and to avoid the criticism that commissioned security brokers have an incentive to "churn" accounts by making recommendations designed simply to create brokerage commissions.

Some wrap accounts provide other services as well. Professional asset management services are provided by a professional financial adviser assigned to the client to determine the best portfolio strategy and then assist in the selection of appropriate money managers to implement the strategy.

What does the wrap cost? For a simple "avoid the commission wrap," about 2.00% to 2.50% of total assets in the account. This type of wrap provides the customer with the ability to buy and sell securities without paying commissions on each transaction. Additional advisory services can increase the fee to 3.00%. These fees are for modest accounts of $100,000 to $300,000. Above that amount, fees do fall. By mid-year 1993, wrap accounts were estimated to exceed $50 billion.

Source: "What's the Wrap?" *Economist,* July 31, 1993, p. 72.

How

it

Really

Works

long-term potential. The asset management business, especially that of mutual funds, has grown rapidly in the last decade.

- *Portfolio management service fees:* Mutual fund asset managers, managers of real estate investment trusts, general partners in limited partnerships, and specialized asset management companies derive their revenue from pure portfolio management services. These organizations and individuals, like the trust companies, manage assets for a fee. Many larger financial institutions provide asset management services through subsidiaries.

- *Credit and debit card annual maintenance fees:* Most providers of credit and debit cards charge an annual maintenance fee to offset the cost of account servicing.

- *Mortgage servicing fees:* A mortgage sold in the secondary market is serviced by the seller or another agent. This activity involves collection, statement production, payoff handling, and processing delinquencies and foreclosures. It is typical for the servicer to earn an annualized fee of 25 to 50 basis points on the outstanding loan balance. A number of large financial institutions have mortgage banking subsidiaries that specialize in servicing mortgages in order to generate mortgage servicing fee income.

- *Corporate loan syndication and participation servicing:* Large corporate loans are frequently sold, in part, to other lenders in the form of a syndication or participation. The originating institution, or lead lender, may sell off one or more participations in the loan to other lenders. The lead institution will earn a servicing fee by selling the loan to another lender at an interest rate that is somewhat below the loan contractual rate paid by the borrower. This creates servicing income for the selling institution.

SERVICING FEES THAT ARE TRANSACTION RELATED

Financial institutions operate the nation's payment system. The cost of operating the payment system involves the assessment of many fees to users of the system. Depositories are the major recipients of these fees. Some of the most important include those discussed below.

- *Credit and debit card transaction servicing income:* Credit and debit card issuers earn transaction income related to the use of the card. Financial institutions earn a fee from the merchant that accepts the card. This fee is split two ways, with a portion going to the card-issuing institution and another going to the institution that converts the card receipts to cash for the merchant (merchant fee).

- *Checking account servicing fees:* Financial institutions earn a number of different types of fees on checking accounts. They include monthly maintenance fees, per-check use fees, nonsufficient fund (NSF) fees, and other fees for assisting the customer in using and maintaining the account.

- *Lock-box services:* The lock-box is a service involving mail-receiving boxes. Financial institutions that provide this service have local payment-processing centers that ensure that the checks are received and deposited into the receiving firm's account in a timely manner. This cash management service assists the firm in minimizing its float.

- *Cash management services:* Related to lock-box services is a full range of cash management services offered primarily by commercial banks. These include such activities as accounts receivable collection, payment of accounts payable, investment of excess liquidity, and developing pro forma cash flow statements.

- *Automated transaction machines services:* Many financial institutions offer automated transaction services through automated transaction machines (ATMs) and earn fees.

- *Computerized banking and brokerage services:* Although relatively new, computerized banking and brokerage are now being offered. These services allow the customer to review account balances, shift funds between accounts, implement security purchases and sales, and access an array of informational services.

BROKERAGE SOURCES OF FEE INCOME

Brokerage activities are another cateory of fee-generating sources for financial institutions. Some financial institutions, such as small broker-dealers, rely on brokerage fees for virtually all their revenue. Others, such as commercial banks and large investment bankers, rely on brokerage for varying percentages of total revenue. The variety of brokerage income sources is discussed below.

- *Correspondent brokerage services:* The services larger commercial banks provide for smaller institutions include brokerage services. Larger banks with security and foreign exchange trading departments provide security and foreign exchange purchase and sale services, as well as the safekeeping of securities, for smaller banks and thrifts. Larger banks also act as brokers, arranging for purchases and sales of Fed funds, between depositories.

- *Security brokerage services:* Investment banking firms and other institutions provide security brokerage services to commercial customers and consumers. The primary revenue from this activity is the brokerage commission associated with each transaction.

- *Foreign exchange brokerage and advisory services:* Financial intermediaries provide foreign exchange services to their clients. This involves buying and selling foreign currencies that earn brokerage income.

- *Insurance brokerage services:* Financial institutions other than insurance companies also sell insurance, including property and casualty and life insurance. The income on this activity is in the form of insurance commissions. The pure brokerage of insurance is not available to all financial institutions. Since 1967, federally chartered savings and loans have been able to broker commercial property and casualty and life insurance through subsidiaries. Although BHCs can offer credit life insurance to customers,

IF YOU CAN'T BEAT THEM, JOIN THEM!

How

it

Really

Works

The rapid growth of mutual funds has forced many commercial banks and thrifts to respond by providing competitive services to their customers. The response of these institutions has been to set up brokerage subsidiaries within their holding company structures. Typically these in-house brokers offer a variety of stock, bond, and mutual fund sales. In some cases, they also sell insurance annuity products. All these products have accounted for large deposit withdrawals.

In 1983, several commercial banks went one step further by establishing BHC Financial. This firm provides trading and clearing services for brokerage firms owned by bank holding companies. The purpose of setting it up was to develop the economies of scale expected from setting up one firm to service nearly 50 banks. In April 1993, the banks that jointly own BHC sold some of the stock to the public. The growth in brokerage activities offered by banks and thrifts is expected to give BHC a bright future.

because this insurance has been determined to be closely related to banking by the Federal Reserve, legislation still prohibits the sale of most insurance by BHCs with assets over $50 million.

Insurance sales today are also a major activity for many retail broker-dealers. Insurance policies with a major investment element, such as variable-rate policies and single-premium annuities, are typically sold by licensed security brokers who also obtain an insurance license to market insurance to their customers.

- *Interest rate swap brokerage:* Financial institutions sometimes act as brokers for arranging interest rate and foreign currency swaps between two parties. These brokerage activities generate income which is usually the difference between what the two parties pay the broker institution and the lesser amount the broker institution remits to the other party. This income is pure "brokerage" income so long as the broker institution does not accept any risk due to defaulting counterparties.

PORTFOLIO MANAGEMENT FEE SOURCES

Although portfolio management activities are usually accounted for by interest income and expense, accounting conventions don't always provide for it this way. Financial institutions that require portfolio risk management engage in several activities that earn revenues typically not included in interest income. These are discussed below.

- *Loan commitment fees:* Loan commitments are issued by most financial institutions involved in portfolio management activities. A loan commitment is a legally binding contract between a lender and borrower which specifies the amount of funds, time period, and price for a loan to be taken down in the forward market. Five common uses of loan commitments are detailed below:

1. A mortgage borrower is preparing to purchase a house and desires to obtain the promise of a loan now (called a *mortgage loan commitment*), even though closing of the transaction will be several months in the future.

2. A corporate issuer of commercial paper (called a *standby letter of credit*) wants to have a backup source of short-term financing should the commercial paper market become unsettled and the firm find it difficult to rollover the paper.

3. A builder-developer is looking for a short-term mortgage (called a *real estate take-out commitment*) to insure that a temporary form of permanent financing is available when the real estate project is completed.

4. A corporate borrower engaged in a business acquisition (called a *credit letter of intent*) wants to prove to the management and directors of the target company that it has sufficient funds lined up to complete the transaction.

5. A corporation or foreign government obtains a line of credit for several years to insure it will be able to sell its short-term securities in the open market and, if not, be assured that the lender will guarantee to purchase the securities (called a *note issuance facility*).

To the borrower, a loan commitment represents a form of guarantee that financing will be available to meet an offsetting obligation. This makes the loan commitment a form of insurance. For other types of insurance, the insured would expect to pay a premium, as with a loan commitment. But in lending, the fee is generally called a *loan commitment fee,* negotiated between borrower and lender.

• *Loan guarantees:* Occasionally, a financial institution will guarantee the timely payment of principal and interest on notes or securities issued by a third-party. The third-party usually has a low credit rating and without the guarantee would be forced to pay a high interest rate. The guarantor institution must view the guarantee as part of the credit risk it maintains in its portfolio, even though the guarantee does not show up on the balance sheet. The guarantor institution typically will be paid a fee for providing the guarantee.

• *Acting as principal in swaps:* Commercial banks and investment bankers are active as participants in currency and interest rate swaps. These transactions do not show up on the balance sheet but do involve credit, interest rate, and settlement risks, as discussed in Chapter 18. As a principal in a swap transaction, the financial institution will earn a fee usually priced as a percentage of the notional principal of the swap.

✓ Checkpoints

23-6 Which sources of noninterest income relate to the origination, servicing, and brokerage functions of financial institutions?

23-7 Which major sources of noninterest income relate to portfolio management?

SUMMARY AND REVIEW

1. **Explain why noninterest income is becoming more important for many financial institutions.**

   The **declining net interest margin** experienced by most financial intermediaries engaged in portfolio management activities has caused many financial institutions to develop noninterest income-generating activities.

2. **Explain the advantages and disadvantages of developing noninterest income sources.**

   The principle advantages of noninterest income sources include the lack of regulatory equity requirements, lower business cycle fluctuations, diversification, and cross-selling potential. The principle disadvantages include higher operating risk and, for smaller institutions, possible existence of economies of scale.

3. **Describe the sources of noninterest income for most financial firms.**

   The primary sources of noninterest income relate to the **origination, servicing, and brokerage** activities of financial firms. In addition, some sources of noninterest income are related to the portfolio management function but are typically off-balance sheet.

CHAPTER 24

Distribution Channels for Financial Products

Learning Goals

After studying this chapter, you should be able to:

1. Explain how and why financial institution distribution channels are changing, the primary distribution channels used, and the use of market segmentation including the concepts of credit rationing and adverse selection.
2. Describe electronic transfer systems and the major types of electronic systems used.
3. Discuss the importance of branches for distributing financial products and know why and how to use the model discussed in the chapter to analyze their profitability.

Basic marketing textbooks cover all aspects of the marketing mix for goods and services. This chapter transfers, condenses, and applies what you learned in your basic marketing course to the financial services industry. As with nonfinancial products, many changes have occurred in the types of distribution channels that financial service companies use. Twenty years ago, firms relied on large sales forces based in company facilities. Cost considerations and improvements in telemarketing and direct mail technologies have caused a relative decline in the use of the traditional brick-and-mortar and direct sales channels of distribution.

Contributing to the changes has been the use of electronic systems for handling financial transactions. Electronic funds transfer systems have become a well-established means of servicing customers and have helped spur the development of new types of financial products, leaving depository institutions, brokerage firms, and insurance companies with significant investments in branch offices and established sales forces. As pressures for consolidation within these businesses continue, financial firm managers will need better methods for assessing the effectiveness of traditional channels of distribution.

Alternative Channels of Distribution

Every business must determine the most cost-effective channels of distribution for its products and services. The channel of distribution is the method chosen to market the product to the desired potential customer base. During the last 20 years, the financial service business has experienced major changes in the types of distribution channels used. Mutual funds proved that direct mail and telemarketing could be an effective way to distribute the money market mutual fund against strong competition from commercial banks and thrifts. Direct mail has been the most effective distribution channel for credit card issuers. Telemarketing and direct mail have also been the distribution channel of choice for discount brokerage firms.

There has also been an increase in the use of agents. Insurance companies selling single-premium annuities and variable life policies have used retail brokerage firms and subsidiaries of commercial banks and thrifts to sell their products. Also, during the 1980s, brokerage firms have become major distributors of certificates of deposit for banks and thrifts. These are known as *insured brokered deposits*.

For the management of financial institutions, the choice of distribution channels has become very important. Because of the high cost of brick-and-mortar facilities and direct sales forces, commercial banks, life companies, and thrifts have been threatened by competitors in the mutual fund and brokerage businesses as telemarketing and direct mail have grown in use. Indeed, the banks and thrifts have increased their own use of direct mail and telemarketing as the effectiveness of these channels of distribution has become more evident.

The old line brokerage and insurance companies have also been threatened by the use of new distribution channels. These firms traditionally have relied on direct sales forces to distribute their products and services. Some insurance companies have competed against these companies by using direct mail and sales through agents of brokerage and depository institutions. Telemarketing and direct mail have been used effectively in the discount brokerage business. Electronic methods of servicing and distributing financial products have become more popular as well. The following are the primary channels of distribution.

- *Direct sales:* Direct sales is still the primary channel of distribution chosen by most sellers of financial products and services. Most depositories rely on a direct sales force for distributing most saving and loan products. This is normally done within the offices of the institution. Direct sales forces solicit financial product sales from larger businesses and other institutional customers. Brokerage firms and most life companies still rely on direct sales forces to distribute their products as well. Usually, the more sophisticated the financial product or service, the more likely direct sales will be used.

- *Telemarketing:* Telemarketing, one of the fastest-growing marketing distribution channels in the last decade, is mostly used for products that are relatively simple to understand and frequently used. The security brokerage business uses telemarketing to develop prospect lists for sales of securities. Depositories also use telemarketing to sell certificates of deposit and a host of other products.

- *Direct mail:* Direct mail has also become an important distribution channel during the last decade. Many of the most common savings, investment, and loan products are offered through direct mail. Direct mail dominates in the distribution of credit cards. A number of lower-cost insurance products such as credit life, mortgage life, and term life insurance are also marketed through direct mail.

- *Dealer:* A number of financial institutions have developed relationships with dealers who market products that are financed with debt. Automobile, boat, recreational vehicle, mobile home, and heavy-equipment dealers frequently have lending relationships with one or more lending institutions. Consumer and commercial finance companies are major users of this distribution channel.

  Financial institutions cultivate relationships with dealers because financial products can be marketed at the point of sale. This is also good for the dealer since it eliminates one potential obstacle that could cause a sale to be lost. The point-of-sale advantage in marketing auto loans through a dealership is a prime example of this type of relationship.

- *Agents:* The high cost of direct sales and brick-and-mortar facilities has caused a number of financial service companies to use agents to distribute their product. The use of agents is common in the credit card business, in which many small banks and thrifts offer credit cards that are serviced by another institution. It is also common for retail direct sales forces of brokerage firms to distribute the products of other financial firms, including stocks, bonds, and other traditional products. For example, many retail brokerage firms sell investment life insurance products, like annuities and variable life policies, as well as certificates of deposit issued by banks and thrifts. Brokerage firms also distribute mutual funds and limited partnerships.

- *Affinity groups:* Credit cards are sometimes offered to members of affinity groups. An **affinity group** is an association, club, or other organization having a large membership that is targeted by a financial institution to solicit financial products. The affinity group receives financial compensation for lending its name and membership list to the distribution effort. Similar arrangements are common in the life insurance business. Many organizations make their membership lists available to sponsor sales of low-cost term insurance.

Table 24.1 shows the major financial service distribution channels and the extent to which they are used by financial service providers for a variety of financial claims. Managers of financial service intermediaries must continually reassess their distribution channels. Changes in life-style, product design and complexity, distribution costs, and pricing all influence which channel is selected. Generally, the larger and more complicated the transaction, the more likely that direct sales will be used. As products become well established in the market, distribution channels that do not require interpersonal sales attention become more cost effective.

TABLE 24.1

Major Distribution Channels Used by Intermediaries by Type of Loan or Investment

Financial Claim	Direct Sales	Tele-marketing	Direct Mail	Dealer	Agent	Affinity Group
Consumer loans						
Auto	X			X		
Boat	X			X		
Credit cards	X	X	X	X	X	X
R/V	X			X		
Mobile home	X			X		
Mortgages						
Single-family	X	X	X		X	
Apartment	X					
Commercial	X					
Commercial loans						
Business	X					
Equipment	X			X	X	
Insurance policies						
Property and casualty	X	X	X	X	X	X
Life	X	X	X	X	X	X
Investments						
Mutual funds	X	X	X	X	X	X
Retail security brokerage services	X	X	X			
Savings accounts and CDs	X	X	X	X	X	X
REITs	X					
Limited partnerships	X	X	X			

A FRAMEWORK FOR SELECTING DISTRIBUTION CHANNELS

The selection of the most cost-effective distribution channels for a given financial product is a complex process because there is usually no objective measure for determining which distribution channel will maximize profitability. Multiple distribution channels are frequently used. These can be especially effective when firms are expanding into new markets and want to avoid high-cost permanent offices or sales forces.

Some of the factors that bear on the selection of a distribution channel include:

- The financial product's complexity.
- The saleability of the product without sales input.
- The distribution channel's fixed versus variable costs.
- The impact of new distribution channels on existing channels.
- The product's cross-sale appeal.

A brief discussion of each of these factors follows.

- *Financial product complexity:* More complex financial products typically require more direct sales effort. Such products as commercial loans, mortgages, and most investment life insurance policies normally require significant sales effort. Consequently, direct sales forces are used.
- *Sales effort needed:* A number of financial products typically require more sales effort than others. Full-service, full-commission security brokers use their sales forces to sell products rather than stand ready to receive orders. These brokers sell investment ideas. Discount brokers, on the other hand, appeal to investors who make their own investment decisions and want lower transaction costs.
- *Channel cost structure:* Full-time sales forces and physical offices have high fixed costs compared to direct mail, telemarketing, and agents. The channels with high fixed costs may be less cost-effective for expansion into markets with established competitors. These channels are also less cost-effective for products with strong cyclical demand volatility and products with low profit margins.
- *Interaction between channels:* The financial firm with a well-established sales force or branch system will find it difficult to sell its products in the same market using competing distribution channels. The established sales force and branch personnel can become alienated.
- *Cross-sale appeal:* Some products are best sold in conjunction with other financial products. An ATM card service is most easily sold to the financial firm's transaction account customers, as is an overdraft credit program. Mortgage customers are good candidates to buy property risk insurance.

The branch office is still the primary distribution channel for depository institutions and retail security brokers. As a result, special consideration should be given to evaluating the cost-effectiveness of this distribution channel. A model for accomplishing this analysis is provided later in this chapter.

MARKET SEGMENTATION IN LENDING

In the distribution of loan products, it is common to use **market segmentation,** the process lenders use to discriminate between two groups of borrowers using different loan programs or distribution channels. This is because the pricing of loan products has two dimensions: the interest rate charged and the credit underwriting risk the lender is willing to accept. The problem is that in many lending situations both of these factors are established simultaneously. Once an interest rate is established for a given level of credit risk, it is necessary to discriminate against customers whose credit risk profile exceeds the level appropriate to the interest rate set. Exhibit 24.1 shows the relationship between the interest rate charged and the creditworthiness of three hypothetical customer classes. The pricing algorithm used is the one discussed in Chapter 21.

EXHIBIT 24.1

Relationship between Interest Rate and Credit Worthiness

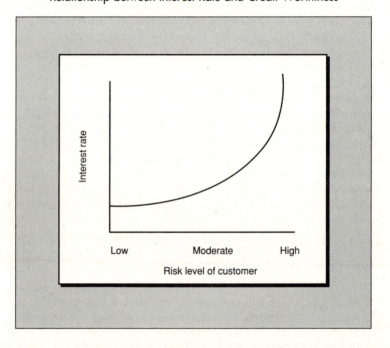

In most lending situations where high volume is common, it is impossible or uneconomic for lenders to price each customer individually, based on the customer's unique risk characteristics. As a result, the lender will determine an acceptable risk profile and then establish the profitable interest rate for that risk level. Having done this, the lender is put in a position to accept all customers whose risk level is equal to or below the maximum risk level chosen.[1] The problem is that if a lender chooses to offer credit to relatively high-risk customers priced at a high rate, the low-risk customers who can obtain loans from low-risk

---

[1]The market segmentation framework used in this section is based on: Anthony Saunders, "The Interbank Market, Contagion Effects, and International Financial Crises," in *Threats to International Financial Stability*, edited by Richard Portes and Alexander K. Swoboda (Cambridge: Cambridge University Press, 1987).

lenders charging a lower interest rate will avoid the higher-risk lenders. Only the higher-risk customers who cannot qualify for loans at institutions that have established lower-risk credit limits at lower rates will be attracted to the high-risk lender. As you know, the tendency for only the high-risk customers to frequent high-risk lenders is called *adverse selection*. While the high-risk lender would like to attract low-risk borrowers, adverse selection will guide low-risk borrowers to low-risk lenders which charge lower interest rates.[2]

This phenomenon also means that low-risk, low-rate lenders will face the prospects of a large fallout from underwriting. High-risk borrowers will approach the low-risk, low-rate lenders and face denial. At high-risk, high-rate lenders, only the high-risk borrowers can be expected to apply. Consequently, lenders likely to serve both groups must use *market segmentation* to develop programmatic distinctions or multiple distribution channels to capture two or more different risk-class customer groups. Exhibit 24.2 shows a graph of the profit-maximizing behavior for lending to two customers with high- and low-risk characteristics. On the vertical scale is the expected return, after the cost of credit losses, for high-risk borrowers shown as Group A and low-risk borrowers shown as Group B. On the horizontal scale is the contract rate charged on the loan. This rate includes the credit risk premium (*crp*) discussed in Chapters 14 and 21. The humped curves for Groups A and B represent a type of demand curve for each group. Consider Group A: at price *ra*, all high-risk customers willing to pay this rate will be charged that rate. If the lender charged less, say rate *rc*, it would be charging high-risk customers less than they were willing to pay. At rates over *ra*, only the highest-risk customers are willing to pay the high rate, many customers are priced out of the market, and profitable volume is lost. Rate *ra* is the rate that will produce the highest expected return, *E(ra)* for the high-risk customer Group A. Rate *rb* is the rate that will maximize the expected return, *E(rb)*, for the low-risk customer Group B.

If the lender has no way to discriminate through programmatic differences between Groups A and B, then the following possibilities will occur:

1.   Credit rationing or discrimination will result for Group A if the lender charges the price *rb* using low-risk credit guidelines designed for Group B.

2.   Adverse selection will result if price *ra* is charged since only high-risk customers in Group A can be expected to be attracted to the lender's program.

3.   At the price *rc*, the lender would be losing many low-risk Group B customers and would be forced to ration many customers from Group A.

The most common ways to segment markets are through using different distribution channels to appeal to different types of customers and by developing special loan programs for different risk-class customer groups. Retail consumer

---

[2]Adverse-selection risk is a well-developed concept in the insurance business. An insurer willing to insure higher-risk groups will have to price the contract's premium higher than if more-restrictive risk underwriting were used. This higher premium will cause the lower-risk groups to seek insurance from insurers who underwrite to avoid the higher-risk groups and charge lower premiums. Thus, the higher-risk insurer will face adverse-selection risk resulting from the fact that primarily the higher-risk groups will use the higher-risk underwriter.

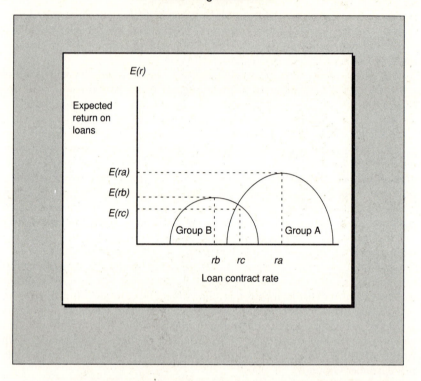

EXHIBIT 24.2

Market Segmentation

finance companies commonly locate their offices in lower-income neighborhoods and small cities while commercial banks locate in wealthier areas.

Lenders also typically offer different loan programs for different customer groups at auto dealers. First-time auto buyers with little credit history generally pay higher interest rates and obtain shorter-term loans than more creditworthy customers. Mortgage loan programs typically discriminate between programs that meet the underwriting guidelines of the government sponsored enterprises, FNMA and FHLMC, from those that do not. The former loans carry a lower rate.

✓ Checkpoints

24-1   What are the five most important distribution channels for financial products?

24-2   Why do some financial intermediaries rely less on physical branches as their primary distribution network and develop other channels of distribution?

24-3   What new channels of distribution have become popular in the insurance industry in the last decade?

24-4 How have the channels of distribution for brokerage services changed?

24-5 Why is the marketing of mutual funds so successful?

24-6 What factors should managers consider when selecting distribution channels?

24-7 Why—and how—do lenders segment the loan market?

Electronic Banking

Electronic banking, sometimes referred to as *electronic funds transfer systems (EFTS),* refers to a number of computer and telecommunication systems that are designed to permit financial transactions with little or no human interface. EFTS was actively discussed in the 1970s and early 1980s when a number of analysts made bold predictions about how electronic systems would replace checks, currency, and tellers in depositories. These systems would pay bills, deposit paychecks, and dispense information and cash. To be fair, many electronic systems have been developed and implemented. However, checks and currency have not gone away. They continue to grow in use, with electronic transactions still representing a fairly small percentage of total transactions.

Where electronics have had an impact, however, there have been clear advantages to businesses, employees, and consumers. The benefits have been a reduction in float available from a payer at the expense of the payee, a reduction in transaction costs (such as postage), and greater convenience. Where these benefits have been significant, electronic systems have replaced paper and human-based systems. The more successful electronic systems firmly established in the marketplace offer the following advantages:

1. Direct deposit of paychecks, social security checks, and other recurring payments through the automated clearing house offers the payee the potential to reduce payer float.

2. Automated tellers and cash-dispensing machines found in financial depositories and offsite locations offer convenience.

3. Point-of-sale systems offer lower transaction costs and convenience.

4. **Electronic data interchange (EDI)** offers better controls, cash management, and data processing efficiencies for companies.

5. Home banking systems offer convenience.

DIRECT DEPOSIT SYSTEMS

Direct deposit systems were the first major electronically based systems to become popular. They allow for individuals and businesses to preauthorize payments to be made directly into and out of a transaction account in a commercial bank or thrift. These transactions usually occur on a specified date.

Direct deposit transactions are accomplished through **automated clearinghouses (ACHs)**, jointly owned associations made up of larger financial institutions in regional areas. They are responsible for clearing checks and making electronic transactions between financial depositories. ACHs are electronically tied together by the Federal Reserve's Fedwire system, which makes electronic transactions between ACHs in roughly 38 regions.

These systems permit employees to have their paychecks deposited directly into their checking accounts, thereby reducing float costs. ACHs also allow retirees to electronically deposit their social security and other government payments directly in their checking accounts. This provides security against lost or stolen checks. These direct deposit systems are also designed to make recurring payments, such as mortgage payments, utility bills, and insurance bills, that the individual preauthorizes, thus helping to reduce the cost of checks and postage.

AUTOMATED TELLERS (ATMS) AND CASH DISPENSERS

Automated tellers and cash dispensers have become a major service in the last 15 years. ATMs eliminate the need for routine manual transactions and improve service by reducing lines and extending hours. ATMs and the less versatile cash dispensers have become very popular. Recent estimates are that the number of commercial bank ATMs reached 90,000 in 1992. That is up from 2,000 in 1973. The 90,000 figure compares to 52,400 commercial bank branches.[3] They have become so popular that financial depositories have joined together to create shared ATM networks, which permit individuals to obtain cash or perform an account inquiry at a machine at any institution that is a part of the network. Some of these networks cover large regions and others the entire country. The Board of Governors of the Federal Reserve System reports that in 1991, 86% of total ATM transactions were cash withdrawals, 10% deposits, 3% account transfers, and 1% bill payments.[4] ATMs are also used by nonbank financial institutions, such as American Express, to provide 24-hour service to account holders.

The appeal of ATMs to depositories is straightforward: if the service is priced properly, the ATM will allow for fewer employees at teller stations, possibly shorten hours, and produce fee income. The fees are charged by some institutions as a service charge on the account activating the ATM. Some fees are for transactional usage, and others are for the use of machines owned by others that are part of the network. The primary fees are assessed on transactions performed at foreign machines—machines not owned by the bank where the customer has an account relationship. Foreign transactions are estimated to account for more than 50% of all transactions.[5] Although the growth in use of ATMs continues, research to date does not indicate that financial firms with ATMs experience lower average costs of operations. Instead of reducing costs, the evidence suggests

---

[3]These data taken from: David B. Humphrey, "Delivering Deposit Services: ATMs versus Branches," *Economic Quarterly,* Federal Reserve Bank of Richmond, 80, no. 2. (Spring 1994), pp. 59–81.

[4]Board of Governors of the Federal Reserve System, *Functional Cost Analysis* (Washington, D.C.: Board of Governors, 1991).

[5]J. McAndrews, "The Evolution of Shared ATM Networks," *Business Review,* Federal Reserve Bank of Philadelphia, May/June 1991, pp. 3–16.

that consumers who use ATMs tend to process more transactions than they did when limited to in-branch transactions.[6]

POINT-OF-SALE (POS) SYSTEMS

Point-of-sale systems are designed to allow consumers to transfer funds directly from an individual's account to a merchant's account. These systems have been more a subject of discussion in financial circles than a reality. From the consumer's perspective, most of these systems have a serious disadvantage. They eliminate the float advantage a consumer receives by charging the purchase on a credit card. There is simply no good economic incentive for consumers to use POS systems as the service is now typically offered.

An offshoot of POS systems are systems designed to reduce credit card fraud. These electronic systems are used by merchants to obtain credit card authorization for purchases above a certain amount. The POS system is likely to expand when merchants decide on the type of incentive that would overcome consumer resistance. In the meantime, the electronic capital investment to run such systems is being put in place.

ELECTRONIC DATA INTERCHANGE (EDI)

EDI is an electronic system which allows corporations to share information electronically. An EDI business can hook up to a supplier or customers to electronically transfer invoices, query a supply catalog, check on a delivery date, look up prices, and create purchase orders. In addition, the financial aspects of EDI allow businesses to make payments electronically to one another. In recent years, the EDI has become a significant alternative to writing paper checks. As a result, it is already having an impact on corporate cash management techniques and on the transaction account products offered by commercial banks. EDI is replacing the paper-based transaction services of depositories.

Growth in EDI is also affecting cash management services of commercial banks. Many firms have been users of bank-operated lock-box services which expedite the clearing of checks by using bank-operated payment-processing centers near paying customers to reduce transit time. As EDI develops, the need for these services is reduced.

HOME BANKING

In the late 1970s and early 1980s **home banking** by telephone became a subject of heated competition among depositories. The primary services offered under home banking included telephone bill paying, account transfers, and inquiries. Interest in home banking was higher when Regulation Q was still in effect, and depositories looked for any type of competitive advantage to differentiate their services from the next institution. The home banking service was implemented by several hundred depositories as a value-added service.

---

[6]Humphrey, "Delivering Deposit Services."

How

it

Really

Works

LARGE CORPORATIONS PUSH EDI

In 1993, an estimated 35 million invoices were paid electronically by businesses using the electronic data interchange. This was up an estimated 59% from 1992. With this kind of growth, it's no wonder that commercial banks are wondering how to deal with the business-to-business growth in EDI.

EDI promises a number of benefits. Some estimate that each check costs businesses $.75 to print, handle, and mail. These costs can be reduced using EDI. Moreover, businesses can agree on when to remit to one another, which improves cash management and eliminates unanticipated float. Moreover, electronic impulses don't get lost, stolen, or delayed in transit. Chevron USA makes more than 5,800 EDI payments a month, or 14% of the checks it once wrote. General Electric Corp. estimates it receives 40% of its revenue electronically.

Commercial banks are being forced to rethink their cash management and transaction services for business. If they don't expand their electronic networks to accommodate all the uses of EDI, they will lose another major market.

Source: Fred R. Bleakley, "Electronic Payments Now Supplant Checks at More Large Firms," *The Wall Street Journal*, April 13, 1994, pp. A1–A8.

Home banking systems have also been adapted to the home personal computer during the last few years. To date, however, neither telephone nor personal computer systems are widely used. Consumers have not been willing to pay the fees attached to these services.[7]

Depository institutions are not the only institutions using telephone- and personal computer-based systems. Stock brokerage firms offer account inquiry and security services from both telephone- and personal computer-based systems. Mutual fund management companies also offer telephone-based services.

Overall, the economics of electronic financial transactions will continue to improve. Paper-based transactions continue to require physical movement and handling. Good cash management procedures require searching for new ways to reduce float. As postage costs continue to rise, electronics will find its way into the design of more payment systems. One interesting new variant of EFTS is the electronic filing of income tax returns with the IRS. Several banks have piggybacked onto this system with a loan program that lends the taxpayer the refund due on the return. In summary, EFTS is here, but it simply has not lived up to its proponents' early dreams.

✓ Checkpoint

24-8 What is electronic banking, and what are the primary systems used?

---

[7]In recent years, nonbanks have also jumped into the home banking business. Several firms are offering telephone-based bill paying systems in competition with systems run by commercial banks. One infrequently mentioned service of the home-banking-service providers is to gather and analyze the consumer spending habits of customers who use these electronic systems.

A Model of Retail Depository Branch Profitability[8]

This section develops a theoretically sound and practical way for depository institutions to measure the profitability of deposit-gathering branch offices. Special emphasis on branch offices is necessary because they remain the primary distribution channel for depositories and other intermediaries. Exhibit 24.3 shows the number of banks and branches of FDIC-insured commercial banks and trusts from 1960 through 1993. Note that while there has been a pronounced reduction in the number of banks in the 1990s, there continues to be a large increase

EXHIBIT 24.3

FDIC-Insured Banks and Offices 1959 to 1993

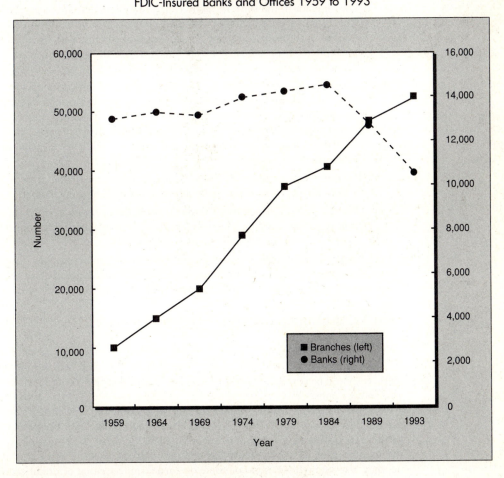

Source: Federal Deposit Insurance Corporation, *1993 Statistics on Banking,* 1994.

[8]This section describing the branch profitability model is taken with permission from Kenneth J. Thygerson, "Modeling Branch Profitability," *Journal of Retail Banking,* Fall 1991, pp. 19–24.

in branch offices. The increase in branch offices is primarily the result of commercial bank acquisitions of weak and failed savings and loans.

WHY A BRANCH PROFITABILITY MODEL IS NEEDED

The need to measure accurately the profit contribution of a branch is greater today than ever before. Consider the following six reasons:

1. The deregulation of the deposit-rate ceilings has made the cost of retail deposit gathering from commercial branches more expensive.

2. The deregulation of deposit rates has forced a change in the competitive service mix. In the days of Regulation Q, depositories competed with convenience in the form of many offices, free services, and a psychological feeling of safety that manifested itself in the form of large costly permanent facilities. Competing on the basis of interest rate or price was prohibited. These institutions need to evaluate the profitability of their branch networks.

3. The Financial Institution Reform Recovery and Enforcement Act of 1989 has resulted in thousands of branch offices being offered for sale by the Resolution Trust Corporation. The RTC has been aggressively trying to sell many of the offices of institutions that have gone into receivership. Institutions wanting to bid on them will need to value these branches.

4. Measuring branch profitability is necessary because of the growth and availability of other types of insured deposit distribution channels.

5. There is an established trend among insured depositories to buy, sell, and trade existing facilities. The feeling is that in many markets consolidation is necessary to restore and enhance profitability.

6. A branch profitability measurement model assists in developing a branch personnel compensation incentive system that encourages behavior that is consistent with the profit measurement objectives of the model.

MODEL OF BRANCH FUNCTIONS AND ACTIVITIES

The retail branch should be looked at fundamentally as a distribution channel for financial products and services. In this respect, it is no different from a retail store. It should be considered one of many alternative distribution channels available to the depository.

The major functions of the branch are the origination and servicing of various asset and liability products of the firm (as discussed in Chapter 7). Because of the substantially different operating strategies used by financial depositories around the country, each institution must perform this analysis for itself. Branch personnel may also be involved in a complete or partial underwriting or credit-scoring activity. Some depositories delegate branches to complete the underwriting as well as to see to the funding of certain loans. Others use the branch simply as a distribution channel, with the branch personnel acting as a direct sales force but not a loan-processing or underwriting unit.

The servicing activities of the branch involve payment processing, deposit processing, and transaction processing to the extent that these activities occur within the branch. The branches of some institutions might also serve to distribute products and services not produced by the firm. In this case, the measure of profitability is based on the commission or service fee cash flows derived from the sale of safety deposit boxes, mutual funds, insurance, and agent-based credit card programs.

MEASUREMENT MODEL OF BRANCH PROFITABILITY

The model for a branch's income statement is total branch profits (*TBP*), equals branch servicing income (*BSI*), plus branch origination income (*BOI*), plus branch fee and commission income (*BFC*), minus branch total costs (*BTC*), as in Equation 24.1:

$$TBP = BSI + BOI + BFC - BTC \qquad [24.1]$$

Branch servicing fee income (*BSI*) includes an allocation provided to the branch from any servicing groups within the firm that receive services performed by branch personnel, such as loan posting, payment processing, and collection. A branch that collects and posts loan payments for mortgages may receive a revenue allocation of $.25 per payment, for example.

Branch origination income (*BOI*) is the largest and most important source of income for most branches. Origination income cash flows come in two forms. The first relates to financial products and services that the branch successfully markets to the public on behalf of the firm's asset managers. Asset managers can be thought of as product managers who market specific loans or other financial service products. Asset managers look at the branch as one of several alternative distribution channels available to them.

Here, the branch should be allocated revenue based on what the asset or loan manager feels it can pay to obtain additional sales of the product. The revenue will be in the form of commissions, say $12 per credit card issued, 0.25% of the funded dollar amount of any first or second mortgage originated through the branch, and so forth. Each loan or service sales unit that wants to use the branch to distribute a product must determine what type of commission and processing fee it can afford to pay the branch to market their product.

The second form of *BOI* relates to the origination of deposit products. This is typically the largest portion of *BOI*. The branch-generated retail deposit is but one of a number of alternative funding sources for the firm. The firm's asset and liability managers monitor prices for all alternative funding sources. These prices, along with monitoring the competition, form the basis of the pricing used by the retail branch system.

This analysis also forms the basis for developing the cash flows for the branch relating to deposit origination. These cash flows are based on the assumption that the goal of the branch is to maximize the present value of the difference between the marginal cost of raising funds through the branch and the next-lowest-cost alternative for raising funds through other distribution channels. These alternative sources of funds might be negotiable CDs, brokered insured deposits, federal funds, or repos.

The branch management can maximize profit by successfully marketing a large volume of deposits at a price that is below the cost of raising funds through alternative distribution channels. Because the cost savings may occur in the future, it is necessary to take the present value of these interest savings. The present value of these cash flows is computed on all deposits new to the depository and on all deposits repriced during the period under analysis. The appropriate discount rate would be the firm's weighted cost of capital (coc). This analysis assumes that deposits such as demand deposits, money market demand accounts, and savings accounts are repriced each day. While having chosen to reprice transaction and passbook accounts daily, alternative assumptions should be based on the institution's experience. Many commercial banks, for example, have analyzed their transaction and passbook accounts and have concluded that an average effective maturity of one to three years is a good approximation.

This analysis will produce the present value of the interest savings cash flows (PVIS). To compute it, we take the difference between the interest rate on the alternative deposit source ($AR_{i,t}$) for account type i for period t and subtract the interest cost of the branch deposit interest rate ($DR_{i,t}$). The resulting interest spread is then multiplied by the amount of deposits of each type i originated or repriced by the branch during the current measurement period. The present value ($PV_{coc,t}$) of this series is then taken for cash flows over the number of periods the deposit is outstanding, t. The firm's weighted cost of capital is used as the discount rate. The weighted cost of capital is assumed to be 9%. The firm with a pre-tax cost of equity of 25% and an average cost of liabilities of 8%, with a 6% equity-to-asset ratio, would have a coc of approximately $[(25\% \times 6\%) + (8\% \times 94\%)] = 9.02\%$, as in Equation 24.2.

$$PVIS = [PV_{coc,t} (D_i \times (AR_{i,t} - DR_{i,t}))] \qquad [24.2]$$

where:

$PVIS$ = Present value of interest savings for period t discounted at the cost of capital coc

$PV_{coc,t}$ = Present value with discount rate of coc for t periods

D_i = Deposits dollar amount of account type i sold or repriced at rate $AR_{i,t}$

$DR_{i,t}$ = Deposit rate for account type i for t periods

$AR_{i,t}$ = Deposit rate for alternative funding source i for t periods

Table 24.2 shows how data might be organized to create the model input. The deposit cost data DR and AR must include the cost of deposit insurance.

TABLE 24.2

Example of Deposit Cost Comparisons for All Deposits Sold by a Branch in One Month

Branch-Generated Deposit	Rate DR_i	Alternative Funding Source	Rate AR_i	$AR_i - DR_i$
Demand deposits	0.00%	Federal funds	5.75%	5.75%
Savings accounts	4.25	Federal funds	5.75	1.50
3–12-month CDs	7.85	Negotiable 3–12-month CDs	8.58	.73
12–24-month CDs	8.24	Brokered 12–24-month CDs	8.90	.66

The cost of Regulation D reserves (reserves held in vault or Federal Reserve deposits that earn no interest), and brokerage commissions, if applicable, must be included. The term structure of alternative funding sources must be properly identified. The cost of alternative funding sources represents the next-lowest cost of funding sources for the institution performing the analysis. These costs will vary from firm to firm. Exhibit 24.4 shows the difference between rates paid on retail, negotiable, and brokered insured deposits by banks from May 1989 through April 1990, as reported by *The Wall Street Journal*. The graph shows high volatility in the spreads, which translates directly into branch profit volatility. The alternative funding source cost is compared to the interest cost of the new deposits and repriced deposits sold during the reference period, *t*.

Table 24.3 provides all the information necessary to calculate the present value of the interest savings on funds renewed and those brought in as new funds into a hypothetical branch for a one-month period. An example will help to illustrate how the calculations are made. Take the case of the one-year deposits: these funds will stay on account for one year and save the firm 0.25% as compared to the next-lowest cost of one-year money. This 0.25% translates into a quarterly positive cash flow of $[(.25\%/4) \times \$2,000,000] = \$1,250$ received at the end of each of the next four quarters. Discounting this quarterly savings at a weighted cost of capital of 9% gives a total of $4,837.

TABLE 24.3

Present Value of Interest Savings Calculated at the Firm's Weighted Cost of Capital (9.00%) for all Deposits Rolled Over and New Deposits Received for the Month of July 1991

	Amount of Deposits Rolled Over or New	Term	Interest Rate	Next-lowest Rate	Present Value of Savings at 9.00%
Checking	$2,100,000	Daily for a month	0.0%	5.75%	$ 10,063
Negotiable order of withdrawal accounts	4,000,000	Daily for a month	4.5	5.75	4,167
Money market demand accounts	3,500,000	Daily for a month	5.25	5.75	1,458
90-day CDs	4,800,000	90-day	6.25	6.75	6,000
Six-month CDs	14,000,000	Six-month	6.50	7.00	34,615
One-year	2,000,000	One-year	7.00	7.25	4,837
Four-year	2,000,000	Four-year	7.25	8.50	51,046
Total revenue for interest savings					$102,186
Less cost of transaction accounts					13,300
Total revenue after transaction account costs					**$88,886**

EXHIBIT 24.4

Retail Cost of Deposits Less Negotiable CD Cost of Deposits and
Retail Cost of Deposits Less Brokered Insured Cost of Deposits
May 1989 to April 1990
(differences in average monthly rates)

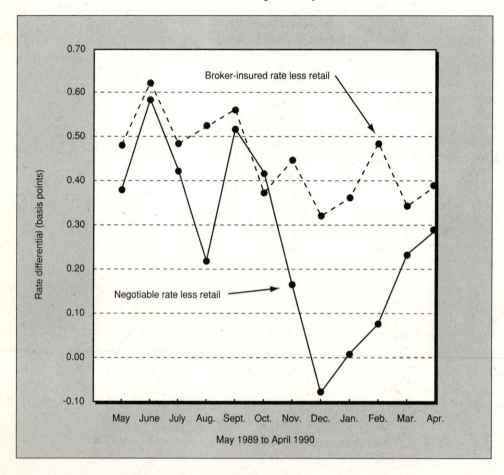

Source: Banquote Online, Reported in *The Wall Street Journal*, various issues.

The value of the checking account deposits is determined by taking the interest savings of 5.75% for a month and multiplying it times the average weekly balance to get $[(.0575/12) \times \$2,100,000] = \$10,063$. The NOW account balances
are handled in the same manner. It is necessary to identify the extraordinary marginal costs associated with transaction accounts such as checking, NOW, and

MMDA. In this example, the depository has determined that the monthly cost of servicing these accounts is $3.50 for activities performed outside the branch. The depository in the example has the following number and associated costs for these accounts:

Type of Account	Number of Accounts	Cost per Month at $3.50
Checking	1,800	$ 6,300
NOW	1,200	4,200
MMDA	800	2,800
Total Cost per Month		**$13,300**

Table 24.4 provides an example of the detailed schedules for branch fee and commission income (*BFC.*)

TABLE 24.4

Schedule of Fee and Commission Income for a One-Month Period
(BFC)

Product Type	Number Sold	Compensation per Unit	Total Income
Credit cards	23	$ 12	$ 276
Second mortgages	5	80	400
First mortgages	12	120	1440
Safety deposit income	20	12	240
Checking fees	120	6	720
Auto loans	12	25	300
Other loans	8	30	240
Annuities	10	80	800
Total BFC			**$4,416**

TABLE 24.5

Monthly Direct and Indirect Costs of Operating a Retail Branch
(BTC)

Heat, light and rent	$ 15,200
Maintenance	1,290
Advertising and promotion	1,000
Staff costs plus benefits	8,765
Training and human resource allocation	765
Data processing allocation	32,453
All other allocations	12,776
Total BTC	**$72,249**

Branch total costs (*BTC*) include the direct costs of running the branch system (see Table 24.5). This includes personnel, heat, light, space, telephone, mail, maintenance, and upkeep as well as all supervisory branch personnel, branch advertising, and branch back-office costs. Many of these costs will be allocated on a per-account or per-employee basis. Branch space costs can best be uniformly estimated by charging the branch the rental cost at the current cost per square foot for commercial space in the locale of the branch. Otherwise, branch space costs could be unduly influenced by whether the firm owns the branch, or if it rents, by when the lease may have been signed. These represent sunk costs or benefits.

Added to this must be the allocation of all indirect costs related to running the branch system. Allocations for data processing, human resources and training, communication, accounting, space management, and executive time must be included. Typically, these allocated costs can be estimated quite accurately by making allocations on a per-account basis or per branch employee.

TABLE 24.6	
Income Statement for Hypothetical Branch **(*TBP*)**	
Income	
Deposit origination	$88,886
Fee income	4,416
Total income	93,302
Costs	
Direct and indirect	72,249
Income or (loss)	$21,053

Table 24.6 provides a summary of each of the revenue and cost estimates assembled for the hypothetical branch. This branch was profitable during the month shown in the example.

USING THE MODEL TO ANALYZE BRANCH PURCHASES, SALES, CLOSURES, AND SWAPS

This model has been used very successfully for analyzing the profitability of branches available for purchase and for valuing existing branches for possible closure, sale, or swap. To use it, it is necessary to forecast expected average spreads between the rates paid on deposits attracted through the target branch and alternative funding sources. The target branch expenses can usually be fairly estimated by using actual historical data. Then, a forecast of future deposit growth is made along with estimates of commission and fee income. By discounting these pro forma cash flows over a five- to ten-year period, the analyst is able to determine the maximum deposit premium that might be offered to buy, sell, or swap a target branch.

Using this model, it becomes very easy to determine which branches might be candidates for purchase or sale. It also makes very clear the special advantages of branch purchases, in which the purchased branch can be merged into an existing branch office. This situation provides a large increase in deposits without a commensurate increase in costs. Branch swaps with other institutions that provide the same result for both parties are also very rewarding.

RTC SELLS S&L BRANCHES

How it Really Works

The Resolution Trust Corporation has been the largest seller of financial institution branches in recent years. These are branches of failed savings and loans. The largest number of acquisitions are known as *purchase and assumptions* in which deposits, certain other liabilities, and a portion of the assets are sold to acquirers.

The largest number of acquirers of former S&L branches (65%) through July 1993 were commercial banks. Most of these institutions were located in Texas, but other states with high branch sales included California, Louisiana, Illinois, and Florida.

Acquiring institutions paid an average premium of 2.44% of total consumer deposits, excluding large denomination CDs and brokered accounts. This average premium probably underestimates branch values since a number of institutons sold valuable branches just prior to being seized by the RTC.

Source: Resolution Trust Corporation, *RTC Review* 4, no. 8 (Aug. 1993).

✓ Checkpoints

24-9 What is the primary function of a branch office for a financial depository?

24-10 The primary contribution to profit for a financial depository typically comes from what activity or product?

24-11 What types of activities do depository branch offices perform for which they should be compensated or credited?

24-12 Why have branch sales and purchases become important activities for financial institutions?

24-13 Do you expect the number of depository offices to increase or decrease in the years ahead? Why?

SUMMARY AND REVIEW

1. **Explain how and why financial institution distribution channels are changing, the primary distribution channels used, and the use of market segmentation including the concepts of credit rationing and adverse selection.**

    The traditional distribution channels of depository institutions, insurance companies, and retail brokerage firms, consisting of **branch offices** and **direct sales forces,** are being relied on less today than in the past. Financial institutions now actively use **dealers, agents, telemarketing,** and **direct mail.** Some financial institutions use product design features and alternative distribution channels to segment markets. **Credit rationing** occurs when institutions set loan rates for low-risk customers. **Adverse selection** occurs when lenders accept high-risk borrowers and charge high rates to cover the higher credit risk.

2. **Describe electronic transfer systems and the major types of electronic systems used.**

    Electronic funds transfer systems have grown to be an important means for financial institutions to service and distribute their products. **Direct deposit systems** are well established, as are **automated tellers** and **cash dispensers.** These systems provide economically proven ways to reduce float and provide added convenience. **Point-of-sale systems** and **home banking** have been less popular, because the benefits are less obvious and the costs of providing them higher. The primary reasons for the acceptance of these systems are reduction of float, reduced transaction costs, and greater convenience.

3. **Discuss the importance of branches for distributing financial products and know why and how to use the model discussed in the chapter to analyze their profitability.**

    Branches and the personnel that operate them represent major costs for depository institutions. One way to determine the profit contribution of a branch is to develop a model to compute the cash flows related to operating the branch. The model given in this chapter relies on estimates of fee and commission income and cash savings, represented as the difference between the cost of funds generated by the branch and that available from other sources. This model is also used to evaluate **branch sales, purchases, closures,** and **swaps.** The primary data inputs in the model include cash flows derived from origination and servicing less the total cost of operations. For depository institutions, the primary source of cash flow is the present value of the interest savings on branch originated deposits as compared to the next-lowest-cost alternative.

CASE 24.1

CASE STUDY IN BRANCH PROFITABILITY: TO KEEP OR TO SELL

Erie Bank is in the process of reviewing its retail branch network. It opened a number of branches during the early 1980s in a major expansion. Many of these branches performed very well. Several, however, did not live up to expectations. Their growth seemed to stall out as competitors with stronger locations and market shares were able to outperform the Erie locations.

The president of Erie has asked the financial officer and the head of the branch system to analyze the Crossroads branch. The bank has received an offer to buy the branch from a competitor for a deposit premium of 1.5%, which will be paid in cash and will represent 1.5% of the deposits in the branch at the time of the sale closing. This is a very small premium, but Erie has little confidence that this branch will perform well in the years ahead.

The financial officer and the head of branch operations put together the following data that they consider relevant to making the decision. Table C24.1 shows the marginal out-of-pocket costs of operating the branch and the expected increase in costs over the next four years. Table C24.2 shows the deposit base for the branch and the expected growth over the next four years, the average expected spread between the cost of retail deposits from this branch and the alternative of raising wholesale money through negotiable CDs or other borrowings, and the profit contribution of the branch from sales of loan products and the fees earned on other services provided.

TABLE C24.1

Estimated Annual Cost of Operating Crossroads Branch

Costs	1995	Expected Annual Change
Personnel	$73,000	4%
Heat, light, and rent	48,000	3
Other operating costs	37,000	4

TABLE C24.2

**Deposit Base, Growth Forecast, and Spread
between Deposit Costs and Wholesale Funding Source**

Type of Account	1995	Annual Growth Rate	Spread to Wholesale Alternative
Transaction accounts	$ 3,500,000	2%	4.00%
Number of accounts	1,500		
CDs and savings	$ 20,500,000	2	0.25
Fees and loan profits	$ 13,000	0	
Total	**$24,000,000**		

The cost of processing transaction accounts is $24 per year per account.

The two executives decided to do 1996 to 1999 pro forma income statements for the branch to determine whether the branch would show improving or worsening profit performance. The branch profits to date have been very unsatisfactory. The $40,000 cost of selling the branch will involve providing severance pay, notifying the customers of the sale, and performing the computer conversion to the seller's computer. In addition, the bank will have to buy its way out of the remaining lease on the branch for a payment of $25,000. The bank estimates its pretax weighted-average cost of capital at 9%.

Questions

1. Using the data provided, develop a four-year pro forma including 1995 as the base and 1999 as the last year. Show all costs and revenues developed by the branch. Ignore taxes in this analysis.

2. If the trends in costs and revenues continue beyond 1999, would you sell the branch at this low deposit premium? Why or why not?

CASE   24.2

DETERMINING THE APPROPRIATE BRANCH PREMIUM TO PAY FOR ACQUISITION

The Resolution Trust Corporation has taken over several savings and loans in your market. They have put a number of branches of these institutions out for bid. First Bank is considering bidding for one of these branches located across the street from one of its existing offices. By purchasing the branch from the RTC, they can close it and shift the deposits to their existing branch without much increase in operating costs.

The branch for sale has deposits of $22 million. The purchase would occur on January 1, 1996. It has been declining in size since the RTC took over management. If First Bank purchases the branch on January 1, 1996, and assumes the deposits without assuming assets, it can repay some of its wholesale deposits and lower its cost of funds. However, it expects to lose deposits because of customer confusion about the closing of the branch and the firing of personnel.

The president of First Bank has asked the head of retail banking and the financial officer to come up with a bid that will provide a solid profit. It will be necessary to determine the net present value of the investment in the branch assuming a pre-tax weighted cost of capital to the bank of 10%. The two executives have come up with the following data for analysis. Table C24.3 shows the expected deposit balances for the next four years through 1999 and their best guess beyond 1999. It also shows the expected average spread between the cost of funds for the deposits purchased in the RTC branch transaction and the expected cost of wholesale funds.

The revenue from additional fees and product sales from the new customers is assumed to be zero. The additional one-time and ongoing costs of the addition to their customer base of the $22 million in deposits is also shown in the table.

TABLE C24.3

Estimated Deposit Balances and Average Spread Compared to Wholesale Funding Source for 1995 to 1998 and Beyond
(dollars in millions)

Year (January)	Average Balance	Spread Versus Wholesale	Number of Accounts
1995	$22	.45%	5,200
1996	17	.40	4,500
1997	14	.45	3,500
1998	12	.50	3,300
1999–2004*	10	.50	2,200

*No value ascribed to accounts after ten years.

The added costs of servicing the additional accounts are shown in Table C24.4. Converting the account files to First Bank's computer system and notifying all the new customers also involve some major costs, which are also shown in the table.

TABLE C24.4

Account Servicing and Conversion Costs
Costs of Conversion

Computer costs	$12,000
Moving files	5,000
Closing out safe deposit boxes	5,000
Personnel for transition	5,000
Promotion and advertising	3,000
Total	$30,000

Costs of Servicing Accounts

Cost per account: $12 per account per year

Question

Construct a cash flow statement using the costs and revenues discussed in the case study. The statement should show the cash outflow representing the conversion and one-time customer costs of assimilating the new deposits. Then calculate the present value of the deposit cost savings less the servicing costs. The discount rate should be that of the firm's weighted cost of capital. Ignore any possible value of the deposits after ten years. All cash flows should be assumed to occur at the end of each year. Determine the maximum discount First Bank can pay for the deposit base. Ignore taxes.

(Hint: The initial cash outflow plus the maximum premium paid on the deposit base should equal the net present value of the interest savings.)

CHAPTER 25

Mergers and Acquisitions

Learning Goals

After studying this chapter, you should be able to:

1. Discuss recent trends in the mergers and acquisitions of financial service companies.
2. Describe the basic sources of value and other rationales used in determining the value created by a consolidation.
3. Explain the primary techniques used for the valuation of acquisition targets.
4. Describe the most important nonfinancial factors to be considered in consolidations.

The 1980s and 1990s have been periods of considerable structural change in the financial services business. These changes have caused most observers to argue that there is excess capacity in the financial services industry, meaning simply that there are more institutions with capacity to provide more financial products and services than there is demand. This provides a strong inducement to reduce capacity. Two effective ways to do this are through failure and mergers and acquisitions. The latter is the subject of this chapter.

Trends in Mergers and Acquisitions

Mergers and acquisitions have accelerated for virtually all types of financial service providers, a trend most apparent in the depository industry. The numbers of
commercial banks, savings and loans, savings banks, and credit unions have all
dropped significantly in the last ten years. A sharp rise in the number of failures
is one explanation. The other is a sharp rise in mergers and acquisitions. Exhibit
25.1 shows the number of FDIC-insured commercial banks and the number of
unassisted mergers of commercial banks for selected years from 1982 to 1993.

EXHIBIT 25.1

Number of FDIC-Insured Commercial Banks and Unassisted Mergers: Selected Years 1982 to 1993

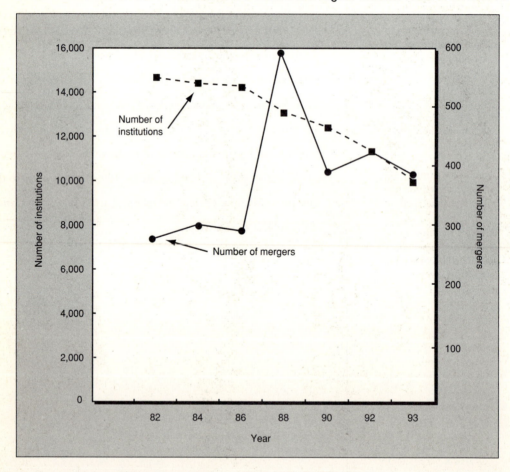

Sources: Federal Deposit Insurance Corporation, *Statistics on Banking 1990*, (Washington, DC.: FDIC, 1991); and Federal Deposit
Insurance Corporation, *The FDIC Quarterly Banking Profile*, various issues.

The number of savings and loans, savings banks, and credit unions have experienced similar—and, in some cases, more significant—reductions in numbers. In all cases, the number of mergers increased significantly. Mergers and acquisitions have occurred in all size groups of financial institutions. For strong, profitable, and well-capitalized institutions, periods of stress provide the opportunity to expand through acquisition at a relatively low price. For a weak institution, regulatory pressures to raise capital provide a very strong inducement to become a willing target of an acquisition.

✓ Checkpoints

25-1 Why has the number of mergers increased so much in the last decade, especially among depository institutions?

25-2 How do regulatory capital requirements affect the pace of mergers and other consolidations?

Rationales for Financial Intermediary Consolidation

The best way to understand the acquisition process is to understand the sources of value of ongoing financial institutions and other rationales for consolidation. These sources of value are what acquirers are purchasing and what the board of directors of a target institution is selling. The most important of these factors are discussed below.

INCREASE CUSTOMER FRANCHISE VALUE

The easiest factor to understand in assessing the value of a financial institution is the value of existing customer account relationships. This is called the firm's *customer franchise value.*[1] It is axiomatic in marketing that it is easier to resell an existing customer than it is to attract a new customer with no previous relationship to the organization. Many mergers and other consolidations are justified on the basis that existing consumer franchise value can be expanded and/or enhanced. This can be done by expanding the number of products and services offered to existing customers. Generally large institutions purchase smaller institutions for this reason. In addition, some services, such as automated teller machine networks, are more valuable the more machines that are tied into a network.

The discussion of retail deposit branches in chapter 24 quantified these sources of value for depository institutions. The discussion developed a model that es-

---

[1] The concept of franchise value is not straightforward in practice. One aspect of franchise value is the notion that banks have a degree of monopoly power in the consumer markets it services. This power only creates value to the extent that it gives the bank some degree of control over price and the ability to earn greater-than-normal profit margins. Other sources of franchise value that may give rise to excess profits include a positive reputation of the acquired, a successful trade name, and a strong market presence.

tablished the value of retail deposits as being derived primarily from the lower price elasticity of retail versus wholesale customers, meaning that retail deposits can be sold at a lower rate and experience less volatility than wholesale deposits. We then quantified this lower cost.

A similar rationale can be used to value relationships of loan, brokerage, asset management, and any other customers that have relationships built over long periods with the organization. So valuable are these customer franchise relationships that even failed institutions have customer franchise value. The Resolution Trust Corporation sold the branches and deposits of hundreds of failed savings and loans in the 1990s, typically by having the acquiring institution assume the book liability value of the deposits and receive offsetting loans, securities, or cash equal to that value. However, most of the branches of the failed institutions had well-established customer franchises which were valuable to the acquiring institution. On average, the acquiring institution actually would receive 2% less in assets than the amount of liabilities it assumed. This translated into a 2% premium for the customer franchise value.

This franchise value can be even more valuable for firms seeking to expand into new markets where they have no name recognition. When BHCs purchase commercial banks out of state under reciprocal state bank acquisition agreements, the purchases often include a significant premium representing the franchise value of the acquired firm.

EXPAND USE OF EXPERTISE IN ORIGINATION, SERVICING, BROKERAGE, AND PORTFOLIO MANAGEMENT

Another principle reason to acquire another firm is to expand an activity that the firm does well. We know from Chapter 2 that each financial firm has to select the origination, servicing, brokerage, and portfolio management functions to perform and the financial assets on which to perform them. Some financial firms have developed substantial expertise in originating business, consumer, or mortgage loans and would like to expand into new markets. The same goes for servicing, brokerage, and portfolio management.

The acquisition of medium-sized to large institutions by other similar-sized institutions is generally rationalized by the fact that these firms have developed valued expertise in one or more financial service functions which, when combined with the other institution, provides an increased scope of operations.

ENHANCING GROWTH

Financial institutions generally develop within relatively small geographic areas. Only a few of the largest commercial banks, thrifts, and broker/dealers have operations nationwide. Consequently, the market a financial institution has developed is of value to another institution seeking to expand. The growth prospects for the geographic areas served by each financial institution also vary considerably, making a financial firm serving a relatively fast-growing market highly desirable to organizations located in slow-growing markets.

Mergers and acquisitions are also motivated by the fact that small financial firms cannot provide all the services large commercial customers need. Limits set by regulators and management on loans to one borrower make it nearly impossible for a small bank to lend to a large corporate borrower. It is not at all uncommon for a corporation to establish a relationship with a local small bank only to discover that several years later it must move its accounts and lending business to a larger bank that can handle its now larger loan request.

TAKING ADVANTAGE OF ECONOMIES OF SCALE—CUT COSTS

In the 1990s, the single biggest rationale used to justify mergers and acquisitions was cost savings. According to this rationale, the merger or acquisition of a financial firm would provide significant opportunities to eliminate redundant operations and improve efficiencies by taking advantage of potential economies of scale.

Some of the most common areas of potential cost efficiencies are in the areas of:

- Servicing and other back-office operational cost savings.
- Elimination of overlapping branch offices.
- Supervisory and middle-management reductions.

INCREASING MARKET POWER

Another strong incentive to consolidate is to lessen competition. Of course, efforts to monopolize markets or substantially lessen competition are illegal under the nation's Sherman Antitrust Act of 1890 and Clayton Act of 1914. The Bank Merger Act of 1960 added a regulatory hurdle for consolidations of commercial banks. To seek approval of a consolidation, banks must apply to appropriate regulator's who must consider the impact on local market competition in the approval process. Thus, while reducing competition is a strong temptation, there are limits as to how much market concentration is allowed in consolidations. What are the limits? One technique used to measure overall competitiveness is called the *Herfindahl-Hirschmann Index (HHI)*.[2]

The *HHI*, used by the U.S. Department of Justice to determine if a consolidation is anticompetitive, is an index of the degree of concentration within a well-

[2]The merger approval process is considerably more complicated than simply calculating the *HHI*. In the case of mergers requiring approval from the Fed, the following actions are taken: (1) the district Fed banks are delegated responsibility over data gathering, analysis, and initial recommendation; (2) data used include contacts with affected bankers and surveys of affected businesses and consumers; and (3) calculation of the *HHI*. A good discussion can be found in Christopher L. Holder, "Competitive Considerations in Bank Mergers and Acquisitions: Economic Theory, Legal Foundations, and the Fed," *Economic Review*, Federal Reserve of Atlanta, Jan./Feb. 1993, pp. 23–36.

defined geographic market. For depository institutions, it is used to define the degree of competitiveness for a defined market of the consolidating firm's deposits. The *HHI* point value is defined by Equation 25.1:

$$HHI = \sum_{i=1,n} MS_i^2 \qquad\qquad [25.1]$$

where:

HHI = The HHI point value

MS_i = Market share for deposits of depository i

i = Number of depositories in market.

HHI point values vary from zero, if there are no institutions in the market, to 10,000 if one institution has 100% ($100 \times 100 = 10,000$) market share. According to regulatory and Justice Department guidelines, there are two considerations. First is the 1,800 rule. Simply put, markets with overall *HHI* point values over 1,800 are considered highly concentrated. The second rule is to question any consolidation that increases the market *HHI* by more than 200 points. Sometimes the *HHI* is calculated with both commercial bank and thrift assets combined. When this is done, the thrift's assets might be weighted only 50% as compared to the commercial bank's.[3]

DEMONSTRATION PROBLEM **COMPUTING THE *HHI***

Situation

Consider the depositories and their respective market shares which are defined by the Department of Justice in the hypothetical market of Western North County. These institutions and deposit market shares are shown in Exhibit 25.2.

Using these data, you have been asked to determine whether the Department of Justice might challenge a merger of any of the institutions in this market. The thrifts in the above table will be weighted at 100% of their market share.

Results

Using the data in Exhibit 25.2, the *HHI* point values were calculated. The data show that the Department of Justice would consider this market concentrated under its 1,800 rule. These data indicate that if the Justice Department's 200-point increase rule could not be waived, no merger among any two of these

---

[3]The use of 50% weight for thrifts has evolved over time. Including thrifts in some *HHI* calculations first began following the passage of the Depository Institutions and Monetary Control Act of 1980 and the Garn-St. Germain Act of 1982. By 1987, the 50% rule was adopted. Today, the Fed will sometimes use a 100% weight for thrifts when it determines that thrifts exercise banklike powers.

EXHIBIT 25.2

Institutions, Deposits, and Market Shares in Western North County
(dollars in millions)

Institution (i)	Deposits in County	Market Share (MS_i)	Market Share Squared (MS_i^2)
County Bank	$ 55.5	11.0%	121
National Bank	123.9	24.5	600
Regional Bank	67.9	13.4	180
City Bank	78.9	15.6	243
Western S&L	123.4	24.4	595
North Savings	56.7	11.2	125
Total	$ 506.3	100.1	1,864

Western North County institutions could take place. For example, if the two smallest institutions, County Bank and North Savings, were to merge, the resulting market share would be 22.2% (11.0% + 11.2%). The new *HHI* point value for the combined institutions would be 493 (22.2²), which is higher than the addition of the two institutions' *HHI* point values of 246 (121 + 125) by more than 200. This means the only consolidation within Western North County would have to involve an institution without any offices in the county.

One way to reduce the concentration level is to agree to sell offices of the combined institution shortly after the consolidation takes place in those markets where a large increase in *HHI* occurs. When Bank of America merged with Security Pacific Bank in California in 1992, it had to sell offices in certain markets in order to reduce the level of concentration in those areas. Although the *HHI* is still used in making determinations about consolidations, the competitive climate among depository and nondepository financial institutions has become so competitive that regulators and Justice Department officials no longer rely on a strict formula-driven *HHI* assessment of market concentration.

INCREASING DIVERSIFICATION

In recent years, diversification of asset credit risk and geographical funding risks have become significant justifications for consolidation. In Chapter 11, we saw that minimizing credit risk is the cornerstone of the development of asset strategies for all intermediaries. Similar arguments can be made for diversifying funding sources from single to multiple markets. Such diversification of funding risk can help avoid local and regional economic cycles which could adversely affect funding availability and cost if it is undiversified.

Some depository regulators have encouraged the large number of consolidations among very large commercial banks in recent years as a method to reduce overall risk of failure in the financial system. Large failures in areas of the coun-

How

it

Really

Works

COMMUNITY REINVESTMENT ACT AND BANK MERGERS

The Community Reinvestment Act (CRA) was first implemented in 1978. The purpose of the CRA is to make certain that insured depository institutions serve "the convenience and needs" of the communities in which they are chartered to do business. As a practical matter, CRA relates to the lending activities of financial institutions. The act requires that the four principle depository examiners—the Federal Reserve Board, the Office of the Comptroller of the Currency, the Federal Deposit Insurance Corporation, and the Office of Thrift Supervision—encourage depositories to meet local credit needs, assess their local lending activities, and take the institution's local lending record into account when seeking approval for mergers, acquisitions, branches, and office relocations. Some lenders argue that CRA fosters unsafe and unsound lending practices and increases regulatory costs and paperwork burdens. Consumer groups, especially in low-income and minority areas, argue that CRA is the only leverage available to eliminate discrimination.

CRA has taken on additional importance since 1989, when Congress amended it to require public release of each institution's examination assessment. The ratings, from best to worst, include outstanding, satisfactory, need to improve, and substantial noncompliance. Institutions with the highest two ratings (80%–90% of all institutions) qualify for special treatment by regulators, such as expedited approval procedures for opening new branches.

Over all, the CRA provides a very big stick for encouraging depositories to meet local credit needs. Any group can make protests of applications for branches, mergers, and acquisitions on the grounds that CRA requirements are being violated. Frequently, a protest, or threat of one, will cause the institution to negotiate a settlement with a community group. Given the sharp increase in mergers and acquisitions, it is clear that CRA will play a growing role in the years ahead. This conclusion was reinforced in November 1993 when the Federal Reserve Board denied a planned acquisition of a bank by the large Shawmut Bank in Boston. Shawmut ultimately settled with the Justice Department and ended the dispute.

Source: Kenneth H. Bacon, "Shawmut Decision Shows Fed's Division over Adequacy of Fair-lending Records," *The Wall Street Journal*, Nov. 22, 1993, p. A4.

try suffering from regional economic dislocations have convinced regulators that geographical diversification of credit risk is a worthy objective.

ENHANCING MANAGEMENT INCOME

Increasing firm value is not the only factor affecting consolidation decisions of managers and directors. Some have argued that management salaries and perks and director fees are highly correlated with the institution's asset size.

Consequently, increased insider benefits are another factor that could provide an impetus to increasing firm size.

TAKING ADVANTAGE OF PROBLEM AND ASSISTED ACQUISITION OPPORTUNITIES

The record number of financial institution failures in the last decade has provided many opportunities for healthy financial institutions to expand by taking over failed institutions or purchasing branch systems. These transactions vary considerably depending on the goals of the regulators, relative supply and demand for failed institutions, and overall industry health.

When the regulators have few failed institutions, demand is high, and the general health of the industry good, the regulators can extract a good price for failed institutions, which provides the acquirer the opportunity to expand into new markets. This was the case in the early 1980s when failed thrifts were sold to out-of-state savings and loans and bank holding companies at large premiums over their core deposit values. Many savings and loans in California acquired failed thrifts in Florida and other parts of the country. During this period, Citicorp began to assemble an interstate network of savings and loans through holding company acquisitions in states from Maryland to California. Many of these early 1980 sales of failed S&Ls were done at well above these firms' liquidation values. The high prices were the result of interstate branching restrictions which restricted out-of-state deposit taking authority to BHCs, thus forcing the BHCs to agree to operate out-of-state thrifts as separate entities from their commercial banks. The small supply and strong demand led to high prices.

The opposite supply-demand balance occurred by the late 1980s and early 1990s. The passage of FIRREA in 1989 gave regulators sufficient resources to close hundreds of institutions. FIRREA-directed higher capital requirements resulted in the need for even healthy institutions to control growth in order to maintain or enhance capital ratios. Now, with the number of failed institutions for sale substantial and the number of potential buyers reduced, prices fell substantially. The average premium obtained by the Resolution Trust Corporation in the sale of core deposits of failed thrifts was 2.57% from the inception of the RTC until December 31, 1993.[4] Of those acquisitions, approximately two-thirds were purchase and assumption transactions, in which the RTC sells the deposits, certain other liabilities, and a portion of assets. In other cases, deposits were transferred to healthy institutions even though they remained liabilities of the RTC. The assisting institutions paid for only those deposits that were retained. However, the premium eventually paid was a lower .67% of the initial deposits. The balance of the institutions were resolved by direct payoff of depositors.

What the experience of this period showed was that the value of these failed institutions was almost exclusively their core deposits. There was little else in terms of valuable origination, servicing, or brokerage skills that could be sold.

---

[4]Data are available in Resolution Trust Corporation, *RTC Review*, various issues.

However, mortgage servicing portfolios were a notable exception. Some failed institutions had mortgage servicing activities that generated considerable revenue, and the regulators sold these profitably.

TAKING ADVANTAGE OF TAX LOSS CARRY-FORWARDS

Occasionally acquisitions of financial institutions are motivated partly by advantageous tax loss carry-forwards that can be used by a profitable acquiring firm. Many of the acquisitions of failed or near-failed institutions in recent years were affected by the presence of tax advantages for the acquirer.

✓ Checkpoints

25-3   What are the primary rationales for mergers and other consolidations?

25-4   Why is increasing market power important to a financial institution? What is the Herfindahl-Hirschmann Index, and how is it used to assess market concentration?

25-5   What opportunities do the sales of failed banks and thrifts provide for healthy financial institutions?

Acquisition Valuation Techniques

Establishing a value of another financial institution is a difficult activity. The price paid must encourage the existing shareholders of the acquired institution to sell and at the same time make the shareholders of the acquiring institution better off. This is easier said than done. The first part of the problem *is* easy: there is almost always some premium that can be paid to existing shareholders of the acquired institution that will coax them to part with their stock. However, once that new high price is paid, the newly consolidated institution must be able to show that its initial shareholders will be better off. This is difficult due to a process called *dilution* which results when the shareholders of an acquiring firm receive a low enough percentage of the shares in the newly consolidated firm. This section considers the process of dilution and the most common valuation techniques used in the valuation of financial institutions.

FINANCIAL BASIS FOR CONSOLIDATIONS

Have you ever seen the following scenario occur? First, an institution announces an acquisition in which it makes an offer to the shareholders of the target at a substantial premium above the target institution's share price. Then, the newspaper reports that the price of the target institution's stock went up in the day's trading following the announcement but the share price of the acquiring institution's stock fell? This is the process of dilution at work. Some shareholders of the acquiring institution obviously felt that the price offered the target institution's shareholders was too high. Too much of the added value of combining the two firms was going to the target institution's shareholders and not enough to the acquiring institution's shareholders.

There are several ways to better understand this process. Consider first what drives one institution's acquisition of another. It would make no financial sense to consolidate two firms if the combined value were not higher than the value of each of them traded separately. In algebraic terms, the post-combination market value of the consolidated firm, MV_{a+b}, must be greater than the pre-combination initial value of the acquiring institution, MV_a, plus the pre-combination market value, MV_b, of the target institution as shown in Equation 25.2:

$$MV_{a+b} > MV_a + MV_b \qquad [25.2]$$

In theory, the amount of the difference between MV_{a+b} and $(MV_a + MV_b)$ defines the maximum premium, P_{a+b}, together with transaction costs, that can be paid to the shareholders of target institution b. That is shown in Equation 25.3:

$$P_{a+b} = MV_{a+b} - (MV_a + MV_b) \qquad [25.3]$$

Put simply, an acquisition only makes sense to the shareholders of both firms if the market value of the consolidated firm, MV_{a+b}, is equal to the initial market value of firm a, MV_a, plus the initial market value of firm b plus the maximum premium $(MV_b + P_{a+b})$.

The next job is to determine the size of the premium generated by the consolidation of two firms. This premium is based on an assessment of the factors that were discussed in the previous section of this chapter. The methodologies used to determine these values is the next subject.

DISCOUNTED CASH FLOW

The most basic model of valuation is the **discounted cash flow model.** Although it is theoretically sound, in practice it is hard to estimate the input variables that are needed to compute it. One simplifying variation of a full-blown discounted cash flow model is the **Gordon constant growth model,** shown in Equation 25.4:

$$MV = D_1 \div (k - g) \qquad [25.4]$$

where:

MV = Market value of one share of equity

D_1 *= Dividends paid per share in the next period*

k = Market discount rate of similar risk class firms

g = Long-term growth rate of per share dividends

This model is discussed fully in corporate finance texts. Consequently, only a brief review is given here. This is best done by a demonstration problem.

DEMONSTRATION PROBLEM	USING DISCOUNTED CASH FLOW TO DETERMINE AN ACQUISITION PREMIUM

Situation

Valley Bank (VB) is considering the acquisition of its nearby competitor Mountain View Bank (MVB). Valley believes that acquisition would be worthwhile since it has invested in new operations software and has considerable unused capacity. It feels it could decrease the combined cost of data processing by 40% of the costs now borne by the two firms. It also feels that by eliminating overlapping branches it can reduce staff and occupancy costs by 20%. The acquisition of Mountain View would also increase Valley's growth rate of assets since Mountain View is located in high-growth markets. The offer will be made for cash. The market discount rate, k, is 12%. The growth rates in dividends for Valley and Mountain View are 3% and 6%, respectively. The next year's dividends for Valley and Mountain View are expected to be $1.20 and $.90, respectively. There are 1,000,000 Valley and 500,000 Mountain View shares outstanding. The reduction in competition, costs, and higher growth potential is expected to result in a consolidated New Valley Bank's (NVB) dividend rate growing to 5%, with next year's dividend remaining at $1.20. This assumes 1,500,000 shares of NVB stock will be outstanding.

VB management is interested in determining (1) what the relative distribution would be of NVB stock assuming MVB shareholders receive no premium over current value and (2) the highest premium that can be paid to MVB shareholders that would not reduce the market value held by existing VB shareholders.

Results

Using Gordon's growth model, it is possible to calculate the value of Valley Bank, Mountain View, and the combined bank called New Valley Bank. The value for NVB initially will be determined assuming no premium is paid:

$$VB = \$1.20 \div (.12 - .03) = \$13.33$$

$$MV = \$.90 \div (.12 - .06) = \$15.00$$

$$NVB = \$1.20 \div (.12 - .05) = \$17.14.$$

In the case of a merger of equals, in which both VB and MVB shareholders receive stock in direct proportion to their current market values, the current market valuations would be:

$$VB + MVB = (\$13.33 \times 1,000,000) + (\$15.00 \times 500,000) = \$20,830,000$$

The expected value of NVB after the merger is expected to be $(1,500,000 \times \$17.14) = \$25,710,000$. Shareholders of both banks expect to experience a sharp increase in the value of their holdings in the post-merger environment. The proportion of stock in a merger of equals that would go to VB stockholders would be ($\$13,330,000 \div \$20,830,000 =$) 64% and to MVB stockholders $(7,500,000 \div \$20,830,000) = 36\%$. VB shareholders would have $(.64 \times 1,500,000 \text{ shares}) = 960,000$ shares valued at $17.14.

Now consider a merger in which the MVB shareholders receive the entire increase in value resulting from the consolidation. The acquisition percentage, *AP*, of total NVB stock for MVB shareholders that would leave VB's shareholders no worse off from a market value perspective can be solved using the following equation, assuming the total number of shares in NVB is 1,500,000 and the number of NVB shares going to MVB shareholders would be *Y*.

$$[(1,000,000 \times \$13.33) + (1,500,000 \times AP \times \$17.14)] = 1,500,000 \times \$17.14$$

$$\$13,330,000 + (1,500,000 \times AP \times \$17.14) = \$25,710,000$$

$$AP = (\$25,710,000 - \$13,330,000) \div (\$17.14 \times 1,500,000)$$

$$AP = \$12,380,000 \div \$25,710,000 = 48.2\%$$

$$Y = .482 \times 1,500,000 = 723,000 \text{ shares}$$

The 723,000 shares is the most that could go to MVB shareholders without reducing the market value of current VB shareholders. Of course, this price also must cover the transaction costs associated with an acquisition.

In this example, VB shareholders receive lower gross dividends in the near future for higher growth prospects in the future. They will have fewer shares in NVB $(1,500,000 - 723,000 = 777,000)$, paying $1.20 per share, than they had in VB (1,000,000). In a present value sense, they are no better off and have no incentive to do the transaction. However, if they could obtain MVB's stock for less than 48.2% of total NVB shares, they would theoretically be able to obtain an increase in value.

In actuality, few if any acquisitions take place which result in such a severe decline in gross dividends going to one party as in this example.

DILUTION IN ACQUISITIONS

The demonstration problem above indicates how an acquisition can lead to lower gross dividends for the stockholders of the acquiring firm. This was called dilution. Dilution relates typically to earnings per share rather than dividends. However, dividends are usually a stable function of earnings so that the difference is usually not significant. The degree of dilution (*DOD*) of acquiring firm *a* stemming from a consolidation with firm *b* is defined as shown in Equation 25.5:

$$DOD = (\textit{Pro forma EPS}_a - \textit{Pro forma EPS}_{a+b}) \div \textit{Pro forma EPS}_a \qquad [25.5]$$

Dilution is generally considered a short-run phenomenon. That is, the shareholders of the acquiring firm expect to experience a lower *EPS* for only a few years if the consolidation is deemed successful.

DEMONSTRATION PROBLEM

CALCULATING THE DEGREE OF DILUTION (DOD)

Situation

In the case of Valley Bank shareholders in the last demonstration problem, there is significant dilution. The VB shareholders experience a significant decline in gross dividends from $(1,000,000 \times \$1.20) = \$1,200,000$ to $(775,963 \times \$1.20) = \$931,156$. Assuming that dividends are a fixed percentage of *EPS*, then what would the degree of dilution be in this case?

Results

DOD would be calculated by using Equation 25.5

$$DOD = (\$1,200,000 - \$931,156) \div \$931,156 = 28.9\%$$

Most analysts would consider a dilution of 28.9% extremely high—so high, in fact, that the acquisition would likely be rejected. Typically, dilution over 5% is considered high.

How it Really Works

BANKAMERICA PAYS DEARLY FOR SECURITY PACIFIC

The 1991 announcement that BankAmerica Corp. would acquire its largest statewide competitor, Security Pacific Corp., was a recordbreaker: it would be the largest bank merger ever. Moreover, the negotiations for the transaction took only about a month and had a $4.6 billion price tag. This is a very short time in which to assess the books of one of the nation's largest bank holding companies.

Looking back, many analysts question whether good judgment was at work. Since the acquisition, BankAmerica has had to take accounting writedowns of approximately $3.5 billion stemming from weaknesses at Security Pacific. The result is that BankAmerica stockholders experienced less than one-third of the price appreciation that holders of other large bank holding companies experienced in the two years following the merger.

While the merger is expected to result in a future payoff for shareholders, due to high dilution of BankAmerica stockholders, the price paid for Security Pacific appeared to have benefited Security shareholders more than BankAmerica.

Sources: Ralph T. King Jr, "BankAmerica Finds It Got a Lot of Woe with Security Pacific," *The Wall Street Journal*, July 22, 1993, pp. A1–A10; "Too Much at the Wrong Time?" *Fortune*, Aug. 9, 1993, p. 71.

PRICE-TO-BOOK VALUATION

Many financial institutions involved in mergers and acquisitions use a **price-to-book value model** as a standard of valuation from which to compute market value. Historically, this has been done for financial intermediaries more than commercial and industrial firms because the book values of financial firms are assumed to be close to market values. This historical convention is less valid today given the growing importance of noninterest income-generating activities which do not preserve the historical relationships between assets and capital values. A financial institution with major servicing, trust, or asset management activities will be undervalued using a simple book value multiple model.

The book value multiple valuation model simply states that the value of the controlling interest in a financial firm is equal to the market's recently established prices paid in relation to book values for similarly situated firms. The only information needed to use the model is the market price-to-book value ratio, *MPBR*, and the target firm's book value per share, BV_a. The acquisition price of firm a's stock, AP_a, would then be calculated using Equation 25.6:

$$AP_a = MPBR \times BV_a \qquad [25.6]$$

Consider the following demonstration problem.

PRICE-TO-BOOK VALUE	DEMONSTRATION PROBLEM

Situation

Bayhaven Bank has identified a bank that it is interested in acquiring. Management has asked Brian, a financial analyst, to review recent acquisitions of similar banks to determine a price-to-book valuation for the target, Sea Breeze Bank (SBB). The per share data below summarize recent acquisitions.

Acquired Firm (i)	Book Value (BV_i)	Acquisition Price (AP_i)	Price-to-Book Ratio ($MPBR_i$)
1st National	$56.00	$74.00	1.32
County National	23.50	35.90	1.53
Winston City	12.87	15.67	1.22
New Hampton	45.00	62.25	1.38
Average			1.36

SBB's book value per share is $45.00. What is a average acquisition price that Bayhaven should consider?

Result

Using the market *MPBR* of 1.36 and Equation 25.6, the acquisition price would be expected to be near

$$AP_{SBB} = 1.36 \times \$45.00 = \$61.20.$$

In light of the fact that many noninterest-earning activities are not reflected on the balance sheet, it has become customary to adjust book value ratios to account for these factors. This is known as the **adjusted book value valuation approach.** The adjustments to stated accounting book value normally considered would include recognition of such factors as:

- *Appraised value of servicing and off-balance sheet portfolio activities:* Such activities include mortgage servicing, swaps, and other profitable off-balance sheet activities.
- *Differences between market and book value for major assets:* Such assets may include real estate or securities.
- *Value of core deposits:* This factor is important when the target firm has a much higher or lower core deposit percentage as compared to the industry norms.

If upon review of Sea Breeze Bank it was determined that adjusted book value should be $51.00 instead of $45.00 per share, the new acquisition price would be $(1.36 \times \$51.00) = \$69.36$ per share.

PRICE/EARNINGS MULTIPLE (MARKET COMPARABLES)

Another approach to valuation focuses on earnings in relation to market price. This ratio is called *price/earnings multiple model.* Viewed simply, it is the dollar amount that investors are willing to pay for a dollar's worth of current earnings. The price/earnings ratio (PE) per share is calculated as shown in Equation 25.7:

$$PE = E \div MV \qquad\qquad [25.7]$$

where:

$PE = Price\ earnings\ ratio$

$E = Latest\ 12\text{-}month\ lagging\ earnings\ (or\ expected\ future$
$earnings\ can\ be\ used)$

$MV = Market\ value\ per\ share\ of\ equity$

This equation computes the *PE* ratio using the last 12 months' lagged earnings. Often analysts compute relative *PEs* using forecasts of the next 12 months' earnings. Also, any unusual aberrations that may have affected earnings can be adjusted for by using adjusted earnings amounts. The demonstration problem below will explain how the *PE* is used in valuations.

PE RATIOS USED FOR VALUATIONS	DEMONSTRATION PROBLEM

Situation

Bayhaven National has decided to consider relative *PE* ratios in their analysis of the valuation of SSB. Brian has been asked to determine an estimate of SSB's value using relative *PE* ratios for recently acquired banks shown in the table below. SBB's earnings in the last 12 months were $4.10 per share.

Acquired Firm (i)	Earnings (E_i)	Acquisition Price (AP_i)	Price/Earnings Ratio $(PE_i) = (AP_i / E_i)$
1st National	$4.72	$74.00	15.7
County National	2.20	35.90	16.3
Winston City	1.02	15.67	15.4
New Hampton	3.98	62.25	15.6
Average			15.8

Result

Using the average *PE* ratio for the recently acquired group of institutions, Brian estimated that an acquisition price, AP_{SBB}, for SBB would be close to

$$AP_{SBB} = \$4.10 \text{ per share} \times 15.8 = \$64.78 \text{ per share}$$

✓ Checkpoints

25-6 Financially, how would you explain the justification for consolidating two financial firms?

25-7 What is the role of dilution in the merger process?

25-8 What are the discounted cash flow, book-value multiple, and P/E multiple valuation models, and how are they used in acquisitions?

Nonfinancial Factors in Consolidations

Although considerable time is spent on the financial characteristics of mergers, there are many nonfinancial factors that should be considered. These involve the banks' human resources, customers, and consolidation processes. We will consider each of these.

CONSOLIDATION'S IMPACT ON HUMAN RESOURCES

Consolidations rarely provide jobs of comparable positions for directors, officers, and other personnel of the combined bank. **Mergers of equals,** frequently heard as a goal in many merger announcements, are rarely achieved. Different skills, work ethics, and demographics usually cause the management of one institution to dominate the other. There is rarely room on the board of directors for the directors of the two merged organizations, usually leading to disgruntled directors. Some organizations handle this by offering valuable early retirement programs and creating **advisory boards,** groups that provide advice to management without legal standing the firm. At lower organization levels, consolidation leads to tension which hurts productivity and may cause very capable staff to seek employment elsewhere. Organizations in turmoil frequently are targets of raids by competitors.

Organizations that combine also rarely have the same wage and salary structures or benefit packages. Bringing the lower wage, salary, and benefit package up to the higher of the two organizations can be costly and may be inappropriate. Yet, uniformity will need to be achieved at some point.

The cultures of two organizations are never the same. Work ethic and styles differ. One style may be preferred over another. This usually means altering behavior of staff who are used to doing things differently and recognizing that these people will likely depart.

CONSOLIDATION'S IMPACT ON CUSTOMERS

Customers are almost always affected by consolidations. This can take the form of customers having to adjust to new employees in a branch or to statements of different designs. Practitioners will tell you that it takes a very unhappy customer to move a transaction account from one institution to another. However, a certificate of deposit is easy to move. Consequently, management of consolidated institutions typically develop customer retention programs in order to retain as high a percentage of customers as possible. It is also common for competitors to target merged institutions for special programs to attract unhappy customers. Customers who experience the moving or closing of a branch are easy targets for such programs.

Larger customers, such as business borrowers, also must be targeted for possible special consideration during a consolidation. Frequently, two lenders have different lending guidelines, resulting in some borrowers finding that they do not meet the new requirements of the combined entity. This can lead to losses of valued customers.

Another group affected by mergers comprises community leaders and social organizations dependent on the firms. Usually a merger means that a corporate office has been lost in a community. Such a loss can be significant for the social organizations that rely on that firm for donations and other support. Management must be very mindful of these relationships because civic groups can challenge mergers under such authority as the Community Reinvestment Act. Even if the challenge is unsuccessful, the process can hold up a merger for a long time.

CONSOLIDATION'S IMPACT ON OPERATIONS

Consolidations always involve major changes in operations for the combined organizations. Computer systems must be merged, policies and procedures for the new organization decided upon, and marketing programs revamped. Virtually every report and customer statement must be changed for at least one of the institutions' customers.

Pricing is another major issue since two organizations rarely have the same fee schedule. This necessitates a careful analysis of how any revision of pricing or services will affect the firm's customers. All these changes require difficult changes in operating systems and notification of customers.

✓ Checkpoints

25-9 What are the primary nonfinancial factors to consider in a merger?

25-10 What are the most difficult issues to deal with in terms of human resources in a merger?

SUMMARY AND REVIEW

1. **Discuss recent trends in the mergers and acquisitions of financial service companies.**

   The deregulation of the financial service industry in the 1980s combined with rising capital requirements for most depository institutions in the 1990s have given rise to a significant increase in the number of acquisitions and mergers.

2. **Describe the basic sources of value and other rationales used in determining the value created by a consolidation.**

   The primary operating rationales prompting consolidation include **expanding markets, extending expertise** in origination, servicing, and brokerage, **increasing market power, cutting costs** through economies of scale, and **increasing diversification.** In addition, the **large number of failed institutions** has provided many acquisition opportunities. These sometimes provide valuable **tax loss carry-forwards.** Finally, **management is motivated** to grow institutions since salaries and other benefits are related to size.

   One of the complicating aspects of consolidating firms is to avoid an antitrust challenge. The **Herfindahl-Hirschmann Index** is used to assess the presence of excessive market power.

3. **Explain the primary techniques used for the valuation of acquisition targets.**

   The primary technique for valuation of financial institutions is **discounted cash flow.** This can be used to value firms prior to consolidation and then on a pro forma post-consolidation basis. A major concern for an acquiring institution is to avoid **dilution** of its current shareholders. In addition, less-complicated techniques, such as **price-to-book multiple** and **P/E multiple,** can be used.

4. **Describe the most important nonfinancial factors to be considered in mergers.**

   The most important nonfinancial factors in the merger process relate to handling **human resource, customer,** and **operational** issues.

PROBLEMS | **HERFINDAHL-HIRSCHMANN INDEX**

25-1

Southwestern County Bank is considering acquiring Williams Bank. They will unite to become a major institution in a three-county area. The Justice Department and the banks' regulator are looking into the merger to determine whether it could monopolize the market in these three countries. The following data have been assembled on deposit market shares in this market. Using the Herfindahl-Hirschmann Index and the 1,800/200 rule, assess the impact on competition stemming from the merger. Assume savings and loans and savings banks are weighted equal to commercial banks.

Institution	Deposits in Three Counties
First Bank	$123.9
Riverside Bank	9.0
Southwest Bank	23.9
Highline S&L	101.9
Williams Bank	65.8
South Savings	12.0
Southwestern City	123.5
Total	$460.0

BOOK AND P/E MULTIPLES

25-2

Mainland Federal is considering an acquisition of Hartland Savings. Marion Wells, the financial officer, has obtained data on a number of recent acquisitions of institutions similar to Hartland. These data are shown in the table below. Using the price-to-book and P/E multiple valuation approaches, Marion has asked you to come up with a ballpark estimate of Hartland's stock value.

Acquired Firm	Earnings	Acquisition Price	Book Value
Brisbane Savings	$6.75	$91.13	$68.00
Bayside National	.90	12.78	9.00
Big City National	3.45	44.51	34.50
New Cairo Savings	5.87	79.83	57.43
Hartland	3.12	?	34.12

DILUTION

25-3

Springvalley National Bank is considering acquiring City State Bank in a stock for stock transaction. The pro forma earnings per share for Springvalley

National Bank next year are forecast to be $3.25 per share. The post-merger earnings per share are forecast to be $2.95 at the stock exchange ratio contemplated. Mr. Washington is concerned about dilution. What degree of dilution is anticipated in this transaction?

CASE 25.1

STRUCTURING A MERGER PROPOSAL

Sheila was excited. Mary Fairberg, vice president of Colonial First Bank (CFB), had asked her to be the principal analyst for a possible acquisition. CFB had grown from $3.2 billion in total assets to $5.7 billion in a little over three years. This growth took place through a series of seven acquisitions of small to medium-sized banks in the Midwest.

Today, senior management of CFB has its sights set on the possible acquisition of Upper Arlington National Bank (UANB). UANB was an old-line institution that was controlled by the Williamson family trust. Brian Williamson, Sr., now deceased, founded the bank in 1937. Over the years, conservative management created a bank that today has $1.35 billion in assets. UANB is primarily a retail institution, which derives a very high 87% of total liabilities from transaction, time, and savings deposits from 35 branches. The bank's loan and investment portfolio consists of a higher-than-industry-average percentage in U.S. government and agency securities, mortgage-backed securities, collateralized mortgage obligations, and a lower-than-industry-average percentage of commercial, mortgage, and consumer loans. The bank is proud of its "tough underwriting policies" and "by the book" philosophy of lending. UANB's conservative lending policies make it difficult to attract business customers, so the bank emphasizes retail consumer products and services. It has a very large automated teller network, and most of its branches have costly drive-up windows.

CFB management felt for years that UANB would be a good acquisition, but the Williamson family did not consider a sale until recently. Estate problems have made a sale virtually essential. CFB managers feel that an acquisition could substantially improve UANB's performance. After the acquisition, CFB plans to absorb eight of UANB's branches into existing CFB branches. The objective is to cut overhead and reduce investment in brick and mortar. They estimate savings of over $400,000 per year. CFB also plans to eliminate all of UANB's middle and senior management because they do not have the same business philosophy as CFB management and are redundant—an action that would save $2.1 million per year. CFB also plans to alter UANB's ultra-conservative investment strategy by adding more business loans, real estate, and consumer loans, which could increase the net interest margin by up to $450,000 per year. A more aggressive marketing program and expanded business and consumer loan product line are expected to add 3% to UANB's historical growth rate.

Sheila began her analysis by assembling data on recently acquired commercial banks near the size of UANB. The date of the merger, asset size, book value per share, acquisition price per share, and previous 12 months earnings per share are presented in Table C25.1.

TABLE C25.1

Selected Data on Recent Bank Acquisitions

Bank Acquired	Date of Acquisition	Asset Size (in millions)	Book Value per Share	Acquisition Price per Share	Previous 12 Months' Earnings per Share
Pleasant Valley Bank	Oct. 1, 1995	$ 543	$20.25	$ 36.45	$1.78
Merchant Bank	Nov. 15, 1995	1,420	17.75	29.28	1.69
Second National Bank	Jan. 10, 1996	982	47.50	90.25	4.10
Meridian County Bank	Feb. 12, 1996	1,130	82.75	144.81	8.77
Mountain Valley Bank	Feb. 15, 1996	700	90.00	166.50	5.15*

*Mountain View experienced an extraordinary loss of $3.05 per share after taxes related to a tax dispute dating back to 1987.

CFS stock sells for $35.50 per share, its book value is $29.75, and its previous 12 month's earnings are $4.10 per share. CFS has 15.3 million shares outstanding. It has experienced a 5.5% growth in dividends over the last three years, which is expected to continue. Next year's dividend will be $2.75 per share. UANB sells for $40.25 per share, has a book value of $37.50, and earned $3.90 per share last year. There are 3.3 million UANB shares outstanding. UANB, by contrast, has a dividend growth rate of 2% and will pay $3.20 per share next year. This rate is likely to continue given the bank's current management and strategy.

CFS senior management told Sheila that changing CFS's marketing program and investment strategy and cost cutting can result in a combined CFS-UANB growth rate in earning and dividends of 6.5% per annum. The market discount rate for banks similar to CFS is 11%.

CFS management would like to make an acquisition using CFS stock. If the acquisition is made with stock, CFS would keep the dividend at $2.75 per share, but it expects the growth rate to increase. However, they are prepared to make a cash offer if necessary, which would necessitate an issue of new common stock.

Problems

1. Based on average acquisition price-to-book valuation, what price would represent a reasonable bid for UANB?

2. Based on recent price/earnings multiples of recent acquisition, what would represent a reasonable bid for UANB?

3. CFB management is interested in determining what the relative distribution would be of UANB stock assuming UANB shareholders receive no premium over current value. Then they would like to determine the highest premium that can be paid to UANB shareholders that would not reduce the market value held by existing CFB shareholders.

References

Chapter 1

Arthur Andersen & Co. *Business Ethics Program: Finance Materials.* 1992.

Bauman, W. S. "Standards of Professional Conduct." In *The Financial Analyst's Handbook.* Edited by S. W. Levine, 1809–20. Homewood, Ill.: Dow Jones-Irwin, 1988.

Chemmanur, Thomas J., and Paolo Fulghieri. "Investment Bank Reputation, Information Production, and Financial Intermediation." *Journal of Finance* (March 1994): 57–80.

Fisher, Irving. *The Theory of Interest.* New York: The Macmillan Co., 1930.

Flannery, Mark. "Asymmetric Information and Risky Debt Maturity." *Journal of Finance* (March 1986): 19–38.

Friedman, Benjamin M. "Effects of Shifting Savings Patterns on Interest Rates and Economic Activity." *Journal of Finance* (March 1982): 37–62.

Henning, Charles, William Pigott, and Robert H. Haney. *Financial Markets and the Economy.* Englewood Cliffs, N.J.: Prentice-Hall, 1988.

Hoffman, M. W., and J. M. Moore. *Business Ethics.* New York: McGraw-Hill, 1990.

Jensen, M. C., and W. Meckling. "Theory of the Firm: Managerial Behaviour, Ownership Costs and the Ownership Structure," *Journal of Financial Economics* 3 (1976): 305–360.

Kaufman, Henry. *Interest Rates, the Markets, and the New Financial World.* New York: Times Books, 1986.

Loab, S. E. "The Evaluation of Outcomes of Accounting Ethics Education." *Journal of Business Ethics* (Feb. 1993): 77–84.

Metzler, L. A. "Wealth, Saving, and the Rate of Interest." *Journal of Political Economy* (April 1951): 93–116.

Smith, C. W., Jr. "Economics and Ethics: The Case of Salomon Brothers." *Journal of Applied Corporate Finance* (Summer 1992): 23–28.

Veit, E. T., and M. R. Murphy. *Ethics in the Investment Profession: A Survey* (Monograph). The Research Foundation of the Institute of Chartered Financial Analysts, 1992.

Walter, I. *Deregulating Wall Street.* New York: John Wiley & Sons, 1985.

Chapter 2

Allan, Franklin. "Information Contracting in Financial Markets." In *Financial Markets and Incomplete Information.* Edited by Sudipto Bhattacharya and George M. Constantinides. Savage, Md.: Rowman and Littlefield, 1989.

Baron, D. P. "A Model of the Demand for Investment Banking, Advising, and Distributions Services for New Issues." *Journal of Finance* 37 (1982): 955–76.

Baron, D. P., and B. Holmstrom. "The Investment Banking Contract for New Issues under Asymmetric Information: Delegation and the Incentive Problem." *Journal of Finance* (Dec. 1980): 1115–58.

Benston, George J., and Clifford W. Smith, Jr. "The Transaction Cost Approach to the Theory of Financial Intermediation." *Journal of Finance* (May 1976): 215–33.

Campbell, T. "Optimal Corporate Financing Decisions and the Value of Confidentiality." *Journal of Financial and Quantitative Analysis* (1979): 913–25.

Campbell, T., and M. Kracow. "Information Production, Market Signalling and the Theory of Financial Intermediation." *Journal of Finance* 35 (1980): 863–82.

Chan, Y. "On the Positive Role of Financial Intermediaries in Allocation of Venture Capital in a Market with Imperfect Information." *Journal of Finance* 38 (1983): 1543–68.

Deshmukh, Sudhakar D., Stuart I. Greenbaum, and George Kanatas. "Lending Policies of Financial Intermediaries Facing Credit and Funding Risk." *Journal of Finance* (June 1983): 873–86.

Diamond, Douglas. "Financial Intermediation and Delegated Monitoring." *Review of Economic Studies* 51 (1984): 393–414.

———. "Asset Services and Financial Intermediation." In *Financial Markets and Incomplete Information.* Edited by Sudipto Bhattacharya and George M. Constantinides. Savage, Md.: Rowman and Littlefield, 1989.

Fama, Eugene. "Banking in the Theory of Finance." *Journal of Monetary Economics* (1980): 39–57.

Greenbaum, Stuart I., and Bryon Higgins. "Financial Innovation." In *Financial Services: The Changing Institutions and Government Policy.* Englewood Cliffs, N.J.: Prentice-Hall, American Assembly, Columbia University, 1983.

Gurley, J. G., and E. S. Shaw. *Money in a Theory of Finance.* Washington, D.C.: Brookings Institution, 1960.

Leland, H., and D. Pyle. "Information Asymmetries, Financial Structure and Financial Intermediation." *Journal of Finance* 32 (1977): 371–87.

Pesek, Boris P. "Banks' Supply Function and the Equilibrium Quantity of Money." *Canadian Journal of Economics* (Aug. 1970): 357–83.

Pyle, David. "Descriptive Theories of Financial Institutions." *Journal of Financial and Quantitative Analysis.* (Dec. 1972): 2009–29.

Ross, Stephan A. "Institutional Markets, Financial Marketing, and Financial Innovation." *Journal of Finance* (July 1989): 541–56.

Sealey, C. W., Jr. "Valuation, Capital Structure, and Shareholder Unanimity for Depository Financial Intermediaries." *Journal of Finance* (June 1983): 857–71.

Tobin, J. "Commercial Banks and Creators of Money." In *Banking and Monetary Studies.* Edited by D. Carson. Homewood, Ill.: Richard D. Irwin, Inc., 1963.

Tobin, J., and W. Brainard. "Financial Intermediaries and the Effectiveness of Monetary Control." *American Economic Review* 53 (1963): 383–400.

Towey, Richard E. "Money Creation and the Theory of the Banking Firm." *Journal of Finance* (March 1974): 57–72.

Chapter 3

Allen, Everett, J. Melone, J. Rosenbloom, and J. Vanderhei. *Pension Planning.* Homewood, Ill.: Richard D. Irwin, Inc., 1988.

Arnott, Robert, and Peter L. Bernstein. "The Right Way to Manage Your Pension Fund." *Harvard Business Review* (Jan.–Feb. 1988): 95–102.

Babble, David F. "The Price Elasticity of Demand for Whole Life Insurance." *Journal of Finance* (March 1985): 225–39.

Baldwin, Ben G., and William G. Droms. *The Life Insurance Investment Advisor.* Chicago: Probus Publishing, 1988.

Barth, James R., and Philip R. Wiest. "Consolidation and Restructuring of the U.S. Thrift Industry under the Financial Institutions Reform, Recovery, and Enforcement Act." Office of Thrift Supervision, Research Paper 89-01 (Oct. 1989).

Benston, George J., ed. *Financial Services: The Changing Institutions and Government Policy.* Englewood Cliffs, N.J.: Prentice-Hall, 1983.

————. "U.S. Banking in an Increasingly Integrated and Competitive World Economy." *Journal of Financial Services Research* (Dec. 1990): 311–39.

Bloch, Ernest. *Inside Investment Banking.* Homewood, Ill.: Dow Jones-Irwin, 1986.

Federal Financial Institutions Examination Council, Federal Deposit Insurance Corporation. Trust Assets of Financial Institutions, 1988. Washington, D.C.: The Council. 1989.

Credit Union National Association. *The Credit Union Report.* Madison, Wis.: Annually.

Flannery, Mark J. "Credit Unions as Consumer Lenders in the United States." *New England Economic Review.* Federal Reserve Bank of Boston (July/Aug. 1974): 3–12.

Furlong, Frederick T. "Savings and Loan Asset Composition and the Mortgage Market." *Economic Review.* Federal Reserve Bank of San Francisco (Summer 1985): 14–24.

Goudreau, Robert E., and B. Frank King. "Recovering Bank Profitability: Spoiled Again by Large Banks' Loan Problems." *Economic Review.* Federal Reserve Bank of Atlanta (May/June 1990): 30–43.

Haight, G. Timothy, and Deborah Ann Ford. *REITs: New Opportunities in Real Estate Investment Trust Securities.* Chicago: Probus Publishing, 1986.

Haraf, William S., and Rose Marie Kushmeider, eds. *Restructuring Banking and Financial Services in America.* Washington, D.C.: American Enterprise Institute for Public Policy Research, 1988.

Heaton, Gary G., and Constance R. Dunham. "The Growing Competitiveness of Credit Unions." *New England Economic Review.* Federal Reserve Bank of Boston (May/June 1985): 19–34.

Hendershott P. H., and J. D. Shilling. "The Impact of the Agencies on Conventional Fixed-Rate Mortgage Yields." *Journal of Real Estate Finance and Economics* (June 1989): 101–15.

———. "Reforming Conforming Loan Limits: The Impact on Thrift Earnings and Taxpayer Outlays." *Journal of Financial Services Research* (Dec. 1989): 311–31.

Industry Outlook on Property/Casualty Insurance. New York: Standard & Poor's Corporation, 1990.

Jesse, Michael A., and Stephen A. Seelig. *Bank Holding Companies and the Public Interest: An Economic Analysis.* Lexington, Mass.: D. C. Heath, 1977.

Kane, E., and C. Foster. "Valuing Conjectural Government Guarantees of FNMA Liabilites." *Proceedings of the Conference on Bank Structure and Competition* (May 1986): 347–68.

Kaufman, George G. "Security Activities of Commercial Banks: Recent Changes in Economic and Legal Environments." *Midland Corporate Finance Journal* (Winter 1988): 14–23.

Kaufman, H. M. "FNMA's Role in Deregulated Markets: Implications for Past Behavior." *Journal of Money, Credit and Banking* (Nov. 1988): 673–83.

Keeley, Michael C. "Deposit Insurance, Risk, and Market Poser in Banking." *American Economic Review* (Dec. 1990): 1183–1200.

LeCompte, Richard L. B., and Stephen Smith. "Changes in the Cost of Intermediation." *The Journal of Finance* (Sept. 1990): 1337–46.

Leibowitz, Martin L. "Total Portfolio Duration: A New Perspective on Asset Allocation." *Financial Analysts Journal* (Sept./Oct. 1986): 18–29.

Masulis, Ronald. "Changes in Ownership Structure: Conversions of Mutual Savings and Loans to Stock Charter." *Journal of Financial Economics* (March 1987): 29–54.

McGee, Robert T. "The Cycle in Property/Casualty Insurance." *Quarterly Review.* Federal Reserve Bank of New York (Autumn 1986): 22–30.

Mengle, David L. "The Case for Interstate Branch Banking." *Economic Review.* Federal Reserve Bank of Richmond (Nov.–Dec. 1990): 3–17.

Neely, Walter, and David Rochester. "Operating Performance and Merger Benefits: The Savings and Loan Experience." *Financial Review* (Feb. 1987): 111–30.

Neihengen, Raymond, Jr., and Mark L. McClure. "Analysis of Finance Company Ratios in 1984." *Journal of Commercial Bank Lending* (Sept. 1985): 40–49.

Pearce, Douglas K. "Recent Developments in the Credit Union Industry." *Economic Review*. Federal Reserve Bank of Kansas City (June 1984).

President's Commission on Housing. *The Report of the President's Commission on Housing*. Washington, D.C.: U.S. Government Printing Office, 1982.

Public Policy in Flux. Cambridge, Mass.: Ballinger, 1986.

Rose, Peter S. *The Changing Structure of American Banking*. New York: Columbia Univ. Press, 1987.

————. *The Interstate Banking Revolution*. New York: Quorum Books, 1989.

Thygerson, Kenneth J. "Privately Owned Federally Sponsored Credit Agencies Impact Depositories." *Journal of the School of Business, San Francisco State University* (June 1992): 33–38.

U.S. Congress Congressional Budget Office. *Controlling the Risks of Government Sponsored Enterprises*. Washington, D.C.: U.S. Government Printing Office, April 1991.

————. *A Framework for Limiting the Government's Exposure to Risks, Report to Congress*. Washington, D.C.: U.S. Government Printing Office, May 1991.

U.S. Department of Housing and Urban Development, Office of Policy Development and Research. *Report to Congress on the Federal Home Loan Bank System*. Washington, D.C.: The Department, April 1994.

U.S. Department of the Treasury. *Report of the Secretary of the Treasury on Government Sponsored Enterprises*. Washington, D.C.: The Department, May 1990.

————. *Report of the Secretary of the Treasury on Government-Sponsored Enterprises*. Washington D.C.: The Department, April 1991.

U.S. General Accounting Office. *Government Sponsored Enterprises: A Framework for Limiting the Government's Exposure to Risks*. Washington, D.C.: U.S. Government Printing Office, May 1991.

————. *Government Sponsored Enterprises: The Government's Exposure to Risks*. Washington, D.C.: U.S. Government Printing Office, Aug. 1990.

————. *Government Sponsored Enterprises: System of Internal Controls at Freddie Mac, Fannie Mae, and Sallie Mae*. Washington, D.C.: U.S. Government Printing Office, May 1991.

Wall, Larry D., Alan K. Reichert, and Sunil Mohanty. "Deregulation and the Opportunities for Commercial Bank Diversification," *Economic Review*. Federal Reserve Bank of Atlanta (Sept./Oct. 1993): 1–15.

Warshawsky, Mark J. "The Funding of Private Pension Funds." *Federal Reserve Bulletin* (Nov. 1987): 853–54.

Weicher, John C. "The New Structure of the Housing Finance System," *Review*. Federal Reserve Bank of St. Louis (July/Aug. 1994): 47–66.

Williamson, J. Peter. *The Investment Banking Handbook*. New York: John Wiley & Sons, 1988.

Zarb, Frank G., ed. *Handbook of Financial Markets,* 2nd ed. Homewood, Ill.: Dow Jones-Irwin, 1986: 462–84.

Zimmer, Steven A., and Robert N. McCauley. "Bank Cost of Capital and International Competition." *Quarterly Review*. Federal Reserve Bank of New York (Winter 1991): 33–59.

Chapter 4

Benston, George J. "Federal Regulation of Banking: Analysis and Policy Recommendations." *Journal of Bank Research* (Winter 1983): 216–44.

———. "Mortgage Redlining Research: A Review and Critical Analysis." In *The Regulation of Financial Institutions*. Federal Reserve Bank of Boston, Conference Series no. 21 (Oct. 1979): 144–95.

Benston, George J., and George G. Kaufman. "Risk and Solvency Regulation of Depository Institutions: Past Policies and Current Options." Federal Reserve Bank of Chicago, Staff memorandum SM 88-1, 1988.

Buser, Stephen, Andrew H. Chen, and Edward J. Kane. "Federal Deposit Insurance Regulatory Policy, and Optimal Bank Capital." *Journal of Finance* (March 1981): 512–60.

Chan, Y. S., S. I. Greenbaum, and A. V. Thakor. "Is Fairly Priced Deposit Insurance Possible?" *Journal of Finance* 47 (1992): 227–46.

Flannery, Mark J. "Deposit Insurance Creates a Need for Bank Regulation." *Business Review*. Federal Reserve Bank of Philadelphia (Jan./Feb. 1982): 17–27.

Holmes, Andrew, and Paul Horvitz, "Mortgage Redlining: Race, Risk, and Demand," *Journal of Finance* (March 1994): 8–100.

Horvitz, Paul M. "Reorganization of the Financial Regulatory Agencies." *Journal of Bank Research* (Winter 1983): 245–63.

Kane, Edward J. "Accelerating Inflation, Technological Innovation, and the Decreasing Effectiveness of Banking Regulation." *Journal of Finance* (May 1981): 355–67.

———. "Good Intentions and Unintended Evil: The Case against Selective Credit Allocation." *Journal of Money, Credit and Banking* (Feb. 1977): 55–69.

———. "Principal-Agent Problems in S&L Salvage." *Journal of Finance* (July 1990): 755–64.

Keeley, Michael C. "Deposit Insurance, Risk, and Market Power in Banking." *American Economic Review* (Dec. 1990): 1183–200.

Maisal, Sherman J., ed. *Risk and Capital Adequacy in Commercial Banks*. Chicago: Univ. of Chicago Press, 1981.

McDowell, Banks. *Deregulation and Competition in the Insurance Industry*. New York: Quorum Books, 1989.

Meier, Kenneth J. *The Political Economy of Regulation: The Case of Insurance*. Albany: State Univ. of New York Press, 1988.

Peterson, Manferd O. "Regulatory Objectives and Conflicts." In *Handbook for Banking Strategy*. Edited by Richard C. Aspinwall and Robert A. Eisenbeis. New York: John Wiley & Sons, 1985.

Stigler, George J. "The Theory of Economic Regulation." *Bell Journal of Economics and Management* (Spring 1971): 3–21.

Todd, Walker F. "FDICIA's Emergency Liquidity Provisions." *Economic Review* 29, no. 3 (1993): 16.

Wheelock, David C., and Paul W. Wilson. "Can Deposit Insurance Increase the Risk of Bank Failure? Some Historical Evidence." *Review*. Federal Reserve Bank of St. Louis (May/June 1994): 57–71.

Chapter 5

Chuppe, Tery M., Hugh R. Haworth, and Marvin G. Watkins. "Global Finance: Causes, Consequences and Prospects for the Future." *Global Finance Journal* (Fall 1989): 1–20.

Clarke, William M. *How the City of London Works: An Introduction to Its Financial Markets.* London: Waterlow Publishers, 1986.

Emerging Stock Markets Factbook 1990. Washington, D.C.: International Finance Corporation, 1990.

Francke, Hans-Hermann, and Michael Hudson. *Banking and Finance in West Germany.* London: Helm Ltd., 1984.

Graham, Edward M., and Paul R. Krugman. *Foreign Direct Investment in the United States*, vol. 10. Washington D.C.: Institute for International Economics, 1989.

Grauer, R., and N. H. Hakansson. "Gains from International Diversification: 1968–85 Returns on Portfolios of Stock and Bonds." *Journal of Finance* (July 1987): 721–38.

Grundfest, Joseph A. "Internationalization of the World's Securities Markets." *Journal of Financial Services Research* (Dec. 1990): 95–125.

Hirtle, Beverly. "Factors Affecting the Competitiveness of Internationally Active Financial Institutions." *Quarterly Review.* Federal Reserve Bank of New York (Spring 1991): 38–51.

Lessaw, S. "World, Country and Industry Relationships in Equity Returns: Implications for Risk Reduction through International Diversification." *Financial Analyst's Journal* (Jan.–Feb., 1976): 32.

McCauley, Robert N., and Lauren A. Hargraves. "Eurocommercial Paper and U.S. Commercial Paper: Converging Money Markets?" *Quarterly Review.* Federal Reserve Bank of New York (Autumn 1987): 24–35.

Pardee, Scott E. "Internationalization of Financial Markets." *Economic Review.* Federal Reserve Bank of Kansas City (Feb. 1987): 3–7.

Pavel, Christine, and John N. McElravey. "Globalization in the Financial Services Industry." *Economic Perspectives.* Federal Reserve Bank of Chicago (May/June 1990): 3–18.

Rosenbaum, Amy. "Coming to America: Foreign Products Hit U.S. Shores." *Futures* (May 1990): 50.

Rowley, Anthony. "Asian Stockmarkets: The Inside Story." *Far Eastern Economic Review* (1987).

Securities and Exchange Commission. *Internationalization of the Securities Markets: Report to the Senate Committee on Banking, Housing, and Urban Affairs and the House Committee on Energy and Commerce* (July 1987).

Solnik, B. *International Investments.* (Reading Mass.: Addison-Wesley), 1988.

Strongin, Steven. "International Credit Market Connections." *Economic Perspectives.* Federal Reserve Bank of Chicago (July/Aug. 1990): 2–10.

Third-World Finance. *The Economist.* (Sept. 25, 1993): 15–44.

Viner, Aron. *Inside Japanese Financial Markets* Homewood, Ill.: Dow Jones-Irwin, 1968.

Watson, Maxwell, et al. *International Capital Markets: Developments and Prospects.* Washington, D.C.: International Monetary Fund, 1988.

Chapter 6

Barth, James R., R. Dan Brumbaugh, Jr., and Robert E Litan. *The Future of American Banking.* Armonk, N.Y.: M. W. Sharpe, Inc., 1992.

Benston, George J., Robert A. Eisenbeis, Paul M. Horvitz, Edward J. Kane, and George G. Kaufman. *Perspectives on Safe and Sound Banking: Past, Present, and Future.* Cambridge, Mass.: MIT Press and American Banking Association, 1986.

Bernard, Victor L., Roger C. Kormendi, S. Craig Pirrong, and Edward A. Snyder. *Crisis Revolution in the Thrift Industry.* Boston: Kluwer Academic Publishers, 1989.

Cargill, Thomas F., and Gillian C. Garcia. *Financial Reform in the 1980s.* Stanford, Calif.: Hoover Institution Press, 1985.

Carron, Andrew S. *The Rescue of the Thrift Industry: Studies in Regulation of Economic Activity.* Washington, D.C.: The Brookings Institution, 1983.

Hendershott, Patric, and J. D. Shilling. "The Impact of the Agencies on Conventional Fixed-rate Mortgage Yields." *Journal of Real Estate Finance and Economics* (June 1989): 101–15.

———. "Reforming Conforming Loan Limits: The Impact on Thrift Earnings and Taxpayer Outlays." *Journal of Financial Services Research* (Dec. 1989): 311–31.

Kane, Edward J. "Accelerating Inflation, Technological Innovation, and the Decreasing Effectiveness of Banking Regulation." *Journal of Finance* (May 1981): 355–67.

———. "Deregulation and Changes in the Financial Services Industry." *Journal of Finance* (July 1984): 759–72.

———. *The Gathering Crisis in Deposit Insurance.* Cambridge, Mass.: MIT Press, 1985.

Kaufman, George G., and Larry R. Mote. "Is Banking a Declining Industry? A Historical Perspective." *Economic Perspectives.* Federal Reserve Bank of Chicago (May/June 1994): 2.

Keeton, William R. "Causes of the Recent Increase in Bank Security Holdings." *Economic Review.* Federal Reserve Bank of Kansas City, 79, no. 2 (1994): 45–58.

National Commission on Financial Institution Reform, Recovery and Enforcement. *Origins and Causes of the S&L Debacle: A Blueprint for Reform.* Washington, D.C.: U.S. Government Printing Office, July 1993.

Pierce, James L. *The Future of Banking.* New Haven: Yale Univ. Press, 1991.

Samolyk, Katherine A., and Rebecca Wetmore Humes. "Does Small Business Need a Financial Fix?" *Economic Commentary.* Federal Reserve of Cleveland (May 15, 1993).

Taylor, Jeremy F. *The Banking System in Troubled Times.* New York: Quorum Books, 1989.

Walker, David A. "Effects of Deregulation on the Savings and Loan Industry." *Financial Review* (Spring 1983): 94–110.

White, Lawrence J. *The S&L Debacle: Public Policy Lessons for Bank and Thrift Regulation.* New York: Oxford Univ. Press, 1991.

Chapter 7

Andrews, Suzanna, and Henny Sender. "Off Balance Sheet Risk: Where Is It Leading Banks?" *Institutional Investor* (Jan. 1986): 75–84.

Bennett, Barbara. "Off-Balance Sheet Risk in Banking: The Case of Standby Letters of Credit." *Economic Review.* Federal Reserve Bank of San Francisco (Winter 1986): 19–29.

Kopcke, Richard W. "The Federal Income Taxation of Life Insurance Companies." *New England Economic Review.* Federal Reserve Bank of Boston (March/April 1985): 42–48.

Wall, Larry D. "Nonbank Activities and Risk," *Economic Review.* Federal Reserve Bank of Atlanta (Oct. 1986): 19–34.

Chapter 8

Aggregated Thrift Financial Report. Office of Thrift Supervision, annual.

Annual Statistical Digest. Washington, D.C.: Board of Governors of the Federal Reserve System.

Brunner, Allan D., John V. Duca, and Mary M. McLaughlin. "Recent Developments Affecting the Profitability and Practices of Commercial Banks." *Federal Reserve Bulletin.* Washington, D.C.: Board of Governors of the Federal Reserve System (July 1991): 505–27.

Finance Facts Yearbook. Washington, D.C.: American Financial Services Association.

Life Insurance Fact Book. Washington, D.C.: American Council of Life Insurance.

Mutual Fund Fact Book. Washington, D.C.: Investment Company Institute.

REIT Fact Book. Washington, D.C.: National Association of Real Estate Investment Trusts, Inc.

Statistics on Banking. Washington, D.C.: Federal Deposit Insurance Corporation, annual.

Year-End Statistical Report. Washington, D.C.: National Credit Union Administration, annual.

Chapter 9

Aspinwall, Robert, and Robert Eisenbeis, eds. *Handbook for Banking Strategy.* New York: John Wiley & Sons, 1985.

Booker, Irene, and Robert Rogowski. "Long-Term Bank Management." *Bankers Magazine* (May/June 1987).

Gregor, William T. "Strategic Planning of Consumer Financial Services." In *The Emerging Financial Industry: Implications for Insurance Products, Portfolios, and Planning.* Edited by Arnold W. Sametz. Lexington, Mass.: Lexington Books, 1984.

Kane, Edward J. "Accelerating Inflation, Technological Innovation, and the Decreasing Effectiveness of Banking Regulation." *Journal of Finance* (1981).

———. "Microeconomic and Macroeconomic Origins of Financial Innovation." In *Financial Innovations*. Federal Reserve Bank of St. Louis. Boston: Kluwer Nijhoff Publishing, 1984.

Kauss, James. "A Guide to Strategic Planning for Banks." *Bank Administration* (Aug. 1987).

Merton, Robert C. "The Financial System and Economic Performance." *Journal of Financial Services Research* (Dec. 1990).

Miller, Merton H. "Financial Innovation: The Last Twenty Years and the Next." *Journal of Financial and Quantitative Analysis* (Dec. 1986).

Prasad, S. Benjamin. "The Paradox of Planning in Banks." *The Bankers Magazine* (May/June 1984).

Silber, William L. "Towards a Theory of Financial Innovation." In *Financial Innovation*. Edited by William L. Silber. Lexington, Mass.: D. C. Heath, 1975.

Chapter 10

Ben-Horim, M., and W. Silber. "Financial Innovation: A Linear Programming Approach." *Journal of Banking and Finance* (1977): 277–96.

Brewer, Elijah, III, and Cheng Few Lee. "How the Market Judges Bank Risk." *Economic Perspectives*. Federal Reserve Bank of Chicago (Nov./Dec. 1986): 25–31.

Buser, Stephen A., Andrew H. Chen, and Edward J. Kane. "Federal Deposit Insurance, Regulatory Policy, and Optimal Bank Capital." *Journal of Finance* (March 1981): 51–60.

Cooper, Ian A. "Financial Innovation." In *The Handbook of International Financial Management*. Edited by Robert Aliber. Homewood, Ill.: Dow Jones-Irwin, 1989.

Finnerty, John D. "Financial Engineering in Corporate Finance: An Overview." *Financial Management* (Winter 1988): 62–79.

Greenbaum, Stuart I., and Bryon Higgins. "Financial Innovation." In *Financial Services: The Changing Institutions and Government Policy*. Englewood Cliffs, N.J.: Prentice-Hall, 1983.

Kane, Edward J. "Accelerating Inflation, Technological Innovation, and the Decreasing Effectiveness of Banking Regulation." *Journal of Finance* (1981): 355–67.

———. "Microeconomic and Macroeconomic Origins of Financial Innovation." In *Financial Innovations*. Federal Reserve Bank of St. Louis. Boston: Kluwer Nijhoff Publishing, 1984.

Keeton, William R. "The New Risk-based Plan for Commercial Banks." *Economic Review*. Federal Reserve Bank of Kansas City (Dec. 1989): 40–60.

Marcus, Alan J. "The Bank Capital Decision: A Time Series–Cross Section Analysis." *Journal of Finance* (Sept. 1983): 1217–32.

Merton, Robert C. "The Financial System and Economic Performance." *Journal of Financial Services Research* (Dec. 1990): 263–300.

Miller, Merton H. "Financial Innovation: The Last Twenty Years and the Next." *Journal of Financial and Quantitative Analysis* (Dec. 1986): 459–71.

Podolski, T. M. *Financial Innovation and the Money Supply.* Oxford: Basil Blackwell Inc., 1986.

Ross, Stephen A. "Institutional Markets, Financial Marketing, and Financial Innovation." *Journal of Finance* (July 1989): 541–56.

Silber, William L. "The Process of Financial Innovation." *American Economic Review* (May 1983): 89–94.

———. "Towards a Theory of Financial Innovation." In *Financial Innovation.* Edited by William L. Silber. Lexington, Mass: D. C. Heath, 1975.

Thomson, James B. "Using Market Incentives to Reform Bank Regulation and Federal Deposit Insurance." *Economic Review.* Federal Reserve Bank of Cleveland (1990–1991): 28–40.

Van Horne, J. "Of Financial Innovation and Excesses." *Journal of Finance* (July 1985): 621–31.

Chapter 11

Altman, Edward. *Corporate Financial Distress: A Complete Guide on How to Understand, Predict, and Deal with Bankruptcy.* New York: John Wiley & Sons, 1983.

———. "Financial Ratios, Discriminant Analysis and the Prediction of Corporate Bankruptcy." *Journal of Finance* (Sept. 1968).

Altman, Edward, R. G. Haldeman, and P. Narayanan. "Zeta Analysis: A New Model to Identify Bankruptcy Risk of Corporations." *Journal of Banking and Finance* (1977).

Argenti, John. *Corporate Collapse.* New York: McGraw-Hill, Inc., 1976.

Beaver, W. H. "Financial Ratios as Predictors of Failure." *Journal of Accounting Research,* Supplement (1968): 71–127.

Donaldson, T. H. *Credit Risk and Exposure in Securitization and Transactions.* New York: St. Martin's Press, 1989.

Hale, Roger H. *Credit Analysis: A Complete Guide.* New York: John Wiley & Sons, 1983.

Chapter 12

Alexander, Walter. "What's the Score?" *ABA Banking Journal* (Aug. 1989).

Altman, Edward I. "Revisiting the High-Yield Bond Market." *Financial Management* (Summer 1992): 78.

Compton, Eric N. "Credit Analysis Is Risk Analysis." *The Bankers Magazine* (March/April 1985).

Eichengreen, B., and R. Portes. "The Anatomy of Financial Crises." In *Threats to International Financial Stability.* Edited by R. Portes and A. K. Swoboda, 10–51. Cambridge: Cambridge Univ. Press, 1978.

Fabozzi, Frank J., and Frank G. Zarb, eds. *Handbook of Financial Markets,* 2nd ed. Homewood, Ill: Dow Jones-Irwin, 1986.

Flow of Funds Accounts. Washington, D.C.: Board of Governors of the Federal Reserve System.

Goldberg, Michael A., and Peter Lloyd-Davies. "Standby Letters of Credit." *Journal of Bank Research* (Spring 1983).

Handbook of Securities of the United States Government and Federal Agencies. New York: The First Boston Corporation, 1988. (Published biennially.)

Logan, John, and Richard Dongan. "Asset-based Lending: You're Doing It, but Are You Doing It Right?" *Journal of Commercial Bank Lending* (June 1984).

Newburgh, Conrad. "Character Assessment in the Lending Process." *Journal of Commercial Bank Lending* (April 1991).

Reavis, Charles G., Jr. "Lending on Income Property." In *The Banker's Handbook,* 3rd ed. Homewood, Ill. Richard D. Irwin, 1989.

Saini, K., and P. Bates. "Statistical Techniques for Determining Debt-Servicing Capacity for Developing Countries: Analytical Review of the Literature and Further Empirical Results." Federal Reserve Bank of New York. Research Paper no. 7818 (Sept. 1978).

Sorenson, Richard. "Why Real Estate Projects Fail." *Journal of Commercial Bank Lending* (April 1990).

Stigum, Marcia. *The Money Market.* Homewood, Ill: Dow Jones-Irwin, 1983.

Tannenbaum, Carl. "The Changing Face of Corporate Debt." *Bank Management* (Nov. 1990).

White, Larry. "Credit Analysis: Two More Cs of Credit." *Journal of Commercial Bank Lending* (Oct. 1990).

Chapter 13

Clarke, Peter S. *Managing Problem Loans.* Homewood, Ill.: Dow Jones-Irwin, Inc., 1989.

Greenawalt, Mary Brady, and Joseph F. Sinkey, Jr. "Bank Loan-Loss Provisions and the Income-smoothing Hypothesis: An Empirical Analysis, 1976–1984." *Journal of Financial Services Research* (1988): 301–18.

King, Arnold. "The Rise in Bank Failures from a Macroeconomic Perspective." *Journal of Financial Services Research* (1988): 353–64.

Lea, Michael, and Kenneth J. Thygerson. "A Model of the Asset Disposition Decision of the RTC." *Journal of the American Real Estate and Urban Economics Association* 22 (1994): 117–33.

Scheiner, J. H. "Income Smoothing: An Analysis in the Banking Industry." *Journal of Bank Research* (Summer 1981): 119–23.

Chapter 14

Boskin, Michael. "Taxation, Savings, and the Rate of Interest." *Journal of Political Economy* (April 1978): 3–27.

Campbell, John Y. "A Defense of Traditional Hypotheses about the Term Structure." *Journal of Finance* (March 1986): 183–94.

Fama, Eugene F. "Forward Rates as Predictors of Future Spot Rates." *Journal of Financial Economics* (Oct. 1976): 361–77.

————. "Term Premiums in Bond Returns." *Journal of Financial Economics* (Oct. 1976): 509–28.

Fisher, Irving. *The Theory of Interest.* New York: The Macmillan Co., 1930.

Hamburger, Michael J., and Elliot N. Platt. "The Expectations Hypothesis and the Efficiency of the Treasury Bill Market." *Review of Economics and Statistics* (May 1975): 190–99.

Homer, Sidney. *A History of Interest Rates.* New Brunswick, N.J.: Rutgers Univ. Press, 1963.

Kaufman, Henry. *Interest Rates, the Markets, and the New Financial World.* New York: Time Books, 1986.

Keynes, John Maynard. *The General Theory of Employment, Interest and Money.* New York: Harcourt Brace Jovanovich, 1936.

Meiselman, David. *The Term Structure of Interest Rates.* Englewood Cliffs, N.J.: Prentice-Hall, 1962.

Modigliani, Franco. "Debt Management and the Term Structure of Interest Rates: An Empirical Analysis of Recent Experience." *Journal of Political Economy,* Supplement (Aug. 1967): 569–89.

Siegel, Andrew F., and Charles R. Nelson. "Long-Term Behavior of Yield Curves." *Journal of Financial and Quantitative Analysis* (March 1988): 105–10.

Taylor, Herbert. "Interest Rates: How Much Does Expected Inflation Matter?" *Business Review.* Federal Reserve Bank of Philadelphia (July–Aug. 1982): 3–12.

Chapter 15

Becketti, Sean. "The Role of Stripped Securities in Portfolio Management." *Economic Review.* Federal Reserve Bank of Kansas City (May 1988): 20–31.

Fabozzi, Frank J., ed. *The Handbook of Mortgage-backed Securities,* 2nd ed. Chicago: Probus Publishing, 1988.

————. *The Handbook of Treasury Securities.* Chicago: Probus Publishing, 1987.

Fabozzi, Frank J., and Frank G. Zarb. eds. *Handbook of Financial Markets,* 2nd ed. Homewood, Ill.: Dow Jones-Irwin, 1986.

Handbook of Securities of the United States Government and Federal Agencies. New York: The First Boston Corporation, 1988. (Published biannually.)

Hendershott, Patric, and Robert Van Order. "Pricing Mortgages: An Interpretation of the Models and Results." *Journal of Financial Services Research* (Sept. 1987): 19–55.

Ingersoll, Jonathan E. "An Examination of Corporate Call Policies on Convertible Securities." *Journal of Finance* (May 1977): 463–78.

Livingston, Miles. *Money and Capital Markets: Financial Instruments and Their Uses.* Englewood Cliffs, N.J.: Prentice-Hall, 1990.

Stigum, Marcia. *Money Market Calculations: Yields, Breakevens, and Arbitrage.* Homewood, Ill.: Dow Jones-Irwin, 1981.

Stigum, Marcia, and Frank J. Fabozzi. *The Dow Jones-Irwin Guide to Bond and Money Market Instruments.* Homewood, Ill.: Dow Jones-Irwin, 1987.

Thygerson, Kenneth J., and Dennis Jacobe. *Mortgage Portfolio Management.* Chicago: United States League of Savings Institutions, 1978.

Chapter 16

Black, Fisher, and Myron Scholes. "The Pricing of Options and Corporate Liabilities." *Journal of Political Economy* (May–June 1973): 637–59.

Bookstaber, Richard M. "The Option Pricing Formula." In *Readings in Investment Management.* Edited by Frank J. Fabozzi. Homewood, Ill.: Richard D. Irwin, 1983, 267–81.

Brown, K. C., and D. J. Smith, "Recent Innovations in Interest Rate Risk Management and the Reintermediation of Commercial Banks," *Financial Management* 17 (1988): 45–58.

Dubofsky, David A. *Options and Financial Futures.* New York: McGraw-Hill, 1992.

Fabozzi, Frank J., and T. Dessa Fabozzi. *Bond Markets, Analysis and Strategies.* Englewood Cliffs, N.J.: Prentice-Hall, 1989.

Financial Derivatives: New Instruments and Their Uses. Federal Reserve Bank of Atlanta (1993).

Goodman, Laurie. "New Options Markets." *Quarterly Review.* Federal Reserve Bank of New York (Autumn 1983): 35–47.

Ingersoll, Jonathan E. "An Examination of Corporate Call Policies on Convertible Securities." *Journal of Finance* (May 1977): 463–78.

Kolb, Robert W. *Understanding Futures Markets.* Glenview, Ill.: Scott, Foresman and Co., 1988.

Kopprasch, Robert W. "Early Redemption (Put) Options on Fixed Income Securities." In *Readings in Investment Management.* Edited by Frank J. Fabozzi, 97–110. Homewood Ill.: Richard D. Irwin, 1983.

MacBeth, James D., and Larry J. Merville. "An Empirical Examination of the Black-Scholes Call Option Pricing Model." *Journal of Finance* (Dec. 1979): 1173–86.

Merton, Robert C. "Theory of Rational Option Pricing." *Bell Journal of Economics and Management Science* (Spring 1973): 141–83.

Stapleton, R. C., and M. Subrahmanyam. "Interest Rate Caps and Floors." In *Financial Options: From Theory to Practice.* Edited by S. Figlewski. Homewood, Ill.: Business One-Irwin, 1990.

Thygerson, Kenneth J. "Futures, Options and the Savings and Loan Business." In *Savings and Loan Asset Management under Deregulation. Proceedings of the Sixth Annual Conference of the Federal Home Loan Bank of San Francisco* (Dec. 8–9, 1980): 118–47.

———. "Hedging Forward Mortgage Loan Commitments: The Option of Futures and the Future of Options." *Journal of the American Real Estate and Urban Economics Association* (Winter 1978): 357–69.

Whaley, Robert E. "Valuation of American Futures Options: Theory and Empirical Tests." *Journal of Finance* (1986): 127–50.

Williams, Jeffrey. "Futures Markets: A Consequence of Risk Aversion or Transactions Costs?" *Journal of Political Economy* (Oct. 1987): 1000–23.

Chapter 17

Bierwag, Gerald O. *Duration Analysis.* Cambridge, Mass.: Ballinger Publishing, 1987.

Flannery, Mark J., and Christopher M. James. "The Effect of Interest Rate Changes on the Common Stock Returns of Financial Institutions." *Journal of Finance* (Sept. 1984): 1141–53.

Kaufman, George. "Measuring and Managing Interest Rate Risk: A Primer." *Economic Perspectives.* Federal Reserve Bank of Chicago (Jan.–Feb. 1984): 16–29.

Macaulay, Frederick. *Some Theoretical Problems Suggested by the Movement of Interest Rates, Bond Yields, and Stock Prices in the U.S. since 1856.* National Bureau of Economic Research, 1938.

Samuelson, Paul A. "The Effect of Interest Rate Increases on the Banking System." *American Economic Review* (March 1945): 16–27.

Weil, Roman L. "Macaulay's Duration: An Appreciation." *Journal of Business* (Oct. 1973): 589–92.

Chapter 18

Arak, M., A. Estrella, L. Goodmand, and A. Silver. "Interest Rate Swaps: An Alternative Explanation." *Financial Management* (1988): 12–18.

Brewer, Elijah. "Bank GAP Management and the Use of Financial Futures." *Economic Perspectives.* Federal Reserve Bank of Chicago (March/April 1985): 12–22.

Goodman, John L., Jr., and Charles A. Luckett. "Adjustable-rate Financing in Mortgage and Consumer Credit Markets." *Federal Reserve Bulletin* (Nov. 1985): 823–35.

Goodman, Laurie. "The Uses of Interest Rate Swaps in Managing Corporate Liabilities." In *New Developments in Commercial Banking.* Edited by Donald H. Chew, Jr., 236–48. Cambridge, Mass.: Basil Blackwell Ltd.

Haley, Charles W. "Interest Rate Risk in Financial Intermediaries: Prospects for Immunization." In *Proceedings of a Conference on Bank Structure and Competition,* 309–17. Chicago: Federal Reserve Bank of Chicago, 1982.

Kolb, Robert W., Stephen G. Timme, and Gerald D. Gay. "Macro versus Micro Futures Hedges at Commercial Banks." *Journal of the Futures Markets* (1984): 47–54.

Marshall, John F., and Kenneth R. Kapner. *Understanding Swap Finance.* Cincinnati, Ohio: South-Western Publishing Co., 1990.

Rawls, S. Waite. "The Evolution of Risk Management Products." In *New Developments in Commercial Banking*. Edited by Donald H. Chew, Jr., 144–52. Cambridge, Mass.: Basil Blackwell Ltd.

Smith, Clifford W. "Managing Financial Risk." In *New Developments in Commercial Banking*. Edited by Donald H. Chew, Jr., 166–87. Cambridge, Mass.: Basil Blackwell Ltd.

Smith, Clifford W., Jr., Charles W. Smithson, and Lee Macdonald Wakeman. "The Evolving Market for Swaps." *Midland Corporate Finance Journal* (Winter 1986): 20–32.

Whittader, J. Gregg. "Interest Rate Swaps: Risk and Regulation." *Economic Review*. Federal Reserve Bank of St. Louis (March 1987): 3–13.

Chapter 19

Bilson, John F. O., and Richard C. Marson, eds. "Exchange Rate Dynamics." In *Exchange Rate Theory and Practice*. Chicago: Univ. of Chicago Press, 1984.

Frankel, Jeffrey A., and Richard Meese. "Are Exchange Rates Excessively Variable?" In *NBER Macroeconometrics Annual 1987*. National Bureau of Economic Research (1987): 117–62.

Grabbe, J. Orlin. *International Financial Markets*. New York: Elsevier Science Publishing Co., 1986.

International Monetary Fund. *Annual Report,* various issues.

Lewent, Judy C., and A. John Kearney. "Identifying, Measuring, and Hedging Currency Risk at Merck." In *New Developments in Commercial Banking*. Edited by Donald H. Chew, Jr., 188–97. Cambridge, Mass: Basil Blackwell Ltd.

Marrinan, Jane. "Exchange Rate Determination: Sorting Out Theory and Evidence." *New England Economic Review*. Federal Reserve Bank of Boston (Nov./Dec. 1989): 39–51.

Pavel, Christine, and John N. McElravey. "Globalization in the Financial Services Industry." *Economic Perspectives*. Federal Reserve Bank of Chicago (May/June 1990): 3–18.

Chapter 20

Bender, Roxanne. "Bank Liquidity: Learning to Love It." *Bankers Monthly* (Dec. 1985).

Brewer, E. "Bank Funds Management Comes of Age—A Balance Sheet Analysis." *Economic Perspectives*. Federal Reserve Bank of Chicago (May/June 1980): 13–18.

Cotes, David. "Liquidity Lessons for the 90's." *Bank Management* (April 1990).

Cross, Howard, and George H. Hempell. *Management Policies for Commercial Banks*. Englewood Cliffs, N.J.: Prentice-Hall, 1980.

Kaufman, D. J., Jr., and D. R. Lee. "Planning Liquidity: A Practical Approach," *Magazine of Bank Administration* (Feb. 1977): 55–63.

Luckett, Dudley G. "Approaches to Bank Liquidity," *Economic Review*. Federal Reserve Bank of Kansas City (Dec. 1969): 11–27.

Rosenbaum, M. S. "Contemporaneous Reserve Accounting: The New System and Its Implications for Monetary Policy." *Economic Review*. Federal Reserve Bank of Atlanta (April 1984): 46–57.

Temple, W. Robert. "Bank Liquidity: Where Are We?" *American Banker* (March 8, 1983).

Chapter 21

Haraf, William S., and Rose Marie Kushneider. *Restructuring Banking and Financial Services in America*. Washington, D.C.: American Enterprise Institute for Public Policy Research, 1988.

Mahoney, Patrick I., Alice P. White, Paul F. O'Brien, and Mary M. McLaughlin. "Responses to Deregulation: Retail Deposit Pricing from 1983 through 1985." Working Paper of the Board of Governors of the Federal Reserve System (January 1987).

Napoli, Janet, and Herbert L. Baer. "Disintermediation Marches On." *Chicago Fedletter*. Federal Reserve Bank of Chicago (Jan. 1991).

Pavel, Christine. *Securitization*. Chicago: Probus Publishing Company, 1989.

Chapter 22

Bailey, John M. "Regulating Capital Adequacy." *Bank Management* (Feb. 1990): 3–33.

Bardos, Jeffrey. "Risk-based Capital Agreement: A Further Step towards Policy Convergences." *Quarterly Review*. Federal Reserve Bank of New York (Winter 1987/1988): 26–34.

Brady, Thomas F. "The Role of the Prime Rate in the Pricing of Business Loans by Commercial Banks, 1977–1984." Board of Governors of the Federal Reserve System. Staff Paper no. 146. (Nov. 1985).

Bryan, Lowell L. "Structured Securitized Credit: A Superior Technology for Lending." In *New Developments in Commercial Banking*. Edited by Donald H. Chew, Jr., 55–68. Cambridge, Mass.: Basil Blackwell Ltd.

Cole, G. Alexander. "Risk-based Capital: A Loan and Credit Officer's Primer." *Journal of Commercial Bank Lending* (Aug. 1988): 4–20.

Crowley, Donald. "The Impact of Risk-based Capital on U.S. Banking." *Bank Administration* (Nov. 1988): 16–20.

Graddy, Duane B., and Austin H. Spencer. *Managing Commercial Banks*. Englewood Cliffs, N.J.: Prentice-Hall, 1990.

Kane, Edward J. "Incentive Conflict in the International Risk-based Capital Agreement." *Economic Perspectives*. Federal Reserve Bank of Chicago (May/June 1990): 40–50.

Kelly, J. Robert. "Risk-based Capital Guidelines for Banks." *Journal of Accountancy* (Jan. 1990): 115–18.

Nadler, Paul S. "Risk-based Capital Standards and the Cash Manager." *Journal of Cash Management* (July/Aug. 1988): 54–60.

Ocampo, Juan M., and James A. Rosenthal. "The Future of Credit Securitization and the Financial Services Industry." In *New Developments in Commercial Banking*. Edited by Donald H. Chew, Jr., 129–39. Cambridge, Mass.: Basil Blackwell Ltd.

Wall, Larry D. "Capital Requirements for Interest-Rate and Foreign-Exchange Hedges." *Economic Review*. Federal Reserve Bank of Atlanta (May/June 1990): 14–27.

Chapter 23

Brewer, Elijah, III, Diana Fortier, and Christine Pavel. "Bank Risk from Nonbank Activities," *Economic Perspectives*. Federal Reserve Bank of Chicago (July/Aug. 1990).

Burns, Merrill O. "The Future of Correspondent Banking." *Magazine of Bank Administration* (May 1986).

Hirtle, Beverly. "The Growth of the Financial Guarantee Market." *Quarterly Review*. Federal Reserve Bank of New York (Spring 1987).

Holland, Kelley. "Banks Mull Special-purpose Corporations." *American Banker* (Sept. 28, 1990).

Merrill, Peter. "Correspondent Banking and the Payments System." *Economic Review*. Federal Reserve Bank of Atlanta (June 1983).

Roosevelt, Phil. "Fee-income Boom of the Eighties Cools Off." *American Banker* (Jan. 7, 1991).

Shafton, Robert M., and Donald D. Gabay. "The Banking Outlook for Diversification into Insurance." *Bankers Magazine*. (Jan./Feb. 1985).

Chapter 24

Bradley, M. D., and D. W. Jansen. "Deposit Market Deregulation and Interest Rates." *Southern Economic Journal* (Oct. 1986): 478–89.

Brewer, E., III. "The Impact of Deregulation on the True Cost of Savings Deposits: Evidence for Illinois and Wisconsin Savings and Loan Associations." *Journal of Economics and Business* (Feb. 1988): 79–95.

Cherin, A. C., and R. W. Melicher. "Branch Banking and Loan Portfolio Risk Relationships." *Review of Business and Economic Research* (Sept. 1987): 1–13.

Davenport, T. O., and H. D. Sherman. "Measuring Branch Profitability." *Bankers Magazine* (Sept.–Oct. 1987): 34–38.

Davis, R., and L. Korobow. "The Pricing of Consumer Deposit Products—The Non-Rate Dimensions." *Quarterly Review*. Federal Reserve Bank of New York (Winter 1987): 14–18.

Davis, R., L. Korobow, and J. Wenninger. "Bankers on Pricing Consumer Deposits." *Quarterly Review*. Federal Reserve Bank of New York (Winter 1987): 6–13.

Faust, W. H. "The Branch as a Retail Outlet." *Bankers Magazine* (Jan.–Feb. 1990): 30–35.

Jilk, L. T. "Strategies for Pricing Core Loans and Deposits." *Bankers Magazine* (Nov.–Dec. 1988): 47–52.

Thygerson, Kenneth J. "Modeling Branch Profitability." *Journal of Retail Banking* (Fall 1991): 19–24.

Chapter 25

Bullington, Robert A., and Arnold E. Jensen. "Pricing a Bank." *Bankers Magazine* (May/June 1981).

Cates, David. "Prices Paid for Banks." *Economic Review*. Federal Reserve Bank of Atlanta (Jan. 1985).

Heggestad, Arnold A. "Fundamentals of Mergers and Acquisition." In *Handbook for Banking Strategy*. Edited by Richard Aspinwall and Rober Eisenbeis. New York: John Wiley & Sons, Inc., 1985.

Holder, Christopher L. "Competitive Considerations in Bank Mergers and Acquisitions: Economic Theory, Legal Foundations, and the Fed." *Economic Review*. Federal Reserve Bank of Atlanta (Jan./Feb. 1993).

King, Ralph T., Jr. "BankAmerica Finds It Got a Lot of Woe with Security Pacific." *The Wall Street Journal* (July 22, 1993).

Neely, Walter. "Banking Acquisitions: Acquirer and Target Shareholder Returns." *Financial Management* (Winter 1987).

Srinivasan, Aruna. "Are There Cost Savings from Bank Mergers?" *Economic Review*. Federal Reserve Bank of Atlanta (March/April 1992).

Svare, J. Christopher. "The New M&A Market." *Bank Management* (Feb. 1990).

Varian, Hal R. "Symposium on Mergers." *Journal of Economic Perspectives* (Winter 1988).

inancial Tables

TABLE B.1

Present Value of $1: $\dfrac{1}{(1 + k)^n}$ $PVIF_{r,n}$

Period	1%	2%	3%	4%	5%	6%	7%	8%	9%	10%
1	0.990	0.980	0.970	0.962	0.952	0.943	0.935	0.926	0.917	0.909
2	0.980	0.961	0.943	0.925	0.907	0.890	0.873	0.857	0.842	0.826
3	0.971	0.942	0.915	0.889	0.864	0.840	0.816	0.794	0.772	0.751
4	0.961	0.924	0.888	0.855	0.823	0.792	0.763	0.735	0.708	0.683
5	0.951	0.906	0.863	0.822	0.784	0.747	0.713	0.681	0.650	0.621
6	0.942	0.888	0.837	0.790	0.746	0.705	0.666	0.630	0.596	0.564
7	0.933	0.871	0.813	0.760	0.711	0.665	0.623	0.583	0.547	0.513
8	0.923	0.853	0.789	0.731	0.677	0.627	0.582	0.540	0.502	0.467
9	0.914	0.837	0.766	0.703	0.645	0.592	0.544	0.500	0.460	0.424
10	0.905	0.820	0.744	0.676	0.614	0.558	0.508	0.463	0.422	0.386
11	0.896	0.804	0.722	0.650	0.585	0.527	0.475	0.429	0.388	0.350
12	0.887	0.788	0.701	0.625	0.557	0.497	0.444	0.397	0.356	0.319
13	0.879	0.773	0.681	0.601	0.530	0.469	0.415	0.368	0.326	0.290
14	0.870	0.758	0.661	0.577	0.505	0.442	0.388	0.340	0.299	0.263
15	0.861	0.743	0.642	0.555	0.481	0.417	0.362	0.315	0.275	0.239
16	0.853	0.728	0.623	0.534	0.458	0.394	0.339	0.299	0.252	0.218
17	0.844	0.714	0.605	0.513	0.436	0.371	0.317	0.270	0.231	0.198
18	0.836	0.700	0.587	0.494	0.416	0.350	0.296	0.250	0.212	0.180
19	0.828	0.686	0.570	0.475	0.396	0.331	0.277	0.232	0.194	0.164
20	0.820	0.673	0.554	0.456	0.377	0.312	0.258	0.215	0.178	0.149
21	0.811	0.660	0.538	0.439	0.359	0.294	0.242	0.199	0.164	0.135
22	0.803	0.647	0.522	0.422	0.342	0.278	0.226	0.184	0.150	0.123
23	0.795	0.634	0.507	0.406	0.326	0.262	0.211	0.170	0.138	0.112
24	0.788	0.622	0.492	0.390	0.310	0.247	0.197	0.158	0.126	0.102
25	0.780	0.610	0.478	0.375	0.295	0.233	0.184	0.146	0.116	0.092
30	0.742	0.522	0.412	0.308	0.231	0.174	0.131	0.099	0.075	0.057
35	0.706	0.500	0.355	0.253	0.181	0.130	0.094	0.068	0.049	0.036
40	0.672	0.453	0.307	0.208	0.142	0.097	0.067	0.046	0.032	0.022
45	0.639	0.410	0.264	0.171	0.111	0.073	0.048	0.031	0.021	0.014
50	0.608	0.372	0.228	0.141	0.087	0.054	0.034	0.021	0.013	0.009

Period	11%	12%	13%	14%	15%	16%	17%	18%	19%	20%
1	0.901	0.893	0.885	0.877	0.870	0.862	0.855	0.847	0.840	0.833
2	0.812	0.797	0.783	0.769	0.756	0.743	0.731	0.718	0.706	0.694
3	0.731	0.712	0.693	0.675	0.658	0.641	0.624	0.609	0.593	0.579
4	0.659	0.636	0.613	0.592	0.572	0.552	0.534	0.516	0.499	0.482
5	0.593	0.567	0.543	0.519	0.497	0.476	0.456	0.437	0.419	0.402
6	0.535	0.507	0.480	0.456	0.432	0.410	0.390	0.370	0.352	0.333
7	0.482	0.452	0.425	0.400	0.376	0.354	0.333	0.314	0.296	0.279
8	0.434	0.404	0.376	0.351	0.327	0.305	0.285	0.266	0.249	0.233
9	0.391	0.361	0.333	0.308	0.284	0.263	0.243	0.225	0.209	0.194
10	0.352	0.322	0.295	0.270	0.247	0.227	0.208	0.191	0.176	0.162
11	0.317	0.287	0.261	0.237	0.215	0.195	0.178	0.162	0.148	0.135
12	0.286	0.257	0.231	0.208	0.187	0.168	0.152	0.137	0.124	0.112
13	0.258	0.229	0.204	0.182	0.163	0.145	0.130	0.116	0.104	0.093
14	0.232	0.205	0.181	0.160	0.141	0.125	0.111	0.099	0.088	0.078
15	0.209	0.183	0.160	0.140	0.123	0.108	0.095	0.084	0.074	0.065
16	0.188	0.163	0.142	0.123	0.107	0.093	0.081	0.071	0.062	0.054
17	0.170	0.146	0.125	0.108	0.093	0.080	0.069	0.060	0.052	0.045
18	0.153	0.130	0.111	0.095	0.081	0.069	0.059	0.051	0.044	0.038
19	0.138	0.116	0.098	0.083	0.070	0.060	0.051	0.043	0.037	0.031
20	0.124	0.104	0.087	0.073	0.061	0.051	0.043	0.037	0.031	0.026
21	0.112	0.093	0.077	0.064	0.053	0.044	0.037	0.031	0.026	0.022
22	0.101	0.083	0.068	0.056	0.046	0.038	0.032	0.026	0.022	0.018
23	0.091	0.074	0.060	0.049	0.040	0.033	0.027	0.022	0.018	0.015
24	0.082	0.066	0.053	0.043	0.035	0.028	0.023	0.019	0.015	0.013
25	0.074	0.059	0.047	0.038	0.030	0.024	0.020	0.016	0.013	0.010
30	0.044	0.033	0.026	0.020	0.015	0.012	0.009	0.007	0.005	0.004
35	0.026	0.019	0.014	0.010	0.008	0.006	0.004	0.003	0.002	0.002
40	0.015	0.011	0.008	0.005	0.004	0.003	0.002	0.001	0.001	0.001
45	0.009	0.006	0.004	0.003	0.002	0.001	0.001	0.001	*	*
50	0.005	0.003	0.002	0.001	0.001	0.001	*	*	*	*

TABLE B.2

Present Value of an Annuity of $1 for n Periods: $\left[\sum_{t=1}^{n} \dfrac{1}{(1+k)^t} \right] PVIFA_{r,n}$

Number of Payments	1%	2%	3%	4%	5%	6%	7%	8%	9%	10%
1	0.990	0.980	0.971	0.962	0.952	0.943	0.935	0.926	0.917	0.909
2	1.790	1.942	1.914	1.886	1.859	1.833	1.808	1.783	1.759	1.736
3	2.941	2.884	2.829	2.775	2.723	2.673	2.624	2.577	2.531	2.487
4	3.902	3.808	3.717	3.630	3.546	3.465	3.387	3.312	3.240	3.170
5	4.854	4.713	4.580	4.452	4.330	4.212	4.100	3.993	3.890	3.791
6	5.796	5.601	5.417	5.242	5.076	4.917	4.767	4.623	4.486	4.355
7	6.728	6.472	6.230	6.002	5.786	5.582	5.389	5.206	5.033	4.868
8	7.652	7.325	7.020	6.733	6.463	6.210	5.971	5.747	5.535	5.335
9	8.566	8.162	7.786	7.435	7.108	6.802	6.515	6.247	5.985	5.759
10	9.471	8.983	8.530	8.111	7.722	7.360	7.024	6.710	6.418	6.145
11	10.368	9.787	9.253	8.760	8.036	7.887	7.499	7.139	6.805	6.495
12	11.255	10.575	9.954	9.385	8.863	8.384	7.943	7.536	7.161	6.814
13	12.134	11.348	10.635	9.986	9.394	8.853	8.358	7.904	7.487	7.103
14	13.004	12.106	11.296	10.563	9.899	9.295	8.745	8.244	7.786	7.367
15	13.865	12.849	11.938	11.118	10.380	9.712	9.108	8.560	8.061	7.606
16	14.718	13.578	12.561	11.652	10.838	10.106	9.447	8.851	8.313	7.824
17	15.562	14.292	13.166	12.166	11.274	10.477	9.763	9.122	8.544	8.022
18	16.398	14.992	13.753	12.659	11.690	10.828	10.059	9.372	8.756	8.201
19	17.226	15.678	14.324	13.134	12.085	11.158	10.336	9.604	8.950	8.365
20	18.046	16.351	14.877	13.590	12.462	11.470	10.594	9.818	9.129	8.514
21	18.857	17.011	15.415	14.029	12.821	11.764	10.836	10.017	9.292	8.649
22	19.661	17.658	15.937	14.451	13.163	12.042	11.061	10.201	9.442	8.772
23	20.456	18.292	16.444	14.857	13.489	12.303	11.272	10.371	9.580	8.883
24	21.244	18.914	16.936	15.247	13.799	12.550	11.469	10.529	9.707	8.985
25	22.023	19.523	17.413	15.622	14.094	12.783	11.654	10.675	9.823	9.077
30	25.808	22.396	19.600	17.292	15.372	13.765	12.409	11.258	10.274	9.427
35	29.409	24.999	21.487	18.665	16.374	14.498	12.948	11.655	10.567	9.644
40	32.835	27.355	23.115	19.793	17.159	15.046	13.332	11.925	10.757	9.779
45	36.095	29.490	24.519	20.720	17.774	15.456	13.606	12.108	10.881	9.863
50	39.196	31.424	25.730	21.482	18.256	15.762	13.801	12.233	10.962	9.915

Number of Payments	11%	12%	13%	14%	15%	16%	17%	18%	19%	20%
1	0.901	0.893	0.885	0.377	0.870	0.862	0.855	0.848	0.840	0.833
2	1.713	1.690	1.668	1.647	1.626	1.605	1.585	1.566	1.547	1.528
3	2.444	2.402	2.361	2.322	2.283	2.246	2.210	2.174	2.140	2.107
4	3.102	3.037	2.975	2.914	2.855	2.798	2.743	2.690	2.639	2.589
5	3.696	3.605	3.517	3.433	3.352	3.274	3.199	3.127	3.058	2.991
6	4.231	4.111	3.998	3.889	3.785	3.685	3.589	3.498	3.410	3.326
7	4.712	4.564	4.423	4.288	4.160	4.029	3.922	3.812	3.706	3.605
8	5.146	4.968	4.799	4.639	4.487	4.344	4.207	4.078	3.954	3.837
9	5.537	5.328	5.132	4.946	4.772	4.607	4.451	4.303	4.163	4.031
10	5.889	5.650	5.426	5.216	5.019	4.833	4.659	4.404	4.339	4.193
11	6.207	5.938	5.687	5.453	5.234	5.029	4.836	4.656	4.487	4.327
12	6.492	6.194	5.918	5.660	5.421	5.197	4.988	4.793	4.611	4.439
13	6.750	6.424	6.122	5.842	5.583	5.342	5.118	4.910	4.715	4.533
14	6.982	6.628	6.303	6.002	5.725	5.468	5.229	5.008	4.802	4.611
15	7.191	6.811	6.462	6.142	5.847	5.576	5.324	5.092	4.876	4.676
16	7.379	6.974	6.604	6.265	5.954	5.669	5.405	5.162	4.938	4.730
17	7.549	7.120	6.729	6.373	6.047	5.749	5.475	5.222	4.990	4.775
18	7.702	7.250	6.840	6.467	6.128	5.818	5.534	5.273	5.033	4.812
19	7.839	7.366	6.938	6.550	6.198	5.878	5.585	5.316	5.070	4.844
20	7.963	7.469	7.025	6.623	6.259	5.929	5.628	5.353	5.101	4.870
21	8.075	7.562	7.102	6.687	6.313	5.973	5.665	5.384	5.127	4.891
22	8.176	7.534	7.170	6.743	6.359	6.011	5.696	5.410	5.149	4.909
23	8.266	7.718	7.230	6.792	6.399	6.044	5.723	5.432	5.167	4.925
24	8.348	7.784	7.283	6.835	6.434	6.073	5.747	5.451	5.182	4.937
25	8.422	7.843	7.330	6.873	6.464	6.097	5.766	5.467	5.195	4.948
30	8.694	8.055	7.496	7.003	6.566	6.177	5.829	5.517	5.235	4.979
35	8.855	8.176	7.586	7.070	6.617	6.215	5.858	5.539	5.251	4.992
40	8.951	8.244	7.634	7.105	6.642	6.233	5.871	5.548	5.258	4.997
45	9.008	8.283	7.661	7.123	6.654	6.242	5.877	5.552	5.261	4.999
50	9.042	8.304	7.675	7.133	6.661	6.246	5.880	5.554	5.262	4.999

TABLE B.3

Future Value of $1: $(1 + r)^n$ $FVIF_{r,n}$

Period	1%	2%	3%	4%	5%	6%	7%	8%	9%	10%
1	1.010	1.020	1.030	1.040	1.050	1.060	1.070	1.080	1.090	1.100
2	1.020	1.040	1.061	1.082	1.103	1.124	1.145	1.166	1.188	1.210
3	1.030	1.061	1.093	1.125	1.158	1.191	1.225	1.260	1.295	1.331
4	1.041	1.082	1.126	1.170	1.216	1.263	1.311	1.361	1.417	1.464
5	1.051	1.104	1.159	1.217	1.276	1.338	1.403	1.469	1.539	1.611
6	1.062	1.126	1.194	1.265	1.340	1.519	1.501	1.587	1.677	1.772
7	1.072	1.149	1.230	1.316	1.407	1.504	1.606	1.714	1.828	1.949
8	1.083	1.172	1.267	1.369	1.478	1.594	1.718	1.851	1.993	2.144
9	1.094	1.195	1.305	1.423	1.551	1.690	1.839	1.999	2.172	2.358
10	1.105	1.219	1.344	1.480	1.629	1.791	1.967	2.159	2.367	2.594
11	1.116	1.243	1.384	1.540	1.710	1.898	2.105	2.332	2.580	2.853
12	1.127	1.268	1.426	1.602	1.796	2.012	2.252	2.518	2.813	3.138
13	1.138	1.294	1.469	1.665	1.886	2.133	2.410	2.720	3.066	3.452
14	1.150	1.320	1.513	1.732	1.980	2.261	2.579	2.927	3.342	3.798
15	1.161	1.346	1.558	1.801	2.079	2.397	2.759	3.172	3.643	4.177
16	1.173	1.373	1.605	1.873	2.183	2.540	2.952	3.426	3.970	4.595
17	1.184	1.400	1.653	1.948	2.292	2.693	3.159	3.700	4.328	5.054
18	1.196	1.428	1.702	2.026	2.407	2.854	3.380	3.996	4.717	5.560
19	1.208	1.457	1.754	2.107	2.527	3.026	3.617	4.316	5.142	6.116
20	1.220	1.486	1.806	2.191	2.653	3.207	3.870	4.661	5.604	6.728
21	1.232	1.516	1.860	2.279	2.786	3.400	4.141	5.034	6.109	7.400
22	1.245	1.546	1.916	2.370	2.925	3.604	4.430	5.437	6.659	8.140
23	1.257	1.577	1.974	2.465	3.072	3.820	4.741	5.871	7.258	8.954
24	1.270	1.608	2.033	2.563	3.225	4.049	5.072	6.341	7.911	9.850
25	1.282	1.641	2.094	2.666	3.386	4.292	5.427	6.849	8.623	10.835
30	1.348	1.811	2.427	3.243	4.322	5.743	7.612	10.063	13.268	17.449
35	1.417	2.000	2.813	3.946	5.516	7.686	10.677	14.785	20.414	28.102
40	1.489	2.208	3.262	4.801	7.040	10.286	14.974	21.725	31.409	45.259
45	1.565	2.438	3.782	5.841	8.985	13.765	21.002	31.920	48.327	72.890
50	1.645	2.692	4.384	7.107	11.467	18.420	29.457	46.902	74.347	117.391

Period	11%	12%	13%	14%	15%	16%	17%	18%	19%	20%
1	1.110	1.120	1.130	1.140	1.150	1.160	1.170	1.180	1.190	1.200
2	1.232	1.254	1.277	1.300	1.323	1.346	1.369	1.392	1.416	1.440
3	1.368	1.405	1.443	1.482	1.521	1.561	1.602	1.643	1.685	1.728
4	1.518	1.574	1.631	1.689	1.749	1.811	1.874	1.939	2.005	2.074
5	1.685	1.762	1.842	1.925	2.011	2.100	2.193	2.288	2.386	2.488
6	1.870	1.974	2.082	2.195	2.313	2.436	2.565	2.700	2.840	2.986
7	2.076	2.211	2.353	2.502	2.660	2.826	3.001	3.186	3.379	3.583
8	2.305	2.476	2.658	2.853	3.059	3.278	3.512	3.759	4.021	4.300
9	2.558	2.773	3.004	3.252	3.518	3.803	4.108	4.436	4.786	5.160
10	2.839	3.106	3.395	3.707	4.046	4.411	4.807	5.234	5.695	6.192
11	3.152	3.479	3.836	4.226	4.652	5.117	5.624	6.176	6.777	7.430
12	3.499	3.896	4.335	4.818	5.350	5.936	6.580	7.288	8.064	8.916
13	3.883	4.364	4.898	5.492	6.153	6.886	7.669	8.599	9.597	10.699
14	4.310	4.887	5.535	6.262	7.076	7.988	9.008	10.147	11.420	12.839
15	4.785	5.474	6.254	7.138	8.137	9.266	10.539	11.974	13.590	15.407
16	5.311	6.130	7.067	8.137	9.358	10.748	12.330	14.129	16.172	18.488
17	5.895	6.866	7.986	9.277	10.761	12.468	14.427	16.672	19.244	22.186
18	6.544	7.690	9.024	10.575	12.376	14.463	16.879	19.673	22.901	26.623
19	7.263	8.613	10.107	12.056	14.232	16.777	19.748	23.214	27.525	31.948
20	8.062	9.646	11.523	13.744	16.367	19.461	23.106	27.393	32.429	38.338
21	8.949	10.804	13.021	15.668	18.822	22.575	27.034	32.324	38.591	46.005
22	9.934	12.100	14.714	17.861	21.645	26.186	31.629	38.142	45.923	55.206
23	11.026	13.552	16.627	20.362	24.892	30.376	37.006	45.008	54.649	66.247
24	12.239	15.179	18.788	23.212	28.625	35.236	43.297	53.109	65.032	79.497
25	13.586	17.000	21.232	26.462	32.919	40.874	50.658	62.669	77.388	95.396
30	22.892	29.960	39.116	50.590	66.212	85.850	111.065	143.371	184.675	237.376
35	38.575	52.780	72.069	98.100	133.176	180.314	243.503	327.997	440.701	590.688
40	65.001	93.051	132.781	188.884	267.864	378.721	533.869	750.378	1051.668	1469.772
45	109.530	163.988	244.641	363.679	538.769	795.444	1170.479	1716.684	2509.651	3657.262
50	184.565	289.002	450.736	700.233	1083.657	1670.704	2566.215	3927.357	5988.914	9100.438

Glossary

Action planning: The itemization and prioritization of specific actions to be accomplished, identification of who is responsible, and determination of when these actions should take place. (9)

Add-on loan: A loan in which the amount of interest computed for the life of the loan is added to the loan balance before the monthly payment is determined. (3)

Adequately capitalized: Depositories that meet the regulator's second-highest of five levels of capital adequacy. (4)

Adjustable-rate mortgage (ARM): A mortgage whose interest rate, maturity, and/or payments are subject to change based on the movement of an index. (A12)

Adjusted book value valuation approach: A method to estimate a firm's value based on a set of systematic adjustments to the firm's stated book value. (25)

Adjustment period: The period between adjustments to the interest rate on an adjustable-rate loan. (18)

Adverse self-selection: A condition in which the inability to discriminate results in a high percentage of customers whose characteristics are likely to result in a loss to the seller. An insurance program that charges the same price to high- and low-risk customers and does not discriminate will appeal to the highest-risk class of customers. (4, 11)

Advisory board: A board of individuals constituted to advise a company, which does not have the legal standing of a true board of directors. (25)

Affinity group: A defined group used to market certain products. (24)

Agency costs: Costs incurred in agency relationships to ensure that agents are performing in the principal's best interest. Such costs include reporting, auditing, shareholder meetings, and costs of maintaining a board of directors. (1)

Agency relationship: The use of paid professionals to manage savings of individuals and assets held by institutions. Examples of agents are the managers and directors of publicly owned corporations. (1)

Agency status: A government-chartered enterprise with a special implicit backing of the government which gives it higher standing by investors. (6)

Agency theory: A financial theory describing the relationship between owners of assets and those hired by the owners to manage the assets. (1)

Agent: One who makes investment decisions for firms and financial institutions on behalf of investors. (1)

American depository receipts (ADRs): Financial claims issued by U.S. banks holding foreign securities in trust. (3)

American option: An option that can be exercised at any time before its expiration date. (16)

American term exchange rate: The dollar price of one unit of a foreign currency. (19)

Amortizing loan: A loan that combines interest and principal payments to pay off the principal by the end of the loan's term to maturity. (11)

Annual debt service: The amount of interest and principal due on a mortgage or installment loan. (11)

Annuity: An insurance contract paying the owner a specified sum of dollars for a specified period of time on a regular periodic basis, usually for life. (15)

Arbitrage: A group of financial claims that allow the owner to invest no money and earn a risk-free return. Actual arbitrage transactions involve some risk. (16)

Arbitrageur: The party involved in an arbitrage transaction. (6)

Ask price: The price sellers are willing to accept to sell a financial claim. (14)

Asset and liability transformation: The process of converting liabilities with one set of characteristics into assets that may have entirely different characteristics. (2)

Asset-backed claims: Financial claims created by using other financial claims as collateral for a new claim. (3)

Asset-backed financing: Borrowing money using real or financial assets as collateral. (22)

Asset/liability committee (ALCO): A committee in a financial firm responsible for determining the asset and liability structure, pricing, and liquidity management. (10)

At-the-money option: An outstanding option that has an exercise price equal to the cash market price. (16)

Automated clearinghouse (ACH): An organization used to clear checks and electronic payments between financial institutions. (24)

Automated tellers and cash dispensers: A machine used to dispense cash and process a variety of common financial transactions. (24)

Average collection period: A financial ratio defined by dividing accounts receivable by average daily sales. (12)

Average payment period: A financial ratio defined by dividing accounts payable by average daily purchases. (12)

Automated clearing house: An organization owned by a group of depositories to facilitate check clearance. (24)

Balance sheet: A financial statement disclosing a firm's assets, liabilities, and shareholder's equity. (7)

Bank discount yield (*BDY*): An interest rate calculation that is used for discounted bonds. (15)

Bank holding company (BHC): A corporation that owns all the stock in one or more commercial banks. (3)

Bank Insurance Fund (BIF): The deposit insurance fund for commercial banks created in 1989 and administered by the FDIC. (4)

Banker's acceptance: A short-term obligation guaranteed by a commercial bank and used to assist corporations involved in international trade. (3)

Barbell liquidity strategy: A method of selecting liquid investments based on the relative yields of different classes of liquid assets. (20)

Barter: A system of exchange that involves trading real goods without the benefit of a medium of exchange such as money. (1)

Basis: In the futures market, the cash market price less the futures price for a specified financial claim. If the cash price is higher (lower) than the futures price, it is a positive (negative) basis. (16)

Basis point: One one-hundredth of 1%, .001. (15)

Basis risk: Financial risks created when the price changes of the futures contract and cash market position are not stable. (18)

Basel agreements: A series of agreements among foreign central bankers regarding uniform regulation of banks internationally. (10)

Best efforts underwriting: A contractual agreement between the issuer of a security and a security dealer in which the security dealer agrees to sell a newly issued security but with no obligation of success in selling the entire issue. (3)

Bid price: The price buyers are willing to pay to purchase a financial claim. (14)

Binomial distribution: A statistical probability distribution. (11)

Black-Scholes option pricing model: A formula used to price various types of European and American call options. (16)

Breakeven risk adjusted yield (*BERAY*): The yield an asset must equal or exceed to cover the firm's weighted cost of capital and all risks and costs associated with the asset. (21)

Bretton Woods Agreement: An international agreement among the major nations to facilitate foreign trade and stabilize foreign exchange rates. (19)

Brokerage: A service related to bringing buyers and sellers together. (2)

Brokered deposits: Deposits of government-insured depositories sold through broker/dealers. (4)

Bulk sales: The sale of distressed financial or real assets in large portfolios. (13)

Business risks: Conditions within a business that are unrelated to capital structure and that give rise to volatility in earnings. (10)

Call option: An option to buy a financial claim at a specified price on or before a specified time. (11)

Call option premium: An amount of interest charged by a lender to compensate for the reinvestment risk inherent in a callable or prepayable debt instrument. (14)

Call or prepayment risk: The risk faced by the owner of a callable financial claim relating to the likelihood that the funds paid off before maturity can only be reinvested at a lower yield to maturity than prevailed on the bond at the time of purchase. (14)

Call provision: A contractual clause in a debt instrument allowing the borrower to pay off the debt before the maturity date. (A12, 14)

CAMEL ratings: A regulatory system of evaluating the safety and soundness of commercial banks. (21)

Cap: A financial option providing the owner the right to receive interest on a fixed amount of notional principal in the event of a rise in an agreed-upon index. (18)

Cap on adjustable-rate loan: The highest rate the index plus margin can rise to, regardless of the rise in the index. (18)

Capital adequacy: A general expression to describe the financial leverage of a firm. (8)

Capital deficit unit (CDU): An economic unit in need of loanable funds. (1)

Capital structure: The relationship between the amount of equity and debt used to finance a firm's assets. (1)

Capital surplus unit (CSU): An economic unit with loanable funds to invest. (1)

Cash flow schedule: A table showing the amounts and dates of the cash inflows and outflows from a specified investment. (15)

Cash flow statement: A financial statement indicating the sources and uses of cash over a specified period of time. (7)

Central bank: A government owned or chartered bank which typically is responsible for implementing a nation's monetary policy.

Certificates of deposit: Fixed-rate and fixed-term deposit accounts of depositories. (3)

Charge-offs: Charges taken to the loan loss reserve account after evidence of a loss is made available and its dollar amount can be established. (13)

Churning: The action of a broker with responsibility over an investor's funds generating excessive commissions from an unnecessarily high level of security trading. (1)

Closed-loan ratio: A measure of determining the percentage of loans to hedge based on the expectations of the loan commitments being drawn down. (18)

Collar: A combination of a financial cap and floor purchased and written by a firm. (18)

Collateral: The asset that is transferred to the investor if the borrower defaults under the obligation. (A12)

Collateral trust bond: A secured bond using common stock as collateral. (A12)

Collateralized bonds: Bonds issued with assets that transfer to the holder in the event of default. (3)

Collateralized mortgage obligations (CMOs): A hybrid series of mortgage-backed bonds created by altering the cash flows on a mortgage pass-through security. They provide several classes of bonds with different expected repayment periods. (15)

College Construction Loan Insurance Corporation (Connie Lee): A government-sponsored firm used to guarantee debt issued by colleges to finance buildings. (A3)

Combined ratio: The sum of a property and casualty company's expense and underwriting loss ratios. (8)

Commercial banks: The largest group of depositories with broad asset and liability powers. (1)

Commercial finance company: A nondepository financial intermediary that specializes in loans to businesses primarily for financing inventory and equipment. (3)

Common-size statement: An income statement or balance sheet modified so that each item is expressed as a percentage of total revenue for an income statement or total assets for a balance sheet. (7)

Community banks: Banks of small to medium size servicing small to medium-sized cities or neighborhoods of large cities. (3)

Compensating balance: An amount of funds or investments that must be held with the lender in relation to the size of a loan as a condition for receiving the loan. (22)

Competitive offer: A method of selecting an investment banker in which the investment banker providing the highest bid price performs the underwriting. (3)

Compliance examination: A regulatory exam, focusing on the extent to which the firm fulfills its reporting responsibilities and requirements under various social lending laws. (4)

Compounding interest: A situation in which interest is accrued more than once per year. (15)

Compounding 360 over 365: The equation that uses the interest factor for a 360-day year and compounds for 365 periods. (15)

Conforming mortgages: Home mortgages that qualify for purchase by the FHLMC and FNMA. (A3)

Consol: A bond issued in the United Kingdom that pays a fixed interest rate and has no maturity. (15)

Constant prepayment rate (CPR): A rate that is based on the assumption that mortgages will prepay by some predetermined percentage each month based on the existing principal outstanding after the previous month's prepayment. (15)

Consumer finance company: A nondepository financial intermediary that specializes in loans to individuals. (3)

Consumer loans: Loans made to individuals secured by the purchase of personal property or on an unsecured basis. (3)

Consumer receivables: A portfolio of consumer loans. (8)

Contingent claims: Financial claims whose cash flows are dependent on those of other financial claims. (16)

Contingent liability: A liability of a financial firm that is not reflected on its balance sheet. (7)

Continuous or infinite compounding: A method of compounding in which the compounding periods per year approach infinity. (15)

Contractual savings: Savings that occur on a specified periodic basis, such as the payment of life insurance premiums and pension fund contributions. (14)

Convergence: The economic process by which the price in the futures market and in the cash market eventually equalize at the maturity of a futures contract. (16)

Conversion privilege: The right to convert a bond into stock. (A12)

Convertibility feature: An option included in a financial debt contract providing that the owner may convert the debt into another type of financial asset. (16)

Convertible currency: Currency that is permitted to be exchanged for currencies of other countries. (5)

Convertible debenture: A bond issued by a corporation that has a provision allowing the owner to convert the bond into shares of stock. (A12)

Core deposits: Deposits generally in small denominations attracted from consumers and small businesses. (8)

Corporate bond: A financial claim representing an obligation of a corporation. (3)

Correspondent services: A variety of services offered by a commercial bank to other financial institutions. (23)

Cost of carry model: A model used to establish the value of futures contracts. (16)

Countercyclical: An economic activity that moves in the opposite direction from the general economy. (14)

Country (or sovereign) risk: The risk that a foreign government will seize property or renege on its own financial obligations or require that individuals and organizations within its jurisdictions renege on outstanding debt. (5, 11)

Coupon rate: The interest rate on a financial debt claim used to calculate the interest payments. (15)

Coupon stripping: The process of creating a group of hybrid financial claims by converting each interest and principal payment of a bond into a new financial claim. (15)

Covenant: A contractual provision of a financial debt claim designed to reduce the probability of loss. (11)

Credit analysis: The process of analyzing the probability of default and loss on a loan or investment. (11)

Credit or default risk: The probability of loss of principal and interest on a financial debt claim. (14)

Credit or default risk premium (*crp*): An amount of interest charged by the lender to cover the expected loss of principal and interest on a portfolio of a specific type of loan. (14)

Credit risk transformation: Issuing liabilities with one level of credit risk and purchasing assets with another. (2)

Credit scoring: The use of a number of attributes to help determine the creditworthiness of potential borrowers. (11, 12)

Critically undercapitalized: Institutions having the regulator's lowest level of capital adequacy that are subject to significant regulatory sanctions. (4)

Cross rates: The relationship between any three exchange rates. (19)

Cross-sectional analysis: Presentation of specified financial ratios for two or more institutions for comparison purposes. (8)

Currency swap: A financial transaction in which two parties agree to exchange currencies immediately and then to reverse the exchange at a point in the future at a fixed exchange rate. (16)

Currency transformation: Issuing liabilities denominated in one currency and purchasing assets denominated in another. (2)

Current ratio: A financial ratio determined by dividing current assets by current liabilities. (12)

Dealer markets: A market for financial markets operated by security dealers. (5)

Debenture: An unsecured debt of a borrower. (3)

Debt coverage ratio: The ratio of a borrower's principal and interest payment to total gross income. (12)

Debt-equity ratio: A financial ratio of financial leverage defined by dividing long-term debt by stockholders' equity. (12)

Debt ratio: A financial ratio of financial leverage defined by dividing total liabilities by total assets. (12)

Debt rescheduling: The action of a government to force the creditor to accept lower interest payments or delayed payment of principal. (12)

Debt service: The amount of cash needed to meet the principal and interest payments on a loan. (12)

Debt-to-income ratio: A ratio used to underwrite consumer loans and mortgages defined by dividing the mortgage principal and interest, taxes, and insurance by the borrower's monthly gross income. (12)

Defined benefit pension plan: A pension plan that has a contractually predetermined retirement payment regardless of the investment results of the pension plan. (3)

Defined contribution pension plan: A pension plan that has a contractually predetermined contribution of the employee and employer in which the retirement payment is affected by the investment results of the plan. (3)

Delegated monitoring: The monitoring of the intermediary's investments as a service to the owners of those investments. (2)

Delivery option premium: The additional interest rate charged on a loan to compensate for the option given the prospective borrower to deliver a loan once the rate has been agreed to. (21)

Demand deposit: A transaction account issued by insured depository institutions that is used as a medium of exchange. (3)

Denomination transformation: The act of converting liabilities of one denomination into assets of another. (2)

Depository institutions: A group of intermediaries whose principal activity is to issue financial claims against themselves in order to purchase financial claims of others. The principle depositories are commercial banks and thrift institutions. (1)

Derivative claims: Financial claims whose value depends on another financial claim or commodity's value, such as a futures contract or option. (3, 16)

Dialectical process: A process in which an action by one party results in a response by the other party that in turn produces an off-setting response by the first party, and so forth. (4)

Dilution: A situation in which a firm purchasing another with its own stock causes its stockholders to receive a lower amount of future earnings and dividends due to the fact that it paid an excessive price for the acquisition. (25)

Direct deposit systems: Electronic systems used to shift funds from the payer to the payee's deposit account. (24)

Direct investment: Investment in physical assets for purposes of generating future income. (5)

Dirty float: Central bank intervention into the market for foreign exchange. (19)

Discount: The amount by which the market price of a financial claim is valued at less than the par value of the claim. (15)

Discount broker: A security broker dealer that offers limited services compared to full-commission brokers and charges lower commissions. (3)

Discount rate: The rate charged by Federal Reserve district banks to their members for short-term loans. (14)

Discount window: The lending activity of regional Federal Reserve banks. (8)

Discounted cash flow model: A valuation model based on present value theory. (25)

Discriminate analysis: A statistical methodology that establishes the strength of relationships between several independent attributes and two or more independent variable classifications. (11)

Disintermediation: The action of intermediary depositors withdrawing funds to invest directly in money and capital market securities. (6)

Distress costs: Increasing costs borne by a firm as financial leverage increases; estimated to be the probability of bankruptcy times the cost of bankruptcy. (10)

Doctrine of comparative advantage: A theory of trade used to explain the optimal division of the production of goods among countries. (5)

Downward-sloping yield curve: A situation in which short-term interest rates are above long-term interest rates. (2)

Dual banking structure: A system under which federal and state governments charter certain financial institutions. (3)

Due diligence: A process designed to establish the veracity of information given to a lender or security buyer regarding financial conditions and prospects. (12)

Dumping: A multinational corporation that sells its product at a price lower than average outside its country of domicile. (5)

Duration: A measure of maturity calculated by dividing an investment's time-weighted discounted cash flows by its nontime-weighted discounted cash flows using a market interest rate. (17)

Early withdrawal penalty: A fee assessed by a depository institution on a customer that withdraws funds from a fixed-term certificate of deposit before its maturity. (16)

Earnings per share (EPS): The after-tax earnings of a firm divided by the number of common shares outstanding. (7)

Economies of scale: The relationship of cost per unit to the number of units produced. (5, 21)

Economies of scope: The relationship of cost per unit of a related group of financial products that share a common production system to the number of units produced. (21)

Efficient financial markets: The degree to which markets operationally provide low transaction costs and price assets to reflect all available information. (2)

Electronic data interchange (EDI): An electronic system that provides information on inventories and prices, facilitates ordering, and transfers funds. (24)

Electronic funds transfer systems (EFTS): A general classification for a wide variety of electronic systems that are able to complete monetary transactions. (24)

Employee Retirement Income Security Act of 1974 (ERISA): Legislation designed to protect an employee from losing benefits if terminated after many years. (3)

Equilibrium real rate of interest: The stable interest rate adjusted for expected inflation that equates supply and demand. (14)

Ethics: An agreed-upon set of standards of behavior or moral judgments. (1)

Equipment trust certificate: A bond secured by equipment, usually railroad rolling stock or aircraft, as collateral. (A12)

Equity multiplier (*EM*): A measure of financial leverage defined as the ratio of total assets to shareholders' equity. (8)

Equivalent annual yield (*EAY*): The annual interest rate, assuming no compounding, an investment would have to earn to produce the same future value that the same investment earns when compounding takes place at a specified coupon rate. (15)

Eurodollar certificates of deposit: Deposits issued by U.S. banks in Europe and denominated in U.S. dollars. (3)

Eurodollar market: The acceptance of dollar deposits and the offering of dollar-denominated loans by European banks. (19)

Euromoney index: A measure of country risk published by *Euromoney* magazine. (12)

European option: An option that can only be exercised on the expiration date. (16)

European term exchange rate: The foreign exchange value of one U.S. dollar. (19)

Exchange rate: The price of foreign currencies measured in domestic prices. (19)

Exchange rate risk: The risk that investing or borrowing in foreign currencies could alter expected yields or costs due to adverse changes in exchange rates between the domestic country and the foreign country. (14)

Exercise date: The date when an option matures. (16)

Exercise (or strike) price: The agreed-upon price in an option contract. (16)

Expectations theory: A theory that holds that long-term interest rates represent the market's expectation of what future short-term interest rates will be. (14)

Expense ratio: The relationship of property and casualty operating expenses to premiums earned. (3)

Expropriation: The action of a government to assume ownership of assets held by others without compensation. (5)

Factor: A financial transaction involving the purchase of a firm's accounts receivable by another firm. (A12)

Fallacy of composition: A term in logic meaning that what may be good for a small group is not necessarily good for a large group. (6)

Fallen angels: Bonds of a corporation that now hold a noninvestment grade rating but that held an investment grade rating when they were issued. (A12)

Farm Credit Banks: A group of GSEs that lend to farmers for housing, equipment, land, and supplies. (A3)

Federal Agricultural Mortgage Corporation (Farmer Mac): A GSE that provides a secondary market for loans to farmers. (A3)

Federal Deposit Insurance Corporation (FDIC): The regulator of state-chartered insured banks and savings banks and administrator of the Bank Insurance Fund and Savings Association Insurance Fund. (4)

Federal Deposit Insurance Corporation Improvement Act of 1991 (FDICIA): Legislation designed to strengthen the authority of depository institution regulators. (4)

Fed funds: A short-term loan of reserves held as a deposit in a Federal Reserve bank from one Fed member to another. (3)

Federal Home Loan Bank Board (FHLBB): The former regulatory agency for savings and loans. It was replaced in 1989 by the Office of Thrift Supervision. (3)

Federal Home Loan Banks (FHLBs): A system of 12 banks, primarily owned by savings and loans, that lend to savings and loans and commercial banks for mortgage investment. (4)

Federal Home Loan Mortgage Corporation (FHLMC): One of the two large secondary-market mortgage finance GSEs. (4)

Federal Housing Administration (FHA): A department within the Department of Housing and Urban Development that provides an insurance program for single- and multifamily mortgages. (A3)

Federal National Mortgage Association (FNMA): One of the two large secondary-market mortgage finance GSEs. (4)

Federal Savings and Loan Insurance Corporation (FSLIC): The former deposit insurance fund for savings and loans. (4)

Fedwire system: A major electronic system operated by the Federal Reserve System used for making monetary wire transfers. (24)

Fee-based income: A portion of noninterest income received by financial institutions. (23)

FHA prepayment experience: A payoff schedule used to determine when mortgages in a pool are likely to pay off based on experience gathered by the Federal Housing Administration on insured mortgages. (4)

Fiduciary responsibilities: A situation is which one person has responsibility for the assets or well-being of another. (1)

Finance companies: A nondepository financial intermediary that lends to businesses and consumers. (1)

Financial asset or claim: A contract evidencing ownership of a stream of cash flows. Bonds, stocks, or deposits are examples of financial claims. (1)

Financial claim/function matrix: A chart describing the financial claims that represent the assets and liabilities of an intermediary and those brokered by the firm and the financial functions the institution performs with those claims. (1)

Financial engineering: A process by which financial experts alter the cash flow or credit risk characteristics of an existing financial claim in order to create new types of financial claims with different cash flow or credit characteristics. (15)

Financial futures contract: A derivative financial claim obligating the party to buy or deliver a financial claim at a predetermined price and time. (16)

Financial guarantee: A third-party that adds its obligation to fulfill the terms of a financial debt in the event that the creditor is unable to fulfill its obligations. (A12)

Financial Institution Reform, Recovery, and Enforcement Act of 1989 (FIRREA): Legislation designed to reform the regulatory structure of savings and loans and organize the Resolution Trust Corporation to sell and liquidate failed savings and loans and savings banks. (4)

Financial institutions: A financial firm involved in one or more of the functions of origination, servicing, brokerage, and portfolio management. (1)

Financial intermediaries: A financial firm that has a major portfolio management activity. (1)

Financial leverage: The extent to which a firm uses debt in relation to equity in its capital structure. (10)

Financial markets: Organized and dealer markets for financial assets. (5)

Financial plan: The development of financial pro forma statements representing the objectives of management for an upcoming period. (9)

Financial restructuring: The action of a firm to alter its financial leverage. (A12)

Financial swap: A financial contract in which two parties agree to make payments to one another. (16)

Firm commitment underwriting: A security underwriting in which an investment banking firm agrees to purchase the securities and accepts the risk of distributing them. (3)

Fisher Effect: The theory that the nominal interest rate is equal to the real interest rate plus market inflation expectations. (14)

Fixed-rate mortgage (FRM): A fully amortizing fixed-payment mortgage. (11)

Flat yield curve: A situation in which interest rates on all maturity bonds are nearly equal. (2)

Float: The availability of funds in a checking account until the check is cleared by the receiving depository. (20)

Floating exchange rates: The value of one country's currency in terms of another as determined by a currency's supply and demand. (19)

Floor: A financial option contract giving the owner the right to receive interest payments on a stated amount of notional principal in the event the index falls below an agreed-upon level. (18)

Floor in adjustable-rate loan: A limit below which the interest rate on an adjustable rate financial claim is not permitted to fall. (18)

Flow of Funds Accounts: A set of financial statistics produced by the Federal Reserve Board showing the borrowing, lending, and assets of the major economic units in the United States. (5)

Foreign direct investment (FDI): Investment of individual or firms in one country in real assets of another. (1)

Forward cash market: The market for financial claims in which settlement occurs in the future. (16)

Forward cash-market transaction: The purchase or sale of a financial claim with delivery occurring in the future. (16)

Forward rate: The interest rate on a loan to be obtained at some future time. (14)

Franchise value (customer): The value of having developed a group of existing customers who can be expected to be repeat purchasers of the firm's products and services. (25)

Fraud: Willful deceit to obtain an advantage. (1, 11)

Front-running: A situation where a trader purchases or sells a financial asset prior to a known large transaction with the expectation that the large transaction will affect the price in a predictable fashion. (1)

Funding risk: The extent to which a financial firm's liabilities are sensitive to interest rates and to concerns about the firm's financial strength. (8)

Future value: The amount of dollars that will be received in the future if a certain sum of dollars is invested today for a specified period of time at a specified rate of interest. (15)

Futures option: An option written to buy or deliver a specified futures contract. (16, 18)

GAAP capital: The capital of a financial institution computed using generally accepted accounting principles (GAAP). (10)

GAP buckets: Periodic *GAP* statistics of a firm computed over different segments of maturity or repricing. (17)

General obligation bonds (GOs): Bonds of states and municipalities whose repayment depends on the taxing authority of these government units. (4, A12)

Generally Accepted Accounting Principles (GAAP): A set of rules for producing the financial statements of business firms which is based on policies developed by the Financial Accounting Standards Board. (7)

Glass-Steagall Act: A law prohibiting commercial banks from underwriting securities and investment banks from accepting deposits. (4)

Gordon constant growth model: A model to determine the value of a firm based on the discounted value of future dividends. (25)

Government National Mortgage Association (GNMA): A federal government department within the Department of Housing and Urban Development that provides a full faith and credit guarantee to securities issued by financial institutions that are collateralized by mortgages guaranteed and insured by FHA and VA. (A4, 4)

Government sponsored enterprises (GSEs): Government chartered financial intermediaries that purchase or guarantee loans deemed to be worthy of government support. The largest GSEs are the Federal Home Loan Banks, Federal National Mortgage Association, Federal Home Loan Mortgage Corporation,

Student Loan Marketing Association, and Farm Credit Banks. (A3)

Grace period: The period of time between a loan payment's due date and a later date when the investor will accept the payment without taking adverse action. (20)

Graduated payment mortgage: A mortgage with a rising payment feature that does not fully amortize the loan in the early years of its life. These are used to assist buyers with growing income prospects. (3)

Grantor trust: A special legal form used to hold loans for purposes of creating pass-through securities. (9)

Guaranteed investment contract (GIC): An unsecured liability of a life insurance company typically sold to pension funds. (8, 22)

Haircut: The different between the amount of a collateralized loan and the value of the underlying collateral. (20)

Hedge ratio: In the futures market, the number of futures contracts needed to provide the highest offsetting price change to the cash market position. (18)

Hedging: A financial transaction that is entered into to reduce risk of price change. (16)

Herfindahl-Hirschmann Index (*HHI*): A mathematical model used by the U.S. Department of Justice to determine whether a consolidation of two or more companies will lead to a substantial lessening of competition. (25)

Highly concentrated market: A geographic area in which the potential customers have few competitors. (4)

Home banking: A group of telephonic and computer-based banking services. (24)

Home mortgage: A financial claim in which residential property serves as collateral. (3)

Hostile takeover: The acquisition and control of a firm over the objection of its board of directors. (A12)

Hybrid claims: Financial claims created by altering the cash flows and/or credit characteristics of an existing financial claim. (3)

Implied forward rate: The interest rate that must prevail in the future, given any specified yield curve, for an investor to be indifferent toward investing for a specified period or alternatively investing for a lesser period and reinvesting the proceeds for the remainder of the initial specified period. (2)

Income approach to appraisal: A method of establishing real estate value by discounting future cash flows on the property. (12)

Income simulation: A model used to forecast changes in income and other financial measures based on specified financial strategies and economic environments. (17)

Indicative bid: The price at which an investment banker expects a security to be sold. (3)

Indirect investment: Investment in financial claims of intermediaries. (5)

Industrial development bonds (IDB): Bonds issued by a state or local development agency which are the obligation of a company using the facility financed by the bond. (A12)

Inflation: A rise in the general price level of a country's goods and services. (2)

Inflation expectations: The tendency of CDUs and CSUs to consider the prospects for future price changes of goods and services in their borrowing and savings decisions. (14)

Informational asymmetries: A condition in which one party has more information than the other party. (1)

Informational efficiency: The valuation characteristics of a market that describe the process by which prices are influenced by information. (1)

Initial margin: The amount of money or assets required to establish a position in the futures market. (16)

Insider trading: A situation in which corporate officers and directors, illegally profiting from not-yet-public knowledge expected to affect the value of a company, trade company stock. (1)

Institutional Investor risk index: A measure of country risk published by *Institutional Investor* magazine. (12)

Insurance companies: A financial intermediary that pools risks related to the probability of death, and health, property, and casualty losses. (1)

Insured (or noninsured) pension programs: A pension plan whose pension obligations are insured (not insured) by a life insurance company. (3)

Interest expense: Interest costs of a financial firm. (7)

Interest income: Interest earned by a financial firm. (7)

Interest-only (IO) security strips: A hybrid financial claim created by using the interest payments from a mortgage pass-through security to create the cash flows on a newly issued security. (15)

Interest rate cap: A limit on the rise of an interest rate for an adjustable-rate loan. (17)

Interest rate elasticity of lendable funds: The relationship of the supply offered and demand for loanable funds to changes in interest rates. (14)

Interest rate index: The index used to adjust the interest rate on an adjustable-rate loan. (18)

Interest rate margin: The difference between the interest rate index and actual rate charged on an adjustable-rate loan. (18)

Interest rate price elasticity of debt: The change in the price of a debt financial asset resulting from a 1% change in the asset's interest rate. (14)

Interest rate risk: The impact on earnings and solvency of a financial firm related to changes in open market interest rates. (8, 17)

Interest rate swap: A derivative financial claim in which two parties agree to make interest payments to one another based on a stated amount of notional principal and at specified fixed or adjustable interest rates. (16)

Intermediation: The process of issuing financial claims issued by firms that use the funds to make investments in other financial claims. (1, 5)

Internal rate of return (*IRR*): The yield calculated for an investment. (14)

International Monetary Fund: A financial intermediary that lends foreign currencies to countries to facilitate foreign trade. (19)

Intertemporal: A transfer of consumption from one time period to another. (3)

In-the-money option: An outstanding option that has an exercise price above

(below) the cash market price in the case of a call (put) option. (16)

Intrinsic value: The positive difference, if any, between the value of a option exercised immediately less the cash price of the option. (18, 16)

Inventory turnover: A financial ratio defined by dividing cost of goods sold by inventory. (12)

Investment banking firm: A specialized financial intermediary that is primarily involved in issuing, brokering, and trading securities. (3)

Investment grade rating: One of the four highest ratings by the major private credit-rating firms. (A12)

Investment opportunity schedule (IOS): A schedule ranking from highest to lowest the internal rate of return for investments available to a firm. (14)

Investment-oriented intermediaries: A group of intermediaries that provide specialized investment services for individuals and institutions, including mutual funds, limited partnerships, and real estate investment trusts. (1)

Investment-oriented policies: A group of life insurance policies used to accumulate and invest funds. (3)

Junk bond: A bond granted a rating below one of the four top ratings by the major credit-rating firms. (A12)

Ladder of maturities liquidity strategy: A method of liquidity asset management involving equal-sized investments in a series of different maturities. (20)

Law: A state or federal provision that spells out required actions or prohibits certain actions. (1)

Law of large numbers diversification: The probability that a specific lender's credit loss experience on a portfolio of a particular type of loan will deviate from the actual loss experience for the population of loans from which it is drawn. (11)

Law of one price: An arbitrage process that states that, adjusted for exchange rates, goods will have the same price in different countries. (19)

Legally binding contracts: The existence of a legal system upholding the rights of individuals to make agreements with one another to own and transfer real and financial assets. (1)

Lender of last resort: A central bank with the authority to lend to financial institutions and others in order to prevent a disruptive withdrawal of funds. (14)

Life cycle income pattern: A theory of how individuals' preference for consumption changes over the course of their life. (5)

Life insurance annuities: A life insurance policy that provides a fixed monthly payment to the beneficiary. (3)

Life-line banking: The requirement that insured depositories provide a low-cost checking service to low-income households. (4)

Life-of-loan cap: A loan contract provision spelling out the maximum interest rate that can be charged on an adjustable-rate loan. (18)

Life-of-loan floor: A loan contract provision spelling out the minimum interest rate that can be charged on an adjustable-rate loan. (18)

Limited partnerships: A group of investment intermediaries that invest funds in intensively managed investments, primarily in the real estate and corporate markets. (3)

Line of credit: A credit commitment agreement that allows the borrower to draw down up to a specified maximum amount during the commitment period. (A12, 20)

Liquidity preference theory: A theory to describe the term structure which holds that differences in interest rates for bonds of various maturities are caused by CSUs' preference for less-risky short-term investments. Thus, the yield curve tends to have an upward-sloping bias. (14)

Liquidity premium: The high-interest return as compensation for accepting maturity substitution. (2)

Load funds: Mutual funds that charge a fee upon sale or redemption of shares. (3)

Loan commitments: A financial contract requiring the lender to lend funds if the borrower demands it. (8)

Loan correspondent: A financial intermediary that purchases a participation in a loan originated by another firm. (22)

Loan covenant: A provision in a loan or investment that establishes a requirement that must be met by the borrower as a condition of keeping the loan out of default. (11)

Loan loss provisions: Expenses taken against the current income of the firm based on estimated losses from default on loans held. (13)

Loan sold with recourse: A loan sold in which the buyer can sell it back to the seller if the loan does not perform as expected. (8)

Loan-to-value ratio: A financial ratio defined by dividing the loan amount by the market value of the mortgaged property. (12)

Long cash: Owning or having an obligation to purchase a financial claim. (18)

Long futures: The purchase of a futures contract obligating the owner to accept delivery. (18)

Loss ratio: The relationship of property and casualty claims paid to premiums earned. (3)

Macro-hedge: A hedge of interest rate risk based on the interest rate elasticity of the firm's entire portfolio of assets and liabilities. (16)

Maintenance margin: A specific amount of cash or securities to be held by a broker in relation to the price of a futures contract. (16)

Margin requirement: Cash or marketable securities maintained in an account by the holder of a futures contract to ensure that the conditions of the contract will be fulfilled. (16)

Mark-to-market technique: A process to establish the current market value of financial assets. (7)

Market comparable appraisal: A method of establishing property value based on comparisons of similar properties. (12)

Market making: The purchases and sales of financial claims by market participants. (14)

Market segmentation: The process of marketing to groups of customers using different products or distribution systems. (24)

Market value: The current market price for a financial asset. (7)

Marketability risk: The risk that financial claims will have to be sold in a market that has a large spread between prices offered and prices bid or in which a purchase or sale may influence the price. (14)

Marketability risk premium (*mrp*)**:** An amount of interest charged by a lender to compensate for the probability that a financial claim may lose value due to the need to sell it at a low bid price in an inactive market. (14)

Marketability transformation: Issuing liabilities of one degree of marketability and purchasing assets of another. (2)

Marketable securities: Securities that are easy to sell or buy as a result of an active secondary market. (3)

Maturity: The date of the last cash-flow payment on a debt financial claim. (14)

Maturity transformation: Issuing liabilities of one maturity and purchasing assets of another. (2)

McCarran-Ferguson Act of 1945: Legislation that gave states the regulatory and chartering authority for insurance companies. (4)

McFadden Act: A law limiting nationally chartered banks from branching to a greater extent than state chartered banks. (4)

Medium of exchange: A thing or system used to make financial transactions. (2)

Medium-term notes (MTNs): Claims with maturities of 1 to 30 years and of varying interest rates. They are offered to investors on a daily basis. (12)

Mergers of equals: The consolidation of two companies of nearly equal market value where shareholders receive stock in a new company. (25)

Micro-hedge: A financial hedge transaction that specifically identifies the financial asset to be hedged. (16)

Model of competitive markets: A theory of pricing behavior of firms in which competition is normal. (4)

Money center and international banks: Very large commercial banks with domestic and international operations. (3)

Money market deposit account: A depository account that provides limited access by negotiable draft and typically pays a floating market interest rate. (3)

Money market mutual fund: A mutual fund that invests in short-term, highly marketable money market investments. (3)

Monitoring: The need for the principal in an agency relationship to collect and evaluate information about the actions of the agent. (2)

Moral hazard: A condition in which a participant to a transaction does not have an economic incentive to avoid risk or doing business with firms that take exceptionally high risks. (4)

Mortality risk: The risk related to insuring the lives of people using life insurance. (3)

Mortality tables: Statistical probability data about the number of deaths in a population of people of similar age. (3)

Mortgage bond: A secured bond using a mortgage on commercial property as collateral. (A12)

Mortgage-backed securities: Financial asset-backed claims using mortgages as collateral. (11)

Multibank holding companies: A bank holding company that owns banks in more than one state. (3)

Multinational corporation: A firm having business activities outside its country of domicile. (5)

Mutual funds: A group of investment intermediaries that invest shareholders' funds in a professionally managed diversified pool of securities in which the shareholders hold a pro rata share. (1, 3)

Mutual-stock conversion: The conversion of a mutually chartered financial institution to a stockholder-owned firm. (3)

Naked option: A writer of an option that agrees to delivery without owning the claim on which the option is written. (16)

National Association of Insurance Commissioners (NAIC): An organization made up of insurance regulators of the various states. (4)

National Credit Union Administration (NCUA): Regulator of federally chartered and insured credit unions. (4)

Near monies: Financial claims that perform most of the functions of a medium of exchange. (2)

Negotiable certificate of deposit: A fixed-rate and fixed-term deposit account of depositories that may be sold in a secondary market and transferred to a new owner. (3)

Negotiated offer: A method of contracting for the underwriting of a new security which involves one underwriter rather than a competitive bid. (3)

Net after-tax income: A firm's income after all expenses and taxes have been subtracted. (7)

Net asset value: The value of the securities in a mutual fund or other investment portfolio computed using the market value of each security in the portfolio. (3)

Net income before taxes: A firm's income after all expenses have been subtracted but before taxes have been subtracted. (7)

Net interest income: A financial firm's interest income less interest expense. (7)

Net interest income after provision for credit losses: A firm's net interest income after an amount for expected credit losses is subtracted. (7)

Net interest margin: The total of a financial firm's interest income less its interests costs. (7, 8)

Net interest spread: The total of a financial firm's interest income, divided by average interest-earning assets, minus the interest expense, divided by average interest-bearing liabilities. (10)

Net operating revenue: A commercial or industrial firm's sales less cost of goods sold. (11)

Net profit margin: A financial ratio defined by dividing net profit after taxes by total sales. (12)

Net working capital: A measure of corporate liquidity defined by the dollar amount of current assets less current liabilities. (12)

Nominal interest rate: The interest rate observed in the market. It is composed of a real interest rate and a premium for market inflation expectations and other risk and cost factors. (14)

Nondepository institutions: All financial intermediaries that do not accept deposits, including insurance companies, investment companies, finance companies, and trust companies. (1)

Noninterest expense: The noninterest expenses of a financial firm. (7)

Noninterest income: Revenue of financial institutions that is not interest or capital gains. (7, 23)

Noninvestment-grade ratings: A bond rated below the top four ratings of S&P's and Moody's private rating firms. (12)

Nonpecuniary rewards: Rewards to management that are not monetary, such as short working hours or reduced stress. (10)

Normal or upward-sloping yield curve: A yield curve in which interest rates on short-term maturity bonds are less than long-term maturity bonds. (14)

Notional principal: The amount on which interest payments are based in a swap transaction. (16)

Off-balance sheet risks: Liquidity, credit, or interest rate risks related to financial obligations not shown on the balance sheet. (8)

Off-balance sheet transactions: Outstanding financial obligations that are not shown on a financial firm's balance sheet. (7)

Office of the Comptroller of the Currency (OCC): The regulator of federally chartered banks operating as a department within the Treasury. (4)

Office of Thrift Supervision (OTS): The regulator of savings and loans created in 1989 as a department within the Treasury. (4)

Open-end mutual fund: An investment fund that sells shares with the proceeds used to purchase investments. This type of fund typically has no limit on the number of shares it will sell. (3)

Open market operations: The purchase and sale of securities by the Federal Reserve System. (14)

Open outcry system: A market where brokers representing buyers and sellers physically buy and sell in a face-to-face market setting. (16)

Operating efficiency: The relationship of the firm's operating expenses to other measures of the firm's activity. (9)

Operating plan: An itemization and prioritization of objectives and action steps to be accomplished that are consistent with the firm's goals. (9)

Optimal capital structure: The relation of debt to equity in a firm's capital structure that maximizes the firm's market value and minimizes its weighted average cost of capital. (10)

Option: A contract allowing the owner to buy or sell a specified quantity of a specified financial claim on or before a specified date at a specified price. (14)

Option premium: The difference between the option exercise price and the current market value of the optioned financial claim. The difference between the option price and its intrinsic value. (16)

Option writer: The party to an option contract that agrees to buy or sell the financial claim on which the option is written.

Ordinary annuity: A financial contract that pays the owner a specified sum of dollars for a specified period of time on a regular periodic basis with each payment occurring at the end of each period. (15)

Organization for Economic Cooperation and Development (OECD): An international organization that shares economic data and analyses. (4)

Organized market: A financial market that utilizes a central location and agreed-upon set of rules. (5)

Origination: The creation of a new financial claim. (2)

Out-of-the-money option: An outstanding option that has an exercise price below (above) the cash market price in the case of a call (put) option. (16)

Overnight repo: A repurchase that takes place in one day. (15)

Over-the-counter (OTC) market: A market for financial assets operated by a group of unrelated security dealers. (5)

Par value: A legal value established for a new security. (7)

Participation: A portion of a loan sold to one or more financial intermediaries. (21)

Participation seller's yield (PSY): The yield on the retained portion of a loan sold in part to another investor giving consideration to any difference between the yield paid by the borrower and the yield paid the participation investor. (21)

Pass-through security: A financial claim collateralized by assets that amortize in which the owner receives a pro-rata share of the principal and interest payments of the pool of collateral, usually mortgages. (3)

Passbook (or savings) accounts: Nontransaction accounts issued by depositories that provide for withdrawal at any time. (3)

Payment system: A group of paper-based and electronic systems used to make transactions using money. (1)

Pension Benefit Guarantee Corporation (PBGC): A guarantee fund covering the assets held by private pension plans for beneficiaries. (3)

Pension funds: Private and public organizations that provide professional management of assets maintained for the benefit of working members for purposes of supplementing retirement income. (1, 3)

Performance standards: The establishment of financial and operating measures used to determine the success of the firm in achieving objectives and action steps. (9)

Periodic capital standards review: A regulatory evaluation of a financial firm's capital adequacy based on a specified schedule. (4)

Periodic GAP: A measure of interest rate risk computed by taking the firm's dollar amount of maturing or repricing assets and subtracting its maturing or repricing liabilities for a specified period of time. (17)

Periodic rate: The interest rate that applies for the portion of a year when compounding takes place. (15)

Perpetual preferred stock: A corporate equity issue that has no maturity and pays a specified dividend return. (15)

Perpetuity: A financial claim that pays a fixed periodic amount indefinitely. (15)

Planning: A process used to direct resources within a firm. (9)

Point-of-sale systems: Electronic systems used by retailers to pay for goods electronically. (24)

Policy acquisition costs: Costs of selling and originating a new insurance policy which are amortized over the expected life of the insurance contract. (7)

Portfolio management function: The process of managing assets and liabilities. Includes credit risk, interest rate risk, and liquidity management. (2)

Preauthorized payment programs: An agreement between a payer permitting the payee to withdraw funds directly from the payee's account to meet the payer's financial obligation. (20)

Preferred habitat theory of the term structure: A theory to describe the term structure holding that differences in interest rates for bonds of various maturities are based on supply-and-demand conditions for various maturities but that interest rates on bonds of other maturities can be higher by an amount sufficient to induce shifts in maturities for CSUs and CDUs. (14)

Preferred stock: Equity in a firm which has preference in liquidation over common stock. (15)

Premium: The amount by which the market price of a financial claim is valued at more than the par value of the claim. (15)

Prepayment penalty (or option): A fee charged a mortgage borrower on a mortgage assessed when the mortgage is paid off before maturity. (15)

Prepayment provision: A contractual clause in a debt instrument allowing the borrower to pay off the debt before the maturity date. It is a form of call provision and is commonly found in home mortgages and installment loans. (A12, 14)

Present value theory: A methodology to convert dollars received in the future into their value measured in terms of today's dollars. (15)

Price/earnings multiple model: A system for estimating the value of a company based on using comparable relationships of price to earnings ratios of recently completed acquisitions. (25)

Price-to-book value model: A system for estimating the value of a company based on using comparable relationships of the firm's market price to its book value. (25)

Primary dealers: A group of security dealers used to help distribute newly issued U.S. government bonds. (15)

Primary financial debt: Debt issued to purchase real assets or finance business operations. (12)

Prime rate: An interest rate depositories use as an index for many loans. (A12, 21)

Principal: The owner in an agency relationship, such as a stockholder. (1)

Principal-only security (PO): A hybrid financial claim created by using the principal payments from a mortgage pass-through security to create the cash flows on a newly issued security. (15)

Private pension plans: A pension plan sponsored by a nongovernmental entity. (3)

Privatization: The process of converting government-owned firms to privately owned firms. (5)

Prompt corrective actions: A group of actions available to regulators to force a financial firm to act in a manner desired by the regulator. (10)

Property rights: A governmentally granted opportunity for individuals to own and transfer property and other real goods. (1)

Proprietary trading: A firm that trades securities for its own account. (3)

Prospectus: A legal document describing a new security offered for sale and the organization issuing it. (3)

Provision for credit losses: An expense taken against income for a financial institution which reflects expected losses of principal and interest on loans and investments held. (7)

Public good theory of regulation: A theory that uses judgments of what is in the public's best interest to justify regulation. (4)

Public security association standard prepayment model (PSA): A set of mortgage prepayment cash-flow assumptions in which the prepayments begin slowly in the early years and increase to 6% per year. (15)

Purchasing power parity: An arbitrage process that determines the relationship between prices of goods and services between countries and their exchange rates. (19)

Put option: A financial contract allowing the owner to sell a specified quantity of a financial claim on or before a specified date at a specified price. (16)

Put-call parity: A mathematical relationship between a put and call option written on the same financial asset. (16)

Qualified thrift lender test (QTLT): A law limiting the investment authority of savings and loan associations primarily to home mortgages and consumer loans. (4)

Quick ratio: A financial ratio used to measure corporate liquidity defined as the amount of cash and marketable securities divided by current liabilities. (12)

Real Estate Investment Trust (REIT): A trust organized to own or finance real estate which meets certain federal tax requirements. (3)

Real estate lending restrictions: Regulatory requirements defining unpermissible types and amounts of real estate loans and methods of real estate lending. (4)

Real estate mortgage investment conduit (REMIC): A tax trust entity that permits the creation of collateralized mortgage obligations which are not required to be shown on the balance sheet of the issuer. (9, 15)

Real interest rates: The rate of interest that reflects the interaction between the demand for loanable funds related to the productivity of savings used by CSDs and the supply of loanable funds relating to the time preferences of CSUs. It is an interest rate determined in the absence of inflationary expectations. (14)

Recourse: The sale of assets with a provision allowing the buyer to sell them back if they do not perform as expected. (13)

Recoveries: Revenue generated for disposing of distressed assets which exceeds the estimate made at the time loan loss reserves were established. (13)

Redemption fee: A charge assessed at the time of redemption of the shares of a mutual fund. (3)

Redlining: A discriminatory practice by financial institutions that excludes certain geographic areas for making loans. (4)

Regional banks: Large banks servicing an entire state or large portion of a large state. (3)

Regulation Q: A regulation of the Federal Reserve System that prohibits payment of interest on demand deposits formerly used to limit the interest paid on time and savings accounts. (4)

Regulatory Accounting Principles (RAP): A set of guidelines for developing the financial statements of financial institutions which meets requirements established by their regulatory institution. (7)

Regulatory arbitrage: A decision of a financial firm to change its charter so that it can be regulated by a more favored regulator. (4)

Regulatory capital: The capital of a financial institution computed using a formula provided by the firm's regulator. (7)

Reinsurance: The process whereby an insurance company transfers a portion of the insurance risk exposure and premiums to one or more insurance companies. (11)

Reinvestment risk: The risk that cash flows received before the maturity of a debt claim cannot be reinvested at a yield to maturity as high as that of the claim that produced the cash flows. (14)

Replacement value: A method of property appraisal which establishes value of determining the cost of replacing the property. (12)

Repurchase agreement (repo): An agreement under which one party sells a financial claim to another party with the stipulation that the first party repurchase it at a specified price on a specified date in the future. (3)

Reputation: Nonfinancial qualities of a firm related to its behavior with customers, such as the firm's trustworthiness. (1)

Reserve requirements: A percentage of certain deposit liabilities, or deposits, that must be kept in the form of vault cash and deposits in a Federal Reserve bank. (14)

Resolution Trust Corporation (RTC): An organization created by Congress in 1989 to manage and liquidate the assets of failed savings and loans. (4)

Restrictive covenants: Provisions in debt contracts required by lenders that restrict the actions of management and shareholders and reduce the potential for financial loss. (12)

Restrictive monetary policy: A monetary policy that constrains the growth in the money supply and increases interest rates. (14)

Retail funding sources: Liabilities sold in small denominations to less-sophisticated investors thought to be less price sensitive. (22)

Revenue bonds: Bonds issued by states and municipalities whose repayment is backed by a specified revenue fee base. Revenue bonds are used to finance revenue-producing investments such as tollroads, airports, and seaports. (A12)

Reverse repurchase agreement (reverse repo): The position of the purchaser of the security in a repurchase agreement. (3)

Revolving credit agreement: A loan commitment allowing a borrower to draw down funds on an ongoing basis as needed. (A12)

Riding the yield curve strategy: A liquidity management technique that involves selling short-term liquid assets to buy longer-term liquid assets. (20)

Risk pooling or sharing: A process of aggregating many similar financial claims to increase the predictability of credit loss. (3)

Risk-based capital requirements: A set of regulator-directed capital requirements that relate the amount of required capital to the types of assets held and to off-balance sheet risks. (10)

Risk-based insurance assessments: A system of assessing deposit insurance premiums based on each institution's risk of failure. (4)

Risk-free rate: A nominal interest rate on a bond, which is considered to have no chance of credit loss. Typically a U.S. government bond is considered credit-risk free. (14)

Return on assets (*ROA*): A financial ratio measuring profitability, defined by dividing net profit after taxes by total assets (or average assets). (10)

Return on equity (*ROE*): A financial ratio measuring profitability, defined by dividing net profit after taxes by total shareholders' equity. (10)

Safety and soundness examination: A regulatory exam focusing on the financial soundness of the firm. (4)

Savings Association Insurance Fund (SAIF): The deposit insurance fund for savings and loan associations created in 1989 and administered by the FDIC. (4)

Search costs: Costs incurred in finding the other party to a transaction. (2)

Secondary claims: Financial claims issued by intermediary financial institutions. (3)

Secondary market: The market used to sell loans and investments after they have been originated. (A3)

Secondary marketing: The process of determining the best place to sell loans originated by a financial intermediary. (12)

Secondary mortgage market: The markets for previously originated mortgages. (3)

Securities and Exchange Commission (SEC): An agency of the federal government that regulates security dealers, issuers of securities, and publicly traded companies. (7)

Securities Investor Protection Corporation (SIPC): An insurance fund that insures funds and securities held in security broker dealer accounts. (4)

Securitization: The use of loans to collateralize and issue securities. (22)

Segmentation theory of the term structure: A theory that holds that the differences in interest rates for bonds of various maturities are based solely on supply-and-demand conditions prevailing in specific markets representing different bond maturities. (14)

Selective hedging: Hedging the price risk of a specific asset, liability, or outstanding forward transaction. (18)

Self-dealing: The action of profiting unfairly from transactions with a firm, made possible because of an insider relationship. (1)

Selling group: The group formed when more than one investment banking firm participates in the distribution of a newly issued security. (3)

Senior-subordinated pass-through security: A series of financial hybrid claims created using pass-through securities as collateral. It involves creating two securities, with the subordinated class experiencing loss of principal first before the senior class suffers loss. (3)

Senior-subordinated security: A series of securities that redistribute the credit risk on the collateral underlying the securities. (15)

Sensitivity analysis: A model of a financial firm used to determine changes in financial statistics and ratios from specified changes in certain economic variables. (17)

Serial bonds: Bonds that have a specified principal amount of their par value come due at a predetermined date. (A12)

Servicing: The process of collecting payments, accounting, collateral management, and ensuring the adherence of all covenants by the borrower. (2)

Servicing cost (sc): The cost expressed as an interest rate to cover the cost of performing the various functions of owning a financial claim. (14)

Servicing income contract: A financial contract that compensates the organization that collects payments on primary financial claims and forwards them to the investors in the financial claims. (15)

Shared ATM networks: Automated teller machines and cash dispensing systems used jointly by financial institutions. (24)

Shelf Registration Rule 412: A Securities and Exchange Commission provision allowing firms to issue a large amount of securities at different times with one registration. (22)

Short cash: The position of a firm that needs to acquire a financial claim in the future. (18)

Short futures: The sale of a futures contract. (18)

Significantly undercapitalized: Institutions that are in the regulator's fourth-lowest of five levels of capital adequacy. (4)

Single-payment note: A loan made by a financial firm which provides a specified amount to be taken down at the time the loan is written and repaid in a single lump sum. (A12)

Sinking fund provision: A provision of a bond that provides that a specified percentage of the principal value of the bonds be redeemed or paid off prior to maturity. (A12)

Small Business Administration: A department within the Department of Commerce that provides guarantee programs for loans to businesses. (A3)

Sources and uses of funds statement: A financial statement showing what a firm spends cash on and what it receives cash for. (7)

Specialized financial institutions: Financial institutions with charters that restrict their activities to specific financial assets and functions. (3)

Speculators: Economic units that profit through the purchase of financial contracts on the basis that favorable price changes will occur within a short period of time. (16)

Spot market: A market in which financial claims can be bought and sold for immediate delivery. Delivery is typically required in two to five business days. (16)

Stakeholders: Those people and groups who have a stake in an organization's well-being, such as stockholders, employees, community, and creditors. (1, 8)

Standby letters of credit: A loan commitment allowing the borrower to draw down funds in the event that another financing technique does not work. (11)

State and local government pension plan: A pension plan sponsored by a state or local government agency or department. (3)

Statement of cash flows: See: Sources and uses of funds statement. (7)

Statement of income: A financial statement showing the revenue and costs of a firm. (7)

Statement of retained earnings: A financial statement that explains changes in a firm's shareholders' equity between two periods. (7)

Statutory Accounting Principles: A set of guidelines established by insurance company regulators for development and presentation of their financial statements. (7)

Stimulative policy: A macroeconomic policy designed to increase income and employment. (14)

Strategic plan: A program to establish a firm's mission and goals, assess the firm's external environment, and evaluate the firm's strengths and weaknesses. (9)

Stripped Treasury security (strip-T): The process of creating new securities from the interest and principal payments of an existing Treasury security. (15)

Student Loan Marketing Association (SLMA): A GSE that specializes in purchasing and servicing federally guaranteed student loans. (4, A3)

Subordinated debenture: An unsecured debt of a borrower that in event of default will not be repaid until general and secured creditors are repaid. (A12)

Super-regional banks: Large banks servicing an entire state or group of states. (3)

Swaptions: A option written on a swap contract. (16)

Syndication group: A group of security broker dealers that jointly sell a newly issued security. (11)

Systematic risk: A factor or set of factors that contribute to the risk of a class of investments. (12)

Tariffs: A government tax on imports. (5)

Taxable equivalent yield (*TEY*): The interest rate that would have to be earned to provide the same after-tax yield as a tax-exempt investment, assuming the interest were fully taxed. (14)

Tax-preferenced investment: An investment whose income is not taxed at ordinary income tax rates. The income may be tax free or tax deferred. (15)

Teaser: An adjustable-rate mortgage whose initial rate is below the index plus margin. (18)

Term insurance: A life insurance policy with no cash value buildup. (3)

Term loans: Loans with maturities of approximately two years or more. (11)

Term repo: A repurchase that takes place over more than one day. (15)

Term structure of interest rates: The relationship of the yields on a specific class of bonds of different maturities. (14)

Thrift institutions: Specialized depository institutions including savings and loans, savings banks, and credit unions. (1)

Time deposits: A deposit in a financial institution that is typically not withdrawable on demand at par value. (3)

Time preference: An individual's trade-off between consumption today and consumption tomorrow. (5)

Time series analysis: Presentation of specified financial ratios over time for comparison purposes. (8)

Time value of option: The amount by which the price of an option exceeds its intrinsic value. (16)

Times interest earned ratio: A financial ratio defined by dividing earnings before interest and taxes by interest payments. (12)

Too-big-to-fail (TBTF) policy: A policy of depository regulators to support large financial institutions that experience financial distress. This policy is based on the idea that a failure of a large bank will create major economic dislocations and financial runs and panics. (4)

Trade debt: Loans extended by the seller of goods and services to its customers in order to induce sales. (A12)

Traders: Individuals involved in market making that execute orders to buy, sell, and broker financial claims for a financial firm. (3)

Tranches: The number of different securities created in a collateralized mortgage obligation or real estate mortgage investment conduit. (15)

Transaction account: Any type of deposit used to make transactions, such as demand deposits, money market demand accounts, share drafts, and negotiable order of withdrawal accounts. (3)

Transaction costs: The costs related to making financial transactions. (5)

Transformation: The process of a financial firm issuing financial liabilities with one set of attributes and creating financial assets with another set of attributes. (2)

Treasury bills: Debt issued by the U.S. government with maturities less than one year and no interest payment. They are issued at a discount from par value. (15)

Treasury bonds: Debt issued by the U.S. government with maturities of ten years or more that pay interest semiannually. (3)

Treasury notes: Debt issued by the U.S. government with maturities of two to ten years that pay interest semiannually. (3)

Trustee: A person with the legal responsibility of safeguarding assets or insuring that one party to a financial transaction carriers out its responsibility to the other. (A12)

Truth-in-lending legislation: A law that defines how financial institutions must quote the rates and other fees on loans. (4)

Undercapitalized: Institutions that meet the regulator's third of four levels of capital adequacy. (4)

Underwriting: A process of establishing the credit risk of a financial asset. (2)

Underwriting guidelines: A set of policies and procedures for determining whether an investment is satisfactory for investment. (12)

Underwriting ratio: A guideline used to establish the riskiness of a loan. (8)

Unit banking: A law limiting banks in a state to one location. (4)

Unsecured short-term loans: A loan made to a borrower that is not backed by collateral. (A12)

Unsystematic risk: A factor contributing to the risk of an investment which is unique to that investment. (12)

Variation margin: The amount of cash or securities that must be kept with a broker in relation to changes in the price of the futures contact. (16)

Vertical integration: A firm's effort to control where it obtains its supplies and raw materials and final sales. (5)

Vesting: A contractual requirement that a pension plan provide a portion of the actuarially determined value of the pension plan to the beneficiary if the beneficiary leaves the employment of the firm sponsoring the plan. (3)

Veterans Administration (VA): An organization that provides a guarantee program for mortgages taken out by military veterans. (A3)

Warrant: A financial claim offered by a corporation permitting the holder of the option to buy the company's common stock. (16)

Well-capitalized: Institutions having the regulator's highest level of capital adequacy. (4)

Weighted average cost of capital (WACC): The cost of debt and equity for a financial firm weighted by each source of capital's relative contribution to the firm's capital structure. (21)

Weighted average life (WAL): A calculation of the expected timing of the cash flows for a group of mortgages based on weighting the cash flows over the life of the mortgages. (15)

Whole life insurance policies: A level-payment life insurance policy that provides mortality insurance and an investment creating cash values. (3)

Wholesale funding sources: Liabilities sold using public security markets and security dealers. (3, 22)

Wire transfer: An electronic system for transferring funds from one depository to another. (24)

Writer of the option: The party to an option who agrees to buy or deliver. (16)

Yield curve: A graph of the nominal interest rate on the vertical axis and maturity on the horizontal axis for specific bonds, usually U.S. government bonds, of different maturities on a specified date. (14)

Yield to maturity: The interest rate that will cause the discounted future cash flow's value to equal the amount of the investment measured in current dollars. (14)

Z score: The mathematical statistical relationship based on the output of a discriminate analysis. (11)

Zero coupon: A bond that pays no periodic interest payments and whose market value is below par value. (9)

$\mathcal{I}$ndex